AF512761

LOKAMANYA TILAK

Father of The Indian Freedom Struggle

DHANANJAY KEER

Popular Prakashan

www.popularprakashan.com

Published by
Harsha Bhatkal for
POPULAR PRAKASHAN PVT. LTD.
301, Mahalaxmi Chambers
22, Bhulabhai Desai Road
Mumbai 400 026
www.popularprakashan.com

First Published September 1959
Second Edition September 1969
Third Edition 2016

(4420)
ISBN: 978-81-7991-861-6

Typesetting: India Printing Works, Mumbai

PRINTED IN INDIA
by Thomson Press (India) Ltd.
New Delhi

Tilak Statue at Chowpaty, Girgaum, Mumbai

Dedicated to
The Memory of
My Parents
Devaki and Aba

LOKAMANYA BAL GANGADHAR TILAK

These, O Men, Shall Ye Honour, Liberty Only And These.

— SWINBURNE

PUBLISHER'S NOTE

'NIRMALA SADANAND SERIES' is being published under Popular Prakashan imprint to commemorate Nirmala (1924-2011) and Sadanand Bhatkal (1922-2011), who along with G.R. Bhatkal (1896-1972) laid the foundation of Popular Book Depot (established in 1924) and its publishing division Popular Prakashan.

Sadanand was the president of the Federation of Publishers and Booksellers Associations in India and put Indian publishing on the world map. He edited a three-volume Marathi 'Encyclopaedia of Marathi Literature', the first of its kind. Apart from their sterling contribution to the book world, particularly as editors of the Journal Indian Publisher and Bookseller (1950-1985), they played a leading role in community and cultural work. Before 1947, they had both participated in India's freedom movement.

Keer's biography of *Mahatma Jotirao Phooley* was brought out with important additions as the first book in the series. The second title in the series, *Bal Gangadhar Tilak* was first published by the author in 1959 and is now being reissued with some useful appendices.

Dhananjay Keer (b.1913), the foremost biographer in India, had the privilege of personal dialogue with the protagonists when he wrote on Vinayak Damodar Savarkar (1883-1966) and Bhimrao Ambedkar (1888-1956).

When Dr Ambedkar expressed regret at his not being able to write a biography of Mahatma Phooley, whom he considered his Guru, Keer promised to take up this task.

Keer's biographies have enabled scholars from different parts of India, not familiar with Marathi, to explore sources not hitherto available to them. Keer's biographies of Mahatma Jotirao Phooley, Chhatrapati Shahu Maharaj and Dr Baba Saheb Ambedkar complete the trilogy, that played an important role in rewriting social history of India. Of these works on Bal Gangadhar Tilak, Mahatma Gandhi and Veer Savarkar have provided a different perspective on the political history of modern India.

All these biographies are being reissued to mark the birth centenary of Dhananjay Keer.

— **Ramdas Bhatkal**

Mumbai
March 28, 2016

PREFACE

It is with great pleasure that I present this new edition of my biography of Lokamanya Tilak. I may humbly mention that when it first appeared in 1959, men of learning and the reviewers accorded a favourable reception to it. Most of them considered it 'to be about the best of the books on Tilak, from the viewpoint of both historical and literary treatment.'

Tilak was the Father of the Indian Freedom Struggle, the Maker of the Indian National Congress and one of the Architects of Modern India. Above all, he was a great fighter whose relentless struggle against British Imperialism had wide repercussions on the Asian Freedom Movement.

Since the publication of the original biography, a lot of important material has come to light. After studying it, I selected some vital facts from it and used them chronologically at the proper places. They heighten the grandeur of the story and add to the beauty of the picture.

I have made slight changes in the content of the original biography. The new material throws much light on the weak-kneed policy of the Moderate or Liberal leaders and gives the correct appraisal of Tilak by the British statesmen. It unfolds the unknown fact how Gokhale threw into the sea the letters of Ranade and Wacha. It also reveals that there had been a plot against the life of Lord Curzon, the Governor-General of India, and men of note were involved in it.

There is now more than adequate evidence, brought forth even by the Russian historians, to prove that Tilak was thinking of organising an armed revolt against British rule.

Yet the most thrilling revelation is the story of the diamonds which the Indian revolutionaries in Germany had secretly sent him. Without touching the diamonds, he sent them over to his lieutenant to be utilised for patriotic purposes, especially for undermining the loyalty of some of the important officers of the Maratha Infantry stationed at Belgaum.

In addition to the new material mentioned above, there is, some new information regarding Tilak's early school life, the Indian political institutions that existed in his student days and the questions asked in the British Parliament about his transportation.

The sub-title of this biography has been changed from 'Father of Our Freedom Struggle' to 'Father of the Indian Freedom Struggle'.

I express my gratitude to my readers and friends and the reviewers of my biographies, who all have encouraged me in my work. My debt of gratitude is to all the authors and publishers from whose works I have drawn excerpts.

My publisher's patriotic and sympathetic attitude towards national literature has played an important role in the production of my biographies. Without any exaggeration I should say that he deserves the praise of the readers and admirers and the author.

To V. D. Limaye, the printer, I am grateful for the personal interest he takes in the printing of my works.

— **Dhananjay Keer**

77, Bhageshwar Bhuvan
Near Shri Cinema
Bombay-16
January 21, 1969

PREFACE TO THE FIRST EDITION

As announced in 1954 in my biography of Dr. Ambedkar, I am presenting with great pleasure the life of Lokamanya Tilak. In his lifetime Tilak was a subject of bitter and long controversies. Now that the dust raised by those controversies has settled down and almost all the actors in the scene have departed this life, the time has arrived to study the life of this great man and to look at the events concerning his life, with an objective and dispassionate view.

I have tried in my usual way to keep the hero of the biography at the central place and have used history as the background against the picture. In conformity with the trends of modern biography I have selected out of the wealth of material only the most authentic information and facts, taking every care that the biography is not swollen with long, dull and unilluminating passages. And without violating the chronology of Tilak's life I have portrayed the evolution of his mind, the progress of his career and the impact of events and personalities on his mind. While thus fully delineating the development of his character and personality, I have also dealt with the various contributions he made in different fields of politics, journalism, philosophy and the national struggle for freedom. In short, this biography depicts all the lights and shades which mingled in the grand composition that the Lokamanya was.

Recently a few biographies have been published to commemorate the birth-centenary of Lokamanya Tilak. It is, however, felt that they are the refurbished versions of the older ones and have, as usual, subordinated the personality of Tilak to history. Besides, their perspective differs from mine. Most of them have, in their zeal to make Tilak and Gandhi appear alike, strained to shape Tilak in such a way as to fit him in Gandhian mood and methods. This is surely a great injustice to Tilak. It is history that Tilak, whose sole aim was to win back independence, cared more for the ends than for the means whereas Gandhi strove more after the purity than for the ends. That is why Tilak never condemned the revolutionaries using physical force against the British regime.

This biography differs from the foregoing biographies in another vital aspect. Some of them have made passing references to Tilak's social views while others are silent upon this point. This book alone has fully dealt with this aspect of Tilak's life in its proper perspective.

My humble opinion therefore is that this book provides a number of new points and facts, gives many fresh glimpses of Tilak's character, thoughts, and personality, and thus presents a truthful picture of the whole man, which is necessary to understand him rationally.

I am sincerely grateful to my friends who have gone through the manuscript, especially to Mr. Nissim Ezekiel. I am deeply indebted to Annarao Gothoskar for carefully reading the manuscript and the proofs. I am deeply indebted also to Bhide Guruji for minutely reading the manuscript and the proofs, and for his unfailing support to me in whatever literary work I undertake. I must gratefully mention here that but for the moral and active support of Appasaheb Tinaikar and Dr. S. D. Mujumdar my works would not have seen the light.

I acknowledge my debt to all the authors, journals and publishers from whose books and publications I have drawn excerpts. I am also thankful to the workers of the India Printing Works and its able proprietors for the excellent printing.

— **Dhananjay Keer**

Bhageshwar Bhuvan
Lady Hardinge Road
Mahim, Bombay 16
August 15, 1959

CONTENTS

Tilak's Ancestral Home in Chikhalgaon, District Ratnagiri

Tilak's Father,
Gangadharpant Ramchandra Tilak

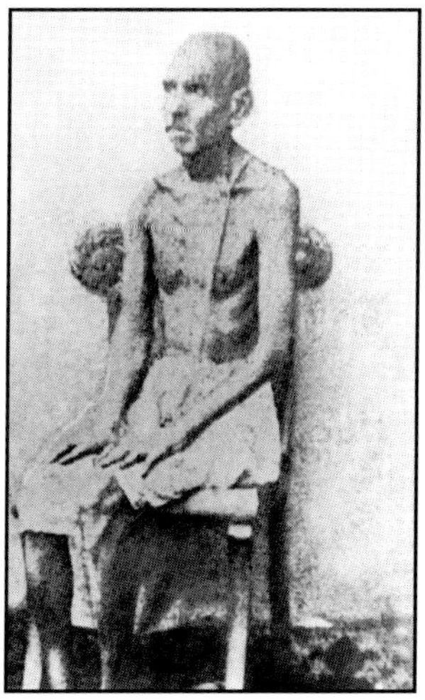

Tilak's Grandfather,
Ramchandra Keshav Tilak

Bal Gangadhar Tilak with
His Wife Satyabhamabai

Tilak Family: Sitting from L to R: Smt. Ramabai Vaidya (daughter),
Lokmanya Tilak with His Son B. Tilak, R. B. Tilak (son),
Smt. Satyabhamabai Tilak, Smt. Parvatibai Ketkar (daughter)
with her son A.V. Ketkar, Smt. Ramabai Sane (daughter)
Standing: Dhondopant Vidwans

Deccan College, Pune (1873)

New English School, Pune (new building)

Vinchurkarwada, Tilak's Residence and Kesari Office till 1905
Swami Vivekanand met Tilak in this house

Gaikwad Wada, purchased from Sayaji Rao, Maharaja of Baroda
Headquarters of Tilak's Freedom Movement and Office of the Kesari

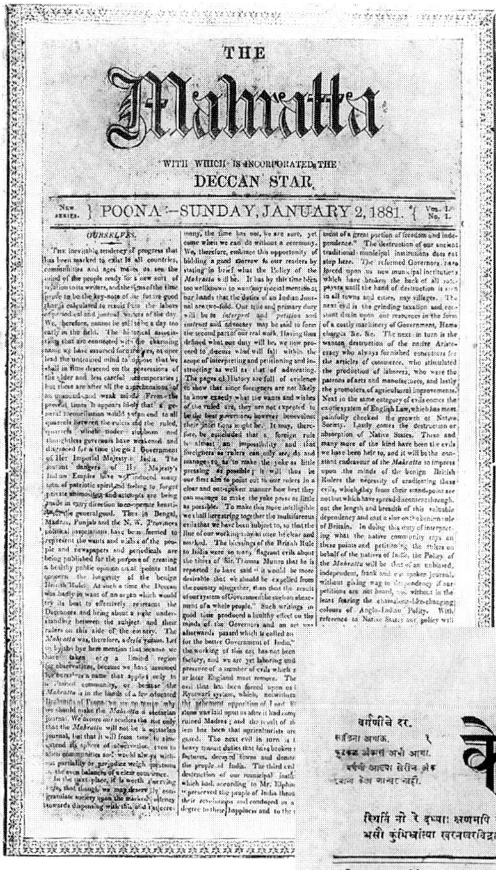

THE
Mahratta
WITH WHICH IS INCORPORATED THE
DECCAN STAR.
NEW SERIES. } POONA :—SUNDAY, JANUARY 2, 1881. { Vol. I. No. 1.
OURSELVES.

Mahratta, 1st issue
January 2, 1881
Editor: Bal Gangadhar Tilak

केसरी.
वर्ष १. पुणें:—मंगळवार तारीख ४ जानेवारी १८८१. अंक १.

Kesari, 1st issue
January 4, 1881
Editor: Gopal Ganesh Agarkar

Tilak addressing a meeting in connection with Ganeshotsav at Shantaram Chawl in Mumbai (1890)

Tilak busy in writing

Ganesh Shrikrishna alias
Dadasaheb Khaparde
Born: August 27, 1854. Death: July 1, 1938

Gopal Ganesh Agarkar
Born: July 24, 1856. Death: June 17, 1895

Indian National Congress, Surat, 1907
(Standing L to R): Dr. B. S. Munje, Ramaswamy, K K. Cooverji Desai
(Sitting on chair L to R): Sardar Ajit Singh, Arvind Ghosh, Tilak, Syed Hyder Reza
(Sitting on the ground L to R): Dadsaheb Khaparde, Ashwini Kumar

Babamaharaj Satarkar

Taimaharaj Satarkar

Tilak with Jagannath Maharaj Pandit

(L to R) Lala Lajpat Rai, Bal Gangadhar Tilak, Bipinchandra Pal
(Known as the triumvirate Lal-Bal-Pal)

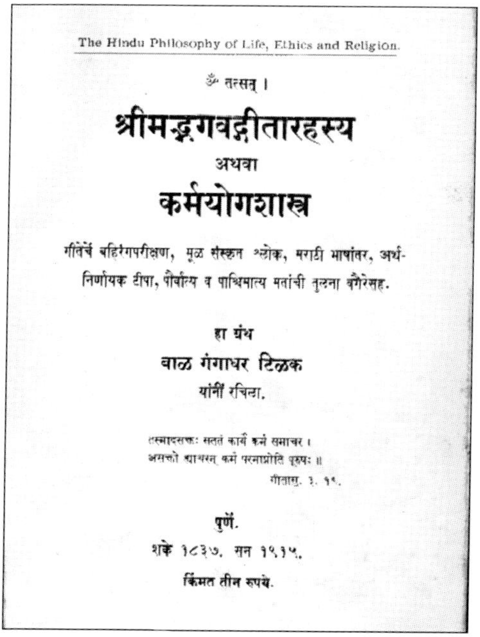

The Hindu Philosophy of Life, Ethics and Religion.

ॐ तत्सत् ।

श्रीमद्भगवद्गीतारहस्य

अथवा

कर्मयोगशास्त्र

गीतेचें बहिरंगपरीक्षण, मूळ संस्कृत श्लोक, मराठी भाषांतर, अर्थ-
निर्णायक टीपा, पौर्वात्य व पाश्चिमात्य मतांची तुलना वगैरेसह.

हा ग्रंथ

बाळ गंगाधर टिळक

यांनीं रचिला.

तस्मादसक्तः सततं कार्यं कर्म समाचर ।
असक्तो ह्याचरन् कर्म परमाप्नोति पूरुषः ॥
गीतासु. ३. १९.

पुणें.

शके १८३७, सन १९१५.

किंमत तीन रुपये.

Gitarahasya Manuscript

National Delegation to England
(L to R): N. C. Kelkar, Vithalbhai Patel, Dadasaheb Khaparde
Lokmanya Tilak, Dr. V. J. Mehta, Bipinchandra Pal

Tilak in England, 1918

Last Glimpse of Tilak

Tilak's Funeral Procession outside Sardar Griha,
Mumbai, August 1, 1920

बाळ गंगाधर टिळक

CHAPTER I

Childhood and Youth

I

THE TILAKS FORM one of the families belonging to the Chitpavan Brahmin community. The Chitpavan Brahmins are known as Konkanasthas because they hail from Konkan. During the seventeenth century some Brahmin families were oppressed by the Muslim Head of the Janjira State in Konkan, and so they moved to Satara to seek their fortune. From one of these families called Bhats sprang able and brave leaders known as the Peshwas, who transformed Poona into the political centre of India in the later half of the eighteenth century.

Ratnagiri is the nerve centre of Konkan, and is the chief town of Ratnagiri District. It had a population of 30,000 and has a port which is closed in the rainy season. Crowned with the ranges of the Sahyadri, the District is hilly and is the nursery of the famous Alphonso mangoes. Its sea-side is lined with tall, green coconut and betelnut trees. As the hilly region does not yield products other than intellect, mangoes, coconuts and mill-hands, neither the British Government nor the Swarajya Government thought it profitable to connect it to other parts of India with the railway. People living in this strip of land are sturdy and hardworking. They are peasants, artisans and fishermen. They wrest a hand-to-mouth existence from the sea, coconuts, mangoes and fragments of their tiny narrow rice fields. The hard brown shell of the coconut with its sweet copra and silver milk inside is symbolic of the character of these people. The roughness of the sea and the hardiness of the Sahyadri have rendered their life a constant, hard struggle, strengthened their bones, sharpened their brains, and kindled their ambitions.

A hundred years ago Ratnagiri had earned a niche for its Marathi, Sanskrit and English education in the educational world of Maharashtra. Another point worth noting about the place is that it is the home of the Chitpavan intelligentsia although their place of origin is supposed to be the part of the District surrounding Chiplun which is about sixty miles to the north of Ratnagiri.

The place of origin of the Tilaks is Chikhalgaon in the Dapoli Taluka of Ratnagiri District. The Tilaks, it seems, were not a family of much importance during Peshwa rule except that they held the Khoti rights of the village. Khoti was a 'Vatan' granted by ancient kings to persons who either had taken a pioneering part in colonisation or had brought fallow land under cultivation. The Khots carried on the administration, collected the land taxes in their villages, and paid them to the Government treasury. The Tilaks belonged to one such leading family in the village. However, there are some documents to show that a certain Dhondopant Tilak fought in the battle of Panipat in 1761, and, while escaping as a fugitive from the debacle, died in Central India on his way home.

This soldier had three brothers at Chikhalgaon. One of them was called Krishnaji, who had a son named Keshavrao. Born in 1778, Keshavrao was a skilful rider, a gifted marksman, a fine swimmer and an expert cook. A man of ready pen, he rose, during the last days of Peshwa rule, by his ceaseless efforts and inflexible determination to the position of the Mamlatdar of Anjanwel near Dabhol. With the end of Peshwa rule in 1818, he threw up the post and spent the rest of his life at Chikhalgaon in virtual retirement.

By his first wife, Keshavrao had two sons, Ramchandra and Kashinath. The eldest son Ramchandra, with what little education he had, took service as a surveyor under the new British regime. His marriage took place, as was the custom in those days, at an early age, and he had a son in 1820 when he was hardly twenty. This son Gangadhar, he left to the care of his father, as he himself was required to be on duty away from his native place. Gangadhar learnt the rudiments of Marathi from his grandfather, and a few days later he was sent to school at Dabhol. After completing his studies in that primary school, the boy took the road to Poona to prosecute further studies on his own account and responsibility. This resolution made by the young boy to go up a hundred miles partly on foot and partly in a bullock cart, illustrates an unbending mind, an ambitious nature and an untiring industry.

While Gangadhar was thus striving to receive an English education in Poona at a school kept by one Mr. Bhavalkar, his mother, Ramabai, who was on her way to pilgrimage to Nasik, a holy city in Maharashtra, came to Poona to get a glimpse of her son. She left for Nasik, but died of cholera before reaching the place of pilgrimage. Ramchandra was totally upset by this calamity. He got his daughter Durga married to a youth from a certain Joglekar family of Karanjani in Dapoli Taluka, and leaving his two sons Gangadhar and Govind, he went to Chitrakut in the Banda District of Uttar Pradesh where the family of the brother of Bajirao II lived.

This sad event changed the course of Gangadhar's life. He gave up his education and returned to his native place. He married a girl from the family of one Mr. Achwal. The problems of and difficulties about the Khoti rights worried him considerably. Realising that the income from the Khoti would not be much helpful in the maintenance of his family, he accepted in November 1841 the post of a teacher in a Marathi Primary School at Malvan on a salary of Rs. 10 a month. Malvan is a small town at the southern end of the Ratnagiri District. Thence, he was transferred to Chiplun on a salary of Rs. 15 a month. In those days, the teachers took deep interest in their noble profession. They laboured hard and conducted their classes to the best advantage of the pupils, imbuing them with a desire to acquire knowledge by the active exercise of their own faculties.

Finally, Gangadharpant was posted to Ratnagiri on a monthly salary of Rs. 20 as Headmaster of the Marathi School. In the meanwhile his father had left the service of the Peshwa family. So he supported his father by sending money regularly to him at Banaras. Gangadharpant could maintain his family on such a low income without much difficulty because in those days living was cheap. One could get rice at one rupee a maund.

II

GANGADHARPANT WAS AN orthodox Brahmin, devoted to rigid performance of religious rites and observances. His wife Parvatibai, too, was intensely religious. She had grown weaker and more delicate. She had three daughters Kashi, Ambu and Awada. She was sorely disappointed in the birth of three daughters in succession, of whom the first was already married. So she took, at the instance of one Narmadabai Soman, to rigid observances and profound worship of the Sun god. A typical Hindu mother, she longed to have a son and intensified her prayers and penance in spite of her failing health. At last, on undergoing the Sunday fasts and observances for over a year, she gave birth to a son on July 23, 1856, in Gore's house at the middle alley in Ratnagiri, about nine months before the War of Independence of 1857. After the birth of the child, both the mother and the baby were unconscious. A few minutes later she regained consciousness and the child also gave its first cry after fifteen minutes. Gangadharpant, who was very anxious to know the result, was told by the superstitious ladies in the house that the new-born was a girl. Terribly disappointed at this result, he angrily exclaimed that if it were a girl she should be thrown on the dunghill.[1] At this, his eldest daughter ran to him and whispered that it was a son and not a daughter!

The new-born was weak in health. His legs were flaccid; his head was somewhat flabby. On the sixth day it was declared that Parvatibai had a son. He was named Keshav after the name of the family deity or perhaps after his great-grandfather, who had passed away that year. His sister called him Bal, and later he was known as Balwantrao, his cradle name being altogether dropped somewhere in the primary school.

Gangadharpant was now Headmaster of the Marathi School at Ratnagiri. Industrious, stern, aspiring and self-respecting, he had acquired the habits of strict economy and reasonable liberality. He helped deserving students and kept one or two at his house. The warmth of his hospitality extended to his guests and relatives. What is more, he had not given up his studies though he had left school long before. Undeterred by the anxiety for the maintenance of his household with the meagre salary he earned as teacher, and the responsibility attached to his post, he continued his studies at home, not for the sake of mere promotion but for the love of knowledge. He was an example of the axiom that the best part of every man's education is that which he himself acquires; for, knowledge acquired by labour becomes a possession. By his indomitable perseverance Gangadharpant gained a remarkable mastery over the Marathi and Sanskrit languages and also over Mathematics. He was known as Nana and was respected as Guruji. People also called him Shastri. The collector used to call him a treasury of clerks. He had written a book on Trigonometry for which he received a prize from the Director of Public Instruction, who arranged also for the purchase of two hundred copies of the book. He wrote a Marathi Grammar which continued as a prescribed text-book until 1877.

However, Gangadharpant got into trouble on account of the Trigonometry book. A disciple of his, who was now serving as his assistant

1 Guruji, K. A., *Life of Lokamanya Bal Gangadhar Tilak,* p. 24 (Marathi).

at Ratnagiri Marathi School, wrote to the Director that he should get half of the prize as Gangadhar Tilak's book was not original but was a translation of an English book which had been translated for Tilak by him. But the jealousy was discovered and he was silenced. Later, when this disciple-teacher was imprisoned for his article on ' Nanasaheb Peshwa' during the 1857 War, Gangadharpant interviewed the Collector of Ratnagiri, explained to him his disciple's thoughtless behaviour, and procured his release. Overwhelmed with gratitude, the disciple fell at his Guru's feet!

Meanwhile, Ramchandra, who had gone to Banaras, wandered there in search of a Guru. No Guru would initiate him into the fold of hermits. Those were the days of the revolt of 1857 and Government, which was bent on suppressing it, had passed strict orders that no mutineer should escape under one or other pretext or under the garb of a hermit. Maybe he thought it his duty to catch the last glimpse of his home, or maybe with a desire to secure an eligibility certificate, Ramchandra came back to Ratnagiri where his son was serving, and was mightily pleased to see the grandson.

Parvatibai's health had now completely broken down. She gave up her rigorous worship of the Sun god after a due fulfilment of the vow.

Bal was now two years old. He had not put on much flesh as yet. By constitution he was lean and weak, by complexion swarthy, and his look was simple but intelligent. He was outspoken and obdurate. He pulled out the books of his father's wards, tore their notebooks, and soiled their slates with urine. Bal now found a new playmate in his grandfather. He bathed with him, he prayed with him; and he sang songs with him. He dabbed his forehead as his grandfather did and took meals with him. Sometimes Bal showed signs of his obdurate disposition. On the day of changing the thread, he would not allow the thread to be taken out which his grandfather had put on him to please his infant fancy. A person who has not undergone a thread ceremony cannot wear it and cannot have his meals with the thread on. Bal was offered sweets and was given other little promises, but he would not allow anybody to touch the thread on his body. He exasperated all. Enraged at this Gangadharpant slapped him and threw away the thread. Bal's sobbing echoed for hours. As he grew up Bal enjoyed himself in his pranks. He shook his mother's head, stroked his sister's face, and hung upon the neck of the Kunbi maid -servant Rukmini. He pulled the tails of calves and made them gallop!

An educationist and a disciplinarian, Gangadharpant naturally wished to give his son a scholarly grounding in his early childhood. He taught him some songs and poems which the child recited even near the lavatory when his father could hear him from inside! He taught him some simple arithmetical problems and rules of grammar and made him recite short Marathi poems and Sanskrit verses. He also took him to listen to the stories from the *Mahabharata* related in his discourse by a priest in a temple nearby.

When Bal was six, he was sent to school in Ratnagiri in October 1861. The servant, who accompanied him to the school, was strictly prohibited from carrying Bal on his shoulders to the school. Attendance at school was very strict. Bal could not play truant. One morning he avoided going to school after enjoying a two-day holiday. When he went to the school in the afternoon, his Guruji, Bhikaji Krishna Patwardhan, who was afraid of incurring the displeasure of Gangadharpant if he let off Bal without punishment, beat him soundly. Under the attentive eye of his father Bal made good progress, which was precocious for his age. Even the priests, who performed his thread ceremony in 1864, were astonished to note his progress and the priest Harshastri Sathe remarked that he would be like the *Karanik* * in the *Guru Puran*. At this Gangadharpant bowed in reverence to God and said the priest's prophecy might come true. The father, however, added with a smile that he would have to labour a little more to make the idol perfect.

About this time Gangadharpant came in contact with Mr. Arthur Crawford, who was then the District Collector of Ratnagiri. Because of his sparing habits Gangadharpant had money enough to lend at interest. Crawford persuaded him to invest some money in the Saw-Mill Company which he proposed to start at Ratnagiri for the benefit of the poor classes. Crawford's was a very charming personality with a sweet flowing tongue. He was a grand spendthrift and an able administrator with very irregular habits. Yet at times he worked at his office with a marvellous tenacity. For some time the saw-mill prospered, and in one year a dividend of 9% was paid to the shareholders.

Gangadharpant belonged to the orthodox school of thought and a little breach of conduct on the part of his friends or relatives or a little departure from religious observances would badly upset him. Those were the days when a person using socks was cursed as an infidel and the orthodox used to take a bath on their return home from office to wipe away the

---

* Karanik = Chief Minister

pollution contracted by contact with persons of other religions and their co-religionists from the lower classes. Such a breach of conduct on the part of a friend worried him a great deal, when Gangadharpant read the shocking news that Rao Saheb Mandlik had received a bouquet at the hands of a Christian at the end of a meeting in Bombay. Mandlik was then a well-known public figure in the Bombay Presidency. Mortified at this news Gangadharpant wrote to him expressing his firm belief that the report was false and wished him to prosecute the newspapers that had published it. Mandlik simply replied that he attached no importance to such reports.

Gangadharpant was strictly methodical and regular in his work. As he could not tolerate any deviations from his mode and methods of instruction or turn away from his experience in the school, he sometimes expressed disagreement with the inspecting officers on the spot. This challenging attitude brought him into clash with Madhavrao Barve, the then Deputy Educational Inspector, who afterwards became the Dewan of Kolhapur. There were frequent clashes and also exchanges of harsh words in official correspondence. Once Gangadharpant's superiors asked him to secure an undertaking from his assistant teachers to the effect that they would not leave the service. He got their signatures on the bond; but in his forwarding letter he remarked that the service conditions and pay scales, under which the teachers were made to work, were worse than the conditions of the Negroes in Africa. For such quips he was suppressed and his juniors were allowed to supersede him.

Gangadharpant had now served for over twenty-three years with patience and unswerving conscientiousness. In a letter written to Rao Saheb Mandlik he lamented the fact that during his service of the past ten years he had enjoyed leave for only three months. He knew no holiday, rest, excursions or vacation. Duty had been his sole friend and he had been toiling like a coolie! His meritorious work was, however, finally appreciated by his superiors, and he was promoted to the post of Assistant Deputy Educational Inspector at Poona and he joined the appointment[2] at the end of June 1865.

On the eve of his departure for Poona, friends in Ratnagiri held farewell parties in honour of Gangadharpant. At one of the functions no less a dignitary than R. G. Bhandarkar, who had been appointed Headmaster[3] of

2 *Report of the Director of Public Instruction 1865-66*, Appendix A, p. 4.

3. *Report of the Director of Public Instruction 1865-66.*

the Ratnagiri High School at the beginning of the official year 1865-66, was invited to preside. Paying a glowing tribute to his friend for his high qualities such as erudition, originality, generosity, and independence of mind, Bhandarkar said that in the transfer of Gangadharpant, Ratnagiri had lost a repository of Marathi, a master of Grammar and Mathematics, and an exemplary teacher. Gangadharpant took his family to Poona towards the middle of October 1865, for his son seems to have studied in the Marathi School at Ratnagiri till October 10, 1865.[4] His father Ramchandra had left for Banaras a few days earlier.

This was a well-deserved promotion, a change for the better. Financially, he was in good circumstances, and from the viewpoint of the well-being of his son he was now in a city which was the intellectual centre of Maharashtra. No other place in India was more surcharged with the spirit of ancient works and echoes of the holy scriptures, and pulsated more strongly with studies in grammar and logic than the city of Poona. In those days, Poona was also developing into a centre of modern literature and science.

III

Favoured with the unique opportunity for educating his son on proper lines, Gangadharpant had his son admitted to a Marathi School in Poona. It was not far from his residence at Gadrewada near Tulsibag. Bal wore a short dhoti, a folding cap with a tuft on it, and an old-fashioned garment with strings. Everything went well with the family for some time and suddenly a sad event disturbed it. Bal's mother could not survive long to see his intellectual progress. Long periods of fasting and the rigours of asceticism had reduced her to a skeleton, and she at last died on July 24, 1866. There after, Bal was brought up by his aunt. Older than Bal by fifteen years, Govindrao, his uncle, had spent most of his life in the country. With the little schooling he had, he had worked at first as a teacher at a school in Konkan and was now a teacher at a Marathi School in Poona. The Khoti income the family received had, after having been divided into different family branches, now dwindled into a paltry pittance. The Khoti land inherited by Bal's father was assessed at Rs. 8-9-0 and the other land owned by him was assessed at Re. 1-8-0.

4 Admission Register of the school at Ratnagiri.

Bal was now about to complete his primary education. His knowledge was far advanced. He had to brush up some lessons here and there. His food was as simple as his dress! He took only boiled rice with ghee or curds. But with all this simple life and advanced studies of Bal, the class-teacher found him rather a stubborn boy. An incident took place that revealed his strength of mind.

One day some boys ate roasted ground-nuts in the absence of the class-teacher and threw the husks on the floor. The sight of the husks made the class teacher angry. He said that those who had eaten the ground-nuts should sweep the floor. Most of the culprits obeyed but they did not clean the space near Bal's seat. The teacher asked him to clear away the husks near his seat but he pertly refused to do so as he had not eaten ground-nuts. The teacher said that whatever might be the facts, as the husks were near his seat he must clear up the space. But Bal would not obey. Enraged at this seemingly impudent gesture of Bal, the teacher roared that Bal might be the son of an influential man, but he must behave in the class as a student, otherwise he should get out. Saying so, he took up the cane, but instantly Bal, too, took up his satchel and went straight home. On inquiry the class-teacher learnt from Gangadharpant that his son had not been supplied with ground-nuts nor was he in the habit of eating outside the house.

Bal joined the City School where he completed three standards in two years. There too an occasion for friction with a teacher arose when he wrote the Sanskrit word " Sant" in three different ways. The teacher treated the first version as correct and the other two as incorrect. Bal insisted that all the three versions were correct. This led to a hot quarrel and the matter was referred immediately by Bal to the Headmaster, who expressed his opinion in favour of Bal. The decision set his mind at rest. It was not that he was not amenable to discipline. As his studies were comparatively advanced in the free atmosphere of home life, he did not conform to the rigid formalities of class work. Perhaps he could not come across anything worth noting in the class.

If the class-teacher set a problem in arithmetic, he would do it mentally and write down the answer on the slate. If the teacher asked the boys to use slates, Bal questioned the necessity for it. However, it became known to the teachers that Bal was a brilliant, independent, and promising student, but he was rather quarrelsome and obstinate.

Bal then joined the Poona High School. He could not easily fit in with the routine work of the school and had occasional clashes with his teachers.

He was weak by constitution and showed signs of a stubborn will. His eyes gleamed and his head was full of hairless patches made by scabbies. His strong sense of independence, his shining intellect, and the inborn stubbornness, however, challenged the little world of the teachers. He would not go to the black-board at the teacher's bidding to solve a problem mechanically. Instead, he answered it straightway. In Bal's opinion the history of India written by Morrison was a biased one!

An incident occurred which must have confirmed the opinion of the teachers that Bal was by nature a tough fighter. This time he had a tussle with his Sanskrit teacher. Mr. Jacob, the Headmaster, who was a strict disciplinarian, decided the issue in favour of the teacher. Consequently, Bal bade good-bye to the school and joined another. He returned to this school after Kunte succeeded Jacob. Meantime he studied at the school conducted by one Mr. Baba Gokhale. These were brief rehearsals of the great battles the boy was destined to fight in future with the authorities and the long-drawn litigations he was to face with unbending will-power.

Thus the little rebel asserted himself in the school world against its rigid and mechanical routine. His opinion of the Government was also taking shape at this early age. Once while he was taking an evening walk in company with his friends, they struck down some mangoes from a tree. The watchman of the mango-grove chastised them. Thereupon Bal asked him quietly the name of the owner of the grove. He replied that it belonged to Government. Thereupon Bal exclaimed that then it belonged to the public! This intelligent answer would not satisfy the watchman. In the end they passed over a coin to him. While parting, Bal remarked: "But do not pay this to the Government!"

Bal's father did not feel happy in his new post. Serious, stern and irascible by temperament, he came into conflict with the Deputy Educational Inspector, who was also a Brahmin by name Sitarampant Patwardhan. Gangadharpant applied for a transfer to Thana. Shortly afterwards he was again posted back to Poona. Owing to his strong sense of independence he could not get on well with Patwardhan, his immediate superior. It was said that as an officer Patwardhan was strict and overbearing whereas Gangadharpant was less strict and more favourably inclined to his subordinates.

In spite of his father's transfer, Bal's progress in his studies was very satisfactory. He believed in self-help. It was his watchword. He hated over-guardianship or over-drilling in the class. Whatever he did, he did it thoroughly. He never crammed notes, but mastered his lessons. From his boyhood a peculiar bent of his mind was noticeable. It was always to attempt the most difficult. He never solved simple problems from mathematics papers. He treated simple questions as child's play. That is why he could not shine in the first rank in the class. He never cared much for it although he must have aspired to it. Eagles never vie with parrots! Routine work and daily composition were not the things to his liking. He loved thinking more than writing. He put his pen to paper only when it was unavoidable. His memory was developing the qualities of a photographic film!

When Bal was in Std. VI in 1871, his father settled his marriage in consultation with his grandfather who was still alive at Banaras. Seventy years ago, most of the boys in the upper classes of a high school and even some boys in primary schools, were married and a few of the high school students were already fathers. An unmarried college student was an unusual occurrence. Gangadharpant was now in need of money, and so he thought it a good opportunity to get some money out of his investments in the Saw-Mill Company at Ratnagiri. In an appealing letter he wrote to Arthur Crawford that he had settled the marriage of his son and as the day of the marriage was drawing near, he urged him to be kind enough to remit him at least Rs. 800 on receipt of the letter. Crawford by then had risen to the post of the Municipal Commissioner of Bombay. A few months earlier he had informed all the shareholders of the Saw-Mill Company that the Company was irreparably involved in a loss amounting to Rs. 24,000. He also tried to graft the company on a Government scheme, but failed. So Crawford could do nothing in the matter. This meant that Gangadharpant had lost his hard-earned money.

Thus, Madhavrao Barve was the first official and Crawford was the second who had troubled Bal's father and it was a freak of destiny that a decade later Bal also should come in collision with them.

Bal's marriage was performed at Chikhalgaon. The bride's name was Tapi. She was ten years old. Her father's family lived at Ladghar, a village about ten miles from Chikhalgaon. Both the bride and the bridegroom were motherless. The surname of the bride's family was Mahajan but they were called Bals. They were a family well known in their village for hospitality and religious charities. Once a gold trinket was found in the grain brought for a beggar, and the head of the family insisted upon giving the article to the beggar. It is said that the bridegroom preferred good books to a gold ring as a present from Ballalrao, his father-in-law. And the father-in-law fulfilled the desire of his son-in-law. The bride was rather well-built and looked stouter than the bridegroom. She was renamed Satyabhama. The weaker constitution of Balwantrao became the butt of his class-mates and colleagues.

Bal passed his annual examination and entered the Matric class. Seven months later, Bal was deprived of the paternal shelter also. Gangadharpant was taken ill and on August 31, 1871, he died of dropsy in Poona. He had done everything he could for his son and set him properly on the journey of life. In his Will he had divided his property between his son and his brother. He had bequeathed Rs. 5,000 to his son and about Rs. 2,500 to his brother and appointed his brother the executor of his estate till his son attained majority. Considering the time and place, this was not a poor patrimony.

Left without parents, Bal continued to study as before. Nobody was now required to guide him. He passed his matriculation examination of Bombay University in December 1872. As usual he could not win any distinction in the examination, for he never studied with a view to scoring high marks. Among the other successful candidates were Behramji Malbari, Nanasaheb Deshmukh, Krishnarao Sharangapani, Dadasaheb Khaparde and others.

CHAPTER II

Aims and Ideals

BALWANTRAO JOINED DECCAN College in Poona and six months later became a resident student. His girl-wife stayed at his uncle's in Poona. The same year G. S. Khaparde, D. A. Khare and V. S. Apte also joined the college. It was the only college in Maharashtra outside Bombay. The first thing Balwantrao did after joining the college was to improve his health. Health is the basis of all success in life. So he took assiduously to physical exercise and went in for all sorts of exercises. He had no love for British games like cricket and tennis. He spent his mornings in the gymnasium doing exercises such as wrestling, boating or swimming and spent his evenings in other outdoor games. For the whole year these exercises had become his pastime.

Tilak had a genius for swimming. It was his favourite practice to float in water for hours together, keeping a loaf of bread in his hands entirely dry. His love for swimming sometimes overflowed even in old age when he saw young men struggling to master swimming or when, once in a blue moon he snatched a moment out of his crowded life to have a dip. During one of his later-day visits to Banaras, he once swam across the Ganges. At Sinhagad, during his restful days, he sometimes taught young men swimming by taking a series of somersaults himself and explained to them the trick of it. They were astonished at his excellence in the sport.

At the gymnasium he wrestled with Daji Abaji Khare with whom he had formed at this time a lasting friendship. They strove with each other till either of them bore the palm. At table their competition often ended in finishing almost all the dishes in the kitchen of the college club. Prior to this, Balwantrao's food consisted of rice, ghee and dal. Now the menu broadened into dishes prepared from wheat, grain and other cereals, plenty of milk and fresh vegetables. His appetite was so much stimulated that when he went to Bombay for some time for his studies the owner of the boarding-house told him that if he were required to provide one man with so much food he would have to close down his boarding-house!

There is one point worth noting about the mess-room. When Balwantrao took his meals he wore silken sacred dhoti in an orthodox manner. His love for this silken dhoti was so over-powering that when after five years he again stayed for his studies in the Deccan College residency he became a member of the sacred club where meals were taken in this orthodox manner. In later life even in the extreme cold of December he doggedly took his meals in this orthodox style during the days of the Lahore and Banaras sessions of the Congress. If anybody ridiculed the idea, he hotly argued that the practice was observed for the preservation of the traditions, and he added that there was no harm in doing it since Europeans too wore a particular dress when they had dinner.

During the first year, studies thus did not occupy much of his time. Balwantrao attended lessons worth listening to, but generally after the roll-call he deserted the lecture-room. One day, caught by the Principal while playing truant, he straightway replied that he was not going to appear that year for the examination. Neither was there any change in the method of his study. He read for acquiring knowledge and whatever subject he touched he digested thoroughly. That does not mean that like Vishnushastri Chiplunkar, he neglected his text-books. He had a great liking for the classical literature of India and he waded through it to his heart's content. Asked by Franz Kielhorn, Professor of Sanskrit, why he did not attend the Sanskrit lectures, he quietly replied that his professor had nothing to add to his knowledge! While he was studying in the college, one Mr. G. W. Forrest was appointed Professor of History and Political Economy. Forrest subsequently taught Mathematics, but turned out to be a poor mathematician. The students therefore clamoured for a change. They made a representation to the Principal, all putting their signatures to it in a circle so that the Principal might not be able to detect the ring leader. Balwantrao and Khare were the inventors of this artifice!

Balwantrao failed in his First year Arts Examination in 1874, but he succeeded in changing his physique beyond recognition. The foundations of sound health so essential to any political leader in his stormy life were thus laid by Balwantrao in one year devoted to physical exercise. When he entered the college he was a lean, spare figure with twinkling eyes and a massive head shaven to the back where the hair grew in a long black tuft.

With his large, round, red turban, flowing long coat with strings and the red Deccani shoes, Balwantrao was now a fine figure, robust, well-built, energetic and healthy. Sometimes he wore a special shirt with buttons on the shoulders, which kept it tight on the chest. He used this shirt at the time of taking bar exercises. At times he was found wearing a dhoti only, his body bare above the waist.

Balwantrao often indulged in innocent pranks in his college days. Those of his friends who were delicate in health and fashionable in dress were his special targets. He forced them to take open air exercise. He undid their cosy beds and threw away their patent medicines and toilet sets; he locked their rooms from inside and jumped out over the walls. One night during a discussion on historical topics, they asked one another how they would disappear at that very moment if occasion arose. Everyone scratched his head but in the twinkling of an eye Balwantrao jumped out of the window! His colleagues ran down to see if he had broken his ribs and legs! To their amazement they saw him coming upstairs in his usual gait! Because of these interesting pranks and harmless mischief his companions called him 'Devil', and for his dissecting bluntness and smashing directness in speech and action they had nicknamed him 'Mr. Blunt' which was the name of a character in Sir Walter Scott's *Kenilworth*.

In the second year Balwantrao turned his attention to his studies. He pored over choice books in Sanskrit and Marathi, and important books on History, Astronomy, Anatomy and Physiology. His method of reading was different from that of ordinary students. Reading is the royal road to intellectual eminence. His knowledge gave him power of thinking and equipped his mind with the greatest intellectual energy of his times. It fitted him for the role he was destined to play so heroically.

Another point worth noting about his reading was that he did not accept anything as established. Whatever he read, he first weighed, scanned, dissected and then digested thoroughly. His thirst for experimental knowledge also was insatiable. He brought once into his study at home a bull's head and heart for study. As far as possible he did not make notes, but when he did so it was to understand the kernel of a very hard question or a very difficult subject. And so carefully were these references treasured by him that later in life when men of learning, priests, essayists, doctors, or authors approached him for his opinion on their works or for the solution to their doubts and difficulties, he readily suggested improvements, or corrections. If any further proof was required, he would step into his study and produce a tattered old note from one of his treasured books or from one of his exercise books as if he had kept it only a day or two earlier. The visitors would marvel at his prodigious memory. On these profound and varied studies rested the foundations of his future volcanic and varied journalism and the fame of his myriad-sided personality.

II

TWO PROFESSORS IMPRESSED Balwantrao with their learning and character. They were Principal William Wordsworth and Professor Kero Laxman Chhatre. William Wordsworth was Principal from 1862 to 1874. He was the grandson of the famous English poet Wordsworth. He belonged to the old school of liberalism and had faith in education and belief in progress. He was devoted to learning and was quite unmindful of his dress. He was kind-hearted and helped students; but when they failed to answer his questions in the class-room, he sometimes abused them in language neither measured nor dignified. He was later transferred to Bombay as Principal of Elphinstone College. Balwantrao held him in high esteem. A self-educated and self-made man, Chhatre was professor of mathematics, and although not a graduate, he was raised to the position of acting Principal of the college during the absence of Oxenham. Chhatre was an embodiment of plain living and high thinking. He was simple, sympathetic, unassuming, and in his homely presence every student felt assured. He was a mathematician of repute and was a recognised authority on astronomy.

There was another gentleman by name Jinsiwale, who worked as a Fellow in the college. He was known as a walking encyclopaedia. He insisted that students should take down notes of his valuable lectures which were a feast of knowledge to students other than Balwantrao. So he did not take down notes. This indifference on the part of Balwantrao angered Jinsiwale. But Balwantrao proved his worth when R. B. Pendse, a Fellow, who taught Sanskrit, asked his students to compose a poem on a mother's sorrow. Balwantrao composed one. The depth and originality in his poem surpassed the poems submitted by his classmates among whom were reputed scholars like Vaman Shivram Apte. Although he wrote some poems, Balwantrao was no poet. His nature did not favour poetry, and music left him cold.

Balwantrao's proficiency in mathematics and Sanskrit became known to all in Deccan College. His striking originality and compendious methods were noted with pride by Chhatre. He predicted with confidence that Balwantrao would keep up his reputation. When teachers or professors came to Chhatre for solutions of knotty problems, the old professor directed them to his disciple saying that Balwantrao would cut the Gordian knot. And indeed he would do it in his terse way.

Balwantrao studied for one term at Elphinstone College, Bombay, in 1875. William Wordsworth was then the Principal of the College. Hawthornwaite, Professor of Mathematics, one day gave Balwantrao some knotty problems from the Cambridge journal and to his surprise he solved them all. His method at once impressed the professor. He frankly admitted that he never thought that Tilak would be able to solve them all in such an original manner. Hawthornwaite, however, could not get credit for the proficiency of Balwantrao when he heard the latter's displeasing remark that he was a disciple of Professor Chhatre. Balwantrao did not feel interested in the atmosphere of Elphinstone College, and he returned to Poona during the second term.

Although Balwantrao was revolving patriotic thoughts in his mind, he never showed or tolerated any emotional extravagance in those days. A college youth full of patriotic exuberance one day trampled upon the picture of the Queen-Empress of Britain and expected Balwantrao's approval and appreciation of his patriotic deed. He chastised the flamboyant patriot saying that instead of displaying his love of freedom in an unworthy manner the student-patriot should, like Sadashivrao Bhau who hammered the Mogul throne, cherish an ambition to hammer the throne of England, or at least he should work keeping such a goal constantly before his mind.

Another characteristic of Balwantrao was noted by his friends. He was a queer blend of softness and hardness of heart. When a student friend, whom he had nursed with the loving care of a mother, died and one of his legs dropped down from the pyre, Balwantrao, to the embarrassment of his colleagues, cut it up and threw the pieces into the blazing pyre! Balwantrao did his First B.A. in 1875, and appeared in 1876 for the B.A. Examination of Bombay University from Deccan College, Poona, passing in the first class. He then turned his attention to Law. As he was not enamoured of Government service, he thought the profession of a lawyer would enable him to lead an independent life. The roaring practice and good name of the Bombay leader, Rao Saheb Mandlik, was an example before him. Mandlik was a friend of his father and was on cordial terms with the Tilak family. Balwantrao had continued to make courtesy calls on Mandlik even after his father's death.

Tilak's independent and self-respecting mind was deeply influenced by the tremor of revolt through which Maharashtra was passing in those days. The Sarvajanik Sabha, which was founded at Poona by Ganesh Wasudeo Joshi and Sadashivrao Govande on April 2, 1870, had begun its work under the guiding spirit of Mahadev Govind Ranade. It had daringly arranged in 1875 for the defence of Malharrao Gaikwad, the Maharaja of Baroda, who was threatened with deposition on a charge of poisoning the British Agent. The petitions and memorials on public grievances addressed by Ranade to the British Government and the Queen-Empress through this Sabha, and the public and patriotic activities of Joshi, popularly known as Public Uncle—Sarvajanik Kaka—were not less encouraging. This Sarvajanik Kaka was the first leader to take the vow of Swadeshi and propagate its use; and he had been practising it himself since 1869. The dhoti, the long flowing coat and the turban he wore, were all made of home-spun cloth. He once saved the lawyers of Surat from the wrath of Government. He had also offered his services to the Government of India on the eve of the Afghan War, apprising Lord Lytton of his desire to lead a Peace Mission to Afghanistan.

The Sarvajanik Sabha, however, was not the first political institution in Poona. Early in the year 1852 Poona had established its first political institution called the Deccan Association. It was mostly dominated by sardars, jagirdars and patriotic young men. Their aim was to represent the grievances of Indian people to the authorities in England. But the patriotic men were in government service and on their transfer the Association died within four months. Another political institution called the Poona Association was founded in 1867, but it had ended its life without much stir, giving place to the Sarvajanik Sabha. In Bombay the Bombay leaders, Jagannath Shankarshett, Dr. Bhau Daji Lad, Naoroji Furdoonji and Dadabhai Naoroji had formed the Bombay Association on August 26, 1852, to represent the demands of Indian people to authorities in England and India and to work in collaboration with similar organizations at Calcutta and Madras. Much later Dadabhai Naoroji founded on May 22, 1869, in Bombay another political institution called the Bombay Branch of the East India Association.

Tilak applied himself for two years to the study of Law. His preparation for the LL.B. examination was not confined to text-books only. He studied almost all the Smritis. This study armed him with powerful arguments and this knowledge proved useful to him when, a few years after, he entered the social reform controversy with eminent authorities on Hindu Scriptures and Hindu Law like Bhandarkar, Ranade and Telang. Well has it been said that study with thought is a power whereas thought without study is perilous or powerless.

While Tilak was for some months staying at the residency of Deccan College preparing for the LL.B. examination, he met Gopal Ganesh Agarkar, who was then studying for the M.A. in Deccan College. He was a student of moral philosophy and logic and had lost his faith in religion. The works of Spencer and Mill had tremendously influenced his mind. One of the leading men of thought of his generation, Agarkar had almost completed his university education, struggling with dire penury and encountering crushing misery from his earliest years. In his boyhood he pounded drugs, did some other odd jobs to support himself, and trotted miles and over hills in search of support for his education. While at college he could not afford to have two shirts at a time. The one he had, he used to wash in the night and wear in the daytime. Subsisting upon little subscriptions, scholarships, prizes and the earnings of his pen, he took the B.A. degree in 1878 through the same college.

But no sooner did Agarkar obtain the degree than he wrote to his mother that she might be expecting her son to become an M.A. and to bring in wealth, but she should not expect much of him by way of money and ease. He had decided, he added, to turn his back upon money and happiness and to dedicate his life to the uplift of his countrymen. He told his maternal uncle about his future plan of starting a college; the latter jeered at him and laughed away the idea! Agarkar told him that Shivaji's ambition to free Maharashtra from Muslim domination was likewise ridiculed by his compatriots as a mad venture. And true to his aim Agarkar soon stood out as one of the founders of a college and rose to the position of its Principalship.

Just at this time Wasudeo Balwant Phadke had risen, with the help of Ramoshis and Bhills, in armed revolt against British rule. His revolt rocked Maharashtra to its bottom from March to May 1879 and struck terror into the hearts of the British rulers. The news of his revolt thrilled the Indian and European newspapers. For some time Tilak had attended the athletic classes of Phadke, who had been, four or five years prior to his revolt, striving to infuse the military spirit in Poona youth. One of Tilak's relations had participated in the revolt of Phadke. Naturally Phadke's revolutionary deeds, the failure of his armed revolt, and his arrest in the last week of July

1879, must have tremendously influenced the strong minds and patriotic souls of Tilak and Agarkar and ignited the flame of patriotism in their minds that were independently pondering over the deplorable state to which their country had been reduced by foreign rule.

Men of like views gather together. When Tilak and Agarkar knew each other's mettle and mind they discussed as to what should be done for the uplift of their countrymen. It was Agarkar's belief that India would not rise unless she was free from casteism and religious superstitions and unless she adopted a pattern of society based on rationalism. Tilak, who represented essentially the Indian mind, opined that social reforms could only be a growth from within and hasty methods would retard their growth. It was his confirmed view that the ills of the nation demanded political reforms and not immediate social reforms. Even in the matter of social changes, he observed, reformers would be compelled to fight with the foreign Government. At last they agreed to stand on a common platform. It was the education of the people, and they made a resolve to take up the problem.

Tilak was of the opinion that there would be no genuine progress until the education of the people was taken up by the representatives of the people. It was the belief of Agarkar that they would reach their goal only through that kind of education which helped them to put an end to casteism and create a sense of equality among the people.

There were about a hundred students receiving higher education in that college, but these two students alone were alive to the miserable and shameful condition under which their countrymen were groaning. They would often take long walks on the moonlit hills of Sadilbova in the neighbourhood of the college, thinking not of their own prosperity, but of the destiny of their countrymen. It is one thing, although useful in its own way, to turn to the service of the nation after amassing money and enjoying the feel of happiness to the brim, or after being involved involuntarily or helplessly by pressure of events; and it is another thing to take up spontaneously the cudgel for a downtrodden people without a thought of the self.

III

THE QUESTION WHETHER social reform should take precedence over political reform, arose in India after the conquest of India by the British. The new pattern of Government, the new kind of education, the new branches of science, the new types of machines, which accompanied British rule, deeply impressed the first Indian generation under that regime. These emblems of European civilisation filled Indians with awe. They believed that British rule was a divine dispensation. As a result of this a violent reaction set in against Hinduism and against all the meaningless accretions of customs and prejudices it had hugged for centuries.

The men of learning from the new generation with their knowledge of Western culture and of Christian religion suffered from an inferiority complex, and attacked their own religious and social institutions which encouraged for centuries Sati, upheld child marriage, forbade widow re-marriage, allowed self-immolation on the bank of the Ganges, and continued infanticide and sacrifice of men to propitiate the gods.

They therefore ascribed their political servitude to these conditions. This conflict of two civilisations ended in confusing the first generation and to some extent dazzled it. The Christian missionaries, who established Bible Societies and educational institutions, unfurled the flag of Christianity in India through the wilful connivance and indirect support of the Christian rulers. The aim of the American Marathi Mission as described by one of its leaders was "the language of the Marathas, as well as the people themselves, must be Christianised."[1] Frederick John Shore, describing the situation, wrote in his *Notes on Indian Affairs*: "I believe there is a very general feeling among the people that some great crisis is at hand in their religious polity; and that the common belief is, that Hinduism will be supplanted by Christianity."[2] Falling a victim to missionary propaganda, some of the new pundits went over to Christianity, and later on some of them yearned to return to the Hindu fold, being disillusioned about the greatness of Christianity.

All, however, were not worshippers of everything that was British and haters of all that was Indian. The missionary tide began to ebb when Raja Ram Mohun Roy introduced a reformed church in Hinduism for its rejuvenation, when Balshastri Jambhekar, the first Marathi journalist and reformer in Maharashtra, stood up for reforming Hinduism and when the first missionary Hindu leader, Vishnubuva Brahmachari, met the missionary challenge in the social and religious field, vanquishing them in debates and discussions. It is surprising to note that the writings of this virile Vishnubuva dwelling on the Vedic Philosophy are tinged with some

1 Reverend Bruce: *The Literary Work of the American Marathi Mission*, p. 13.

2 Frederick John Shore: *Notes on Indian Affairs*, Vol. II, p. 467.

ideas of Communism. During this period another social revolutionary, Mahatma Jotirao Phooley, raised the standard of revolt, declaring that social equality and spread of education among the masses constituted the real solution of the people's ills. Jotirao Phooley rang the bell of social reform in Maharashtra. He was, in the history of India, the first Indian who started in 1848 a school for the Untouchables and Girls' schools in Maharashtra in 1851. He strove for the liquidation of the power, privileges and prestige of the Brahmins and for the liberation of the lower classes from social slavery. To propagate his mission he established an institution named the Satya Shodhak Samaj.

Another reformer Lokahitwadi Gopalrao Deshmukh, author of a number of books and pamphlets, fearlessly attacked Brahmins who were, according to him, stagnant, decadent and unprogressive. He welcomed the machine age, favoured swadeshi, and appealed to Brahmins to revise their knowledge in the light of modern sciences. His vision was clear enough to foresee Indians liberating themselves when they would be prepared to accept the responsibility of Government, and if at that time the British denied them freedom they would free themselves from the shackles of slavery by following the examples of the people of the U.S.A.

The doyen of these reformers was M. G. Ranade. He was a mighty intellect, a man of great vision, broad mind, prodigious industry and vast learning, an eminent economist and historian, and one of India's greatest thinkers of his day. He aimed at reorganising Hindu society on the basis of justice and reason, which implied a freedom from race, creed and prejudices, and a devotion to all that seeks to do justice between man and man. Long before the birth of the Indian National Congress, he had, as we have already noted, begun to educate the public on Indian affairs by submitting petitions and memorials to the British Parliament and the Queen-Empress through the Sarvajanik Sabha, Poona. He was one of the pioneers of the Prarthana Samaj, which in those days, like its sister branch, the Brahmo Samaj of Keshub Chandra Sen, had more or less Christianity as its pattern.

But unlike Dadabhai Naoroji, Ranade, who aimed at revitalization of Indian economy, laid more stress on industrialisation which depended on British capital. He thought that "we have reason to be thankful that we have a creditor who supplies our needs at such a low rate of interest."[3]

3 Ranade, M. G., *Essays on Indian Economics*, p. 177.

Dadabhai was persistent in showing that political slavery was the root cause of economic slavery, and he often declared that British statesmen and capitalists were draining India under the opiate of the liberal ideas of English social philosophers. About this time Dayananda Saraswati also started his Arya Samaj to infuse a new life into the Hindus. All these institutions contributed to the national awakening. In short, the teaching of these reformers, Lokahitwadi, Mahatma Phooley and Ranade had some points in common. They welcomed the new machine age, secular education, the spirit of enquiry; they propagated abolition of casteism and child-marriage, and encouraged widow re-marriage.

The most striking point, however, in respect of these social reformers of the past two generations under the British regime was that except Phooley every one of them was a Government servant. Lokahitwadi Deshmukh was a judge. So was Ranade. The works of Lokahitwadi could not create in those days a favourable impression upon the Brahmins to whom most of his writings were addressed, as his writings were brutally frank and direct, although his diagnosis of the social disease was correct. Ranade had introduced multifarious activities; but being a Government servant he had to be cautious and moderate, and so he could not be popular with the masses. It was not that he was liked by the Government either. The essay 'On Shivaji's system of Administration and British system of Administration' which he wrote in one of his college examinations, and his various public activities had given cause for suspicion. His loyalty was suspected also at the time of Phadke's revolt. But the emphasis laid by Lokahitwadi and Ranade on the introduction of social reforms and their harping on the defects of Hindu society without their leading an active social movement had an irritating effect upon the educated men of the younger generation. Most of the leaders of social reforms neither practised what they preached, nor made any sacrifice for their principles.

One energetic man from the younger generation came forward to challenge both the Christian missionaries and the social reformers. His name was Vishnushastri Chiplunkar. He was the son of Krishnashastri Chiplunkar, who was an eminent scholar and one of the recognised leaders of the intellectual world in Poona and whose house was the refuge of learned men. Born in 1850, Vishnushastri obtained the B.A. degree in 1872. His mastery of the Marathi and English languages was remarkable. He was a student of English literature and compared Western education to the milk of the tigress, as it imbued the students with the priceless virtues of freedom, patriotism and science. While serving as a teacher he started in January 1874 a magazine called *Nibandhmala* and launched through its columns a frontal attack on Christian missionary activities. He mercilessly criticised the social reformers who found fault with Hinduism and its institutions and whose ideas were more or less influenced by Christianity. The *Nibandhmala* was a great success.

At this juncture some other events occurred that also fanned the fire of patriotism in the minds of the young generation. The resistance to Russian aggression by Turkey, the rout of the British Army in Afghanistan, the glory of the ancient Indian scriptures sung by European scholars like Monier Williams, Max Muller, William Jones, Henry Colebrook, Charles Wilking, Goethe and Schlegel, and the assumption of the new title Kaiser-i-Hind by Queen Victoria amidst the yells of the famine stricken masses, inflamed the minds of young men who were seized with a gnawing restlessness over their shameful condition. A writer of great power and brilliant abilities, Chiplunkar gave an impetus to this feeling and stirred the hearts of the young by his volcanic writings. He was deeply influenced by the styles of Addison and Johnson and attacked the social reformers with a force, incisiveness and violence that was unprecedented in Maharashtra. The Rao Sahebs, the Rao Bahadurs and the Reverends quivered under the lashes of his pen. By appealing to the glorious past, Chiplunkar imbued young men with a fiery patriotism that soon inspired numerous patriots with intrepid courage to fight for the emancipation of their motherland.

The result was that although no equal of Ranade in greatness of vision, profundity of thought, and depth of erudition, Chiplunkar, with his forceful, fiery and unstinted personality, ushered in a mental revolution in Maharashtra. But as his appeal to the young, sprang from his love of tradition and history, Chiplunkar, in his extreme opposition to the social reformers, often defended and sheltered the defects of Hinduism and Hindu institutions, and went to the length of saying that the Hindus were reduced to slavery not because they had any defects and deficiencies, but because of their ill-luck. Ranade aimed at reforming society; Chiplunkar wanted to rouse the people. Chiplunkar preached a cult, whereas Ranade prescribed a cure from within. Ranade's qualities had more light than heat in them, whereas Chiplunkar had more heat than light in his writings. Ranade had before him the ideal of Britain that had evolved a great Democracy. Chiplunkar had before him the history of countries that had fought for their independence and become free nations. In the light of his noble principles,

Ranade wanted to prepare the people for the coming Swaraj, whereas Chiplunkar always harked back to the Swaraj of the past with an eye on future independence. Both Ranade and Chiplunkar were instructors and inspirers of the two schools of thought they founded.

CHAPTER III

The Trio

IN CONFORMITY WITH their resolve Agarkar and Tilak began to think out ways and means of establishing private schools on the model of missionary institutions. They wrote to Ranade, who had been summarily transferred to Dhulia on suspicion that he had a hand in the revolt of Phadke, requesting for his advice and support. Ranade suggested to them either to take over a certain Bhave School which was not working properly or to give a serious thought to their proposal for at least six months before they started a new school. Though their object was a laudable one, he observed, people would not come to their assistance until they had done some actual work. He added that the country would not be emancipated unless it had, like America, its national press, national education and national church.

At this time Tilak and Agarkar came to know that the celebrated Vishnushastri Chiplunkar was thinking of starting a school in Poona. Upon his father's death Chiplunkar had come on leave to Poona in May 1879 from Ratnagiri where he was serving as a teacher in the Government High School. He had now resolved to snap asunder the chains of Government service and to start a school of his own with a view to preparing a generation that would devote their lives to the uplift of their motherland. Tilak and Agarkar met him first some time in July or August 1879. After some meetings they tendered their proposals in September for joining him in the enterprise and requested him to take the lead.

Chiplunkar welcomed the idea and agreed. He had decided to resign his post from 1st October 1879 and informed the Government educational authorities accordingly. So eager was he to bid farewell to his job that towards the end of September 1879 he wrote to his brother: "The memorable 1st of October is approaching. I shall enjoy the pleasure of kicking off my chains that day. Agarkar (going for M.A.), Tilak (going for LL.B.),

Bhagwat and Karandikar (appearing for B.A.) have tendered proposals for joining me in the enterprise. This they have done of their own accord. We have settled 1st of January for the hoisting of the standard. Such a battery must carry the High School instantaneously before it!"

In the meanwhile Wasudeo Balwant's historic trial took place at Poona from October 22, 1879 to November 7, 1879. It was witnessed with patriotic emotions and helpless anger by thousands of people, and followed with anxious hearts all over India, and with interest by the press and political leaders in Britain. Sarvajanik Kaka came forward daringly to defend Wasudeo Balwant in the Lower Court, and then an eminent Maharashtrian lawyer, Mahadeo Chimnaji Apte, defended him in the Sessions Court. But Wasudeo Balwant was sentenced to transportation for life. He later passed away in jail at Aden on the 17th February 1883.

Thus, one revolt came to an end and another was about to break out. Having broken the chains of his service, Chiplunkar issued a prospectus over his own signature on December 15, 1879, supplying people with the details of the proposed school. As announced, Chiplunkar formally opened the New English School on January 1, 1880, and hoisted the standard! The school started its work next day at the Wada of Morobadada Phadnis. Agarkar could not join it on account of his failure in the M.A. examination. Tilak, at first, it seems, was not firm in his resolve. It is not known why he was hesitating; it might be due to the failure of Agarkar in joining the school. But he joined on the first day as promised, and others like Dharap, Damle and Khare joined the school as teachers. Amongst them was also Namjoshi who, being a resourceful, energetic and intelligent man, proved to be an asset to the school. He was a matriculate but made good his deficiency in academic qualifications by the power of his pen and tongue, and above all, by his outstanding ability as an organiser.

Chiplunkar unfurled the standard of the New English School with 35 students on its roll. It was a New School in every sense of the term. It was a new school of thought, of action and of energy! The unfurling of the standard implied the declaration of war, the will to fight against the existing conditions and particularly against the submissive attitude on the part of the people to foreign rule. There were other schools in Poona conducted by private individuals. But this school specially started to infuse self-respect in the youth, a sense of patriotism and love for industry and enterprise and to prepare them for the service of the nation. Another important point was that the young teachers established a new tradition in Maharashtra, a tradition of selfless work, whereas the leaders of the first two generations served Government as best and as long as they could do so. Thus in Poona a new centre of patriotic, fearless and selfless men was created that would challenge the lukewarm policy of Ranade, would stand erect before the British bureaucrats and talk and behave with them with a sense of equality.

Tilak had passed his LL.B. examination, and the degree of Bachelor of Laws was conferred on him in January 1880. He had started an independent establishment at Tambe's Wada in Shaniwar Peth, Poona. During the first term of the school, his mind, however, was gauging the situation very carefully. Maybe for being a little disappointed in his surroundings, or may be as a matter of precaution, Tilak paid visits with Upasani, who was his former classmate, to some places in Maharashtra with a view to settling as a lawyer if need arose. He also applied on 25th May 1880 to the Governor of Bombay for the post of a sub-judge. Mr. Hart, Private Secretary to the Governor, wrote to Tilak: "In reply to your application of the 25th instant the Governor desires me to inform you that your name has been entered in the list of the candidates for the appointment of sub-judges."[1] He was thereupon asked to call upon the Governor at the Government House, but he was, it appears, not in a position to avail himself of that opportunity. It is a historical fact that every man is unconsciously influenced by the traditions in which he is born and by the surroundings in which he is brought up. Tilak was going the way the educated men of the two generations before him had gone. But the greatness of a man lies in manfully overcoming those influences and surroundings. And Tilak did it selflessly and valiantly!

In July 1880 Sarvajanik Kaka died and his son-in-law Vaman Shivaram Apte was forced by circumstances to stay in Poona. A fatherless and penniless lad, Apte had struggled hard to complete his education. On pressing requests from Tilak, this renowned scholar now joined the New English School, though only six months earlier he had declined to do so. After a few days he was appointed Superintendent on a slightly higher salary as a special case, Chiplunkar himself remaining the Head-master of the school. As he was a born teacher and a strict disciplinarian, he could raise the tone of the school to a high standard. One important feature of the school, besides its patriotic atmosphere, was the development of physical culture. The number on the rolls began to rise by leaps and bounds. Boys who were enamoured of the great writer and patriot in Chiplunkar,

1 N. R. Phatak in the *Vividhadnyan Vistar* of September 1924.

abandoned even their scholarships in other schools to join his school, and some did so on winning the consent of their parents with a struggle.

On the eve of the closing of the school for the summer vacation Chiplunkar observed that his school had made tremendous progress and was now "an accomplished fact amidst a thousand difficulties, amidst apathy, in utter disregard of desponding opinions, in contemptuous indifference to showers of epithets like 'mad', 'hopeless', 'chimerical', 'Utopian', the invariable lot of everyone who would be so bold as to disturb the dull routine of things in spite of mean device and disappointed malice."

They were men of undying faith determined to carry out their mission at all cost; and nothing is impossible for men of faith!

Agarkar joined the school in January 1881, the beginning of the second year. A few days earlier all the colleagues were invited by Apte to dine at his house on the occasion of the death anniversary of his father. On this occasion they fully discussed the possibility of launching two weeklies—one in Marathi and the other in English—to educate the people on public affairs. How keen was Chiplunkar on this project also is seen from a letter written by him about this time to one of his teacher-colleagues. He said: "I am to try what might be done for public good with the instrumentality of a press establishment worked by a vigorous hand." Chiplunkar had already purchased on instalments, the press of Namjoshi, who was conducting the *Deccan Star*, his own paper. It was decided to name the Marathi weekly the *Kesari*—the Lion, and to name the English weekly the *Mahratta*, for a 'Mahratta' has been known as an indefatigable fighter for the honour of his country. In the public announcement about the weeklies it was declared that the aims and objects of their weeklies were to give a fearless account of the existing condition of the country, to give reviews of Indian books and to give correct estimates of political affairs in Britain.

At that time there were about two hundred newspapers in India. Of them the *Dnyanprakash*, established in 1849, the Induprakash, in 1862, the *Native Opinion* and the *Subodh Patrika* were important provincial papers and had some influence on the public in the Bombay Presidency. There were 28 Indian language papers in Bengal, 71 in Bombay Presidency, 19 in Madras and about 60 in other provinces. Lord Lytton, the Viceroy of India, who wanted to silence all criticism of Government in the Press had promulgated in 1878 the Vernacular Press Act. This had provoked bitter opposition. To avoid the clutches of the law the *Amrita Bazar Patrika* was converted into an English daily overnight. In Southern India *The Hindu* had made its appearance and the agitation against Lytton's Vernacular Press Act spread. When Macaulay drafted the Indian Penal Code, "sedition" had already crept into the body of the law, and editors came within the mischief and purview of the Act.

The Anglo-Indian newspapers served as spokesmen of British Imperialism and amongst them were the *Times of India*, Bombay; the *Madras Mail*; the *Pioneer*, Lucknow; the *Statesman*, Calcutta; and the *Civil* and *Military Gazette*, Lahore.

Chiplunkar, Tilak and Agarkar decided to start their weeklies on the 2nd and 4th of January 1881. On the eve of the publication of the *Kesari* and the *Mahratta* Tilak and his colleagues, on account of their differences with the owner of the building in which the press was housed, carried the type cases on their heads to Moroba's Wada, and on the morning of the publication of these papers, Tilak and his friends distributed the copies of the papers to the subscribers. The Editor of the *Kesari* was Agarkar and the editor of the *Mahratta* was Tilak. The *Deccan Star* of Namjoshi was incorporated in the *Mahratta*. The office of the editors was quite bare, where blankets served as writing tables. Thus by starting a school, Chiplunkar, Tilak and Agarkar had begun to educate the younger generation, and by launching the papers they now set out to educate the older generation on public affairs.

II

THE SCHOOL WAS going on well. It was making progress in many directions. In order that children should attain a certain intellectual standard by the time they reached the high school stage, these young men started, in the beginning of 1882, a preparatory class. They made the instruction of that class more interesting and more systematic and less rigid. Tilak taught Mathematics and also Sanskrit. Although a brilliant mathematician, Tilak never took the trouble to use the blackboard. He sat on his chair, his grave dignified face looking always downward. His teaching, according to some of his students, although intelligent, was not easily intelligible and interesting. The notable point as regards Tilak as a teacher was that he always considered the demands of students favourably. They, therefore, flocked to him, consulted him on important matters, and even returned home in the company of their teacher. Nevertheless, he examined neither the exercise books nor the answer books in time.

Agarkar taught in an attractive manner. Apte was a brilliant teacher. The mind of Chiplunkar was distracted gradually from his school. He had to manage his Chitrashala, Kitabkhana and his *Nibandhmala*. As a teacher he seldom kept to the text-books, and dwelt on many other topics in his peculiar vein. By nature he was reticent and industrious; but now he looked spent and distracted concerning the school affairs.

The group had now to conduct a school, two weeklies and a press. Everything had to be done anew. The work was heavy and it put a great strain on the energies of all. But the working became smooth as the members were full of youthful energy and everyone of them was given work suited to his temperament. The Society needed good school books and in the first year Tilak wrote a book on Mechanics. He had also accepted the Secretaryship of the Inamdar's Association. One thing deserves mention here, that Tilak obtained a lawyer's sanad in July 1881 to practise at Poona Courts. It was a formative period and it must have been a logical step taken as a matter of course.

The fearless champions of the people's cause watched the administration of the native States as well as that of the British Provinces. During the first year most of the articles in the *Kesari* and *Mahratta* dealt with the affairs in the native States of Baroda and Kolhapur. The *Mahratta* appealed to Lord Ripon to set about reforming the Political Agents and try to give constitutional Government to the Indian States. The *Kesari* launched an attack on Sir T. Madhavrao, the Dewan of Baroda, for having neglected the interests of the Maharaja, who was a minor, and for the Dewan's rank partiality for British rule.

The affairs of the Kolhapur State also engaged the minds of the young editors. Since 1877 the adopted Prince Shivajirao had been showing signs of suspected insanity. It was rumoured that the Dewan, Madhavrao Barve, spurred by the Maharani, was concocting plans to remove him from the Gadi by deposing him or by administering dangerous drugs to him. The people of Kolhapur had given vent to their feelings at a meeting, and a similar big meeting was held at Poona in November 1881 under the presidentship of Lokahitawadi Gopalrao Deshmukh. The meeting demanded that the Prince should be placed under a new guardianship.

The *Kesari* published a series of articles accusing Barve of taking underhand measures to cause the insanity of the Maharaja, and thus exposed Barve as the villain of the piece. An editorial in the *Kesari* by Apte challenged him to prove his innocence before a Court of Law. These editors also sent to Government a petition against Barve praying Government to keep a watch on him, so that he might not commit suicide to avoid a public enquiry. But in spite of this Barve was made a C.I.E.! Barve sued the editors and publishers of the *Kesari* and *Mahratta* and that of the *Dnyanprakash* contending that the published letters were mere fabrications got up in order to defame him. Barve's arch-opponent was one Nana Bhide, who had been refused permission by Barve to practise as a lawyer at Kolhapur on account of his not having passed the qualifying examination. So he had an axe to grind and fabricated the plot in collaboration with the natural mother of the Prince.

The case came up for hearing on February 8, 1882, before Mr. Webb, the Chief Presidency Magistrate of Bombay, and on February 29, 1882, two men came forward to stand security for Tilak and Agarkar, the editors. One was a Bombay businessman Annasaheb Nene and the other Ramshet Uravane, the latter being prompted to do so by Mahatma Phooley.

At this time another calamity overtook the young editors. They suffered a severe shock on March 17, 1882, when Chiplunkar, the prime founder and originator of the New English School, died, having nursed it up for two years and three months. A great literary figure, he really deserved the self-coined title "the Shivaji of the Marathi language". Since Dnyaneshwar he was one of the greatest literary figures and ushered in an epoch in the history of the Marathi language. He was only thirty-two when he died, and although he left behind no issue, the child institution he left behind grew into a vast institution that produced several leaders and journalists. It was his devout wish that no white feet should ever touch his institution and indeed no white feet did touch it in his lifetime. His famous essay *The Present Condition of our Country* had thrilled the hearts of patriots and some years later this essay was proscribed by the Government! The *Kesari*, bewailing the loss of Chiplunkar, observed: "Our good friends sometimes used to call the five of us in jest by the name of Graduate Panchayatan—Graduate Quintette or Graduate Pandavas. Cruel death has carried to his domain our eldest brother Dharma; the head-bead of the string is lost. But we are hopeful that our firm and deliberate resolve to strive to elevate our country will not relax." It added: "Nothing preyed upon the heart of Vishnushastri so much as our country's political bondage and poverty."

In the Barve defamation case Tilak and Agarkar were committed to Sessions and the hearing of the case commenced in the Bombay High Court from July 16, 1882. There were two cases against Tilak. In one he was alone and in the other he was co-accused with Agarkar. European Barristers appeared for Barve, and Branson and the rising Bombay legal luminary

Telang defended Tilak and Agarkar. Those leading men on whose scrutiny and approval the accused had published the so-called original documents and those who had supplied them with the information, appealed to the accused not to disclose their names during the proceedings. Meanwhile Nana Bhide, Keshav Bakhale, and Wamanrao Ranade of *Dnyanprakash* were found guilty, and on July 7 Tilak and Agarkar tendered an unqualified apology to Barve for the false statements they had made concerning him in their papers, stating that " it was established at the trial that the letters were fabricated and that their greatest punishment would be the feeling they had been the cause of so much undeserved pain and anxiety to Barve." Invarity read the apology in the Court; but Barve was adamant and did not withdraw the case.

Telang defended Tilak, but the jury found him guilty; and on July 17, he was sentenced to four months' imprisonment. Branson, who stood for Agarkar, advised him to plead guilty. He did so. And he too was sentenced to four months' imprisonment and Tilak being a co-accused was sentenced to an equal term, but his two terms were to run concurrently. The Judge, however, declared them free from malignity but not from recklessness.

Tilak and Agarkar were at once taken from the court in a closed carriage, and were lodged at Dongri Jail in Bombay. Anglo-Indian papers like the *Times of India* were hostile to these editors. They defended Barve and averred that the Kolhapur Prince was really insane. The public was sympathetic and admired the courage of the young leaders in defending the Prince who belonged to the dynasty of Shivaji the Great. People subscribed to the fund which was collected for their defence; students also did their utmost to collect funds. And it was a strange freak of fate that G. K. Gokhale, who later became Tilak's political opponent, should have acted a female part in a play staged by the students of Rajaram College, Kolhapur, the proceeds being sent to the fund raised for the defence of Tilak and Agarkar.

The agitation for collecting funds did not stop even after the conviction of Tilak and Agarkar. It took the form of a movement for their release. William Wordsworth, the then Principal of Elphinstone College, and Rao Saheb Mandlik forwarded a petition to Sir James Fergusson, the Governor of Bombay, to save the young editors from the rigours of gaol life, but the Government turned it down. The Government of Sir James Fergusson had kept mum about this and had neither helped the defence side in any way in compelling the Kolhapur witnesses to attend the Bombay Court nor had intervened in the proceedings. People were full of sympathy, and the *Deenabandhu*, the mouthpiece of Jotirao Phooley, declared that the public should accord a magnificent welcome to the young patriotic editors on their release.

Both the prisoners lived in the same cell which measured 13x13 feet.[2] The prison food was nauseating. Agarkar, who was an asthmatic, could not digest some part of the food. Moved at this, Tilak requested the jail superintendent's permission to give Agarkar that portion of his food which his colleague could digest, and himself took the remaining portion from both the plates. The prison walls were full of bugs and fleas. So they passed sleepless nights. In spite of these discomforts they sat till late in the night discussing future plans, comparing notes, reviewing past mistakes, exchanging their opinions of men and social problems. In the heat which the discussion engendered over social problems they often lost sight of jail rules, and the warder would mildly remonstrate with them to curb their loud voices.

Jail life hung heavily upon both. About a month later they were, however, allowed the use of pen and paper. That was a soothing factor more to Agarkar, who had a liking for writing, than to Tilak, who put pen to paper only when it was unavoidable. Jail life impaired their health. Tilak lost twenty-four pounds and Agarkar fared no better! The only outcome of jail life was a translation of Shakespeare's *Hamlet* in Marathi by Agarkar, and Our *101 Days in Dongri Jail*, another book written by Agarkar after their release which occurred on October 26, 1882.

On the morning of 26th October one benefactor took a barber into the jail to give a refreshing look to the heroes. After their release both editors were taken out in procession by about two thousand people who were waiting outside the gate of the jail since early morning. Phooley's lieutenants, Lokhande, the editor of the *Deenabandhu*, and Damodar Yande took a leading part in honouring the heroes. While the procession was going on, people garlanded and honoured the heroes at different places on the way. Poona also planned to present the returning heroes with an address of welcome. A batch of about seventy Deccan College students went ahead to Kirkee, and greeted their leaders with grateful tears in their eyes. A vast crowd thronged the Poona station. A procession was taken out, and Tilak and Agarkar were made the recipients of tributes at many

---

2 Now a slab is fixed there in memory of the illustrious prisoners

places on the way. In the evening a special function was held under the auspices of the Sarvajanik Sabha to accord them a grand reception. It was at one such function that Mahatma Phooley honoured the two great patriots. Responding to the overwhelming kindness of the people, they said that although they had undergone trials and tribulations they would not deviate from their righteous path and sought co-operation from the younger generation in their efforts. A few days after the Deccan College students invited the young editors to a party, which they attended. They thanked the students for the honour, advised them to think over the helpless condition of their country, and added that life was meant for better and higher things and not for mere enjoyment.

III

TILAK AND AGARKAR resumed their work on October 28, 1882, and were glad to see that through the unflagging exertions of Karandikar and V. B. Kelkar, their school had kept up its position intact. Tilak and Agarkar were now celebrities. People said they were proud of the young lions. With their names spread the names of their institutions. The spirit of self-reliance displayed and sacrifices made by the members of the society, their moral courage, the brilliant success of their students in winning the famous Nana Shankershet Sanskrit Scholarship, the spirit of discipline, and the patriotic atmosphere in the school, greatly impressed the visitors. The Hunter Commission, appointed by the Government of India to examine into the prevailing educational system in India, paid a visit to the School, on September 8, 1882, and expressed supreme satisfaction over the wonderful spirit and progress shown by the School. Praising the work of the zealous, able and intelligent educated youth actuated by ideas of self-support and self-dependence, Dr. Hunter, the Chairman of the Commission, further remarked: "I can with certainty affirm that throughout the whole of India I have not yet witnessed a single institution of this nature which can be compared with this establishment. This institution, though not receiving any aid from Government, can rival and compete with success, not only with the Government High Schools in this country, but may compare favourably with the schools of other countries."[3] *The Times of India*, the sentinel of the British Empire, foretold that the institution was destined to have a momentous effect on the future of India.

3 Limaye, P. M., *The History of the Deccan Education Society*, p. 7.

V. S. Apte, the superintendent of the school, while giving evidence before the Hunter Commission, submitted a statement which was prepared by Tilak and Agarkar just on the eve of the judgment in the Kolhapur case. It embodied the ideas and ideals of the promoters of the school. The statement said that they had undertaken the cause of popular education "because, of all agencies of human civilisation, education is the only one that brings about material, moral and religious regeneration of fallen countries and raises them to the level of the most advanced nations by slow and peaceful revolutions", and so it should be in the hands of the people themselves.

The statement protested against the teaching of the *Bible* in aided missionary schools and colleges as militating against the principle of religious neutrality enunciated in the Despatch of 1854, and added that the Bombay Government itself had declined to give grants to missionary schools for more than ten years after 1854, but a complete reversal of policy then took place, and grants were given freely even to the institutions that made attendance at the Bible class compulsory.[4] The missionary institutions, the statement proceeded, did not represent indigenous enterprise, nor were their objects purely educational, and they should not be admitted to grants if they did not stop the teaching of the *Bible* or any other scriptural books and impart purely secular education to the students. The chief aim of this body of workers, continued the statement, in the New English School was the establishment of a native Educational Mission to provide a network of national system of education. In the end the statement expressed a hope that Government would transfer the secondary education and, if possible, college education also to popular control and aid solidly the popular institutions.

The object of these young educationists was evident. In those days the Government always stated that it did not invest Indian people with political rights because the people were not sufficiently educated. When the people clamoured for education, it put forth the plea that it was short of funds. Tilak and his colleagues were determined to resolve that stalemate.

The New English School, which had started with thirty-five pupils, had on its rolls 501 pupils by the end of 1882. On their release Tilak and Agarkar took to consolidating the position of their institutions. The chief members formed themselves into a body, and formulated their future plans. It is true that the Kolhapur case had plunged them in debt; yet the members

4 Ibid, p. 43.

were as firm and energetic as before. They needed funds and help was now coming gradually. Four gentlemen from Akola donated a sum of Rs. 1,200.

In January 1883 the New English School was shifted to Gadre Wada, at Shaniwar Peth. Its old building, Morobadada's Wada, had no accommodation enough for six hundred pupils. The task of securing another building for the school was entrusted to Tilak. For carrying on negotiations in this connection he had to visit different places, and, dealing with the persons concerned with tact and patience, he succeeded in securing Gadre Wada for the school. They had lost the Kolhapur case, but they had gained the sympathies of all the native States. As a manifestation of that sympathy, Jaysingrao Abasaheb Ghatge, Chief of Kagal and Regent of the Kolhapur State, paid a visit to the school on September 18, 1883, and donated five hundred rupees for the foundation of the Kagal Prize.

The Maharaja of Baroda also paid a visit to the New English School and gave a donation. When the stock of sweetmeats purchased for distribution through that gift ran out, Tilak, in his characteristic way, spent money from his own pocket, and distributed sweets among the elderly students. Tilak had an opportunity of calling on the Maharaja of Baroda and in the course of their talk they discussed the possibility of Tilak's studying the various developments in modern sciences in Europe. But the plan did not materialise.

IV

BY NOW THE school had attained such an important position in the field of education that even H.E. James Fergusson, Governor of the Province, thought it worthy to preside over its annual prize distribution ceremony which was held on February 13, 1884, at Gadre Wada. Sir William Wedderburn and Rao Bahadur M. G. Ranade were present on the occasion. In the report which Apte read, the managers of the school reiterated their aims and objects, that on a small yet decent remuneration they were prepared to establish a network of schools throughout Maharashtra, and that it was their ambition to start a private college to secure a continuous supply of graduates, actuated by the same motives as their teachers.

After giving away the prizes the Governor announced the intention of the Government to aid private educational enterprise with a more liberal hand. As regards the New English School he said that within a few years it had achieved a standard of excellence comparable to institutions more highly favoured, and so it had established a claim to public assistance. "It would be not only unjust to it," he added, "but discreditable to ourselves were we not to extend a helping hand, and share the credit which the promoters had achieved for themselves." He gave a concrete shape to his appeal by announcing a donation for the foundation of a prize, and Sir James became the first patron of the New English School and subsequently of the Deccan Education Society. Commenting upon this function, the *Times of India*, in fearful forebodings for its imperialist masters observed: "No doubt, these enthusiastic men will preach love of country to these disciples, but it is better after all to have patriotism preached by educated men than wandering mendicants. We have given the people of India education and now it is for us to do all we can to have the moral energy created on our side and not against us." Mr. Lee Warner, the then Director of Public Instruction, described the society as a patriotic society and added that the experiment had no parallel in any other city in India and was interesting from many points of view other than the educational.

At last the long cherished day dawned. The preliminaries being over, a meeting was called on October 24, 1884, under the Chairmanship of Sir William Wedderburn, and the Deccan Education Society was formed with a Provisional Council consisting of Sir William Wedderburn, Prof. R. G. Bhandarkar, K. T. Telang, Rao Bahadur M. G. Ranade, Rao Saheb S. V. Patwardhan, Prof. F. G, Selby and Rao Bahadur N. B. Dandekar, William Wordsworth and Vishwanath N. Mandlik as Trustees; and seven life-members—Tilak, Namjoshi, Apte, Agarkar, Kelkar, Gole and Dharap. His Highness Shri Chhatrapati Shahu Maharaj of Kolhapur, who had given a magnificent donation to the Society, became the first President of the Deccan Education Society. The Provisional Council raised the necessary funds. Tilak's friend Namjoshi wrote to the secretary to the Governor for permission to name their proposed college after Sir James Fergusson. Two years and a half earlier, Tilak, Agarkar and Namjoshi had made speeches at the condolence meeting held at Poona on behalf of the general committee of the Poona Sarvajanik Sabha and the public to mourn the death of Lady Fergusson. So it was not very difficult for them to obtain the Governor's consent. There was also a move for naming the proposed college, " Shri Shivaji College" or " New Poona College", but the idea was dropped. The view of Tilak and Namjoshi prevailed.

In November 1884, the resolution was passed. Sir James Fergusson, who was described by the *Kesari* as the blend of Lord Ripon and Lord Lytton for his conservative policy in regard to the development of Local Self-Government, signified his consent. Immediately the application was made to

Bombay University for permission to start Fergusson College, and the Senate granted, at its meeting held on December 15, 1884, provisional recognition to the College in the Faculty of Arts for three years. The success and history of the New English School by now spread far and wide and evoked deep interest in Lord Ripon, the then Governor-General of India. He became a patron of the Society. In the meanwhile, Tilak, who always liked efficiency and a high standard in every field, tried to raise himself academically to the highest standard. He studied for some time in Bombay, and then appeared for the M.A. examination with mathematics but failed miserably. Tilak's fee for the M.A, examination was paid by the Deccan Education Society.[5]

On January 2, 1885, Fergusson College was formally inaugurated by Principal William Wordsworth as requested by Sir William Wedderburn, the Chairman of the Provisional Council. Wordsworth wished the institution a long, useful and honourable career. Bhandarkar and Telang thanked Wordsworth and Wedderburn.

Except Dharap and Namjoshi all the five life-members, were elevated to professorship. Tilak became Professor of Mathematics. It was found that Gadre Wada was not sufficient for the accommodation of the New English School and the college. Negotiations had, therefore, been going on since October 1884 with the Government and it promised to hand over to the Deccan Education Society the Shaniwarwada, but soon they perhaps felt that it was too inspiring a place, being the residence of the rulers of the Mahratta Empire. They, therefore, proposed to give the Faraskhana Building and Budhwarwada Garden.

Sir James Fergusson, the retiring Governor, laid, on March 5, 1885, the foundation stone of the college building at the new place and expressed gratitude for naming the college after him. Concluding his speech, he said: "That this institution has developed is due to the self-denying patriotism which actuated the teachers of the college. True patriots are they and well worthy of all the praise that can be given them." It was a rare tribute paid by the retiring Governor to the self-denying patriotism of true patriots; for it is a historical truth that self-denying patriotism is the source and spring of liberty. The site was, however, abandoned for some reasons and the same foundation-stone was laid in 1892 by Lord Reay at the place where the present Fergusson College building stands.

5 Limaye, P. M., *The History of the Deccan Education Society*, p. 111.

CHAPTER IV

The Angels Quarrel

SOON AFTER THE Society was registered on August 13, 1885, under Act XXI of 1860. According to its rules life-members were to receive equal pay, and had equal rights, but as the monthly salary fixed was not very high, it was proposed that under special circumstances, gratuities might be granted in addition to their monthly salaries. A further provision was made by assuring the life of every member for three thousand rupees.

But some members felt the pinch of poverty, and they began to talk of the growing needs of their families. They asked for an increase in pay. The first step towards the equalisation of pay and rights was taken in October 1885 when inequalities were removed by making up the account of each life-member since 1880, and accounts were so adjusted as to make the sum drawn by each proportionate to the period of service. Tilak was opposed to this revision and new policy. This was the first note of rupture in the Society.

During this period Tilak and Agarkar stayed at Tambe's Wada. Their differences now led to an exchange of hot and bitter words and expressions, and as each of them talked at the top of his voice, their voices could be heard from a distance. It was at this place that Tilak's little son Waman died in infancy. He rolled down one day from the staircase, and his illness which was the result of an acute attack of diarrhoea became worse. The whistle of the train had a peculiar attraction for this infant boy, and when its shrill note fell on his ears, he toddled up to Tilak saying, "Dada, the train has whistled!" Tilak, though by nature a taciturn and grave man, had developed a special fondness for his infant son, and when he returned home in those days he called to him and asked whether the train had whistled! The child succumbed one night in the arms of a boy relative, who whispered to Tilak about it. He quietly asked the boy to keep the son by the side of the sleeping mother, without a word. When the mother awoke she said that the baby son was fast asleep. "Yes, only to wake up after a new birth if he desires," said Tilak. The meaning flashed across her mind and she burst into tears.

Satisfied with the mission of the Deccan Education Society, the Government now came forward with a new offer. They wrote in October 1885 to the Society requesting them to take over the Deccan College and amalgamate its own college with it. They were contemplating to make over their High Schools and Colleges to private bodies. Meanwhile, Lord Reay paid a visit to the New English School. While taking a round he asked the students in one of the classes, whether they would like to take up Government service. And to the utter surprise of the management, the majority raised their hands in assent! The negotiations with the Government, however, broke down in January 1887, as the Society was opposed to Government interference in the management and to the engagement of European professors whose salaries would be exorbitant.

The harmony in the Society was now disturbed owing to differences that had arisen over two issues, viz. the policy of the weeklies and the taking up of outside work by the life-members. Agarkar was editor of the *Kesari* and Tilak was editor of the *Mahratta*. Agarkar supported social reforms, taking sides with Ranade, and Tilak replied to Agarkar in the *Kesari*, attacking Ranade and other reformers.

The first disturbance was caused by the social reform sought to be introduced by Behramji M. Malbari, a Parsee poet and litterateur, to raise the age of "consent" of Hindu girls to the consummation of marriage. This was the second occasion when a storm raged over the issue of social reforms in India, the first being the Widow Remarriage Act of 1856. A wave of protest passed through the country when the orthodox Hindus and their supporters came to know that the age of consent was about to be raised from 10 to 12. The agitation was given a fillip by an event which shook Maharashtra. A woman named Rakhmabai refused to stay with her husband who was a poor illiterate man and to whom she had been married without her consent. The High Court, setting aside the judgment of the Lower Court, upheld in 1886 the right of the husband to compel his wife to stay with him. Tilak, Namjoshi and Apte expressed their views in favour of the husband whereas Agarkar, Ranade and Bhandarkar defended the woman's right.

An entire hell of abuse was let loose on reformers and men like Malbari. Englishmen like Wordsworth and Wedderburn were of the opinion that reforms should grow from within. Tilak, who also subscribed to this view, missed no opportunity to attack Ranade and other reformers for their views on social reforms.

On the occasion of the annual gathering of Deccan College in May 1885, Ranade had a passage-at-arms with the young professor Agarkar and others on account of their over-emphasis on the philosophies of Mill, Spencer and Kant to the neglect of their own Hindu religion. Immediately after this gathering an article appeared in the *Kesari* under the caption "Rao Bahadur Ranade converted", having a tilt at Ranade that he was veering towards Hinduism from his Samajist opinions. This angered Bhandarkar and he pulled up the young professors at a meeting of the Managing Board of the Deccan Education Society. Agarkar now openly took sides with the social reformers. He supported them on grounds of rationalism, although he differed from Ranade fundamentally; for he was an out-and-out rationalist. Ranade searched for the justification of his social reforms in the ancient scriptures, whereas Agarkar did not care for their support. Had the controversy between Ranade and Agarkar continued, Maharashtra would have been provided with a new light.

About this time the Indian political leaders were thinking of forming an All-India organisation to voice the people's grievances. Prior to 1885 different associations in different provinces were educating the people on public affairs through petitions, memoranda and deputations. But their efforts were spasmodic and sporadic. Just then the Ilbert Bill was introduced in the Central Assembly to remove the bar against the Indian Magistracy trying European and likewise American offenders. Enraged at this move, the anti-Indian Europeans launched a vociferous opposition against the Bill and consequently it was withdrawn. So disgraceful was the surrender that every moment a disturbance was feared in Calcutta, the then capital of India; but the popularity of Lord Ripon averted it. The Anglo-Indians and Europeans in India had actually planned to capture and send back Lord Ripon for his sympathy with the Indians and his liberal ideas about equity and equality; and they displayed their hatred by decorating the walls of an English Club in Bombay with brooms when Lord Ripon left Bombay for England amidst the admiration and gratitude of many Indians.

The failure of the Ilbert Bill impressed upon the leaders of different associations the necessity of an All-India organisation, and they decided to band themselves into a body which was to form the germ of a National Parliament. So they formed an Indian National Union and under the auspices of that Union decided to convene a conference at Poona in the last week of December 1885. The conference was to be held at the Peshwa Garden near Parvati Hill in Poona. Originally, the conference was meant to be more or less a social conference, but owing to divergent opinions on religion and customs, A. O. Hume and Lord Dufferin decided that it should be a body to point out to the administration its defects, and provide a 'safety valve'[1] for the escape of great and growing forces in India. Besides Hume, who worked as the General Secretary for a good many years, Dewan Bahadur Raghunath Rao, M. G. Ranade, Subramania lyer, K. T. Telang, Rao Saheb Mandlik, Dadabhai Naoroji, Surendranath Banerjee and Charuchander Mitter were the conveners of this proposed conference.

Owing to an outbreak of cholera the conference could not meet at Poona. It was held in Bombay at Gokuldas Tejpal Sanskrit College at 12 noon on December 28, 1885. Seventy-two delegates attended it and thirty Government servants were present as friends. It was Ranade who named the conference[2] "Congress". For the first time in modern history the best brains in India assembled together to think over the deteriorated condition of their motherland. A great force was born eventually to challenge British Imperialism, a force that was the first of its kind in Asia. The first session of the Congress was presided over by W. C. Banerjee. Tilak did not attend this Congress. His colleagues Agarkar and Apte did.

Indian newspapers welcomed the Congress and congratulated its leaders on the bold step they had taken.

II

THE MALBARI PROPOSALS gave a fresh impetus to the question whether social reform should take precedence over the political. At a Bombay meeting K. T. Telang, who was a profound thinker, a Napoleon of scholarship, an eminent lawyer, and a matchless orator of his day, gave in an eloquent speech his opinion on the controversy. He observed that Shivaji and subsequent Mahratta rulers were examples to show that the theory that a nation socially low could not be politically great, was not supported by history. He, however, added that it was not possible to sever political from

1 Wedderburn, W., *Allan Octavian Hume*, p. 77.

2 Washikar, S. S., *Hindi Rajkaran*, p.28.

social reform altogether and hence the two must go hand in hand although the march might not in the case of both be with absolutely equal celerity.

Just at this time Tilak read a paper on the age of consent at the annual gathering of Deccan College in which he scathingly attacked all the supporters of the Malbari proposals. On the eve of the gathering some friends knew that he had used violent language in his paper and so they requested Mahadeo Chimnaji Apte to persuade Tilak to tone down his invective. Apte declined point-blank saying that nobody could persuade the obdurate man. For some days past Ranade and his lieutenants had given up their evening sittings at the Sarvajanik Sabha and instead met at a certain club in Budhwarpeth. One day Tilak happened to visit that club and had a hot discussion with Ranade. There was a scene and each party called the leader of the other a demagogue!

The tension created by the Malbari proposals was growing. The opposition was taking active steps to compel Government to abandon them. The orthodox and conservative sections of the public in Bombay called a meeting at Bombay on September 5, 1886, under the presidentship of Rao Saheb Mandlik. The meeting condemned the age of consent proposals on the ground that they interfered with their religion. Tilak and other opponents had sent a letter to the leaders of this meeting, supporting their stand. On September 13, 1886, a deputation of Shastris of Poona led by Ramshastri Apte called on the Governor at Poona and stated that Malbari was a stranger and he did not know the internal state of Hindu society. They added that the religious rules and injunctions ought not to be altered even in compliance with the opinions that might be held by a majority. Any such legislation, they concluded, would amount to a breach of promise solemnly made by the Empress of India in the Royal Proclamation of 1858.[3]

While this question was being hotly discussed, Gokhale joined the Deccan Education Society as life-member in June 1886. He concurred with Agarkar in this opinion. The question of the revision of the salary of life-members was coming to a head. The differences now degenerated into heart-burning and sharp repartees, and ultimately led to an acrid controversy. Tilak now left Tambe's Wada where Agarkar also stayed and moved into Mande's Wada at Narayan Peth.

As Professor of Mathematics Tilak had a place of his own in the college. An expert mathematician and reputed Sanskrit scholar, he

3 Interview of the Poona Shastris with H.E. the Governor, pp. 2, 6.

displayed thoroughness, originality and profundity in his teaching. He had a natural aptitude for mechanics. Gole, Professor of Science, constructed a small balloon, but his theoretical knowledge could not succeed in flying the balloon. To the amazement of all Tilak corrected the mistake and the balloon flew up. There was, however, one defect that marred Tilak's great gifts as a teacher. He sometimes could not adapt the range of his teaching to suit the understanding of average students. It swept over them like a hurricane. Like Chiplunkar, he taught them, not how to remember, but how to develop their powers. He had no love for tasteless repetitions and tiresome reiterations.

Tilak was quite indispensable to the Society from another point of view. He had boundless energy, and he worked untiringly for the Society and was largely responsible for its rapid development and success. Taciturn, grave and efficient, he was a tower of strength to the Society. There was something imperious in his air which suggested that he regarded no one as his superior and few his equals. Nature had blessed him with a personality which had limelight, panache and power sufficient for the work of all the members of the Society. The practical bent of his mind and his quick grasp of the intricacies of any problem made him the fittest man to carry on negotiations on behalf of the Society. He successfully dealt with legal matters and set right the financial affairs pertaining to the Society.

Yet signs of discord were appearing one after the other. Owing to growing differences over the policy regarding the management of the institutions, Tilak's personal defects and deficiencies were attacked at this time. He was sometimes late in going to classes and was not punctual in leaving classes at the sound of the gong. Neither did he, his colleagues grumbled, check exercise books in time. Apte and Agarkar expressed their displeasure at this irregularity on the part of their colleague. Tilak never took things lying down. He retorted that it might be that he was sometimes late in going to and leaving the classes; but his teaching did not suffer in any way in quality and quantity. It compared well with that of those who boasted of their regularity.

In February 1887, Agarkar brought forth a draft of bye-laws intending to increase the pay of the life-members by Rs. 5 a month. Tilak was opposed to these proposals which demanded that pay should be regulated according to necessities. He held that members should stop working outside and if they worked outside such income should go to the common fund of the Society. The meeting ended in confusion as the members demanded an apology for Tilak's "disorderly and disrespectful conduct towards the other members." He, however, refused to give it on the plea that the Chairman was not a duly elected one. These episodes led to deep estrangement. The recess time was also punctuated with sharp digs and bitter words.

When the life-members sat together during the recess, at Gadre Wada, Tilak criticised Ranade and other reformers. He shouted that it was not given to Ranade alone to serve the people and be in the limelight. He would also do that. In May 1887, at an elocution prize distribution ceremony a youth criticised the social reformers for having failed to practise what they preached. Ranade, who was presiding at the function, asked the youth to keep to the point. Heckling began. Tilak, who was in the audience, roared: "Rao Saheb, let the young man have his say. You cannot gag him like that!"

After the meeting of 18th February, Tilak informed his colleagues that it was not possible for him to devote his attention to the work of the Society unless matters were set right. There upon Agarkar said that Tilak wanted to defy the majority, set rules at naught, and cow down opposition by threats of resignation. A compromise, however, was effected in January 1888, and Tilak was authorised to conduct the institutions; but the compromise broke down in April 1888. It was patched up by appointing the junior members to look after the management. In June 1888 the Managing Board prescribed an arithmetic book by Gokhale as a text-book. This was a new point that added to the growing discontent, because the Board had not called for arithmetic books from other members.

From the middle of 1886 the Deccan Education Society severed its connection with the *Kesari and Mahratta*. On Agarkar's refusal to take over the ownership of the press and newspapers, V. B. Kelkar accepted the responsibility and took them over with the help of H. N. Gokhale. This naturally restrained Agarkar's pen, and it was announced in the *Kesari* in October 1887 that Tilak would be responsible for the publication of the *Kesari*. Still Agarkar wrote in the *Kesari*, but the replies to his articles were also published in the same or in the next issue of the *Kesari*. This was rather inconvenient for Agarkar. So he thought it wise to start his own paper, and he launched the *Sudharak*, the Reformer, an Anglo-Marathi weekly, the English section of which was penned by G. K. Gokhale.

Agarkar's fearless articles in his new paper against the opponents of social reforms widened the gulf between Tilak and Agarkar, the *Kesari* now replying to Agarkar with the same vehemence. In December 1888 further enstrangement followed. Maharaja Shivajirao Holkar of Indore called for

Agarkar and Tilak, and presented them with a gift of seven hundred rupees for being distributed among the life-members for their dresses. On their way home, Tilak went to some other place. Agarkar handed over the sum to the clerk of the Society.

On the same day when Agarkar learnt that the Maharaja was going to purchase books for distribution amongst school boys, he submitted 300 copies of his book *Vakya Mimansa* and 39 copies of *Vikarvilasit* to the Maharaja. He was mightily pleased with Agarkar's books and so he, instead of remunerating Agarkar independently, ordered Gupte, his personal secretary, to present Agarkar with a dress of honour and to write to the Society to pay Rs. 400 out of Rs. 700 to Agarkar as an appreciation of his books and to divide Rs. 300 among the other members for their dresses. Gupte carried out both the orders. It, however, appears that Tilak kept the letter in his possession for some time. Meanwhile, the clerk of the Society at the instance of Tilak made an entry in the Account Book that the money was handed over to the Society by Tilak and Agarkar jointly. In reply to Gupte's letter Tilak informed him that the amount had been already distributed among the members of the Society.

According to Agarkar both the statements of Tilak were false, and so he was mad with righteous anger at this distrust. He wrote to Tilak that his statement was a downright falsehood and unworthy, he must say, of a gentleman of honour. Even Tilak's friends did not side with him in this affair. Agarkar, however, did not touch a pie from that gift. Agarkar, who in his previous letter[4] had said to Tilak that "I know it is your way to denounce everybody who goes beyond you," now in righteous indignation hit harshly Tilak back saying that Tilak was playing on words to cover his mean despotic and selfish conduct under a cloak of Jesuistical casuistry or legal sophistry,[5] A wounded mind, like broken glass, is never mended! Now a rupture was inevitable. The feeling of bitterness was too much for Tilak, and he consulted his friends like Bapusaheb Athalye whether he should resign. Athalye persuaded him to pull on for some time. He, therefore, proceeded on leave for six months from January 1889.

The first thing Tilak did after proceeding on leave was to go to Chikhalgaon, his native village in Konkan, for about a week to look into the affairs of his estate and to make some arrangements, and to renovate

---

4 Agarkar's letter, 24 December 1888.

5 Ibid, 25 December 1888

the village temple of Laxmi-Keshav. His family was with him. It may be mentioned here that by now his wife, who was illiterate at the time of marriage, had learnt the rudiments of Marathi at the house of her husband's uncle with the help of the latter's school-going children, and her self-study enabled her to read the *Kesari*. In those days it was not customary with an educated man to teach his wife when there were elderly persons in the house.

On his return from Chikhalgaon, Tilak devoted the remainder of his leave period to public service. The Poona leaders were intent upon holding the Congress session in Poona. They found in Tilak the proper leader to conduct negotiations with the Bombay leaders regarding the venue of the Congress. Accordingly, Tilak and his friend Namjoshi went to Bombay and extended an invitation to the Congress leaders. The Bombay leaders were particularly enthusiastic about holding the session in Bombay. Meanwhile Bombay's veteran leader Rao Saheb Mandlik passed away. The Poona leaders then gave up their attempt; for it was their intense desire to see Mandlik installed in the Gadi of Congress Presidentship.

III

JUST THEN AN event occurred which gave Tilak an opportunity to make his mark in Maharashtra as an agitator and an independent leader. It was the Crawford Case in which he played a leading part in defending certain unfortunate Mamlatdars who were thrown out of employment, as a result of an inquiry instituted by Government against Arthur Crawford. This former Collector of Ratnagiri District had by now risen to the post of a Revenue Commissioner. His reckless and squandering habits had brought him to the verge of ruin. For a considerable time there had been rumours that he had accepted illegal gratification for appointing Government servants to the posts of Mamlatdars and Deputy Collectors. Crawford's enemies moved in the matter. So Government suspended him and launched a prosecution against one Hanamantrao Jagirdar who was his agent.

During the course of Hanamantrao's trial at Poona, Tilak wrote some articles on the Crawford affair, and urged Government officers to come forward to give evidence before the District Magistrate of Poona since Government had promised not to take any action against those who would give such evidence in the case. Accordingly, a few Mamlatdars and Deputy Collectors gave such evidence in which they deposed that they had given money to Hanamantrao for securing promotions at the hands of Crawford.

Hanamantrao was found guilty and was sentenced to two years' imprisonment. Alarmed at this, Crawford tried to escape from India incognito. He was, however, arrested at Bombay; was taken back to Poona, and an Inquiry Commission was set up to investigate all the charges levelled against him. But the Commission, nervous about the declining prestige of a Britisher, found Crawford guilty of extracting money only in the form of loans, and acquitted him of the other charges of corruption and bribery. The confessions given by Mamlatdars on solemn assurances, however, recoiled on them. Twelve Mamlatdars were dismissed summarily; a few of them were demoted and others were threatened with the same fate.

About this time the second Bombay Provincial Conference was held at Poona under the presidentship of Rao Bahadur G. H. Deshmukh. The first Conference was also held at Poona, but Tilak had not taken part in it. These Provincial Conferences were, in fact, Congress sessions in miniature. At this Conference, at the instance of Tilak a resolution was passed, congratulating Government upon doing its duty by instituting an inquiry into the Crawford affair. In a speech at this Conference Tilak appealed to Government to consider leniently the cases of the Mamlatdars. This was Tilak's first important public speech in the true sense of the term. Tilak, Namjoshi and Gokhale were appointed Secretaries of the Provincial Conference to organise its next session.

For a whole year Tilak led a furious agitation against the injustice inflicted upon the officials. In September 1889 he convened in Poona a meeting at which resolutions were passed, urging Government not to break their promise to the Mamlatdars. Tilak further tried to bring the case of the Mamlatdars before the British Parliament through William Digby, Secretary of the Congress Agency, in London, and Charles Bradlaugh, who was a Member of Parliament. They appreciated Tilak's work and promised to move Parliament; but finally nothing came out of it, there being an equally strong counter-propaganda against Tilak's move. Ultimately an Act of Indemnity was passed by the Government of India under which the officials were saved from further prosecution and persecution. The Mamlatdars, however, expressed their gratitude to Tilak for having championed their cause untiringly. At a meeting they publicly honoured him and presented him with a silver watch and a scarf.

It may be noted here that although Tilak defended the Mamlatdars valiantly, he also condemned them roundly for resorting to corrupt methods in securing their promotions. He observed sadly that it was a painful fact that however highly Indians might boast of their advancement in education, their qualities of truthfulness and honesty which elevate a nation were not up to the mark.

Meanwhile Tilak had returned, in July 1889, to work in the College when there was some sort of compromise regarding the question of outside work of the life-members. In October 1889 Gole was appointed the sole authority, but the permission granted by the University of Bombay for starting the 1st B.A. classes put an end to this arrangement. All were gladdened by the news for a while and matters looked improved. In the last week of December, Tilak and Gokhale went to Bombay to attend the fifth session of the Congress.

This session of the Congress was indeed an epoch-making event in Indian history. So far the Congress had held four sessions. The second session was held in 1886 at Calcutta in the Town Hall under the presidentship of Dadabhai Naoroji. The Chairman of the Reception Committee of the Congress declared in no uncertain words that "We live, not under a National Government, but under a foreign bureaucracy." The President of the Congress, Dadabhai Naoroji, said that the Congress should concentrate on political matters on which they were united and should not deal with social problems on which they were not united.

"A national Congress must confine itself to questions in which the entire Nation has a direct participation, and it must leave the adjustment of social reforms and the class questions to class Congresses." The Viceroy received some of the delegates of the Congress and also invited them to a garden party, not as delegates but as distinguished visitors to the capital. *The Times*, London, however, described the Congress merely as "an affair of discontented place seekers—men of straw, with little or no status in the country." For the third session Congress had met at Madras in the last week of December 1887. It was presided over by Badruddin Tyabji who laid stress on the representative character of the Congress. He endorsed the view of Dadabhai to keep aloof from social problems. B. C. Pal made his first speech at this Congress.

The fourth session of the Congress was held at Allahabad in December 1888. Sir Auckland Colvin, the Governor of the United Provinces, tried to prevent the Congress leaders from holding the session at Allahabad and the Viceroy, Lord Dufferin, branded it as seditious. Sir George Yule presided over the Congress session. He was the first Englishman to preside over the Congress. In his presidential address he pleaded for the right of representation in the administration of India. During the course of a speech Eardley Norton said that as an Englishman he was ashamed of England's broken promises to India. It was at this Congress that Lajpat Rai made his first speech.

But the Congress of 1889 was very important. Charles Bradlaugh, M.P., who was contemptuously called in England a Member for India, was a guest of the Congress, and Sir William Wedderburn, who was associated with the Deccan Education Society, was to preside over the Congress. It was in this session that Tilak and Gokhale took an active part for the first time. Tilak made special arrangements for the publication of the *Kesari* in Bombay during the Congress session. Speaking for the first time in the Congress, Tilak moved an amendment to the Resolution on the personnel of the Imperial and Provincial Legislative Councils demanding that the Imperial Council should be elected by the Provincial Councils instead of by the electoral colleges. Gokhale, seconding the amendment, made his maiden speech in the Congress. Bepin Chandra Pal, Lajpat Rai, G. Subramania lyer and Malaviya made speeches supporting the resolution. This was the first and last occasion when Tilak and Gokhale concurred with each other in the Congress proceedings! The amendment, however, was lost.

A lively little incident then occurred, when one of the Muslim delegates, making a violent speech, claimed that Muslims should be elected in Councils in equal numbers with the Hindus although the Muslim population was smaller. This amendment was, of course, lost.

Tilak was now more and more attracted to public activities. Early in the new year a committee was set up at Poona to commemorate the services of His Royal Highness the Duke of Connaught, the Commander of the Bombay Forces, who was about to retire. The proposed memorial on the occasion was to take the form of a military school for training Indian youth. A deputation consisting of some Sirdars with Tilak and Namjoshi as its Secretaries was elected to wait upon His Royal Highness. The Deputation accordingly waited upon him on March 12, 1891. He was presented with an address when he accepted the offer to name the school after him. A representation was consequently made to the Government of India in the light of the address presented to His Royal Highness. The scheme, however, was not approved by the Government of India, and ultimately it was dropped.

Tilak also took an active interest in the third Provincial Conference which was held at Poona in May 1890, under the presidentship of the Hon'ble Kazi Shahbuddin. In this Conference Tilak moved a resolution attacking Government Excise policy and demanding the application of the principle of local option. He felt happy over the progress achieved by Temperance Associations in the country, but at the same time asserted that the very existence of such organisations in India was reprehensible since riotous drunkenness was unknown in India. Tilak and Gokhale were again elected Secretaries.

The agitation made by Tilak for securing justice to the Mamlatdars had already had a far-reaching effect on the Sarvajanik Sabha. Sitaram Chiplunkar, Secretary of the Sarvajanik Sabha, being on friendly terms with Crawford, refused to say or write anything on the Crawford affair, and was, therefore, pulled down from the Secretaryship by the members. And G. K. Gokhale, who was taking lessons in politics and public problems at the feet of Ranade, was elected Secretary of the Sarvajanik Sabha in place of Chiplunkar. Tilak now came forward as a public figure and a vigorous independent agitator who rebelled against all wrongs, and his boundless devotion to whatever cause he championed was witnessed by an admiring public.

The elevation of Gokhale to the Secretaryship of the Sarvajanik Sabha proved to be the last stroke in precipitating the crisis, and the relations of Tilak with the Deccan Education Society broke down. Tilak requested the Secretary of the Managing Board to hold a meeting to consider Gokhale's acceptance of the Secretaryship of the Sarvajanik Sabha. The meeting was called but it ended in angry scenes. Another meeting was called on October 14, 1890, at which after a hot discussion the Managing Board passed a vote of censure against Tilak. Tilak tendered his resignation while the meeting was going on and left. On October 22 the Managing Board accepted his resignation "recording their sense of the irreparable loss which would be sustained by the Society by the severance of his connection with the Society, and of the high value of his services for the last ten years".

On December 15, 1890, Tilak submitted to the Deccan Education Society a detailed statement explaining the causes that led to his resignation. It contained thirty-two articles which spread over thirty-three pages. From the text of the resignation of Tilak it seems that there was nobody amongst the Managing Board "who by virtue of his personal character commanded respect from the rest". They were all equals. The second thing was that the principles of Jesuits were not laid down specifically as articles of faith. As regards the charges levelled against Tilak that he was haughty and violent, and that a cloak of divine disinterestedness and stoicism, self-assertion and self-glorification had been his aim throughout, Tilak said: "I have alienated the sympathy of almost everyone and rendered myself extremely unpleasant; so much so, that I am regarded almost an obstacle in the way of others and every fault of mine, however trifling, is at once caught hold of, and magnified to an incredible extent. I should not have cared for this, but even when my capacity had come to be questioned, and a vote of censure passed against me, it was impossible to pull on any longer; and I was obliged to resign. I might be haughty or violent... but for all that, if the Board had arrived at some final settlement of the great questions at issue, I should not have minded the charges at all."

"The chief fault," Tilak continued, "that I am aware of mine is my manner of expressing myself in strong and cutting language. I am, I think, never violent in the beginning; but being a man of very strong feelings, I often fall into the error of giving sharp and stinging replies when aroused, and of being unsparing in my criticism. Sharp words do cause an amount of mischief; but I can assure, as I have done before this, that I spoke strongly because I felt strongly for the interest of the Institution."

However disagreeable it might be, he said, he could not do better than ask their permission to part company. "I assure you," he proceeded, "that it was only after a great struggle with my own feelings that I have come to this resolve. In fact I am giving up now my life's ideal; but the only thought that by separating myself from it I shall serve it best, is my consolation." "In the end I bid you," Tilak concluded pathetically, "my dear colleagues, a good-bye, with my heart burdened with a load of sorrow; but in the hope that by severing myself from you, I may perhaps be able to help you in preserving harmony, so very essential to the welfare of our Institutions, as it is for the sake of that harmony I am making this sacrifice of myself. With my best wishes for the continued prosperity of the Institutions with which I had the honour of being connected for the last eleven years... I remain."

The resignation affair went on for some time. Dr. Bhandarkar had taken a serious objection to a remark made by Tilak in his resignation imputing dishonesty to his colleagues, who, Tilak had stated, were prepared to show worked-up accounts to suit the Grant-in-aid rules! In February 1891 the Managing Council passed a resolution condemning Tilak's charges imputing dishonesty to the members of the Society as baseless. Tilak again replied but the managing committee confirmed its previous resolution.

Chiplunkar conducted Chitrashala and Kitabkhana of his own and nobody complained that it was a breach of rules. Tilak himself had written a book on Mechanics, had taken an active part in the election propaganda of his friend Namjoshi, had taken an active lead in the defence of the aggrieved Mamlatdars, and had worked for the Congress also. It was Tilak's devout wish to run the Institution on the principles of self-sacrifice, self-negation and Jesuistic ideals which were not laid down on paper. Tilak himself had written in his letter of resignation that "our aim, as has been declared so many times, is to make liberal education indigenous". But he expected his colleagues, who had their families and relatives, to lead, within their meagre means, the life of Jesuits. It is a well-known fact that the Jesuits have no family responsibilities.

Tilak's colleagues had not in the least deviated from the principles of self-sacrifice, but they perhaps thought that the rigours of the strict and stringent Jesuistic principles would be impracticable for married Hindu men and feared that it would involve the Society into a life of constant inquisition. Tilak felt unhappy over this and resigned. But from the recollections of his son Shridharpant, it appears that Tilak repented in his heart of hearts for having lost his hold on a big institution.[6] It is difficult for a man to regain a position which he loses in his thirties, and never could Tilak do so. However, the spirit of selflessness shown by Tilak was praiseworthy. When the Deccan Education Society offered him his insurance, he stoutly refused to touch it!

Tilak was hardly thirty-four then, and he had played a leading role in the field of education. One of the founders of the foremost educational institutions in India when he was twenty-four, he had unceasingly worked for it for eleven years!

6 Tilak. S. B., *Maza Vyasang*, p. 145 (Marathi).

CHAPTER V

War on Social Reformers

I

HAVING RESIGNED THE life-membership of the Deccan Education Society, Tilak was now free to enter upon a life to his liking. The principle of Jesuistic poverty had now to be set aside; for he had to serve the people and in the world of politics and public life it keeps your backbone straight if you are not dependent upon others for the livelihood of the members of your family. A man of Tilak's obliging nature must necessarily possess some such means of livelihood as would provide for all his activities and his family. Some of his admirers and friends suggested that he should practise at the Bombay High Court, but he refused to do so. A few ambitious souls approached him with a proposal for starting a rival college to Fergusson College, but he silenced them by saying that no sensible man would cut down the tree which he had planted.

The thought of becoming a professional lawyer was of course out of the question. He never appeared in any Court except perhaps once in the Court of the District Judge of Poona in connection with a civil suit, and that too he conducted free of charge. He, therefore, started from June 1891 at his residential quarters a Law Class, a new idea in the Bombay Presidency, for the purpose of preparing students for the High Court and District Pleaders' Examinations. This created a great opening for the middle class intelligentsia to make an independent living. From this class sprang some of Tilak's lieutenants who afterwards rose as leaders in mofussil areas.

One Mr. Waknis was Tilak's assistant at the class. The class met in the morning from 7 to 9 o'clock. This class brought him an income of about one hundred and fifty rupees per mensem. Tilak taught the class Hindu Law, Equity, Law of Evidence and Law of Contract with special interest. One morning, while he was teaching Equity to the class Ranade entered the class unnoticed from the other end and sat on one of the back benches. Tilak was so much absorbed in his lecture that he did not notice his arrival. When somebody drew Tilak's attention to it, he stopped the lecture; but Ranade asked Tilak to continue the lesson. The great legal luminary in Ranade expressed satisfaction at the proficiency with which Tilak dealt with the subject.

Partly to augment his income and partly to promote the Swadeshi industry Tilak invested money in a ginning factory which he started at Latur with the help of two other partners. Latur was a cotton centre in the Hyderabad State. For further investment in this enterprise he could secure a loan of five thousand rupees through the influence of his friend V. S. Bapat, who was an influential officer at Baroda. Bapat arranged for it through a money-lender's firm in Baroda. Tilak sent his nephew D. V. Vidwans to Latur as his representative to look after the management of the factory.

Tilak was now free to utilize his phenomenal energy and his unswerving industry for solving the problems of his country. A man of strong views and a lover of traditions and ancient history, he decided to launch a vigorous campaign against those who were concentrating their energies on social reforms. At this time news came that Malbari, who had been to London a few months earlier to win support for his proposals, was successful in bringing sufficient pressure to bear upon the Government of India to consider his proposals. The *Kesari* warned the people against the imminent danger to their religion and traditions, and appealed to them not to give their support to the Malbari proposals.

Some of the Malbari proposals were:

(1) Cohabitation by a husband with his wife, under twelve years of age, should be made penal.

(2) In case of infant-marriages, the wife should be entitled to cancel the marriage, if she liked, on attaining majority.

(3) Suits by husbands for the restitution of conjugal rights should not be allowed. and

(4) A widow should continue to hold her first husband's property even after her remarriage.

This problem of reform was, however, given a fresh impetus by an event that happened in Bengal. A grown-up man committed rape upon his child-wife and she died. This event impressed upon the Government the necessity for moving in the matter of the Age of Consent, and the result was that consideration of one part of the Malbari proposals was accelerated.

It was the confirmed opinion of the orthodox Hindus that raising the Age of Consent struck at the very root of Hindu society and nullified at one stroke the sanctity and indissolubility of the marriage tie. Their leader Tilak challenged the right of a foreign bureaucracy to sit in legislative judgment on Indian society. He asserted that a foreign Government should not be trusted with the power of making social changes. In his view social conditions could not be improved until political conditions were bettered. He held that slow and spontaneous action by society would bring about the desired result; education and consciousness of social evil would eradicate the defects.

The spokesman of the orthodox Hindus had at the beginning of the controversy, written in the *Kesari*, deprecating Government interference in social customs: "If we want Acts and Resolutions to regulate child-marriage, why then, not have 'Dinner Acts', 'Sandhya Adoration Acts' and 'Bathing Time Acts'?"[1] In short, it was the confirmed belief of the opponents of social reformers that because the latter laid too much stress on India's inferiority, they were trying to imitate English life, diet and habits. They wished to Westernise India and hence they said that women should be educated, widows must remarry and castes must go. Instead of fighting for their political independence they were pining for social reforms!

Ranade, the leader of the reformers, replied to Tilak and his party on all counts. He observed: "Whenever there is a large amount of unredressed evil suffered by people who cannot adopt their own remedy, the State has a function to regulate and minimise the evil." Those who welcomed the State regulation of *Sati* and widow marriage, of infanticide, of the self-murder of Jogees on the Ganges and hook-swinging before idol shrines, observed Ranade, should not object to this regulation of the Age of Consent because the regulation of marriageable age had been a part of national jurisprudence in all countries. The old

1 Limaye, P. M., *The History of the Deccan Education Society*, p. 102.

argument that sufferers themselves did not complain of the evil was no defence. It was urged as an argument against the abolition of slavery. It was urged that a foreign Government could not be trusted with that power. This objection would have a meaning and significance had the foreign interests overridden native interests. But in social matters the foreigners had no interest to serve. So the interference was not of foreign initiation but Indian.

The history of the suppression of Infanticide and of *Sati* showed, Ranade asserted, that those institutions were checked, and could be checked, only by the strong arm of Law, and once they were denounced as crimes, they disappeared from the face of the country. The sharp surgical operation, and not the homoeopathic infinitesimally small pill, concluded Ranade, was the proper remedy for the first class of disorders.[2]

K. T. Telang was of the opinion that "We must and ought to devote the greater portion of our energy to political reform ... let us keep alive our sympathies with social reform and those who undertake them and let us all help them to the extent of our powers". "At all events for God's sake," he continued, "let us not set ourselves in antagonism to social reform. In this way only, shall we best discharge the whole of the duty which lies upon us, the duty of reform in social as well as political matters." "I entirely agree," he observed, "that the remedy for removing India's social ills does not lie in Anglicising India. But to say or suppose, as so many at present do, that those who desire social reform want to Anglicize the country socially, is at least as great and as injurious a misapprehension as to say that those who want political reforms want to Anglicize the country politically." [3]

The opponents of the Age of Consent Bill held a meeting at Tulsibag in Poona in October 1890 when the Tilak party-men rather purposely put forth their counter-proposals which were to be brought into force by law for the reformers alone, who clamoured for the Age of Consent Bill. They were as follows:

1 and 2 Girls and boys should not be married until they reached the age of 16 and 20 respectively.

---

2 Miscellaneous Writings of the Late Hon'ble Mr. Justice Ranade, pp. 78-81.

3 S. N. Karnataki: *Namdar Nyaymurti Kashinath Trimbak Telang (Marathi)*, pp. 438-439.

3 and 4 Unless they were prepared to marry widows, men should not marry after they were 40 years old.

5 There should be absolute prohibition of liquor.

6 Acceptance of dowry in marriages should be prohibited.

7 Disfigurement of widows should be forthwith stopped.

8 One-tenth of the monthly income of every reformer should be devoted to public purposes.

It was very strange that those who opposed a little thing like raising the age of consent from ten to twelve now themselves offered to confer a greater benefit on society! But their action belied their intention! As these proposals were meant for a few persons and were not to be applicable to the Hindus in general, they were not considered at the meeting. At this stage it appeared on the surface that Tilak, their leader, did not want the foreign Government to interfere in social matters and that he objected to social reforms being enforced by law. He had roundly condemned Malbari's suggestions for Indian Marriage Laws as absurd and as involving an interference with Hindu religion.

As mentioned above, by signing the abovementioned proposals Tilak was willing to break Shastric Laws himself, but he could not bear the idea of Ranade and Bhandarkar agitating for the enhancement of the age of consent from 10 to 12 years. Tilak made a speech at this meeting showing how ruinous would be the consequences of the Age of Consent Bill on Hindu society, and then the meeting decided to appeal to Government not to legalise it.

Another meeting was held in November to discuss Tilak's proposals. At that meeting Tilak asserted that there had been much tall talk but little action in bringing about social reform, and that the reformers did not consider what reforms were required and practicable. They must carry public opinion with them and secure sanction of religion for their reforms. Ranade, who was present at the meeting, said that they found that there was no support for Tilak's proposal. He was, however, glad that Tilak had brought himself to accept legislation for himself.

II

DECEMBER 1890 CAME and that year the session of the Congress was held at Calcutta. It was on the eve of this session that Government had issued the Risley circular prohibiting Government officials from attending the Congress session. This arrested the patient and silent work of M. G.

Ranade who had been the real power and in spite of this circular also, was for many years behind the Congress and was the one source of inspiration to Congressmen, preparing and drafting its resolutions, going over its presidential addresses, and guiding its proceedings. The Congress vigorously criticised the Risley circular.

Tilak attended this session of the Congress. He was then an ordinary delegate, and Gokhale was advancing gradually in the Congress hierarchy. The only thing Tilak did in this session of the Congress was to convey to the Congress President, Pherozeshah Mehta, a resolution passed at a Poona meeting by the Poona Shastris requesting the Congress President not to allow the Social Conference the use of the Congress pandal for its session. Tilak did nothing more than to hand over the resolution to the President. The Social Conference had been held in the Congress pandal since the second session of the Congress without any break. No province had taken any objection to the holding of the Social Conference in the Congress pandal.

It was true that leaders like Dadabhai Naoroji and Pherozeshah Mehta never took an active interest in the activities of the Social Conference, but they never opposed or discouraged the social reformers. Dadabhai Naoroji and Mehta did this for two good reasons. Firstly, they sprang up from a minority community and so they shrewdly took the precaution of not interfering in the social reformers' activities which were mainly discussed with a view to reforming Hindu society. Secondly, they, in public life, favoured the principle of division of work, but to them division of work did not mean opposition. So no leading Congressman took note of the message of the Poona orthodox Hindus. It might be that Tilak was not then inclined to create a crisis over this issue. There had appeared also a note of disagreement in the *Kesari* over the resolution passed by the Poona Shastris. Notwithstanding this Tilak took part in the proceedings of the Social Conference, and supported the resolution on child-marriage and widow remarriage.

During the days of the Congress session Tilak and his friends had taken lodgings at the premises of the *Amrita Bazar Patrika* and the proprietor, Motilal Ghose, provided accommodation for the Poona guests. In those days delegates to the Congress used to carry their own utensils, cooked their own food, took their meals in the orthodox manner even at these distant places, and the Poona delegates were no exception to this practice.

The Congress session over, Tilak and his colleagues visited Gaya, Raniganj, Prayag, Lucknow and Agra, seeing holy places, and industrial centres from the point of national growth. At Agra, Tilak came to know that the Age of Consent Bill was coming up for consideration in the Central Legislature. With an eager look he told his colleagues that he was going direct to Poona as agitation over the Age of Consent Bill was to be renewed with greater force and enthusiasm.

On January 9, 1891, the Age of Consent Bill came up for consideration before the Central Legislative Council. Sir Andrew Scoble, Law Member, in moving for leave to amend the Indian Penal Code and the Code of Criminal Procedure, said that it was considered an offence of rape when a man had sexual intercourse with or without the consent of the woman when she was under ten years of age. It had been the law in India under that Code for more than thirty years. The proposal in the Bill, he observed, was to raise the age of consent, both for married and for unmarried women, from ten to twelve years. He did not suppose, he added, that anyone would question the right and duty of the State to interfere for the protection of any class of its subjects where a proved necessity existed for such interference.

He observed that the object of the Bill was two-fold. It was intended to protect female children (1) from immature prostitution and (2) from premature cohabitation. The Bill affected all classes of children, Europeans as well as natives.

As regards the second aspect of the proposal, he said that the sages enjoined and the institution of many castes required that a girl should be given in marriage before she attained puberty; and the second, that the Shastras denounced in the strongest terms and awarded the most terrible punishments, both here and hereafter, to the sin of connection with an immature girl. He, however, pointed out that the question of child-marriage was left untouched by his Bill.

"I am justified in saying that the teachings of the sacred books of the Hindus are not in conflict with the proposals of the Bill. To put it crudely, I shall say that a law which permits a full-grown man to violate with precaution a little girl of ten years' age cannot be considered sufficient, except from the ruffian's point of view."[4] Speaking on the Bill, the Hon'ble K. L. Nulkar supported the Bill, saying that it

4 *The Times of India*, 13 January 1891.

simply sought to remove a glaring defect in the Criminal Law of India. Sir Ramesh Chander Mitter, the solitary opponent of the Bill in the Council, said that the Bill interfered with Hindu religion, and it was against the spirit of the Queen's Proclamation.

On his return to Poona from Agra, Tilak sounded a warning to the opponents of the Bill of the impending danger. He declared now war on Ranade, Telang and Bhandarkar, the leaders of the social reformers. Telang expressed his opinion that those who broke scriptural rules for the advancement of political power could not object to the breach of such rules for saving Hindu women from inhuman cruelty. They should be compelled by law, asserted he, to do away with evil practices. He cited an example saying that because it was the tradition of a thief to rob, he should not be allowed to rob and preserve his tradition.

As regards protection granted under the Queen's Proclamation, Telang stated that its rigid application would involve a condemnation of all political and educational regulations, and lead them nowhere. Just at this time Bhandarkar published a pamphlet replying to the objections raised by Sir Ramesh Chander Mitter to the Bill. Referring to Tilak's interpretation of certain scriptures, Dr. Bhandarkar remarked that Tilak was at sea as regards the meaning of some words. Ranade also supported Bhandarkar in his scriptural interpretation and defended the Bill vigorously. Tilak took up the cudgels on behalf of the orthodox Hindus and the battle was joined!

Replying to both Bhandarkar and Telang, in the *Times of India*, Tilak observed that both of them had failed to grasp the real meaning of the Hindu Law texts. He stated that every writer of note on Hindu Law, Raghunandan, Kamlakar, Vijnaneshwar, Anantdeo and a host of others were on his side. Thus both the written law and the unwritten, he proceeded, enjoined consummation of marriage on the first attainment of puberty, and the Bill, if passed into law, would interfere with the religious custom.[5] He did not think that because certain exceptions were allowed in the Shastras, Government would be justified in going beyond them. Even though the precepts were obligatory or recommendatory, Government had no right to violate them. He asked Telang whether or not it would be an interference if a foreign Government proclaimed in England that no girl should marry when she was below twenty-five,

5 *The Times of India*, 2 February 1891.

and further asked him whether or not it would be a clear interference if Government were to abolish idolatry in India or restricted it in favour of certain idols alone.[6]

Tilak further said that though their English education had slackened their faith in the religious precepts, it ought not lead them to speak in such derisive words of the feelings and sentiments of the great majority even though they wished to reform them. He concluded his letter by expressing regret at the attempts made by the reformers to tune the *shastras* to the wishes of the rulers.

Tilak, who believed in the direct forceful attack, doubted, in the heat of the controversy, the depth of Bhandarkar's knowledge of Sanskrit although it was he who during the days of this controversy over the Age of Consent Bill went to Dr. Bhandarkar for references and to get to know the meaning of some technical terms in scriptures! He further said that Telang was a busy lawyer when, in fact, he was a judge and so his scriptural interpretation was not correct! He did not care to pay heed to the reply of his opponents who taunted him on the fact that Yeshwant Wasudeo Athalye whom Tilak tried to range against Bhandarkar, was also a busy lawyer. Moreover the authority of Athalye was cast to the winds as he finally certified that the interpretation of Bhandarkar was correct! The truth is that leaders of positive and forceful natures always drown their opponents' replies and rejoinders in the great din they create by their vociferous propaganda.

The controversy now reached a climax. Meeting upon meeting was held, some in support of the Bill, others in protest against it. On the opposition side were prominent pundits and leaders like Pundit Sesadhar Tarkachudamani, W. C. Banerjee, Babu Surendranath, G. S. Khaparde and others. A meeting of Hindu leaders in Bombay was called at Madhavbag, and it was decided to hold a meeting on February 8. At Poona the Shastris held a meeting which vehemently voiced its opposition to the Bill and declared that it interfered with religion and broke the solemn promise contained in the Queen's Proclamation. Such meetings were also held by the opponents of the Bill at Nagpur and Banaras. It may be noted here that A. O. Hume, who was for a number of years the Congress Secretary, declared that he would sever his connections with the Congress if he found that the majority of the

---

6 Ibid, 29 January 1891.

Congress leaders were opposed to the Bill. At the Bombay meeting held on February 8, 1891, Tilak was present and he congratulated the meeting on behalf of the Poona orthodox Hindus on the bold stand they had taken in regard to the Bill. At Shaniwarwada the Poona opponents of the Age of Consent Bill held on February 8, 1891, another meeting wherein they denounced the Bill.

Shortly after this, a meeting of the supporters of the Bill was held at Krida Bhuvan in Poona. It was sponsored by Dr. Bhandarkar and others. Admission to the meeting was confined to the supporters of the Bill only. Tilak and his party leaders had planned at a private meeting on the previous night to capture that meeting. Accordingly Tilak and Wasukaka Joshi, who acted as Tilak's right-hand man on such occasions, and also Tilak's followers, turned up at the appointed time one by one at the gate. Tilak was not allowed to go in; he had to wait outside for some time. But he got in saying that he wanted to make arrangements for the reporter of the *Kesari*.[7]

Tilak's partymen and students had entered under one or other pretext one by one. Soon the uproar from inside and pressure from outside increased terribly. This resulted in rowdyism, students and other hooligans slinging mud and pelting the reformers with stones at the meeting, and cursing Dr. Bhandarkar in unspeakable terms. Despite these attacks the meeting went on and extended its support to the Bill. The meeting concluded and Dr. Bhandarkar the old man had to seek shelter in a neighbouring house. The police then escorted him to his residence.

As a result of rowdyism, Wasukaka Joshi and others were arrested. Mahadeo Chimnaji Apte, a famous lawyer from Bombay, was briefed to defend the accused. The police failed to produce proper evidence and all the accused were acquitted. During the proceedings Dr. Bhandarkar was severely heckled by Apte, and he turned pale when Apte asked him to name the man who had wired to the *Times of India* about the meeting!

Tilak and Namjoshi then attended a meeting of the opponents of the Age of Consent Bill at Sholapur. But despite this agitation and opposition the Age of Consent Bill was passed on March 19, 1891, by the Central Legislative Council at Calcutta. The Law Member, Sir

7 Deogirikar, T. R., *Wasukaka Ani Tyancha Kal (Marathi)*, p. 213.

A. R. Scoble, said, while winding up the debate, that the balance of arguments and authority was in favour 0of the supporters of the Bill. "Even if it were not so," he observed, "were I a Hindoo, I would prefer to be wrong with Prof. Bhandarkar, Mr. Justice Telang and Dewan Bahadur Raghunath Rao than be right with Pundit Sesadhar Tarka-chudamani and Mr. Tilak." [8]

Tilak did not leave the leaders of the social reform at that. He wrote furiously in the *Kesari* that Ranade, Bhandarkar and Telang were not the leaders of the people. They were the men who had brought destruction on the people. People should not put their faith in such leaders. They must be cut off, as a deceased limb of the body is done away with![9] With the help of a Sanskrit quotation he described Ranade, Bhandarkar and Telang as wicked men adorned with learning![10]

This remark hurt Dr. Bhandarkar to the quick and he sadly remarked: "I have been carrying on literary controversies since 1864 but never did I hitherto meet with an opponent who treated me with such studied discourtesy as Mr. Tilak has been doing. This circumstance has rendered my task disagreeable and even painful."[11] "But this invcctivc of Tilak could never provoke the men of balmy fragrance, Ranade, Bhandarkar and Telang to use abusive epithets about Tilak.

Yet the opponents of the Age of Consent Bill in Poona made a final attempt by appealing to Government to abrogate the legislation. They held a mass meeting at Shanwarwada, voiced their opposition to the legislation and collected funds on the spot to carry on agitation and to present a representation in connection with the legislation.

In May of the same year the Bombay Provincial Conference was held at Poona under the presidentship of Govindrao Limaye where Tilak denounced Government for passing the Age of Consent Bill against popular opinion. There was a spirited discussion on the definition of the expression "popular opinion". The meeting passed a resolution expressing its dissatisfaction to Government for having passed the Bill against popular opinion. G. K. Gokhale, who had been upto this time one of the Secretaries with Tilak, resigned his post as Secretary of the Bombay Provincial Conference.

---

8 The *Times of India*, 23 March 1891.

9 The *Kesari*, 24 March 1891.

10 The *Kesari*, 7 April 1891.

11 Karnataki, S. N.: *Dr. Sir R. G. Bhandarkar*, p. 256 (Marathi).

By the next month the agitation over the Age of Consent Bill died down, and the acrimonious war of words ended. Strictly speaking, it had nothing to do with religion. The orthodox Hindus had dragged religion into it. It was concerned with the Indian Penal Code. The age-limit was to be raised from ten to twelve. Government had already by law abolished *Sati* and Infanticide and legalised widow-remarriage. Anyhow Tilak fought against it, and therefore he came to the forefront as a champion of Hindu institutions and traditions, and a group of leaders in small towns was being formed all over Maharashtra to support him in his future campaigns.

Apart from the outdated nature and reactionary fervour of its opponents the Age of Consent Bill exposed, it proved a pyrrhic victory for the foreign Government; for thereafter it never of its own accord touched any social matters. The agitation over it attracted the keen attention of the people and created a wave of popular opposition to social reforms. Reformers are always in a minority; traditionists are always in a majority! Tilak preferred to be with the majority. He said he must respect their prejudices and try to make the humblest of them feel that he was one of them. "If I adopt the heterodox ways," he observed, "I would not be in a position to influence them to the same extent as I could do by keeping to my orthodox ways." [12]

In private conversation Tilak often expressed to his friends concurrence in the views of the reformers. But his friends were surprised to hear Tilak opposing the reformers in public. When once he privately endorsed the views of the reformers, his daughter asked him why Dada[13] then opposed the reformers.[14] He replied that he was not prepared to go in the wilderness!

Another feature of the agitation was that people appreciated Tilak's courage in defying the British Government. Once again his remarkable quality displayed itself, and it confirmed the popular belief that when Tilak took upon himself any responsibility or undertook any public work, he untiringly laboured for it and carried it out, facing, struggling with and overcoming all difficulties.

---

12 Reminiscences and Anecdotes about Lokamanya Tilak, compiled and edited by S. V. Bapat, Vol. II, p. 7 (English Section).

13 Tilak was called Dada by his children.

14 Ibid, Vol. II, p. 30.

III

In October 1890 Tilak, the defender of orthodox Hindus, got himself unwittingly involved in an affair which brewed trouble for him for a year or two. The storm originated in a cup of tea which he had taken on October 4 along with forty-six men including Ranade and Gokhale. The prime mover in this affair was one Gopalrao Joshi. This gentleman had served in the postal Department for some years. He was no doubt a man of progressive views, but was rather a turbulent social worker. Queer, daring and energetic, he sent his wife to school and later sent her to Philadelphia, a great educational and political centre in America. He worked hard to make provision for her education, and she obtained there the degree of Doctor of Medicine. But unfortunately on her arrival in India she could not live long to give the benefit of her education to her countrymen. After her death Gopalrao Joshi went to England, but returned soon to Poona. Having travelled in foreign countries, he was now accustomed to the ways of other religions and customs. One day he decided to tease the Poona Christians by proving that the sprinkling of water and reading a chapter of the Bible could not convert one to Christianity. He received baptism at the hands of a priest, and a few days after he performed some religious rites and averred, to the surprise of the people, that he was still a Hindu.

Not satisfied with this achievement, Gopalrao Joshi devised a mischievous plan to expose the raw reformers and to twit rabid reactionaries. He engineered through the Panch Howd Mission at Poona an invitation to local leaders like Ranade, Tilak, Gokhale and others to deliver lectures at the Mission. The leaders came and spoke. After the lectures were over, as previously planned, the leaders were served tea. Hindu leaders taking tea publicly at a Christian House was in those days a monstrous idea! The whole gathering was embarrassed! All were trapped and nobody suspected that it was a trap laid with great care. Ranade did not drink tea, but took a sip in a spoon! Tilak, the boldest of them all, said that he would take it if a Brahmin served it! And the brother of Gopalrao Joshi served him tea in a cup from the mission kitchen. G. K. Gokhale and some others took tea without a word. Some Hindu women were also present, but they did not even touch the cup. Just imagine their consternation! The names of all those persons were published in a Poona weekly in January 1891 as the perpetrators of sin!

Though the sensational news was read by the orthodox leaders, they could not take immediate action against those violators of their religion!

The Age of Consent Bill had taken the time of the defenders of Hindu religion, and Tilak was fighting their battle. When the Age of Consent Bill became law, this new event came up before the public for discussion. Balasaheb Natu, the leader of the Sanatanists, referred the case to the Ecclesiastical Court of Shri Shankaracharya. Fortunately for the reformers and unfortunately for the orthodox, this time their defender and spokesman Tilak was thrown on the side of the reformers. During the discussion he attacked in his usual vitriolic way, Natu the orthodox leader, saying that the man who came of a family that was responsible for the ruin of the Peshwas and therefore whose seven generations were condemned to hell, was not the proper person to teach him what was and what was not conducive to the good of the nation; what was religion and what was duty!

At the aforesaid Court it was proved beyond doubt that Tilak had taken tea, but then he said he had undergone an expiation for his religious deviation. When he was attacked for his confession he replied that the tea affair was not before his mind when he performed *prayaschitta*. Gokhale did not care for the curses of the orthodox leaders and treated them with scant notice. So the arm of their Ecclesiastical Court did not reach him. The Ecclesiastical Court gave its judgment in the case in May 1891, pronouncing various punishments on those who were found guilty of transgression of Shastric laws. A few days after, to the astonishment of the orthodox and to the consternation of his admirers and lieutenants, Ranade, the leader of the reformers, too, on a mature consideration, decided to bend down to the decision of the Court of the religious Head. Not satisfied with the decision, Natu and others made an appeal to Shankaracharya, and Tilak and Ranade put up a vigorous defence at the Court. Tilak said that taking tea at the hands of non-Brahmins did not amount to losing one's caste. In return he asked the orthodox leaders whether it was proper on their part to eat potatoes which were never mentioned in the scriptural texts! Ranade's wife expressed disapproval of her husband's unqualified surrender to the orthodox Hindus. She resented it, she wept, she agitated in vain! Ranade performed *prayaschitta* in order to save his friends and lieutenants from being harassed by their relatives. No doubt he did it as a matter of policy and not on principle. For this kind of religious work he had patronised a Brahmin priest to perform religious rites at the houses of his friends.

The clash between the orthodox reactionaries and Tilak was not of Tilak's making. It was not due to any change in his convictions, but due to a chance. Had Tilak been as usual on the side of the orthodox reactionaries, he would have made Poona too hot for Ranade. Indeed his opposition to Ranade verged on hostility. This storm in the tea cup did not soften it; for, when the Nagpur Congress met in December 1891, he vehemently attacked Ranade during the session of the Social Conference. He nearly collided with Ranade, the father and leader of the Social Conference. Tilak had a tussle with Ranade's lieutenants in the morning and in the afternoon he had a passage-at-arms with Ranade during the session. Against Ranade he dashed with the force of the tidal waves of a rough sea. But like a rock in the sea, Ranade was placable and tranquil amid the raging billows! The questions came on direct like arrows, and the replies repelled their attacks, Ranade giving written replies through Dadasaheb Khaparde, President of the Social Conference. The violence of the tone and tempo of Tilak irritated even Khaparde who threatened Tilak with bodily removal if he did not observe decorum. Yet Tilak persisted in his questions and Ranade silenced him with smashing replies! The bitterness evoked was so sharp that one of Ranade's lieutenants exclaimed that their differences would not vanish during Tilak's lifetime!

At the Congress session which, as stated above, was held in a very beautiful pavilion in Nagpur, Tilak made a speech on a resolution urging the Government to conciliate Indian public opinion on matters concerning the defence of the country and to encourage and qualify Indians to defend their homes and their Government by modifying the rules under the Arms Act.

As the British Government defended Indians, observed Tilak in the course of his speech, some asked Indians why they wanted arms. The Government undertook to defend two hundred and fifty millions of the people against wild beasts and the wild bear of the north. As their own returns showed, proceeded Tilak, they did not defend the people against wild beasts and as for the northern enemy, they would doubtless do their best when the time came, but meanwhile their preparations were crushing the life out of the country. They did not wish the people to be starved to death, because the Russians might make a raid twenty-five years hence, he concluded.

As a result of the decision of the Appellate Court of Shankaracharya Tilak was ex-communicated. Brahmin priests would not perform religious rites at his house. Tilak doggedly sat with a sacred book in one hand and performed his rites with the other. The boycott was so complete that even the playmates of his children boycotted them. Tilak, in whose dictionary of life the word surrender was not found, did not mind this social boycott. At home there was no elderly person who could press him to yield to the social boycott. Self-respecting and unbending, he did not yield, as was his wont, to the threat. The thread ceremony of his eldest son and the marriage ceremony of his daughter were occasions when Tilak, too, felt the pinch of the boycott. A protege of Ranade was available for performing the religious rites at those functions, but Brahmin cooks were not available! One of his friends serving in a State sent help from his State and the difficulty was overcome.

It was quite strange that Tilak was thrown on the side of the reformers who blamed him for not being courageous enough to denounce the orthodox, while the orthodox leaders were offended by the defence he put up on behalf of the men who had taken tea at the hands of Christian Missionaries. Agarkar, therefore, described Tilak as a bat hanging in an inverted position between the reformers and the orthodox! More than that, Agarkar wrote an article in his *Sudharak* declaring that Tilak had taken food at the hands of a Muslim at a railway station. Tilak challenged Agarkar either to prove his allegation or to withdraw it unconditionally, and was about to take up the matter in the court when Ranade intervened and a compromise was arrived at. Of course, Agarkar had to eat humble pie.

IV

The second occasion that led to a complete breakdown of Tilak's relations with the reformers was the bitter controversy over an institution established by a woman named Pandita Ramabai, who was a Hindu convert to Christianity. She was the daughter of a Chitpavan Brahmin, who conducted a Sanskrit Academy at a secluded place. Her father was a promoter of women's education. He taught his wife Sanskrit and she too became a Pandita. After the death of Ramabai's parents she went to Calcutta with her brother and impressed with her Sanskrit learning all those who came in contact with her. She married her brother's Bengali friend by name Babu Bepin Biharidas, a Shudra who was a lawyer and a Brahmo. She lived in Assam with her husband. Soon after her husband died. She, therefore, came back to Calcutta, and thence returned to Bombay with her little daughter. Such was her courage and learning that her name and fame had preceded her.

She soon removed to Poona and decided to give herself up to the uplift and emancipation of women. To achieve her goal she established an institution called 'Arya Mahila Ashram'! She was a poor woman and she found it difficult to run the Ashram. The apathy shown by the Poona leaders to her institution totally disappointed her. By nature she was an ambitious woman and her ambition did not let her sit with folded hands. She turned her eyes for sympathy in another direction. She was favourably inclined to Christianity, and eventually she turned to Christian missionaries for help. She went to London accompanied by her daughter and there embraced Christianity in 1883. A woman of great moral force, she was endowed with untiring energy and great organising ability. She joined Cheltenham College to prosecute her studies. She also served as professor of Sanskrit in the same College. Her fame reached the farthest corners of America. She was thereupon invited by the authorities of the medical college at Philadelphia, to attend its convocation ceremony at which Anandibai Joshi was to receive the degree of Doctor of Medicine in 1886. Accordingly she went to America at the instance of Gopalrao Joshi and Anandibai Joshi. There she secured the help of missionaries, founded some institutions in America and then returned to India.[15]

With the solid support of American Missionaries she started her welfare activities in Bombay by establishing an institution called Sharada Sadan in March 1889. The Board of advisers consisted of reformers such as Ranade and Bhandarkar, and influential men like Nulkar and Dandekar. Soon she shifted her Sharada Sadan to Poona, the home of public institutions. The Sharada Sadan was a residential school for Indian girls, especially for widows. A Hindu woman converted to Christianity and working for the uplift of Hindu women from uninterested motives was regarded with suspicion. Tilak and his party did not believe in her disinterestedness, and they kept an eye on the activities of Ramabai. A few months after some reports appeared in American papers conducted by Missionaries praising Ramabai's missionary work at Poona. Tilak read one such report in the *Illustrated Christian Weekly* of New York and he threw a searching light on Ramabai's missionary work by publishing extracts from those reports.

Meanwhile Pandita Ramabai went to Mangalore for some days. In her absence earthen pots containing Tulsi-plant were handed over to a Christian woman, the acting Head of the Sharada Sadan, for the use of the religious rites of the Hindu girls and women in the Sadan. This was done purposely to test whether the institution was giving religious freedom to its occupants.

15 Thakare, K. S., *Pandita Ramabai.*

It had the desired effect. On her arrival in Poona from Mangalore, Pandita Ramabai kicked away those tulsi-pots. This was learnt from one Gadre, her clerk, who was a Prarthana-samajist. Nulkar resigned his membership when it was proved that Ramabai had converted to Christianity Gadre's own daughter who was also a student at the Sadan.

Tilak published a block of Ramabai's letter which she had addressed to Gadre, and there was a widespread uproar in Poona. Wasukaka Joshi played a very useful role in all the manoeuvres connected with the Ramabai affair. A man of robust common sense, he was a ready help to Tilak in his day-today public work and was a faithful colleague. Ramabai, with equal force, retorted that because the Hindus did not care for her institution she had to approach the missionaries on bended knees. The Hindu leaders should come forward, she added, to take charge of the Sharada Sadan if they did not want the missionaries to run the school. At this juncture Tilak published further extracts from Ramabai's American speeches and from her books published in America, and proved how she had promised the American missionaries that she would throw open the door of salvation through Christianity to the emancipated Indian girls and widows. Tilak likened her action to that of a woman who locked her neighbour's children and set fire to the roof, and who then said to God: "Oh! Almighty, I have done by humble part! Now it is in your hands to complete my mission!"

Tilak, editor of the *Kesari*, and V. B. Kelkar, editor of the *Mahratta*, differed in their views on this affair of the Sharada Sadan. When friends twitted Tilak pointing to the articles in the *Mahratta* which favoured the stand taken by Ramabai, Tilak wrote bluntly that it was ingrained in his blood to criticize fearlessly anybody from a judge to the editor of *Subodh Patrika* disregarding the opinions of father, uncle, maternal uncle, wife and sons. The separation between the two editors became inevitable and Tilak took over the ownership of both the *Mahratta* and *Kesari* accepting liability of seven thousand rupees over the two papers, the Press being taken over by his two partners, V. B. Kelkar and H. N. Gokhale.

Ranade and Dr. Bhandarkar pulled up Ramabai for her unreasonable attitude, but she set their authority at naught by securing plenary powers from her Head Office in America. Ranade and Bhandarkar protested against her unjust attitude; but they failed to evoke in her any unbiassed feelings and to make her eschew her ulterior motives. So they severed their connection with the Sadan. At last they declared that the Sadan was conducted as an avowedly proselytizing institution and that Ramabai had departed from the lines of strict neutrality. Guileless as they were, they came round at last to the views of Tilak after being thoroughly disillusioned.

Later, Ramabai removed the Sharada Sadan from the purview of the Poona leaders to Kedgaon where she changed the name "Sharada" to "Mukti" —salvation—and it became a Christian centre for proselytizing activities. So complete was the metamorphosis Ramabai underwent that she refused to let her daughter learn Sanskrit.[16]

Tilak rightly and ruthlessly attacked the Sadan because it had developed into a centre for proselytism. However, it must be noted here that a notice was given in 1893 over the signatures of Tilak and other leaders in the *Kesari* to the effect that a school would be opened for Hindu girls and widows, but nothing came out of it. It had been the charge laid against Tilak by his critics that Tilak made only destructive criticism and never took up the consequential responsibility for constructive work. Tilak had a genius for organisation and if he had a mind to establish a school for girls and widows, he would have seen the scheme through. He had his own ideas about women's education, but he had no time to give practical shape to them, and so none knew exactly what they were like! Later D. K. Karve, who started women's education on the basis of Indian traditions, too, could not win any support from Tilak.

While engaged in the controversies over social reforms, Tilak's mind had been labouring patiently for the previous three years on determining the hoary age of the *Vedas*. While reading the *Gita* in 1889, one day it occurred to him that "we might derive important conclusions from the statement of Krishna that 'he was Margashirsha of the months'." This led him to put his intellectual telescope to the Vedic Calendar. In those days Deccan College provided a platform for intellectual giants. A few months earlier Tilak had made a speech at the College on " the sacred thread and the Thread Ceremony "in which he suggested that the idea of the sacred thread must have originated in the astronomical positions of the planets in the sky and through various changes the idea must have assumed the present form.

This time Tilak read a paper on the subject of the Antiquity of the *Vedas* at Deccan College under the presidentship of Principal Selby and also delivered a lecture on the same subject in Poona. Arriving at some conclusions, he decided to submit a paper to the Ninth Oriental Congress

---

16 Zacharias, H. C. E., *Remanescente India*, p. 21.

which was to be held in London in 1892. With that end in view he took up the work in hand and shut himself for a month in a room on the third floor of his residence at Vinchurkar's Wada and, dictating page after page, he completed the paper in one month, working day and night, hardly having time to sleep. As a result of this continuous sleeplessness, his mouth and tongue were covered thickly with red and sensitive spots, and he could not take his usual diet for a month or so.

The paper was submitted to the Oriental Congress and was published in October 1893 under the title *The Orion* or *Researches into the Antiquity of the Vedas*. The originality of the work lies in the fact that so far the Western scholars had carried their research through purely language methods. Tilak abandoned it and adopted the astronomical method. The Western scholars had come to the conclusion that the *Vedas* were not the most ancient scriptures, and they hesitated to place the commencement of the Vedic civilization earlier than 2400 B.C. Tilak pressed all his knowledge of Sanskrit and astronomy, and traced the Greek origin of the Orion and also the name of that constellation to Sanskrit Agrahayani or Agrahayan. The latter word means the beginning of the year. He, therefore, based his conclusions on what is known as the precession of the equinoxes, the phenomenon associated with the crossing of the meridian by the Sun.

He, therefore, concluded that all the hymns of the *Rigveda* containing references to that word, i.e. the equinoxical point, or the various traditions clustering round it, must have been completed before the Greek separated from the Hindus and at a time when the vernal equinox was in the Orion, or, in other words, when the year began with the Sun in the constellation of Orion or Margashirsha, i.e. before 4000 B.C. In support of his conclusion he quoted many of the Vedic texts and legends, and showed how these legends were strikingly corroborated by the legends and traditions of Iran and Greece.

As every new research is subjected to a gruelling test before it is accepted by scholars, Tilak's new theory* was also examined; and gradually Western scholars like Max Muller, Weber, Jacobi and Whitney acknowledged the learning and originality of the author. Whitney, with a thought-provoking article on Tilak's book in the journal of the Oriental Society, paid glowing tributes to the author. Dr. Bloomfield of Johns Hopkins University, in an anniversary address, described the book as "an event which is certain to

* Russian research scholars have upheld most of the points in Tilak's thesis.—The *Soviet Land*, Bombay, issues Nos. 12 and 13 of July 1968.

stir the world of Science and Culture." He applauded at the leonine way in which the author had marshalled the Vedic literature and other occidental works. "The book is unquestionably," opined the famous scholar, "the literary sensation of the year; history, the chronic readjuster, shall have her hands uncommonly full to assimilate the result of Tilak's discovery and arrange her paraphernalia in the new perspective."

Long before, Dr. R. G. Bhandarkar and K. T. Telang also had unfurled the flag of Indian scholarship and research. Bhandarkar's different papers, Telang's great thesis on Shankara-charya and his brilliant essay on the *Ramayana*, which he wrote at the age of twenty and twenty-three respectively, had cast a halo round Indian scholarship and research. Their intellectual peer Tilak came forward now to carry on the torch of the light with his great illuminating scholarship. The days of Tilak were the days of scholar-politicians. These leaders Ranade, Bhandarkar, Telang and Tilak were the peaks of erudition and research. Government also could not resist its admiration for the great work. It purchased some copies of Tilak's book to help defray the expenses of its publication. It may be noted that H. Jacobi, a German scholar, had at the same time sought to date the Vedic literature with the help of astronomical data. Both Tilak and Jacobi independently and simultaneously arrived at nearly the same conclusion, just as Darwin and Wallace evolved the theory of natural selection without knowing of each other's work.

VI

The fight in the social field being over, Tilak now turned his attention to Congress propaganda. He had now much leisure. He taught in his Law Classes in the morning, and editing of the weekly *Kesari* would take him two days at the most. The rest of the week was utilised by him for public work.

The Congress leaders in those days were busy lawyers. A. O. Hume was General Secretary of the Congress for many years, and he worked very hard to attract able men to it. After the annual session everybody forgot the work of the Congress; for the delegates made speeches and passed resolutions with the eyes fixed towards Government quarters. It was Tilak who first saw the futility of those appeals and realised that the Congress would be able to ameliorate the condition of the people if the masses were attracted to it and their power was harnessed to the chariot of the Congress.

It was the main role in his life to stir up the people against their poverty, degradation and slavery.

Tilak naturally turned his attention to the peasants who had been harassed by the constant visitations of famine. It was the responsibility of the Government to look after the interests of the peasants in times of famines. But Government was not performing its duty properly. He therefore began to criticize Government policy fearlessly. He laid emphasis on economic troubles, dwelt on the selfish policy of the foreign Government that had dislocated Indian nascent industries and had hampered their growth with a view to favouring the imports of British goods.

Tilak pleaded that unlike America where there was fresh, fertile and plenty of land for cultivation, the Indian soil was worn out and had grown less fertile having been under cultivation for centuries. Heavy pressure on land further made the life of the peasants poorer. The failure of rains drove them to desperation with the result that their houses, lands and cattle were encumbered with heavy debts. More than that, about fifty millions of the population dragged on a miserable existence remaining on the verge of starvation and in every decade millions died of starvation. Intensely sympathetic with the masses for their unbearable sufferings, Tilak protested against the laws and administration that were reducing the peasantry to hopeless poverty.

It was at this time that Hume addressed a confidential circular letter to the Congress leaders, saying that the cup of misery of scores of millions of the Indian masses was well nigh full and that a terrible rising was at the door. He, therefore, warned the leaders that Government would not be able to protect the people or itself. The circular created an uproar. Some Indian journals and Englishmen described Hume's circular letter as a symbol of treason, and Mr. Maclean, Member of the British Parliament, declared that under a less mild rule than the British Hume would be hanged or shot as a traitor. Some of the Congressmen took fright and dissociated themselves from that circular.

Tilak's own articles bore the title: "Will the Peasants have to revolt?" Pointing out that the people were burdened with taxes, that the population was increasing and trade was declining, and that Government was becoming costlier and land growing less fertile, he emphatically remarked that these factors presented a very horrible picture, and it was not impossible that there would be a revolt!

Tilak's articles in those days were full of anxiety about the future of the Congress organisation, although he was sure that the Congress would go down in history as a monumental institution. But to make it a power he said it should be organised on a firm basis so that it might grow from strength to strength. He was restless over the indifference on the part of moneyed men and educated classes to the Congress. In its early stages the Congress organisation always suffered from want of men and money. Tilak persistently wrote that Congress must continue to hold its annual sessions with greater enthusiasm. He urged the rich classes to subscribe to the Congress fund and lend support to the Congress and appealed to the educated classes to lend liberal support to the Congress. He was, however, glad that the movement was gradually spreading and hoped that the ignorance of the people about the Congress would be decreased with growing propaganda.

In November 1892, the Bombay Provincial Conference was held at Poona. The successive successful sessions of the Provincial Conference now attracted the bosses of the Congress like Pherozeshah Mehta, and he presided over that year's Conference. Lively interest was taken by the delegates in discussing the form and constitution of the proposed Councils under the New Act of 1892. Tilak moved the important resolution on this subject and suggested that the Municipalities and such other institutions should be the electorates of the proposed Legislative Councils. This Conference was important from another point of view. Delegates from other parts of the Bombay Province attended it for the first time. At the end of the Conference Tilak was again elected Joint Secretary of the Provincial Conference along with D. E. Wacha and Chimanlal H. Setalwad.

CHAPTER VI

A National Awakening

I

DURING THE FIRST quarter of the year 1893 Tilak was busy with two problems. The first was the demand for the extension of the system of trial by jury. The Congress had been voicing that demand through its resolutions since its second session. The jury system was introduced in India in 1862; but it was almost nullified by Government in 1872 by depriving the verdicts of juries of all finality, and by investing the Sessions Judges and High Courts with the power to set aside the verdicts of acquittal by the juries.

At this time K. T. Telang, giving his opinion on the issue, said that the system of trial by jury in murder cases should not be applied to areas like Belgaum, Ahmedabad and Surat. Tilak severely criticised Telang's stand and declared that however cultured a man might be by learning and gentlemanliness these qualities might not necessarily inspire him with confidence and courage to express his opinions fearlessly and would not lead him to any substantial achievement. And Telang was an example of this! That Telang the Judge, the first Indian to be appointed Vice-Chancellor of an Indian University, the orator and the author should have expressed such an opinion was very strange. Tilak, therefore, said that it would indeed be a great day when people began to understand the difference between an able and learned executive and a leader of the people. The title of Tilak's article was a sharp Marathi proverb used to depict a traitor: "One who assists the enemy is injuring his own people."

The second problem that occupied Tilak's mind this year was the resolution of Government modifying the Public Service Commission's Report. All Congress leaders opposed it vociferously. Dadabhai Naoroji, who was now an M.P., pressed upon the attention of the British Parliament the injustice done to India by not holding simultaneous examinations in India and England for the Indian Civil Service. It was the consensus of opinion among Indian leaders that, as the service was to be performed in India, the examinations should be held in India alone.

Tilak also wrote in his weeklies asking people to send petitions to Parliament, and himself submitted a memorial defending the natural right, the inalienable right of Indians to serve their motherland. He explained to the people how the Government policy of employing Europeans in the higher ranks of public services was responsible for draining away India's money and was the cause of the growing poverty of India. He told the people that it was a pity that the sons of India should be required to serve the British masters in the capacity of subordinate officers, such as assistants, deputies and sub-officers. The appellation "Head" could be connected with Indians only when they were police constables and teachers. He added that the popular belief that under British rule even a blind man could travel from one end of the country to the other with gold tied to his staff without being robbed was no longer true, as the prevailing regime itself had rendered them paupers.

Speaking on simultaneous examinations before the Congress, Gokhale, too, had indignantly remarked that if the rulers did not carry out their promises, they should openly and publicly fling into flames all those promises and pledges as so much waste paper, and should tell their subjects once for all that, after all, they were a conquered people and they could have no rights or privileges. Thereafter Gokhale was looked upon as an enemy of the Government and was followed by police spies!

While this propaganda was going on, an event took place that proved to be a turning point in Indian politics. On August 11, 1893, communal disturbances occurred between the Hindus and Muslims. Communal disturbances had occurred before this, but there was a difference now in that the recent disturbances had a method in their madness. Sudden outbreaks of great fury broke out between the Hindus and Muslims when temples and mosques were stormed; localities were given up to pillage and slaughter, and peace was restored only by military troops. Such riots had taken place at Banaras in 1809, at Bareilly, and at other places in the United Provinces in 1871; and in 1885-87 serious clashes took place throughout the Punjab culminating in the great Delhi riots of 1886 when there was an overlapping of festivals.

To understand the background of these disturbances it is necessary to go back a little. The birth of the Congress was not taken too happily by the leaders of Muslims. At Lucknow, on December 28, 1887, while the National Congress was holding its third session at Madras, Sir Syed Ahmed Khan warned the Muslims of the evils which they would suffer from majority rule and of the bloody consequences of political agitation.[1]

The wave of these communal clashes spread from Prabhas Pattan in the Junagadh State to Bombay, although grave outbreaks had already occurred in the Azamgarh District of the United Provinces because cow killing was allowed on the Bakri-Id day near temples. Much earlier serious riots had broken out at Rangoon between the Hindus and Muslims because cows were not allowed to be slaughtered near the temples. The Junagadh State was in those days ruled by a Muslim Prince. There the Muslims broke the idols of the Hindus and poured boiling oil on innocent saints and hermits, gosavins and pilgrims.[2]

Gujarati Hindus in Bombay held a meeting to express sympathy for the oppressed Hindus at Prabhas Pattan; Muslims in Bombay also held a meeting and expressed their support to the Muslims at Prabhas Pattan. This created tension, and the Muslims in Bombay started a riot on August 11, 1893, at Hanuman lane breaking the temple of Hanuman. The Muslims in neighbouring localities simultaneously sprang out at the appointed time and pounced upon the Hindus, who were taken unawares. Such was the ferocity of the rioters that guns had to be fired to quell the rioters.

Next day, at the instance of Laxmidas Khimji, a Bombay millionaire, who was a very influential man well known for his magnanimous heart, the Mahratta Hindus attacked the Muslims and literally reduced them to a position between the devil and the deep sea, the Muslims from some localities seeking shelter at the seaside mosque at Mahalaxmi. In order to restore peace in the city the Police Commissioner took a round in company with the leaders of both the communities.

The news of the riots spread to Poona and Hindu leaders there were perturbed and the masses were disturbed. Tilak took up his pen and attacked the British officials holding them responsible for the butchery of Hindus. The main point of his attack was that Government was partial, and was not performing its duty in a just and fearless, impartial and ruthless manner.

---

1 *Political India*, edited by Sir John Cumming, p. 89.

2 Kelkar, N. C., *Life of Lokamanya Tilak* (Marathi), p. 395.

When Tilak took up the question, a controversy started. The Anglo-Indian newspapers and Government spokesmen attributed these riots to the cow-protection societies established by the Hindus. Some said mischievously that the Hindus were safe under British rule, otherwise Muslims would have harassed them. This anti-Hindu propaganda carried on by interested groups provoked Tilak, and he replied that nobody so far had heard any complaint made by any Muslim that because of the work of the cow-protection societies there was paucity of beef. Tilak observed that there was a ban on cow-slaughter in the pre-British period also, and repudiating the charge that Hindus were safe from Muslim attack under British rule, he stated the fact that the British captured India not from the Muslims, but from the Mahrattas and Sikhs, who had brought the Muslim rulers to their knees.

Elucidating these points, he further observed that the false notion that Government was afraid of the Muslims gave rise to these riots, and its partiality emboldened them to attack the Hindus. He held that because Government could not curb the aggressors, Hindus had to resort to violence in self-defence. The Hindus had no other alternative but to beat back the Muslim aggression when Government protection failed. In his opinion the Hindus were a tolerant people; they were not rude and wild like the Muslims. They had to resort to violence only under provocation. He was glad to note that the Hindus had not so far fallen a victim to the spirit of the adage, "resist not but yield to the aggressor." He was glad that the Mahratta Hindus had not developed that cowardice which would ask them to suffer meekly the miseries inflicted by others without retaliation!

Immediately after the Bombay riots, the Poona Hindus led by Tilak called a meeting of Hindus to represent their case to the Government. Ranade and Mehta asked Tilak to drop the idea of the meeting as they feared that such Hindu meetings would aggravate feelings. It was not that they did not believe in the justness of the Hindu side. The *Dnyanprakash*, the mouthpiece of the Ranade Party, said two weeks later: "Some of the Government officials may think it to be an agreeable pastime to put one race against another and to make political capital out of the whole affair. But how dangerous this procedure is can now very well be realised when we have experienced this year a frightful succession of disturbances."

Tilak replied to the Ranade Party that if Government were to be plainly told that Muslims rioted because of its partial attitude, the meeting should be a purely Hindu affair. Ranade had sent a written message to one of his lieutenants advising him to root out the idea of a Hindu meeting in its early stage. But the meeting did take place, as Tilak was determined to hold it. Another feature of the meeting was that not only the Ranade Party, but also those who had supported Tilak's agitation against the Age of Consent Bill were now on the opposite side. So Tilak took every precaution not to give any chance for misreport or misrepresentation of the speeches that would be made at the meeting. Every speaker read his speech before the audience.

Tilak made a vitriolic attack on Ranade and his Party and wrote with ostentatious piousness that had Ranade the sweetness of Telang he would have been installed in judgeship long before; had he one-fourth of the courage possessed by Mandlik or Mehta he would have been hundred times more useful than what he was. Tilak acknowledged the vastness of Ranade's intellect and its sharpness, but, he proceeded, it did not mean that Ranade had been born with a charter of righteousness and infallibility.

In this attack on Ranade Tilak explained his theory of leadership. His first principle was that leaders were not masters, but servants of the people. As long as the views of the leaders did not differ much from those of the people, the leaders deserved their homage. When they differed, there was bound to be a divorce! He pointed out that Government valued the opinion of the Sarvajanik Sabha not because it was the mouthpiece of Ranade, but because it represented public opinion.

In another article in the *Kesari* Tilak observed that differences on political and social problems were bound to prevail, and such differences were welcome to some extent; just as it was dangerous to say that God was reachable by only one particular way of worship, so also it was very dangerous to plead that one particular method or one particular opinion alone was conducive to national progress. Everyone was more or less proud of his views and depended on the people for their support. Naturally one whose views captivated the masses at a particular time must be regarded as a leader of the people. He concluded that Ranade's views would have been people's views had the leaders of different groups accepted them.

This was how Tilak influenced public opinion. According to those principles it was easy, his critics held, to rouse the people, but those principles were not useful for controlling, educating and guiding public opinion as the leader who followed such principles would not show courage to differ from the people. No other leader was a better or more perfect symbol of this philosophy of leadership! By his agitation over the Age of Consent Bill Tilak captured the sympathies of orthodox Hindus and the haters of British Raj; by his agitation over the Crawford affair he won the hearts of many others. Tilak was now coming to the forefront as a leader of the Hindus in Maharashtra, overcoming all opposition to his leadership offered by the Ranade Party.

These controversies could not distract Tilak's attention from the session of the Bombay Provincial Conference. Its sixth session was held at Ahmedabad in the first week of November 1891, where he moved a resolution opposing the increased land assessment in Maharashtra. The Conference put on record its opinion that the separation of the Executive and Judicial functions should be effected as early as possible, and it appointed a committee under the Hon'ble Mr. Pherozeshah Mehta to work out a scheme for the various districts in the Presidency. Tilak was a member of that Committee. At this juncture Hume paid a visit to Poona. Impressed by the zeal, sacrifice and sincerity of Hume for the uplift of India and his ability in active propaganda for bolstering up the Congress, Tilak praised Hume as the Mahatma who showed the Indian leaders the key to political progress, and he hoped that some Indian leaders would come forward to carry on vigorously the work of the Congress. A few days later Tilak was elected Fellow of Bombay University by the students, and Ranade, genial and placable, had supported his candidature.

About this time Dadabhai Naoroji, who had been elected to the British Parliament in 1892 by the electors of Central Finsbury, came to India on an invitation by the Congress leaders to preside over its Lahore session which was to be held in the last week of December 1893. He was given a great ovation on his arrival in Bombay on December 16, and next day Poona accorded him a grand welcome at a public meeting which was held at Hirabag. Paying glowing tributes to Dadabhai, Tilak said that they had received the guest in as fitting a manner as they could and added that those of the Bombay friends who had come to see how the Poona people performed their duty would take favourable news to Bombay. Upon this Pherozeshah, who in response to a call from the audience rose to make a speech, said amidst laughter that he had not come to Poona as a spy as stated by Tilak but as an Indian to join in co-operating with them at the national gratification for the election of Dadabhai.

Soon after this function Tilak went to Amritsar to attend the annual session of the Congress. In this session he spoke on the resolution asking Government to fulfil their thirty years' old promise to grant permanent settlement in land revenue in India. He pointed out that the increase in land revenue amounted to thirty per cent in the Bombay Presidency.

Just then riots between the Hindus and Muslims occurred at many places in Maharashtra, disturbing intermittently the tranquillity of the Province for over two years. During the course of the riots idols were broken and cows were killed in temples. In February 1894 Tilak visited Akola where riots had broken out for the second time and brought to light the mischief of Government officers, blaming the Government of Lord Harris for not taking proper precautions in the matter. Riots had been threatening to break out in Poona since June 1894, but were averted. At last a riot broke out at Poona also in September 1894 during the Ganesh festival which Tilak had started as a means of propagating nationalism among the masses and in which people enthusiastically participated. The Hindus at Poona retaliated severely, and as a result some Hindus were arrested and prosecuted; but later were acquitted in November 1894 by Mr. Jacob, the judge in the Sessions Court, Poona. Jacob was thereafter privately honoured by Poona Hindus; and while he was presiding over a school function, the Poona Hindus showered flowers on him! At a public meeting the leaders were publicly congratulated on their acquittal, and Government was blamed for wrong prosecutions and for their negligence in the matter. Tilak demanded an apology from Lord Harris for running down the Poona Brahmins.

Tilak said there should be a peaceful and just settlement of the issue. With that end in view Muslims should not be allowed to kill cows near Hindu localities, and Hindus should be allowed also to carry on cow protection in Muslim localities. Muslims should not object to the playing of music by Hindus near mosques and should carry on their prayers as they did when in trains and steamers!

As regards the advice tendered by the Christians, who asked the Hindus to have brotherly relations with all, he replied that it would happen when all other people also behaved well towards the Hindus. He further declared that it would be good if the Hindus and Muslims understood that they would not be profited by rowdyism and brutalities. The third party, the Government, was dividing them and setting one against the other. He further pointed out that the Britishers took sides with the Muslims not because they loved the mosques more than the temples, but because it helped them to perpetuate their rule by creating divisions among Indians.

These views led the British officials to believe that Tilak's agitation was directed more against the British Government than against the Muslims. Indeed, his leadership did not aim at opposing the Muslims or at arousing the animosity of the Hindus towards them, but he opposed vehemently their fanaticism. To foster opposition to British rule in India, to bring people into conflict with Government, and to make Government unpopular was the sole aim of his speeches, writings, and leadership, although the inner man must have felt sure that the view that communal differences were deliberately fomented by the British on the principle of *divide at impera* was not wholly true. Yet Tilak would not have missed an opportunity to win over Muslim sympathy and direct the Muslims against the Government had they shown such a gesture.

Out of this tension and trouble, some good, however, came out. Tilak utilised the enthusiasm and vigour of the people for keeping up their pride in the doings of their ancestors and used it as a means of educating the common people. The Hindus, who had been so far participating in the Moharram celebrations, now gave it up. He harnessed their energy for organising the Ganesh festival and thus people got a substitute. Before the advent of Tilak, the Ganesh festival was not a public affair. It was a private one. It was his organising ability and lead which transformed it into a public festival. He aroused in the people a sense of corporate feelings. And Ganesh or Ganpati festival societies were founded all over Maharashtra. Youths organised themselves into bands of singers. Gymnastic societies were encouraged, and deeds of self-denial and valour were put forth for emulation before the young by fiery speakers and priests during the days of the festival. For some time a band of Hindu youths acted as bodyguard of Tilak to protect him against any possible attack by Muslim ruffians.

Tilak realised that the British rulers took sides with the Muslims because their policy turned upon selfishness and self-aggrandizement! They sided with the Muslims because they saw a danger in the Hindu majority who were gradually awakening. The Muslims thought that they were in a minority and backward in education, and they feared that because the Hindus were going ahead in every field, they would capture all political power!

The Act passed by the British Parliament in June 1893 on the civil service was not less responsible for confirming that belief of the Muslims. A few enlightened Muslims like Badruddin Tyabjee took part in the Congress movement. Congress leaders were taking steps very cautiously and tactfully lest they might wound the susceptibilities of the Muslims. That is why a proposition on cow-protection was dropped during the Madras Congress[3] when Badruddin Tyabjee presided over the Congress

3 Athalye, D. V., The Life of Lokamanya Tilak, p. 76.

in 1887. Despite such caution, now the Muslims were showing signs of a slight departure from the national stand. The Aligarh school of thought ushered in by Syed Ahmed to preach boycott of the Congress was gradually gaining ground. At the time of the last Provincial Conference, which was held at Ahmedabad, some Muslims there had held a separate meeting and declared that they had nothing to do with that Provincial Conference.

While the Congress was holding its session at Lahore, at Aligarh Sir Syed Ahmed and Mr. Beck, the Principal of his College at Aligarh, were exhorting Muslims to keep aloof from the Congress and impressing upon the Muslim mind the importance of establishing a separate organisation for the British and Muslims to counteract Hindu domination. Tilak watched these activities and wrote an article in which he described Beck as an enemy of Hindusthan. A few months before, the Bombay Provincial Conference had met at Bombay under the presidentship of a Muslim gentleman, and Tilak therefore felt great relief. He expressed a hope that the national-minded Muslims would not fall a victim to communal feelings. When, therefore, two years later the Muslims held a separate conference at Karachi while the Bombay Provincial Conference was going on in that city, Tilak deplored the move and the object behind it.

II

DURING THE LAST quarter of the year 1894 Tilak was engaged in the defence of his friend V. S. Bapat who was an Officer in the Land Alienation Department of Baroda. While the Maharaja of Baroda was on a tour of Europe and the British officer who was the well-wisher of Bapat had proceeded to England on leave, the British Resident at Baroda, the Land Alienation Settlement Commissioner and the Dewan of Baroda decided to bring an action against Bapat for corruption. Bapat was suspended and a Commission was appointed to try him. Bapat was brought to Bombay by Wasukaka Joshi by giving the police the slip, and Bapat lay for some time in hiding. A few days later he was produced at Baroda through his legal advisers. He was charged with having received thirty-six bribes. It was the allegation of the prosecution that in fifteen of the original charges Mr. Bapat had himself received the bribes, and in the remainder agents had been employed.

Tilak, who was as ruthless in crushing his opponents as he was sincere in helping his friends, went to Baroda to defend his friend. It was his belief that Bapat was absolutely innocent of the charges laid against him. Tilak and M. C. Apte defended him. 'Pursue an object with all your might, with all the power of your mind, with all the force of your will' was Tilak's motto. Tilak sat day and night preparing all papers of the case, arranging evidence and doing clerical work also. On the other side was a European Barrister, Branson, and for some days Pherozeshah Mehta also worked for the prosecution. Apte was an experienced lawyer and he was powerful enough to make even Pherozeshah Mehta uneasy on the other side. Tilak, the editor and lawyer, sometimes suggested some points which were not relevant or appropriate! And Apte said to Tilak with a meek smile: "Balwantrao, this is a court affair and not a matter to be howled after in an editorial!" While the proceedings were going on, Apte died and his place was taken by Tilak's friend D. A. Khare.

Tilak worked at Baroda under many disadvantages. Bapat, who had full power to do a good or an evil turn to anyone who had dealings with the Alienation Office, found now that his influence had totally waned. Tilak could not get even accommodation for his office at Baroda. Police spies dogged his footsteps, and he had to write to the Dewan of Baroda that if he so desired he would send his day-to-day diary for his perusal.

Tilak returned to Poona after recording the statement of the accused, and reopened his Law Class from March 1895. Engrossed in the proceedings of Bapat case, he could not find time to attend the Bombay Provincial Conference which was held in Bombay in November 1894, nor could he attend the Madras Congress which met in December 1894. Although Bapat was originally charged with having received thirty-six bribes, only twelve of those charges were investigated. Finally he was sentenced by the Commission to six months' imprisonment, and, in addition, was fined ten thousand rupees.

His Highness the Maharaja of Baroda just then returned to Baroda. He called for the papers of the Bapat case, and took counsel with his judges and ministers. On the unanimous advice of those officers the Maharaja made a decision. He "freed" the accused of the whole eleven charges of which the Commission had found him guilty, but ordered that Bapat's services be dispensed with. Bapat, however, was pensioned off. Some papers highly criticised the decision, asking why the Maharaja did not use the expression "acquitted" instead of "freed".

In serving his friend, Tilak had served the Maharaja of Baroda also whose administration his ill-wishers wanted to censure. Tilak had indirectly defended the administration of Baroda and on many points frustrated the plans of the clique that wanted to cast aspersions on the Maharaja! The Maharaja called him and requested him to translate a work for his State. Tilak was a symbol of self-respect, and he was confident that his pen and power were meant for higher achievements. He, therefore, did not stoop to conquer. When he returned home, he told his nephew that he had flatly declined the offer of the Maharaja, and added: "I am not born to earn my bread by making mere translations for others. I am actuated with the spirit of some century work for the age I live in!"[4]

No sooner did Tilak return to Poona than he was drawn into another controversy. It was the time of retirement of Lord Harris, the Governor of Bombay, and his admirers wanted to erect a public memorial to him. Lord Harris had said that the leaders of the Province needed more commonsense and had also called them mean-minded. So Tilak expressed his indignant disapproval of the remark and was grieved to see that people had grown so devoid of self-respect as to erect a memorial to a ruler who had insulted them and had failed in performing his duties. He attacked the servile attitude of those leaders who had developed the habit of flattering the rulers by erecting a memorial to every retiring Governor or Viceroy, just as they performed every year the anniversary rites of their deceased father with studied regularity! The result was that the idea of a public memorial was given up! Nobody but Tilak could write in such a ruthless manner. He was a synonym for courage! He despised the cowards and loathed the abject flatterers who fawned on the Governor.

It was the practice of Tilak to congratulate and encourage anyone who faced or pulled up bureaucrats for some reason or other. He bestowed his hearty praise on Pherozeshah Mehta, who had attacked the Government in the Council in connection with the Police Act Amendment.

III

TILAK'S FRIENDS AND admirers now strove to raise their leader to a still higher status in his political career. The time for the elections to the reformed Legislative Councils, which were expanded under the Indian Councils Act of 1892, had come. Under that Act, the Bombay Presidency got six seats for its elected representatives, Madras seven and Bengal also seven. Tilak had not contested a seat at the time of the first election. Six Districts in the Bombay Presidency then were not given elective rights, Poona District

---

4 *Reminiscences and Anecdotes about Lokamanya Tilak*, Vol. I, p. 200, compiled and edited by S. V. Bapat.

being one of them, but now the Districts were invested with elective rights. Tilak decided to contest a seat and entered the arena; and it turned into a battle.

There were two rivals. One was Garud, who was a well-connected and well-to-do young man. Another rival, Jathar, was also a very influential man. He was a Rao Bahadur and former Director of Public Instruction in Berar, and was supported by the Ranade Party. Government servants, who abhorred Tilak, were on the side of Jathar. However, some Government officers who were Tilak's friends and worked for him silently. The propaganda on both the sides soon reached a climax. Tilak was now an outstanding leader in Poona, and Ranade was the only leader in Maharashtra whom he could not outshine so far.

In the meanwhile Tilak stood for the Poona Municipal election also. Till then, he had helped his men to capture municipal seats. Now he desired to do it himself. It was easy for him to win success and he was elected in March 1895 on behalf of the doctors, engineers, and graduates. He served the city in that capacity for about two and a half years. During this term he prepared, as requested by the Municipality under special resolutions, the welcome speeches to be made on the occasions of the visits of the Governor and the Governor-General and on the Diamond Jubilee Day of Queen Victoria.[5] He was now riding the popular wave. Triumphs came one after another as the reward of his selfless service in the public cause. Tilak succeeded in the election to the Legislative Council, routing his formidable rivals. This victory of Tilak must have made Government and the Anglo-Indian newspapers very uneasy. Tilak was not yet in open revolt against Government, and those officers who came in contact with him were surprised to know that he was an extraordinarily intelligent and very straightforward man. The Anglo-Indian papers were nervous about the whole affair, and some suggested to Government to cancel Tilak's election on the plea that he was a journalist! Notwithstanding the clamour and ill-will, Tilak received the approval of Government to his election on June 12, 1895. This was indeed a victory of the people, a victory of the principle of election.

Tilak's success was an event of joy to all patriotic-minded men. The Brahman Sabha of Bombay held a meeting at Bombay to congratulate Tilak on his victory. Presiding over the function, Sir Bhalchandra Bhatavdekar

---

5 Mangudkar, Dr. M. P., *Poona Municipality Centenary Vol.* (Marathi), pp. 508-09.

proudly narrated that it was Tilak's complaint that a day's time was not sufficient for his daily work. His activities were spread over a vast field, and it would be better, said the President, if he were blessed with a day lasting for more than twenty-four hours.

It was at this time that the idea of a Shivaji Memorial was being discussed by the public. The origin of the Shivaji Festival was in Mr. Douglas' *Book of Bombay* which was written in 1883, in which he referred to Shivaji, saying that people had neglected him. The Governor of Bombay some time thereafter paid a visit to Raigad and saw the tomb of the great liberator of the Hindus in a dilapidated condition. With great generosity he sanctioned a grant of five rupees a month for the upkeep of the tomb. Then someone wrote in the *Times of India* about the condition of the tomb. This gave an impetus to the question of a Shivaji Memorial at Raigad. Tilak's *Kesari* supported the idea of a memorial, and in May he held a meeting in Poona to find ways and means to give the idea a practical shape. Similar meetings were held in important towns all over Maharashtra, and a Memorial Fund was collected.

When Tilak was thus working and shining with a lustre of his own, his one-time colleague G. G. Agarkar, who had risen to the Principalship of Fergusson College, wound up his mortal coil when he was thirty-nine. He had been suffering from poverty and asthma since his early youth. Many took in the past a vow of leading a life of extreme poverty for the uplift of their nation, but few stuck to it as nobly and valiantly as did Agarkar.

Tilak was moved at the death of his whilom colleague. A few days before Agarkar's death, Tilak had been to his residence to have a last glimpse of his former brilliant and brave colleague; but the dying man turned his face aside! He had turned into an inveterate opponent. They had mercilessly attacked each other in their papers, and when feelings ran high, both had written crude and often censorious articles about each other. During the last five or six years Tilak and Agarkar were not even on speaking terms! When the news came to Tilak that the great man had passed away, he was filled with memories of his youth, and he sobbed as he dictated an obituary in which he paid glowing tributes to his great ability as an editor and appreciated his solid contribution to Indian journalism. He praised Agarkar for his selfless aim in life and asked the youth to emulate his example.

In August 1895 Tilak led a deputation to wait on the Maharaja of Kolhapur and discussed the question of a Shivaji Memorial with him. It must be noted here that the Shivaji festival was first started by men like Ranade as early as 1885, but when Tilak transformed it into a national festival they opposed it, thinking perhaps that it would estrange the non-Hindus and possibly bring the promoters into conflict with the Government, although apparently they said they were against idol-worship!

Meanwhile the fight between the Ranade Party and the Tilak Party had come to a head over the management of the Sarvajanik Sabha, and Tilak was making preparations for administering a final blow to the followers of Ranade. In July 1895, at the annual meeting of the Sarvajanik Sabha, the Tilak Party captured it, electing their own office-bearers and retaining the Secretary Prof. G. K. Gokhale, who was allowed to remain in the hope that being stifled in his voice he would in course of time voluntarily send in his resignation! He had held that post for about seven years. Another outcome of the new leadership was that the Muslim members of the Sarvajanik Sabha resigned.

Gokhale eventually resigned in August 1895, and Justice Ranade founded the Deccan Sabha when he went to Poona during the Diwali vacation. In order to give Gokhale an opportunity to work independently and to have a rallying centre for the Moderates to work smoothly, Ranade founded this institution. It was a queer freak of destiny that compelled Tilak to resign from the Deccan Education Society, whereas it was now Tilak who drove the Ranade Party out of the Sarvajanik Sabha. Ranade started another rival institution to Sarvajanik Sabha through which he had done useful work for many years and which he had himself brought up. Democratically, this attitude, according to some critics, did not befit Ranade.

This gave an opportunity to Tilak, who ferociously attacked Ranade, saying that Ranade had done it because his senses had ceased functioning in his old age. The idea of starting an institution was discussed by Ranade at a garden tea-party, and Tilak retorted that it was surprising that the idea of starting a new institution should have occurred to Ranade during his discussion with his followers on the day of the new moon, and that too under toddy trees!

This time Tilak surpassed his vitriolic performances in the past. As Ranade tried to kill what he had himself brought up, he compared Ranade with Bacon and said that Bacon was a great but mean-minded man. He further described Ranade as a Kautilya and a Shukracharya. But the last twinge of conscience gripped Tilak's mind, and he expressed a hope that there might not arise an occasion for him to denounce Ranade so caustically. When feelings run high, even great men lose their balance and sense of proportion.

Tilak was never satisfied until his rival went down reeling. He would not shrink from lacerating his enemy even if he was half dead! He was a queer combination of hard-heartedness and softness. Later when someone reminded Tilak that his attacks on Ranade were cruel and sordid, unbecoming and uncharitable, he would point out that the Anglo-Indian papers too had attacked Ranade, and nobody complained against them.[6] How can one bad thing justify another? He defended himself saying that it was modern warfare, and as he believed that in such warfare success rested with those who could use boldly guns of longer range than those of their enemies.[7] He gave no quarter and asked for none! Ranade, who, while grounding his disciple, told Gokhale that there should be more light than heat, thus experienced the sting of Tilak's tongue and the scorpions of his bitter pen. This attack, however, failed to provoke Ranade. Ranade was called a Socrates; Tilak the Blunt, not in vain! What of Ranade, in fact, no contemporary Indian leader entirely escaped the wrath of Tilak's pen! 'When arguments fail, try abuse' goes an adage. And Tilak sometimes used both, arguments and abuse!

With the foundation of the Deccan Sabha, Poona had now two Sabhas, two symbols for two schools of thought, two Parties, two clubs, two types of leaders, Moderates and Extremists—two appellations or nomenclatures that were soon to divide India politically into two groups. The Party of Ranade remained all along radical in social reforms and moderate in politics. Tilak's Party remained to the end of his life extremist in politics and conservative in matters of social reforms.

IV

Poona was going to hold the Congress session in December 1895, and the preliminaries were being discussed. A new issue was now developing around it. The opponents of social reformers in Poona declared that they would oppose the Congress allowing the Social Conference the use of its pandal. They raised a hue and cry against the Social Conference. The orthodox reactionaries organised a crusade against the reformers and it was declared through leaflets that the promoters of the Social Conference

---

6 Tilak-Paranjpye Controversy, p. 19.

7 Ibid, p. 3.

were the corruptors and destroyers of Hindu religion. Some educated men also allied themselves with them to cry down the social reformers. The opponents of the Social Conference said they would not subscribe a pie to the Congress unless the leaders promised them that the Social Conference would not be held in the Congress pandal, whereas the friends of the Social Conference said that they would not subscribe a pie to the Congress unless they were promised that the Social Conference would be held in the Congress pandal. At first Tilak denounced both and said they both were enemies of the Congress.

The Reception Committee was manned mainly by the Ranade Party, and the Tilak Party was in a minority. Tilak, Gadgil and G. K. Gokhale were Secretaries. Tilak appointed subcommittees without the sanction or the knowledge of the Working Committee, and when the Working Committee suggested some names to be added to the personnel of the sub-committees, he left that body and convened a meeting to explain his stand. The requisition of that meeting was signed by Tilak and his party-men, and not by his co-Secretaries.

A bid for compromise having failed, the meeting then was held as decided by Tilak. It was a big meeting and was attended mostly by orthodox Hindus, green-grocers, and school-boys. It was addressed by Tilak, Namjoshi and by others. The meeting was very disorderly throughout, and the police had difficulty in maintaining order. It was proposed by Tilak that the work in connection with the meeting of the eleventh National Congress should be entrusted to persons who had its welfare at heart, and therefore a Reception Committee of sixty-five persons was elected. Another resolution was moved by Namjoshi declaring that as the general opinion of Poona inhabitants was against the Social Conference, the time had arrived to sever the connection of the Social Conference with the National Congress. This was also passed.

At the meeting Tilak said that the Congress work should be entrusted to those persons who were prepared to work for the Congress and for the Congress alone. As regards the Social Conference, he said that he was not himself in its favour, as it stood then, and cared little where it was held. He exhorted the people to work for and support the Congress irrespective of the other questions.

But the new Reception Committee was not recognised by the Working Committee, and so the point was referred by G. K. Gokhale to the Bombay Standing Committee. Accordingly a meeting of the Bombay Standing

Committee was held at Bombay on October 26, in the rooms of the Bombay Presidency Association under the Chairmanship of Pherozeshah Mehta. Printed representations submitted by Tilak and Gokhale were read by the Chairman of the meeting. Then Tilak addressed the meeting in explanation of his representation. The meeting did not recognise the Reception Committee formed by Tilak at the Reay Market meeting, and they said that they recognised only the existing Congress Committee. Tilak acquiesced in the propriety and justice of the circumstance. He was, however, allowed to continue by the Bombay Standing Committee as a joint Secretary to the existing Committee, and D. E. Wacha, Daji A. Khare and Chimanlal H. Setalvad were requested to work as additional Secretaries. Tilak asked the Committee that he should be allowed a day to consider whether he should continue as Secretary or not. Defeated, he returned to Poona. The Bombay leaders did not know what they were doing! They were sending back a leader who was, as his opponents themselves called, a living god of the Poonaites. The lion of Bombay was running down the lion of Poona!

Some letters appeared in the *Times of India* against Tilak's move in connection with the Congress session. One said that, like an ambitious man, Tilak sacrificed principles at the altar of popularity and organised an agitation against social reformers whom he wanted to crush by forming an unholy alliance with the orthodox and ignorant people, and that the crusade was fomented by a few educated men. Another said that he was at once the apostle and leader of the reactionary party in the Deccan and the writer of that letter was sorry that the man who called the Social Conference an imposture or a farce should be allowed to take a leading part in the Congress.

Tilak replied to these critics in the *Times of India* saying that the Party which opposed the Social Conference being held in the Congress pandal, though not very strong, was certainly stronger numerically than the social reformers' Party. It was his main complaint that the friends of the Social Conference worked for the Congress in such a way as would accord best with the interests of the Social Conference, and their predilections for social reform necessarily limited the scope of their work, because they served two masters. Hence their work for the Congress did not receive undivided attention. "Personally, I do not approve of the method of social reform adopted by the promoters of the conference," he continued, "nor am I prepared to admit that any want of supreme admiration for this conference means, at least so far as I am concerned, opposition to real social reform." "We only wish that whether orthodox or heterodox, reformers or reactionaries, all should join in and support the Congress movement as every inhabitant of India is entitled to do. No efforts, in my opinion, should be spared to induce the large masses of Poona and other places in the Presidency to take an interest in the forthcoming session of the Congress and thus to place the Congress on a popular basis."

"If masses are drawn to the Congress," he explained, "it is possible that they may not lend their support directly or indirectly to the Social Conference. It is this apprehension that makes the friends of the social reform restrict the scope of their work for Congress within a safe narrow circle,"

He, then, stated that if the Congress aimed at being a Congress of the people, the object could not be achieved unless they approached the artisans, the working men as well as the educated classes. In the end he promised all the well-wishers of the Congress that he would not persist in claiming recognition of the views of the majority of the public and hamper the Congress work.[8]

So he resigned on November 4, and then openly attacked the social reformers and the Social Conference in the *Kesari*. This strengthened the hands of the reactionaries like Balasaheb Natu and S. V. Date, the latter of whom had advanced money for the Congress to keep up Tilak's prestige if he were to accept the responsibility of holding the Congress session. Balasaheb Natu and S. V. Date were ultra reactionaries. Natu had more hate for the Social Conference than love for the Congress. S. V. Date, a dismissed Mamlatdar, was a rich man with a ribald tongue and was an admirer of Tilak. All the opponents of the Social Conference held a mass meeting where the passing of every resolution was declared in a crude and riotous way by blowing trumpets! At this meeting Date gave the Congress leaders the rough side of his tongue and added threateningly that, if they did not pay heed to what he said, the Congress pandal would be burnt, and Poona would repeat the scenes it had created during Dayananda's visit to Poona; and with the Social Conference would go down its supporters and protectors! As regards the Social Conference, he said it was a disease, a lap-dog, and if kicked out of the Congress pandal at this stage, the other cities would be freed from its poison. S. V. Date soon visited the Congress

8 *The Times of India*, 1 November 1895.

pandal and said to the passers-by pointing his finger at any part of the pandal, that it could be easily burnt down from that corner.

The President-elect Surendranath Banerjee informed the Congress leaders that he could not agree to preside over the Congress unless the dispute was settled. He, however, wrote to Ranade that the request of the other side was very unreasonable; but they had sometimes to submit to unreasonable demands to avert greater evils. Ranade thereupon declared that the Social Conference would be held in a separate pandal although the majority of the Standing Committees, of course, being manned by followers of Ranade, had supported the proposal for holding the Social Conference in the Congress pandal.

It was the policy of Tilak to show up the leaders who, in his opinion, adversely criticised the people. In one statement issued on behalf of the Congress, Gokhale charged Tilak with capturing the Congress with "brute force". Tilak at once twisted the expression, and, putting it before the public, said that Gokhale stigmatized the people as brutes; and gentle Gokhale felt nervous about it! He approached Selby, the Principal of the Deccan College, for the meaning of the expression, and the latter said to Gokhale: "To say that in attributing to certain people a desire to carry their measures by 'brute force' you intended to call them brutes, is nonsense." Yet Tilak wrote an editorial under the caption "Who are the animals?" on the subject defining "popular opinion". He observed that popular opinion meant opinion of the people who were well-to-do or of those who could read and write and maintain their families by working hard and honestly, irrespective of their high or low qualifications, wealth or authority. He added that the really educated man who was interested in the uplift of the nation should win over to his side the merchants, sirdars, landlords, inamdars, peasants and workers; true leadership lay in doing that, and not in calling them brutes!

It may be remembered that it was Tilak himself who had handed over to the President of the Calcutta Congress in 1890 a resolution passed by the Poona orthodox requesting that the Congress should not lend its pandal to the social reformers for the use of the Social Conference. Thus the Poona reactionaries, who had launched the opposition to the Social Conference being held in the Congress pandal, at last succeeded in their objective. Shortly after this, Tilak declared in one of his articles in the *Kesari* that the very idea that the Social Conference could be national was ridiculous.

Another by-product of this Congress muddle was that Tilak was going to bring an action against Subramania Iyer, the editor of the *Hindu*, for publishing a report of a Poona meeting under the title "a disgraceful squabble" in the issue of the *Hindu* of the 21st October 1895, in which it was said that the students from the Law Classes of Tilak were riotous at the meeting which elected the delegates to the Congress. Tilak's master technique in capturing a meeting or institution was to ask his party-men to outnumber his opponents and spring on them a surprise. This technique he always used, and he had used it at this meeting to the embarrassment of Gokhale although he himself did not attend the meeting. It can be seen how Morley later on correctly judged Gokhale when he said that as a party manager Gokhale was a baby. Tilak was supreme as an organiser and party boss! There was nothing wrong in Tilak's winning his object in a democratic way. Yet according to Tilak the report in the *Hindu* misrepresented the Tilak Party. It seems the motive behind this proposed legal action was to teach a lesson to Subramania Iyer, because being a man of broad views and a social reformer, the latter was disposed to agree with Gokhale's views. The suit, however, was not filed in the court.

The Congress pandal was erected in Poona at a convenient spot on the road leading to Ganeshkhind. Three pandals were erected for serving meals, with kitchens belonging to the various castes! Tilak received the Congress President Surendranath Banerjee just two stations short of Poona while the official reception awaited him at Poona station. The Congress was held with great enthusiasm. The Social Conference pandal was put up near Fergusson College.

Surendranath Banerjee, who was India's first political leader to make a political tour of India as early as 1876, delivered his address for more than three hours. Physically and intellectually it was a marvellous performance. He went through the whole solid speech without a mistake, without hesitation, altering no fact, changing no figure, never for once looking into the printed copy of his speech. A brilliant editor and a first-rate orator in India, he was capable of addressing thousands of his countrymen at an open air meeting in pre-microphone days. He declared that it was the Congress of a united India, of Hindus, of Muhammedans, of Christians, of Parsees, of Sikhs, of those who would reform their social customs and those who would not. They stood on a common political platform and had agreed to bury their social and religious differences. "We have called forth this Congress into existence," he added, "with a view to safeguarding and extending our rights and redressing our grievances."

The Social Conference met and Ranade delivered an address in which he said that as time and tide wait for no man, so also social revolution would not allow the people to rest where they were. He observed that the existing friction had proceeded through the method of the social reformers in Maharashtra under which, unlike the social reformers in other parts of India, worked on all lines with others, and above all they wanted not to break with the past and cease all connection with the society.

Tilak spoke at the Congress on the resolution concerning Civil and Medical services and the fixity of land tenure. The Congress session over, Tilak's friend, Sardar Baba Maharaj, gave a party in honour of the Congress President and Congress delegates. Then Tilak took the President and delegates to a Shivaji Memorial meeting where Babu Surendranath and Pandit Malaviya delivered speeches praising the role of Shivaji as the liberator of the nation.

Yet the impression many Congress leaders carried with them was that Tilak was a leader of great ability and courage, but was a defender of the reactionaries and a deadly opponent of the social reformers.

A small incident that happened during the Congress session is worth mentioning. A picture of a famine-stricken man holding a placard in his hand stood before the Congress pandal. The placard asked the congregation whether there were at least twenty men who were really interested in the welfare of the peasants.

Tilak expressed great satisfaction at the grand success of the session which just concluded amidst great rejoicings and an inspiring atmosphere, but he alone took notice of that picture and the placard. He wrote that the resolutions passed by the Congress during the last ten years indicated what political reforms were required in the administration; but the time had come when the Congress should have a definite programme for the next ten years, and think out ways and means for bringing the peasants and workers under the Congress fold, and see with their backing and support how best its resolutions could be given effect to.

Tilak was now busy with the Shivaji Memorial work. In April 1896 he organised the celebrations of the Shivaji birthday anniversary at Raigad on a grand scale. Government was hesitating to grant permission to hold the function, but the Hon. Mr. Tilak had a personal interview with the

Governor, who was then at Mahabaleshwar, and obtained the necessary permission. British statemanship must not have naturally been happy over this revival of the memory of this Great Saviour of India.

Statesman that he was the Governor must have granted permission with great difficulty; for Tilak had written in the *Kesari* on the eve of the celebrations that people should be moderate in their speeches at Raigad! A notable point about the statesmanship of the British rulers was that it was their unwritten policy to neglect all Hindu emblems of heroism and glory and keep intact the historical places of Muslim association or domination. So Government did not show any interest in the Shivaji Memorial agitation.

People of all classes and castes assembled to celebrate the anniversary. Collateral descendants of Tanaji Malusare and of other famous Sirdar families were invited to the function. Youth of all cults, gymnastic and patriotic, forming choirs, sang inspiring songs. Fervent speeches were made, and there was an exciting atmosphere. People took meals in files of hundreds.

It was very sad and rather surprising that the reformers belonging to the Ranade Party should have dissociated themselves from this festival and taken an unfavourable view of it. Mass contact was their bugbear! With Tilak it was the breath of his life.

To Maharashtra, said Tilak in a brilliant article, Shivaji was a symbol of courage, self-respect, heroism and nobility, and a great figure in modern history who immortalised Maharashtra and India. It was not in the hands of human beings to create such extraordinary men of great talents, great courage and great aims, in every generation. Another aspect of the Shivaji celebration was that the revival of Shivaji's memory was an attraction to all communities in Maharashtra as no other force was as unifying in Maharashtra as was the name of Shivaji. Tilak wanted to arouse the pride of the people about the great patriots in their history and to enkindle their minds with patriotism and love for freedom. The Ganesh festival and the Shivaji festival were the most important celebrations that provided Maharashtrian Hindus, high and low, a common platform for work, unification and organisation!

Nations that live and nations that survive never forget their heroes. Those heroes provide every generation with inspiration, patriotism, and courage! This is how Tilak connected the worship of great men and the revival of religious festivals with the slumbering hatred in the people's minds against British rule! He was awakening the dormant spirit of nationalism in the peasants and other lower classes. Tilak may not be an originator of new ideas; he may have, according to some critics, favoured cultural revivalism and by-passed social reforms; but he was doubtless the one great leader of his generation who gave practical shape to ideas and transformed them into active volcanoes by his extraordinary zeal, sublime courage and selfless work.

It may be said here that Shivaji celebration was in keeping with the spirit of the age. During the last quarter of the nineteenth century, throughout the civilized world anniversary celebrations of great men and great events were held. Catholic Europe celebrated the Jubilee of its Pope; Protestant Europe celebrated the quarter-centenary of Luther's birth. Portugal commemorated the fourth centenary of Vasco da Gama's triumph in the East; Spain and America did the same for Columbus. England held the centenary celebrations of Johnson and Edward Gibbon.

As a Legislative Councillor, Tilak took the customary oath of allegiance to Her Majesty the Queen Empress, in August 1895. He could do nothing extraordinary in the Council. The Act of 1892 gave the Members the right to discuss the annual finance statement, the major portion of which would be brought into force by the time the Council opened. The Members often said that making a speech on the Budget was doing post-mortem dissection or flogging a dead horse! Another notable feature was that the foreign Government had just shown gestures of generosity by offering the Indian representatives the democratic privilege of interpellations during the ten days in a year when the Council met.

In many ways Tilak's presence in the Council was unique. He was elected against the wish of those persons who called themselves politicians. The Governor had confirmed his election to the Council despite the suggestions made by the Anglo-Indian Press to the contrary. Above all, Tilak was a leader who had foiled the attempts of the *elite* to raise a public memorial to a Governor, the representative of British rule over a Province. Councillor Tilak wore strictly Indian dress; his peculiar flowing long coat with strings, his dhoti and his crimson-red turban, and red shoes on his feet. He always kept his shoes outside the entrance. When taunted by his friends that he had to keep his shoes outside, he retorted with a smile that he was the first Indian whose shoes were looked after by an English guard! He refused to wear the Western type of dress. He was the most simple but the most fearless, outspoken, dreaded and detested Member in the Legislative Council.

At the time of the Budget discussion Tilak asked for the Advocate-General's notes and he was told to refer to the Printed Budget and to the statement of accounts. He criticised the Government saying that it had raised the taxes by Rs. 5½ crores during the last twenty-five years, but was spending a very small portion of the revenues to alleviate the miseries of the people and on the material improvement of the Province. The right of Interpellation also was exercised by him. During August and September 1895 the Council met for one day each. He asked questions regarding the number of licences granted or renewed each year under the Arms Act in the Districts of Belgaum and Karnatak and asked why the election of the Vice-President of Wai Municipality was disapproved when he was chosen by election. He asked Government whether they would be pleased to direct the District Officers to take the initiative in bringing about a settlement of the question of music before mosques as had been done in the Aundh State. He inquired whether Government would make an industrial survey of the Province as was done by the Kolhapur State and why the rate of perennial irrigation on the Krishna Canal was raised. He brought to the notice of Government that in some criminal cases undue delay occurred causing harassment to the people.

It was not easy to work in the Council; for the representatives of the bureaucracy were still rough and they treated the Members with scant respect. Some Members were told that they were riding their hobby horse and turning the house into a circus; one was told to submit a printed copy of his speech so that it might be taken as read! Tilak neither flattered the bureaucracy, nor did he spare it.

In the vanguard of Indian politicians Tilak had now reached a position which no other Indian politician of his generation had dreamt of. India's first full-time politician, he made his mark in Maharashtra by his selfless work and sublime courage, but these great qualities were sharpened and his personality was rendered more invincible by his great journalism. His editorship was as fiery as his leadership. Tilak was India's foremost editor, who was the exponent of the new spirit in India. He had now created a political force behind him.

A loud, daring, scathing critic, Tilak was a terror to bureaucrats and to his opponents. He had the four chief qualities of a great journalist: readability, irreverence, individuality, and courage! He wrote impeccable prose, simple, direct, effortless and clear and made it attractive by the impress of his vast learning. He courageously used his resourceful erudition. He fearlessly exposed Government officials by unearthing their secrets and by ruthlessly attacking their high-handed policy. He irreverently attacked the weak points of those who toadied Governors and bureaucrats and who spoke or acted against people's interests. His stinging notes, his echoing phrases, his selfless service, his spotless patriotism, and the note of defiance in his speeches and writings made his position unrivalled in the world of Indian journalism.

Journalism in the native languages being then a new type of literature in India, Tilak had to coin Marathi words and phrases in political terminology. He thus made Marathi rich, pulsating with new vigour and power. Here and there his arrowy writings sometimes smacked of crude journalism, but every pioneer has his ways and weapons imperfect in some way. His pen had such a destructive power that with one stroke of a short heading he would shoot his opponents! Direct and piercing, it struck the target, like a bullet!

His vast learning, the carefully treasured cuttings of important informative articles and commitments of his opponents were pressed into service. His head, saturated with ideas for a week, was relieved at the end of the week when he poured down his thoughts in an editorial and his weekly miracle was performed!

His advice to his young assistant editors is worth mentioning. He asked them to read important books. Party spirit in an editor, he observed, was more an asset than a defect. The article should be free of any unwanted commitments and an editor's views should be definite, unfailing and straight, and must hit the target like a bullet. An editor in his chair was like a judge in his court. He must therefore assume perfect knowledge like a judge who decides his case confidently. An editor's chair was a place where the decisive voice was more effective than the nature of a doubting Thomas!

On another occasion he said to a young journalist: "Whoever has something to achieve in this world must brush aside or run down the opposition of his opponents. An arm-chair thinker can do his thinking without having any occasion for wounding the feelings of others or without disturbance to or from anybody. He can tender advice on a higher plane in high-sounding phrases and with philosophical geniality; but it is impossible for a man of mission or man of action to assume that sort of geniality and perfection when he is at grips with those who strive to blow up or annihilate his cherished goal. It is difficult, if not impossible, to have dealings with a person who opposes your mission which has been the breath of your nostrils!"

Although now a formidable leader and a public figure, Tilak's mode of living remained unchanged. His dress and house were as simple as before. Neither English games nor English imitation in any field was tolerated in the house. His eldest son, who was now a high school boy, one day secured a badminton net and a racket. Young N. C. Kelkar, who was a good player, became his companion at the net. But when Tilak noticed it, he asked his servant to remove the net and told his son to abandon the game. Such games in his opinion were to be played by women! He asked his son to take manly exercise as he himself had done in his college days. In those days Tilak himself did not take any exercise. He usually went to see persons on business, and his long walks served him as an exercise. His favourite posture was to lie and relax in an easy chair, cutting and chewing betel-nut while having a chat with his friends or visitors. He never cared to handle his purse, not even his own things. Yet his guest chamber hospitality was widely known! He had a special liking for soda-water and in summer he took it with a little ice.

There was sometimes a lighter side to the grave scene. Tilak was hard of hearing. He had contracted that defect through an excess of quinine he took during one of his illnesses when he was down with high fever. His loud talk was the subject of jokes among his friends and admirers. One day somebody suggested different roles for different politicians. Pherozeshah Mehta to play the Rakshas, Shridhar Date a dare-devil, Gokhale to play a female role, Gopalrao Joshi to play a buffoon, Wasukaka Joshi to be in charge of curtains! But nobody mentioned Tilak in his presence. It might be because drama was a subject he disliked or because they had a great respect for his status; but the hesitation was overcome and Wasukaka Joshi said that Balwantrao, i.e. Tilak, was a prominent politician and it would not be proper to exclude him! Thereupon one Mr. Hardikar remarked that if it was announced that Tilak was to play a role in a drama, people would not purchase tickets because his voice could be easily heard from a distance!

So far Tilak's admirers or friends mixed freely with him, and he also did not prevent them from enjoying his company! His orthodox friends sometimes also observed their Holi traditions in his compound. In those days the native princes enjoyed his hospitality. On occasions there were close and confidential talks between him and his friends. If fits of cutting humour or country jokes emerged during the talk, he did not pay attention to them, but he never uttered foul words himself. His house was always open to anybody and the visiting room was always alive with the presence of a lingering visitor. At dead of night Tilak's real work began when his personal assistant was almost tired out or was dozing. He then dictated an article chewing betel-nut, striking the right arm of the chair with his fist; or stroking the crown of his head with the palm.

It would not be out of place to state here that Tilak had no time nor love for drama. Yet at the instance of the famous Kirloskar Theatrical Company, which he held in high esteem, he prevailed upon Narayanrao Jogalekar, then a student of his Law Class, to take to acting, and Jogalekar became a famous singer-actor.

CHAPTER VII

India's First Mass Leader

I

While the Ganesh festival and Shivaji festival were utilised for organising the middle and lower classes and rousing in them a sense of national self-respect, Tilak now resolved to connect the poverty of the peasants with the patriotism of the middle classes, to create a powerful public opinion in support of their grievances, and to make them feel confident that they would some day be able to regain the power of governing themselves.

Tilak caught another opportunity to rouse in the middle classes a sense of self-respect and self-reliance and to encourage them to fight against the oppressive laws of the Government. Excise duty on Indian cloth was raised in order to balance the customs duty imposed on British cloth. He, therefore, raised a storm of criticism against the new tax and appealed to the people to boycott foreign cloth and to use swadeshi cloth. He cited examples of Americans who threw tea-boxes into the sea and refused to pay taxes to the British Government.

In a moving appeal he further observed: "People must fight for the vindication of their rights. If we are unmoved at the sight of injustice and high-handed policy of the Government, we should not be regarded as human beings. The days are gone when the left cheek was turned to the aggressor if the right was smitten! If you are fit to be called human beings, if you are really perturbed at the injustice at the hands of Government or anybody, if your hearts do flutter at insults, if you truly wish the country well, if you really take pride in your brave ancestors and heroes, then boycott foreign cloth." "If you want to teach a lesson," he continued, "to the merchants of Manchester, if you have self-respect and qualms of conscience, carry this into effect. Government will not pay heed to your grievances unless you show grit, courage and resolution. Government will not respect your representatives in the Council unless they are backed by action!"

Meetings were held at Bombay, Poona, Satara, Nagpur and Amraoti, and resolutions were passed exhorting people to take a vow of using swadeshi cloth. Tilak said that most of the educated men were consumers of foreign cloth, and it was they who must take a vow not to use foreign cloth. He cited the example of Ganesh W. Joshi alias Sarvajanik Kaka who had taken a vow to use swadeshi cloth twenty years earlier.

There were people who, on this plea or that, did not like Tilak's idea of boycotting foreign goods. D. E. Wacha, a well-known Congress leader and an economist of repute, wrote a letter in the *Times of India* that the vow of swadeshi and the movement against foreign cloth were not practicable because India could not produce cloth sufficient for her people. Replying to Wacha, Tilak said that Wacha's argument was based on unsound understanding. The Congress movement and the Industrial and Social Reform movements were not given up because they could not fructify immediately. Another mistake committed by Wacha was that he assumed that all the people would take to using swadeshi cloth from the next day. Tilak said that the popular demand for swadeshi cloth would induce Indian millowners to produce more cloth, and this would promote the national nascent industry.

The economic condition of the people had vastly deteriorated. There was acute and widespread poverty. The British Government had dislocated Indian industries and had destroyed Indian fine arts in order to favour the import of cheap foreign goods. The British Government had neglected irrigation and sanitation. The land revenue was high and the indebtedness of the agricultural classes increased day by day.

After the Provincial Conference which was held at Karachi in May 1896, Tilak said that it was high time that the Provincial Conference was galvanized into action. The same type of resolutions were moved every year by the same set of leaders; Gokhale moving and Wacha seconding them. He therefore tried to impress upon the organisers of the Provincial Conference at Satara that it was necessary to attract the agricultural classes to the Provincial Conference and expressed the hope that the next Provincial Conference which was to be held at Satara would attract the peasants and help them solve their problems in respect of land revenue, salt, forest and excise duties under which they had been crushed. They should be taught what those rights were, and how they should get their grievances redressed. This was the way to increase the influence of the Congress and the Provincial Conference with the illiterate and common people.

In the last quarter of the year 1896 a famine broke out in Maharashtra. This was not, however, the first visitation of famine. Famine had followed British Rule in India, and there had been twenty famines from 1770 to 1880 and four since 1880. Sir William Hunter had observed that forty million people in India went through life with insufficient food, and Sir Charles Elliot had declared that half the agricultural population in India did not know from one year's end to another what it was to have a full meal. In twelve years twenty million people had perished. The British blessed India with peace, but had killed her prosperity.

As a real representative of the people, Tilak put questions to Government in the Council in October 1896 asking them whether in view of the impending famine the Government had watched the condition of the crops, had any idea of rainfall, had maintained any records of the accumulated store of grains in the areas likely to be affected by famine, and what measures they were contemplating for giving relief in case of the occurrence of an actual famine. He further asked Government whether they were contemplating to grant suspension of revenue in regard to the first instalment of land revenue which fell due, and whether they were going to throw open the protected forests in each village for the use of the villagers. Government said they had no idea of the accumulated stores, and added that the Famine Code contained explicit directions regarding the suspension of revenue instalments which could be put in force as soon as occasion arose!

In 1896 famine played havoc also in North India and the peasants rioted and looted property at places like Kanpur, Agra and Nagpur.

The agricultural classes in Konkan deserted their homes, sold or gave away their cattle, and became incurably depressed in body and estate. The Governor had made a frank admission at Surat that the famine was already upon the Deccan and the distress was likely to increase and not decrease in the Deccan and Southern Mahratta country; and he thought that it might possibly invade Konkan. He had also declared that no effort would be spared to relieve the distress of the people so far as it was in their power to do so.

Tilak decided to secure the agricultural masses an exemption from or remission of land revenue. The *Kesari* roared that in accordance with the Famine Code it was the duty of Government to mitigate the sufferings of the peasants. He seriously but sarcastically explained in his terse and plain language that, when the Queen Empress had pronounced that none should die of starvation, when Government was going to perform its duty by helping the people and when there was money deposited with Government in the form of insurance, it would be the people's fault if they died from starvation. They should only see that Government acted up to its promises. He pointed out that the Famine Code contained certain provisions under which it was laid down to what extent and when the assessment was to be reduced, when forests should be thrown open, and what should be the daily wages of workers.

They should also bear in mind, said Tilak, that they had a moral claim upon the Government for their livelihood. In these matters if the subordinate officers behaved with highhandedness, they did so because they had been acting in that manner in the past and people had tolerated their doings. Another important fact Tilak asked them to note was that the Famine Code clearly stated that land revenue should not be collected by making people sell their cattle or land.

Tilak deplored and denounced food riots, and exhorted the people to give organised resistance to hooligans. He warned them against fighting amongst themselves, against looting Banias or merchants, or bazaars. That would lead them to disaster. But he purposely published news of food riots so that the altruistic impulses of charity might move the rich, at least through fear of safety of their life and property, to help the people who were in great distress. They should boldly approach the Collector whose duty was to provide them with food and work. He said the Government was their own, its money was their own, and if remission of land revenue was granted to them that time, they would make it up next time!

"If you have money to pay Government dues," declared he, "pay them by all means. But if you have not, will you sell your belongings only to avoid the supposed wrath of subordinate officers? Can you not be bold even when in the grip of death? We can stand any number of famines, but what shall we do with such sheepish people? Had such a famine broken out in England and had the Prime Minister been as apathetic as Lord Elgin, his Government would have, in less than a week, collapsed like a house of cards!"

II

A similar famine had visited Maharashtra in 1876 when Ranade had tremendously helped Government by making concrete suggestions through the Sarvajanik Sabha about the methods of relief. He had sent his emissaries to different famine-stricken places and culled and collated the information received, finally editing it under the title "The Famine narratives" in the Quarterly of the Sarvajanik Sabha.

Tilak's work was on the same lines, but on a broader basis. By pointing to the Famine Code he pressed Government to do their duty by the famine-stricken people. He sent forth a Memorial on behalf of the Sarvajanik Sabha appealing to Government to declare the famine-stricken districts to be famine districts and to undertake relief work as directed in the Famine Code.

A reply came from the Government to the effect that all practicable measures were being taken for the preservation of agricultural cattle, that the Famine Code then in force made no provision for an official declaration of famine, and that the question of the extent to which land revenue should be suspended or remitted was one to which the fullest attention would be given at the proper time.

Tilak then published on behalf of the Sarvajanik Sabha a pamphlet containing a summary of the Famine Code in Marathi and requested the District Collectors to distribute the copies among the general public. They did not like him to interfere in their work, and so some of them returned the copies without any remark. Tilak addressed meetings of the students, who had been to Poona for the University examination, and advised them to drive their villagers to clamour for food and fodder. He, therefore, sent the representatives of the Sarvajanik Sabha to different places in Thana, Kolaba and Ratnagiri Districts to infuse courage into the people. They advised the peasants to claim remissions of land revenue and to withhold the payments of taxes. They explained and distributed the pamphlets among the peasants, acquainted the people with their rights, and impressed upon them that it was not necessary for them to sell away their lands and cattle to pay off Government dues. These lieutenants sent their reports or people's applications to the Sarvajanik Sabha, and they were forwarded to Government. Furthermore, Tilak published translations of Government notes and explained in his papers various rules relating to the problem for the use of the people. He started a co-operative movement for weavers, who could not do anything else for their livelihood. He started also cheap grain shops in Poona.

Tilak had attacked the Indian bureaucracy on several occasions and also the then Governor in his papers. So they replied to his memorials, or queries, with great reluctance, and when they did so it was a formal affair. Government were perturbed by this propaganda, and more so when Tilak published their secret orders to the Mamlatdars to interpret clauses in such a way as to whittle down claims of sufferers for relief. Tilak wrote furiously and fearlessly in his paper that the people should not tolerate high-handedness at the hands of subordinate officers. He observed that those were the days of Government by law and not by high-handedness. He exhorted the local leaders to form local committees and to teach people how to fight for their rights peacefully, but fearlessly and lawfully. It was the duty of the Government to make laws and the duty of the people to see that they were properly given effect to.

Tilak further stated that it was very likely that some of the local leaders might be prosecuted for this propaganda, but they should not be afraid of it. On the contrary they should not mind suffering imprisonment for the good of the people.

This movement, systematic and well organised, had a wonderful effect on the people. They took heart, attended meetings organised by the Committees set up at the instance of the Sarvajanik Sabha, and approached Government officers for relief. One such meeting was held at Khattalwad in Kolaba District. Addressing that meeting, Prof. A. S. Sathe, emissary of the Sarvajanik Sabha, made a fiery speech in the presence of the Assistant Collector. The meeting was surrounded by a posse of soldiers who had been stationed there to undermine the morale of the people and to cow down the lecturer.

Lord Elgin was then making a tour of some Indian States. Tilak felt enraged at the apathy shown by Lord Elgin to the sufferings and hardships of the people. He scathingly criticized the Viceroy for choosing a time of distress in order to parade before the States and the public the unjust grandeur of Her Imperial Majesty. He censured the people who spent money on the reception of Lord Elgin and remarked that they could have better expended the money on charitable relief of the starving millions! During Lord Elgin's stay at Baroda some people died at the Public Gardens as a result of an accident, and still the State feasts and banquets went on. Tilak wrote in a challenging mood that fifty persons were lying dead, and the Viceroy, without condescending even so much as to give a moment's thought to them, plunged himself into hearty enjoyment. "But the prevailing situation is such," observed Tilak indignantly, " that there is absolutely no one to bring the Viceroy, who is practically the Emperor of India, to book!"

The *Times of India*, then guardian of the British Empire over India and naturally the sworn enemy of Indian nationalist leaders, described this furious article of Tilak as the usual spurtings of the disaffected and disloyal section of Mahratta politicians. That was a tribute to the Mahratta politicians, the champions of freedom, who, though defeated, were never subjugated and consequently constituted a real thunder under the throne of the *Times*' Imperial Majesty! *The Times of India* suggested that the Governor should take serious note of these defiant and disloyal attacks by Tilak on the Viceroy, and taking his record into consideration, set aside his future nomination. And there was a rumour also at this time that Government was seriously thinking of prosecuting Tilak for these fiery articles which it considered seditious. The power of a newspaper is so great that even Napoleon said that four hostile newspapers were more to be feared than a thousand bayonets. To leave the press, Napoleon held, to its own devices, was to sleep next to a powder keg.

How formidable a personality and leadership Tilak had by now developed can be easily imagined by the estimate which Gandhi formed about him when he went to Poona in the middle of November 1896 with a view to organising a meeting on the "grievance of Indians in South Africa". When Gandhi called on Tilak he told him that there were two Parties in Poona, one represented by the Sarvajanik Sabha and the other by the Deccan Sabha. If a man of the position of Prof. Bhandarkar consented to preside, Tilak observed, then he was sure that both Parties would see to it that a good meeting was held. He assured Gandhi of his fullest help in his struggle in Africa. This was the first time when the two makers of history talked to each other.

The meeting was held on November 16, 1896, under the auspices of the Sarvajanik Sabha when Prof. R. G. Bhandarkar presided. Gandhi addressed the meeting, and it passed a resolution moved by Tilak sympathising with the Indians in South Africa and authorising a Committee composed of Bhandarkar, Tilak, Gokhale and six others to submit a memorandum to the Government of India on the disabilities imposed on the Indians in South Africa.[1]

---

1 The Publications Division, Government of India: *The Collected Works of Mahatma Gandhi*, Vol. II, p. 136.

Later, in his recollections, Gandhi said that Tilak appeared to him like the ocean on which one could not easily launch forth and Gokhale appeared like the holy Ganges which invited one to its bosom. To have evoked such a tribute symbolising loftiness in a mighty heart was indeed a glorious achievement. In his later life, Gandhi, relating to Dr. Rajendra Prasad his reminiscences of Poona of those days, said that Poona was a place of pilgrimage for a person who wanted to devote himself to the service of the people and added that no other place in the country had so many public institutions run entirely by a selfless body of workers.[2]

III

TILAK THEN ATTENDED the Congress session of 1896, which was held at Calcutta. There pointed references were made to famine as a recurring trouble and to impoverishment of the country by excessive taxation and by over-assessment. The Hon'ble Mr. Tilak, who had published in the Quarterly of the Sarvajanik Sabha an article on the "Decentralisation of the Provincial Finance" demanding greater fiscal responsibility for the Provincial Government, in a short but effective speech said that the Supreme Government was like an intemperate husband who came to the wife, the Provincial Government, asking her to surrender all her savings. He, therefore, urged limiting the power of the Supreme Government to draw on provincial resources to a fixed amount, levied on a definite and just basis.

Tilak's movement upset the bureaucrats, and Government launched a prosecution against Sathe and Apte, who were working in Kolaba District, and against three other workers who were agitating in Thana District.

A telegraphic message was sent to Tilak's Calcutta address about the arrests of the representatives of the Sarvajanik Sabha. He hurried to Poona, studied the cases and ran, like an eagle to protect his little ones, to Pen where Prof. Sathe was being tried. The situation was tense and explosive. A mob had surrounded the tent of the Magistrate, who requested Tilak to ask his people to maintain order and peace. Tilak rose, and the mob spontaneously accorded him a thundering ovation. One sentence from his lips and the mob was silenced. In the end the prosecution against Sathe failed, and he was set free. G. V. Apte, however, was sentenced to one year's simple imprisonment and was fined two hundred rupees.

---

2 Prasad, Dr. Rajendra, At the Feet of Mahatma Gandhi, pp. 66-67.

The prosecution against the representatives of the Sarvajanik Sabha in Thana District failed when the District Magistrate referred to an extract from the *Kesari* saying that though the writer was very subtle, the statement that peasants should not pay off Government dues by getting into debt was very likely to have an undesirable effect upon the agricultural classes! The report made by Mr. Logan, Commissioner, Central Division, observed: "Tilak had flooded the country with proclamations against payment of land revenue, urging resistance to any attempt to collect it."[3] He added that there was a partial mutiny against the police, and the village officers were almost passive or active connivers with the disturbances. Maratha colleagues of Tilak like Ram Rao Jambre and the then Maratha Patil of Poona also were in black books of Government.

While the representatives of the people were thus prosecuted, the people themselves fared as badly at the hands of the Government. Proper relief was not given to them. Undue and harsh measures were taken to collect Government dues, and Magistrates prosecuted and summarily punished men who were trying to approach Government officers, not with weapons, but with humble petitions.

While an intense agitation was thus being carried on in the famine-stricken districts, the Hon'ble Mr. Tilak put questions in February 1897 to Government in the Council on the same subject. He asked whether the Government of Bombay was asking the Imperial Government for a revision of their policy in respect of help they were to receive from the Central Government in case of a severe famine like the one prevailing, and whether their officers inspected the conditions of crops preliminary to giving relief by way of remission of the land revenue under the Famine Code. Government said they were unable to comply with the request. He further asked whether Government intended to grant any suspension of land revenue to superior holders like Khots, mortgagees and others with directives to pass them on to their tenants. Government said they had no intention of granting any general suspension of land revenue to superior holders with directions to pass it on to the tenants.

Tilak wanted to stir up the people against Government, and to make the superior holders also conscious of their rights. He wanted both the sections to stand up for their rights. In the heat of the discussion he could not therefore foresee how his demands would ultimately affect the harassed

---

3 *Source Material of a History of Freedom Movement in India*, Vol. II, p. 196.

tenants. Tilak further asked Government whether they were making provision for paying compensation for dearness from the general budget to the low-paid teachers in vernacular schools in the affected areas who had been refused so far any compensation for the dearness of grain by local bodies on the plea that they had no funds. Government said that it was for the Local Bodies to decide what they should do. He asked some questions also regarding the information on the loss of cattle, statistics of relief work, about the ill-treatment meted out to a Bengali author by a Railway servant and other questions.

Government was now seeking an opportunity to break its connection with the Sarvajanik Sabha, and when one of the representatives of the Sabha at Dharwar distributed a pamphlet which was based on rumours current in the city, Government asked the Sarvajanik Sabha to prove the validity of the statements. Government was also furious with Tilak for publishing some of their secret orders. The Sabha prevaricated, and the result was that the Government withdrew the right of the Sabha to petition to Government. Thereupon Tilak remarked that it was his firm opinion that whenever Anglo-Indian papers and Government officers expressed an adverse opinion of a leader, he should take it for granted that he had rendered the best service to the public and served the cause of the country properly!

Thus this splendid agrarian movement was the first of its kind in India. It was full of new spirit, new energy, new leaders, and new technique 'Pay the Government dues if you have money, but don't do it by contracting debt' was its watchword which almost amounted to a no-tax-campaign, and was compared by some with the similar no-tax-campaign launched in Ireland by Irish revolutionary leaders in their struggle for freedom.

The collision of the Sarvajanik Sabha with the Government was not, however, in the opinion of old leaders, a happy sign. Dadabhai wrote in April 1897, that he was much grieved that an institution built up by the efforts of the Poona people for more than a generation should be swept away in a breath. He hoped that Tilak would do all he could to save the Sabha from the blow that had come down upon it.[4]

Formerly, when Ranade was the guiding spirit of the Sarvajanik Sabha, he voiced through its memorials and petitions the people's grievances.

---

4 Masani, R. P., *Dadabhai Naoroji, the Grand Old Man of India*, p. 450.

Explaining the object of such memorials, Ranade once said to Gokhale when the latter doubted their effect: "You don't realise our place in the history of our country. These memorials are nominally addressed to Government, but in reality they are addresses to the people, so that they may learn how to think over these matters. This work must be done for many years, without expecting any other result, because politics of this kind is altogether new in this land. Besides, if Government notes the contents of what we say, even that is something." [5]

Ranade taught public workers how to think over such matters, and move Government in regard to people's grievances. Tilak, the man of action, went one step ahead and taught people how to act fearlessly but peacefully and lawfully, and how to get their grievances redressed by Government. He did not send memorials for mere perusal, but to press Government to give effect to their promises and laws. In fact he was preparing his people to be bold enough to fight for their rights. The foreign yoke is overthrown by such a type of leadership which is discontented and rebellious; for, when people are awakened and discontented, it is not possible for a foreign Government to hold them long under its sway!

Tilak's subtle, forceful arguments, the note of defiance and the challenge in his speeches and writings, his spotless sincerity, his untiring efforts in relieving the distress of the people, and unflinching courage marked him out as the first militant mass leader of modern India. He struck terror into the hearts of the bureaucracy and instilled a new spirit and a new life into the people.

---

5 *Speeches of Gopal Krishna Gokhale*, published by G. A. Nalesan & Co., p. 929.

CHAPTER VIII

Cock's Crow of Revolution

I

WHILE TILAK WAS thus engaged in the struggle for the amelioration of the agricultural classes, he had to plunge himself into another vortex to save the people from a visitation which followed in the wake of the fetid famine. Plague broke out in the Bombay Presidency. It had travelled a long way from Calcutta to Bombay. The famine had exacted a heavy toll of more than two crores. When plague broke out in Bombay in the last quarter of the year 1896, medical men at first did not take serious notice of it, nor did the Government worry themselves about it. But when mortality increased and European trade languished, Government took drastic action to stamp out the epidemic. As the epidemic was new and its nature hitherto unknown, the people could not gauge the enormity of its horrible consequences. Soon the plague stretched its tentacles over Poona, and at other places it spread like wildfire!

In order to make amends for their neglect, Government now gave a push to their belated steps against plague by investing the District Collectors with military powers; and plague committees were speedily established.

Such a plague committee was established in Poona and Walter Charles Rand was appointed Plague Commissioner in February 1897, and Lieutenant Owen Lewis was put in charge of the Segregation Camp.

Previously Rand was an Assistant Collector at Satara and had acquired a sort of notoriety for prosecuting, convicting and ruthlessly sentencing some Hindu leaders of Wai in connection with a riot in that town. It was the opinion of Tilak that Rand had wrongly convicted the Hindu leaders, and reminding the people of it, he wrote in his paper that the appointment of such an officer in Poona was perhaps a significant indication of the determination of Government to show no mercy and no hesitation in enforcing the preventive and remedial measures. Rand was known to be a thoroughly firm and determined official who doggedly adhered to his orders irrespective of public opinion.

Rand sent his soldiers round the city of Poona to conduct a house-to-house search. Terror-stricken and dumbfounded, the people could not give the search officers proper information about their plague-stricken relatives. Nor did they desire that their relatives should be taken to the plague hospital and themselves put into a segregation camp.

British soldiers were employed instead of native soldiers to enforce the precautionary sanitary measures which were detestable to the prejudices and customs of the people. Tilak wanted Government to move and improve the situation by taking the people into confidence. So it was his opinion that if the Municipality was left to adopt measures to eradicate plague, the people would not dread the new machinery.

Tilak infused courage into the people. He himself took rounds in the city with the soldiers who conducted the searches. "I went," said Tilak later, "from house to house myself with the search parties, sometimes with them and sometimes without them, but mostly with the English soldiers to see that they did not go to any excess, and when we found that they would not heed our requests we gave up the practice of accompanying them." Tilak wrote articles in his paper censuring the people for hugging their orthodox observances in the matter of facing the dangerous disease. He said that their fear that admission to a plague hospital was departing this life was erroneous. He wrote severely about their slums and slovenliness in respect of hygiene.

Tilak's fears came true. In their maddening zest for combating the plague the British soldiers took no notice of the sacred places, kitchens and the privacy of the people. A healthy man from the street, a woman in the kitchen, a child from the cradle, were seized and thrown into the hospital on a mere shadow of suspicion. Thus the Government measures for stamping out plague were carried out by the agency of British soldiers with greater energy and ruthlessness than thoughtfulness, and were instrumental in accentuating popular misery, discontent and harassment.

Patients complained to the Hindu leaders that they were badly and carelessly treated at the hospital. In the segregation camp there was no proper arrangement for boarding. Prominent people led a deputation to Government and to the plague officers to explain to them how the rules should be modified and how searches might be made. But nothing came out of it.

People were now exasperated, and Tilak warned Government week after week against harassing the people with the ruthless measures. He criticized the plague administration and explained how as soon as a patient was taken to hospital, his relations were taken to the segregation camp; the property of the infected was either destroyed or his house was kept open without anybody to take care of the property. Describing the pitiable condition of the people under the plague administration, the *Mahratta*, Tilak's English weekly, observed indignantly: "Plague is more merciful to us than its human prototypes now reigning in the city. The tyranny of the Plague Committee and its chosen instruments is yet too brutal to allow respectable people to breathe at ease." In a word, the people found themselves between two menacing dangers!

Unlike other Poona leaders who ran away for their lives, Tilak took a courageous stand, and stood irrevocably by a suffering people, making efforts to relieve them from distress. He worked unremittingly and selflessly. He was as dauntless as he was daring in his energetic rounds in the localities where the fell disease was raging.

At last the indignation of the people reached white heat, and Tilak described Rand's administration as a reign of terror. He also averred that Government would not have dared act so thoughtlessly and remorselessly had the educated men co-operated with the workers in stamping out the evil and had the people shown a little courage and grit.

To alleviate the sufferings of the people Tilak started with the help of other Hindu leaders a Hindu hospital where Hindus were treated at their own expense. He started a free kitchen for the use of the poor in the segregation camp which he had organised. This was a brave attempt at easing the tension and allaying the fears of the distressed people. Those leaders who had clamoured to reform the people socially did not care to see whether people lived or perished in their agony; they left them in the lurch. But Tilak stood unflinchingly at the burning post! This is the difference between a leader and a pleader!

II

SINCE THE FIRST week of April 1897 plague began to die down, and by May it disappeared from Poona. The Rand regime ended, the administration was dismantled, and amidst great joy cables were sent to London declaring that they had achieved success in the end! But the evils that Rand did lived behind and lingered in the minds and ears of the people. At this juncture Tilak paid his meed of praise to Dadabhai, who was in London, and to D. E. Wacha and G. K. Gokhale, who had been to London to give evidence before the Welby Commission. He said that all of them had done their best to serve the cause of the nation and bitingly added that Gokhale proved a worthy disciple of his Guru whose ideas he reproduced and represented faithfully! He, however, severely criticized Gokhale for his statement in which the latter had said, "I am the Honorary Secretary of the Deccan Sabha, an Association established in Poona for promoting under British Rule the political interests of the Indian people."

The object of this display of an undivided loyalty to British rule on the part of Gokhale was, Tilak inferred from Gokhale's intentional emphasis on the expression 'under British rule', to insinuate that the other institutions in Poona like the Sarvajanik Sabha subscribed to political views of a different character, although Gokhale had said that the Sarvajanik Sabha was of a similar character. Tilak observed that the question before the people was not whether independence, which the people were to achieve, should be under British rule or whether it should be the full splendour of the glowing and inspiring Sun of *Swaraj*! So there was no occasion for Prof. Gokhale, he concluded, to lay emphasis on loyalty or disloyalty to British rule! This was a pointer to Tilak's mind and goal. It was here that Tilak first used the term "Swaraj".

The Diamond Jubilee of Queen Victoria of England was shortly to be celebrated on June 22, 1897. Preparations were going on everywhere. Here Tilak was busy making preparations for the Shivaji festival. The *Kesari*, however, was not indifferent to the Diamond Jubilee Celebrations. It eulogised in a series of articles the greatness of Queen Victoria's vast empire and hoped that nothing would be done to mar the auspicious occasion by reminding the rulers of any other thing than the Proclamation of 1858. The *Kesari* applauded the meritorious career of the Queen, and with great appreciation mentioned the expansion of her Empire.

The Shivaji festival began on Saturday the 12th June in Poona at the temple of Vithal, near the Lakdipool. The temple was decorated in excellent style for the occasion. An image of Shivaji on horse-back was placed therein, and several pictures of Shivaji Maharaj drawn by different artists were displayed.

This year's Shivaji festival had a special significance. Prof. Karkaria read an essay at the Royal Asiatic Society, Bombay, on Shivaji. It was published in February 1896, and the controversy over the killing of Afzulkhan started. A reply to Karkaria was expected at the Poona celebrations. On the first day of the celebration some students recited songs at the beginning in praise of Shivaji, and Prof. S. M. Paranjpe read the *Puran*. Paranjpe was another revolutionary leader who was coming to the forefront in Maharashtra. He had for the text of his discourse two axioms from the *Mahabharata*: "Discontent is the root of prosperity, but contentment destroys prosperity." He compared the Rajasuya sacrifice with the Diamond Jubilee of Queen Victoria, and said by way of an exordium that it was not an attempt to lay before them what Duryodhan did, but only "to lay before them the differentiating principles mentioned in the *Mahabharata* as to the potency of ambition which inspires all beings and the innate power it has of elevating a country or party." He concluded that the two maxims were the sum and substance of his discourse!

After the discourse by Prof. Paranjpe, Prof. Jinsiwale, in a touching speech, said that the reason why Shivaji Maharaj should be considered superior to Caesar and Napoleon was that whereas like Duryodhan, the great men of Europe were actuated by ambition alone, the superhuman attributes displayed by Shivaji were not enkindled by ambition or discontent, but were the outcome of the terrible irritation at the ruination of his country and religion by aliens. Then followed the *kirtan* by the pious Matange Buva. On Sunday morning there were athletic sports at Vinchurkar's Wada where Tilak resided. Students of the New English School and the Nutan Marathi Vidyalaya acquitted themselves creditably in their performance with Indian clubs.

On Sunday night, a lecture on the 'Killing of Afzulkhan' was delivered by Prof. Bhanu, when Tilak presided. Bhanu refuted the charge of "murder" which the British historians had levelled against Shivaji. How was it possible for Shivaji to imagine that Afzulkhan, who had undertaken an oath either to seize him and bring him alive, or to kill him and bring his head to Bijapur and who had on his way trodden under foot the image of the goddess of Tuljapur and that of Vithoba of Pandharpur, really meant to make peace with him? What treachery did the Maharaj commit if he went to meet Afzulkhan after making every preparation for the battle and for his own safety?

The English historians' assertion, continued Bhanu, that Shivaji was the first to strike was baseless. It was Afzulkhan who first struck Shivaji. Even if they assumed for argument's sake that Shivaji was the first to strike Afzulkhan, what right had any writer to call that man a murderer who had divine inspiration in his early age not to bow before the Mussalman Emperor? How could English writers who refrained from calling Washington a rebel, call Shivaji a rebel? How could they have the audacity to belaud such men as Clive and Warren Hastings who were incomparably inferior to Shivaji and whose careers were fraught with foul deeds, and yet call Shivaji a rebel? The history of Europe could not show even a single upright man of Shivaji's type. History might find fault with Shivaji, but from the point of ethics his act did not merit censure. How could the European system of ethics that had the greatest good of the greatest number as the basis, condemn Shivaji for abandoning a minor duty for accomplishing the major one? In the *Mahabharata* a man of this type, he observed, was called a "Buddha".

"Every Mahratta, every Hindu," proceeded Bhanu, "must rejoice at the Shivaji celebration. We are all striving to regain our lost independence, and the terrible load is to be uplifted by us all with joint efforts." After this speech Prof. Jinsiwale said that if no one blamed Napoleon for committing two thousand murders in Europe, and if Caesar was considered merciful, though he needlessly committed slaughter in Gaul (France) many a time, why should so virulent an attack be made on Shivaji for killing one or two persons? The people who took part in the French revolution denied that they committed murders, and maintained that they were only removing thorns from their path. Why should not the same argument be made applicable to Maharashtra?

Then rose Tilak, the president of the meeting, and in his concluding remarks said, "It was needless to make historical researches in connection with the killing of Afzulkhan. Let us assume that Shivaji first planned and then executed the murder of Afzulkhan. Was this act of the Maharaj right or wrong? This question should not be viewed from the standpoint of the Penal Code or the *Smritis* of Manu or Yadnyavalkya, or on the principles of morality laid down in the Western and Eastern ethical systems. The laws which bind society are for common men like yourselves and myself. Great men are above the common principles of law. These principles fail in their scope to reach the pedestal of great men."

"Did Shivaji commit a crime in killing Afzulkhan? The answer to this question can be found in the *Mahabharata* itself. Shrimat Krishna's teaching in the *Gita* is to kill even our teachers, our brothers. No blame whatever attaches to any person if he is not actuated by a desire to reap the fruit of his deeds. Shri Shivaji Maharaj did not commit the deed for mercenary motives. He killed Afzulkhan from disinterested motives for the public good. If thieves enter a house and we have not sufficient strength in our wrists to drive them out, we should without hesitation shut them up and burn them alive. God has not granted the mlenchas (a generic term for a foreigner) a copper plate (sanad or charter) to rule India. Shivaji was not guilty of coveting what belonged to others, because he strove to drive them out. Do not circumscribe your vision like a frog in a well. Get out of the Penal Code, enter the sublime sphere of the *Bhagwad Gita*, and consider the achievements of great men."

Tilak then referred to Bhanu's appeal for unity and said, "A nation that can't unite even on a few occasions should never hope to prosper. Bickerings will go on at all times, but it is most desirable that on one day out of 365 we should unite and respect one another. For quarrelling are all other days. Rama and Ravana felt no difficulty to meet in the same temple on the occasion of worshipping Shiva."

On this occasion a spirited youth sang a poem called 'Shivaji's Utterances'. The central idea of the poem was that Shivaji observed that he could not bear the heart-rending sight of India in which the cow, the mainstay of the agriculturists, the imparter of strength to the people, the foster-mother of babes, was ruthlessly slaughtered; women were molested, native Princes were deposed under flimsy pretexts, and still the Hindus brooked those insults and injustice. In the imaginary utterances Shivaji further asked the people to convey his message to the Britishers that they should make their subjects happy and discharge the debt of gratitude they owed to him for not having driven them back to their country when it was possible for him to do so. In the end Shivaji asked the people how they tolerated the ills under the foreign Raj like imbeciles.

The youth who composed and sang this poem was Damodar Hari Chapekar. A young man of twenty-seven, he was the eldest son of a famous religious preacher. Damodar was an out-and-out orthodox Hindu, and to him religion was politics and vice versa. He had assaulted in Bombay a Professor who had embraced Christianity, and had thrashed Tilak's reformist opponents also in a Poona street! He had tried to get himself enrolled in the army, but he could not succeed. He then founded a secret revolutionary organisation in Poona. His soul was disturbed when he heard about the excesses committed by Rand's ruthless soldiers, and, therefore, he was seeking an opportunity to take revenge upon Rand. To that end he had collected some weapons. He had been dogging Rand's footsteps for the past two months and had shadowed him on his way to office, club, church and gymkhana. Tilak knew Chapekar to be a spirited youth. When the day's programme was over, Tilak took him aside and remonstrated with him for calling the speakers imbeciles at the meeting. He added that had the youth like Chapekar been themselves brave and manly, Rand would not have been alive in Poona! A caustic rebuke indeed![1]

The report of the Shivaji festival was published in the issue of the *Kesari* of the 15th June 1897. The poem and the speeches appeared in that issue. The proofs of the article were seen by Tilak although the report was from the pen of K. P. Khadilkar, assistant editor to Tilak.

About this time Tilak was again elected to the Bombay Legislative Council in June, and the election awaited confirmation at the hands of the Governor. Anglo Indian papers were hinting that the Governor should disapprove of it!

III

On June 22 the Diamond Jubilee of Queen Victoria's rule was celebrated all over India, at all Government places, with great pomp and jollity, without any mention being made of the hardships of the people, who were harassed by famine and plague. The Jubilee was celebrated in Poona at the Government House situated at Ganeshkhind. All officers and title-holders were invited to dinner by the Governor. Tilak was of course among the invitees, and he attended the function with his friend Appasaheb Pendse. He had also made a speech in honour of Queen Victoria at the Poona Municipality.[2] Among the visitors were Lieutenant Ayerst, W. C. Rand, and Lieutenant Owen Lewis, who were connected with the plague administration. Crowds had gathered in the neighbourhood of Government House to witness the fireworks and the illuminated neighbouring hillocks with heaps of enkindled hay. It was a scene of rare brilliancy.

At twelve o'clock Lord Sandhurst's guests were making their way home from the State Reception and Dinner. Ayerst and his wife in a

1 Joshi, V. S., *Mrityunjayancha Atmayadnya*, p. 88 (Marathi).
2 Mangudkar, Dr. M. P., Poona Municipality Centenary Vol. (Marathi), p. 509.

hurry occupied the carriage which had brought Lieutenant Lewis to the Government House. Then followed the carriage which carried Lewis and his friend Sergeant. And the third carriage carried Rand, who was in a very happy mood, as no untoward incident had happened although he was given threats through private letters. The two Chapekar brothers with their friends Mahadeo Ranade and Vinayak Apte lay in ambush. When Rand's carriage began to trot down, Wasudeo Chapekar who was following it, made a signal by shouting, and Ayerst was shot by his brother Balkrishna thinking that he was shooting Rand. Lieutenant Lewis, who was following in another carriage, heard a shrill cry of a woman and her groans in the carriage that was running before theirs. He jumped down and overtook it. But he found Ayerst almost dead and his wife horrified. He thought that there might be a doctor in the carriage that was following. Yet Wasudeo was making a signal! Damodar realised the mistake and understood that Rand was coming down in the carriage that was following. The carriage passed by. He ran behind it, leaped on to it, fired a shot at the man inside, and jumped down. Frightened at the shot, the horse galloped, and it reached the place where Lewis was standing. Lewis anxiously stopped it and peeped into the carriage hoping to find a doctor inside, but to his horror he saw Rand fatally wounded. In the vicinity there were big sounds of fireworks, and these coachmen could not distinguish the sound of the pistols from the sound of the fireworks outside.

Ayerst and Rand were taken to hospital where the former was found dead, and the latter, unconscious. The young men parted in batches, and walked slowly back to their houses. Crowds witnessing the fireworks knew nothing about it.

Next morning clouds of horror spread over Poona. The wrath against Indians reached its climax. Though murder of any person is a horrible and despicable act, the people of Poona thought that it was the proper punishment meted out by God to Rand for his evil deeds.[3] The murderer was unknown. At dawn Tilak got a message from Damodarpant Chapekar that the Ganapati from Ganeshkhind had been propitiated the night before! He at once grasped the meaning and exclaimed, "Is it so? Then be cautious now!"

3 Kelkar, N. C., *Gata Gosthi* (Autobiography), p. 274.

The investigation of the murder of Rand was entrusted to Brewin, Superintendent of Police from Bombay. He was an Anglo-Indian known to be a very intelligent officer. On his arrival in Poona he started the investigation. Houses were searched, some streets blockaded, and a punitive police force was imposed on Poona owing to the so-called misconduct of the inhabitants. Mr. Lamb, the Collector of Poona, summoned a meeting and made a significant speech. He began by expressing surprise and regret that no expression of abhorrence of the crime had emanated from Poona. Having detailed the circumstances connected with the murder, he said that the fact that the Jubilee time was chosen pointed to a deliberate intention on the part of the miscreants to darken the celebration and convert it into days of mourning. He asked the citizens to be up and doing, that the deeds of the sedition-mongers and murderers might be held up to universal ridicule. He saw there was a tendency to misuse the liberty allowed under British rule to mislead the young generation with crude and impracticable notions of political liberty.

Lamb referred to the extravagant history of Shivaji then being taught to the youth, to the dissemination of a school-boy leaflet denouncing the Diamond Jubilee, and to petty insults to the pictures of Her Majesty the Queen-Empress. He intended his words to reach, not only those present, but those of a different character to whom he had alluded. If the advice and exhortation he had given remained unheeded, they would all find themselves undergoing an experience to which they had not been accustomed!

The Anglo-Indian papers were seized with panic and desperately raised a hue and cry against the Poona papers, and especially the Poona Brahmins. As the day chosen for the murder by the murderer was the day of a worldwide rejoicing, they thought that it was a deep-laid conspiracy hatched by the Poona Brahmins. The Secretary to the Governor-in-Council, however, wrote to Tilak on the next day of the murders that his election had been confirmed. The Anglo-Indian papers blamed Lord Sandhurst for having failed in taking their concrete suggestions into consideration and vetoing the very recent election of Tilak to the Legislative Council. They remarked that such action on the part of Government would place good citizenship at a discount and would create an impression that disloyalty was no disqualification for nomination by Government to places of honour.

Extracts from the Poona papers were published by malicious Anglo-Indian papers through men who were antagonistic to Tilak's Party. One mischievous man, under a pen-name 'Justice', with the venom of Junius, attacked Tilak through the *Times of India* quoting extracts from writings that had appeared in the *Kesari*, and asked whether or not those writings amounted to preaching political murder.

Quoting the title of Tilak's article 'Futility of mere clamour' the *Times of India* said: "Though we do not offer any suggestion as to the view that a jury might take of the Hon'ble Mr. Tilak's discourse on the 'futility of mere clamour' against Mr. Rand and his assistants, still someone with a pistol in his hand seems to have been in hearty agreement with the Honourable Member's distrust in the efficacy of 'mere clamour'."

The reaction of the English papers was mostly provocative. The news of the murders caused a shock and sensation in conservative circles in London, and they were seized with a tremendous feeling of popular uneasiness. *The Times*, London, declared that there were not wanting signs that the whole native community were well aware that a disaster of some sort would occur to some of the Europeans visiting Ganeshkhind that night. There was an air of expectation and suspense, not unmixed with certain triumphant aggressiveness of bearing towards Europeans. The *Daily Chronicle* frankly blamed the Bombay Government for imposing punitive police on Poona. The teethless Arthur Crawford blossomed into a booklet and poured out vials of his wrath upon Chitpavan Brahmins. The *Englishman* of Calcutta said that if the object of the instigator of the murder was to give a shock to the whole country, then he had certainly succeeded.

Rand's death occurred on July 3, and it added fuel to the fire. So panic-stricken were the Anglo-Indians that they did not allow men like Dr. Bhandarkar and some Parsees, who had joined the funeral procession, to enter the cemetery. They were sent back. On July 4, under the presidentship of Bhandarkar a meeting of sirdars, merchants, servants and pensioners residing in Poona expressed in the presence of the District Collector its utter abhorrence and detestation of the dastardly murder.

The *Times of India*, in an angry editorial, made a fervent appeal to Government to give immediate effect to section 124A of the Penal Code and to put on trial the editors of the Deccan papers which had led a campaign of vituperation and especially one of the Poona papers which said that the British Government in India was the worst Government in the world; it had charged British soldiers with deeds more cruel and coldblooded and its writings were an instigation to murderous acts.

Tilak was not cowed down at all! He was undisturbed although he knew the storm was gathering over his head. He wrote in the *Kesari* that as nobody thought that there was any possibility of such a horrible event happening, immediately it came to the ears, it filled the hearts of all with sorrow and surprise. As an editor he further observed that at such a time every man must render such assistance as might be required by the police in detecting the murderer; otherwise, for the folly of one man a dark imputation and calamity would come over all without any reason. He admitted that it was equally dangerous and disgraceful to all that such horrible crimes should have remained undetected. On June 26 he wrote a letter to the *Times of India* saying that in his paper he had done nothing to excite feelings of disaffection among the people, and it was foolish to condemn a community as a whole simply because a fanatic took it into his head to perpetrate a horrible deed which they all deplored.

And yet he thundered in an article against the punitive police and asked whether 'Government's head was on its shoulders'. He compared the Government with a mad elephant trampling under foot everything to dust that came in the way. He wrote another article in which he declared that 'to rule was not to revenge'. He denounced the *Times of India* and such other papers and persons who attributed the murder to the Brahmins of Poona and added that Lord Sandhurst should not condemn or punish the whole society or community for the misdeed of one man.

In the meanwhile the news of the Chitpur riots aggravated the situation in London. Hindus and Muslims were reported to be acting in sympathy and murdering or assaulting Englishmen in India. Letters and articles appeared in the British press saying that disaffection and disloyalty were rife in India. The condemnation of the educated classes in general and of the Poona Brahmins in particular was for a time universal, and suggestions were made to the British Government to undertake repressive legislation immediately.

This anti-Indian propaganda provoked even the gentle G. K. Gokhale, who was then in England. He granted an interview to the representative of the *Manchester Guardian* with a view to counteracting the malicious propaganda that harped on the falsehood that there was a deep-laid conspiracy of the Poona Brahmins behind the murder. In the course of the interview Gokhale remarked that the plague administration was responsible for the Indian atrocities and added that two women were violated by British soldiers forming the search party and one of the women had since then committed suicide. This came as a veritable bombshell on Britain. British newspapers and leaders clamoured for an explanation from George Hamilton, the Secretary of State for India. He demanded an explanation from Lord Sandhurst, the Governor of Bombay. Lord Sandhurst telegraphically stated that the accusations were a tissue of falsehood from beginning to end. Thereupon the British House of Commons condemned Gokhale's remarks as malevolent inventions.

A volley of questions was put to Lord Hamilton by Members of Parliament. Sir E. Ashmead-Bartlett asked him "whether the Governor of Bombay had confirmed the nomination of Bal Gangadhar Tilak, and whether he was aware that the person, besides publishing attacks upon the British authorities in his newspapers, had himself made speeches inciting people to rebellion, and if so, whether the Government of India proposed to take any action in this matter." Another Member Howell asked Hamilton whether he was aware that "Bal Gangadhar Tilak was some years ago sentenced to a double term of imprisonment for being concerned in a conspiracy to defame a distinguished native statesman, Rao Bahadur M. Barve, Minister of an influential Native State."

In a studiously brief written reply Hamilton said that the nomination of Tilak had been confirmed by the Governor of Bombay. "But the question," he added, "whether the articles which appeared in those papers were seditious, and whether that speech contained an incitement to rebellion, was a matter of law as to which the Government of Bombay has not at present arrived at any final opinion."

British leaders wanted to punish Gokhale. So some asked how he had secured the appointment of a teacher of political economy in a college that received a grant from Government.

Tilak understood what these questions and replies meant for him and, referring to them, he wrote an editorial under the title ' What is sedition?'. It was the duty of a paper to acquaint the people with their rights and to educate them how to get their grievances redressed lawfully. To bring to the attention of the people that European culprits were let off without proper punishment, that people could not receive proper relief in times of famine, that the native Princes were deposed on any pretext without enquiry, that the Government expended money on the Indian military although the army was engaged outside India, was no sedition. It was merely attracting the attention of the people to the unjust state of affairs.

IV

THE GOVERNMENT HAD set the wheels of vengeance moving against Tilak, and the time for an explosion was drawing nearer. All the past clashes with bureaucrats had now accumulated into a thundering storm, and the whole atmosphere was charged with electricity waiting to burst forth any moment. There were rumours that Tilak's imprisonment was imminent. Tilak wanted to prosecute the *Times of India* for its mischievous articles. So he went to Bombay on the morning of July 27, to consult his lawyer friends in the matter and also to scent the move of the Government as regards his arrest. It was also said that he intended to publish some material in the *Champion*, a Bombay English paper, supporting Gokhale's statements, although he had opined in his own paper the *Kesari* that there was a little exaggeration as to two of Gokhale's statements and that there was no evidence for the third.

But on the very day of his arrival in Bombay a warrant of arrest was issued under Section 124A of the Indian Penal Code by the Presidency Magistrate, and the police went to serve it on Tilak. Tilak was staying with Daji Abaji Khare in the latter's house on Girgaum Back Road. Sirdar Abdul Ali Khan Bahadur, Superintendent of the Criminal Investigation Department, Bombay, experienced some difficulty in identifying Tilak. So he took with him Mr. James Guider who knew Tilak. He surrounded the house with a strong police party, and served the warrant of arrest on Tilak. Tilak asked his servant for his bedding, and he quietly surrendered himself to the police. He was arrested on the charge of exciting and attempting to excite disaffection towards the Government by law established in British India, by publishing inflammatory articles in the *Kesari*. He was taken into custody and locked up in a separate cell at the Esplanade Police Court Chowkey. Khare immediately saw the Presidency Magistrate, but he refused to release Tilak on bail. Khare returned to the cell and found Tilak snoring! This gave proof of his extraordinary coolness in danger. Khare, however, knocked at the door and he woke up. They then decided about the next day's proceedings, and Khare returned.

The news of Tilak's arrest spread in Bombay with remarkable rapidity, and the next noon the police court and all approaches thereto were crowded as Tilak was to be produced before the Magistrate. There was, however, no disorder or any demonstration. An application for bail was made before Mr. Sanders-Slater, Chief Presidency Magistrate. Russel, Bar-at-law, instructed by M. R. Bodas, appeared for Tilak. He appealed to the

Magistrate to let Tilak on bail as he occupied a prominent position, and there could be, he added, little ground for supposing he would not appear to take his trial at the proper time. Nicolson, the Public Prosecutor, opposed it on the ground that the Magistrate had no power to grant bail if there was sufficient ground to prove the accused guilty. Therefore, the Magistrate refused the application, and Tilak was removed to Police custody.

Tilak's arrest on charges of sedition was the first of its kind in modern India after the birth of the Congress, and, therefore, it came as a volcanic shock to Maharashtra and India! One editor was prosecuted in Bengal under section 124A, but his was an ordinary trial. Here the murder of Rand had made the atmosphere very dangerous, and the arrest of Tilak made the trial colourful and explosive!

At Poona police arrested Keshav Mahadeo Bal, Printer of the *Kesari*. There was also a warrant for the arrest of Hari N. Gokhale, the owner of the Press, but he was not in Poona. The house of the Natu Brothers, the elder of whom had sent written complaints to Government against forcible intrusion of soldiers during the plague administration, was carefully searched, and arms and other things found therein were taken possession of. They were arrested under the very old Regulations of 1827 which empowered Government to deal with political offenders. One brother was put in Thana Jail, and the other in Sabarmati Jail. More arrests followed. The Editors of the *Poona Vaibhav*, *Modavritta* and *Pratod* were arrested. The editors of the *DnyanPrakash* and *Sudharak* were also arrested, but they were afterwards let off. Thus Lord Sandhurst established a reign of terror by making Poona undergo experiences of which they never had any taste since British rule began.

On July 29 an appeal was made to the High Court for the release of Tilak on bail, and it was heard by Mr. Justice Parson and Mr. Justice Ranade. Tilak's friend Daji Abaji Khare, Chimanlal H. Setalwad and M. R. Bodas appeared for the defence; the Advocate-General Lang appeared for the Crown. Khare said that he would furnish bail to any amount for his client and added that justice would not be served by keeping his client in custody. Mr. Lang opposed the application for bail and said that it was not a bailable offence. Mr. Justice Ranade simply inquired if some corrections were made afterwards in the original articles of the *Kesari*. Khare replied in the positive. As the case was going to commence in the Presidency Magistrate's Court only two days after, Mr. Justice Parson refused to release Tilak on bail. He, however, told Khare to make a further appeal to the High Court in the matter if any adjournment was made in that Court and his client was detained any further.

Crowds had thronged the High Court, and some had expected that Ranade would at least release Tilak, the leader of the people, on bail, although Tilak was his chief opponent in Maharashtra. They murmured that Ranade was afraid to grant bail to Tilak. Ranade was known for his impartial judgment and had once chastised his father for bringing undue pressure on him in one case. Ranade was not free from British suspicion either. During the trial of Tilak detectives were hovering about the residence of Ranade in Bombay.

While Tilak was taking his trial, Gokhale arrived in Bombay on July 30. Vacha, according to Mahatma Gandhi, met him on the steamer and requested him to tear the particular letters as none was coming forward to give evidence. So Gokhale threw the letters of Ranade and Vacha into the sea.[4] The Police Commissioner of Bombay, too, met him on board the steamer and desired to have a talk with him in connection with the charges he had made against the Plague Committee. Finding that the promised evidence was not coming forward, Gokhale soon tendered an unconditional apology to Lord Sandhurst, stating that he withdrew all the allegations unreservedly which he had made on the strength of letters received from persons whose general trustworthiness he had no reason to doubt. An infuriated public believed that the charges were entirely true, and it was said that sulky, gloomy Gokhale would not live down the retraction.

The hearing of Tilak's trial was resumed on Saturday, and it continued on July 31 and August 2, 1897, before Mr. Sanders-Slater. D. D. Davar, Bar-at-Law, boldly complained in the Court against the confiscation of the registers of subscribers of the *Kesari* and *Mahratta* and said that the Government would be charged with unlawful conduct and malicious vindictiveness if they gagged the papers in that way! The Magistrate committed the case to the Sessions.

Davar made an application again for the grant of bail on August 4. He pleaded his case with great force of argument and told His Lordship that his client would be put to great difficulties in the preparation of his defence. Believing that the accused would be handicapped by being kept in jail, Mr. Justice Badruddin Tyabji let off Tilak on bail by directing that two

4 *The Diary of Mahadev Bhai, Vol. III*, p. 248, (Hindi) published by the Navajivan Trust, Ahmedabad.

sureties worth twenty thousand rupees each and a personal surety of fifty thousand rupees should be furnished. As soon as His Lordship rose, people assembled inside the Court and outside, commenced cheering Badruddin Tyabji for his independent spirit and liberal attitude!

Annasaheb Nene, a big landlord, and Dwarkadas Dharamsey, a businessman, the latter at the instance of Laxmidas Khimji, boldly came forward to stand surety for Tilak. Dr. Bhajekar, who had expressed his willingness to stand surety for Tilak even upto five lacs, was nominated by Government to the Council and his name was dropped. Tilak was made to wait in the Prothonotary's office till the bail amount was produced. Annasaheb Nene and Dwarkadas Dharamsey produced the necessary amount and Tilak was released on bail at night on the 4th August. Next day Tilak went to Poona. Besides Mr. Khare and Bodas, Dr. M. G. Deshmukh, Bhajekar, Setlur, Keshavrao Deshpande, Gajananrao Vaidya, and Wasukaka Joshi were the men who took keen interest in the defence of Tilak. It was reported in the press that Eardley Norton was coming from Madras to defend him.

Two days after his arrival at Poona, Tilak, the protector and defender of his friends, agreed to be an executor of the will of a dying friend, Shri Baba Maharaj. He was a first class Sirdar and also Raj Guru of the Kolhapur Maharaja. He had established his claim on his property after struggling in the Court for a number of years and was now dying in debt. He was dangerously ill and Tilak could not displease his dying friend. In accordance with the wish of his friend Tilak agreed to be one of the trustees. Had he not been released on bail for two days more, Tilak would have been spared the money, energy and time which would have enriched the nation in many other respects. For he had to struggle relentlessly through fire of calumny for over nineteen years to fulfil the pledge he gave to his dying friend.

During Tilak's stay in Poona Harry Brewin, the officer in charge of the investigation of Rand's murder, had long talks with Tilak. Suave and subtle, he was a man of charming manners and could talk Marathi fluently. But his subtle intellect failed to fathom Tilak's depth. Great men are seldom deceived by soft and gentle words. When at last Brewin asked Tilak why he did not help Government in finding out the culprit, Tilak bluntly said, " Well, I don't think that I can help you in this matter. None is expected to give me information. But, Mr. Brewin, you should rest assured that even if I come to have such information, I will never pass it on to you. Though I believe that an offender should be punished adequately, never will I agree to be anybody's spy and never will I betray anyone in the world. Certainly, I will not put obstacles in your path. I resent Mr. Lamb's allegation that the murder is a blot upon Poona. Yet I do not deny that the offender, if and when found, should be sentenced according to the dictates of law."[5]

The time for departure to take his trial at Bombay came near, and Tilak was deeply moved by the thought of his financial difficulties. The Latur Mill was a burden on the income from his law-classes, and he had hardly paid down the debt which he had accepted with the ownership of the *Kesari* and *Mahratta*. Conviction and sentence was a foregone conclusion. He had his children to provide for, and his papers to be looked after. In life money had no interest for him.Austerely contemptuous of all personal advantage, he knew his financial position was utterly unsound. Reluctantly he reviewed the position and saw that the other side of the ledger was not balanced even with the heavy debts he had contracted. For a few moments he was stung by a strange pang. He then dictated his will. Having fixed, settled and arranged all things, he started for Bombay with what money he could manage to borrow through the efforts of his colleague Wasukaka Joshi.

Tilak's friends and admirers knew this difficulty, and an announcement for public subscription was made through newspapers. All provinces responded well to the appeal and especially the Bengali leaders Shishir Kumar Ghose and Motilal Ghose, editors of the *Amrita Bazar Patrika*, and Babu Surendranath Banerjee took keen interest in collecting the defence funds. Tilak and Ghose had great affection for each other. They stood by each other in their journalistic attacks and victories. The Bengal leaders raised the necessary funds and engaged two leading barristers from the Calcutta Bar, L. P. Pugh and William Garth, who were then to leave for England via Bombay. The Calcutta solicitors Bhupendranath Basu and Hirendranath Dutt established contact with Messrs. Bhaishankar and Kanga, Tilak's Bombay solicitors, and the Calcutta leaders enthusiastically wired to the friends of Tilak in Bombay their decision promising to take up responsibility for the defence of Tilak. They added that they undertook to pay the fees of Pugh and Garth. J. Chaudhari, Bar-at-Law, tendered voluntary help and accompanied the barristers.

Some persons hinted at an apology, and Motilal Ghose also wrote in that vein. Tilak replied to him that Government was bent upon humiliating

---

5 Kelkar, N. C.. Life of Lokamanya Tilak, Vol. I, p. 659 (Marathi).

the Poona leaders, and as the other side expected him to do what amounted to pleading guilty, he was not prepared to do so. He added that Government would not find him a *Kuccha* reed as they did in some others. "My position among the people entirely depends upon my character; and if I am cowed down by the prosecution, in my heart of hearts I know the case for the prosecution is the weakest that was ever placed before a jury. I think, living in Maharashtra is as good as living in the Andamans."

"Such risks, however, we must take if we dabble in politics. They are all the risks of our profession,"[6] he concluded.

Pugh, Garth and Chaudhari, the barristers from Calcutta, reached Bombay in time. Pugh was allowed to defend Tilak. But Garth, who was a powerful cross-examiner, was not allowed to do so by the High Court on the ground that there were many senior lawyers at the Bombay Bar. D. D. Davar was engaged as Pugh's junior. Russell and Branson were retained. Garth and Chaudhari were allowed to sit next to Pugh to take down notes and instruct him. When Pugh and Garth had long consultations with Tilak and his solicitors, they were greatly impressed with the great ability, keenness of intellect, strong common sense, the spirit of independence, and the remarkable knowledge of law that Tilak displayed during the course of consultations. Curiously, they asked Tilak whether he desired Self-Government for India and not absolute Independence, and Tilak replied, " Desire for independence on the part of a subject people is nothing dishonourable and is no crime."

V

AT LAST THE day of the trial dawned. Tilak and the printer K. M. Bal stood in the dock of the Bombay High Court before Mr. Arthur Strachey on September 8 upon the charge of exciting disaffection towards the Government established by law in British India.

The Court and the galleries were packed. On either side of the judge on the desks, accommodation was provided for some prominent ladies and gentlemen. A swarm of pleaders and representatives of vernacular journals occupied seats which were set apart for those actually concerned in the case. Worried by the demand for seats, the Clerk of the Court said amidst laughter that those representatives of the vernacular press who could not be accommodated might seat themselves in the dock!

6 *All About Lokamanya Tilak*, B. G. Paul & Co., p. 35.

And thus commenced the trial of Tilak upon which the attention of all educated India was concentrated and which was being watched with interest, not only throughout the British Empire, but over a considerable portion of the civilized world!

Both the accused pleaded not guilty. Then the trial began before a jury consisting of six Europeans, two Hindus and one Parsee.

All reports on the Shivaji festival were taken as the objectionable articles. The first article constituted Shivaji's utterances, the production of a poetaster, and the other was the report of Tilak's speech at the close of the function defending Shivaji's killing of Afzulkhan. The oriental translator and other witnesses were examined regarding the correct meaning of the sentences. Rules of Grammar, denotations and connotations of words in Tilak's sentences were discussed. At last Strachey called on Tilak to explain certain words and their grammatical relationship. The Advocate-General said that Tilak's speech was calculated to impress upon the minds of the readers of that article that the British Government had no right to be in India, and that his hearers were perfectly justified in adopting any means they liked, even murder, for the purpose of attaining that object.

Pugh submitted to the jury that had it not been for the murder of Rand, they would never have heard about this prosecution at all. The persons were charged with certain writings in Marathi, and it would have been monstrous to have asked the jury for a conviction upon an offence for which the accused was liable for transportation for life, relying upon the meaning of Marathi terms which the majority of the jury and of the counsels did not understand. He also brought to the notice of the jury that Government had confirmed Tilak's nomination to the Legislative Council after the murder of Rand. The Shivaji festival was celebrated just in the same way as they celebrated the memory of Robert Bruce and Wallace in Scotland, where many things were said which outsiders might not think justifiable and still the Scots were loyal to the British throne. The same case was with the Shivaji festival. It was a resume of Carlyle's Heroes and Hero Worship. Political assassination was not thought of at the meeting, as was conveyed to the jury by the prosecution, because there was no evidence to show that there was any connection between the reference to the assassination of Afzulkhan at the meeting and the assassination of Rand. If Government had thought that the murder of Rand was due to the incident in question, they would not have brought action against Tilak under section 124A, but they would have certainly proceeded under some other section of the Penal Code.

The hearing of the case lasted six days, and on September 14 the judgment was delivered. A large crowd assembled outside before the opening of the Court; a holiday helped to swell the crowd. The Judge commenced summing up at eleven o'clock and continued till five with an interval of three quarters of an hour for tiffin. His Lordship explained to the jury the meaning and scope of section 124A. He observed that he did not wish to suggest in any way that there was the relation of cause and effect between either of those articles and that abominable murder, and he added that even the Advocate-General had admitted that he could not prove that those murders were caused by those articles.

The question, then, before them was whether the accused had excited or attempted to excite feelings of disaffection towards the Government. Disaffection, he said, meant hostility or ill-will of any sort towards Government, feelings of ill-will, great or small, intense or mild, and any attempt to excite such feelings brought the offender within the purview of the section. It was not action but feeling was the test. The attempt to excite feelings of hatred against or disaffection towards the Government was enough to constitute the offence. Absence of affection, the Judge observed, amounted to presence of hatred against the Government in a man's mind. The jury, in considering the articles, must always bear in mind the time, the place, and the circumstances of the case. They were not to take a philosophical view of those utterances, but were to consider the intention that the prisoner had in his mind when he wrote the article, and the effect he intended then to produce on the minds of his readers.

At five o'clock the jury retired to consider their verdict, and their return was awaited with keen anticipation. In the meanwhile an application was made to the Judge on behalf of Tilak to reserve for the consideration of a full bench certain parts of law arising from the charge to the jury, but this was not granted. At twenty-minutes-to-six they reappeared in the Court. The foreman announced that six out of nine considered Tilak guilty of attempting to excite feelings of disaffection towards the British Government, but they were unanimous in acquitting the Printer Bal. The three Indian jurors returned a verdict of not guilty. Then the Judge asked Tilak if he had anything to say before the sentence was passed upon him. "In spite of that verdict," declared Tilak, "I still maintain that I am innocent, and for this reason I think the verdict has been arrived at owing to the misunderstanding of certain Marathi texts. In fact, there was not a single intelligent Marathi gentleman put in the witness box by the prosecution. It seems to have been lost sight of, and not pressed on the attention of the jury, but whatever it is I still hold that the writings themselves are not seditious. They were not written with a seditious intention, and I do not think they have produced that effect on the readers."

The Judge then said that he concurred with the verdict of the jury. The young British Judge said that in fixing the sentence he bore in mind the good work Tilak had done in connection with the plague and attempted to enforce a reasonable policy upon his countrymen. Furthermore he was influenced by the fact that this was the second prosecution under section 124A and that the absence of any proceedings under the section had led journalists to believe that there was no kind of writing in which they might not indulge with impunity.

"You are not an ordinary obscure editor and publisher," continued the young Judge, "but are one of the leading members of your community, and being a man of influence many of your people look for their guidance to you a man of intelligence, a man of remarkable ability and energy, and who might under other circumstances have been a useful force in the State. Instead of adopting the course which could have brought you credit, you have allowed yourself to publish articles of this kind, which, if persisted in, could only bring misfortune upon the people."

He, then, passed upon Tilak half the full-term of imprisonment allowed by the section, namely, a sentence of eighteen months' rigorous imprisonment.

In the afternoon an enormous crowd had gathered in the precincts of the Court, and it was only by the aid of mounted guard that egress could be obtained. Tilak was taken to the judges' entrance to the Court, and was quietly driven away to the prison in a private brougham. Meanwhile public attention was concentrated on the prison van which had been ostentatiously driven up to the general entrance, and it went away empty.

Writing on the judgment, the Times of India felt glad that Strachey acquitted himself of the heavy responsibility with ability and dignity, and added that the sentence did not err on the side of severity. Tilak had, it remarked, a fair trial and the punishment carried an impressive lesson with it for those who had need for it.

The Times, London, also observed that Tilak had had a fair and patient trial and, making a wrong statement that half the jury consisted of Tilak's countrymen, said that Tilak's very able and distinguished Counsel Pugh had no solid evidence. *The Times* added that the purport and drift of the articles were to impress upon the people that it would be justifiable to overthrow British rule and to justify political murder. "The Brahmins of the Deccan," proceeded the editorial, "have been adepts in the art of stirring up sedition and discontent without committing themselves to phrases of so definite a kind. The conviction of a man of Tilak's birth and rank will probably teach them to be a little more cautious for the future." *The Times*, London, concluded that if that failed, the Government of India would be obliged to have recourse to more stringent measures of a legislative order!

A European accused could have a European jury in India, but an Indian could not demand an Indian jury! This was the British Law in India. On top of it all the jurors were unacquainted with the Marathi language. The nationalist press declared that the decision was a foregone conclusion. "The case was," said the *Indian Mirror* of Calcutta, "one of the greatest importance and involved the settlement of a grave issue. It was too much to expect so young and inexperienced a judge as Mr. Arthur Strachey to rise equal to the importance of the issues before him. It seemed that the judge and the Advocate-General had interchanged places." Indeed the Advocate-General had made a very sober speech, and it was a mild affair between him and Pugh.

The *Daily Chronicle* of London highly criticised the new definition of disaffection enunciated by Strachey and observed: "We feel confident that such an interpretation of the law would not be tolerated in England and if not speedily overruled, may produce mischief in India." For some days the interpretation put on the word 'disaffection' by Strachey as 'want of affection' was a matter of jokes in the Indian High Courts. Sir Charles Paul, the then Advocate-General of Bengal, laughed at Strachey. Mr. William Jackson nicknamed Tiger Jackson, who was the leading lawyer at the Calcutta Bar, always chafed Mr. J. Chaudhari, who had assisted Mr. Pugh at Bombay during Tilak's trial, about the Bombay canons of interpretation, and asked him why he did not ask his leader Pugh to tell the Bombay Judge that 'dissension' might as well mean 'absence of tension'. Referring to the Tilak case, Dadabhai remarked in London that gagging the Press was simply suicidal, that there never was a greater mistake than to prosecute

Tilak and that the British Government was introducing the Russian system of Government.

The sentence raised Tilak in the estimation of the people. What they loved most was that he preached with deeds and not with mere words. The millhands fasted spontaneously; and the student world was indignant. Newspapers published special issues praising Tilak as the martyr to liberty. The *Advocate of India* brought out a supplement giving a big photograph of Tilak. C. Y. Chintamani wrote later that he had framed that picture and bowed before it every morning in those days! Efforts were made by interested groups to bend Tilak before Government, but he refused to tender an apology like Gokhale. Government knew that he was a hard nut to crack. Government had great powers and resources at its command while Tilak had courage, self-control, faith and sympathy of the people. Tilak was changing now the idea of leadership in India. The role of a leader in a slave country was being transformed or remodelled, and a type of new leadership was being born with powers of suffering and courage, driving politics from academical to practical methods. A subject nation always marches ahead through the trials and tribulations of her great men. Thus this trial of Tilak proved to be the first cock's crow of Indian revolution.

The Tilak Defence Committee did not lose courage. They decided to move the High Court for leave to appeal to the Judicial Committee of the Privy Council. Next morning Tilak's solicitors and counsels had a meeting at the Byculla Club. A messenger was to see Tilak and bring his suggestions from Jail. While they were discussing the transcript of the Judge's charge, the messenger brought a bundle of papers from Tilak with a lot of writing on sheets in pencil. On finishing their reading of the charge, they opened the bundle of papers from Tilak. Pugh went through it carefully from top to bottom, and they all found to their unspeakable surprise that it was a draft of the petition for leave to appeal to the Privy Council which they had met to draw up. Tilak at once rose higher in their estimation, and Pugh and Garth remarked that during their professional careers they had not come across any layman or even a lawyer who could draw up a petition of appeal so accurately and exhaustively in absence of any notes or a copy of the charge or judgment! Perhaps they were not aware that Tilak was a teacher and guide to law-students and counsel for lawyers.

The application was made to the High Court, Bombay, for leave to appeal to the Privy Council against Tilak's conviction. A full bench of the High Court comprising the Chief Justice, Justice Candy and Justice

Strachey heard the application on September 24. The grounds for the application, said Tilak's Counsel, Russell, were briefly that the sanction for prosecution was inadequate, and, therefore, the Court which tried him had no jurisdiction, and that the learned judge had misdirected the jury both as to the scope of the section and the meaning of the word 'disaffection' and also as to what was meant by British Government.

The Chief Justice said that there was no misunderstanding as to the jurisdiction or the construction put on the section or to the meaning of the British Government, and added it was going too far to assert that the section could not be said to be contravened unless there was a direct incitement to stir up disorder or rebellion. Touching upon the objection raised to Strachey's summing up, the Court said that although 'contrary to affection' and not 'absence of affection' should have been used in connection with reference to Sir Comer Petheram's decision, the jury could not have been misled by it. On these grounds the application was refused.

CHAPTER IX

A Nation is in Tears

I

THE GRIM SENTENCE passed on Tilak was a grave warning to all politicians and editors, and to all those who had business connections with him. The self-centred among his circle lost no time in dissociating themselves from him and his activities. Calamity is a mirror wherein we see ourselves and our friends reflected in true colours. Gokhale, one of the proprietors of the Aryabhushan Printing Press, refused to print Tilak's papers. Tilak's nephew Vidwans managed to get the papers printed at the Vithal Press owned by a pensioner by name Bhide. A declaration of both the papers was made in the name of N. C. Kelkar, Tilak's assistant editor, who was a young man of twenty-five with an old head on his young shoulders.

Another lieutenant of Tilak, K. P. Khadilkar, a brilliant journalist, stood by Kelkar and they started the office of the papers at Tilak's residence by putting together two empty oil-tins to serve them as a table. Amidst the panic-stricken atmosphere, the publication of Tilak's *Kesari*, in the absence of Tilak, made great news. People felt glad to know that the *Kesari*, the lion, continued to roar and the *Mahratta*, to show fight! *The Times of India*, therefore, thought it to be an important piece of news that Tilak's papers were published in the name of a young man named N. C. Kelkar. Time had now arrived for Kelkar to prove his mettle on the touchstone of difficulties, to prove himself worthy of the trust his leader had reposed in him; for when a year before Tilak offered him the editorship of the *Mahratta* he had written to the young man: "I want in you not a servant but a friend for the last days, as it may be, of my life."

The news of the sentence passed on Tilak rendered a severe shock to his wife. She wriggled with pain on her bed for two days without taking a morsel of food. This was the second time she was facing such an affliction. She trembled at the thought of the hard labour and the rigours of jail life her husband was undergoing. It drove her to despair. Her soul writhed in terrible agony. Amidst the crushing sorrow she groaned, “Send in a petition praying the Government to put me also in jail with him. I, too, am his co-partner.”

Tilak had not attended the session of the Bombay Legislative Council which had met on August 4, 1897. His friend Khare asked a number of questions which stood in the name of Tilak. Threatened with imminent imprisonment, Tilak had sent in his resignations of the membership of the Poona Municipality and the membership of the Legislative Council. He had not resigned his membership of the Senate of Bombay University. Government seized that opportunity and struck his name off the register of the fellows of the University. The panic-stricken Anglo-Indian devils clamoured for their pound of flesh, and they demanded cancellation of Tilak’s University degrees also!

By now the investigations regarding the murder of Rand had met with success. Damodarpant Chapekar was arrested in Bombay on September 30, 1897, and he confessed that he had shot Rand. The clue to the mystery of that murder was given by one Ganesh Dravid who was undergoing imprisonment in Yeravda Jail for forgery. The Government offer of a reward of twenty thousand rupees roused this criminal’s proclivities and prompted him to this treacherous act. After Chapekar’s arrest detailed investigations were carried on in the case.

The Tilak Defence Committee had not given up their struggle. They decided to make an application to the Privy Council itself for leave to appeal to the Privy Council. It was the penultimate stage, and if the application was granted, the final stage would be the appeal to the Judicial Committee of the Privy Council which had powers to revise, under special circumstances, the operations of the Criminal Courts in India. Tilak’s friend Khare sailed for England on October 2, on that mission, with papers pertaining to the case, and Kanga, solicitor, followed him. They engaged Umeshchandra, the big gun at the Calcutta Bar, Blair, Pugh and Garth to assist Mr. Herbert Asquith, then an eminent Liberal leader. Asquith was known as a marvel of precision, and he argued well without any enthusiasm. They had also engaged Mr. J. D. Mayne, who was an authoritative text-writer on the Indian Penal Code and a practised hand at the Privy Council Bar.

The case was prepared with great labour giving English synonyms for Marathi words and phrases, and then the meaning of the whole paragraph in English.

The application came up for hearing before the Judicial Committee of the Privy Council, the highest Tribunal in the British Empire. The Tribunal consisted of the Lord Chancellor Lord Halsbury, Lord Hobhouse, Lord Davey, and Sir Richard Couch. They heard the application. Mr. Asquith laid great emphasis on the interpretation of Section 124A of. the Indian Penal Code, dealt with Strachey's meaning of the word disaffection, and tried to impress upon their minds the need for going minutely into the proceedings of the case, especially the meaning of Section 124A as it was likely to hit badly the Indian Press and Platform if the interpretation were not revised. Counsel for the Crown, Mr. Cohen, who was assisted by Mr. Spring Branson, simply read to the Judicial Committee the latest resolution passed by the Privy Council as to when the Privy Council could take up appeals in criminal cases for revision. The Judicial Committee held that there was not even a *prima facie* case for revising the proceedings of the Bombay High Court, and Lord Halsbury briefly gave judgment, rejecting the appeal without entering into details. The decision was a shock to the well-wishers of Tilak. The *Kesari* gave vent to the people's feelings, and expressed the view that the confidence of the people in the justice and fair play of the British Judiciary was completely shaken on account of that decision.

The *Times of India*, Bombay, with sardonic satisfaction, sang the praises of the Judicial Committee of the Privy Council. It observed sarcastically that Tilak's friends had made as good a fight as was within their power, but they should now accept the failure, in good temper and in a spirit of good citizenship.

The editors, who were arrested after Tilak's arrest, were dealt with severely or leniently as the tone and temperament of the persons concerned merited punishment. A reign of terror was thus experienced by educated men and political agitators.

The jail life of Tilak commenced at Dongri gaol in Bombay. Fifteen years before he had passed 101 days in that gaol with his colleague Agarkar. Prison rigours told upon Tilak's health very severely. He was treated as an ordinary criminal and was given food which was dross. To him food cooked with onion and garlic was anathema, and in prison the curry was dressed with nothing but onion and garlic. He liked boiled rice, but he had to live on pieces of dry bread with the result that he was terribly reduced in health and sank down from 135 lbs. to 104 within a short time. In addition to his worries, he was given coir work which was arduous. The news of his declining health disturbed his well-wishers and friends outside, and they felt anxious for his safety. A few days later Tilak was removed to Byculla Jail in Bombay.

To the people Tilak was a symbol of sacrifice and selflessness. The Indian officers in jail showed secret sympathy for his sufferings. They sometimes under this or that pretext sought opportunities to see him and offer him bits of betel-nut under some cover. They took him to the jail hospital on the slightest pretext indifferent health. The watchmen and the other menial staff displayed reverential devotion towards him and tried to alleviate his sufferings whenever they could.

A Muhammadan watchman was intensely grieved at the declining health of Tilak. He hailed from a village in Poona District. At night he threw towards Tilak pieces of copra and jaggery. Grateful for his kind gestures, Tilak warned him against the danger he would expose himself to. Tilak meticulously observed jail rules, and gave the jail officers no cause for anxiety or trouble. So he tried to dissuade the Muslim warder from acting against the rules, but he would not listen to him. Purposely Tilak then told him that he was suffering from a sore throat. Bent upon helping him, he then gave Tilak almond nuts and pieces of sugarcandy.

Tilak was overwhelmed with the unquestioned devotion of the people. The Muhammadan warder was going to resign his post, but Tilak told him that in future patriotic leaders would be often coming to jails and servants with a sympathetic heart like him would be a sort of help during their privations in jail life. After his release Tilak presented this Muslim with a gift and a dhoti which his family superstitiously used as a divine pain-reliever from any disease. Tilak experienced another phase of mental relief in Byculla Jail. His friend, Sirdar Tatyasaheb Natu, had just then been shifted from Thana Jail to Byculla Jail. Being in detention he was allowed to have home food in the jail. Some part of that food somehow secretly reached Tilak's cell.

II

But these pieces of sugarcandy and silent gifts by Natu, which were rare occurrences, could not check the deterioration in Tilak's health. His declining health was causing deep anxiety to his friends and admirers. S. S. Setlur, an advocate of Bangalore, who had taken an active interest in the work of the Tilak Defence Committee, wrote a letter in November 1897 to William Tallack, the Secretary of the Howard Association in London, about the jail life of Tilak. The main objective of this institution was to endeavour to reform prison life all over the world. The Secretary of the Association interviewed George Hamilton, the then Secretary of State for India, and invited his attention to the condition of Tilak's health. Hamilton replied to him that Tilak was given treatment in conformity with the rules of the jail. He, however, instructed the Bombay Governor to arrange for Tilak's medical examination. The result was good. One day the jail medical authorities stood before Tilak asking him whether the jail food had done him any harm. Tilak replied calmly that his sinking weight was itself a reply to their query.

The Secretary of the Howard Association wrote to Setlur a sympathetic letter in which he said: "If any serious thing happens to Tilak you may let me know of it in detail. But I hope he will survive his detention. In my letter I reminded Lord George Hamilton that if Tilak should die in jail, it would attract widespread criticism, both in this country and in India, of the Indian prison-regime, and that this of course would be very undesirable from the point of view specially of Government."

The criticism of Strachey's judgment fully brought out the inadequacy of Government measures to condemn and crush a fearless patriot like Tilak. Even so imperialistic-minded a British Judge as Strachey had to strain the law to suit its purpose. So it was now proposed to amend Section 124A of the Indian Penal Code.

Tilak's incarceration had repercussions also on the Congress session which was held at Amraoti in December 1897. Seized with suspicion and hatred consequent on the Poona murders, the bureaucracy tried to smother it by putting every possible difficulty in the way of holding the Congress session. The hosts of the Congress moved cautiously lest they should incur the displeasure of the bureaucracy on an issue connected with Tilak. There was also a hot discussion on the suggestion whether or not a picture of Tilak should be hung in the Congress pandal. There was also a suggestion that a resolution should be passed at the session expressing disapprobation of the Government attitude towards Tilak. Both the suggestions were ultimately abandoned. To sympathise with Tilak, who had been convicted of sedition and to do either of those things was tantamount, in the opinion of the Congress bosses, to upholding sedition, and nobody was prepared to risk the tranquillity of the session on that issue. Another question that disturbed the Congress leaders was whether G. K. Gokhale should address the Congress or not. It was decided that Gokhale should, as far as possible, be kept out. Gokhale on his own part was not in a mood to take any active part in the Congress proceedings.

C. Shankaran Nair, an honoured and illustrious leader of the Congress movement, presided over the Congress. In the course of his address Nair said that to deny Indians the freedom of the press and to deny them representative institutions, England would have to ignore those very principles for which the noble names in her history had toiled and bled. It was impossible, he proceeded, to keep out of India eloquent orations on patriotism by men like Mr. Chamberlain—a Cabinet Minister holding up to admiration the memory of patriots like Wallace whose head was stuck up on the traitor's gate of the city of London, of Bruce guilty of foul murder in a church, of Emmet and other Irish leaders executed or hanged for treason by the British Government.

He referred to the plague operations in Poona and told his audience how, after the murder of Rand, the Anglo-Indian press drove the Anglo-Indian community into unreasoning panic, and the result was that Lord Sandhurst tried to take measures which, it was believed, he would never have sanctioned if he had remained a free agent.

Then protesting against the arrest of Natu brothers, the President referred to the condition under which Tilak was convicted after the farce of a trial. He expressed his opinion that the offence of sedition should be tried by a native jury. He further observed that in England a man convicted of sedition was not treated as an ordinary criminal, sedition being regarded as a political offence, but in India apparently one was subject to the ordinary hardships of prison life. This was obviously an indirect reminder to Government to give proper treatment to Tilak in jail.

On the third day of the session Surendranath Banerjee moved a resolution urging Government either to try or release the Natu brothers whom Government had kept in detention for five months. Speaking on the resolution, he observed with great force of heart: " We regard the quartering of the Punitive Police at Poona as a mistake. We regard the imprisonment of Tilak and of the Poona editors as a still greater mistake. For Tilak my heart is full of sympathy. My feelings go forth to him in his prison house. A nation is in tears. . . ." At these words the whole congregation stood up, and the pandal resounded with thundering applause for Tilak. But no separate resolution was passed expressing sympathy for Tilak and disapproving of the policy of Government. The Congress by another resolution protested against the proposed changes in the law of sedition as dealing an irreparable blow to the liberty of speech and the freedom of the Press.

The Imperial Legislature, however, legalised Strachey's arbitrary and wrong interpretation of Section 124A of the Penal Code by amending on February 18, 1898, the notorious section in the face of public opposition.

Gokhale, who much reluctantly attended the session, did not make any speech, nor was he asked by anybody to do so. There was no question of honouring him for his great services rendered through his evidence before the Welby Commission. With the pangs of an internal conflict in his mind, he sat there unconcerned, uncared for. Had the Moderates liked his apology they would not have treated him as an untouchable.

III

THE ANXIETY EXPRESSED by the outside world over Tilak's health indirectly impelled Government to take care of his health. The jail officers now gave him a little milk and ghee. Just then plague paid its yearly visit to Bombay. Tilak had no faith in the efficacy of inoculation. But in conformity with jail rules he offered himself for inoculation although it was not yet supposed to be a remedy of provin efficacy. Seeing that Tilak offered himself for inoculation, all other prisoners without any trouble submitted themselves to it. The inoculation hit Tilak hard, and in two days' time high fever reduced his weight considerably. The danger from plague in Bombay and the growing anxiety and agitation outside about Tilak's health, led Government to free themselves from the responsibility that devolved upon them for Tilak's life. Government, therefore, decided to remove him to Yeravda Jail at Poona. The decision was kept a secret, but somehow the news leaked out, and at Kalyan Station a vast crowd awaited the arrival of the train to have a glimpse of their great leader.

The facilities he had been given in Bombay were continued in Yeravda Jail also. Here the work was less arduous, he being assigned the work of painting walls and furniture. Tilak went to the root of the theory of the mixing of paint and became well-versed in it. While Tilak was thus preparing paints and caning chairs, one day the Governor's Councillor Mr. Nugent paid a visit to the jail and saw Tilak in the cell. Whether the Councillor had a good or a bad motive in paying the visit is not known. Tilak, who could at will look at the world with a detached view, must have been oblivious to the arrogant presence of the bureaucrat!

By now the agitation for the release of Tilak had struck root. The clouds of suspicion were dispersing. On his arrest Damodar Chapekar was inveigled into confiding all the details regarding the Rand murder. His case was committed to Sessions, and he was sentenced to death on February 3, 1898. When the judge passed the capital sentence upon him, Chapekar roared: " You may hang me tomorrow, but my soul will at once pass into another body, and in sixteen years it will be fighting against the English again!"[1] Chapekar thereafter expressed his wish that his application to the High Court should be drafted by Tilak. The request was granted, and Tilak drafted his application sitting by the side of Chapekar for nearly three hours in the presence of the jail and C.I.D. Officers who were all ears and all eyes to discover any clue to the remotest connection between the two.

In the High Court, Branson, the famous lawyer, tried to save Chapekar's neck from the gallows, but his sentence was confirmed by Mr. Justice Parson and Mr. Justice Ranade. Chapekar again expressed his desire to see Tilak in the jail. He was granted that privilege. He expressed his intense desire for two things. The first was the request for a copy of the *Bhagvad Gita* which Tilak had with him. He said he would die with the *Gita* in his hand. The second was a request for the disposal of his dead body in accordance with Hindu rites, and that it should not be defiled by the touch of non-Hindus.

At this juncture some of Tilak's friends and admirers contacted Prof. Max Muller and moved him to take an active interest in the release of Tilak whom he knew to be a man of great learning. The learned man was moved by the thought of the privations Tilak was undergoing in jail. He had already had some correspondence with Tilak after the publication of Tilak's thesis *The Orion*, and he had sent a copy of the translation of the *Rigveda* to Tilak in jail with a Bengali gentleman. Max Muller expressed deep anxiety for Tilak's life, and obtaining the signatures of Sir William Hunter, Sir Richard Garth, William Caine, Dadabhai Naoroji, Romesh Chandra Dutt and some Members of the British Parliament, he sent a petition to the British Government entreating them to release Tilak on the grounds that by nature he was a scholar; being unused to hard labour he was completely shattered in health and that as the ends of justice had been served by his imprisonment he should be now released. Tilak wrote a very courteous letter to Max Muller, expressing his gratitude to the great scholar for the interest he was taking in his release and for the copy of the *Rigveda* he had received from him.

1 Nevinson, Henry W., *The New Spirit in India*, pp. 49-50.

Sir C. H. Setalwad writes in his Recollections and Reflections that he also had called on Lord Sandhurst, the Governor, and tried to persuade him to commute Tilak's sentence and create good feeling in the minds of the public who undoubtedly, he added, held Tilak in great esteem.

The rare gift for Tilak from a world-famous man of learning, Max Muller, created sympathy in the heart of Solomon, the Jail Superintendent. He allowed the distinguished prisoner some facilities in the jail, such as light for reading and writing, pencil, and some such small concessions. There were rumours that Tilak was to be released in a day or two, but nothing came of it. Tilak, the born scholar, was absorbed in studying the translation of the *Rigveda*, and his vision extended itself to the far ends of the universe! Once while reading the *Rigveda* a second time, he came upon a certain stanza, and he paused and sat far into the night revolving his thoughts over it! It dawned upon his mind that the home of the *Vedas* was the Arctic region! Like Archimedes, who, when the idea of the principle of specific gravity struck him, ran from the bath-tub into the street without clothes, dancing with joy and crying out, "Oh it is found!", Tilak was entranced with joy, and he could not sleep that night for joy when he knew the real meaning of the verse: "Many days passed before the Sun rose." Thus he utilised the enforced leisure to enlighten the misty paths to the antiquity of the Aryans! It is only such men as live beyond the plane of worldly joy or sorrow that can cherish such great thoughts even amidst misery!

Damodarpant Chapekar heroically mounted the gallows on April 18, 1898, amidst a serene atmosphere, holding in his right hand the copy of the *Gita* he had borrowed from Tilak, and singing and chanting hymns in Yeravda Jail which was guarded by armed police on that day. The little book which he held in his hand was lying in the grip of his fingers! Tilak fulfilled Chapekar's last wish by arranging to dispose of his dead body in accordance with Hindu rites. One Bhausaheb Gokhale, who resided near the temple of Umbrya Ganapati, a locality of Poona, fulfilled Tilak's desire and did all the funeral obsequies of Chapekar. Describing the impressions and emotions of that generation, no less a personality than Lala Lajpat Rai observed that the younger generation admired Chapekar although they did not know whether they approved of the deed or not, and it was an admiration of the motive behind the deed, not of the deed itself.[2]

---

2 *Reminiscences And Anecdotes about Lokamanya Tilak*, Vol. II, p. 659.

After the retirement of Solomon, another Jail Superintendent Colonel Jackson came. He did not disturb the jail life of Tilak, but his insolence and menacing attitude sometimes blustered forth. Tilak was allowed to wear his shoes in prison, and so he asked for a new pair. When it came to the jail office, Jackson did not like its crimson-red colour. He got it painted black and sent it over to Tilak. He must have been amused to see that Government officers were so attentive even to his shoes!

In spite of this drastic and stringent discipline, the jail authorities felt sometimes flabbergasted! If Tilak happened to go to a place where prisoners were working in the presence of the jail authorities, the prisoners, to the utter surprise and anger of the authorities, spontaneously got up as a mark of respect to their popular leader. Those poor souls hailed him as a great man, and it was their duty, they thought, to pay him due respect. The jail authorities on their part sometimes utilised Tilak's moral force to tame the uncontrollable prisoners, and his name or words had a magic effect upon them. It was at this time that Tilak had to pass some anxious days about the publication of his papers as the press in which his papers were printed was destroyed by fire. But he was relieved of the anxiety when the guardian of the other partner of the Aryabhushan Press accepted the work on a note from Tilak.

At last Government now began to think seriously about Tilak's release. Brewin, who had been in touch with Tilak for some months, now discussed with Tilak the terms of release. Government put forward two conditions for his release. The first was that he was not to participate in any functions which would be held after his release, and the second demanded that he should not take part in politics! A selfless patriot, Tilak was willing to accept the first, but was not prepared to yield to the second. The Governor's Council passed a resolution imposing on him the foregoing conditions. D. A. Khare was specially brought to Poona to negotiate with Tilak the terms of his release in Yeravda Jail. Khare and Brewin discussed the proposed conditions with Tilak in the jail. Tilak would not accept the second condition. A day was spent in wording the conditions of release. Spent, fagged out, Khare was about to leave Poona when Government also modified their resolution to suit the new conditions of release. The conditions were as follows:

"That Tilak will not countenance or take part directly or indirectly in any demonstration in regard to his release or in regard to his conviction or sentence.

"That he will do nothing by act, speech or writing to excite disaffection towards the Government."

Tilak gave an undertaking that he accepted the conditions, and added that if, as laid down in the second condition, a Court of Law announced that by act, speech or writing he excited disaffection towards the Government, the Governor of Bombay in Council, might cancel the remission of his punishment, and he might be remanded to jail to undergo the unexpired portion of his original sentence.

Thus there was no apology, no repentance, no exit from politics. That was the bold characteristic of Tilak who marched ahead regardless of consequences.

At last on the night of 6th September 1898, as a special case, the gate of Yeravda Jail creaked, and Tilak, the prisoner No. 1445 with 55 books and the balance of Rs. 9-4-3 from his deposits, was released after fifty-one weeks of hard labour. His friend Khare brought him to his residence at Vinchurkar Wada. Tilak, however, did not come home straight. On his way home he visited a temple, and although not much of a devotee, he said his prayers to God Ganapati, paid his respects to Annasaheb Patwardhan, an old and venerable man, and then made his way to his house. Tilak was very weak, weighed about 113 Ibs. with his cheeks pale and hollow, his eyes sunken, and his lips dry and black, and his chest measured 31 1/4 inches and height five feet two inches and a half.

At night the whole city of Poona was agog, and the news spread with the rapidity of lightning throughout India. Crowds of people poured in, and Tilak's house was turned into a place of pilgrimage. Next day bells rang in temples which beamed, as it were, with the joy of the people. People celebrated the event with prayers of thanksgiving, illuminations and distribution of sweetmeats. Tilak's picture was exhibited at all meetings and also taken out in processions. And suddenly from behind the dark clouds the sun came forth and shone brightly on Poona. Congratulatory telegrams and letters rained upon Tilak. Newsmen flocked at Tilak's residence to obtain details of his prison-life, his future programme, and the conditions of release, but they were disappointed. Yet they made up news out of guesswork and gossip and issued special supplements. Shortly after Gokhale also paid a courtesy call on Tilak.

Congratulations came also from England. Sir Romesh Chandra Dutt wrote from London, "I cannot describe in words what feelings rise in my heart when I remember the hardships you have borne. The courage and the power of suffering you have so far shown are worthy of admiration. Those nations alone rise whose people possess such qualities and bear such sufferings. I do not doubt that the effect of your example will be permanent. Your hardships will lead the nation to victory."

Mr. William Caine expressed his mind in the following touching words: "You are coming out from your ordeal of jail-life with a fuller and brighter lustre. The future historians of India will record your achievements in the proper place, and posterity will ever be justly grateful for the enormous hardships you bore for the nation's political liberty."

Thus the murder of Rand turned out to be a landmark in the history of India. Two things arose from it. The emergence of Tilak as a hero of Maharashtra and a rising leader of Modern India. Tilak glowed like fire, and he now outshone Ranade. The second thing was that it marked, to quote Lala Lajpat Rai, the beginning of a revolutionary movement in India. Referring to this fact, the Sedition Committee later observed: "It is among the Brahmins of the Poona District that we first find indications of a revolutionary movement."

IV

It was suggested by his doctor friends and well-wishers that Tilak should take rest at Sinhagad and recoup his health. Sinhagad is the name of a mountain fortress which has attained a great name in Mahratta history. Tilak had purchased a plot there and in 1890 built a small villa. There, with his friend Daji Abaji Khare, he used to stay in summer and sometimes even in winter!

Accordingly Tilak had rest at Sinhgad. He always advised his colleagues to have rest once a year at such secluded places. Always busy like a bee, Tilak had no rest at his residence in Poona. Amidst the historic environment and beautiful scenery around the fort, he now felt better, his health showed quick improvement, and his soul, which sometimes loved seclusion amidst the ruins of Sinhagad felt reinvigorated. October and November 1898 were thus spent in leisure. But to men of action leisure is not inaction. Change of work is rest for great men. Tilak wrote some chapters of his new book The *Arctic Home in the Vedas* which he had outlined in jail. Tilak, with his long, flowing white coat, red turban, crimson-red shoes and the usual staff in hand, became ready for resumption of public activities although his doctors opined that the recovery of his health was satisfactory, but not complete, and that for some time he should avoid work and public engagements involving great strain.

There were pressing invitations from Madras requesting Tilak to attend the Congress session in December 1898. The news of his proposed visit enlivened the hearts of the younger leaders in Madras and in Bengal. Tilak and his colleagues travelled to Madras by the same train by which Ranade and Gokhale did. On the way huge crowds gave an ovation to Tilak at every station while men of note and position turned to the compartment of Ranade and Gokhale. One graduate at a station in the Madras Province expressed his superstitious mind by exclaiming that as Tilak's feet had touched the Madras Province plague would disappear in no time. Tilak was sorry that educated men should hug to such beliefs. He was reminded of the story about the Peshwa Bajirao I. A batch of men from Karnatak acclaimed him a divine personality and entreated him to recruit them for his infantry. He declined their request saying that those who meekly called him God were unsuitable for such jobs!

During the Congress session Tilak stayed in the historic building called Carnan Castle which stood on the beach. The building was owned by a leading solicitor Bilgiri lyengar, but it was the former residence of Lord Clive, and Swami Vivekananda had also resided there during his stay in Madras. Tilak's friend Gangaprasad, editor of the *Advocate of India*, Lucknow, too, stayed there with Tilak.

Tilak did not take much interest in the proceedings of the Congress. As was his practice, he took interest in the proceedings of the Subjects Committee where he had a tussle with Surendranath Banerjee on the use of the word 'gratitude' used in the resolution expressing grief over the death of Gladstone. Tilak insisted upon the use of the expression 'satisfaction' and said with a smile that the word 'gratitude' did not sound well to his Mahratta ears! He added that Gladstone did nothing for India beyond uttering sweet words. The resolution passed by the Congress, however, expressed its sense of gratitude for the sympathy which Gladstone uniformly evinced towards the efforts of the Indian people in securing a more liberal and progressive Government in India.

In the open session Tilak did not make any speech. His critics interpreted his silence in many ways. A few critics described him as a skeleton at the feast. Some said that because he had given an undignified undertaking he did not open his lips, while others felt that he did so because he feared that Government would again trap him if he made any violent speech. Pherozeshah Mehta could not attend the Madras Congress for various reasons, and it was rumoured that he did not attend as the sedition-monger Tilak was to attend it. Sankaran Nair had urged on Pherozeshah Mehta to attend the Congress lest it should drift into the hands of the noted extremists, and disloyalty get the upper hand over it! Nair added that if the Congress did not listen to men like Pherozeshah Mehta they would leave the Congress.[3]

In fact some leaders were nervous about mixing with Tilak for they feared that they would be bracketed with Tilak! In those days patriots convicted of sedition were shunned even by public men. The Congress protested against the law of sedition which had been passed in the Imperial Legislative Council against the stubborn opposition of the non-official Members and an unprecedented agitation in the country. The leaders, however, hoped that the new Viceroy, Lord Curzon, who had just arrived in Bombay and whom they had accorded a respectful welcome, would govern India according to the best traditions of British rule, and would repeal the iniquitous legislation of his predecessor. Lord Curzon sent a telegram to the Congress President expressing thanks for their cordial message of welcome.

At Madras, Tilak was given by Maharashtrian residents a grand reception at the house of Sir T. Madhavrao where Tilak and his party were given a feast. Tilak was glad that the Mahratta soul was conscious in the hearts of Southern Brahmins. In return, Tilak gave a feast in the Carnan Castle to all prominent pleaders, leaders and editors who had assembled for the Congress session. That time also caste-wise meals were served, for the Smarths and Vaishnavas of Madras did not take food in one file! The son of Sir T. Madhavrao presented Tilak with the watch chain of his father as a memento of Tilak's visit to his house.

Tilak had planned a tour of Southern India and Ceylon with a view to visiting important places of pilgrimage and living a life of comparative isolation for some time. On his way he gave an interview to a representative of the *South Indian Post* clarifying his position. He said nobody had gagged him; he did not speak because if once he made a speech he would be required to make speeches at other places also, and his indifferent health would not be able to stand that strain. But he added, "I would continue to do hereafter what I have been doing before this."

3 Mody, H. P., *Sir Pherozeshah Mehta*, p. 439.

Tilak had deep veneration for the sacred shrines and places of pilgrimage of the Hindus. Before reaching Madura, he stayed a day or two at Kumbhakonam, Tanjore and Trichinopoly to see the magnificent temples, sacred places, holy Maths and historic monuments of India's ancient learning and culture. He paid a visit to Pondicherry to study the conditions under which Indians lived in that French colony. He noted that Indians enjoyed the privilege of sending representatives to the republican Senate in Paris. He then spent some time at Madura and saw the grand glorious temple of Minakshi. From Madura he proceeded to Rameshwaram in a bullock cart, a journey of ninety miles. He must have been happy to have darshan of one of the four sacred abodes of God and must have gone devoutly through all the rounds of religious ceremonies. Speaking of this tour later at the spring lectures in Poona, Tilak observed seriously: "One cannot have an idea of the ancient grandeur and glory of Hinduism and the temples of the deities without visiting these institutions. Who can say that they are not powerful influences that give substance to the tree of Hinduism and foster the spirit of unity among the Hindus?"

Returning to Madura again, Tilak and his colleague Wasukaka Joshi went to Tuticorin by train, and, embarking a steamer, went to Ceylon—the Lanka. At Kandy they cooked their own food at a Dharmashala and liked the bread-fruit. The different varieties of coconuts, the green gardens of tea and coffee on the slopes of the surrounding hills impressed them much.

In those days the members of a Ceylonese family would follow a religion of their choice—either Buddhism or Christianity. The dress was an indication of their religion, a Christian member of the family using trousers, a Buddhist lungi, and a Hindu dhoti! He realised that one of the important problems which the social reformers in Ceylon had to tackle was how to revive the spirit of self-respect among the masses and how to revive Buddhism for which they had lost their love owing to their close association with or the domineering influences of Christian missionaries for a period of 300 years. He said that Ceylon was a fertile country, rich in mineral wealth, but because the Ceylonese were by nature an easy going, indolent people and were satisfied with little, their wealth was being drained out of their land. During his stay in Ceylon Tilak called on George

CHAPTER X

Resurgam

I

On his return from Ceylon, Tilak found that Poona was again in the vortex of danger. Damodar Chapekar's younger brother, Balkrishna Chapekar, who had absconded, was passing days in hiding in the forest of the Hyderabad State. There he was perishing for want of food and was reduced to a skeleton. Tilak had made provision for his food and medicine through Keshavrao Koratkar,[1] afterwards the Chief Justice of Hyderabad State. At last Balkrishna had now surrendered himself to the Police authorities at Hyderabad. He was arrested and brought to Poona in January 1899. A second 'Rand Murder Trial' opened, and he was committed to Sessions. A few days earlier the youngest Chapekar, Wasudeo, too, had been arrested and released. Harry Brewin, the police officer, had in his subtle, coaxing and coercive manner, persuaded him to be witness at the Sessions Court against his brother Balkrishna. Vinayak Apte, their colleague, passed several years in hiding, but the police could not trace him out. Outwardly, Wasudeo accepted Brewin's advice, but since December 1898 he had been planning the murders of all those who were responsible for his eldest brother's conviction and execution. Curiously enough, just at this time Ganesh Dravid, who had been released from jail by Government for his treachery to his friends the Chapekars, wrote a letter to the *Times of India*, complaining that it was unjust and cruel that he was not awarded the full amount of twenty thousand rupees for helping the police to find out the murderer of Rand. Only half the amount, he said, was awarded and that too was divided between his brother and himself.

1 Bapat, S. V., *Tarun Bharat*, 28 July 1957.

On February 9, 1899, Wasudeo was to be produced in the Sessions Court as a witness against his brother. So he decided to finish before that date Ramji Pandoo, the chief police constable and the Dravid brothers. In a subject country struggling for the overthrow of foreign yoke informants or traitors rarely go unpunished. In utter desperation Wasudeo was seething with vengeance. For a week he and his friend Ranade shadowed Ramji Pandoo and one night tried to shoot him, but there was a misfire. At last they decided to 'award' the Dravids the balance of their prize which they so meritoriously deserved! On the night of February 8, Wasudeo, his friend Mahadeo Vinayak Ranade, who was a college student, and Khanderao Sathe, who was reading in standard VII of the New Poona High School, dressed up as Pathans and left Wasudeo's residence with loaded revolvers.

Sathe waited brandishing a lathi at the mouth of the lane to blocade it. Wasudeo and Ranade went up to the Dravids, and pretending to be sepoys under Brewin, told them that they were wanted immediately by Brewin. The Dravid brothers came down. Quick as lightning Wasudeo and Ranade shot them in the street and ran away. The Dravid brothers died within a few hours. Next day Wasudeo and Ranade were taken to the police station where Wasudeo, who had carried a loaded pistol concealed under his shirt, fired a shot at the chief police constable; but the bullet again missed. Thereupon Wasudeo tried to shoot Brewin, but he was overpowered. This must be a rare incident wherein a police officer was shot at during a police inquiry at the police station itself!

Wasudeo and Ranade openly confessed that they had shot the Dravid brothers for their treacherous act. Wasudeo said that it was necessary for him to do so, so that he might be saved the shame of giving evidence against his brother, and added that had they failed to do so, either of them would have shot down the Dravid brothers in the open Court. Two days after the police went to the New Poona High School and arrested Sathe in his class.

The Dravid murder trial opened, and Wasudeo, Ranade and Sathe were tried amidst an atmosphere of great excitement. Muhammad Ali Jinnah defended Ranade, and D. D. Davar defended Sathe in the Sessions on March 4, 1899. The first two accused were sentenced to death, and Sathe was sentenced to ten years' rigorous imprisonment. Two days later Balkrishna Chapekar was tried for the murder of Rand, and Wasudeo and Ranade were tried as the co-accused. All three were sentenced to death.

Wasudeo, with a sarcastic look, asked the Judge which of their sentences they were to undergo first and whether they would be hanged twice!

In the second week of May 1899, two young Chapekars were hanged in Yeravda Jail as also their great friend Ranade who kept them company till death. The last scene was quite moving, and it heightened the tragedy. When Wasudeo was being taken to the gallows on May 8, he cried out in front of the cell of Balkrishna: “Bapu, I am going, farewell! “Out came the reply: “Farewell!” When Ranade’s turn came he cried out before the cell of Balkrishna, “Bal, I am going, farewell!” “Farewell, my friend! I, too, am following you,” echoed the voice in the cell. And Balkrishna followed his brothers and friend a day after. In this way all the Chapekar brothers died heroically on the gallows avenging the wrong deeds of the British administration. The Sedition Committee described the Chapekars as ultra orthodox and perhaps therefore anti-Muhammadan and anti-British, having no definite political aims but daring in the achievement. The wives of all these Chapekars pulled on their existence for years uncared for. The old father of the Chapekars died broken-hearted in 1899; their mother having breathed her last before the trial of her eldest son commenced.

The Anglo-Indian Papers and bureaucracy were fuming at their helplessness in implicating Tilak in these dreadful crimes. The situation again became dangerous. A note in the *Kesari* on Ganesh Dravid’s letter to the *Times of India* aroused suspicion in the minds of the Anglo-Indians. The *Mahratta* added fuel to the fire of their anger. It described Wasudeo and his comrades as brave and generous youths and praised their extraordinary courage and bravery saying that it was for an unselfish but sentimental end that they manfully bore the consequences. *The Times of India* characterised the remark of the *Mahratta* as a substitute of a garland for ropes and said it was not a little less than scandalous.

On top of this all, the biting and pungent articles in the *Kal*, a paper started in the last week of March 1898, by Prof. Shivaram M. Paranjpe, proved to be a red rag to the Moderates as well as the bureaucracy. The Bombay leaders expected Tilak to hold the reins of the *Kal*, but Tilak would not interfere. Master of satire, Paranjpe was channelling his own path. A magic pen and a marvellous oratory were his weapons. Tilak neither discouraged nor encouraged Paranjpe. During Tilak’s imprisonment Pherozeshah Mehta had called Kelkar, editor of the *Kesari* and *Mahratta*, to Bombay, and threatened him that if the Poona leaders did not bridle the *Kal* he would run his pencil through the name of Poona wherever it might occur. Kelkar politely but firmly told the Bombay lion that Paranjpe had his own opinions and he had a right to express them; but because the *Kesari* did not openly condemn the *Kal* for its views, it was absolutely wrong to presume that they approved of its line of thinking. In practical life such a presumption would lead to chaos, he added.

Tilak had, up till now, neither settled down to his work as editor nor resumed his other activities. He wrote a series of articles in the *Kesari* on the Khoti land system prevailing in Konkan. His well-wishers suggested to him that he should not make the declaration of his papers in his name, for they had apprehensions that on any flimsy pretext Government would endanger his liberty. He calmly said that it was a responsible and exacting job and one should do it oneself. He, therefore, declared, amidst that threatening atmosphere, to have resumed the editorship from July 4, 1899, and wrote the first editorial under the caption 'Resurgam'. He devoutly expressed his debt of gratitude to God for his return to his post. He expressed his grateful thanks to the editors of the *Amrita Bazar Patrika*, the *Hindu* and the *Champion* for their sympathy and support and made a particular mention of the help rendered to him by Max Muller. He wrote in high terms of his assistant editors and expressed his deep gratitude to all those who had rendered him help during his trial.

He, however, deprecated the attempts of some wicked politicians in the opposite camp, viz. Moderates, and added that it was sheer malice to instigate the Government to prove the articles in the *Kesari* to be seditious and enjoy the discomfiture of one's opponent.

Tilak then took a review of the political situation that had developed during the previous twenty-two months, and averred that the disunity between the Moderates and the Extremists had emboldened the bureaucracy to launch on a policy of widespread repression in the Presidency. In an appeal to the Moderates he observed that if they wanted to revive their movement they would have to close up their ranks. It was futile to consider oneself a peacock and regard others as crows when the eagle of bureaucracy was soaring in the sky to pounce upon both. To those who boasted of their moderation because they were not prosecuted in 1897 he said that it was not necessary for him to remind them why and how they had escaped unscathed. Both the parties were demanding rights from Government and educating the people to make such demands. Neither of them was thinking of breaking or transgressing the laws of the land while putting forth those demands. And since Government had restricted their liberty of speech, it would be useless, he concluded, to emphasize their political differences and to call themselves Moderates or Extremists.

It was unbecoming on the part of the Moderate leaders in Poona to instigate the Government against the Tilakites and to drop suggestions to Government officials that the possibility of overthrowing British rule was not an uncommon subject among the Tilak faction in Poona.[2] These Moderate leaders also told the Government officials like Portious,[3] the Commissioner for the Central Division, that the agitation of the Tilakites was directed in reality not against the Muslims but against the Government and that their pretended earnestness on behalf of Hindu religion was only a blind.

Tilak now began to look after his affairs and concentrate his efforts on certain activities. He closed down his Law class which Kelkar had restarted during his incarceration. Intermittent visits of plague and Tilak's visits to different places on public duty disturbed the class. So he had to close it down, although it was not unprofitable.

II

TILAK AGAIN CAME into conflict with the Government over the methods used by it in stamping out the plague. The inoculation which was still an unproved remedy was being rigidly imposed upon the people who were allergic to any such new moves. On July 16, 1899, as resolved at a public meeting held in Poona a week before, a deputation of local leaders was led by Tilak to the plague officers. The plague officers were now more accommodating, listened very politely to the complaints, and discussed the issues patiently. Tilak pleaded that only those who were willing should be inoculated. Arguments for and against the idea of inoculation were hotly discussed in the newspapers. Dr. Bhalchandra Bhatavadekar had a long correspondence with Tilak over the efficacy of inoculation. K. A. Guruji, who had attacked Government by writing in the *Kesari* a series of articles on the subject, was later on brought into trouble at Banaras where he had started a Marathi weekly called *Kalidas*.

In August 1899 Tilak wrote a very fighting article on the detention of the Natu brothers, who were kept still in detention by Government without giving any reasons. Their detention, however, had been transformed into

2 *Source Material of a History of the Freedom Movement in India*, Government of Bombay, Vol. II, p. 204.

3 Karmarkar, D. P., *Bal Gangadhar Tilak, A Study*, p. 81.

internment at Belgaum since May 1899. Pherozeshah Mehta had bombarded the bureaucrats in the Legislative Council for the unjust treatment meted out to the Natu brothers. Government had no satisfactory replies to give, and they gave answers that were evasive, insulting and peremptory.

About this time the *Times of India*, following doggedly the imperialistic policy of ' divide and rule', published a letter from a certain ' historicus' who upbraided the Brahmins of the day with inconsistency and hypocrisy for honouring the memory of Shivaji, because in his opinion their ancestors had set aside Shivaji's successors and ruled in their name and finally lost the state established by Shivaji through their incompetence and vices. Tilak replied that the fact was that the Peshwas had respectfully set aside the weak and incapable kings in the interests of the nation and extended Shivaji's State. He, however, added that a powerful Mahratta general should have set aside the incapable and unworthy Bajirao II and captured the whole power in the interest of the country.

The suspicion that Tilak was indirectly the motive power behind the Poona murders was still haunting some of the British papers as also some Anglo-Indian newspapers. One of these, the *Globe* of London, while writing under the columns 'Notes of the Day' on the appointment of Sir Stafford Northcote as Governor of Bombay advised him to complete the extermination of the seditious conspiracies there and observed: "For some years past, parts of the Western Presidency have been permeated by seditious conspiracies of a most dangerous sort, and although the ringleaders have seen fit to remain quiet since that arch-plotter, Tilak, was imprisoned, sedition is merely in temporary abeyance." It further said that Sir Stafford Northcote was going to his important office with much fuller knowledge of the state of affairs than his predecessor possessed until his mind was informed by the campaign of murder which Tilak directed, if he was not its organiser. The *Times of India* gave wide publicity to the notorious note of the *Globe* in its issue of the 18th November 1899.

Tilak brought immediately in the Presidency Magistrate's Court in Bombay an action on November 23, 1899, against the editor and the proprietor of the *Times of India* and sued them for defamation. Pherozeshah Mehta, though rather displeased with Tilak for his not condemning the bridleless *Kal*, accepted Tilak's brief. Chimanlal Setalwad also was engaged to assist Pherozeshah Mehta. The Magistrate Mr. J. Sanders-Slater tried to sidetrack the issue, and asked Pherozeshah Mehta, Tilak's counsel, whether Tilak was not prosecuted for sedition. But Mehta silenced him by pointing to Strachey's judgment in which he had said that there was nothing to connect Tilak with the murder. Pherozeshah must have had a ferocious look at the Magistrate who could not distinguish between sedition and murder.

Considering now that discretion was the better part of valour, the *Times of India* next day published an apology to Tilak in its editorial columns under the caption "Tilak and the Times of India". Mr. Pherozeshah brought to the notice of the Court that this was not the first time that the *Times of India* had made such an assertion; on a previous occasion when the capture of Balkrishna Chapekar was announced, it had done so, but had disclaimed it next day. Counsel for the *Times of India* stated that they had received some cuttings from the London press and as they expected nothing objectionable in them they were inserted as received, without unfortunately undergoing any revision, and so, now they regretted the insertion of the statements "which we regard as unwarranted, and as doing a serious injustice to Mr. Tilak."

But Tilak was bent upon chastising the *Times of India*, for making an example to others who were carrying on a regular campaign of calumniating him, and to end the controversy once for all. The hearing of the case came up before the Magistrate on December 8, 1899. Macpherson, Bar-at-Law, counsel for the defendants, Bennett, editor and proprietor, and Coleman, Managing Proprietor of the *Times of India*, respectfully reiterated the apology and observed that Bennett during the last five minutes had told him that he did not believe in the statements made in the *Globe* and that he would not have for one moment permitted them to appear in his columns. It had never occurred to his client that there would be anything objectionable to Tilak. Counsel further said that Mr. Bennett was a journalist of thirty years' standing, and that was the first occasion he had been caught tripping in anything that had passed under his eyes. His client absolutely dissociated himself from the injurious imputations and expressions which, very much to his surprise, were contained in the *Globe*. Mehta replied that as Tilak was the victim of insinuations of such character his client thought it was due to himself and the cause he was espousing that he should embrace the first opportunity to subject himself to any hostile cross-examination on those matters. Here was an opportunity for him to do so. Mehta, however, accepted on behalf of Tilak the expression of regret which Bennett and Coleman through their

Counsel had offered, and requested the Court to allow him to withdraw the case.

Tilak then turned his attention to the main offender at London. The *Globe* was served with a notice which it had scornfully thrown into the wastepaper basket. Tilak therefore engaged a London solicitor and lodged a suit against the *Globe* for defamation. Money was advanced from the Tilak Defence Fund, and it was agreed that if the case was decided in his favour, Tilak should pay back the money to the Fund. Later in March 1900, Tilak's solicitor advised him to engage an eminent lawyer and gave Tilak an idea of the enormous cost he would have to bear. The suit was filed in June 1900, Tilak being required to deposit £100 as security. The *Globe* sought here, there and everywhere for information to support its defamatory statements, but could not get a scrap of paper. So it finally surrendered, and although Tilak was authorised to dictate the apology, he left it to his solicitor, and the apology was published in the *Globe* at a prominent place in its issue of the 24th November 1900.

The news that Tilak had brought a British publisher to his knees was welcomed in Indian circles with great relief. Mr. Justice Ranade expressed his appreciation of Tilak's unswerving determination in bringing any work he undertook to an end, overcoming difficulties and dangers. Ranade had high regard for Tilak's courage and ability and so he pulled up an obdurate Moderate at the annual meeting of the Marathi Grantha Sangrahalaya, Bombay. The institution had mentioned in its report the visit of Tilak which he had paid to it after his release from jail. Every party has its black sheep. This Moderate black sheep asked Ranade whether it was proper to take note of the visit of a man who was convicted of sedition. Ranade silenced him by stating that it was a literary institution, and it did the proper thing in honouring Tilak as a great litterateur.

At this juncture Tilak wanted to contest the election to the Legislative Council. He, however, gave up the idea when he found that a number of his supporters had committed themselves to help Gokhale who had already announced his candidature and sent in his nomination. Had Tilak entered the election arena, Maharashtra would have witnessed a grand spectacle of a fight which would have been remembered for many years to come! Gokhale was, therefore, elected and his return to politics after almost two years of dismal silence was welcomed by the Province.

In the last week of December 1899, Tilak's friends the Natu brothers were released unconditionally. Tilak expressed joy over their release and said that Poona was now free from the eclipse which had begun in June 1897, and using an astrological phrase he added that the evil period of Saturn had at long last come to an end!

III

THIS YEAR THE Congress met at Lucknow. Tilak, Ranade, Gokhale and other leaders travelled by the same train to Lucknow. Tilak was going to North India for the first time after his release. His defiant and dignified conduct in the Court and his sacrifices and sufferings in prison had made him the first political hero of modern India. At Bina Station a vast crowd had assembled to accord him an ovation. Amongst them a European Police Inspector with a batch of police was strolling on the platform. When the train steamed into the station, the European Inspector, to the surprise of the travellers, inquired of the passengers about Tilak, and going to Tilak's compartment, said that he had come to pay his respects. Tilak thanked him for his good wishes and said to his colleagues that Europeans could appreciate good qualities and patriotism and that they were admirers of real patriotism.

At Lucknow R. C. Dutt presided over the Congress and declared that there was no better way of creating sedition than by suppressing free discussions, newspapers and meetings. Stating that the cause of the famine was heavy assessment, he further observed that Indians were virtually foreigners in their own land. Miss Garland, a delegate sent by the British Congress Committee, urged that the military forces in India were unnecessarily large so far as India was concerned. She declared that because India was made a convenient military base for Imperial purposes, England should bear part of the cost.

The Moderates were afraid of publicly associating with Tilak because he had been convicted of sedition. One of the Moderate leaders told Swami Shraddhanand during the session that Tilak was a great intellect, but he was horrified by his terrible ambition! So Tilak was not given a seat on the platform. When he entered the pandal the delegates loudly applauded him, and Tilak took his seat among the Maharashtrian delegates. It was at this time that Swami Shraddhanand made his acquaintance with him and had a talk with him on the *Vedas* which was the subject of their common interest.

At the Subjects Committee Tilak and Gokhale had a passage-at-arms, Tilak chuckling at Gokhale's discomfiture and his irritable temper! The intervention of Surendranath stopped further fighting. But there came up the question of passing a resolution condemning Lord Sandhurst for his mal-administration. R. C. Dutt, Mudholkar and other elderly leaders were disturbed about the idea of colliding with the Government. They said the question related to a provincial administration, and so it should not be dealt with on an all-India plane and platform. Tilak silenced them by citing similar questions of provincial importance dealt with in the past by the Congress. The debate began to raise dust and create uneasiness when Tilak quoted chapter and verse to prove his point. Tilak pressed his point and was almost within reach of victory when the President of the Congress R. C. Dutt threatened to resign if Tilak persisted in his resolve to get that resolution passed by the Congress. When matters came to such a pass Tilak withdrew his proposition for the sake of compromise.

A man of iron will, Tilak had a most supple intellect, and at critical moments he himself showed a wonderful elasticity in toning down the pitch of his stand or demands. There was another occasion when Tilak might have ignited a spark. R. C. Dutt moved a resolution from the chair in the Subjects Committee, urging the appointment of Indians to the Executive Council. The resolution was considered to be too radical and it was withdrawn. The elderly leaders, however, were surprised that even Tilak did not press for it.

After the Lucknow Congress Tilak proceeded to Calcutta to board a steamer which was commissioned by Tilak's friend Chhatre to transport his circus to Rangoon. Tilak had a desire to study the political and social conditions of Burma. But before he left Calcutta for Rangoon he wrote to Kelkar asking him to make arrangements to send regular news from Maharashtra to Motilal Ghosh for the *Amrita Bazar Patrika*, to enable him to compete with the *Bengalee* which was to be turned into a daily about that time. He need not add, he observed, that it was their duty to back up "Motibabu". A friend in need is a friend indeed. It may be noted that the editor of *Bengalee* was Surendranath Banerjee.

There was another issue on which a storm was gathering. It was the Sandhurst Memorial agitation which he was going to oppose. Tilak wrote to his lieutenant Kelkar from Calcutta that from the talk he had with Pherozeshah Mehta he was convinced that Mehta must have given his consent half-heartedly to put up his name as Secretary in connection with the Sandhurst Memorial, although Mehta now denied it. Mehta was not for holding the Provincial Conference in February, because he feared that it might be presumed that the Conference was held for expressing disapprobation of Sandhurst's work. Tilak further wrote to Kelkar that they both knew well the spirit of Mehta and the degree to which he could raise his opposition to Government.

Tilak also observed that Mehta was not a man of independent spirit as he appeared, and the Bombay lion expressed his fearlessness and independent view whenever it was convenient for him to do so or was not harmful to him, He, therefore, asked Kelkar to denounce Mehta in the *Kesari* and *Mahratta* for his vacillating attitude, but asked him to add without fail that Mehta's name might have appeared in that connection without his permission. He himself wrote a series of articles on Lord Sandhurst's regime, which were published in the *Kesari* in his absence from Poona. Therein he observed that the alarm raised by the bureaucracy that there were seditious activities was false. What the people demanded was that the Government should be run in the interests of the people. He expressed a hope that an inefficient administrator like Lord Sandhurst would never be appointed. He, however, added that Sandhurst was a man of rank and birth, and as a private individual he was gentle and hospitable.

From Calcutta the party reached Rangoon about January 29, 1900. While on board the ship Tilak and Wasukaka Joshi cooked their own food in the steamer. Tilak always preferred boiled rice to other edibles. Open air schools conducted by yellow-robed Buddhist monks under trees, the leading part played by Burmese women in their household affairs, their magnanimity and munificence, and the economic hold of the Chetties from the Madras Province upon Burmese life, were in those days the special features of Burma. The Chetties were a rich community, and they had built temples in Burma. It was a pleasant surprise to Tilak that they conducted a Veda Shala where he heard all the four *Vedas* being recited! Tilak's colleague-cum-secretary Joshi saw the Private Minister of Theba, the banished king. There they saw no signs of any revolt or revolution. Tilak spent some time in Mandalay.

Tilak's visit to Rangoon and Mandalay was invigorating and was very significant from the point of view of an editor. In his tour he noted with curiosity that Burma did not observe caste division, there was freedom of religion, women were educated, marriages took place at a late age, and divorce and widow-marriage were allowed. He said that in spite of these social reforms, which the Indian social reformers harped upon in season and out and preached that they constituted a condition precedent for the introduction of political reforms in India, there was a feeling of mutual hatred among the Burmese and absence of self-respect, and the result was disunion that led to the destruction of Theba's kingdom. He therefore drew an inevitable conclusion, which, he said, supported his stand in Indian politics in reference to social reforms: that political or national progress was not dependent on social reforms, and that they might even conflict. It was his confirmed view that the qualities required for national uplift were quite different from and independent of those required for social reforms. They were love of one's country, unity in working out national salvation by sinking petty differences, an urge for acquiring even in foreign countries knowledge required for national industry and development, and zeal for preserving national character.

Thus Tilak added the examples of casteless Ceylon and Burma to the one of Ireland which he had been often citing since 1896 in support of his pet theory that political progress was not dependent on social reforms.

Tilak and Joshi returned to Calcutta about February 12. Tilak wrote to Kelkar from Calcutta that he was not satisfied with the mild attack in the *Kesari* on Mehta, since it did not ruthlessly expose Mehta and those who had been connected with the Sandhurst Memorial. On his way back to Poona Tilak made a speech at Jubbulpore in which he reiterated his views on social reforms, citing the example of Burma in support of his theory that political progress had nothing to do with social reforms!

IV

IN THE LAST week of February 1900, Tilak gave an impetus to the historical celebration which was going to be held in honour of Nana Fadnavis, the great Mahratta statesman, whose intellectual excellence is held in high esteem by history. Tilak sent his nephew with an imposing picture of Nana Fadnavis and his written address which was to be read on the occasion at Velas in Konkan. He had a certain weakness for historical monuments and historic families, and whenever he came into contact with things connected with either, his heart was overjoyed, and his head bowed with reverence. In April the Shivaji celebration was held at Raigad amidst great rejoicings. Tilak's presence at the Fort galvanised the neighbouring villages. Of course, Government officers were present to watch over the programme and proceedings. The enthusiasm of the people was so great that at a neighbouring village Tilak and his party took their dinner at three o'clock at dawn because they could not reach the place in time.

It was at this time that the Bombay Provincial Conference was due to be held at Satara. For the last five years the Conference had not been held.

All leaders knew that the question of the Sandhurst regime and memorial would be a bone of contention. Tilak wanted to frustrate the attempts of Sandhurst's admirers and lackeys at raising a memorial to Lord Sandhurst and therefore opened an attack by writing an editorial in the *Kesari* of the 1st May 1900. He declared that it was high time that they boldly named the evil planets that had influenced the Bombay Province during the last four years. The notion that an evil planet assumed a more destructive power, because it was called an evil planet, was erroneous.

On May 12 both the Parties, supporters and opponents of the Sandhurst Memorial, entered the arena of the Conference at Satara. The local leaders had sensed the danger to the Conference. At the instance of Pherozeshah Mehta, Gokuldas Parekh was chosen to preside over the Conference. He was a reputed lawyer, and he made good what he lacked as a public speaker by his seniority at the Bar and moderation in his views. The question of denouncing the administration of Lord Sandhurst came up before the Subjects Committee. Tilak wanted to move that "this Conference desires to place on record its deep sense of regret that during the last few years, the Government of Bombay should have been pleased to adopt a retrograde policy of repression and distrust, as evidenced by the press prosecutions, arrests and imprisonments of persons without trial, widening the powers of the Police . . . and it earnestly prays for a speedy return to the policy of progress which had characterised the best traditions of British rule in India."

This proposition took away the breath of most of the Moderates and there were heated discussions between different groups. The President, true to his party's characteristic, took great precaution against offending Government, and he held out a threat that he would resign if a resolution of that kind was passed. So the matter was given up for the day. The whole night the issue was being discussed at different camps. The next day a requisition signed by 124 out of 175 delegates was handed over to the President requesting him to move the resolution criticising the Sandhurst administration. There was again consternation, and the President finally reconciled himself to the requisitionists by agreeing to record the view of the majority in the proceedings of the Conference. Tilak was making a vigorous attempt to change the tone and philosophy of the Provincial Conference, which was in fact the annual session of the Provincial Congress. His attempt at Lucknow to electrify the Congress into action and make it echo the feelings and grievances of the people had failed. He wanted the Congress leaders to show a little more courage, but so far the result was not satisfactory although it now became evident that Tilak would drive them to the deed some day. Both sides became now very conscious of this. It was the first sign of an open split!

At this time Mr. Justice Ranade read a paper entitled 'Introduction to the Peshwa's Diaries' before the Bombay Branch of the Royal Asiatic Society. Dealing with the caste ascendancy in the course of that paper, he observed that the first half of the seventeenth century was singularly free from racial and caste jealousies; and the infusion of the racial and caste element among the military leaders of the nation was the most distinguishing mark of the latter half of the century. It was during this latter half of that century that the great commanders who acquired fame and territory were, almost exclusively, Brahmins, while most of the great military commanders in the earlier period were Marathas. During the latter half of the eighteenth century Brahmins regarded themselves as a governing caste with special privileges and exemption from the extreme penalty of law which were unknown under the system founded by Shivaji. Ranade, remarking that these features introduced demoralisation, concluded his observations on the caste ascendancy saying that in the hands of Bajirao II, the State ceased to be the protector of all classes and upholder of equal justice.

Tilak held decided views on the caste system. He had been expressing those views on occasion. He had read a paper before the Industrial Conference in 1892 under the title 'The Hindu caste from an industrial point of view'. Therein he observed that "caste must therefore be regarded as a secular and social organisation amongst the members of the Aryan race, for the preservation of hereditary occupations, and for the purpose of mutual help and co-operation," [4] and opined that the Hindus could utilise the already existing institution of caste to improve the moral and material conditions of the working classes.

Criticizing Ranade's views, Tilak put forth his stock arguments and observed that Ranade's opinion that the fall of the Mahrattas was caused by the infusion of caste jealousies which led to disunion was not historically true. Had Ranade cast a look at the history of the downfall of the Moguls, Tilak observed, he could have realised that the Mogul Raj did not go to pieces because there was caste rivalry, but because of the selfish ambition of the Mogul Sirdars to become independent rulers.

---

4 Kulkarni, A. V., *The Last Eight Years of Lokamanya Tilak*, p.194 .(Marathi).

According to Tilak, the downfall of the Mahrattas was not caused so much by the infusion of caste prejudices as by a lack of a dominating statesman who could hold all forces under control and make them work in harmony. What most of those leaders lacked was the quality of serving the country's cause selflessly and of preferring it to self-interest. From all the arguments he put forward in indirect defence of the caste system, it seems he took the view that social justice and social equality would never, by themselves, contribute to national unity and solidarity.

In August of the same year, Tilak expressed his views on Hinduism in one of his speeches in Poona during the Ganapati festival and defined Hinduism as "faith in the *Vedas*, variety in the means and infiniteness of the objects of worship."[5] Religion in the true sense of the word, defined Tilak, meant and included the knowledge of all nature of God and soul and of the ways and means by which the human soul could attain salvation. However, his definition of Hinduism was based on the consistent and positive and matter-of-fact outlook. The Hinduism of his conception excluded its tributaries like Jainism and Buddhism. The other point worth mentioning about Tilak's definition was that while it desired every Hindu to have faith in the *Vedas*, seventy per cent of the Hindus had no right to study and know the *Vedas* the authority of which they were expected to accept or to have social customs and laws ordained by that authority. It was meaningless to say that the people should have faith in the *Vedas* which they had no right to listen to, much less to study.

A little later Tilak therefore supported the rights of the Brahmins who refused to perform worship with Vedic hymns at the palaces of the Maharaja of Baroda and the Maharaja of Kolhapur because, he said, the Brahmin priests followed the commands of their religion. And according to that religion the non-Brahmins were not entitled to the right of performing their religious rites with Vedic hymns! Not only that, but he defended their action and asserted once again his view that it was improper on the part of Marathas to insist on the performance of their religious rites with Vedic hymns. Neither would such an attitude benefit them, he added, nor would it redound to their credit, nor would it be beneficial in any way to the nation. Even though the Marathas performed their religious rites with mantras direct from the *Vedas* they would not be one with the Brahmins; they would remain Marathas. He tried to impress on the Marathas that their position in

5 Pt. Laxmanshastri Joshi, *A Critique of Hinduism*, p. 86 (translated by G. D. Parikh).

society was due to their prowess and not to a particular form of worship.[6] This ungenerous view fomented discontent and for years it polluted the political and social atmosphere in Maharashtra, so much so that some go so far as to attribute to this narrow attitude the terrible atrocities and arson which were venomously inflicted in 1948 on the Brahmin community in Maharashtra.[7]

When S. K. Bole, then one of the topmost non-Brahmin leaders, saw Tilak at Poona in connection with the article which propagated the foregoing view, Tilak told him that its author was one of his lieutenants. This evasive stand was unlike the bold stand Tilak took in Law Courts in respect of his political convictions. It was unfortunate that a first-rate leader of the people should come to propagate this narrow view, but it was a fact. It was not a question of a song here or a hymn there. It was a fundamental question embodying the principles of liberty, equality and fraternity; in fact, social equality, justice and democracy! He appreciated the translation of the *Vedas* by Max Muller, but never supported unequivocally the right of the majority of the Hindus to read or to study the *Vedas*! It may be mentioned here that Shivaji too had similarly to face Brahmin opposition in his day. When after his accession to the throne Shivaji began to learn and recite Vedic mantras, the Brahmins, who were offended by this conduct of Shivaji, boycotted Gaga Bhatt, the Brahmin preceptor who had performed Shivaji's coronation ceremony with Vedic hymns. Shivaji reacted to this boycott severely. He declared that although the Brahmins as religious preceptors were worthy of homage, their employment in Government service, unconnected with priestly functions, was also against the religious tenets. So he removed all Brahmins from Government service.[8] The recital of Vedic hymns by Shivaji, the protector of Hinduism and saviour of Hindustan, was heretical to the Brahmins! The policy of Tilak in this respect was not different from that of the Brahmins of Shivaji's times.

V

DURING THIS YEAR Tilak expressed his views on cow-slaughter and the conversions of Hindus carried on by missionaries. He said the Hindus desired and would welcome total cessation of cow-slaughter in Hindustan, but at the same time they would not prevent the Muslims and Britishers

6 The *Kesari*, 29 October 1901, also 22 October 1901.
7 *Shree Swami Kevalanand Abhinandan Grantha*, p. 65.
8 Sardesai, G. S., *Marathi Riyasat*, p. 494.

from performing cow-slaughter in conformity with their religions provided they did so without being noticed by the Hindus. The Hindus held that everyone should follow his or her religion without offending others. As regards the conversion activities of the missionaries during the famine of that year he grieved at the loss of 25,000 children to Hindu society, and pointing to this calamity he warned the Hindus that if they did not take measures to put an end to it they would have to face annihilation. He also supported and gave a fillip to two other new activities. The first was about the starting of a Fund called 'Paisa Fund', a pice fund for starting national industries. Antaji Damodar Kale was the originator of the idea. The other activity he supported was the preparation of a scientific almanac.

Tilak's profound knowledge of ancient Hindu Philosophy, History, Astronomy and Mathematics had been a source of help to many in those fields. He held in high esteem all those intelligent persons who had made some sort of contribution to the greatness and glory of India. On account of this frame of mind he paid, although there was no love lost between the two Poona groups, a courtesy call on R. P. Paranjpye, who had by his intellectual feats captured the imagination of Indian youth and given a rude shock to Britain's academic world that had so far believed that Indian students shone only where things and facts required memorisation. When Paranjpye addressed the Graduates' Association at Bombay, on the 'History of Mathematics', Tilak the scholar and mathematician was called on to speak at the end, and all were deeply impressed with the profundity and readiness of his scholarship. After this speech, Tilak himself addressed the Association on 'Relation between the Vedas and Assyrian Mythology!' His audience was surprised at his knack of making a difficult subject simple. The facility, originality and depth evoked their great appreciation.

It was this frame of mind that kept him musing over any missing link in his research in spite of the multifarious duties he had to perform. Often he used to discuss a new or difficult point in his research with Shastris whenever he came across them. Once absorbed in such a discussion he forgot has home or work. One evening he had been to attend a meeting. Everyone and even his colleagues went home, but Tilak could not get home till after midnight. The members of the family ran here and there in search of him. At last he was found at a street corner hotly and loudly discussing with a Shastri a point from his proposed book on the antiquity of the *Vedas*. The Shastri had come out in search of a midwife as his daughter-in-law was in labour!

Tilak's sublime love for true seekers-after-knowledge manifested itself when Friedrich Max Muller, the great authority on the sacred books of the East, died on October 28, 1900, at Oxford. Imbued with the true spirit of a research scholar, Tilak wrote a memorable obituary note on the death of the author of *What can India teach us*. Learning commands respect in every country, but a scholar estimating the greatness of a scholar heightened the effect of the tributes to the memory of one who had revealed to the world the greatness of Indian literature. Tilak said he had described Max Muller as a Professor, because the honours and degrees conferred on him sprang from his great scholarship. This shows why Tilak was sometimes tickled when somebody called him a Pandit or a Professor. To him the greatest honour and divine happiness constituted in digging out knowledge and passing it on to posterity.

In December, Tilak went to Latur and obtained first-hand information about the working and management of the ginning factory of which he was one of the proprietors. This could not be so profitable a concern as to be a source of income to Tilak, for it had been for a long time encumbered with debts. He then left for the Lahore Congress.

The Congress met at the Bradlaugh Hall in Lahore. Tilak was not happy over the election of N. G. Chandavarkar as the President of the Congress. He had no high opinion of Chandavarkar. He had criticized him in the *Kesari* when the latter in the course of his tour in Britain, which he had undertaken on behalf of the Bombay Presidency Association in the latter part of 1885, had made some observations which Tilak did not like. In September 1900 he had attacked Chandavarkar, and expressed his disapproval of his election. Chandavarkar was just then appointed a Judge of the Bombay High Court, and it was the opinion of his opponents that he had not shown enthusiasm for the Congress during the last ten years. In those days the influence of a man with Government rather than his zeal for the public good generally brought him the Presidentship of the Congress.

In the Congress, Tilak supported a resolution moved by G. Subramania lyer asking for an inquiry into the economic condition of India, with a view to discovering and adopting remedies for the oft-recurring famines. Tilak said that some blamed the ryot for his poverty, but the ryot was much the same as he had long been. "But if you take away the produce of the land and do not give it back to the land in some form more material than prestige and advice," he added, "the country must grow poorer and poorer." In his recollection Lajpat Rai tells us that "the leaders of the Congress did not like Tilak very much, but the people held him above everyone else." To the student world he was a beacon-light. The students presented him with an address. It was at this Congress session that B. C. Pal, Tilak's future colleague from Bengal, saw Tilak after the Congress. Tilak spoke at a public meeting on the antiquity of the *Vedas*. Lajpat Rai invited him to his house to dine with him and to meet a few friends there. Lajpat Rai inquired of him whether he would take food cooked by his wife or whether it was necessary for him to have it prepared by a particular caste of Brahmin, for Lajpat Rai observed : "he (Tilak) was an orthodox revivalist. I was a social reformer. He was a pucca Sanatanist." Tilak, however, dined with Lala Lajpat Rai. He formed an everlasting friendship with the great champion in Lajpat Rai, and it is history how their common political principles and almost common political ideals with a deep-rooted distrust in foreign rule and disbelief in foreign help, lack of faith in empty promises and pledges of the British statesmen, drove the Congress to active agitation. Another leader of note who came over to Tilak's views in this Congress was Vijaya Raghavachariar.

A fortnight after the Lahore Congress, Ranade, who had patiently plodded on and piloted for the last thirty years the rising destinies of the land, breathed his last. He had just proceeded on leave for six months and in his leave vacancy Chandavarkar was appointed a judge of the High Court. By his intellectual and moral grandeur, his divine restlessness and universal mind Ranade towered above his contemporaries, and so he was characterised by his contemporaries as a Socrates, a great god or an Erasmus.

He was a religious man, but he deemed it his religious duty to work in all directions of public usefulness. He did not isolate himself from humanity and made his own personal or individual spiritual development the ideal of his life. Meeting after meeting mourned the death of this prophet of new India in every town all over India declaring that Ranade was preeminently the best man of his time, was an embodiment of all the best and truest, and deserved to be included in the rosary of great and good saints.

When Tilak heard the news of Ranade's death he was greatly grieved. He grew reminiscent and said, "I felt more grieved over Agarkar's death. That is due to close companionship. At that time tears streamed down for two days and I was rather distressed."

A great obituarist, Tilak, too, wrote a very thought-provoking obituary worthy of his pen. Forgetting the bitter controversies he had with Ranade from political necessity, Tilak, on retrospection, judged of the unique career and character of Ranade on a high plane and laid special stress on the role Ranade played in the regeneration of India in general and Maharashtra in particular. Tilak described him as the first regenerator of Maharashtra during British Rule over Maharashtra which had grown morally, politically and spiritually lethargic, and comparing him with Madhavacharya, who was the preceptor of the Vijayanagar kings, he observed that Ranade was omniscient indeed! This was praise, murmured the Poona Moderates, lavished on the dead.

CHAPTER XI

The Fiery Ordeal

I

THE JAIL HARDSHIPS had their repercussions on Tilak's life. Besides he suffered from hernia for which he had twice undergone minor operations. As a result of this ailment he fell ill in March 1901 for about two weeks; his temperature rose to 103°. During this illness his assistant editor Kelkar chanced to refer to some points raised in a technical speech by a European regarding plague. Kelkar, who was known for his balanced views, must have expressed concurrence with "the views of the European. This enkindled the fire in Tilak and he stormed at Kelkar; it was feared that his fever would relapse.

On the whole Tilak had no doubt a little respite for these two years. He utilized his leisure in ascertaining some points in connection with his proposed book The *Arctic Home in the Vedas*. He was perusing books on geology and holy works on other religions. He was in correspondence on this subject with Max Muller whom he wanted to convince of the new points in his research. Max Muller had worked all his life on a different line; so he would not easily accept Tilak's view and opined that the interpretation of the Vedic passages proposed by him were probable, yet his theory appeared to be in conflict with the established geological facts. Tilak politely wrote in reply that he had examined the question from that point of view also, and he expected soon to place before him entire evidence in support of his view. But in the meantime the great authority on the sacred books of the East passed away. Tilak had discussed this question with many scholars in Madras, Calcutta, Lahore, Banaras and other places, during his travels in different parts of India. He had called for a copy of Dr. Warren's book *Paradise Found* from America and learnt German with the help of Whitker's *Modern Method of Learning German*.

During the early part of 1901 he had completed some chapters of this book. After his illness in March 1901 he wrote a few articles. Writing on Curzon, he said that out of his twelve problems Curzon did only those which helped to fix India, the diamond, in the iron frame of the British Empire—such as the problem of the North-West Frontier, introduction of the gold coin, and expansion of the railways; but he neglected all the vital issues concerning the welfare of the peasants, the common man, indigenous industry and others. Another important article pointed out the danger from the missionary propaganda. The Archbishop of Bombay, then in London, declared at a meeting that the Hindus and Muslims were in favour of Christianity, and that if they desired to develop into a nation they needed only one thing and that was the acceptance of Christianity. Tilak reiterated the principles of nationality such as religion, language, love of one's country, and added that common interest was the most vital factor in the formation of a nation. The view that the Hindus and Muslims were now eager to receive baptism, he concluded, could be held and propagated only by those who depended for their livelihood on proselytism or by those who regarded it as a means of expanding the Empire. He then went to Sinhagad to have a respite where he completed the work in May and June upto the thirteenth chapter. He could neither finish the book, nor have a longer respite as G. S. Khaparde came to Sinhagad with a problem that needed an urgent solution.

That problem was the execution of the will of Baba Maharaj who had appointed Tilak, Khaparde, Kirtikar, Kumbhojkar and Nagpurkar as his trustees and executors. Kirtikar refused to act as a trustee, and the last two were already in the service of Baba Maharaj.

Baba Maharaj died on August 7, 1897. After a few days Tilak was put in jail for sedition in September 1897 for 18 months.

Mrs. Sakavarbai, the widow of Baba Maharaj, was known as Tai Maharaj. At the time of his death she was enceinte and gave birth to a son in January 1898 ; but he died in March 1898.

The will directed that-

'My wife is pregnant. If she does not give birth to a son or if the son after birth is short-lived, then, for the purpose of continuing the name of my family, with the *Vichar* of the trustees a boy should be given, as often as may be necessary, in adoption, on the lap of my wife, in accordance with the Shastras and the *panch* should, on behalf of that son, carry on the management of the immovable and movable estates till he attains majority.'

While Tilak was in jail, he was consulted about the estate affairs, and in January 1898 Dadasaheb Khaparde received the probate for the trustees. He made inventories and arranged about other details.

On his release Tilak attended the trustees' meeting first in October 1898 and again in May 1899. Nothing important took place in 1900. In the last week of May 1901 a meeting of the trustees was held at Sinhagad, and as the estate was encumbered with enormous debts curtailment of expenditure was thought to be the only way out. This was of course an insulting and detestable idea to the young widow, who fancied herself to be the equitable owner of the estate; and her prejudices were fanned by the hangers-on or servile flatterers who had crept into her confidence by whispering agreeable words. In June 1901 the trustees recorded a resolution that Bala Maharaj of Kolhapur was too old, and none of the other boys on the list was approved and that Tilak and Khaparde accompanied by Tai Maharaj should go to Aurangabad in the Hyderabad State to make enquiries as to boys of the Babra branch at Nidhone, and dispose of the matter.

So the party started on June 19, 1901, for Aurangabad and put up there at a Sikh Mandir. Tilak and Khaparde brought boys from Nidhone, a village in the neighbourhood of Aurangabad. A boy was selected. The horoscope and the wishes of Tai Maharaj concurred with the testator's wishes and directions. Thereupon, on June 27, a meeting of the Shastris and of other persons in Aurangabad was summoned. At that meeting it was announced by the trustees to the assembled guests that the boy Jagannath was selected for adoption. The father of the boy was taken to the widow. She asked him to give his son in adoption and he agreed. This fact was announced at the meeting, duplicate deeds of adoption were drawn up, and a letter from the widow addressed to the boy's father informing him about his son's adoption was prepared.

Next morning, before a gathering, the deeds of adoption and the letter were duly executed; the boy was received by the adoptive mother on her lap in performance of the requisite essential rites of adoption. This being done, it was decided that the formal ceremonies and festivals would be performed in Poona. On the arrival of the Party in Poona, Tilak made Tai Maharaj inform Aston, the British Agent to the Sardars in the Deccan States, about the adoption.

But things were taking a turn. A coterie of scheming persons incited Nagpurkar who had on his own part sought adoption of his son. He joined the machinations of those men whom he formerly had described as unscrupulous. The first thing he did to that end was to insert a minute of dissent to the Poona resolution under which the adoption at Aurangabad was done. The records were in his possession. Having done this, he won over the widow to his side as she was displeased with the trustees' strict management of all her affairs. At this juncture Pandit Maharaj, who was striving for his brother Bala Maharaj being adopted by Tai Maharaj, joined hands with these men. Nevertheless they knew that the combined strength of their evil influences was not sufficient to pull down Tilak. So they invoked the bureaucracy to help them in their designs against Tilak who was their common enemy.

These scheming men induced the young widow to see H. F. Aston who was both the Government Agent to the Sardars of the Deccan and District Judge of Poona. The widow saw him privately at his bungalow and sought his protection against the tyranny of Tilak whose name was a red rag to Aston and the bureaucracy. He thought that it was a golden opportunity to remove Tilak, the enemy of the Government, from the field by defaming him in the eyes of the public and making a Parnell out of him.

Tilak discovered the plot against the Aurangabad adoption and reported Nagpurkar to the trustees. On advice from the circles mentioned above, the widow served the trustees with a notice informing them not to interfere in the management of the estate, and wrote to the Kolhapur Darbar for sanction to the adoption of Bala Maharaj. Tilak sent a telegram and a letter to the Dewan of Kolhapur, requesting him to postpone granting permission for adoption in the Tai Maharaj case till he received his letter as trustee. He mentioned in his letter that giving and acceptance of a son by Tai Maharaj had been completed by a registered deed at Aurangabad with the trustees' consent, and added that Tai Maharaj had no power to adopt.

Notwithstanding Tilak's appeal, the permission from the Kolhapur Darbar came telegraphically. Tai Maharaj decided to take in adoption Bala Maharaj, the brother of Pandit Maharaj, on July 13, in spite of the opposition of Tilak and other trustees. The family of Pandit Maharaj and his guests-cum-gymnasts, who had obviously come to effect the adoption under any circumstances, took their lodgings at the big bungalow of Tai Maharaj who was herself living in one part of the bungalow. Tilak came to know about this move, and so he filed a suit in the court of the First Class Sub-judge of Poona for a perpetual injunction to restrain Tai Maharaj from adopting Bala Maharaj and also asked for a temporary injunction which was granted. He, too, addressed a letter to Aston for an interview and informed him that the giving and receiving in adoption of such a boy had already been effected with the full consent of Tai Maharaj at Aurangabad.

Tilak was determined to frustrate the plans of Tai Maharaj, and so in the small hours of July 13, 1901, he went with his men and occupied the third part of the bungalow. Now the two camps faced each other. At first Tilak tried the art of persuasion. He calmly requested Tai Maharaj to postpone the adoption ceremony till the arrival of Dadasaheb Khaparde and Kumbhojkar. This unexpected seeming softness on the part of Tilak inveigled the vain lady into believing that Tilak had given up his opposition. Khaparde arrived in Poona on July 15, and a regular fight began! Persuasion had no effect upon Tai Maharaj, and she gave orders to proceed with the preparations for the adoption of Bala Maharaj which was to take place on July 16. The trustees served a notice on the Kolhapur guests asking them to quit the place at once. Near midnight on July 15, Tilak with his men entered the compound of the bungalow, locked the gate, kept his own watchman who allowed only Tilak's men like Kelkar, Shivarampant Paranjpe editor of the *Kal*, Balasaheb Natu and others to enter the compound. At dawn Tilak's men surrounded Tai Maharaj's apartment to prevent the adoption from taking place and turned out the Kolhapur guests bag and baggage into the street.

Pandit Maharaj appealed to the Police but to no effect. He then laid the information before the City Magistrate, but there too he failed. The police came and went. Aston visited the place and returned! It was so legal an affair!

At last Tai Maharaj, on the advice of her evil-advisers, and as a result of her interview with Aston, filed her application on July 29 for revocation of the probate. She drove away Tilak's men from her house. On August 15, Tilak went to Kolhapur to persuade the Kolhapur Darbar not to sanction the adoption of Bala Maharaj. Shahu Maharaj gave a hearing to Tilak, but did not commit himself to any view. During his short stay at Kolhapur Tilak was honoured at the Sanskrit Pathashala. He went to Miraj and on being informed that the adoption ceremony was to take place on the 18th August, returned to Kolhapur. Just a few hours before the adoption he saw Shahu Maharaj and made a final appeal to him. But the appeal fell flat. Tilak was shrewdly kept engaged in a long talk by Shahu Maharaj till the adoption ceremony was over. Tai Maharaj, who had already reached Kolhapur, thus formally adopted Bala Maharaj on August 18, 1901.

II

Meanwhile, all leaders in the province had concentrated their thoughts on the Bombay Land Revenue Code Amending Bill which aimed at making certain changes, one of them preventing the agriculturists from transferring their land. Under the proposed change land could be heritable but was not transferable. Obviously Government wanted to save the agriculturists from the clutches of Sowkars and the leaders said that Government was establishing State landlordism by reducing the ryots to a status of short-term tenants. But those were not the days of a socialistic pattern of society. An intense agitation had been launched against the Bill. Government denounced it as Sowkar's agitation. Tilak wrote masterly articles and propagated the view that the Bill was ruinous to both the agriculturists and the landlords. A meeting in the Town Hall, Bombay, on July 27, attended by seven hundred delegates representing different institutions voiced their unqualified opposition to the Bill. Government was determined to carry the Bill through, and when the second reading of the Bill was begun, Pherozeshah Mehta moved an amendment seeking to postpone the consideration of the Bill with a request that it should be referred to various officials, associations and individuals. The Amendment was lost. Thereupon Mehta, Gokhale and three other Members left the Council Hall in protest, Gokhale explaining that his departure meant no disrespect to the President of the Council, the Governor!

The *Times of India* described this walk-out of the representatives of the people as a comic scene and dubbed it a risky experiment for public men to take to histrionics! Had Tilak been a Member of the Legislative Council he would have brought a hornets' nest about his ears! Tilak replied to the criticism levelled against the representatives of the people by saying that the autocratic Government should now raise layfigures in the Council Hall and put Mehta's cap on one, Gokhale's turban on another and so on, and carry on the work of the legislature!

This shows how Tilak failed to gauge the problem of peasants correctly. As his chief role was to foment discontent against foreign rule he sometimes failed to support the good laws enacted for the amelioration of the peasants. The aforesaid legislation unmistakably aimed at preventing the money-lenders from seizing the immovable property of the peasants. Tilak misinterpreted it and said that because the power of the moneylenders was made ineffective, the peasants were not given loans; and this led to the worsening of the condition of both parties.

It is not surprising that the Moderate leaders like Mehta and Gokhale were one with Tilak in opposing the Bill that clearly sought the amelioration of the peasants and gave them protection against the money-lenders. These leaders were the spokesmen of the higher urban class and the landed and moneyed interests.

Soon in September 1901, the Provincial Conference was held in Bombay where Tilak supported a resolution moved by Parekh on the work of the Famine Commission which had endorsed the view of the leaders against the famine policy of the Bombay Government in the matter of remissions or suspensions of land revenue. He remarked that it was a distinct triumph of the public over official opinion.

On September 23, 1901, Tilak and the other two trustees filed a suit in the Court of the First Class Sub-Judge of Poona against Tai Maharaj, Bala Maharaj and Pandit Maharaj, stating that the adoption of Jagannath was valid and that of Bala Maharaj was invalid and that Nagpurkar the fourth trustee had colluded with Tai Maharaj to get Bala Maharaj adopted.

In his extreme zeal to crush Tilak, Aston, who had in 1897 sentenced a Satara editor to transportation for life for a seditious article, allowed an inquiry to be made on points which were wholly irrelevant to the question under dispute. Instead of considering whether the grant of Probate to Tilak and others had become inoperative under Hindu Law owing to the birth and death of a son to Tai Maharaj, he also allowed the plaintiff to put in the evidence of the Aurangabad adoption in spite of Tilak's challenge and protest to the contrary.

Tilak was put in the witness-box for no less than sixteen days during the greater part of which he was subjected to a most rigorous cross-examination lasting intermittently from November 16, 1901, to April 3, 1902. Throughout the proceedings Tilak was deliberately teased, provoked, insulted, misunderstood and misrepresented on record by interrupting and twisting his answers.

Although involved in a serious litigation, Tilak was watchful and whenever he noticed leaders acting in a manner devoid of self-respect he lashed at them mercilessly. Such an occasion arose when Mr. Bennett, editor of the *Times of India*, was given a party on the occasion of his retirement by Dr. Sir Bhalchandra whom Bennett had described as an idiot! Tilak said that either the praise bestowed on Bennett was false or Dr. Sir Bhalchandra was indeed an idiot, otherwise he would not have praised a man like Bennett who was a third-rate editor as compared with eminent editors in England and who was not a man of learning, or an orator, or a statesman, or a general.

Tilak went to Calcutta to attend the Calcutta Congress in December 1901. When he appeared in the pandal he received a splendid ovation as a persecuted martyr and a man of the people. During the session Tilak seconded a resolution that dealt with education, urging that education should be made thorough. He also delivered there a speech at a public meeting on Hinduism.

On this occasion of his visit to Calcutta, Tilak and his party paid a visit to Vivekananda's Math at Belur near Calcutta. The grand imposing building and the surrounding natural scenery exceedingly impressed them. Swami Vivekananda, the first Indian to win an international reputation in the modern world, welcomed Tilak and they had a talk. Swami Vivekananda had been to Poona in 1892. Tilak had come across the Swamiji in the train when he was returning from Bombay where he had been on some private work. Some Gujarati gentlemen introduced Vivekananda to Tilak and requested him to take him to Poona. Swamiji stayed for a week or so at Tilak's place in a separate room. He had a few articles which a *Sanyasin* keeps and some selected books. In those days Tilak and his colleagues held weekly discussion at a club in Hirabag, Poona, on a topic on which one of them delivered in English the main speech. At such a meeting one day when the main speech was delivered on a philosophical topic, Swamiji was requested to offer his views on the subject, and to their surprise, in a flowing imposing vein, Vivekananda dealt with the subject. From the next day Poona intellectuals began to pay visits to Swamiji and discussed with him social, religious and philosophical topics.

During this visit Vivekananda asked Tilak to take to Sanyasashram and preach his gospel in Bengal while he would go to Maharashtra to do the same kind of work. Tilak replied that he liked to do all things as a man of the world, and as to the idea of a change of Province he opined that the man who attained leadership in his own Province was likely to influence men in other Provinces. Tilak was conscious of the historic role Swami Vivekananda had played in connection with the evolution and revelation of Hinduism. When the Swami departed this life, Tilak in an obituary observed that there appeared two great men in India who regarded Hinduism as a glorious heritage and treasure. They not only undertook to reveal and expound the real message and glory of Hinduism, but also thought it their sacred duty to prove its abiding greatness and supremacy in the world. One was Shankaracharya, who played his role some 1000-1200 earlier; and the other was Swami Vivekananda, who did it at the close of the nineteenth century! This was an appraisal of a maker of history by another maker of history!

Another important visit Tilak paid during this Congress session was to a lady called Mataji who had started a Girls' School in Calcutta with a view to rendering some service to the nation. She was a widow from Tanjore and could speak Marathi fluently. She felt in the company of Tilak and his party like a lady enjoying the company of persons of her father's place. She revealed a chapter of her mysterious life; how she paid a visit in her widowhood to the holy place of Pashupateshwar at Khatmandu, how her charming personality happened to come in view of the Samsherbahadur, King of Nepal, how she stayed with the royal family and after some time how she came to Calcutta. She expressed her desire to introduce Tilak to the King of Nepal and hoped that the contact would result in the well-being of the nation. Wasukaka and Tilak in fact took the risk and went by railway as far as Patna where they were stopped for want of passes. They had a letter of introduction from Lt.-Colonel Kumar Narsinha to the Chief Minister of Nepal.

Wasukaka and Tilak's lieutenant Khadilkar again got themselves introduced through Mataji to the ruler of the Nepal and in a mysterious way Khadilkar started at Khatmandu a tile-factory for Nepal.[1] Khadilkar was Tilak's assistant editor and one of the able wielders of the pen in Maharashtra. The Chief Minister of Nepal was persuaded to send some Nepali young men to take military training in Japan, and Wasukaka himself went to Japan. Contacts were established with a German firm at Calcutta, and a bullet-preparing machine was purchased in great secrecy. The strain, stress and danger proved too much for Khadilkar, and he gave up the idea when a man named Damu Joshi, who had worked with him at Khatmandu, on being arrested in the Kolhapur Case, disclosed the Nepal affair. The British Government made inquiries of the Nepal Government. So it closed the chapter at once.

Tilak was involved in the Tai Maharaj case, and he had no time to concentrate his mind on such plans! But what price such danger! Later the Nepal students were accorded a reception at Poona on their arrival from Japan.

---

1 Khaparde, B. G., *Dadasaheb Yanche Charitra (Marathi)*, p. 168.

On his way back to Poona from Calcutta, Tilak paid a visit to Nagpur on the invitation of some college students. Their representatives were Madhav Shrihari Aney and others. Tilak delivered a speech on Sanskrit literature and Western philosophy at the Rajaram Tulsiram Theatre, where he was presented with an address on behalf of Nagpur students. The address ended with 'Lead Kindly Light, Lead Thou us on'. It was at this meeting he gave an outline of the fundamentals of his future great work, the *Gita-Rahasya*. At night Tilak's host Gopalrao Butti arranged a music programme in honour of his distinguished guest. When the other people expressed their appreciation in nodding or cheering at the proper time, Tilak sat with his mind absorbed in other things. The Mathematician showed no interest in Music. On being asked why he was inattentive, he said he had no taste for worldly music when he had already heard the *Gita*, the divine song of the Lord. He had no desire to drink lemonade when he had already tasted nectar. Yet it was Tilak who later conferred the title Bal-gandharva, the young celestial musician, on Narayanrao Rajhansa, the king of actors and musicians on the Marathi stage.

III

THE PROCEEDINGS IN the Tai Maharaj case commenced again in January 1902. Sensing the hostile attitude of Aston, Tilak applied in January 1902 to the High Court for the transfer of Tai Maharaj's application to some other Court. But Tilak's application was rejected. Well aware of the turn and twist of Aston's mind, Tilak did not care to produce evidence. Tilak's pleader gave up the fight, but his lieutenant Kelkar held on till the last day, working in conformity with the orders of his master.

While facing a grim trial Tilak was busy in the early part of the year 1902, fixing the new machinery for the *Kesari*. To cope with the demands of the people he had to increase its circulation. Gifted as he was with technical aptitude, he could fix the new machine with the skill of an engineer. Having thus equipped himself with men and material, he started the enlarged edition of the *Kesari* in the new form in February 1902, devoting much space to varied fields of national development, industrial, intellectual, agricultural, religious, social and political. Thus he put the *Kesari* on a satisfactory footing enlarging its circulation as well as its usefulness. Indian journalism has a noble and selfless background behind it. It has been built up by the efforts of patriotic youth and great men who, disregarding the rewards of the legal profession or Government service, devoted their lives to the national awakening. Newspaper enterprise in the country had not then attracted the attention of capitalists and speculators.

On April 3, Aston was to deliver his judgment, and so Tilak was ordered by the Judge to be present in the Court. Sensible men read in his accusing glance the decision he was going to pronounce. He not only revoked the probate and held the Aurangabad adoption disproved, but also committed Tilak next day to the City Magistrate to be dealt with according to law. The Judge, mad with the spirit of an inquisitionist, described Tilak as "a fencing, prevaricating, quibbling witness," with "distinctly untruthful demeanour."

Thus April 4, 1902, was the darkest day in Tilak's life. Aston's vindictiveness armed Tilak's bitter opponents and deadly enemies with poisonous spears. A man of great learning, a leader of great influence, and long service, stood before the world condemned as an unscrupulous character, judicially denounced as a perjurer. A man of iron will and undying faith alone could overcome such a calamity! Tilak filed an application in the High Court against Aston's order of revocation.

The Police Officer, Brewin, made secret inquiries into the matter and reported that the charge of forgery would not stand in the Court, and as the other charges pertained to personal affairs, Government should not take action against Tilak. The High Court considered Tilak's application against Aston's judgment and reversed it. This was a silver lining to the dark cloud. However, the motion made simultaneously with the civil appeal for a stay of the criminal proceedings against him till the decision of the regular adoption suit pending in the Civil Court was turned down by the High Court. Displeased with the decision of the Judge, the Government, it was rumoured, sent him on leave! Yet Government, bent upon ruining Tilak, sanctioned an initial sum of no less than thirty thousand rupees and appointed Mr. Clements Special Magistrate. The City Magistrate transferred the case to Clements, and he commenced the trial on September 15, 1902. The charges formulated against Tilak were:

(1) Mr. Tilak had made a false complaint for breach of trust against Mr. Nagpurkar, one of the trustees.

(2) Mr. Tilak had fabricated false evidence for use by making alterations and interpolations in the accounts of the Aurangabad trip.

(3) Forgery in connection with (2).

(4) Mr. Tilak had corruptly used or attempted to use as genuine evidence known to be false.

(5) Mr. Tilak had corruptly used as genuine the adoption deed.

(6) Mr. Tilak had fraudulently used as genuine the adoption deed containing his interpolation over Tai Maharaj's signature.

(7) Mr. Tilak had given false evidence intentionally.

The hearing of the charge of perjury began on October 23, 1902. Tilak made an application to the High Court for stay of the proceedings in Clements' Court on the plea that it had no proper Government sanction. The Court formally cancelled the proceedings. Tilak again brought a motion in the High Court for stay of proceedings on the ground of illegal transfer of the case from the City Magistrate to Clements, but it was rejected.

At this juncture Nagpurkar was egged on by Government to sue Tilak in the Court of the City Magistrate who had decided the case in favour of Nagpurkar. The Sessions Judge Mr. Beaman, supporting Tilak's stand, observed that Nagpurkar was a salaried servant and agent for the estate and as such a responsible custodian of the valuable jewellery entrusted to him. "It was his clear duty," added the learned Judge, "to allow inspection of the ornaments when demanded by a majority of the trustees, on pain of dismissal, if suspected of dishonesty and criminal misappropriation." The High Court also turned down Nagpurkar's application as Tilak's counsel Branson appealed to the Judges to take into consideration the character of Nagpurkar who had written private letters to the Judges of the Full Bench for an adjournment independently of his Counsel!

To struggle against a Government that had levelled serious charges against him and to face them meant a colossal task. Government had all the resources at its disposal, while Tilak was lonely fighting Government on all fronts. So he could not attend the Ahmedabad Congress which was held in December 1902.

In the midst of such terrible calamities Tilak published his work The *Arctic Home in the Vedas*. This was a sequel to his first book *The Orion* or *Researches into the Antiquities of the Vedas*. Establishing his theory that the original home of the Aryan people was in the far North, in regions roundabout the North Pole, he observed: "We have also seen that our view is supported by the latest scientific researches, and is not inconsistent with the results of comparative philology. We may, therefore, take it as established that the original home of the Aryan people was in the far

North, in regions roundabout the North Pole, and that we have correctly interpreted the Vedic and the Avestic traditions which had long remained misunderstood."

"A primeval Arctic home would have been regarded an impossibility," he asserted, "had not science cleared the ground by establishing that the antiquity of man goes back to the Tertiary Era, that the climate of the Polar regions was mild and temperate in interglacial times and that it was rendered cold and inclement by the advent of Glacial epoch."

"It was the advent of the Ice Age," he continued, "that destroyed the old climate of the original home and converted it into an icebound land unfit for the habitation of man. This is well expressed in the Avesta which describes the Airyana Vaejo as a happy land subsequently converted by the invasion of Angra Mainyu into a land of severe winter and snow. This correspondence between the Avestic description of the original home and the result of the latest geological researches, at once enables us to fix the age of the Arctic home, for it is now a well-settled scientific fact that a mild climate in the Polar regions was possible only in the inter-glacial and not in the post-glacial times."

Written in a lucid, flowing style, the book supports its facts, statements and conclusions by quoting a chain of arguments derived from numerous sources from Mythology, Geology to Archaeology.

The book won high praise. Expressing its views on the work, the *Bengalee* said that *The Orion* and *The Arctic Home in the Vedas* "may be said to have thrown new light upon the antiquity of the *Vedas* and the real meaning of certain Vedic texts which had so long baffled the ingenuity of Vedic commentators from Sayana to his modern successors. Reading those books, one might well exclaim :

'Vedas and Vedic laws lay hid in night'

'God said, "Let Tilak be" and all was light.'"

The most important tribute came from Dr. Warren, the President of Boston University, who in his *Paradise Found* had anticipated Tilak. He observed: "In the judgment of the present writer, the array of evidence set worth is far more conclusive than any ever attempted by an Indo-Iranian Scholar in the interest of any earlier hypothesis. Absolute candour and respect for the strictest methods of historic and scientific investigation characterize the discussion throughout."

The *Times of India* opined: "We are sure that the book will be welcomed as a most learned and valuable contribution to the solution of an extremely fascinating problem. All the arguments are so well arranged and the exposition of the subject is so admirably lucid that *The Arctic Home in the Vedas* may be read with pleasure and profit by the general reader who has little knowledge of astronomy, philology and geology and still, less of Sanskrit lore."

Henry W. Nevinson expressed real appreciation when he said : "In the midst of direct persecution when money, reputation, influence and everything were at stake, few men would have had the courage to spare a thought either for sacred books or Arctic culture."

Tilak attended the Provincial Conference which was held at Dharwar in March 1903 and was presided over by his friend D. A. Khare. During the conference he worked hard on the drafting of the main resolutions with regard to the land problems for which he had examined old reports and records and had collected data with great pains.

IV

YET TILAK'S MIND was not away from the people. He had written some articles in the *Kesari* on the poverty of India, on the greedy expansion of the British Empire and its consequent crushing military expenditure on the Indian people. He explained how the subtle method of flooding the country with Commissions adopted by Lord Curzon was either postponing the vital problems of the nation or making the Commissions echo his plans. He explained how British rule had deliberately killed Indian industries. When the Delhi Darbar was held by Lord Curzon against the almost unanimous protests of all public and representative men both in the press and on the platform, Tilak roared through the *Kesari* that it was against the interests of the country to waste vast sums of money on an empty pageant when famine and pestilence were stalking over the land. Tilak, in a sneering vein, asked the revellers to climb the Kutub Minar and have a glimpse at the surroundings of Delhi where at least seven capitals were long buried.

Misfortune was dogging Tilak's footsteps. His health also was not good. He suffered from an acute pain in his knee, which was the result of an accident. He could walk with difficulty. It was amid this misfortune that Tilak lost his eldest son Vishwanath who was possibly the brightest of his children. He was studying in college and had taken to writing articles and showed great signs of stepping into his father's shoes. His death occurred in February 1903 from plague in a cottage near Fergusson College. Tilak suppressed his feelings, brought some Government reports and wrote articles on them. A day or two after, the second son cried out to the father from the adjoining cottage, in spite of his mother's advice to the contrary, that his younger brother too had fever! Tilak was dictating an article to A. V. Kulkarni, his personal assistant. He heard the call and also the conversation between Tilak's wife and his son. Tilak also must have heard it. But he quietly finished his work and then went to the bedside of his son to inquire after his health.

That little son recovered from his illness. Tilak had, however, suppressed his sorrow over the loss of his eldest son, and the father's heart burst into strange emotions when one day he unconsciously called to him in his usual manner to open the door on the arrival of his personal assistant. He realised his mistake and instantly opened the door himself! When his friends tried to console him, he said with the self-command and coolness which were so dominant in him that there was calamity all over and it claimed victims from his house also. The minds of great men are controlled by a stern sense of realities, and they forget their own suffering and sorrows while engaged in alleviating the sorrows and sufferings of the people.

While the proceedings in the Court of the City Magistrate were going on, there were occasions when Tilak was excited. But his face became crimson when the meanest attack was made on his personal character which ultimately came out untarnished through the stormy attacks. During the course of the examination Tai Maharaj, who was a tool in the hands of the authorities, and her servant, both described an incident in which it was insinuated that Tilak had violated Tai Maharaj during their stay at Aurangabad. Tilak felt grieved that a lady from a Sardar family should have stooped so low as to stain her character with her own tongue which even a prostitute would not do. Another feature of the case was that Tilak demanded that the remaining charges should be proceeded with, but the Magistrate did not pay attention to it.

Tilak had asked for a Commission to examine some witnesses at Aurangabad and Amraoti, and he and his counsels had to move to these places. The people had not lost a whit of their faith in Tilak. Agriculturists and poor people from far and near assembled at Amraoti and accorded an enthusiastic reception to him. During the course of discussions on the fate of agriculturists Tilak observed that the agriculturists constituted the soul of the nation, and there would be no salvation till they were helped out. At

Aurangabad, Tilak had clashes with the Government Counsel, Strangman, who was stern and overbearing. Completing their work at Aurangabad in May and July 1903, the Commission went in July to Amraoti to examine Khaparde and one Mr. Joshi.

The Commission work over, they came back to Poona. Tilak's counsel Karandikar put up a brave defence and Strangman replied with equal force. Amidst these troubles and worries Tilak spared time to write leaderettes and address meetings. Five days before the judgment of Clements, Tilak's friend Prof. Jinsiwale died and in an obituary Tilak impressed upon the youth that it was an irrevocable faith with Prof. Jinsiwale that he was a Hindu, he would live as a Hindu, he would die as a Hindu, and could attain salvation by following the principles of Hinduism. In so doing Western education did not come in his way. Tilak then presided at this time over a meeting at which Gajananrao Vaidya, a Bombay Missionary Hindu leader, spoke on 'the empire of Brahminism'. Tilak told his audience that if the Hindus made common cause with the followers of Buddhism who were their co-religionists, it would be possible to bring one hundred million people of Asia under the influence of Brahminism. At this meeting Tilak could not overcome his feelings and his eyes were full of tears when he said that Prof. Jinsiwale, a scholar and religious man, was the proper authority to have presided over this meeting!

The proceedings in the Court of the Special Magistrate came to an end. August 24, 1903, the day of judgment, dawned. At his residence Tilak was making arrangements and keeping his application ready for bail. There was a dead silence at his residence. His old uncle Govindrao Tilak, who had lost his only son six months before, piteously looked at the faces of Tilak's colleagues, and turning his face aside, he burst into tears! The Government had taken extraordinary precautions at the Court. Police were posted at all the principal entrances to the Court filled with an expectant crowd. Tilak's Brahmin followers and admirers, who had made offerings to God for his acquittal, were anxiously awaiting the decision.

In his judgment Clements said that it was proved beyond doubt that when Tilak said "we never kept her under restraint, nor intended to do so" he made a false statement and one that was false to his knowledge and that his statement that Jagannath was placed on Tai Maharaj's lap was false and false to the accused's knowledge. As regards Tilak's plea that all he did was for the good of the estate, the Judge observed that there seemed to be evidence and reasons sufficient to raise a suspicion that his original motive in working for the adoption of Jagannath might have been composed of feelings of jealousy towards Nagpurkar, of wounded self-esteem, of a desire to continue in a position of power with regard to the estate.

Clements further said that Tilak was egged on by Khaparde in every step he took and the latter discreetly removed himself from the scene when on two occasions the situation gave signs of becoming dangerous, and feeling safe in the witness-box in Amraoti showed his disposition by making cowardly insinuations against Tai Maharaj's character. He found Tilak guilty of the offence of perjury and sentenced him to undergo eighteen months' rigorous imprisonment and a fine of one thousand rupees, with two months' further rigorous imprisonment in case of default. Clements had the last surprise in store for Tilak's counsel. Notwithstanding the usual order of a stay of the sentence pending appeal, he insisted on the recovery of the fine.

After the judgment was delivered, the defence applied for time to appeal to the District Judge to admit the accused to bail, but the Magistrate, who had kept a warrant ready for the police, allowed only ten minutes while he remained in the Court. All this was anticipated by Tilak and his counsel; so they had an application for bail ready to be submitted to the District Judge whose court was in the same building. The District Judge Lucas was then engaged in hearing another appeal, and so D. A. Khare, Counsel for Tilak, was unable to present it. In the meantime Tilak was taken to Yeravda Jail in the company of two European constables. The District Judge admitted Tilak to bail, and he was brought from the Yeravda Jail after two hours. Amid that colossal calamity he was undisturbed. His coolness in danger was unique. On his return home he dictated a brief summary of the decision of Clements for the *Kesari*.

The news of Tilak's sentence was received with profound sorrow all over the country. Almost all leading Indian newspapers expressed disapproval at this persecuting attitude shown by Government towards Tilak. Criticising the judgment, the *Tribune* of Lahore expressed Indian opinion correctly on the sentence on Tilak. "It is needless to say that all-India will await with suspended breath the result of the appeal from the Magistrate's judgment. We must add that the majority of our countrymen are not waiting for the higher Court's verdict in order to rebuild their estimate of Tilak, his work and character. His hold on the minds of his host of friends and admirers is not of a nature to be affected by verdicts of Law Courts. He has lived and worked in full view of the public, as it were, all his days. There is no mistaking such a character; it is unfolded to its inmost depths before the eyes of all who know him. A Court of Law, on the other hand, is liable to errors and misconceptions."

But Tai Maharaj could not live long to enjoy her pyrrhic victory. Having thus played a very notorious part in the life of Tilak, she closed her eyes on September 30, 1903.

The hearing of the appeal before the Sessions Court commenced on October 26, 1903. Counsel for Tilak was Khare. Lucas, the Sessions Judge, was frank, courteous and sympathetic. From this attitude it was presumed that as he differed from Aston and Clements, whom people thought to be the symbols of hate and contempt, his judgment would be in favour of Tilak. The hearing of the case was complete just before the Court broke up for the Christmas holidays. The judgment was to be delivered in the first week of January 1904.

It was the end of the year and the Congress was to be held at Madras on December 28. On the eve of the Congress Hume issued an earnest appeal to Congress leaders to devote themselves to the work of the Congress with undivided devotion, industry and sincerity and carry on the work of ameliorating the condition of the country in the right direction.

"You meet in Congress; you glow with a momentary enthusiasm ; you speak much and eloquently. But the Congress closes and every one of you goes off straightway on his private business! Years ago, I called on you to be up and doing; years ago, I warned you that 'Nations by themselves are made' and have you heeded these counsels ? You have, indeed, ever eagerly clamoured for and vainly clutched at the Crown, but how many of you will touch the cross even with your fingertips?" Tilak endorsed these views and appeal of Hume and said that the time had arrived when Congress leaders should ponder over the ways and means of attaining their objectives. If they found that their means and methods were right, they should carry on their struggle unremittingly, sincerely, selflessly, courageously and resolutely for winning their aims and objects.

Tilak's leaderette in the *Kesari* on this topic began with a Sanskrit quotation which describes frogs with varied colours and sounds and says they croak without fail at the end of the twelfth month! Some papers like the *Indian Opinion,* discussing the causes of failure of the Congress, opined that there were no leaders who untiringly and actively worked for its cause, and pointed out that Congress leaders like Telang, Badruddin,

Chandavarkar, Subramania Iyer and Sankaran Nair accepted Government jobs with the result that Congress work suffered.

V

LUCAS, THE DISTRICT and Sessions Judge, was ready with his judgment on the 4th day of January 1904. Tilak's friends came to the Court with beaming faces and ready with garlands and sweets in their hands with a view to congratulating Tilak on his acquittal in the precincts of the Court. But when over half the judgment was read, the Judge looked slipping off the path of justice. People in the Court gasped and looked flabbergasted! A bolt from the blue fell down on Tilak as the Judge announced him guilty. The only relieving feature of the decision was that Tilak was found guilty only in respect of the statement that the boy was formally placed on Tai Maharaj's lap. The Judge, therefore, said that he reduced the sentence of eighteen months' to six months' rigorous imprisonment. Lucas, however, attributed such an offence to proneness to temptation in weak moments that is sometimes found even in remarkably strong and obstinate characters though actuated by positively virtuous motives.

This time the bureaucracy gave vent to their mean and spiteful joy by publicly handcuffing Tilak in the Court. The Police removed him to the police van outside like an ordinary criminal. Handcuffed he got into the van with great difficulty. He was lodged in Yeravda Jail. The High Court admitted Tilak to bail on January 8, 1904. When Kelkar and Tilak's personal assistant Kulkarni, who went to bring him back to his residence saw him, they were overcome with emotions and so could not utter a word. Breaking the silence, Tilak said, "Look here, Kelkar, they have stamped my name on my scarf. Now there is no possibility of my losing it anywhere!" His lieutenant replied sadly, "God has endowed you with this rare courage!" Tilak did not come home direct. He went to the bedside of his uncle Govindrao, who, like other relatives, had been paralysed with his conviction. The old man had a glance at his nephew, muttered some words, and never came to himself. He passed away. This old man's wife, too, died after a fortnight.

The judgment of Lucas was shocking news to most of the leaders and papers who had implicit faith in Tilak's public and private honesty. Expressing its opinion on the Lucas' judgment, the *Deccan Herald* said that the announcement of the sentence came as a rather unexpected revelation. "The news of Mr. Tilak's imprisonment, it is needless to say," observed the *Amrita Bazar Patrika* of Calcutta, "will create profound sensation in the country. That the case would end in this way was not even dreamt of by anyone. But, it seems, Tilak was born at an unlucky moment, and so it is his lot to suffer." "His only consolation lies in the fact," continued the paper with a touching note, "that there are millions of hearts who will weep for him. If bitter tears can remove miseries, Mr. Tilak will be able to bear up this fresh misfortune with fortitude. We fear, however, this time he will not return alive, for he has not yet been able to fully recover from the effects of his last incarceration. We wish he were not born at all, or he had died long ago; for then his countrymen would not have been subjected to all this excruciating pain on his account."

Another paper from Calcutta described the startling and shameful news of the distinguished native gentleman of Tilak's stature being manacled in the presence of the District Judge as a common felon. "We say at once," it roared indignantly, "and we say with the strongest feeling, shame upon the perpetrators of this foul and disgraceful act." Describing further that only cowards experienced delight by treading on the fallen man, it reminded Government that "it was first but a small matter that set the Indian Mutiny afoot, and it would, we think, be well to avoid a repetition of such unfortunate mistakes."

The *Pioneer*, an Anglo-Indian paper, voiced the feelings of the non-Indians in a peculiar vein. It said sarcastically that Tilak's conviction for sedition did not matter at all as involving any moral turpitude. "The paths of scholarship," it added, "lead but to the gaol."

While the proceedings of the case were going on, simple folks and selfish men troubled Tilak for his advice on their intricate land or estate problems, and Tilak used to advise them or instruct their lawyers, or often draft their applications or representations in those days also.

One day a man came to Tilak seeking legal advice on a long-drawn litigation. He had become desperate. As a last resort, before committing extreme action, he came to Tilak. Government had confiscated his property saying that as long as he was alive it would not be returned. The case was fought on many points, but to no avail. Tilak heard the details of the case and with the speed of lightning a thought struck him. He asked the disappointed legal wreck whether he would act up to his advice. The man readily replied that he was prepared to lay down his life to save his family. Upon this Tilak asked him to turn a sanyasin and to inform the Head of the District about it. According to the Hindu Law a sanyasin is no more an owner of property. He is dead to it legally. It was a sure remedy prescribed by a legal mind. The desperate man returned to his place and informed the Collector through a petition that he had turned a sanyasin. As a result, the property was returned to his sons! Thus the ingenious ruse solved the knotty problem. Such instances are numerous. On another occasion he was dictating an application for someone in trouble. When asked why he was dictating an application even when he was himself worried to death, he replied that there were people who would like to light their cigarettes even on a pyre!

Tilak was determined to fight out the case to the last. An appeal was made to the High Court, Bombay, from the decision of the judgment of Lucas. Branson and D. A. Khare appeared for Tilak when the High Court heard the appeal on March 3, 1904. The Advocate-General stated in the High Court that all other charges except the one in question, i.e. whether Tilak made a false statement intentionally to the effect that the boy was placed by his father on the lap of Tai Maharaj, were withdrawn. Branson raised an objection to the course adopted by the Magistrate and the Sessions Judge who failed to call evidence necessary for the proper determination of the case. He, therefore, said that the reasons given by the Sessions Judge were insufficient to support a conviction.

The Chief Justice, Sir Lawrence Jenkins, and the Hon. Mr. Justice Batty, delivering judgment, said that they upheld the objections so ably urged by Branson. They observed that there was misreading of the documentary evidence, that there were fundamental errors in principle which vitiated the conduct and disposal of the case, and that no attempt at sifting the large body of the Aurangabad evidence was made by the Sessions Judge. The Chief Justice observed that the accused Tilak in the course of his examination, had clearly explained the words 'Datta Vidhan Samarambha' and as the word Vidhan meant the act of giving, though the pleaders by whom he was examined either could not, or would not, understand it, the expression must have meant that there was to be an actual ceremony of giving and taking. "And if that be so, it does away with the idea of an inconsistency with the statement on which the accused is charged." Accordingly they set aside the conviction and sentence, and ordered the fine, if paid, to be returned.

VI

THE NEWS OF Tilak's acquittal ran like wildfire all through Poona City at twelve-thirty in the night. People expressed great relief at this joyful news.

Crowds of people rushed to his residence to felicitate him. They garlanded him, dubbed his forehead with red powder, and made him presents of sweetmeats. The road in front of his house was blocked. Congratulations poured in from all corners of India. Special thanksgiving prayers were said at the principal temples in the city. Tilak visited in the evening the chief Hindu temples in Poona to offer his thanksgiving prayers and was cheered by an enthusiastic crowd on the way.

The newspapers welcomed the High Court decision and thanked it for its soundness and impartiality in administering justice. The *Advocate of India* said that by persistence, considerable expenditure and finally by an appeal to the High Court, justice had been obtained. The *Gujarati* said that the High Court had saved Tilak's character and added that it had done an important service in checking partially the spirit of Lee-Warnerism. "Let us sincerely hope that his recent troubles and misfortunes will now be the last," continued the *Gujarati*, "and that no other countryman of ours will ever be made to undergo such ill-deserved prosecution or be made the victim of such heartless persecution."

The *Oriental Review* remarked that the Tilak case, in its unrevised stages, was one of the most extraordinary miscarriages of justice that had been known in India. It added that Mr. Tilak had to thank his stars that the times had changed and that, although there were probably still in India a plentiful crop of would-be Hastings, the Supreme Courts were no longer dominated by Judges of the stamp of Impey and it might add, of Jeffreys.

"Mr. Tilak's character has shone forth more brilliantly," glowed the *Amrita Bazar Patrika*, "like gold after being tested by fire. But the blot on the character of Government will not so easily be effaced." "He has had to spend large sums of money," observed the *Hindu*, "to defend himself against an unjust and unrighteous prosecution. He was humiliated in all possible ways, even when there was no necessity or justification for subjecting him to humiliation. And the only satisfaction that he can now have is that the attack on his honour has miserably failed. The Government, which dragged him into this prosecution, is not likely to think of paying him a compensation. Yet it cannot now deny that it has inflicted the cruelest hardship and injustice on him."

The *Indu Prakash* blamed Government for its official imprudence in instituting proceedings against Tilak and said: "The punishment which Mr. Clements inflicted on Mr. Tilak was certainly Draconian. But fortunately his decision was subject to revision by two higher tribunals and did nothing more than astound the public by its enormity."

The citizens of Poona showered congratulations on their leader at a public meeting. Expressing his opinion on the decision, Tilak wrote a detailed editorial on the trial reviewing the whole case and exposed Government's vindictiveness. He averred that the day the High Court decisions were influenced by Government, British rule would vanish in no time.

At another meeting in Poona organised by the institution of promoters of good character, he said that Government squandered on his trial sixty thousand rupees and added that the Government which prosecuted him on the false charges that he had not properly carried out his duties as a trustee, itself could not execute the public trust properly.

At a third meeting summoned for the same purpose, speaker after speaker eulogised him for his stainless and sublime character and other great qualities. Tilak said with a touch of humour that to refute the charges levelled against him by Government there was at least the High Court, but to refute the great qualities the speakers attributed to him there was no court to approach! A similar streak of humour he once showed when he was dictating a note on the Tai Maharaj Case for his paper. The name of Tai Maharaj was required to be repeated and it took much space. So he said with a laugh to his personal assistant, "Look here, we have no space for this big 'Maharaj'. Write Tai and put M. every time after it!"

Thus success came after a struggle. Tilak's character was vindicated, and it was seen how a great man respects his abiding friendship. Tilak spent about thirty thousand rupees from his pocket, and the pressure which these hardships must have exercised on his health and mind was unimaginable. He had to prepare arguments for his lawyers, attend the courts, travel with the Commission examining witnesses at different places, without minding his meals, health or private affairs. At one moment, he felt disgusted with the long teasing boredom and despondently remarked that he had several lawyer friends and yet the case remained long undecided; he had many doctor friends, yet the pain in his knee was not cured! But this was a momentary phase. He stood with all his might, fought out the case with an iron will and unflagging determination, and ultimately frustrated the evil designs cherished by a Government which awaited an opportunity to declare to the world at the top of its voice by quoting the example of Tilak thus condemned, that Indian leaders were devoid of public and private character. Tilak was possessed of sufficient evidence, it is said, that could have damaged the reputation of Tai Maharaj, who basely cast aspersions on his character, but he always refrained from publicly uttering a single harsh word against the wife of a deceased friend.

Tilak soon put in his claim to the Government of Bombay for compensation. That claim for damages, however, was turned down on the plea that it was untenable. Tilak moved the Secretary of State for India, but his move had no resposse. It fluttered in a British paper, and although backed by some sympathisers there and in India by men like Gokhale, it ultimately died out.

Anyway Tilak must have felt a great relief over the crushing defeat of the Government and his ill-wishers. In a light mood which seldom comes over such iron men he went to witness a play *Dandadhari* performed at Aryabhushan Theatre, Poona, by Belgaonkar Theatrical Company consisting solely of actresses. The play had a plot which displayed the conflicting roles of Tilak and Gokhale. Vyankamma, the proprietress of the Dramatic Company, played the role ' Tilak' so perfectly and magnificently that Tilak was overjoyed to see her grand performance on the stage. Tilak on the stage walking, talking and chewing betelnut, moving the scarf over his shoulders, and banging the table, perfectly resembled Tilak the leader! During the interval Tilak addressed the audience, and paying a glowing tribute to the proprietress, said, " Today I have seen my role played here. I do not generally go to the theatre nor do I look in the mirror. But I declare that the excellent performance of today deserves our unqualified praise. You have shown your appreciation of the brilliant role played by the proprietress. I also admire her wonderful acting. I hope some day the familiar face of Gopalrao would be displayed on the stage." "He also is depicted in this," interrupted a voice. " No, this Gopalrao (Gokhale) is our friend and I meet him often." "I mean Gopalrao Agarkar," he said with a strange note in his voice.[2]

---

2 Sathe, V. D., Actor, *Dramatist and the Theatre*, p. 43 (Marathi).

CHAPTER XII

Rise of Extremism

I

TILAK WAS NOW free to give a lead to his people. Fearless thinking and fearless action were now released with greater force. Religion, politics, philosophy, festivals, their origin and usefulness, application and aim, were discussed.

There was a discussion on the relation of theosophy to Hinduism. "Theosophy," observed Tilak, "is not a religion by itself. Theosophy teaches that different people from different religions should live in a brotherly manner and follow their own religion without hating the followers of other religions, always keeping before their mind that the occult and mystic principles of all religions are the same. Theosophy does not ask you to abjure your own religion and embrace another. It is an institution of philosophers who preach to the people to follow the principles of their own religions. Some Theosophists are Hindus, others are Buddhists, some are Muslims or Parsees. Mrs. Annie Besant and Colonel Alcott are the two chief promoters of Theosophy. The former favours Hinduism whereas the latter favours Buddhism. Mrs. Annie Besant conducts a Hindu College while Alcott conducts Buddhist Schools in Ceylon."

Tilak was of the opinion that Hinduism must be interpreted in the light of materialism as was done in the case of Christianity.[1] He gratefully mentioned that theosophists could win back to Hinduism those Hindus who had become apathetic to their religion. He, therefore, criticised those who opposed the national song introduced by Besant in the Hindu College at Banaras. He maintained that just as the Catholics, Protestants, Puritans and such other cults regarded themselves as Christians, so also the Vedantists,

1 The *Kesari*, 29 March 1904.

Shaivas, Vedics, Vaishnavas and such others regarded themselves as Hindus and they must be taught to pride themselves on their *Hindutva*.[2] They were but so many canals dug out from one and the same river, Hinduism.

At this time Tilak had discussions with the deputies of Shankaracharya of Sankeshwar. He asserted that the modern Shankaracharya should be a man educated on modern lines. He must march with the times. He must lead a virtuous life, must be a man of resolute determination, must win the hearts of the people, and deliver speeches at big meetings. Just as in England highly educated persons took orders, so also highly educated men must turn sanyasins and preach religion. He pointed to the great part played by Vivekananda. The question of taking *Prayaschitta* was again reopened after twelve years, and Tilak showed his willingness to abide by the decision of Shankaracharya. At the same time he was thinking of starting a new Dharmasabha.

In April 1904, the descendant of the Chhatrapati of Satara died in Poona. Tilak spent a whole night in meeting authorities and arranging for the safe despatch of the corpse to Satara in a befitting manner. An obliging man by nature, Tilak took great pains in making those arrangements, because the deceased belonged to the dynasty of Shivaji. Tilak had made some efforts to link the Nepal Royal family with the family of Satara Chhatrapati by arranging a marriage of this descendant with the princess of Nepal. But the plan failed like some of his other schemes.

At this time an article by R. P. Paranjpye, Principal of the Fergusson College, appeared in *East and West* in which he laid emphasis on the need for secular instruction in India. Tilak was a believer in religious instruction, so he did not like Paranjpye's views. Kelkar wrote a critical editorial on the subject, but Tilak changed the caption to a virile heading which meant that a crow perching on the dome of a palace cannot be mistaken for an eagle! To Tilak controversy was a war in which an enemy was to be mercilessly attacked; the offence was the best defence in war. Defensive arguments, he said, made a case weak. So Tilak made his case stronger, as it were, by this caption! Fourteen years later when somebody reminded him that the caption of the article still rankled in Dr. Paranjpye's mind, Tilak expressed surprise and added that in public life one should not be so sensitive and that one should follow a give-and-take policy. Indeed Tilak seemed to

2 The *Kesari*, 5 April 1904.

think with Addison that it is folly for an eminent man to think of escaping censure, and a weakness for him to be affected by it!

The first place Tilak visited, after a partial victory in the Tai Maharaj Case, was Junnar where people became delirious with joy on seeing him. In those days it took a long time to reach the place. The reception accorded to Tilak by the people of the town was a memorable one. He was taken out in a procession when a rich man showered pearls on Tilak. Next day a blind follower secretly took away one of Tilak's shoes, and a letter came by the next delivery saying that it was for the purpose of worship that he had stolen it. Tilak often protested against this sort of devotion, but people never paid heed to his advice. Tilak humorously told the people that if a rebel raised a revolt at Junnar, he would have two days' rest till the British army from Poona reached it!

He then paid a visit to Konkan with his family. He attended that year the Nana Fadnavis celebrations at Velas where he bowed in reverence before the old man of the Bhanu family which had produced Nana Fadnavis, the great statesman. Tilak bowed down before the old man's wife also, who was an old lady. This sight brought tears of joy to the eyes of the spectators. He regarded such historic families as sacred links between the past and present, and he showed his reverence whenever he came across them. He told the organisers of the celebrations that the object of such historical celebrations was to attract people of all shades and castes and if a temple was inconvenient for the purpose, then such functions should be held at a place where even Muslims could be present. He then visited Ladghar along with his family to pay his respects to his mother-in-law; for his father-in-law had died some time before.

Tilak's mother-in-law murmured that he should now leave the dangerous field of politics and follow a calm and quiet life. She said Nana, Tilak's father, also never wished him to lead such a life. Tilak respectfully replied that events were taking place according to the spirit of the times. Men's destinies were shaped by a higher power than by their inclinations or aptitudes. It was in the hands of men, he said, to act accordingly. From Ladghar he went to his native village, and paying visits to Dapoli, Harnai and Dabhol, he returned to Poona. In summer Konkan is majestic with its varied kinds of fruit and flowers. This must have had an invigorating effect on his mind. He had a nostalgia for Konkan, and he often said that it was his home. This was the last visit of Tilak to Konkan. In May he took rest at Sinhgad. The pain in his knee still continued.

By this time Pandita Ramabai had assumed the role of an iconoclast. She attacked and ridiculed the ideas of God and Heaven, the worship of the elephant-headed God, of Shaligram and such other gods in Hinduism. As a result of this attack, Tilak, who never openly and freely favoured D. K. Karve's mission of female education, became for a while less apathetic to the great cause which Karve had been championing. He gave publicity to a few of Karve's statements in his paper. Some complained about this time that Besant did not arrange for caste-wise meals in her Hindu College at Banaras. In this controversy too Tilak supported Besant saying that although there might be less rigidity in regard to the observance of caste-wise meals, there was better provision for imparting religious education of Hinduism than there was in Government-aided educational institutions. He further remarked that rejuvenation of Hinduism was beyond the reach of a foreigner like Besant; but it would be sheer ingratitude to belittle the efforts of such persons on that count.

Meantime, Tilak paid a visit to Sankeshwar, the abode of Shankaracharya, concerning the social boycott declared on him by the Poona orthodox, but which had almost died much earlier. So his regard for that religious heritage took him there to discuss the question of his *prayaschitta*. Tilak, a popular leader, spending his energy on such matters was a very strange thing! He was trying to rebuild an institution that had decayed and belonged to a bygone age!

Tilak was now gradually shifting to what the Moderates called Extremism. He was smouldering at the apathy shown by the Moderate leaders towards active politics. They were neither allowing the young leaders to go ahead nor adopting active measures to secure the political advancement of India. The Congress was now nothing more than a lifeless body, a resort for retired lawyers and title-holders, who sought relaxation in it. Far from being the faith of the common man, it had degenerated into the fad of the rich. Orators brandished polished phrases like soldiers polishing their swords for a parade. The path of prayers and petitions had landed the people in sterile wilderness. A cry was now developing that the old order must change. Politics must cease to be the pastime of the old orators and title-holders.

During a private discussion Tilak explained this to his followers in August 1904. He was of the opinion that an intense and active struggle should be launched unitedly both in India and in England voicing the demands of Indians. He reminded them of Lord Curzon's speech which he made at the United Club in London. In that speech Lord Curzon had declared that India would be lost on the floor of the House of Commons. Tilak said that those words were a pointer, and, therefore, he asserted that unless they agitated furiously for about twenty-five years in England also and launched a tremendous struggle in India to support it, the Indian people would not be able to gain their political rights.

Asked about the Irish political movement, Tilak said that compared to India, Ireland had some advantages. In the British Parliament there were eighty representatives of Ireland; Irishmen like Lord Roberts could get high posts and could be even Generals in the British Army. But in one respect India had an advantage over Ireland. In Ireland it was the existence of English landlords that was coming in the way of her attaining political rights. There was no question of British landlordism in India. The landlords in India did not belong to the ruling class.

It was during this discussion that Tilak said that the view that the *Gita* was an allegory hinting at the battle of the five senses, was erroneous. The main idea, he added, was to drive Arjun to fight the Kauravas. Another opinion he expressed was on the *Bhavishyapuran*. He said the infiltration of the word Noah and the stories of Adam and Eve clearly showed that the *Bhavishyapuran* must have been written after the eleventh century, and the stories of Adam and Eve must have been taken from the *Koran*.

Then came the Ganesh festival. There was as usual a revision of and reflection on sacred books and historical events. The institution which Tilak had bestowed on Maharashtra had come to stay. Still the reformers, who were Moderates in politics, were voicing their flickering opposition to the Ganesh festival which was now celebrated in far-off lands like China, Japan and Aden where Maharashtrians resided. Tilak gave the last reply to the opponents of the Ganesh festival which had now become a permanent feature of the religious life of Hindu society in Maharashtra. At the outset he said that Art always rested on a deep and steadfast earnestness of mind and "in every country and in every age a religious festival serves as an occasion for the display of the best output of knowledge and the intuition of the people in the matter of the fine and the aesthetic arts."

Tilak admitted that there might be certain defects and habits in the Melewallas, and they might be corrected; but their honest and strenuous faith could not be doubted. "It is said that the Ganesh festival," continued Tilak, "is an imitation of the Moharrum of the Mohammedans. It is a good point for a critic of the festival to be able to taunt with the remark that though the festival was inspired by a spirit of disagreement with and retaliation upon the Mohammedans, still after all what was substituted for the Moharrum was nothing better than a Hindu edition of it. But a little reflection will show that when the organisers of the festival proposed to divert the mind of the Hindus from the Moharrum, they did not step in as reformers of the *fashion* in which the Moharrum was carried on; they did not create a parting of the ways because Mohammedans were hopelessly inattentive to counsels of reform, but because they wanted to give their Hindu followers a religious festival of their own, and it was but natural that the Hindus entered upon the diversion only with their latest tastes and habits." He then asked the reformers whether the conduct of the service at the Prarthana and Brahmo Samajas unhappily was or was not a poor and wretched imitation of Christian worship in Churches.

As regards references to politics in the songs of the Melewallas, he said: "When we know that even ecclesiastics can make references to controversial matters from the pulpit we do not see why Melewallas are to be debarred from saying a thing or two about the political condition that they see all around them." Referring to the objection raised by the reformers that the language of the songs was abusive or filthy, Tilak said that he had not yet established a strict and regular censorship over the poetical literature that flooded Poona during the festival and added: "When reformers, who have not learnt even the ABC of Sanskrit religious literature, can think themselves competent to sit in judgment over them and bestow rank abuse on our Rishis, surely the Melewalla who ridicules the egg-eating and brandy-drinking reformer, ought not to look presumptuous!"[3]

At this time one more objection to the religious awakening of the Hindu was taken by Tilak's opponents. It was their belief that religious awakening or revival would foment hatred of others and in the end it would be destructive to national unity; for the growth of national solidarity either all religions should disappear or one of them should hold sway over the land. Tilak's reply to them was that there was no example in history in which national solidarity or national prosperity became a certainty because religion was destroyed and people became religionless. Moreover, it would be sheer madness, he continued, to think that only one religion would survive and the others would die down. And supposing it did, it might not guarantee national solidarity; for Europe belonged to one religion and still

3 The *Mahratta*, September 1904.

it was divided. Taking all these things into consideration, he held that it was possible to organise and consolidate all the followers of Hinduism into one unit by means of a religious awakening, without creating a sense of hatred for or opposition to other religionists, as he thought that Hinduism was a great means and force to consolidate the majority of the people of India.

During the Ganesh festival Tilak gave a number of lectures on different topics. At one meeting he delivered a lecture on the Bhagawat Dharma and maintained that the view taken by historian Rajwade that the teachings of the saint-poets had emasculated generations of men and had resulted in the downfall of religion and the country, was not a correct one. He said that the *Bhagwat Gita* was the sacred book of the Bhagawat Dharma in which Lord Krishna taught Arjun to do unto others as he would be done by, and added that even saint Tukaram had said that the worshippers of Vishnu were softer than wax, but they were also strong enough to break even steel. Because of their detachment from the practical world, he asserted, their influence was not felt in the practical world. The disinterestedness, the selflessness and the compassion in the saints aroused in common men devotion to religion and duty.

Dwelling on the Vedanta, he said : "Vedanta means end of the Vedas, i.e. the *Upanishads* begin where the *Vedas* end. The Upanishads contain the knowledge and wisdom of the Rishis. The influence of the Vedanta should be useful for annihilating the 'tama' qualities and raising the good qualities in a man."

At this time Shivrampant Paranjpe, the editor of *Kal*, wrote an inflammatory article on the assassination of M. D. Plehve, the Russian Minister of Interior. He explained the facts about the assassination ' because such murders have an educative value'. He endeavoured to differentiate between 'political murders' and common murders and asserted that the assassination of ' a king as an exalted functionary' was a laudable object, a kind of surgical remedy, and in the other half of the article he reverted from the picture of Plehve's oppressions to Lord Curzon's virtues in a satirical vein. The *Times of India*, the watch-dog of the British Empire, did loyal service to the British Government by inviting the attention of Government to the incitements and elusiveness in this article and to some other extracts from the old issues of the *Kal*, a paper of some celebrity and considerable circulation which the *Times of India* had described in earlier days as a rag, and further opined that the time seemed to have arrived when Government could take suitable action against the *Kal* for such writings. There was again a great hubbub in the Anglo-Indian papers, and replies and rejoinders to them appeared in the nationalist papers.

Tilak wrote an article entitled ' The Marathi and the English Times', for in Marathi *Kal* means 'Times'. Tilak devoted a whole issue to this controversy quoting Hyndman's article side by side with Paranjpye's. Tilak observed that he did not subscribe to some of the socialistic views of Paranjpye and added that the *Times of India* and the British rulers might take any view of his socialistic ideas. But the fact remained that Curzonism was day by day tightening the grip of slavery and if that policy continued unopposed, it would no doubt prove harmful to the interests of the British Empire as predicted by the *Kal* or Mr. Hyndman. Tilak described the *Times of India* as a villain who poisoned the ears of Government, and reminded it of its apology to him. He added that a dog's tail cannot be made straight however long it might be kept in a tube. Tilak fearlessly stated that they had not started papers to endorse the likes and dislikes of Government. They would not mind if they incurred displeasure by their severe criticism of Government. The papers would not be able to justify their existence, he said, if they did not frankly and fearlessly criticise Government for its oppressive rule. He warned that if they failed to do so, it would ultimately be prejudicial to the interests of the rulers and the ruled.

The editor of *Kal*, however, was not prosecuted. The elusiveness and the indirect violence of the opinion of Paranjpye must have remained beyond the pale of sedition, and his explanatory article on the situation might have easened the situation. His reference to Curzon, however, was not unintentional. There was a plot to murder Curzon, and Aurobindo, Poet Tagore, Charu Chandra Dutt, his father-in-law Mullik, the famous Japanese author and artist Baron Okakura and Sunren Tagore were involved in it. But it did not materialise.[4] Wamanrao Palande, who was a confidant of Tilak, later confessed in the Nasik Murder Case that he had attempted on the life of Curzon.[5]

As the Congress of 1904 was drawing near, its leaders began to take a lively interest in it. The Congress had not made much progress during the past two years. The message which Hume had sent forth on the eve of the Madras Congress of 1903 had left the Congress leaders unaffected.

4 Dutt, Charu Chandra, (I.C.S.), was then a judge in Maharashtra. His article in the *Mahratta* dated the 1 August 1952.

5 The *Kesari*, 22 June 1967.

Pherozeshah Mehta had already read the address of the President-elect of the Madras Congress and decided to forestall his attack on the old guard of the Congress. So while moving the proposition for the election of the President at the Madras Congress, he assured the Congress delegates that he himself had never been autocratic in his conduct as a leader. The President of the Madras Congress was Lal Mohan Ghose, who was by constitution and temperament a student and a recluse. He said he was not associated with the factions and cliques which had caused and were still causing considerable mischief by sowing dissension and discord among public men. Lal Mohan Ghose further said he was surprised that Mehta should have so readily applied to himself Gibbon's description of the Roman Tribune Baroucelli that "he spoke the language of patriots and trod in the footsteps of despots." The old guard tried their level best to stem the tide of nationalism which they styled extremism; for, Tilak, its Napoleon, was not in the battle-field! He was busy fighting the Tai Maharaj Case and had not attended the Congress sessions of 1902 and 1903.

But on the eve of the Bombay Congress, Tilak came forward and openly declared that if the Congress leaders were not going to take to agitation with unflagging zeal and undivided devotion, they should close down that farce. The effect of Tilak's propaganda in the words of C. Y. Chintamani, was that the majority of the thinking people in Maharashtra refused to subscribe to the Congress fund for the ensuing Congress. Someone brought this to the notice of Dadabhai who was then in London. He appealed in his private letter to Tilak not to attack the Congress leaders in that vein and weaken the Congress in a way that would jeopardize its existence; for, he held that a split in the Congress at that stage meant a disaster for the country. Dadabhai wrote to Hyndman also : "If you write anything to attack and disparage the Congress, you will weaken and discourage the only body through whom India has to work out its redemption!"[6] This was indeed a paradox! Tilak strove to instil life in the Congress, but was deemed to be its destroyer owing to a misunderstanding of his motives.

On the eve of the Congress session which was held in Bombay in December 1904, Sir William Wedderburn also wrote an article in *India* suggesting that there should be a political mission for India in England. Otherwise resolutions alone would not be able to achieve anything; just

---

6 Masani, R. P., *Dadabhai Naoroji*: The *Grand Old Man of India*, p. 442.

as solicitors alone would not be able to do anything unless there was an advocate to defend the arguments made out by the solicitors.

Tilak said that the stand taken by Pherozeshah Mehta was not correct. To assemble for two days, to pass some resolutions focussing the attention of Government on the demands contained in them and to go home, leaving the rest to be done by the newspapers all the year round, was the idea of Congress work conceived by Mehta. Tilak averred that the aim of the Congress could not be accomplished unless they strove ceaselessly for its accomplishment. Before the Bombay Congress met, Tilak again wrote an editorial earnestly appealing to Congress leaders to take up the cause with resolute determination. He said that if they wanted to propagate their cause let them send a deputation to England, and if they wanted to support men like Sir Henry Cotton, Mr. Schwann, Sir John Jardine, let the Congress leaders go to England and strengthen the hands of those benefactors.

Meantime, Tilak visited Baroda on some business where he was pressed to deliver a lecture on Jainism at the Conference of the Shwetambar Jains. He had taken his lodgings at the house of his friend Sharangpani, a Judge of the Baroda Court. The Judge went to the club at night. Tilak had to address the meeting of the Jains, so he took hurriedly a seat and asked his friend's wife to serve him food. Astonished by the unusual familiarity shown by his eminent friend, on his return home the Judge friend asked Tilak why he took his meal in a hurry, and inquired whether he had some urgent engagement. Tilak in a friendly gesture said he had to attend a conference. In the Conference he said that the Jains believed in deities and stories from the *Ramayana* and *Mahabharata* and some principles of the Yogashastras. Formerly several men exchanged their Jainism for Vaishnavism, or Vaishnavism for Jainism. They were not foreigners only because they did not believe in the *Vedas*. They were the brethren of the Aryans. The difference between them was not much from the viewpoint of nationalism; just as there was not much difference between the established Church and the non-conformists of Christianity.[7]

The Congress session was held under the presidentship of Sir Henry Cotton in Bombay in the last week of December 1904. It met under the gloom created by Lord Curzon's policy, rightly characterised in the official report of the Congress as 'repressive' and 'reactionary'. Tilak went to Bombay to attend the session. He met Mehta and Cotton and interviewed

7 The *Kesari*, 13 December 1904.

Wedderburn who had also come to Bombay with Cotton, and discussed the future of the Congress. When Tilak entered the pandal the delegates and visitors accorded him an enthusiastic welcome, the Muslim leader Mahamed Bhimji taking a lead in shouting ' jai' to Tilak Maharaj.

Pherozeshah Mehta, Chairman of the Reception Committee, welcoming the guests, said: "To those who decry the moneys spent upon the Congress as moneys wasted on a show and a 'tamasha', I would say, they are not men of real insight and true imagination. ... If you realise it clearly and fully, there is no purpose more important, no mission more sacred than the one the Congress fulfils in the three short days to which it confines its session. . . . We delegates, representatives of the people, meet together at the end of the year to give voice to the public opinion of the country taking shape and formulating throughout the year, to present our petition of Rights, our Giant Remonstrance, our appeal and our prayer for a firm and unaltering grasp of a policy of wisdom and righteousness.

"But we are told that we have done this for long and we have done this in vain. I absolutely dispute both these propositions. . . . To estimate the position rightly, let me lay before you the confession of faith of a devout and irreclaimable Congressmen like myself. I accept British rule, as Ranade did, as dispensation so wonderful . . . that it would be folly not to accept it as a declaration of God's will." He maintained that the record of the Congress left no room for disappointment or despair, and apart from the material achievement, the greatest triumph of the Congress lay in awakening the soul of the nation.

This was a reply to Dadabhai, Hume, Wedderburn and Tilak!

Sir Henry Cotton in his Presidential address emphasized that the Congress was the voice and brain of the country, and its function was "to give united and authoritative expression to the views on which there is already a consensus of opinion in the country."

The President approvingly quoted Mountstuart Elphinstone who conceived "that the administration of all the departments of a great country can never be contemplated as a permanent state of things." Sir Henry Cotton further declared that the ideal of an Indian patriot was the establishment of a federation of free and separate states, the United States of India, placed on a fraternal footing with the self-governing colonies, each with its own local autonomy, cemented together under the aegis of Great Britain. Bringing his speech to a conclusion, he appealed to the leaders to strive constantly and rely upon themselves for the initiation and development of their schemes, and to take to heart the need for a brotherly feeling towards one another and a spirit of veneration and gratitude to their leaders in the national movement.

This Congress protested against Lord Curzon's policy which set at naught the proclamation of Queen Victoria. Speaking at the Congress session on the employment of Indians in the public services, Surendranath Banerjee denounced the statement of Curzon that by environment, heritage and upbringing the Indians were unequal to the responsibilities of a high office under British rule.

The President asked Sir William Wedderburn to move the important resolution asking the Congress to send a deputation to England to bring the claims of India before the electors in Britain in the ensuing election. Tilak seconded the resolution moved by Sir William Wedderburn and said that they were directing the rays of public opinion to illuminate the hearts of the bureaucracy that ruled India. Tilak urged that an agitation be made in England, for there sat the judges who would decide India's case; and as the Government of India was impervious they must reach the English people, and there should be a permanent political mission in England. "Indian Empire," he concluded, "is a dead body and a foreign body; if that foreign body is not assimilated with the British Empire, we shall have to perform a surgical operation and take out that foreign body from the living Empire. I hope such a time will not come. We want the body to be assimilated into a political body of the British Empire. We should have the same rights and the same privileges as the other members of the British Empire have. India should not be allowed to remain a dead weight and a foreign body; it would trouble the body-politic if it is not assimilated with the system." [8]

The Congress recorded an emphatic protest against the proposed partition of Bengal as it aimed at shattering the unity and undermining the feelings of solidarity. The Congress also demanded that each Province of India should be entitled to return at least two Members to the House of Commons.

During the Congress days Tilak was also busy with the preparation of a common Almanac for India. A conference was held under the presidentship of Shankaracharya near the Babulnath Temple, Bombay. Tilak's friend Madhavrao Bodas had collected some material at different

---

8 Kulkarni, A. V., *The Last Eight Years of Lokamanya Tilak*, pp. 381-82 (Marathi—1909).

places during his tours, in Northern India, which he had undertaken for the purpose. At Banaras, Munshi Madhavlal had called a meeting in October 1904 to consider the question. Astronomers and astrologers from all parts of India attended this Bombay Conference and the decision they took was far-reaching in the preparations of a common Almanac.

Recollecting his memoirs about the Congress session, Sir Henry Cotton later said in his *Indian and Home Memoirs* that " Bal Gangadhar Tilak was there, and he had his following, but there was no division then of the community into extremists and moderates." Sir Henry Cotton, however, forgot to mention that a revolt had broken out against the Congress autocrat Mehta. Lajpat Rai and Lala Murlidhar resented the overbearing attitude of Mehta as he was not in favour of any constitution for the Congress. When the question was being discussed in the Subjects Committee, Lajpat Rai was busy talking with some delegates at a distance. Mehta inquired about Lajpat Rai and said angrily that men like him remained absent at the time of the discussion and afterwards criticised him behind his back. When Lajpat Rai heard of this remark, he rushed to the Subjects Committee and sharp remarks were exchanged. The Punjab lion roared that the Bombay group was opposing the Congress having any constitution.

The Congress session over, Cotton led a Congress deputation to present to Lord Curzon personally a copy of the resolutions passed at the Congress. Lord Curzon, however, declined to meet the Congress deputation led by Henry Cotton on the ground that he was not willing to set a bad precedent for his successors. But Lord Balfour, Prime Minister of Great Britain, in a reply to Dadabhai said that Lord Curzon declined to receive the President of the Congress 'for the purpose of discussing the resolutions'.

The proceedings of this Bombay Congress mark the rise of extremism in the Congress. The mild constitutionalists, who accepted British rule as a divine dispensation, were called the Moderates. They were led by Pherozeshah Mehta and G. K. Gokhale. The militant constitutionalists, who refused to believe in the doctrine of divine dispensation and were fearless spearheads, were called the Extremists. They were led by Tilak and were supported by the virile leadership of Lala Lajpat Rai. This new type of leadership was pulsating with a militant form of agitation and a boundless love of energy, activity and self-sacrifice. The first phase of the Congress life had come to an end. It had served as a school of political education for the whole country and had promoted a sense of national unity. This was the last Congress which kept to its tradition of seeking boons from Britain, with eyes intent on the goodness of British statesmen.

An impetus to this smouldering nationalism was given also by Lord Curzon. Having gained distinctions at Oxford and Trinity, he had won a high reputation for industry, knowledge, self-reliance and power of speech with his classic tongue when he worked as Under-Secretary for India and Under-Secretary for foreign affairs. His pretensions to love of India, its history, its Government, the complexities of its civilization and people, dwindled, and on his arrival in India his real self dominated his policy and actions; his cool insolence and courage in defying public opinion came to the surface. His love of efficiency and exploitation began to have full play. He introduced a change in the currency and reduced the number of members of the Calcutta Municipality against a popular protest. He set up several Commissions. He made new laws such as the Punjab Land Alienation Act which prohibited the transfer of land to anyone but agriculturists, the object being to prevent the expropriation of peasants by money-lenders. He created the North-West Frontier Province, held the expensive Darbar and imposed crushing restrictions upon the press by introducing the Official Secrets Act. He passed the Universities Act and restricted the freedom of Universities.

Yet some of his bold acts won him respect. He denounced a British battalion some privates from which were believed to have outraged a native woman to death at Rangoon and remained undetected. He did more than any of his predecessors to preserve historical monuments, architecture and ancient memorials.

But no other act of Curzon raised such a stormy wave as did his speech which he delivered on February 11, 1905, at the time of the convocation of Calcutta University when he said that truth took a high place in the moral code of the West before it had been similarly honoured in the East. Referring to the Epics of Hindusthan, he added that truth was often found extolled in them as a virtue but very often praise was given to successful deception practised with an honest aim. The *Amrita Bazar Patrika* pulled up the Viceroy by publishing an extract from his book *Problem of the Far East* in which he had colourfully described the lies he told to the President of the Korean Foreign Office about his age, his marriage and other things. The *Amrita Bazar Patrika*, added that in the second edition the interview with the Korean President had been discreetly omitted. Tilak, too, wrote an article saying that it was evident that apart from the incapacity of Lord

Curzon to understand the *Mahabharat*, the maximum good in it could have no effect upon Curzon's mind and like a serpent he took milk and vomitted poison. Referring to Max Müller's essay *India, What can it teach Us?*, Tilak asked whether Lord Curzon had in his mind the expressions 'Machiavellian Policy', and 'Perfidious Albion' meaning 'Treacherous English Nation' when he used the expression 'Oriental Diplomacy'.

In the last week of January 1905, Tilak purchased the famous Gaikwad Wada from the Maharaja of Baroda. The site was known to have been a haunted place although for some time it had been used for a hospital. Tilak spent about thirty thousand rupees on its repairs and made some alterations in it according to his requirements. The stories of ghosts at the place and its general appearance were so terrible that the first watchman at the gate went mad through his fear of ghosts.

A few days after, Tilak performed the marriage ceremony of his youngest daughter Mathubai with Shrirangrao Sane. A large number of people were treated to a party. Some familiar guests took delight in making Tilak angry and laughed at the repartees made by him. While distributing gifts among Brahmins Tilak asked them to recite the *richas* from the *Vedas* and detected their mistakes in accents, omission of words and in other respects, to the surprise of his guests.

When Tilak was in such a good humour he poked fun at children. He felt a peculiar joy in whirling his children or grand-children by their arms and in patting his eldest son when he was inattentive!

Events were now fast moving. Just at this time the Moderates denounced Lord Curzon at a meeting in Bombay and decided to send Gokhale and Jinnah to England as the representatives of Bombay on the Indian deputation. Tilak supported the selection of Gokhale, but expressed his disapproval of the selection of Jinnah as he was politically a raw recruit. In those days it was the ambition of Jinnah to be the Muslim Gokhale of India!

Then came the annual Shivaji festival. It was now celebrated in Bengal and Madras, and its waves reached Japan and China. At Tokyo the Indian students observed the celebrations, and eminent men of Japan and the Philippines made speeches appreciating the spirit of the students and the greatness of Shivaji.

In the first week of May 1905, Tilak spoke at a meeting held in the Ganesh Theatre which was crowded to the utmost capacity by an anxious and enthusiastic crowd. In the introductory remarks he said the real festival was that which helped the progress of the people. People should, at least once a year, think over the condition of their nation and if it was not satisfactory they should work out the remedies for removing the defects. Shivaji anniversary was such a day which provided for political thought.

Tilak maintained that Shivaji had killed Afzulkhan not because he was a Muslim but because he was an obstacle in the way of national progress. Otherwise Shivaji could not have sent back the wife of Afzulkhan to Vijapur with due honour.[9]

Shivaji did not harass the non-Hindus on the count of religion. He fought against the tyranny of the rulers who happened to be the Muslims and whose rule had proved to be oppressive to the Hindus, he concluded.

On the same subject Tilak said at a meeting in Poona that the spirit that guided Shivaji's policy was the love of his country although patriotism and nationalism were the new names for it. The idea of divorcing religion from politics was of recent growth. The main object of Shivaji in founding a new State was not to become a champion of the Brahmins and cow-protection. He neither gave dinners to Brahmins, nor started stables for cow-protection. Protection of Brahmins and cows was the outcome of the establishment of Swaraj. A king could bring about changes. What one man could do, could be done by the people's struggle.

Impressing upon the people the significance of the national role Shivaji played in building up the nation, Tilak now drew their attention to an epoch-making event in the history of Asia, in fact world history! Presiding over a meeting in Poona on June 4, 1905, he congratulated the Japanese on their victory over Russia and dwelt at length upon the effect the war had and would have on affairs in the Far East and on the fact that it exploded the myth of European supremacy over Asia! Gokhale did not attend this meeting as he was not in favour of such a demonstration. The victory of Asiatic Japan over European Russia had had an inspiring effect upon the Indian leaders. Babu Surendranath Banerjee expressed similar thoughts at that time: "The sun has arisen in the East. Japan has saluted the rising sun. That sun, in its meridian splendour, will pass through our country." Tilak had written many articles during the latter part of 1904 emphasizing the point that Japan had shown by her grit and courage that an Asiatic country could cry a halt to the Western powers and defeat them. Tilak had

9 The *Kesari*, 16 May 1905.

also collected money and sent it to the Japanese Relief Fund Committee at Bombay.

A few days later Tilak held discussions with some scholars on the translation of the Vedas. It was his opinion that the Vedas contain Chaldean words as the Sanskrit of later times contains Dravidian words, and he added that the description of magic had much to do with Chaldean thought and culture.

CHAPTER XIII

The Age of Boycott

I

IN JULY 1905, Lord Curzon, the Governor-General of India, finally announced the partition of Bengal and aroused the dormant spirit of nationalism in India. Strong and persistent opposition had been voiced since its inception, but in the face of all opposition Curzon decided to partition Bengal.

Ostensibly, the object of partitioning Bengal was the convenience of administration, but the real object was to cripple the growing solidarity of the Bengalees and to crush the rising movement in Bengal by dividing its political forces, and setting one community against another. Support for the formation of East Bengal was expected from the Muslims in the belief that being in a majority in the new Province they would have considerable advantage.

Curzon's insolent disregard of the wishes of the people and his callous apathy towards their protests goaded them to the verge of madness. The cup of bitterness and humiliation, which had been already filled, now overflowed. In order to attract the attention of the British people to the grievances of Bengal, her leaders launched a widespread agitation and clamoured for the reversal of the proposed partition. August 7, 1905, was observed as a day of mourning all over Bengal, and four meetings protesting against the partition were held in the Town Hall and its compound at Calcutta. The *Bengalee* and the *Amrita Bazar Patrika* issued their numbers with black borders. A large number of meetings were held to denounce the partition of Bengal; petitions were sent to the British Parliament.

Simultaneously, the Indian agitation in England took a new and definite turn when Shyamji Krishna Varma founded in July 1905 his India House which was soon to develop into a hot-bed of the Indian revolutionary movement. Born of a poor family by name Bhansali, this great patriot by sheer force of his energy and industry became the right-hand man of Swami Dayananda Saraswati, went to England through the influence of Prof. Monier Williams, obtained the B.A. degree at Cambridge, was called to the bar, and at the instance of the Secretary of State for India represented India at the Berlin Congress of Orientalists. On his arrival in India he served three Indian States successfully, and upon a tussle with the ruler of Junagadh he left India for good. He was an admirer of Tilak, and although an eminent social reformer, he was greatly influenced by Tilak's fervent nationalism. He started the *Indian Sociologist* in London and became known as the stormy petrel of Indian nationalism in Europe. Few expended money, time and labour on the freedom movement of India as this man of learning and sterling patriotism did.

An obituary note by Tilak in the *Kesari* on Mr. Brewin, the assistant to I.G.P. (C.I.D.), who had been entrusted with the secret inquiry into the Chapekar Case of 1897 and the criminal case in which Tilak was involved by Aston, became the subject of criticism in some circles. On both occasions Brewin had resisted the temptation of incriminating Tilak for the mere gain of higher posts. He held Tilak in high esteem and he had once remarked, "Take away Tilak and Poona is nothing". That had been particularly noted by Tilak and in an appreciative tone, he praised the ability of the Anglo-Indian officer. It was very queer that Tilak should take note of the death of a British Officer. So far Tilak had never favoured intelligent people taking up Government service. Yet he always demanded high posts for Indians. He wanted first-rate men to take up the cause of the nation, and yet he had friends in Government service and was on cordial terms with them. He meant that in whatever field one chose to serve, life should be spent with an eye to the ultimate good of the nation.

The law suit pending in the Civil Court in connection with the adoption of Jagannath Maharaj came up for hearing, and Tilak went with the Commission to Amraoti to examine Khaparde. While in Amraoti, he delivered in the second week of August 1905 a speech on 'Old and New Empires'. Distinguishing the old empires from the new, he said that the ancient Hindu Empires were contented with the acceptance of their sovereignty by the conquered states. The horse sacrifice was a method for establishing this sovereignty. The Hindu Empires never interfered with the internal or local administration of the conquered states. The ancient Roman Empire did not grant equal citizenship to the conquered people.

The modern empires interfered with internal administration. Concluding his remarks, he said that the British Empire was exploiting India ; but one day it would surely vanish and at that time India must not be weak and unprepared, otherwise it would fall an easy victim to the aggression of another nation.

Tilak then visited Yeotmal on pressing invitation from younger leaders. Addressing a meeting for women at Yeotmal, he said that he was not in favour of the Western type of education for Indian women. Western women took service in offices, but it was not proper for Indian women to follow suit. He then paid a visit to the office of the vociferous paper the *Harikishor*. Tilak found that Gosawi, the proprietor of the paper, stood abashed at the poverty of his office. The patriot-proprietor was relieved from embarrassment when Tilak remarked that one should not be ashamed of one's poverty; what one should be ashamed of was one's vices!

At another public meeting in Yeotmal, Tilak impressed upon the audience that the world valued not opinions but resolution. If the people persisted in their struggle with a resolute will God would crown their efforts with success. "God does not appear for the protection of the rightcous and the destruction of the wicked," he said, "unless the people create certain conditions for His work and His deeds. That is the essence of the principle of Hero-Worship. A match alone cannot make a lamp burn. The lamp needs oil and wick as well." In the same month Tilak visited Belgaum on the occasion of the Ganesh festival. He addressed a meeting at the Market. Although rain was pouring down in torrents, people heard him eagerly. It was very characteristic of him that he refused to shelter himself under an umbrella. Tilak had a talk with Gangadharrao Deshpande's father and congratulated him on his bold stand in allowing his son to serve the country.

As regards the Swadeshi movement, Tilak emphasized the point that unless the people began to use articles manufactured in the country there would be no encouragement to the producers. It was foolish to wait till all articles were available in the country. The rulers had two prominent traits in them, the trader and the politician. If the one was pressed, he concluded, the other was bound to be affected.

The agitation over the partition of Bengal stirred up fervent nationalism all over India. It captivated young and old alike. The student community was being galvanized into action by zealous appeals to patriotism, self-respect and self-reliance. Youth began to think of adopting drastic measures against Government, and they clamoured for an active agitation.

This agitation took the form of a boycott of British goods, although it was claimed by its originators that it was not anti-British. Its natural culmination was encouragement of indigenous products. All this resulted in the fall of the prestige of the Moderates, the old leaders of the Congress, and led to the rise of a new leadership. No other leader was so happy over this growing tension caused by the cool insolence of Lord Curzon as Tilak who had described Lord Curzon as Aurangzeb. He saw in Curzon's proclamation a life's opportunity to rouse the nation to a man.

Lord Curzon had sharp differences with Lord Kitchener over the appointment of a new Military Supply Member to the Viceroy's Council. The British Government supported Kitchener's view and Lord Curzon tendered his resignation on August 12, 1905. Yet Curzon decided to give practical effect to the proposal of partition and made a proclamation from Simla on September 1, 1905, appointing Sir Andrew Frazer Lieutenant-Governor in Calcutta and Sir Bampfylde Fuller Lieutenant-Governor in Dacca. The partition came into force from October 16, 1905; and the day was observed all over India as a day of penance, fasting and sorrow.

II

TILAK WROTE ARTICLES discussing the policy of boycott and said it was the duty of Maharashtrians to back up Bengal, endorse their views at meetings in every town, and give support to its agitation. He asked young men not to mind an old man here or a loyalist there habituated to English cloth voicing notes of dissent. A boycott on a national scale was the proper remedy, but its results depended upon their actions and not upon words. In another article in the *Kesari* he said if it was unavoidable to use a foreign article, they should give preference to articles produced in Asiatic countries and the next preference should be given to other European countries and America. Tilak gave an impetus to the Swadeshi movement addressing students' meetings in Poona and saw D. E. Wacha to induce the Bombay millowners to support the movement by providing dhotis at moderate rates to the people.

The Poona students also were roused and Vinayakrao Savarkar, their leader, decided to give a lead to the Swadeshi movement. By now Savarkar, who had established a revolutionary society early in 1900, when he was hardly sixteen, had come to the forefront in Maharashtra as a rising leader of about seven hundred youth initiated into the revolutionary party called the Abhinava Bharat. An inspiring poet, a brilliant writer and a wonderful orator, he was a rare combination of a rationalist thinker and a revolutionary leader. He made great preparations for a bonfire of foreign clothes in Poona. Savarkar stimulated the people into action by his thrilling speeches. A cartload of clothes was taken in procession on October 7, 1905, the Dassera Day, a day that has been observed every year for centuries by the Hindus and especially by the Mahrattas for inaugurating great enterprises and deeds of bravery. The procession terminated at the Lakdi Pool in Poona where fire was set to the heap of clothes.

After Paranjpe had spoken at the meeting in his scorching vein, Tilak too delivered a speech before the bonfire. In that speech he said that according to Hindu rites a deed was to be performed in the presence of sacred fire. It was good that the students took a vow to use Swadeshi clothes. Some might say that instead of burning those clothes they could have been put to a better use by distributing them amongst the poor ; and their suggestion was not entirely wrong. But he held that the effect the bonfire would have upon the minds would be more lasting than the effect the distribution of the clothes would create. Moreover, whatever things they desired to give away to others should be good. It was good to put their sin into the sacrificial fire. On an auspicious day, he observed, they had begun the struggle for the success of Swadeshi manufacturers, and it would be crowned with success in course of time if the youth took it upon themselves to pursue it with unremitting energy. He said it was not proper to expect the old leaders to continue the struggle any more, for they had become tired.

This was the first bonfire of foreign cloth in India. It had far-reaching repercussions on Indian politics. Savarkar the originator and leader of the bonfire was rusticated from the hostel of Fergusson College, and he was fined for this bold venture in order that he should be moderate in his views. The amount of Savarkar's fine was paid promptly by students and the public, and the nationalist press all over India furiously denounced the college authorities, Tilak declaring that "these surely are not our Gurus". At a Bombay meeting which was held in the last week of October 1905, Tilak announced his intention of starting a Co-operative Stores in Bombay for the sale of swadeshi goods, on the next Hindu New Year's day. At a public meeting in Poona he supported the students, justifying the part taken by them in the Swadeshi movement.

The partition came into force from October 16, 1905. As a protest the people had a dip in the Ganges, wore ribbons on their wrists symbolic of their unbroken ties of brotherliness, and observed a fast. But the ribbon proved literally a red rag to John Bull. As a symbol of their undivided brotherliness they laid the foundation of a new building, the Federation Hall, in Calcutta.

In 1889, at the time of the Congress session, students had collected subscriptions for the Congress. Tilak advised the students not to take part in politics and some days after the bonfire he again expressed his opinion that students should devote themselves to studies. His real motive was that students should be imbued with the spirit of patriotism and should be taught to take interest in national movements and obtain knowledge of public institutions; so that they might be able to discharge properly their public duties and manage the affairs of their own country, but at the same time he advised the students not to neglect their studies.

He once told a youth that there were two sides to the political movement; one was the statistical or investigation line wherein facts and figures regarding the condition of the country and the various problems arising annually were to be collected, analysed and evaluated. The other was the propaganda line. For years to come the war with the rulers would continue, on the intellectual plane. What, however, was more important than statistics was readiness to suffer and even to die for the country. "I want young men to develop their will more than their intellect. A combination of these two would be, of course, an ideal thing." [1] He stated that some years before earlier, Lajpat Rai and he wanted to start an institution wherein young men could train themselves for national work. But the idea was given up.[2]

Lord Minto arrived in Bombay on November 18, 1905, to take the place of Lord Curzon, who was so sullen that he had cancelled the military reception to his successor. Minto had been Governor-General of Canada for six years (1898-1904) and wore four war medals on his chest.

Their Majesties the Prince and Princess of Wales were also to come to India for the Delhi Darbar which was to be held on December 12, 1905.

Tilak was compelled at the time to castigate the Bombay leaders for their action which was devoid of self-respect. On the eve of the visit of the Prince of Wales some of the Bombay leaders showed over-enthusiasm and asked the people to whitewash and decorate their houses and celebrate the occasion of the visit of the Prince of Wales. Tilak said that these

---

1 *Reminiscences and Anecdotes about Lokamanya Tilak*, Vol. II, pp. 640-41.

2 Ibid, p. 641.

leaders were going too far, and their conduct did not spring from loyalty but shamelessness. It was unfair, he said, to impose such conditions and burdens on the poor people. He hoped, he said sarcastically, that in their extreme zeal the Bombay leaders would supply the poor with wheat-flour, jaggery and face-powder so that people would present a gay and happy appearance on the occasion of the visit of the Prince of Wales!

III

GOKHALE, WHO HAD then been sent to England on deputation, worked there feverishly. He made forty-five speeches in nine days and impressed the British statesmen. The British newspapers paid tributes to his gift of the gab. This successful mission and his long splendid service to India and the Congress came to be recognised. While he was in England his name was announced in India as the President-elect of the Indian National Congress. Lala Lajpat Rai, who worked with Gokhale, also rendered great service to India. When, therefore, he returned from Europe, Tilak met him in Bombay. " Tilak", said Lajpat Rai afterwards, "was the first to welcome me back to Bombay, and to express an appreciation of the work I had done in England and approval of the views I had expressed there."[3] Lajpat Rai's impression about the English people was that they were busy with their own problems, the Liberal Party declined to make Indian reforms a party question, and the only way to win the consideration of the English people was to prove the determination and self-reliance of Indians themselves.

Gokhale returned to India on December 9, 1905, and Poona accorded him a grand welcome. Tilak was pleased with the work of Gokhale and took an active part in welcoming him back to Poona. Gokhale, therefore, returned the courtesy by paying a visit to Tilak's Gaikwad Wada.

In the evening a mass meeting was held in Poona to congratulate Gokhale on his brilliant mission in England. Gokhale had fearlessly told the British public of the necessity of introducing a change in the outlook on India. This was a rare occasion when Tilak publicly honoured Gokhale. In 1902, they both were present at a meeting held in Poona when Tilak insisted that Gokhale should preside over that meeting. To the pleasant surprise of the people Tilak was seen repeating his request that Gokhale should take the chair and Gokhale saying that Tilak should take it. People were overjoyed to see Tilak honouring Gokhale and paying regard to him.

---

3 *Reminiscences and Anecdotes about, Lokamanya Tilak,* Vol. II, p. 661.

At this meeting Tilak paid a full-throated tribute to Gokhale saying that it was given to Gokhale to turn to account any change in the interests of India with his sweet, flowing tongue and charming methods. Gokhale had successfully refuted the points raised by the British spokesmen of the Indian administration and created a favourable impression on the British people, he added while moving the main resolution congratulating Gokhale.

Tilak and Gokhale had their differences. Gokhale was Ranade's political heir. He derived inspiration from Ranade who believed in social equality and social justice but who welcomed British rule as a divine dispensation. Tilak was self-luminous and self-made. Gokhale criticized the Government in a parliamentary vein, whereas Tilak agitated against it and faced imprisonment. Gokhale sought interviews with the spokesmen of the British Government and its representatives in India and interpreted the aspirations of the people, impressing upon them the necessity of introducing reforms. He cooperated with Government where desirable and opposed it where necessary. Gokhale said to the British Government: "We can understand your difficulties, but these measures are neither proper nor justifiable. It is not good for a Government to violate its pledges to the people and flout their aspirations. This will anger them. So, Sir, open your eyes to the realities and grant our demands."

Tilak fought with Government and said : "These are the rights of the people and they must have them." Gokhale tried to understand the ruler's difficulties. Tilak wore the rebel robe and always guarded the interests of the people at any cost. Gokhale's genius being parliamentary and of constitutional nature, his field of action was confined to the Council Chambers, British Parliamentary Committees and lecture halls. Tilak's field of action spread from the Press to mass meetings. The medium of expression of the one was English, whereas that of the other was Marathi, the mother-tongue of the people. One was the man of the classes and the intelligentsia; the other was a man of the people.

Gokhale later became a C.I.E. and was respected by Government. He objected to his being described as a leader of the Opposition in the Legislative Council [4] while the Government branded Tilak as its inveterate foe and yet he was the idol of the people.

Both were teachers in their early life like their other distinguished contemporaries—Surendranath Banerjee, Dr. Ramkrishna Bhandarkar,

---

4 *Speeches of Gopal Krishna Gokhale*, published by G. A. Natesan & Co., p. 395.

B. C. Pal, Pandit Malaviya and Jagadish Chandra Bose. Neither was ever a Government servant. Both were life-long servants of the people. Both wore turbans. Gokhale's dress more or less inclined to that of modern times; Tilak's essentially belonged to the old order and was simple; he was rather indifferent to his dress.

The one was a parliamentary type of orator, the other was a simple but effective speaker. Gokhale was a studious man whereas Tilak was an eminent scholar. By temperament Gokhale was gentle, polite and full of human kindness, a politician who probably never uttered a wounding word in his life. At an obscene expression uttered in his presence he would hang his head in shame. By temperament Tilak was kind, but his thoughts often verged on extremism or revolution and his pen was vitriolic. He did not take notice of an obscene expression if uttered by his colleagues in his presence. It was Tilak's opinion that as long as the private character of a man did not affect his public work, they need not look into his private character.[5]

The motto of one was love and service, that of the other was action and suffering. The goal of Gokhale was 'Self-Government' for India within the British Empire whereas Tilak's goal was 'Swaraj'.

Gokhale worked untiringly to reform the Government. Tilak fought endlessly to replace it! Gokhale said that rebellion, aiding or abetting a foreign invasion and resort to crime, barring these three things all else was constitutional.[6] Tilak once made a pithy remark that "the only constitution we have is the Penal Code",[7] and he sometimes said that if there appeared even a fifty per cent chance for the success of an armed rebellion he would resort to it trusting God to give success to the extent of the remaining half.[8] Gokhale represented a type of statesmen who are useful in a free country for its development, consolidation and democracy. Tilak represented the type of a revolutionary leader whose role was to win back the independence of a nation. Gokhale said of Tilak that had he been born during Peshwa rule, he would have won new territories.

After visiting some places in the Satara District, Tilak went to Bombay towards the middle of December 1905, to look into the arrangements for

---

5 *Reminiscences and Anecdotes about Lokamanya Tilak*, Vol. Ill, p. 135 (English Section).

6 *Speeches of Gopal Krishna Gokhale*, pp. 1105-06.

7 C. R. Das in *Reminiscences and Anecdotes about Lokamanya Tilak*, Vol. II, p. 623.

8 *Reminiscences and Anecdotes about Lokamanya Tilak*, Vol. I, p. 26.

the defence of the editor of *Bhala*, Bhaskar Balwant Bhopatkar, who was charged with sedition. He was later sentenced to six months' imprisonment. Any man who stood in danger of being punished by the Government because of his political views could naturally look to Tilak for help!

IV

THIS YEAR THE Congress session was to be held at Banaras at a critical moment. The ex-Viceroy Lord Curzon had adopted every possible reactionary measure and gagged the Press. He made education expensive and crippled and mutilated the Universities. Amidst such an atmosphere the Prince of Wales was on a tour of India.

Tilak went to Banaras with his family in the last week of December 1905. He was present at Banaras station to receive the President-elect, Mr. Gokhale, till then the youngest President of the Congress. Tilak's presence at the station attracted an immense crowd and when the President-elect arrived there was a sea of men. Amidst this stifling and crowded atmosphere Sister Nivedita and her companions were striving to have a glimpse of Tilak. They shook hands with Tilak and Sister Nivedita said that upto that time they had heard his name in America but only through his famous works, the *Orion* and the *Arctic Home in the Vedas*. They were happy to see him in person and regarded that day a happy one in their life.

Tilak, now an outstanding figure, ordinarily should have been offered a seat on the dais. But he was not. Tilak's young lieutenants made inquiries into this purposeful insult, but none replied to their queries. To Tilak the cause of the nation was everything; his personal honour was not so important a point.

And when the sky was overcast and the storm was raging, Gokhale took the chair and delivered, to quote Lala Lajpat Rai, an address which was applauded and admired all round as it was the first of its kind from the chair of the Congress ever since it was founded. Like Tilak, he compared Lord Curzon's regime to that of Aurangzeb, indicated the administration of "its utter contempt of public opinion." He cursed British rule, praised the British connection as a blessing and declared that "the goal of the Congress is that India should be governed in the interests of Indians themselves, and that in the course of time a form of Government should be attained in this country similar to what exists in the self-governing colonies of the British Empire".

Gokhale denounced the partition of Bengal as a cruel wrong, inflicted upon the Bengalee brethren, and said it had stirred the country to its deepest depths in sorrow and resentment. "The tremendous upheaval of popular feeling, which has taken place in Bengal in consequence of the partition," he continued, "will constitute a landmark in the history of our national progress." " Bengal's heroic stand against the oppression of a harsh and uncontrolled bureaucracy," he added, "has astonished and gratified all India." As regards the Swadeshi movement, Gokhale observed, it was both a patriotic and an economic movement and that boycott was a political weapon which should be reserved for only extreme occasions.

After this brilliant speech came the time for the real test. The Anglo-Indian papers remarked that even Gokhale had given up Moderate principles, and so they felt despondent. But they breathed somewhat freely when the resolutions were announced. Gokhale was really surrounded by angry billows and the rocks ahead he saw were to be used for the lighthouse of nationalism. Afraid of the rocks, he had wired to Setalwad at Bombay insisting on Pherozeshah's presence at the session. But Mehta could not go.

The Prince of Wales had declined to pay a visit to the Congress, and when the draft of the resolution according a hearty welcome to him came up for consideration, Tilak rose up, like Balaram, with the plough of his opposition. There was a stir among the members of the Subjects Committee when there appeared before them the man with his red turban, swarthy complexion, red Deccan shoes and long flowing white coat with strings. His fearlessness and sincerity were proverbial and were known to all. When he fearlessly opposed the resolution the storm broke out. Munshi Madholal and Pandit Malaviya whose indefatigable exertions had materially contributed to make the session a success "felt that the ground was slipping from under their feet. They saw an abyss which was likely to engulf the Congress and all those who stood by it."[9] Another stout heart arose to support Tilak. It was Lala Lajpat Rai. Tilak and Lajpat Rai were on one side and Gokhale and all the veteran leaders were on the other. The amendments moved by Tilak and seconded by Lajpat Rai were defeated, and so they gave immediate notice of moving them in the open session. There they were sure of their victory.

---

9 Lala Lajpat Rai in *Reminiscences and Anecdotes about Lokamanya Tilak,* Vol. II, p. 662.

The open session was announced for eleven o'clock in the morning. There was an agitation all over the city, both in official and in non-official circles. Rumours of strong action on the part of the Government were afloat, and it was in the air that the Government was going to place a British regiment in close quarters to the pandal for emergency purposes!

Before the commencement of the open session, the compound of the pandal was full of delegates, and visitors were discussing in groups of twos, threes and fives as to what was likely to happen.

President Gokhale came and sent for Lajpat Rai. He appealed to him personally for easing the situation by dropping their amendment to the resolution relating to the Prince of Wales' visit. Although he was not convinced, he agreed to drop it.

"What about Mr. Tilak?" asked Lajpat Rai.

"You are the only person who can manage him. I am confident that you will succeed where others will not," said Gokhale.

"Supposing I manage Tilak, and we manage the Mahrattas and Punjabees, I cannot guarantee about the young leaders of Bengal," answered Lajpat Rai.

"I am sure, you and Tilak can manage the Bengalees," hopefully replied Gokhale.

"All right. I promise you my best support on one condition that the resolution should not be declared to have been passed unanimously," said Lajpat Rai resolutely.

"I agree," said Gokhale.

Upon this Lajpat Rai immediately met Tilak. He suggested to him that as they could not conscientiously be a party to any resolution of that kind, they should not enter the Congress pandal until after the resolution had been passed. Romesh Chandra Dutt also intervened and Tilak agreed to the compromise if the old guard agreed to pass a resolution supporting the boycott measure adopted by the Bengalee leaders. Every time Tilak used his Herculean powers to push the Congress onwards to the goal of nationalism and national struggle. When the leaders showed willingness to meet him halfway he agreed and left them alone. That is why he was praised by all as a democrat of democrats! The Congress passed a resolution declaring that the boycott movement initiated in Bengal was justified under the special circumstances. This was a notable victory achieved by the nascent New Party growing under the banner of Tilak!

In the open session Tilak was asked to move the resolution on Famine, Poverty, Economic Enquiry and Land Revenue. When he came to the dais he was accorded an ovation from all corners of the pandal. Moving the resolution, Tilak said that it was the duty of the Government to deal with the causes of poverty, and to ensure prosperity. "Government," he added, "would not be needed if there were universal well-being, any more than doctors would be wanted if there were no disease."[10]

V

AMONGST THE OTHER activities and meetings at Banaras, Tilak attended a meeting of the Nagari Pracharini Sabha. Expressing his opinions on this vital question, he said at the outset that it was a part and parcel of the National movement to have a common language for the whole of India; for a common language is an important element of nationality. To draw a nation together there was no other force more powerful than to have a common language for all. He pointed out that the opinion of European Sanskritists was that the Devanagari alphabet was more perfect than any which obtained in Europe, and therefore it would bc suicidal to go to any other alphabet in search of a common character for all the Aryan languages in India, and added that its classification and sounds were best suited to represent the different sounds Indians used.

Tilak then emphasized the necessity of introducing in the vernacular school books of each province text lessons in this standard script so that the next generation might become familiar with it from its school days. He hoped that the Government which gave the Indians a standard time and a standard system of weights and measures would not object to lend its help to a scheme which aimed at securing a standard script for all Aryan languages.[11]

Under the auspices of the Bharata Dharma Mahamandala, Tilak addressed a big meeting on the importance of Hindu religion, its existing condition and efforts that were being made to preserve it from decay.

"The word Dharma," explained he, "means a tie and comes from the root *dhru* to bear or to hold. What is there to hold together, to connect the soul with God, and man with man ? Dharma means our duties towards God

10 Besant, Annie, *How India Wrought for Freedom*, p. 430.

11 *Bal Gangadhar Tilak—His Writings and Speeches*, Ganesh & Co., Madras, pp. 27-34.

and duty towards men. Hindu religion as such provides for a moral as well as social tie."

"The term Sanatana Dharma," continued he, "shows that our religion is very old, as old as the history of the human race itself. Hindu religion as a whole is made up of different parts co-related to each other as so many sons and daughters of one great religion. If the idea is kept in view and if we try to unite various sections it will be consolidated into a mighty force."

"A Hindu of this place," observed he, "is as much a Hindu as the one from Madras or Bombay. You might put on different dress, speak a different language, but you should remember that the inner sentiments which move you are the same. The study of the *Gita*, *Ramayana* and *Mahabharata* produce the same ideas throughout the country. Are not these a common allegiance to the *Vedas*, the *Gita* and the *Ramayana*—our common heritage? If we lay stress on it forgetting all the minor differences that exist between different sects, then by the grace of Providence we shall ere long be able to consolidate all the different sects into a mighty Hindu Nation. This ought to be the ambition of every Hindu."

"Buddhism flourished," he proceeded, "and attacks were made on the Hindu religion by Buddhists and Jains. After 600 years of chaos rose one great leader, Shankaracharya, and he brought together all the common philosophical elements of our religion and proved and preached them in such a way that Buddhism was swept away from the land."

"When there is a decay," he remarked, "owing to disunion, when good men are persecuted, then Shri Krishna comes down to save us. There is no religion on the face of the earth except the Hindu religion wherein we find such a hopeful promise that God comes to us as many times as necessary. After Mahomed no prophet is promised, and Jesus Christ comes once for ever. No religion holds such a promise full of hope. It is because of this that the Hindu religion is not dead."

"Our religion," he went on, "is based on truth, and truth never dies. The great characteristic of truth is that it is universal and catholic. It is not confined to any particular race. Hindu religion tolerates all religions. Our religion says that all religions are based on truth, ' you follow yours, I mine'. Shri Krishna says that the followers of other religions worship God though not in a proper form. Lord Krishna does not say that the followers of other religions would be doomed to eternal hell. I challenge anybody to point out to me a similar text from the scriptures of other religions. It cannot be found in any other religions, because they are partial truth while our Hindu religion is based on the whole, the *Sanatana* Truth, and therefore it is bound to triumph in the end."

"There are," explained he, "mainly two forces that are arrayed against us. They are (i) Science and (ii) Christianity. If our religion is threatened with any hostile criticism, it comes from these two. As for the first, a great change is coming over the West and truths that are discovered by them were known to our Rishis. Modern science is gradually justifying and vindicating our ancient wisdom. With the establishment of Physical Research Societies and the expansion of scientific knowledge they have come to understand that the fundamental principles of our religion are based on truth that can be proved. Take an instance, *Chaitanya* pervades everything. It is strictly a Hindu theory. Professor Bose has recently shown that this Vedantic doctrine is literally true according to modern science."

"Take," he declared, "the doctrine of the survival of the soul independent of the body. Doctrines of Karma and Re-incarnation go with it. Spencer never believed in them. But recently it has been one great privilege to see that Sir Oliver Lodge, Mayor and others have declared that the soul does not die with the body; so much now they are convinced of. Modern science accepts the doctrine of Karma if not of re-incarnation. But such is not the belief of Christianity. They hold that God gives a new soul each and every time. Thus it would be seen that a change is coming over the West."

"Now a days," observed he, "Vedanta is not only read but studied by the Americans. No European doctor believes that the beating of the heart can be voluntarily stopped. But it has been proved to the contrary. Vedanta and Yoga have been fully vindicated by modern science and these aim at giving you spiritual union. It is our clear duty, therefore, to follow truth and re-edit our scriptures and place them before the world in the light of modern science that they may be acceptable to all."

"Thus Modern Science," he concluded, "and education are prepared to help you if you take advantage of them, and a time will come when instead of Christians preaching Christianity here we shall see our preachers preaching Sanatana Dharma all over the world."[12]

Tilak visited with his family the famous temple of Kashi Vishweshwar, and as Gokhale did not visit it, people were displeased!

It was the practice of Tilak to meet other provincial leaders during the session and to cement the contact, and political workers were surprised to

12 *Bal Gangadhar Tilak—His Writings and Speeches*, Ganesh & Co., Madras, pp. 35-41.

note that like many a national leader he was not filled with overweening egotism and self-importance. By his courtesy, regard and esteem he held together his compatriots of whatever school of thought or following they might be. In that extremely cold weather of the place he took his meals with only a silken cloth on. When Dr. B. S. Moonje showed a little boldness to take his meal with the usual clothes on, the other leaders followed suit! Tilak had a dip in the Ganges and swam across it. It was here that he took a vow not to use foreign sugar for his tea and he stuck to it.

There was another important meeting at the Town Hall in Banaras to consider a proposal for founding a Hindu College and a Hindu University. Pandit Malaviya was the principal convener of this meeting, and he had prepared a pamphlet containing a passage from the *Mahabharata* describing the object of his proposed university. Promises of a lac of rupees were given on the spot, and Tilak promised to loan the services of Prof. Vijapurkar who was deprived of his post at the Rajaram College, Kolhapur, because he was supposed to have had a hand in the demonstration of the college boys who, in the spirit of the Swadeshi movement, refused to write their answers on foreign paper at the time of their annual examination.

Tilak and his colleague Wasukaka saw Malaviya and asked him about his plans of the proposed university. Malaviya invited them to Allahabad. There they realised that Malaviya was avoiding them. Still Tilak left behind Prof. Vijapurkar, who returned after a few days to Poona when he felt that Malaviya was not responsive. Perhaps Malaviya did not want Tilak to be associated with the proposed University as he was at loggerheads with the Government. At Allahabad Tilak took his lodgings with his son-in-law Dr. S. M. Sane, who was staying at Holkar's Wada. There Tilak came across the Maharaja of Indore. When Holkar asked him why the Congress was not protesting against the sudden deposition of the native Princes by the British Government, he replied that the Congress was there to defend the rights of all; but he asked the Maharaja bluntly why the Congress, the newspapers and other institutions should care at all for the Princes who suppressed the Congress movement in their States!

CHAPTER XIV

Goal of the Congress

I

THE VICTORY OF the Liberal Party at the polls in England raised hopes in the minds of the Indians. When Mr. John Morley became Secretary of State for India, his appointment was received with enthusiasm in India. It was natural that the student of Burke, the disciple of Mill, the friend and biographer of Gladstone should evoke sympathetic ripples in the hearts of educated Indians. It was therefore felt in India that thc philosopher and statesman Morley would act up to his political philosophy. Prior to this appointment Morley had told Parliament that nothing should be done in disregard of the feelings and opinion of the majority of the people. But the Tory Viceroy Lord Minto outran the prudence of the radical Secretary of State for India, and the first statement Morley made removed the illusion. Morley, the apostle of compromise, declared emphatically in the British Parliament that the partition of Bengal was a settled fact, which could not be unsettled; and his recantations were lustily cheered by the Opposition Benches!

Tilak said that Philosopher Morley, who wrote philosophy disinterestedly in a study, was quite a different man from the statesman that he was. Morley was then acting as the Secretary of State for India, and it was preposterous to hope that a statesman, however learned, sympathetic and broad-minded, would do anything towards redressing the political grievances of a nation upon which his countrymen and relatives depended for their livelihood. A man who hoped for such a thing exposed himself to ridicule on account of his ignorance of political morality. People in England might listen with interest to Morley's philosophy in peaceful times, Tilak observed, but if Morley took up the cause of the enslaved people there would break out a fire in which Morley's political life would be burnt to ashes.

Tilak opined that political morality looked to self first and to logic afterwards, if it was convenient for the justification of its policy. So he observed that people would not get their demands and grievances redressed unless they proved to Morley that their capacity for suffering had reached a climax. Nobody ever subsisted on the earnings of a begging bowl. Morley was neither a Tukaram nor a Gladstone who strove for the welfare of Ireland at the risk of his political career.

Tilak encouraged any man whom he considered to be useful for rousing the self-respect of the people. At this time a sanyasin known as Agamya-Guru came to Poona with a European lady disciple to preach the Vedanta philosophy. He was a Punjabee Hindu gentleman who, with the English tongue and sanyasin's dress, had preached his philosophy in Europe, America and Japan. He was the author of a book *Brahmadhara*, and had organised Vedant Committees at some places in England. Although Agamya-Guru made no speech in Poona, his disciple Miss Slade delivered two lectures on Vedanta in Poona. People were attracted more to this cult than to theosophy because the latter had its prophets who were not Indians, and the philosophy propounded by Agamya-Guru was strictly Indian.

This Swami was by temperament an irascible man, who privately upheld the cult of lathi. The students in Poona took some interest in him. So they invited their leader Vinayakrao Savarkar, who was studying law in Bombay, to interview the Swami. But Savarkar and the Swami did not hit it off together. Tilak had a soft corner for this Agamya-Guru and hoped that he would be useful in his struggle in the near future.

In April 1906 the Shivaji festival was celebrated at Raigad on a grand scale. Khare and Tilak went to Mahad in a steamer from Bombay. On the deck Tilak in his dhoti, shirt and cap took a round and made fun of those who were feeling giddy and sea-sick. On reaching Raigad, he had a pleasant dip in the Gangasagar. Among the invitees was a direct descendant of Yesaji Kank who was Shivaji's general. On this occasion a vast audience had gathered to celebrate the festival. Tilak made a stirring speech from the quadrangle where Shivaji was coronated. Hundreds of Mavalas took their meal in a grand long file. The special feature of the function was that a Savarkarian choir sang Vinayakrao Savarkar's famous ballad on Tanaji and when the young men repeated a certain stanza all the audience shouted the war cry of Mahrattas 'Har Har Mahadeo'!

As the vast audience began to show intense animation in the ballads, their bubbling enthusiasm and the indirect political hints in the ballad crossed the limit of Moderate politics, and Khare left the meeting under the pretext of indisposition; Tilak followed suit. Shivrampant Paranjpe then presided over the function till the end. The ballad by Savarkar and his colleague Govind, another revolutionary poet, enthralled thousands in Maharashtra, and their patriotic songs and ballads echoed through hills and dales for two generations.

Another important item connected with the celebration was a public announcement of the audited accounts of the Shivaji Memorial Fund. Tilak was Secretary of the Committee and in his meticulous way kept the records and accounts of the Memorial Fund. He was so much engrossed in this festival that he ordered his men not to show him any letter or telegram concerning his family during the celebrations. His son was ill and at Mahad there was a telegram for Tilak from Poona, informing him about his serious illness. He got it when he had almost reached the Raigad Fort. Duty first, other things afterwards. It was the strict observance of duty that made Nelson apply the telescope to his blind eye and shout out, "England expects every man to do his duty."

A few days after this Tilak signed papers recommending Savarkar to Pandit Shyamji Krishna Varma for the Shivaji Scholarship to study law in England. In his application Vinayakrao Savarkar said: "Independence and liberty I look upon as the very pulse and breath of a nation. From my boyhood, dear Sir, upto this moment of my youth, the loss of Independence of my country and the possibility of regaining it form the only theme of which I dreamt by night and on which I mused by day." Recommending Savarkar's application, Tilak said: "When there is such a rush like that, it is no use recommending anyone particularly to your notice. But, still, I may state, among the applicants there is one Mr. Savarkar from Bombay, who graduated last year and whom I know to be a spirited young man very enthusiastic in the Swadeshi cause so much so that he had to incur the displeasure of the Fergusson College authorities. He has no mind to take up Government service at any time and his moral character is very good." Tilak was to go to Bengal and Savarkar was to sail for London in the second week of June. So Tilak invited Savarkar to dinner and they had a talk. This visit of Savarkar to Tilak is not so widely known. The old lion must have cast a measuring eye at the young lion during their last meeting.

For these two leaders never met thereafter. It is not unsafe to believe that Tilak must have cautioned Savarkar to go slow.

Shortly after the Shivaji festival, Tilak took part in the Marathi Authors' Conference, which was held in Poona. While Tilak was addressing the Conference, the President of the Conference, who was a Moderate, requested Tilak to allude only to literature lest he should attack the Government there also. Tilak told the Marathi authors that a language and its literature were enriched by the varied and vigorous activities of the people who spoke it.

By now the Swadeshi movement had struck root. In Bengal students looked at one another's clothes and they wrangled with those who wore foreign clothes and tore them to pieces. Children threw away exercise books made of foreign paper. Even flags made of foreign cloth were torn at public meetings. People dared not walk in the streets with foreign clothes on. Surendranath's grand-daughter, a child of five, threw away foreign shoes which somebody brought her as a present. A child on her death-bed, half-conscious, refused to take medicine because it was of foreign make.

The student world was intensely agitated over this point and was mainly responsible for the success of the movement. The Bengali leaders threw away their black coats, boots, ties, collars and put on short dhotis, big shirts, big scarves or shawls! Thus there was a powerful swing towards Indian ways prompted not so much by love of everything that was Indian but by a determination to tolerate European things no more. The idea of self-reliance and self-sufficiency was dawning upon the minds of the leaders. So they were directing their enthusiasm to proper channels. Factories were opened to manufacture match boxes, glass, cloth and other articles.

Tilak was invited to Calcutta to address meetings during the Shivaji festival. S. G. Deooskar, a Maharashtrian Bengali, had prepared ground for the celebration of the Shivaji festival. He was born at Ratnagiri in 1869 and was educated at Banaras and at Deoghar in Bengal. During his student days he wrote fiery articles and while a teacher he wrote in *Hitabadi*, a leading weekly in which Bankim Chandra Chatterjea and Poet Tagore also wrote. For his fiery articles he got the sack. Then he became the editor of *Hitabadi*.[1] He was a brilliant journalist and his book *Desherkatha* had earned him name and fame. In the meanwhile the political unrest in Bengal had begun to take a serious turn. Sir Bampfylde Fuller, Lieut.-Governor

1 Bhattacharya Vivek, the *Navahal*, 13 August 1965.

of Dacca, in his extreme enthusiasm to crush the anti-partition movement circularised the teachers and other Government servants against attending public meetings. He issued also an order prohibiting the Bengalees from singing the song 'Bande Mataram'!

In spite of this repression, a Conference was held at Barisal in April 1906. Surendranath Banerjee was arrested and fined, and the police pounced upon the procession, assaulted the delegates and volunteers with lathis and batons, threw one of them into a tank and broke the Conference. The Gurkha soldiers, quartered as a punitive measure, indulged in licence and pillage. The whole town was turned into an opposing camp, and the air was full of the cries of 'Bande Mataram'. This 'Bande Mataram' for which lacs of people later suffered whipping and imprisonment and underwent sufferings was a song from a novel named Anand Math by Bankim Chandra Chatterjee. This revolutionary song inspired two generations of patriots in India, and it acted as a mantra, a power, an inspiration, a revelation. For this ruthless act, Bampfylde Fuller was condemned on all sides, and he was sacrificed at the altar of popular wrath. In his policy he was not supported even by his superiors, and Mr. Fuller resigned. When he later went to England, Morley refused to give him an interview. The news of the atrocious deeds perpetrated by the police converted Bengal into a restless, smouldering camp. Some young students came to Surendranath and disclosed to him their intention of assassinating Fuller, but he dissuaded them from doing it.

At such a time Tilak started by train for Calcutta which was thrilling with the Swadeshi and Boycott movement. He wanted to fuse the strength of the Mahratta will with the resourceful imagination of Bengal and to inspire Bengal with the message of Shivaji, a symbol of Swaraj. Dr. Moonje and Dadasaheb Khaparde, one or two private attendants and a cook were with him. All stations rang with the names of Shivaji and Tilak, morning, day and night! Enthusiastic crowds thronged the stations in advance; devotional groups awaited their deliverer with tea and fruit and garlands in their hands. During the course of the journey the party touched on a lot of subjects. When the topic referred to Gokhale, Tilak said he was rather gentle by temperament and not fearless. In a free India Gokhale would have been an efficient Home Member, but would not have been a successful Foreign Secretary. The fact is that Gokhale would have been an able Finance Minister! When the train reached Howrah station, the platform was so crowded that all passengers were locked up in their carriages, and in the words of Khaparde, not even an ant could have crept in. Tilak was practically lifted out of the carriage. The station resounded with the cries of Bande Mataram and Shivaji Maharaj-ki-jai. The procession began with banners and bands marching ahead; and Tilak and Khaparde were seated in a coach-box. A few minutes after they unyoked the horses and hauled the carriage. The procession went to the celebration grounds where Tilak declared open the Swadeshi exhibition and the Shivaji festival.

On June 5, 1906, Tilak made a speech at the Shivaji celebration under the presidentship of Babu Ashwini Kumar Dutt, pointing out the important role Shivaji had played in the history of India. Stressing the different facets of his noble character, he traced his birth to Rajput stock and praised his tolerance for other religionists. His reference to Shivaji's Bhawani sword appealed very much to the audience. It was at this meeting that Tagore's poem on Shivaji was sung.

On June 7 Tilak delivered a stirring speech under the presidentship of Babu Surendranath at a public meeting attended by twenty thousand people. At the outset he said that the hope that the British would grant the Indians rights and privileges when they were properly educated was lost. Lord Curzon had declared that the Queen's Proclamation was an impossibility. It was useless to expect anything from the rulers. The rulers had developed a system which they were not prepared to alter in spite of the protests of the people. Mere protests, not backed by the people, would not help the people. The days of protests and prayers were gone.

"Do not expect much," he proceeded, "for a change in Government. Three Ps—pray, please and protest—will not do unless backed by solid force. Look to the examples of Ireland, Japan and Russia and follow their methods. We must show that the country cannot be governed well by the present method. We must convince the Government of this." Then he compared Morley's sympathy to a law which provided the punishment of whipping, but allowed the sufferer to be taken to hospital for treatment.

"The partition grievance," he went on, "will be the edifice for the regeneration of India. Do not give up this partition grievance, for the whole of India is at your back. The love of nation is one's first duty. Next comes religion and next to it Government. Swadeshi and Swadeshi alone will be our cry for ever, and by this we will grow in spite of the wishes of the rulers."

Next day, speaking at a meeting at the College Square, Calcutta, he said that Morley's sympathy sounded like a message of condolence, but the

Bengalees would send him condolences, if he was not prepared to undo the partition. "We are black men but not block-heads, and we can see through such arguments," he concluded. Tilak was now turning to good account the frustration which people felt at British rule and was driving the leaders' attention to the people who were the real source of strength.

Tilak was the first Indian leader to receive such a great ovation outside his own province. People were not satisfied with these speeches. They wanted Tilak to sanctify their lives by having a dip along with them in the Ganges. A holy river with the selfless and spotless presence of a mighty man they regarded as a rare opportunity. So they started in a procession to the Ganges with Tilak Maharaj, accompanied by Moonje, Khaparde and B. C. Pal. The procession swelled every minute with volunteers and crowds that entered with banners of Bande Mataram fluttering in their hands! "We went to the Ganges," observes Khaparde, "near the bridge and had the public religious bath. The scene was unique and they worshipped Tilak like a God." In the evening Tilak addressed a meeting of the Marwaris and appealed to them to support the Swadeshi movement.

Tilak paid a visit to Kharagpur near Calcutta where a large number of Maharashtrians lived. He was honoured also by the Sanskrit pandits in Calcutta. One more point to be noted about Tilak's Calcutta tour was that he distributed in Calcutta some pamphlets relating to the Sinn Fein movement in Ireland. Sinn Fein is a Gaelic expression meaning "ourselves alone". This was fuel to the fire in Bengal, to the young men who were smarting under the insults inflicted upon Bengal by British rule.

On his return to Poona from Calcutta, Tilak wrote an article entitled 'Shivaji, a national hero'. "Hero-worship is a feeling deeply implanted in human nature; and our political aspirations need all the strength which the worship of a Swadeshi hero is likely to inspire into our minds. For this purpose Shivaji is the only hero to be found in the Indian history. He was born at a time when the whole nation required relief from misrule; and by his self-sacrifice and courage he proved to the world that India was not a country forsaken by Providence. It is true that the Mahommedans and the Hindus were then divided; and Shivaji, who respected the religious scruples of the Mahommedans, had to fight against Mogul rule that had become unbearable to the people. But it does not follow from this that—now that the Mahommedans and the Hindus are equally shorn of power they once possessed and are governed by the same laws and rules—they should not agree to accept as a hero one who in his own days took a bold stand against the tyranny of his time. It is not preached nor is it to be at all expected that the methods adopted by Shivaji should be adopted by the present generation."

"The Shivaji festival," continued the article, "is not celebrated to alienate or even to irritate the Mahommedans. Times are changed, and as observed above, the Mahommedans and Hindus are in the same boat or on the same platform so far as the political conditions of the people are concerned. Can we not both of us derive some inspiration from the life of Shivaji under these circumstances? That is the real question at issue, and if that can be answered in the affirmative it matters little that Shivaji was born in Maharashtra."

"We are not against a festival," went on the article, "being started in honour of Akbar or any other hero from the old Indian history. Such festivals will have their own worth, but that of Shivaji has a peculiar value of its own for the whole country, and it is the duty of everyone to see that this characteristic of the festival is not ignored or misrepresented. Every hero, be he Indian or European, acts according to the spirit of his times, and we must, therefore, judge of his individual acts by the standard prevalent in his time. If this principle be accepted, we can find nothing in Shivaji's life to which one can take exception." [2]

The British Government was watching these new developments minutely. Morley wrote on June 6, 1906, to Minto that "everybody warns us that a new spirit is growing and spreading over India," and Morley warned him that before long the Mahommedans would throw in their lot with the Congress members against Minto.[3] Fuller, who called the Muslims the favoured wife, sided with the Muslims.

At this juncture the Maharashtra Vidyaprasarak Mandal started the Samartha Vidyalaya in August 1906 at Kolhapur with Prof. Vijapurkar at its head! Tilak, one of its founders, must have cherished great hopes about its success.

Tilak visited Nasik for the thread ceremony of his grandson Gajanan. He told his daughter in a lighter mood that he would make her son editor of the *Kesari*, and later on Gajananrao Ketkar turned out to be a brilliant editor of the *Kesari*.

---

2 The *Mahratta*, 24 June 1906.

3 Quoted by Krishna, K. B., *The Problem of Minorities*, p. 108.

In the month of July, the adoption suit was decided by the First Class Sub-Judge's Court at Poona in favour of Tilak. But the other party was intending to appeal to the High Court from the decision.

A few weeks after this Tilak went to Belgaum to deliver lectures during the Ganesh festival. In one of his speeches he observed that Morley fully knew what India wanted. But on his coming to power the philosopher became a different man. A throne had such a miraculous power! The former Secretary of State talked bitter things, Tilak concluded, but Morley did good and bad things alternately. While one of these meetings was going on, rain was pouring heavily and people listened to Tilak in wet clothes. A local man held an umbrella over Tilak till the speech was over. Tilak resisted but the man persisted.

This umbrella affair gave rise to criticism, and some Moderates and other critics, who would have tolerated persons doing such a thing in the case of British officers, criticised Tilak, and he was rather perturbed at the heinous charge levelled by them that Tilak gave himself the airs of a monarch!

This charge had a certain background. Just on his arrest at Barisal, Surendranath Banerjee reached the meridian of popularity. He was worshipped by Brahmins who showered on his head flowers and chanted some hymns. This was represented by the panic-stricken British officers as the coronation of Surendranath! The *Daily Chronicle*, London, said that the coronation of King Banerjee in Bengal was the climax of political unrest in Bengal. The *Daily Telegraph*, London, described Surendranath Banerjee as a dangerous lunatic, and an imposter. Some other British newspapers described him as Emperor Banerjee![4]

Tilak visited also Nasik during the Ganesh festival. On the station young men belonging to Savarkar's revolutionary society gave a pleasant surprise to Tilak. He was accustomed to the greetings 'Bande Mataram', 'Swadeshi', 'Shivaji Maharaj', but the Nasik revolutionaries greeted him with 'Victory to the Goddess of Liberty'. Tilak asked them to stop at that. During his stay in Nasik he met also the Nasik revolutionaries at a private meeting and asked them about their preparations. He talked in a suggestive way and referred to Russian terrorism; but said that those methods depended for success on certain factors such as preparations, circumstances, time and secrecy. He appreciated their selfless devotion to

4 Savarkar, Veer, *Letters from London*, pp. 13-14 (Marathi).

the country, but said that such attempts were not likely to be crowned with success. That was his experience, he said! So he cautioned them against any hasty and impatient steps.

Tilak wanted to awaken the masses and lead them. So he was shrewd enough never to support the revolutionaries publicly. But he never discouraged or discarded them. He wrote as early as 1897 that "the British rulers believe that the subjects, if entrusted with arms, may one day use them against the Government. The belief is partially well-founded, for the British Government is an alien Government and the subjects in trying to get emancipation will, if constitutional methods fail, have some day to resort to arms." But he never supported dacoities for revolutionary purposes. In 1904, some Bengali young men were thinking of resorting to underground channel for self-expression and said that Tilak was in favour of dacoities. So Sarala Devi Chaudharani who was dissuading those spirited young men from resorting to such acts saw Tilak in Poona. Tilak told her plainly that "he did not approve of the dacoities, much less authorise them, if for nothing else simply on the score of their being practically useless for political purposes. But looking to the differences in human nature and the varying processes of evolution suited to different temperaments, he did not condemn them openly."[5]

Just then some young men who were afire with patriotism emanating from the partition went to him for advice. He asked them to devote unswervingly their life to the uplift of the nation, to follow, like the disciples of Ramdas, the life of a Fakir. This was the time when intelligent Brahmin youth should embrace that cult and begin work in right earnest. If they were prepared to follow such an active, selfless life, the nation was bound to prosper. No use simply coming to him for advice.

On another occasion a youth questioned him whether it was possible for a man to lead a life of celibacy till the end of life; and if that was possible, should he go in for such a life and serve the nation? Tilak at once replied that he should go home and settle his marriage. The man who consulted others on problems which should be undertaken on the strength of his own self-confidence was unfit for such a work. "A really brave man never seeks advice from others as to whether he should do an act of bravery. A bud opens spontaneously and naturally into a flower. It seeks no permission from anybody." One day a graduate asked Tilak what he should do in life.

5 *Reminiscences and Anecdotes about Lokamanya Tilak*, Vol. I, p. 511

Tilak angrily told him that he should not do anything and added that if in spite of his higher education he was not able to come to a decision, he had studied in vain; and from such incidents he was convinced that the existing system of education produced only clerks.

Tilak was doing his best to promote the Swadeshi movement. On September 9, 1906, he addressed a meeting of the Swadeshi Wastu Pracharini Sabha, Bombay, and exhorted them to do all in their power to further the cause of Swadeshism. Being a leader of practical bent, he could not but express sympathy with the Postal strike and deprecated the action of those Bombay gentlemen who induced the peons to resume work before they had derived any benefit from their action. On October 7 he addressed another meeting at the same place and dwelt upon the awakening of Persia, China and Afghanistan and its effects on the Swadeshi movement. At the third meeting he honoured Seth Khemraj Shrikrishna for his practical work in the cause of the Swadeshi movement, and at the fourth meeting he appealed to the Bhatias and other merchants of Bombay to boycott foreign articles with a view to reducing the imports and increasing the exports of India and to encourage the movement without fear and religious scruples.

But the Bombay millowners took advantage of this movement and raised the prices of cloth. This had a very bad effect upon the Swadeshi movement. So Motilal Ghose and Bhupendranath Basu wrote to Tilak requesting him to make a representation to the millowners for keeping down the prices of Swadeshi cloth. Tilak and Wasukaka visited Bombay every week-end to see the millowners. But the millowners were indifferent and often a man of Tilak's eminence and sacrifice had to cool his heels at their places. And if they met Tilak they gave him evasive replies and talked in an insulting manner. Tilak and his colleagues saw Narottam Morarji, a millowner, in Bombay. He asked Tilak to go to his office next day. When they went to his office next day, D. E. Wacha, who was one-time President of the Congress, told them in the capacity of manager that he had neither any information nor instructions from the proprietor in the matter. Tilak expressed his desire to wait till the mill-owner came. Wacha told Tilak and his colleagues not to wait in his office.[6] Capital knows no morality. It talks of the love of country only when it is profitable!

A Swadeshi co-operative stores was soon started in Bombay and Tilak became one of its directors. The stores worked well and gradually

---

6 Deogirikar, T. R., *Wasukaka Ani Tyancha Kal* (Marathi), pp. 354-55.

its branches spread all over Maharashtra. Thus the boycott helped the Swadeshi movement and the Swadeshi movement helped the boycott.

Gokhale had been to England in April 1906 as a spokesman of the Indian National Congress and he returned to India in September. It was about this time Tilak is reported to have interviewed a Russian consular official ostensibly to obtain letters of introduction to firms in Russia and to purchase goods, machinery and such other articles in furtherance of the Swadeshi movement, but confidentially inquired of him whether the Government of Russia would admit Madhavrao Jadhav to their military academy. "His military training in Europe," reported the official to Russia, "is evidently intended to enable him, if ever need be, to assume command of native troops deserting the British, or of rebel forces." Tilak had seen the Russian consulate in Bombay also in the previous year to find out if it were possible for Indian officers to get admission to military schools in Russia. For such admissions the Tilakites had tapped American sources also. The idea behind these requests, declared the Russian historians, was to organise an armed resistance against British rule.[7] As regards the purchase of goods and machinery, this time he was advised not to try Russia and given a letter of introduction to the German Consul whom he subsequently interviewed. He also saw the Austrian Consul and obtained letters of introduction to firms in Austria.

About this time Tilak made a very stirring speech. He said, "We shall not give the Government assistance to collect revenue. We shall not assist them in carrying on the administration of justice. We shall have our own courts and if time comes we shall not pay taxes." [8]

On October 1, 1906, a dark event in the history of India took place. A Muslim deputation led by the Aga Khan waited upon Lord Minto. It presented an address to the Viceroy and prayed for communal representations to the Muslims. Partition of Bengal blessed them with a Muslim majority Province and it whetted their appetite for separate electorates! Minto said that he was in accord with them! From this deputation sprang the terrific child, the All-India Muslim League.

In last week of October 1906, Tilak visited Pandharpur with his family to attend the Swadeshi exhibition. It was opened by the Chief of Miraj.

7 'Editors: Reisner, I. M., and Goldberg, N. M., *Tilak and the Struggle for Indian Freedom,* p. 561.

8 Dange, S. A., *Gandhi vs. Lenin,* Title page.

When Tilak came to the place of the exhibition, Gokhale asked him to occupy a chair which was kept close by. But Tilak refused to come from the audience and said that it was proper for him to have his place among the devotees of Vithoba, the God. His love for the rights of the common people refused to enjoy a preference over other men standing in queues in having a darshan of the image of Vithoba. He was persuaded with difficulty not to cool his heels and waste his precious time. He addressed a meeting under the presidentship of Vishnubuva Jog and to the bewilderment of the audience he said that mere singing of praises to God would not lead them to God if they did not endeavour to eradicate poverty of the millions. He had no love, he concluded, for the Bhakti cult or for cessation of worldly activities.[9] Yet when someone attacked the cult of Bhakti he said that it was not proper to criticize that cult. For it was there that the world-negating attitude was found and he opined that selfless persons should capture that institution and utilise it for national purposes. Tilak was essentially a born Sanskritist and his soul had been nurtured on Sanskrit lore and literature. He was not therefore much impressed by the Bhakti cult or the philosophy of Dnyaneshwar. Nobody has at any time mentioned that Tilak ever visited Alandi where the great saint has his eternal abode.

During the days of the exhibition Tilak addressed a meeting. The people had forgotten, he said, their Swaraj. Shivaji and Ramdas and others had won it back for them. At that time also they had forgotten their Independence. The real danger was the stark poverty of the masses. That condition was the outcome of British rule. To fight poverty, the Swadeshi movement had been started. This movement would bear fruit when the agriculturists realised the point. Just as the struggle for spiritual salvation went on for years, so also that movement must go on for generations and a day would dawn when success would crown their efforts, and God willed it, too.[10]

As the twenty-second session of the Congress was drawing near, the conflict over the question of the ideals and methods of work of the Congress again cropped up. It was a conflict between two ideologies. The difference between the two groups, Moderates and Extremists, had assumed a threatening look. A tug of war began. The nationalists of Calcutta led by Pal wanted Tilak to preside over the Calcutta session of the Congress, and

---

9 Deshpandc, Gangadhar, *Mazi Jeevankatha* (Marathi), p. 128.

10 Kulkarni, A. V., *The Last Eight fears of Lokamanya Tilak*, p. 39 (1909).

so they carried on a regular campaign in favour of Tilak, whereas Tilak's lieutenant Khaparde, after scenting the Moderates' violent opposition to Tilak becoming president of the Congress, suggested the name of Lajpat Rai for the presidentship. Lajpat Rai and Tilak were both disliked by the Anglo-Indian press and they therefore raised a cry of alarm.

To the old veterans, Tilak or Lajpat Rai made no difference; they feared that either of them would give a different turn to the existing ideology of the Congress. So they laid heads together for averting the danger, and their attention turned to Dadabhai Naoroji. In doing so they thought they were choosing the lesser evil. Dadabhai, who had taken a prominent part in the International Socialist Congress, was regarded by the Moderates as less radical than Tilak!

A cable was secretly sent to Dadabhai by Babu Bhupendranath Basu, the right-hand man of Surendranath, requesting him to accept the presidentship of the Congress. Dadabhai expressed his willingness. Surendranath Banerjee wrote on October 25, 1906, to Dadabhai that "those who were canvassing for Tilak have given us the assurance that they will unanimously join in electing you as President."[11] Motilal Ghose also wrote to Dadabhai: "You are aware that a change has come over the people. The Congress as it is cannot satisfy them. The method must be changed and you yourself latterly acknowledged it in many of your speeches."[12]

The nationalists withdrew their opposition as they naturally thought Dadabhai would go a step further. Replying to the criticism levelled by the critics of the Extremists, Tilak said that, according to the Extremists the holding of the Congress for three days in a year, the tepid work of the British Congress Committee and the occasional sending of a deputation to England were not quite sufficient. The Moderates thought they would win political rights by persuasion while the Extremists thought they would not be secured without strong pressure. If that pressure was to be applied, the Congress must shed that holiday character and should develop itself into an energetic, active organisation.

Dadabhai Naoroji, the President-elect of the Congress, arrived in Bombay on December 14, and was accorded a grand reception by the people. The spontaneity and warmth of the demonstration of the people at Calcutta also was unique. Tilak had predicted that a man of Dadabhai's

11 Masani, R. P., *Dadabhai Naoroji, The Grand Old Man of India*, p. 497.

12 Ibid, p. 497.

industry and nature would infuse a new spirit into the Congress. He and his party then started for Calcutta. During the course of the journey Bhave, assistant editor of the *Kesari*, was with him. He was an expert mimic. Tilak persuaded Bhave to mimic him. He did it marvellously. The train reached its destination. Congress leaders and volunteers were present at the station to receive Tilak. Bepin Chandra Pal received him on behalf of the nationalists. As usual the people accorded him a warm reception. Tilak, Khaparde and Moonje took their lodgings at the house of C. R. Das. B. C. Pal and Aurobindo Ghose were leaders who had captivated the imagination of young Bengal. Babu Bepin Chandra Pal was the son of a District Munsiff. While a college student, he became a Brahmo and so his father disowned him. By dint of his strenuous struggle and unbending will he rose to the position of the headmaster of a high school. In the meanwhile his father was reconciled to him, and he started his own school on the patrimony; but afterwards closed it down for want of funds. Just then he lost his wife also. He turned a sanyasin and wandered about.

After some time Pal married the widowed niece of Babu Surendranath Banerjee, launched a counter propaganda to the Christian movement, went to England, studied comparative theology, and travelled widely in England, France and America, lecturing at many places. On his return to India in 1901, he started a weekly called *New India*, and toured South India as a missionary of the Brahmo Samaj. After the declaration of partition he came to the forefront of the political fight, addressed meeting after meeting throughout the length and breadth of Bengal, and started the *Bande Mataram*.

The education of Aurobindo Ghose began in England when he was seven. He failed in the Indian Civil Service Examination as he could not pass the riding test. He thereafter graduated in 1892, securing a first class in classical tripos at Cambridge. Taking service next year under the young and enlightened Maharaja of Baroda, he served as a confidential personal assistant, and during the twelve years of his service he rose to the vice-principalship of Baroda College. Although he was little short of an Englishman in speech, dress and manners, in all the internal aspects of his life he was essentially an Indian.

Gradually Western civilization lost its gloss and glamour for Aurobindo. The call of the motherland proved irresistible, and he gave up the cloistered seclusion of Baroda to join the battle of freedom over the partition of Bengal. He was present at the break-up of the Barisal Conference and witnessed the atrocities committed upon his countrymen by the police. Thereafter he stayed a few days at Baroda and in July took up his abode in Calcutta, the land of his birth, action and vision at a time when Bengal was awaiting the arrival of an inspired personality. He regarded the new movement as a special dispensation of God. The student world of Bengal was in a confused state of mind. Owing to their disobedience to the circulars prohibiting the students from attending meetings, several students were expelled from Government High Schools and aided schools. The nationalist leaders rose to the occasion and took up the responsibility of the education of these young men. They established in Calcutta the National Council of Education and its immediate practical step was to start the National College in Calcutta of which Aurobindo Ghose became the first Principal.

Soon Aurobindo plunged himself in politics with his brilliant pen and noble vision of a free India. His virile nationalism hated the mendicant policy of the Moderates, his inspiring pen and poetic verse and the fluency of his speech infused a new spirit into the hearts of the young and old Bengal. He contributed his moving and fiery articles to the *Bande Mataram* started by B. C. Pal. The complete editorial control of this revolutionary daily passed into Aurobindo's hands in December 1906, and after the Calcutta Congress of 1906, it stirred over a year the innermost heart of Bengal with its message of Swadeshi, Boycott and Swaraj!

On his arrival Tilak accompanied by Dadasaheb Khaparde and Dr. Moonje went to meet Babu Surendranath Banerjee, the maker of modern Bengal, at his office. After a formal talk, the conversation shifted to the main subject and there was a heated discussion :

TILAK: Babusahib, there is no doubt that a resolution on boycott of British goods will come up before the Congress.

SURENDRANATH: Who is going to move it?

TILAK: Of course, you will have to do it. You have sponsored this tremendous agitation and the boycott of British goods has been pushed ahead by you with such resolution and vehemence that I am confident that none but you will be the proper man to move the boycott resolution. We are there to support you!

SURENDRANATH: I shall not be able to bring such a resolution before the Congress and shall have to oppose it if somebody moves it.

TILAK: This attitude will be quite inconsistent. Outside Congress you defend and justify the boycott of British goods and inside Congress you oppose it! How will it look consistent?

SURENDRANATH (a little excited): Tilak, it is too much to expect consistency in politicians; there is some such thing as expediency.[13]

Tilak, Khaparde and Moonje looked at one another in surprise! This was the first round!

On an invitation Tilak went to meet Dadabhai at the residence of the Maharaja of Darbhanga where the latter had taken his lodgings. Dadabhai asked every leader to give his opinion on the question of Boycott. Khaparde and Malaviya gave their opinion on the point at issue. Tilak spoke and Mehta countered him, and D. A. Khare negatived Mehta! This angered the Bombay lion.

On December 23 Tilak delivered a speech on 'Swadeshi' under the presidentship of Lajpat Rai at Beadon Square. Lord Minto had opened the Industrial exhibition and said that honest Swadeshism should be dissociated from politics. Tilak said that the Government of India should impose taxes on imports to protect the infant industries. "If the Indian Government," concluded Tilak, "dissociates itself from the commercial aspirations of the British Nation, then it will be time for Swadeshi workers to consider the question of dissociating their movement from politics. But so long as politics and commerce are blended together in the policy of the Government of India, it will be a blunder to dissociate Swadeshi from politics." As a result of the meeting it was resolved to abstain from patronising the exhibition as its organizers had invited Lord Minto to open it. When Manikrao insisted that he should be present at the sports which were held in the premises of the exhibition Tilak waited outside!

The Calcutta Congress was the largest political gathering witnessed in India up to that day. The Chairman of the Reception Committee Rash Behari Ghose described Swadeshism as the cradle of New India, defended Boycott, and reminded the country that the wounds inflicted upon Bengal were as fresh as ever.

The octogenarian President, whose life was associated with strenuous intellectual labour and political activity spread over fifty years, thanked the Congress sincerely for electing him President for the third time and asked Gokhale to read his address.

---

13 *Reminiscences and Anecdotes about Lokamanya Tilak*, Vol. II, pp. 509-10.

At the outset Dadabhai's address declared that it was the first Congress after its having come of age. The birth-right to be free or to have freedom was the Indian's right from the very beginning of their connection with England when the Indians came under the British flag. "We do not ask any favours. We want only justice. Instead of going into any further discussion or details of our rights as British citizens, the whole matter can be compressed in one word 'Self-Government' or Swaraj like that of the United Kingdom or the Colonies." He declared that although he was a free trader, he opined that Swadeshi was a forced necessity for India.

As regards his faith, Dadabhai, the Grand Old Man of India, said: "Since my early efforts, I must say that I have felt so many disappointments as would be sufficient to break any heart and lead one to despair and even, I am afraid, to rebel." But perseverance was the rule of his life and so he had not despaired. He ended his speech with a fervent appeal for unity. "Be united, persevere and achieve Self-Government."

The key-note of the address was Swaraj. It thrilled the audience and the country from end to end. The tide of this movement of Swaraj must have swept the Moderates! Dadabhai's address voiced the demand of New India and expressed the thought of Tilak. Really it so happened many a time that what Tilak thought and fought for, political leaders expressed and accepted after a struggle. He compared Curzon with Aurangzeb and Gokhale repeated it from the Chair of the presidentship of the Congress in 1905. Since the early nineties of the last century Tilak had been preaching Swaraj and Swadeshi and these two principles had come to stay now. There was a sort of solace to the palpitating hearts of the Moderates as the President advocated the demand for Swaraj under British paramountcy and stood for constitutional agitation.

The address of Dadabhai did not say anything about Boycott, although it brushed aside Swadeshi with a few phrases. But the one point that caused the utmost disappointment was the announcement of his irrevocable faith in the British people's sense of justice and fair play. Besides, he did not recommend any change in methods and tactics. That is why the *Bande Mataram* described it as a great refusal. The *Bengalee* of Surendranath hailed the presidential address as the political gospel of the new era.

The *Englishman*, a typical representative of the Anglo-Indians, blamed Dadabhai who, "being called upon to quench the flames of hatred towards British Rule in India, had only used kerosene for that purpose".

Tilak was striving to get the Congress committed to the boycott of British goods and the Swadeshi movement. All the nationalist leaders were sitting among the delegates, while the old guard of the Congress sat on the platform.

At the Subjects Committee meetings, there were violent scenes over the refusal to submit resolutions for extending the boycott all over India. The Extremists felt strongly about it, and they put forward amendments to eliminate the clause asking for a commission of inquiry. Babu Motilal also opposed the clause. Votes were not counted and the President said the majority was in favour of asking for the commission. Bepin Chandra Pal accepted the ruling on condition that he would be allowed to move an amendment in the open session.

When the Swadeshi resolution came up for consideration, a stormy discussion took place. The President would not consent to divide the house for voting. Thereupon, Khaparde, Pal and Aurobindo left with their followers. Khaparde said to Tilak that there was no use sitting there. Tilak said they should go, his work was in the pandal. Tilak returned late at night to the residence of C. R. Das. He sat up late and prepared four amendments. One he sent to Motilal Ghose and asked him to send it to the Secretary, the second he sent in the name of Khaparde, the third to Pal asking him to send it to the Secretary, and the fourth he sent in his own name. By this statecraft he thought that Surendranath would accept either Khaparde's amendment or that of Motilal Ghosh, and Surendranath was tricked into accepting one of these amendments.

The next day Tilak's friend Khare intervened. He, Tilak, Mehta and others went into a room adjoining the Subjects Committee's meeting. Tilak would not give up his points. "Tilak skilfully paraphrased the word boycott and introduced its elements into his amendment. Mehta, the lion of Bombay, was very much annoyed and roared, "You would not and could not have treated me so in Bombay." Tilak replied, "If provoked to it we would show you a sample even in Bombay."[14] It was not difficult for a lion-tamer to beard the lion in his den! At last a compromise was effected, and Tilak's points were accepted. At the Subjects Committee Tilak made an impressive speech, and the members said it was statesmanlike. Upon this when the resolution was passed, Gokhale is said to have remarked: "No, Mehta, there is no forecasting the capacity of this admirable man."

14 G. S. Khaparde in *Reminiscences and Anecdotes about Lohamanya Tilak*, Vol. II, pp. 588-89.

The Congress passed a resolution declaring that the Boycott movement inaugurated in Bengal by way of protest against the "partition of Bengal, was, and is, legitimate." This resolution proved to be a bone of contention. According to the interpretation of the Extremists, it applied to the whole country, and the Moderates interpreted it as confined to Bengal only. It also passed two more resolutions: one demanding Self-Government, and the other on national education appealing to the people to take up the question of national education for both boys and girls and organise a system of education to suit the requirements of the country, on national lines and under national control.

In the open session, Tilak spoke on the resolution which advocated Swadeshi and called upon the people of the country to labour for its success, by making earnest and sustained efforts to promote the growth of indigenous industries and to stimulate production of indigenous articles by giving them preference over imported commodities even at some sacrifice. Tilak said that the middle classes were the greatest consumers of foreign goods. Self-help, determination and sacrifice were needed. He further said that he was glad that they had arrived at a satisfactory solution, because their Anglo-Indian friends had predicted that the twenty-second Congress would probably be the last Congress, and would meet with premature death immediately on attaining the age of majority. The prediction, however, had been falsified under the able, impartial and judicious guidance of the veteran leader in the chair. All differences, continued Tilak, had been squared; both parties had approached the question in a spirit of conciliation.

C. R. Das, then a legal luminary, had not flung himself into politics but his sympathies were with the Extremists. His wife was a Brahmo and was, in the words of Dr. Moonje, anglicized. She did not take food unless the guests were served with food. During the days of the Congress Tilak often returned to Das' residence late at night. But the venerable woman very cordially served Tilak and his men food even at dead of night!

The twenty-second National Congress dispersed amidst scenes of the wildest enthusiasm and rejoicing, with a swadeshi umbrella from Poona unfurled and held over Dadabhai Naoroji when he said a few words of thanks. Another event of note was that while the Maharaja of Darbhanga was playing the role of informer[15] to the Viceroy, the Maharaja of Baroda visited this Congress session.

15 Das, M. N., *India Under Morley And Minto*, p. 94.

The hopes of the enemies of the Congress were thus falsified by the statecraft of Tilak. There was a marvellous elasticity in his extremism.

Tilak was now far from disappointed. With the passing of the Boycott resolution he knew that the Congress would be no longer a shelter for pleasure-seekers and phrase-mongers. With the declaration of Swaraj from the presidential chair of the Congress the Extremists became now known as Nationalists. The active part of the life of the Congress began.

Now it was time that the Nationalists formulated their principles and so they held a meeting at College Square. Mr. Pal presided. Expounding the new principles in a brilliant manner befitting the leader of a political party, Tilak said: "The Extremists of today will be Moderates of tomorrow, just as the Moderates of today were Extremists yesterday. Every new party begins as extremist and ends as moderate. We must, therefore, study the present and work out a programme to meet the present conditions."

"The old party," he observed, "believes in appealing to the British Nation and we do not. It is the hope of achieving the goal by our own efforts that has brought into existence this New Party."

"You got the Queen's Proclamation. But it was obtained without a Congress. They wanted to pacify you, as you had grown too turbulent and you got the Proclamation without a demand, without Congress and without constitutional agitation. It was after 1858 that constitutional agitation began. A promise was made but you proved too weak to have it enforced. Lord Curzon poohpoohed it. Is Morley going to fulfil it? This is the point at issue." "Whenever there was a grievance," he continued, "we used to hold meetings, make petitions, representations, and complaints in the press; and once the decision of Caesar was known, everything was silent and we accepted it loyally. Morley's councillors are Anglo-Indians, they placed this before Mr. Morley." "The remedy," he went on, "is not petition but boycott. We say prepare your forces, organise your power, and then go to work, so that they cannot refuse you what you demand. We have a stronger weapon, a political weapon in boycott. Self-Government is our goal; we want control over our administrative machinery."

"What the New Party wants," he thundered, "you to do is to realise the fact that your future rests entirely in your own hands. If you mean to be free, you can be free; if you do not mean to be free, you will fall and be for ever fallen. So many of you need not like arms; but if you have not the power of active resistance, have you not the power of self-denial and self-abstinence in such a way as not to assist this foreign Government in ruling over you?"

"This is," he concluded in an appealing tone, "the advice of the New Party. Perhaps we have not obtained a full recognition of our principles. Old prejudices die hard. Neither of us wanted to wreck the Congress, so we compromised, and we were satisfied that our principles were recognised, and only to a certain extent. That does not mean that we have accepted the whole situation. We may have a step in advance next year, so that within a few years our principles will be recognised, and recognised to such an extent that the generations who come after us may consider us Moderates. This is the way in which a nation progresses. This is the way national sentiment progresses, and this is the lesson you have to learn from the struggle now going on. This is a lesson of progress, a lesson of helping yourself as much as possible, and if you really perceive the force of it, if you are convinced by these arguments, then and then only is it possible for you to effect your salvation from the alien rule under which you labour at this moment." [16]

This is one of the best speeches of Tilak. The words are symbolic of his great power and personality! He did not possess the gift of the gab. In short, plain, pithy sentences he expressed a realism that had crystalline clearness and practical exactness. The burning sincerity, courageous action and noble sacrifice behind the speaker heightened the effect and Tilak's speeches became irresistible. Describing Tilak as a speaker, a contemporary observed: "As a speaker, Mr. Tilak has nothing of the demagogue or the impassioned platform orator about him. There are no high-sounding phrases, no flights of rhetoric. His manner is subdued and free from gesticulation. The sentences are terse; the language is simple and direct. What he spoke was perfectly suited to the comprehension of his audience. He appealed, as he himself said, to their intelligence and not to their sentiment. The real power lay in the matter of his speech and not in the manner. There was no generalisation, no enunciation of abstract principles in a flowery language. Every statement was clear and every point was driven home with a readiness of illustration and power of antithesis, that showed the power of the speaker and the subtlety of his intellect. Every issue was put plainly and uncompromisingly." [17]

---

16 *Bal Gangadhar Tilak—His Writings 6- Speeches*, pp. 55-67.

17 Kulkarni, A. V., *The Last Eight Years of Lokamanya Tilak* (1909), p. 478.

In order to make the Congress a living and active force, Tilak, the real spokesman of the people, insisted that the Congress leaders should discard mendicancy and turn to the people to organise them. From this time onwards the name of Tilak became part and parcel of the Indian national movement.

The forces of national awakening stirred and vitalized by the partition agitation gave a stimulus to the growth of national industry. And Tilak had played a very vital role in this great national movement.

CHAPTER XV

The Battle of Surat

I

TILAK LEFT CALCUTTA and visited Allahabad on his return journey. There he addressed one or two meetings and the newspapers there acclaimed him, "the most powerful and the most influential leader of the new Extremist Party". On his way home the citizens of Nandgaon accorded him a tremendous ovation and illuminated the town as a mark of their great joy in his visit. He expressed satisfaction at the temperance movement. The leaders of the *chamar* community were honoured for introducing certain reforms in their community. At a meeting Tilak impressed on the minds of the people the importance of the Swadeshi movement.

The goal of the Congress was now irrevocably settled. The goal was Swaraj and the means were Swadeshi, Boycott and National Education. Tilak was so happy that he expressed satisfaction at the message of Dadabhai and praised him as an angel who had descended from above to give that message. Summarising the work of the Calcutta session, he said, "The Congress has now in effect laid down the Swaraj or Self-Government as the goal to be ultimately and gradually attained by the nation and that, while the nation may pray and petition to government as a part of the constitutional agitation and seek the redress of grievances or the fulfilment of political aspiration, the nation will mainly rely on its own endeavours to accomplish the object. Swadeshi, Boycott and National Education are the three most potent weapons given into our hands by the National Congress, and with these we must establish Swaraj."

The proclamation of Swaraj by the Congress as its goal had far-reaching effects both in India and in Britain. Terrified by this declaration,

The Times, London, blustered that they had won India by the sword and in the last resort they would hold it by the sword!

The Government now was intent on dividing the ranks of the Congress. It began to separate Moderates and Muslims from the Congress movement. In Eastern Bengal, the bureaucracy instigated Muslims to rise against Hindus. The Nawab of Dacca played into the hands of the bureaucracy and harassed Hindus. Muslims plundered the Hindus in Comila and Jamalpur. Tilak endorsed the statement issued by the Bengali leaders including Surendranath Banerjee on those riots. The statement described how "Hindu shops have been looted; Hindu temples have been desecrated; the images of Hindu deities have been defiled; the offices of the Hindu Zamindars ransacked; Hindu women have been outraged." Tilak scathingly condemned both the Muslims and the officers who were responsible for this pillage and outrage.

At Dacca, an Educational Conference was called by the Muslims, and at the eleventh hour it was converted into a political league to support the Bengal partition and to protest against the Boycott and Swadeshi movement. A few days carlier, while Tilak was in Calcutta a Mohamedan from Lucknow met Tilak at the residence of Das. He was displeased with Tilak for his strong views which were causing a split in the Congress. The Muslim politician was of the opinion that there should not be any division in the Congress and asked Tilak whether he was aware that the Muslims were about to launch an agitation for Pan-Islamism against the Hindus. He blamed Tilak for dividing the ranks of the Hindus while the Muslims were planning to crush the Hindus. Tilak exclaimed that the time for attaining India's freedom must be nearer at hand! "If the Muslims unite," he observed, "Government will try to crush them, and when that takes place, the Muslims will join us!" C. R. Das in his recollections asks whether Tilak's foresight was right or wrong.[1]

Government wanted to keep the young generation aloof from Congress politics and especially from the Swadeshi and Boycott movements. So under the Risley circular they wished to keep the students away from any kind of agitation. Tilak said: " Students of today are the citizens of tomorrow," and therefore their duty was to study public questions and to devote part of their leisure to such work as was allotted to them by their leaders. He further said that if the Risley circular was to prevent free

1 *Reminiscences and Anecdotes about Lokamanya Tilak*, Vol. I, pp. 333-34.

expression of thought in youth, if the Government Servants' Rules were to prohibit us from participating in public activities in manhood, and if the Pensioners' Code was to guide our actions in old age, when was a man in India free to think of his nation! He, therefore, opined that in the name of patriotism and self-sacrifice the people should declare their educational independence.

The Swadeshi movement was carried on with full vigour. Tilak appealed to the people to boycott foreign sugar, cloth and other luxuries on the occasion of marriages and on other such religious and auspicious occasions, and a part of the money thus saved should be donated to the Maharashtra Vidya Prasarak Mandal which had started the Samarth Vidyalaya at Kolhapur to impart instruction on national lines. He quoted Arthur Griffith, an Irish leader and editor and one of the founders of the Sinn Fein Movement, who had remarked that the Irish people could do as much damage to England's prestige and trade as was done by the Boer War.

Tilak gave an impetus to the Paisa Fund movement at a meeting held in Bombay on February 10, 1907, and declared that after some more collections, the proposal for starting an industry would be considered, and later a Glass Factory was started at Talegaon in Poona District.

Early in March 1907 Tilak attended the wedding of the daughter of Baba Maharaj at Malkapur where he addressed a public meeting exhorting the State people to render themselves fit for the enjoyment of political rights and asked the people to agitate ceaselessly for a substantial share in the Government of the State. He hoped that questions affecting the Native States would sooner or later find a place in the Congress programme. Soon after Gokhale's return from his tour in Northern India, Tilak called on him to discuss the measures the Congress should adopt to further the cause of the country. But they could not agree.

The Moderates and the New Party leaders now realised that there would be a battle at the next Congress session over the question of the Boycott and Swadeshi movement. So the Moderates began to consolidate their forces. They held Provincial Conferences all over India in the summer. And although no Provincial Conference had been held for the previous twelve years, the Bombay Provincial Conference was held, in March 1907, at Surat under the presidentship of Dr. Bhalchandra, a Moderate.

The President of the Conference worked under the direction of Pherozeshah Mehta, who was now striving his utmost lo suppress the idea of Boycott. In the absence of Tilak, Mehta succeeded in giving the go-by to the Boycott and Swadeshi resolutions although Tilak's party-men led by his lieutenant N. C. Kelkar struggled hard to introduce the resolutions. The President of this Conference said that the Swadeshi movement was not under the jurisdiction of the political conference and it was a concern of the industrial conference! Mehta said he could not make out anything from the term 'National Education'. At Raipur a Moderate presided over the Provincial Conference of Nagpur and Berar where even the Bande Mataram song was taboo; but Khaparde's pressure avoided a rupture. There, too, the Boycott resolution was dropped. Placards at every entrance displayed the motto of the Moderates: "Moderation is our motto!"

At Allahabad, Pandit Malaviya played the role of Pherozeshah Mehta in a successful manner. He refused admission to two hundred delegates of the New Party to the Provincial Conference. Malaviya had declared indignantly at the Calcutta Congress that his Province would never go in for the Boycott resolution! But his joy could not last long. Lajpat Rai came there, and with him spread over the United Provinces the tide of the message of the New Party. The Bengal Provincial Conference too was dominated by the Moderates.

After the Calcutta Congress the nationalist newspapers voiced the new principles of Boycott and Swadeshi at the top of their voice. In Maharashtra a security was demanded from the *Vihari*, a revolutionary weekly with which Savarkar was associated before he went to England. In the Punjab, the editor of the *Punjabee* was arrested, and his trial provoked the people when some policemen and English officers were beaten. News came that at Calcutta some ammunition was stolen by a few young men. Muslims were rioting in Memonsingh District, and Hindu young men were defending themselves. Pal, the orator of Bengal, electrified Southern India with the message of passive resistance, and for six days about thirty thousand persons heard him at the beach of the Madras City. Young men made bonfires and at some places they boycotted schools.

Tilak was at Sinhagad, his resting place. He wrote articles showing how a struggle was going on in the mind of Gokhale who was happy over the new spirit of India, but whose mind was filled with anxieties that the boycott, which according to him meant a vindictive desire to injure others and had unsavoury associations with it, might be applied to all India and might end in disorder. "Gokhale," wrote Tilak, "believes in sacrifice. He calls upon the people to be up and doing. He accepts even passive resistance as a constitutional weapon. He admits that bureaucracy is callous and our efforts have not borne fruit. But when it comes to action he will say: 'My friends, let us wait a little. No use flouting the Government, they will suppress us.' Thus Gokhale belongs in theory to the New Party and in practice to the old one." To support his stand Tilak published Gokhale's old article from the quarterly of the Sarvajanik Sabha in which Gokhale had taken a vow of never purchasing foreign cloth.

While Tilak was resting at Sinhagad, news came that Lajpat Rai and Ajit Singh were deported to Mandalay on May 9, 1907, the real cause of their deportation being that British officers feared that on the day of the completion of the fiftieth year of the 1857 Revolt there would be another revolt for freedom. The spokesman of the Anglo-Indians, the *Englishman*, alleged that Lajpat Rai was, with the help of the Amir of Afghanistan, preparing for a revolt! The Viceroy believed that the 'head and centre' of the entire sedition in the Punjab was Lala Lajpat Rai and his prominent agent in the dissemination of sedition was Ajit Singh. Lajpat Rai and Ajit Singh were lodged in a house in Mandalay jail, but so perfect was the arrangement that neither of them knew that the other was in the same house! After the deportation of his son, Lajpat Rai's old father said: "The chief sin of my son Lajpat consisted in this, that he stood forth a champion of his people and I rejoice that I have a son like him."[2]

Kelkar sent a special messenger to Sinhagad to inform Tilak about the deportation of Lajpat Rai. Tilak came down the same day. When he entered Gaikwad Wada and went upstairs, a gentleman named Mande followed him. Putting his turban on a hanger with one hand and untying the strings of his long flowing coat which he could not take off as usual in that excitement, he roared, "What, a patriot like Lala Lajpat Rai is deported, and is Minto still alive?" After a moment his feelings calmed down, and he exclaimed, "This cannot be expected of a weak nation like India!" [3]

In an article in the *Kesari* Tilak warned Government that if it applied to India the Russian system of Government Indians would be compelled to adopt the methods of the Russian people. The *Kesari* further stated that if there was any charge against Lajpat Rai he should be forthwith tried for it, or the charge must be withdrawn. If he was found guilty of treason, let him be hanged; but if Lajpat Rai was an eyesore to the Government because he was an agitator and fought constitutionally for the rights of

2 *The Indian Nation Builders*, published by Ganesh &; Co., Madras, p. 323.

3 *Reminiscences and Anecdotes about Lokamanya Tilak*, Vol. I, p. 221.

the people, Government should note that the agitation would never stop. On hearing of Lajpat Rai's deportation, people created disturbances at Rawalpindi and Peshawar. Meetings were held at important cities all over India, and in London by Pandit Shyamji Krishna Varma, protesting against the deportation of Lajpat Rai.

Tilak delivered a speech at Nasik on May 31, 1907, and denounced the circular issued by the Government of India which prohibited students from taking part in politics. He warned the Government that if it adopted Russian oppressive methods, people also could learn from the Russian people what to do!

Under this tense situation the Shivaji festival of this year was celebrated at Poona where detectives and police reporters swarmed. In the course of his speech at the festival Tilak said, "The path of duty is never sprinkled with rose water, nor do roses grow on it. It is true that what we seek may seem like a revolution in the sense that it means a complete change in the 'theory' of the Government of India as now put forward by the bureaucracy."

"Your revolution," he observed, "must be bloodless; but that does not mean you may not have to suffer or to go to jail. Your fight is with the bureaucracy who will always try to curb and suppress you. But you must remember that consistently with the spirit of laws and the bloodlessness of the revolution, there are a hundred other means by which you may and ought to achieve your object. . .Though downtrodden and neglected, you must be conscious of your power of making the administration impossible if you but choose to make it so. Let your place be filled by Europeans on the splendid salary of eight annas a day if possible!"

"If one Lala Lajpat Rai is deported," he continued, "another ought to be found to take his place as readily as a junior collector steps into the shoes of a senior. It is vain to hope that your petitions will effect the release of Lala Lajpat Rai though it is well known that the Government do not mean to keep him a prisoner all his life. His deportation is intended not so much to penalise Lala Lajpat Rai as to terrorise those that would follow his example, and if your agitation stopped as soon as one deportation took place, Government would run away with the idea that repression had triumphed."[4]

---

4 *Bal Gangadhar Tilak—His Writings and Speeches*, pp. 76-78.

In different parts of India Government now resorted to repressive measures. In Bengal, the editor of the *Yugantar* was sent to jail, the editor of *Sandhya* refused to conduct his defence because he did not think that in carrying on the God-appointed mission of Swaraj he was in any way responsible to the alien ruler. Babu Aurobindo Ghose was arrested on August 17, on a charge of sedition. Babu Bepin Chandra Pal was called upon to give evidence in the case. When he was put in the dock and questioned, he declared that he considered the prosecution of Aurobindo detrimental to the country, and therefore he had conscientious objection to taking part in the case! For this Pal was sentenced to six months' simple imprisonment. People sent money to Pal's wife, and a huge meeting at Calcutta eulogised him! Aurobindo was, however, acquitted in the case.

In September Tilak again expounded the principles of national education at a meeting in Poona. He emphasized that it was in the interests of the nation that the books by Dadabhai and Dutt should be introduced in Indian schools as the Nationalists had done in Calcutta in national schools. It was true that the schools conducted by Government produced men like Ranade and Gokhale, but it was time that several men of such type should spring up in India. That was not possible unless they introduced national education in schools. It should be taught in schools how the Government was responsible for reducing the country to utter poverty.

It was the firm belief of the advocates of national education that the Government and the people were not actuated by the same ideal of citizenship. The foreign Government wanted to keep the people in bondage and therefore there had arisen the need of national education, which was a means to the attainment of Self-Government.

Tilak was intensely disturbed by the prevailing political situation in India. At a meeting he said that if the Indians did not improve their conditions, no nation would respect them. It would not be proper on the part of the Congress leaders to confine Boycott and Swadeshi to Bengal and to sit at home with folded hands and save their skin when the Punjab was being oppressed. "If the existing situation has not become unbearable to you," he said indignantly, " then it would be better if this nation dies sooner. Instead of being populated by ungrateful people, the land will welcome some worthy people who would bless it with honour and prosperity."

At another meeting during the Ganapati festival, he declared that it was useless for beggars to quarrel among themselves whether they should beg for two crores or two lacs when the giver was not prepared to part with a pie. The time had arrived now to show the world whether they were fit to live in this world. The battle was joined. There was no question of retreating. If not then at least after twenty years somebody should rise from amongst them to declare to the world that the cause where hundreds of people suffered had succeeded.

About this time Henry Nevinson, a British journalist, who was on a study tour of India, came to Poona. He saw Tilak at Sinhagad. Nevinson was indelibly impressed with Tilak's personality. His sincerity, his courageous indifference to his own future; his legal mind, subtle, given to fine distinctions, rather capable of expressing thought than thinking; his full, brown eyes steady with daring, rather aggressive; and his general manner, quiet and controlled, all created a profound impression upon Nevinson's mind.

A few days later another eminent British leader visited India. His name was Keir Hardie. He was a Member of the British Parliament. Born of very poor parents, he had worked in coal mines and raised himself from a common worker to the Membership of the British Parliament. He was received by Tilakites, and Tilak took him to a village nearby so that he might see things for himself.

Belgaum was developing into another storm centre of the Tilakites. So Tilak took much care to nurture it. On repeated invitation, Tilak visited Dharwar, made speeches, and reached Gurl Hossur where he went to attend the yearly function held in honour of Swami Chidambaram. A centre where saintly life and Hindu religion were worshipped was an attraction to Tilak, and so he visited Gurl Hossur. Tilak had a pleasant dip in the river and hundreds of people had a bath in the holy river made still holier, they thought, by the presence of a great man!

Tilak then visited Bail Hongal. There an incident happened which throws light on Tilak the leader. Tilak was to be presented with an address by the citizens of Bail Hongal. When the draft was read to him, he inquired with surprise whether he alone was to be the recipient of the address and whether Paranjpe, the editor of *Kal*, who was with him, was not to receive one. The organisers took a clue from this, and both the leaders were presented with addresses.

Just then a disturbing incident took place in the Punjab. A woman named Viranwali who was waiting for a train at a railway station was outraged both by Anglo-Indian station master and his Mohamedan servant. When Tilak heard the news he became restless, and on his way from Bail

Hongal to Belgaum he spent a whole night in brooding over the incident. He felt ashamed of the helplessness and impotence to which the country was reduced. When a few days afterwards the husband of the woman filed a suit in the court against the station master and his servant, Tilak was mad with anger and he exclaimed, "The prosperity of a country in which a man approaches the court to vindicate the honour of his outraged wife, is distant!"

At Belgaum, on the Dassera Day, Tilak reiterated his views on national education. He said that Government education produced learned men that were useless. So there was a dire necessity for starting as many national schools and colleges as possible.

Tilak expressed his desire to meet Brandon, the Collector of the District, who was then reading Tilak's books. When Tilak, accompanied by S. M. Paranjpe and Gangadharrao Deshpande, went to his bungalow, the Collector in a jolly mood exclaimed : "You are making a regular raid through my district!" Tilak replied with a smile, "It is not your sole monopoly." During the course of the talk the Collector said he was reading Tilak's books, but could not make much progress. Tilak told him that those works were the result of the toil of twelve years, and unless one had some knowledge of astronomy and Sanskrit, one would find it difficult to understand the subject.

After the talks, Brandon bade good-bye to Tilak. He called Gangadharrao Deshpande aside and said, "Really, Tilak is a great man." During the course of the conversation Brandon was very particular not to mention politics!

While this propaganda for national education was going on, preparations for the Congress session were proceeding at Nagpur and the fight between the Moderates and the Nationalists had come to a head. The Reception Committee, which was formed in February 1907, was captured by the Tilakites. The new constitution of the Congress laid down that the Reception Committee had the right to elect the President of the Congress; they were to decide that question by a majority of three-fourths votes. A meeting of the Reception Committee was held at the Town Hall in Nagpur on September 22, and it was found that Tilak could be elected President by the Nationalists. The meeting ended in pandemonium and there was bloodshed, a shoe being hurled at a Moderate leader. The Nationalists sent their representatives to Poona to consult Tilak, but they were surprised to see Tilak's messenger at Nagpur with definite instructions. The Moderates were all leaders without followers. They lacked organising ability and were miles behind in political warfare. Wamanrao Kolhatkar, the Moderate leader of Nagpur, informed Pherozeshah Mehta that if Tilak was not elected President, it would not be possible for them to hold the Congress session in Nagpur.

Mehta called a meeting of his partymen at his house to decide the question at which Kolhatkar and Parekh were present, and also Dr. Moonje, being one of the Secretaries of the Reception Committee at Nagpur. Tilak and Dr. Moonje put up at Sardar Griha. Tilak advised Dr. Moonje to take care not to allow himself to be drawn into arguments with Mehta, who could easily outwit or silence him. He asked him to stick to his point, to speak briefly but fearlessly. When Moonje went to Mehta's, he was lying in an easy-chair. The other leaders sitting by him looked like school-boys. Dr. Moonje narrated to Mehta in detail the episodes that had led to the crisis and boldly said that if Tilak was not elected by the Reception Committee they would abide by its decision; but if Tilak was elected the other Party must abide by the decision. Upon this Mehta made a stir in the chair.

Mehta asked Moonje what he would do if Kolhatkar did not assist him in collecting funds. Dr. Moonje replied that the Moderates would have to surrender the funds to them. "If the Moderates do not surrender the funds?" asked Mehta with a staring look. Dr. Moonje replied that the Nationalists would do without them and added that he was a Brahmin lad and he would beg in the name of Tilak from door to door! [5] Then Mehta indignantly asked him why they wanted Tilak to preside over the Congress. Dr. Moonje said because it was their sweet will. Pherozeshah said in a gruff voice that the question would have to be considered at a meeting of the All-India Congress Committee. Dr. Moonje made his last fervent appeal to Gokhale and Wacha, the Secretaries of the Congress, attached notes worth ten thousand rupees as deposit, and prayed that in any case Nagpur should not be deprived of an opportunity to hold the Congress session of the year.

Gokhale sensed the danger and was sad and fearful. He wrote to Wedderburn on October 11, 1907, that the outlook at the moment was as dark as could be and if a split did come, it meant a disaster.[6]

Tilak again stimulated the Paisa Fund movement. He addressed one meeting in Bombay in the middle of October 1907 at Shantaram's chawls

---

5 Dr. B. S. Moonje in *Reminiscences and Anecdotes about Lokamanya Tilak*, Vol. II, p. 501.

6 Wasti, S. R., *Lord Minto and the Indian Nationalist Movement,* p. 57.

and asked people to subscribe to the Fund for starting national industries. He cited to them the example of missionaries who collected money not in big sums but in pennies.

That meeting of the All-India Committee of the Congress convened at the house of Sir Pherozeshah Mehta met on November 10, 1907, to settle the dispute between the two Parties in Nagpur. The Moderate leader, Wamanrao Kolhatkar, was invited to the meeting, but Dr. Moonje was not called. Gokhale, Vijaya Raghavachariar, Jinnah, Mudholkar, Khaparde, D. A. Khare, Tilak and Ambalal Sakarlal attended the meeting. Khaparde suggested that a five-man committee be appointed to see that the session was successfully held at Nagpur. Mehta and his friends were not in a mood to listen to it. If the question of funds had been raised, it would have been solved as Tilak had kept ready with Dr. Moonje an amount of ten thousand rupees. Dr. Moonje was, however, not called to the meeting, but he had accompanied Tilak to the residence of Mehta in the hope that he should see the members of the Committee if they wanted to ask him any questions. But when Mehta came to know that Dr. Moonje was waiting in the veranda of his bungalow, he asked his servant to drive him away, and Dr. Moonje was driven out! Pherozeshah and his friends were smarting under the humiliation inflicted upon them by Tilak and his Bengali friends. Bhupendranath Basu had written to Mehta, after the Calcutta Congress, giving expression to the deep sense of humiliation which was felt by him and many of his friends at the rudeness displayed by some of the truculent young politicians of Bengal towards "one who was by common consent the leading statesman and politician in India".

While the Committee were thus discussing the question of the venue of the Congress, all at once a delegation from Surat descended upon the scene to extend an invitation to the Congress to hold the annual session at Surat! It may be remembered here that when, at the Calcutta Congress, the leaders of Gujarat had extended an invitation to the Congress to hold its session at Surat, it was not accepted because Pherozeshah himself was not in favour of it. The invitation of Punjab leaders was also discarded for fear of growing extremism there. But now the All-India Committee resolved to hold the Congress session at Surat. Lala Murlidhar from Punjab, C. Vijaya Raghavachariar and Daji Abaji Khare, who were present, voted for it; and Surendranath, Bhupendranath and Gangaprasad, who had expressed their opinions in their letters, favoured Surat as the venue of the next Congress session.

The All-India Committee decided to hold the session at Surat. Tilak and Khaparde did not vote. Pherozeshah Mehta dictated, others said ditto, and the meeting dispersed. Pherozeshah Mehta had played out his role. When a man's role is run out, he cannot read the signs and portents of the new spirit and times. Mehta had been thrown out in the Bombay Civic election. So he girded up his loins to prevent, in the words of his admirer Chirol, the complete triumph of Tilakism in the Congress, right down to the Surat upheaval.[7] In the words of Henry Nevinson, Pherozeshah's achievements as a builder of a model local Government "were nothing to the Nationalists. They belonged to the past, to the scrapheap of dead reputations. The crisis called for other arms, other methods!"[8]

But just at this time news came that Lala Lajpat Rai had been released. At once the Nationalists suggested his name for the presidentship of the Congress. Tilak sent Wasukaka to Lahore to persuade Lalaji to consent to accept the presidentship of the Congress, but Gokhale's pressure proved decisive and Lajpat Rai announced that he could not accept the presidentship. He did not want to take sides with either Party, and so he must have refused it. This was a sore disappointment to Tilak, and he felt grieved that Lalaji should have let down the Nationalists at such a critical moment.

Tilak was now seizing every opportunity to explain to the common people the miserable condition of their motherland. He went to Pandharpur where lakhs of Hindus go on pilgrimage. On November 16, he addressed a large meeting at Pandharpur. "The days are such," he said, "if your hearts are stirred up by the devotion of God, it may be considered that you have infringed Government laws. I can now appeal to you to think over your country's condition with the same vigour, faith and sincerity as you perform your devotion to God. Every village must give a thought to this unbearable condition." "I ask you," observed he, "neither to revolt nor to sit silent." You know who conducts the Government. All officers are from amongst you. Open your mouth; speak out the truth. Do not fear. Tell the Government that you are unhappy under the British regime. You have no arms, but you have an equally powerful weapon—Swadeshi. The Government that depends upon your help, money, toil and information,

7 Chirol, Sir Valentine, *Indian Unrest*, p. 51.

8 Nevinson, Henry W., *The New Spirit in India*, pp. 240-41.

must come to a stop if you so will. Do not be informants. Informants have their abodes in hell!"

At this meeting Tilak twice told his audience that possibly he would not be there to speak next year! Tilak must have sensed the danger of imminent imprisonment.

Pal was in jail, Aurobindo Ghose had luckily escaped the sedition charge. On November 1, 1907, the Seditious Meetings Act was passed despite the opposition of Gokhale and others.

The Nationalists and Moderates were gathering their forces and weighing their strength before they went to Surat, the Kurukshetra. In November of the year the Midnapur District Conference met at Midnapur in Bengal. Aurobindo Ghose, the leader of the Nationalists, had a tussle with the Moderates, and the Nationalists were ejected from the Conference with the help of the police! This was the first open rupture that took place between the Moderates and the Nationalists, and the latter were so much excited that they called Surendranath a 'traitor'!

As the day of the Congress session was nearing, the tension between the two groups was rising and feelings were mounting. They were attacking each other ferociously. The tone of Tilak's *Mahratta* of which Kelkar was the editor was mild as compared to that of Tilak's *Kesari*. Kelkar lacked the ferocity of his master. Tilak's other lieutenants and colleagues were critical of Kelkar. In their opinion Kelkar was less staunch and less fanatic. So Kelkar requested him either to relieve him of the responsibility of the editorship of the *Mahratta* or to accept his resignation. The fact was that Kelkar was one with Tilak as regards principles, but could not be brutal in his attack on Gokhale and other Moderate leaders. Besides, he personally did not like critics to speak ill of Gokhale, who was attacked on a low level by Tilak's followers. Tilak frankly disagreed with Kelkar on many points of tactics, but he was not willing to lose him. And so they pulled together.

At Surat the Reception Committee was formed on November 21, and a meeting was convened to elect the president so that no member from Maharashtra might be able to attend the meeting, almost all of them receiving intimation about it on the very day! Yet the Nationalists in Surat and the neighbouring places fought for the election of Lajpat Rai, but they were in a minority. At first Gokhale coaxed them saying that it would not be possible for the Congress to denounce the Government for his deportation if Lalaji was in the chair, but when Gokhale saw that the Nationalists were still unyielding, he took off the mask and threw down the gauntlet to the

Nationalists to secure Lalaji's election in the face of the opposition of the Moderates. And thus Dr. Rash Behari Ghose was elected President. Tilak had written to Motilal Ghose that if Lajpat Rai was chosen President of the Congress, it would be in a way a great inspiration to the nation and an act of denunciation of the Government. He, therefore, requested him to dissuade Rash Behari from accepting the presidentship of the Congress. Had he been present there, Tilak concluded, he would have, for principle's sake, knelt down before Rash Behari and prayed him not to accept the chair.

Tilak declared in the *Kesari* that the coming Congress would be described as a court assembly of Mehta and Company. He reminded Mehta of his defeat in the civic election and warned him that the same story would be repeated at Surat. He further wrote that Lajpat Rai was a hundred times better than Rash Behari Ghose from the point of view of sacrifice, sufferings and hardship he had undergone for the cause of the nation, and remarked that Gokhale was compromising the stand taken by the Congress and committing it to a policy which was discouraging and prejudicial to national interests. He stated that the Congress was established to wrest rights from the Government. It was not established to placate the Government and the bureaucracy. At this time Tilak received a letter from Sir William Wedderburn asking him to find some compromise and compose the differences between the two Parties. Those who were interested in India's political advancement had fixed their eyes on the Surat Congress.

III

On the eve of his departure for Surat, Tilak addressed a meeting at Chinchpokli, a labour area in Bombay, and told the workers that the Swadeshi movement was beneficial to them. He said that because people were asked to use Swadeshi cloth, the work in the mills would increase and the employees would be benefited. The object of the Swadeshi movement was to provide them with work. The workers in Bombay numbered about two lacs and their strength was greater than the British forces in India. They should think over their own condition and explain it to others. He appealed to them to give up drink and added that though Government was popularising inoculation, it did nothing to minimise the liquor evil.

By now Hemchandra Das had reached India with copies of the Bomb manual, the original of which P. M. Bapat had secured in Germany. Savarkar, the prince of the Indian revolutionaries, was then turning the switch of the revolutionary movement from London. On the arrival of Hemchandra Das, the first bomb exploded at Midnapur as a result of which the Viceroy's train was derailed. In the third week of December 1907, Alien, the retired District Magistrate of Dacca, was shot.

Tilak went to Bombay and made arrangements for the reception of Lala Lajpat Rai in Bombay. He was very particular about it, as he knew that the Moderates would not care much for it. Lajpat Rai was lustily cheered when he came to Bombay. He went to Ahmedabad on the 23rd December 1907, and Tilak reached Surat on the morning of the 23rd of December. People accorded him a grand welcome. There Dadasaheb Khaparde was already addressing meetings and explaining the viewpoint of the New Party.

Passions ran high. The Reception Committee, which was dominated by the Moderates, was not in a mood to do its duty. The volunteers at the station did not give the Nationalist leaders correct information as to their place of sojourn, or arrangements. The Nationalist Party pitched their tent at a distant place from the Congress pandal. Lajpat Rai came and was given a thundering ovation. Tilak studied the situation carefully. He came to know that Khaparde was removing doubts from the minds of the people regarding the aims and objects of the New Party. Tilak addressed a meeting at Balaji's Tekdi in Surat and declared that the Nationalists had not come to Surat to cause a split in the Congress. They wanted to move the Congress on. "Our aim," he observed, " is Self-Government. It should be achieved as soon as possible. . . . We are against autocratic movement. These autocrats want to cripple the Congress and so they are against Boycott and Swaraj resolutions. They don't want to say or rather preach boycott openly. They have no moral courage." Morley and other officials, he proceeded, wanted to make a breach in the Congress camp. If they did not stick up to the idea of Swaraj, they would be considered traitors to the country. Political regeneration was their ideal, and no one had any authority to make the Congress recede from that ideal.

Referring to the opinion expressed by Morley and by *The Times*, London, that self-government was impracticable for India, he said: "Remember, what is impracticable for Mr. Morley and for the Anglo-Indians is practicable for our countrymen because our interests are conflicting." "We are fighting," he concluded, " against foreign autocracy. Why should we allow this home autocracy? The Congress is an organisation of all the people, and the voice of the people ought to predominate. We should not allow any man, high or low, to ruin the cause of the Congress." [9]

In the official announcement of the draft resolutions, the Calcutta resolutions on Boycott, Swadeshi, and National Education did not find place. Naturally the suspicion of the New Party was aroused. What was more, Gokhale took over the drafting of the resolution from the Reception Committee, but somehow he could not supply the New Party leaders with a copy of the resolutions in time. On December 24 the National Party held a meeting under the presidentship of Aurobindo Ghose, and it was felt that the majority were not in favour of a compromise. Tilak calmly said that he believed in compromise and added that his opinion was that the New Party should not leave the Congress fold. Aurobindo, though personally disinclined to a compromise, believed in the practical sense of Tilak. At this meeting a committee consisting of Khaparde, Pillai, Tilak and Moonje was formed to negotiate with the Moderates the terms of the compromise.

Next day the Nationalists held a Conference under Aurobindo's presidentship at Ghee Kanta Wadi where they had a separate camp. Tilak made a very clear and forcible statement at the Conference as regards the aims and objects of the New Party. He said that the difference between the Moderates and the Nationalists was that the Moderates wanted Self-Government on colonial lines, whereas the Nationalists wanted Independence. The methods of the Moderates were prayers, petitions and protests, whereas those of the Nationalists were boycott, passive resistance and self-reliance. The opponents of the Nationalists did not venture to express their goal for fear of displeasing the Government, whereas the Nationalists were prepared to suffer for their convictions. After the Conference they held a meeting at Balaji's Tekdi. The charges that could be easily levelled against any leader were those of communalism or provincialism and it was done in Tilak's case too. Some mischief-monger had distributed pamphlets, written under a *nom de plume* in Surat, alleging that Tilak had made in his papers some remarks indicating disrespect to the Gujarati community, and come to Surat to complete the work of Shivaji, who had raided English warehouses in Surat during the days of the East India Company! None knew what the raids of Shivaji on the English warehouses had to do with Gujaratis at Surat in 1907.

---

9 Bal Gangadhar Tilak: *His Writings and Speeches,* pp. 376-3

So, at this Balaji Tekdi meeting, Tilak challenged his critics either to prove that he meant disrespect to the Gujaratis or to apologise unconditionally. Khaparde gave the Gujarati version of Tilak's speech and the passions aroused were assuaged to some extent. Sirdar Ajit Singh also spoke at the meeting.

On the 25th of December 1907, Tilak and his lieutenants tried to bring about a compromise. They saw Surendranath Banerjee. He gave his consent to the terms of compromise and added that he would let Tilak know about it after consulting Gokhale. Lalaji said he would try to bring about a compromise, but he could do it either on the 25th or on the 26th. At noon the Nationalists held another Conference where Tilak made a masterly speech. Motilal Ghose arrived at night, and the number of delegates and the strength of the Nationalists increased!

The whole day and night the New Party leaders were discussing the situation at Ghee Kanta Wadi where they had camped. It was agreed that if the Moderates did not compromise then an amendment was to be moved to the proposition of the name of the presidentship. For that significant task a powerful man was required, and Tilak himself undertook the task of moving that proposition as none came forward from the Bengali delegates to do it, because it looked awkward for a Bengali delegate to pull down a Bengali from the presidential chair! Tilak admired this attitude on the part of the Bengali delegates. When Tilak asked his lieutenant Kelkar whether he would second the amendment moved by him, he too point-blank declined to do so. All Tilakites were enraged at this refusal of Kelkar. The whole day Tilak would not exchange a word with Kelkar!

On the morning of December 26, Tilak again tried to meet the Moderate leaders, but all of them avoided him. Some Moderate leaders said that they had previous engagements. The Chairman of the Reception Committee Tribhuvandas Malvi, a solicitor of the Bombay High Court, said that he was engrossed in his religious practices! At two-thirty in the afternoon Tilak was in the President's tent. He went there to meet him, but Malvi said he was busy with the President's procession!

The Congress pandal was erected at the old historic French Gardens in Surat. It was now time for the Congress session to commence. The New Party men entered the pandal. The Nagpur delegates were allotted a place at the farthest corner, and care was taken to see that all Maharashtrian delegates did not come together! Just behind the President's chair the members of the Reception Committee from Bombay and Gujarat sat in two rows.

The arrival of the Nationalist leaders like Lajpat Rai and Tilak was greeted with thundering applause. The procession entered the pandal. The President Dr. Rash Behari Ghose, accompanied by Gokhale, Surendranath and Pherozeshah, entered the pandal, but they could not evoke so much warmth as did Tilak and Lajpat Rai. Tilak was given a copy of the draft resolutions at three although the *Advocate of India* got it the previous day. Tilak was not asked to occupy a seat on the dais! The Moderate bosses alone occupied the platform with the President elect. These men of balmy moderation and broad outlook did not care to offer Tilak a seat on the dais!

The Chairman of the Reception Committee read out his speech. None was interested in it, and it looked a long tedious tale. Then rose Dewan Bahadur Ambalal Sakarlal and proposed Dr. Ghose to the chair. He was heckled, but was allowed to finish his speech amidst continual cries of dissent. Surendranath Banerjee, the hero of a hundred platforms, rose to second the proposition. When Surendranath, the Indian Cicero, rose up the Bengalee delegates denounced him as the 'Midnapur traitor'! That cry was taken up by the other Nationalists, and they heckled him. Amidst persistent cries he could not continue his speech. Any new attempt at stilling the raging storm of a violent tumult proved to be of no avail. So Malvi got upon a table and declared that he had suspended the session for the day.

Nevinson went to see Tilak far across the city at his tent. Tilak had taken off his clothes and wore only a dhoti. They had a talk. Tilak told him that the whole thing was a mistake; it had all happened because the undertaking to renew the Calcutta resolutions had reached him too late, not till the Chairman had begun his speech.

At night Chimanlal Saraiya, Vice-Chairman of the Reception Committee, came to Tilak and expressed his intention of bringing about a compromise. Tilak agreed, but Saraiya did not turn up that night. The hostile demonstration staged by Tilak's Party was not prearranged. On their returning to their residence, Tilak expressed his displeasure and said to his men that next day they "must be calm like a block of stone".

Next morning Saraiya came, and Tilak, Saraiya and Khaparde went to meet Dr. Rutherford, Member of the British Parliament, who had come to witness the Congress session; but he could not meet them at the appointed time.

Tilak put forth a fresh proposal to Saraiya. He proposed that the business of the election should be adjourned, and a committee of one leading Moderate and one leading Nationalist from each Province be appointed to consider and settle the differences between the two Parties,

Dr. Rutherford's name being added to the list. Saraiya returned after consulting Mehta and Gokhale and said that nothing could be done in the matter.

At one, the procession of the President-elect entered. Tilak put a small slip of paper into the hands of Malvi. It read:

" Sir,

I wish to address the delegates on the proposal of the election of the President after it is seconded. I wish to move an adjournment with a constructive proposal. Please announce me.

Yours sincerely,
B. G. Tilak
Deccan Delegate (Poona)."

Malvi put this into his pocket with a shadow of anxiety over his face. At the place where the Nagpur batch of delegates was sitting, Muslims were posted with lathis. Dr. Moonje sent out some of them as they had no tickets. Dr. Moonje and his group were ready with lathis as he was told by the man who sold tickets that his group was particularly selected for being hammered! Passions had risen high. The leaders on both sides were on their guard. It may be that the chiefs on either side were unaware of these secret preparations. The session commenced. Surendranath proposed Dr. Ghose to the chair, and he was allowed to finish his speech. Pandit Motilal Nehru supported the motion and it was put to the vote. It was about to be passed. Tilak, who waited to be called upon to address the meeting, now fully realised that the Chairman of the Reception Committee wanted to gag him. So he rushed towards the dais, pushing aside a volunteer who tried to hold him back. There was a sudden uproar in the pandal.

The young Moderates, observes Nevinson in his book, on either side of Tilak, sprang to their feet wildly gesticulating vengeance, shaking their fists and yelling in the air; they clamoured to hurl him down the steep of the platform. The nationalist delegates shouted that he must be heard. The Chairman of the Reception Committee told Tilak that he had ruled him out, and, therefore, he could move neither an adjournment nor an amendment to the election of the President. Dr. Ghose too said that he had ruled out Tilak. Tilak replied that Dr. Ghose was not a duly elected President and said he had a right to appeal to the delegates on the subject. Dr. Ghose and Malvi said that Tilak would be removed from the platform. Tilak said he would not move an inch unless he was bodily removed and added that they should try to do so if they dared! A young man named Gandhi, who was one of the Secretaries of the Reception Committee, touched Tilak's person with a view to carrying out the Chairman's order.

At this, young leaders from the delegates' compartment rushed to the platform. Dr. Moonje jumped upon the dais and stood by Tilak; his friends who followed on to the platform saved Moonje without his knowledge from an assault. Ambalal's son hurled a chair at Tilak, but Madhusudan Bhagat from Punjab caught it and threw it aside. Gokhale stood by his old opponent to protect him from the threatened onset and snubbed Ambalal's son saying that if he touched Tilak there would be bloodshed! And at this moment, in the words of Henry Nevinson, who was present all throughout, "suddenly something flew through the air, a shoe!—a Mahratta shoe! reddish leather, pointed toe, sole studded with lead. It struck Surendranath Banerjee on the cheek; it cannoned off upon Sir Pherozeshah Mehta. It flew, it fell, and as at a given signal, white waves of turbaned men surged up the escarpment of the platform. Leaping, climbing, hissing the breath of fury, brandishing long sticks, they came, striking at any head that looked to them Moderate, and in another moment, between brown legs standing upon the green-baize table, I caught glimpses of the Indian National Congress dissolving in chaos. Like Goethe at the battle of Valmy, I could have said, 'Today marks the beginning of a new era, and you can say that you were present at that.'[10]

But amidst this erupting volcano of violence Tilak stood there with folded arms, defiant, calling upon violence to do its worst. In front of him the white-clad audience roared like a tumultuous sea. A Punjabi leader said that he saw that day the true spirit of a Mahratta on the dais!

The Moderate leaders left the pandal by the back door. Tilak refused to leave the pandal. He sat in a chair and chewed pieces of betel-nut. When Tilak saw women trembling in a corner, he told his men to take them out safely. Dr. Moonje did it immediately. When the women went out, almost all persons in the pandal were about to go when an old Parsee threw his umbrella at Tilak, but it fell aside. Tilak prevented his men from hitting that Parsee. While he was going out, Tilak was pelted with stones. So the followers held their lathis over his head. When the battle was over, Tilak went to the wounded soldiers and made arrangements for the dressing of their wounds and for medicine. In the meanwhile the police entered the

---

10 Nevinson, Henry W., *The New Spirit in India*, pp. 257-58.

pandal and cleared the place. Thus the fight which was to take place in the Gondvans, took place on the banks of the Tapti.

IV

In the evening Tilak, at a meeting of the Nationalists held at Ghee Kanta Wadi, made a very stirring speech for an hour and a half. He dealt with the grave situation extensively and said that the Bombay Moderates, who wanted to please Government by moving the Congress a little backward, took advantage of the exceptional majority of Moderate delegates to force their view on the Congress even at the risk of a split. It was that spirit of intolerance that had led to the present situation. The Nationalists had to devise means to keep up the work of the Congress. He expressed the hope that an opportunity would present itself when both the Parties would unite not only to resist the repressive measures of the Government, but also to advance towards the goal of Self-Government.

Mr. Nevinson was present at this meeting which was held under the presidentship of Aurobindo. Hearing Tilak's bold and correct stand he was deeply impressed, and while putting his note-book into his pocket, he exclaimed, "Here is the man!" Technically, Tilak could have moved any amendment or an adjournment. Moreover, he could have modified the resolutions on the line of his Party's policy had he got a majority in the Subjects Committee. Pherozeshah said that the conscientious conviction of the Moderates was not in favour of the resolutions, and if Nationalists had a majority they could have carried the resolutions in the Subjects Committee and outside also. If there was no majority in favour of altering or modifying the resolution, such an undertaking as was demanded by the Nationalists constituted an outright aggression imposing the will of the minority upon the majority.

Gokhale's whole conduct in this affair was evasive. He did not supply the Nationalist leaders with the draft of the resolutions until it was too late. It was afterwards found that in spite of his Party's profession that they did not want to go back upon the Calcutta resolutions, from the draft resolution on the Swadeshi the phrase "even at some sacrifice" was dropped. The Calcutta resolution said the Boycott movement inaugurated in Bengal 'was and is justifiable', but Gokhale changed it to read as Boycott of foreign goods resorted to in Bengal. The Calcutta resolution on National Education appealed to the people to organise a system of education on national lines and under national control. The draft slyly dropped out the words 'on national and under national control' and said it should be organised as an independent system of education. Motilal Ghose and A. C. Mitra wanted to bring about a compromise to revive the Congress next day. Tilak gave them an assurance in writing as follows:

Surat, 28th December 1907.

Dear Sir,

With reference to our conversation and principally in the best interests of the Congress, I and my Party are prepared to waive our opposition to the election of Dr. Rash Behari as President of the 23rd Indian National Congress, and we are prepared to act in the spirit of forget and forgive provided, firstly the last year's resolutions on Swaraj, Swadeshi, Boycott and National Education are adhered to and each expressly re-affirmed, and secondly such passages, if any, in Dr. Ghose's speech as may be offensive to the Nationalist Party, are omitted."

Yours etc.

B. G. Tilak.

Dr. Ghose's speech had been already published in the Calcutta papers, and the Nationalist leaders had protested against it by telegrams!

Next day, December 28, a Convention was held under the Chairmanship of Dr. Ghose, and only those delegates who agreed to a certain line of action taken by the Moderates were admitted to it. Lajpat Rai said at the Convention that in spite of all misfortunes they were going to prove to the world that with all the internal quarrels they had agreed to serve the country by helping the Congress under whose banner they had been battling for the last twenty-two years. Tilak was not happy over this disaster, and he was about to go to the Convention by signing the pledge.[11] But S. M. Paranjpe and Wasukaka Joshi prevented him from doing so. Recollecting his thoughts about this in 1916 Aurobindo observed : "Many after Surat spoke of him as the deliberate breaker of the Congress, but to no one was the catastrophe so great a blow as to Mr. Tilak. He did not love the do-nothingness of that assembly, but he valued it both as a great national fact and for its unrealised possibilities and hope to make of it a central organisation for practical work." [12]

---

11 *Reminiscences and Anecdotes about Lokamanya Tilak*, Vol. Ill, p. 118.

12 An Appreciation by Babu Aurobindo Ghose in *Bal Gangadhar Tilak: His Writings and Speeches*, p. 13.

And yet Pherozeshah Mehta in an interview that he gave to a representative of the *Times of India*, said that Tilak's influence over reputable people in the Provinces other than his own, rested on the fact that he managed to hang on to the Congress. Now that the split had come people would find him out. The Moderates, he concluded, had managed to avoid the grand mistake of using force against Tilak, which he very much desired they should do, and had so placed the onus of the split on Mr. Tilak.[13] This is, however, one side of the picture, and as to the influence of Tilak it is an uncharitable estimate warped by the partisan view!

The party leaders returned home. Henry W. Nevinson writes in his famous book that "every station rang with the shouts of 'Down with Rash Behari,' 'Down with Gokhale,' 'Down with Surendranath'!"

On reaching Poona, Tilak wrote a reasoned article in the *Kesari*: "Both the Moderates and the Nationalists must remember that persons belonging to both the parties are actuated by a sincere desire to promote the welfare of the country; and none is deliberately working to bring about the ruin of the country." "Neither should try to stamp out the other," he continued, "both should, while exerting their utmost to get the upper hand in the National assemblies conducted by the united efforts of the Moderates and the Nationalists, never abuse their supremacy by trying to crush or cripple their opponents in the other party. Moderates should remember that it is because the New Party has come into existence that the Bureaucracy condescends to 'rally' them. The Nationalists must understand that though the caution and hesitation of the Moderates is often galling to them, still their influence and prestige is not to be despised."

Morley asked for the information regarding the Congress session telegraphically. On having it he said that the Congress had gone to pieces. "For it means, I suppose," he added, "the victory of Extremist over Moderate; going no further at this stage than the break-up of the Congress, but pointing to a future stage in which the Congress will have become an Extremist organization." [14]

For a few days after the Surat Congress, there was a discussion on Tilak's conduct at the Congress, especially from the point of view of the

13 *Some unpublished if Later Speeches & Writings of the Hon. Sir Pherozeshah Mehta*, p. 211.

14 Das, M. N., *India Under Morley And Minto*, p. 99.

general procedure of a meeting. Tilak also wrote articles on the rights of the Chairman. Both sides quoted authorities to support their standpoint.

The Surat Congress became a subject for discussion for the literate and the illiterate. A Poona Moderate said to a friend of Tilak, "Balwantrao was the devil incarnate." During those days the opponents of the Nationalists heaped words of abuse on Tilak, and one morning Tilak said to his grown-up children that they ate something with tea, but he had of late words of abuse with the morning tea!

Aurobindo Ghose paid a visit to Poona in January 1908. He was accorded a great welcome. Poona heard a great Bengalee whose demand for absolute political independence had surpassed that of Tilak. In a speech which he delivered in Bombay he declared in a religious vein and with spiritual fervour: "Nationalism cannot die, because it is God who is working in Bengal. God cannot be killed. God cannot be sent to gaol." Aurobindo then went to make a tour of the Central Provinces. By this time Maharashtra and Bengal had made considerable progress in their preparations for revolutionary deeds. Aurobindo came in contact with the revolutionary forces in Maharashtra. Government was watching the activities of the revolutionaries. Repression was launched by Government as foretold by Tilak. In the Madras Province the Nationalist leaders like Chidambaram Pillay were put in jail on return to their respective home towns.

CHAPTER XVI

Bombs Intervene

I

In the last week of January 1908, the Governor of Bombay, Sir George Clarke, invited press representatives to visit the laboratory where serum was prepared. Tilak attended the meeting at the Haffkine Institute, Bombay, and congratulated the Governor on his taking many precautions against plague. He, however, cautioned Government against making inoculation compulsory as it was then in an experimental stage. Tilak moved a vote of thanks to the Governor. In February 1908 Lala Hardayal met Tilak at Poona. He gave him directions as to the work to be done in the Punjab and hoped that Hardayal would develop into a nationalist leader in the Punjab and would prove a tower of strength to the Nationalist Party.

About this time the Maharashtra Vidyaprasarak Mandal thought it safe to shift their school from Kolhapur to Talegaon. Tilak had also fixed Talegaon as the site for the Swadeshi Glass Factory. But these projects needed funds. The promoters of national education said that mere popularity of their great leader would not be helpful in removing the distress and difficulties of the students. They wanted actual help. Tilak was a man of his word. He decided to raise funds for the school.

Accordingly Tilak addressed a meeting at Sholapur and told his audience that national education was that which made the students conscious of the nation. He said that English was a difficult language and a student had to waste many years to gain knowledge through the medium of English. The younger generation must obtain knowledge upto the age of fifteen years which the old generation could not gain upto thirty-five. He remarked that Government money belonged to the public. Because public funds were in the possession of the Government he had to seek their help.

He further told the audience that Government might not like the idea of national education and it might put an end to it, but that opposition would be met as circumstances would demand. After his speech he met some rich people and collected money.

Tilak visited Barsi on March 3, 1908, and appealed to the rich to help the cause of national education. Addressing a meeting at Barsi, Tilak said that to be able to read and write alone was no education. They were simply the means of its attainment. That which gave them a knowledge of the experience of their ancestors was called education. Want of religious education was one of the causes that had led to the missionary influence over the country. Government wanted engineers, doctors, and clerks. It therefore started such schools which could supply its needs. If the Educational Department had been under their control they could have effected in it the necessary changes immediately. "We are not given such education," he observed, "as may inspire patriotic sentiments in us. In America the Declaration of Independence is taught in the fifth or the sixth class. In this way they train their children in politics."

"Of the many things that we will do," he proceeded, "religious education will first and foremost engage our attention. Secular education alone is not enough to build up character. Religious education is necessary because the study of high principles keeps us away from evil pursuits. Religion reveals to us the form of the Almighty. Says our religion that a man by virtue of his action can become even a God. Hinduism to the Hindus, Islam to the Mussalmans, will be taught in these schools. And it will be also taught there to forgive and to forget the differences of other religions."

He then observed that the second thing that they would do, would be to lighten the load of the study of foreign languages. They could not help learning English; but there was no reason why its study should be made compulsory.

Industrial education would be the third factor. Matches would be manufactured in India and the sugar industry would be run in India if training in the industry was imparted.

Education in politics would be the fourth factor. "Every year some thirty or forty crores of rupees," he went on, "are drained out of India without any return. We have, therefore, fallen into a wretched state of poverty. These things, if understood in the prime of life, can make such a lasting impression on the hearts of our young men, as it would be impossible in an advanced age."

"The will," he concluded, "is wanted. Let the Government be displeased. We should not give up our work for fear of Government displeasure. If perchance any difficulty arises, our young men are to face it. To fear difficulties is to lose manliness. Difficulties do us immense good. They inspire courage in us and prepare us to bear them manly. A nation cannot progress if it meets no difficulties in the way. We do not get this sort of education for want of Self-Government." [1] During this tour Tilak collected a sum of fifty thousand rupees for national education.

From Barsi he came to Bombay direct to give evidence on March 9, 1908, before the Royal Decentralisation Commission. He observed that any further decentralisation would tend to vest greater powers in the lower officials and make the system unpopular by encouraging local despotism which the people had justly learnt to look upon with disfavour. The transfer of authority and power should be not between officials themselves, but from officials to the people, and that too in an ungrudging spirit: "We must begin," he explained, "with the village system the autonomy of which has been destroyed by the growth of departmentalism under the present rule. The village must be made a unit of Self-Government, and the village communities or councils invested with definite powers to deal with all or most of the village questions concerning education, medical relief, justice, police and sanitation." "It is high time," he continued, "that the combination of Judicial and Executive functions in the same officers should be discontinued."

Referring to the partition of Bengal, Tilak further observed : "In this connection I may here state that I advocate a rearrangement of Provinces on considerations of linguistic and ethnological affinities and a federation thereof under a central authority." "English education," he concluded, "has created new aspirations and ideals amongst the people; and so long as these natural aspirations remain unsatisfied, it is useless to expect that the hiatus between the officers and the people could be removed by any scheme of official decentralisation, whatever the other effects may be." [2]

---

1 Bal Gangadhar Tilak: *His Writings and Speeches*, pp. 83-89.

2 Ibid, pp. 93-96.

II

TILAK WAS BUSY with one more plan. He had started collecting funds for launching a Nationalist Marathi daily in Bombay. During his stay in Bombay he addressed two meetings of mill-hands and urged the jobbers to form committees in their respective mills to root out the evil of drink. He told them that the income of Government from Abkari alone exceeded the total revenue of the Mahratta Empire, and so the Government was not discouraging the evil of drink.

Tilak took keen interest in the Poona Municipal election as he wanted to measure the strength of the nationalists in the election, and he succeeded in browbeating the Moderates in the civic election.

In the last week of March 1908, Tilak organised the Poona District Conference which was held under the well-known statistician Rao Bahadur Joshi. The Conference appealed to bring about unity in the National Congress and advocated the Boycott and Swadeshi movement. 'Self-reliance; no mendicancy,' was the watchword of the Conference. It was resolved to take steps to encourage the sugar industry in Poona, to make an industrial survey of the district, to start at least twenty-five schools during the course of one year, to encourage arbitration and discourage the habit of drinking liquor.

Tilak delivered at this District Conference a speech on the 'evil of drink'. He ridiculed the idea of carrying on a temperance propaganda by means of magic lantern performances and other methods. These methods, he said, were all right in countries having the hereditary habit of drink in their blood. But where, as in India, morality, religion, social opinion, instinct and heredity were strongly against the use of liquor, picketing was the only way to rouse the individual.

Appealing to the youth, he concluded: "If you really desire to banish the evil of drink, you must be prepared to lay down your lives for accomplishing it."

Soon the movement spread to Belgaum, Ahmednagar and to some other towns. Youth came forward to take part in the temperance movement started under the auspices of the Poona Temperance Association which was sponsored by Tilak in August 1907. The President of the Association was G. K. Gokhale. The volunteers were selected after careful scrutiny. Work was assigned to them, and they started peaceful picketing before the principal liquor shops in Poona, Thana, Belgaum and Ahmednagar

Districts and tried to check the evil of drink. Within a fortnight, the Poona City almost gave up drink. All leading personalities of Poona, Dr. Bhandarkar, Gokhale and Tilak took an active interest in it. Youth working under the Poona Temperance Association cautiously and tactfully carried on their activities in spite of rebuffs, insults and provocations. The Rev. Dr. MacNickol, a Christian missionary, was so much overjoyed with the work that he exclaimed to Tilak's friend Shankarrao Lavate; "Mr. Lavate, who is supporting this gigantic movement and doing all this? Is it that great man?" A deputation consisting of Gokhale, Tilak and the Rev. Dr. MacNickol and others waited on the then Collector of Poona to discuss the rules, and it was said that in accordance with some of his suggestions, certain changes were introduced thereafter. Some volunteers were arrested and produced before a Magistrate and their cases were fought out. The movement was such a success that one officer in his confidential report to Government said that Tilak ruled over Poona for those two weeks.

In the Court, Tilak stood as a witness on behalf of two picketers who were prosecuted for breach of the rules and for unlawful assembly. During the cross-examination Tilak replied as follows to the questions asked by Davar :

TILAK: I am not an Extremist. You please tell me what you mean by extremist.

DAVAR: Jahal means extremist.

TILAK: Extremist is a vague term. You please ask me what I am and then I will tell you what I am.

DAVAR: Does not your creed preach to raise objections to measures adopted by Government?

TILAK: I am for obstructing unlawful measures adopted by Government.

Tilak's leadership had transferred the temperance movement into a model organisation. He not only defended the volunteers in the Court, but also protected them from drunken ruffians. One day, while on his rounds, he saw a ruffian mishandling a volunteer. Seeing Tilak on the scene, he ran into the liquor shop. And to the amazement of the by-standers Tilak sprang upon him like a lion, seized him by the neck, dragged him out of the liquor shop into the street, and handed him over to the police. When injustice was meted out to his men his blood boiled. There was such an occasion when S. V. Bapat, one of Tilak's confidants, told Tilak that he was to appear the next day before a Magistrate for his trial for picketing. Tilak burst out, "Damn it! Why don't you catch the Magistrate's ears and slap his face? First he does us an injustice and then punishes us! I wonder how youths like you sit silent and why their blood is not up at the sight of injustice!" Upon this Bapat left his house. But Tilak called him back and said: "Look here, you don't do any such thing now. Otherwise you would say you did what Tilak asked you to do. It requires an inborn spirit to react in that way." The arrest of volunteers and the convictions inflicted upon them damped their spirit, and the agitation ended in a tremendous meeting held under the presidentship of Dr. Bhandarkar. The meeting protested against the Government policy of harassment, and a deputation waited on the Governor; but nothing came out of it.

III

SIMULTANEOUSLY, ATTEMPTS WERE made to reach a compromise between the two sections of the Congress. Tilak had not lost heart. He declared that "the real cause of the split was the insistence upon the conditions that the members of the Congress should be only those who profess a particular view, viz. the creed." So he wrote vigorous articles vehemently condemning the Moderates for attempting to modify the Congress creed. He wrote a series of articles, explaining to the people the difference between Independence and Self-Government and stressed the value of Independence! Tilak was not willing to break from the great organisation. His son Shridharpant later wrote in one of his articles that his father was determined not to repeat the mistake of abandoning an organisation. He had drawn a lesson from the affairs of the Deccan Education Society. So he carried on a vigorous campaign in favour of a united Congress. At Pabna, the Bengal Provincial Conference was held under the presidentship of Rabindranath Tagore, and there was a compromise. There the Moderates did not take objection to their passing the Calcutta resolutions. The Bombay Provincial Conference met at Dhulia in April 1908, and there resolutions on Swadeshi, Boycott and National Education were passed. The resolution appointing a committee to bring about a compromise was moved at this Conference by Tilak. He declared that it would be suicidal to leave out of the Congress any Party pledged to peaceful and constitutional methods, only because that Party preached independence.

Pherozeshah Mehta expressed his opinion in favour of the Congress and the *Times of India* piously opined that the Congress would gain in power and influence if it had the courage to amputate the accretion, viz. the Extremists.

Tilak attended meetings or conferences at Amalner, Akola, Khamgaon and Nasik, explaining the principles of the New Party and supporting the idea of unification of both the groups in the Congress. It was at Akola on May 2 that he declared his historic motto 'Freedom is a birth-right' and Khaparde wrote in his diary that "this aphorism of his has been adopted as a motto and repeated everywhere since then."[3]

Tilak secured at this time many well-known works on Russia, and he had a mind to write a series of articles on Russia just to give an impetus to the Indian political movement, but he could not do it as he was soon arrested.

Tilak could have established a *rapprochement* between the parties and unified the Congress, but just at this time the revolutionaries were up in revolt and the whole political atmosphere suddenly changed! Savarkar's colleague, P. M. Bapat, returned to Bombay under a pseudonym in March 1908, with perfect knowledge of the technique of bomb-making. He attended a secret meeting of the Bengal revolutionaries just before the Muzaffarpur incident. On April 30 Khudiram Bose and Prafulla Chakravarti threw a bomb at a car in the belief that Mr. Douglas Kingsford, Sessions Judge at Muzaffarpur, was in it, but it killed instead Mrs. and Miss Kennedy, the wife and daughter of Pringle Kennedy who was an English barrister. This incident created a panic among Government circles, and they arrested a number of youths in Bengal and in Maharashtra. In Bengal four editors were put behind the bar.

In Calcutta young men went to jail as editors as if they were born as prison-editors. The young Bengalis led by Aurobindo must have caused Macaulay and other critics to turn in their graves—critics who had painted them with cowardice and described them as the cowards of the world. "Courage," said a leader in *Bande Mataram*, "is your principal asset. Heroism, says Emerson, feels and never reasons and therefore is always right. If you are to work out the salvation of your country, you will have to do it with heroism." On May 2 a *posse* of constables raided Aurobindo's house, placed irons on his hands, put a rope round his waist, and took him to the central police office in Calcutta like an ordinary criminal. Tilak himself wrote an article under the caption "Country's Misfortune," in the

3 *Reminiscences and Anecdotes about Lokamanya Tilak*, Vol. II, pp. 591-

Kesari of the 16th May and then went to Sinhagad to have a little respite. He was preparing a brief symposium of the work on politics which he had planned. On May 15 there appeared an article in the *Kal* on the Muzaffarpur incident.

On May 22 a statement was issued over the signatures of Tilak and other leading Nationalists in Maharashtra. "We view with deep regret," said the statement, "the recent acts of violence on the part of certain young men in Bengal, resulting in lamentable deaths."

The statement observed that these regrettable occurrences were the result of a continued policy of repression on the part of the Government and that the true remedy for the prevailing state of things lay in making liberal concessions to the legitimate demands and aspirations of the people in a spirit of large-minded sympathy and far-sighted statesmanship.

The Bombay Government, horrified by the explosion of the bomb at Muzaffarpur, laid its repressive hand on the editors of *Hind Swaraj*, *Vihari*, and *Arunodaya*. Having dealt with the small fry, the Government turned its iron hand to the *Kal* and the *Kesari*. Meanwhile S. M. Paranjpe was arrested on June 11 and was taken to Bombay for trial. On June 8 the Indian Newspapers (Incitement to Offences) Act VII of 1908 was passed. And on June 9 the Government decided to prosecute Tilak for his article "Country's Misfortune", in the *Kesari*. When Paranjpe was arrested Tilak was on a private visit to the Ketkars in Nasik. On receiving a telegram, Tilak went direct to Bombay and arranged for the release of Paranjpe on bail. He was released on bail on Saturday the 20th June, and Tilak and Paranjpe both returned to Poona on June 21, 1908. Tilak accompanied Paranjpe to his residence and then he went to Gaikwad Wada.

The *Modern Review*, describing the prevailing political situation, remarked : "It may be easy for arm-chair critics who are incapable of risking or sacrificing anything for humanity, to inveigh in unmeasurable terms against persons who have made terrible mistakes, but who nevertheless were prepared to lose all that men hold dear, for their race and country;—persons whose fall has been great, because perhaps, equally great was their capacity for rising to the heights of being."

On June 20, the Governor of Bombay declared threateningly that certain persons possessing control over the people were exciting hatred and contempt for the Government and that they were playing with fire. The wind of repression had already set in, and the storm was about to burst.

It was during this fortnight that P. M. Bapat met Tilak at his instance. The meeting took place in Poona at midnight. Bapat told Tilak that in accordance with his message he had sent him with Hotilal Varma a copy of a Bomb manual from Paris. Tilak replied that he had received it. N. C. Kelkar, who had about this time seen Tilak's hands sprinkled with picric acid and heard of his presence at a bomb explosion trial, expressed horror at it and is said to have threatened Tilak with his resignation. Tilak gruffly told him that he was not doing it at the *Kesari* office and besides he would not ask Kelkar to defend the cult of bomb; and so he need not worry himself about it.

CHAPTER XVII

Trial and Transportation

I

TILAK AGAIN ACCOMPANIED S. M. Paranjpe to Bombay on June 23, 1908, to assist him in his defence. At Poona station he learnt from a C.I.D. officer that his arrest was imminent, and so he had better go back to Poona to make the necessary arrangements. He refused to go back. Why should he go back home? Was he to give a call to the army, to raise an army, to make ditches at the fortress for its defence? India herself was a vast jail and they could at the most put him in a smaller compartment. On reaching Bombay, next morning, he looked into the arrangements made for the publication of the proposed Marathi daily *Rashtramat* which was to be issued from Bombay. He then went to Joseph Baptista to consult him about the defence of Paranjpe. Baptista told Tilak that the prospects of acquittal were not bright but he added that a political defence would convert the High Court into a corner of Hyde Park. "Hyde Park! What is Hyde Park!" asked Tilak. Ten years later Baptista showed Tilak that Orators' famous Corner in London! Later Paranjpe was, however, convicted in the High Court and sentenced to nineteen months' rigorous imprisonment on July 8, 1908. After seeing Baptista, Tilak returned to the Sardar Griha, his Bombay headquarters. There he was told by someone that the Presidency Magistrate had signed a warrant for his arrest. Tilak said that it made no difference to the leader of a nation which was not strong enough to strike back, whether such news came an hour earlier or later.

In the evening he was discussing with Paranjpe the points of his defence. He then encouraged Paranjpe to conduct his own case in Court. To snatch the independence of a country from foreign rule was a great task and it meant enormous hardships and sacrifices, he added. If he was arrested, he told Paranjpe, he would conduct his own case. Just at this moment the warrant came and he asked the police officer why he took four hours to come to a place which was near their headquarters when the warrant had been signed by the Presidency Magistrate four hours earlier. He said he could have got time to move for bail had the warrant been served a little earlier in the day. He put on his clothes, accompanied the police officer as one would accompany a guest and sat in a victoria. He was arrested under Sections 124A and 153A of the Indian Penal Code for the article "Country's Misfortune" in the *Kesari*. He was taken in custody and was lodged at the Esplanade Police Station.

By now a police party had reached Poona and taken possession of Gaikwad Wada except one room wherein were huddled the members of the Tilak family. Next morning a search was made, and all account books, list of subscribers and other correspondence were seized. A post-card was seized from Tilak's papers and cuttings kept in an unlocked drawer. On the postcard were written in Tilak's handwriting the names of four books on explosives such as *Nitro-Explosives* and *Handbook on Modern Explosives*. While the search was going on, a huge crowd assembled near Tilak's residence, and a *posse* and a party of mounted police were placed near it. Immediately the police went to Tilak's house at Sinhagad, asked the watchman to open the house, forced open the cupboards, and without any person from Tilak's family to witness it, they searched the house.

On June 25, the news spread in every quarter of Poona and Bombay and then throughout India. A dreadful silence enveloped Poona. There was a spontaneous hartal, and suspension of normal activities. In Bombay too the workers struck work.

Davar, Bar-at-Law, appeared on June 25, for Tilak, in the Court of the Presidency Magistrate and moved for bail. But the Court did not grant the application. This Barrister Davar was the son of Mr. Justice Davar. On the morning of 29th June, Government served another warrant on Tilak saying that the article in the *Kesari* of 12th June entitled " These remedies are not lasting" was also objectionable. This article was written by K.P. Khadilkar, Tilak's assistant editor, when Tilak was at Sinhagad. The *Rashtramat's* first issue appeared on June 29. It attacked Government and was all praise for Tilak. It had eminent men on its editorial board and Gangadhar Deshpande, Baptista and Kaka Patil looked to the financial side of it. The party leaders and lieutenants of Tilak, who had run down to Bombay, began to address meetings explaining the stand taken by Tilak. The chawl committees for temperance started by jobbers in accordance with Tilak's advice were now active. This many-sided propaganda turned Bombay into a volcano.

On June 29, Tilak was again produced in the Court. A vast crowd had gathered outside and in the vicinity. Excitement grew as people poured in the Court. Police tried to push them back but failed. At last, mounted police came and so people were provoked. They showered stones on the *posse*. Some men were arrested, and six of them were later tried for creating a disturbance. The case began at three in the afternoon. Davar, Bar-at-Law, brought to the notice of the Court some writings in the *Advocate of India*, the *Bombay Gazette*, the *Times of India*, Bombay, and the Magistrate issued warnings to these papers. Datar, the agent of Tilak's papers, was cross-examined. The case was committed to the Sessions on the same day.

On July 2, Mr. Mohamed Ali Jinnah appeared for Tilak and applied for bail; but Mr. Justice Davar refused it. And yet Davar was himself the counsel who had secured the release of Tilak on bail eleven years earlier but who now refused to release Tilak on bail although the grounds were the same. Tilak sent for Joseph Baptista, and he had an interview with Tilak in Dongri Jail. He asked Baptista to object to a special jury or at least to insist that the majority should consist of Indians.

Baptista appeared for Tilak on July 3. Opposing the grant of special jury, he said that if a special jury was empanelled it would consist of a majority of Europeans, who, besides being ignorant of Marathi, would not be the best judges of articles alleged to have excited disaffection against the Government and the feelings of Indians against Europeans. On the contrary, a common jury would consist of a majority of non-Europeans. Baptista's prayer was not granted, but Mr. Justice Davar promised that a good many Indians would be invited before the jury was empanelled; and yet, eventually only two Indians were empanelled.

The atmosphere was filled with dread and foreboding. Tilak was hard up. The Tai Maharaj case had drained his funds. Fear was haunting everybody. Tilak could not employ a first-rate lawyer for his defence; neither did any first-rate lawyer come forward to defend him. Tilak's lieutenant Kelkar found it difficult to get the papers of the case printed in any of the Bombay presses. It was not even possible to issue a special edition of his weeklies in Bombay.

On the refusal of bail on June 25, Tilak was removed to Dongri Jail, Bombay. Next day Babarao Savarkar, who had been sentenced to one month's rigorous imprisonment on a charge of riotous behaviour in the street at the time of Paranjpe's trial, caught an opportunity to exchange a few words with Tilak. When Babarao Savarkar expressed to him his anxiety for the future, Tilak said if Maharashtra were alive it would take care of itself; if it were dead, an individual would not be able to revive it!

While he was lodged at Dongri Jail, Dr. Moonje and Dadasaheb Khaparde went to see him. The gaoler, who was a Madrasi gentleman, held Tilak in reverence. When Tilak came downstairs the visitors and gaoler stood up! The gaoler placed before Tilak a piece of betel-nut and said sadly that it was unfortunate that Tilak had to face a trial; but out of the evil would come some good. He, however, added that the home of sinners was sanctified by his presence. Next time R. G. Pradhan accompanied Khaparde to the jail, and the young man fell prostrate at Tilak's feet despite the gaol rules! Such was the people's reverence for Tilak. On one of these occasions Khaparde, his intimate and illustrious friend, said in a moving tone to Tilak that he feared it might prove to be the last meeting between them. By his life of service and sacrifice, he added, Tilak had attained his own salvation and there was no necessity for special prayers to God. Tilak calmly replied that when he prayed to God he did not yearn for salvation for himself as long as his countrymen were rotting in the hell of slavery. Moreover, he prayed to God that he might be born in Hindustan again and again with better intellect and strength to struggle for the independence of his country till she was free![1]

His lieutenants and followers were filled with anxiety for his safety. Everyone did his best in his own way for his leader's release. Some prayed for his safety. A follower came with a piece of bread. Always ready to respect the feelings of his followers, Tilak swallowed the piece of bread which his follower had brought from a saint as a blessing.[2] Once he had allowed a simple believing old man to tie on his wrist an amulet which the latter had brought from a holy place!

The Moderates were totally estranged. No help came from them. Their leader Pherozeshah Mehta was being pressed by the Governor to issue a public statement condemning Tilak. Mehta said that whatever might be Tilak's opinions he was prepared to suffer for them. He, therefore, stoutly refused to run Tilak down and added that he would never do such a thing.

---

1 *Reminiscences and Anecdotes about Lokamanya Tilak*, Vol. II, p. 534.

2 Ibid, Vol. Ill, p. 203.

II

GOVERNMENT PREPARED ITSELF for the battle. General Greenfield was consulted for military assistance, and additional troops were brought to Bombay on the eve of the trial. The Police Commissioner issued a notification prohibiting assemblies throughout the city during certain days. A jobber named Deoji and Dr. Salunke, who had great influence on the mill-hands and who were Tilak's followers, were called by the Police Commissioner and warned against creating trouble. The Police Commissioner interviewed almost all millowners and requested them to keep their mill-hands away from strikes and demonstrations.

On July 13 the trial was to commence. Tilak was brought from Dongri Jail to the High Court building the night before, and was lodged in a hall on the second floor. When asked why he was brought there he humorously replied that because he was senior to the Judge he was given the upper storey, and the Judge was sitting in the lower storey!

There were special police arrangements. A large crowd gathered; but it was not allowed to stand on the roads on both sides of the High Court building. The court room was packed to its utmost capacity.

Tilak was brought to the Court at half-past eleven and was allowed to take a seat at Counsel's table where the Advocate-General was sitting. Assisted by Dadasaheb Khaparde, N. C. Kelkar, Dadasaheb Karandikar, Joseph Baptista, Madhavrao Bodas and Bapusaheb Gandhi, Tilak was going to conduct his own defence. It was an irony of circumstances that the Judge was his counsel during his trial of 1897 and Dwarkadas Dharamsey, who had furnished bail during that trial, was now sitting alongside the Judge all throughout the trial as Sheriff of Bombay.

Branson, who had appeared for Tilak in the Tai Maharaj Case, was now the Advocate-General. Assisted by Mr. Inverarity and D. B. Binning instructed by Bowen, Public Prosecutor, Branson appeared for the Crown. It appears that Tilak's friends were persuading Branson to resign and to take up his defence. Branson's son, Major L. H. Branson, writes that Tilak and his friends offered his father £21,000 as one day's fee if he would give up being the Advocate-General and would defend the case.[3]

The proceedings opened with an application by Mr. Branson for a joint trial of the two cases arising out of the two articles. He said that offences

3 Branson, Major L. H., *A Life of Deception*, p. 80.

in both cases were exactly the same. Tilak said that the two cases ought to be tried separately. The Judge ordered that the three charges should be tried together but as to the remaining charge he felt inclined to think that if it was allowed to stay, such stay should mean acquittal. Branson replied that the question of the fourth charge should be held over until after the conclusion of the trial.

Tilak drew the attention of the Judge to the fact that the prosecutor had not specified the objectionable passages from the articles. He was told that the whole articles were objectionable. This increased Tilak's burden and compelled him to explain each and every sentence while conducting his own defence. So the trial of the accused was reduced to three charges, namely under Section 124A in respect of the article of the 12th May, and under Sections 124A and 153A in respect of the article of the 9th June, leaving the question of the fourth charge to be decided thereafter. Tilak was put in the dock, and the charges were read out to him. Tilak pleaded "not guilty"! Then a jury consisting of six Europeans, one Jew and two Parsees was chosen and the trial commenced.

In the absence of the Advocate-General Branson, Inverarity, in opening the case, explained to the jury the sections under which the accused was charged, and he gave information regarding the *Kesari*. Then giving the gist of the article of the 12th May he said: " To understand the real meaning of the bomb, all the following three things should be calmly considered, (namely) what (is the) cause (that) led to the birth of the bomb party in India, and how will this party fare in India and what effect will this party have on the administration and the people."

"All thoughtful people," Inverarity continued to read the article, "seem now to have formed the opinion as to the cause that gave birth to the bomb party. The bomb party has come into existence as a result of the oppression practised by the official class, the harassment inflicted by them and their obstinacy in treating public opinion with recklessness. The bomb exploded owing to the official class having tried the patience of the Bengalis to such a degree that the heads of the Bengali youth became turned. The responsibility for this calamity must, therefore, be thrown not on political agitation, writings, or speeches, but on the thoughtlessness and the obstinacy of the official class."

The whole of the article, observed Inverarity, was devoted to explaining the cause of the outrage which was alleged by the writer of the article to be the iniquitous character of the British Government of India. The writer said that British rule was of an oppressive and tyrannical character and had become unbearable to the people of India. Counsel submitted that the writer in the article attempted to impress upon his readers that British rule was in its self-interest alone. He remarked that it was a gross libel to say so. The writer went on to say that such a rule would not last much long, and must pass into the hands of the people. Coming to the word Swaraj—one's own rule—or Self-Government, he had Tilak's own definition of it, and the accused meant to convey that whenever people would like to upset the Government, they were entitled to do so. The *Kesari* on a previous occasion had warned the Government that Russian methods would be imitated by the people of India if it did not take care. Counsel, therefore, asked whether the article transgressed the limits which the law allowed to a public discussion of the measures of Government.

As regards the article of the 9th June, Counsel proceeded, the writer there properly repudiated all sympathy with the throwing of bombs and murders committed with the purpose of weakening and subverting British rule; but its references about bomb-throwing were most extraordinary. It pointed out that although Government might pass the Arms Act, bombs could be easily manufactured as it required a very few chemicals to make bombs; it was impossible for the Government to prevent their manufacture. The writer suggested, although in a veiled manner, that other countries had the advantage by throwing of bombs and by foul murders, and the result could be achieved in this country by the same means. All the articles, continued the Prosecution, were directed to the same view, namely, that British rule was a curse to the country and that if British rule went on without giving the people the right of Swaraj, Government must expect to have the same state of affairs existing in this country as existed in Russia.

Counsel further called the attention of the jury to the fact that the writer alluded to the murder of the King of Portugal, and to his son as a mad-cap patriot, and according to him bombthrowing there had the desired effect. The same thing happened after bombs were thrown in Russia. The jury, said Inverarity, had to consider, after reading the whole article in a fair manner whether their allusions were not made with a view to holding out a threat to the Government.

As regards the charge under Section 153A, Counsel said that the writer frequently alluded in an article to alien rulers as being white. He submitted that it was intended by these references to stir up racial feelings between

Europeans and Natives by pointing out that the white ' class ' was acting in a manner which was directly hostile to the interests of the natives.

While the case was going on in the Court, detachments of the Northamptonshire Regiment had been posted early in the morning in the neighbourhood of the mills in Bombay. All markets were closed. The morning passed. There was not much trouble in the city. Crowds of mill-hands made their way down to Fort, and at the Greaves-Cotton Company's Mills a considerable number refused to resume work. A section of infantry was sent to those mills, but on its arrival the crowd, which was already being moved by the police, dispersed.

In the evening the streets near the High Court were crowded. Mounted police and a squadron of the 26th cavalry were employed for moving that crowd. People were anxious to have a glimpse of their leader, but they were disappointed as he was kept in the High Court premises during the trial. After waiting for an hour and a half, they dispersed. Tilak's legal advisers and some friends were granted permission to see him while he was in custody.

The assistant oriental translator, one B. V. Joshi, was the first witness called. Binning, Bar-at-Law, conducted his examination-in-chief. Tilak cross-examined the translator in Joshi very closely and severely. He asked Joshi to give Marathi renderings of several English and Sanskrit words. The cross-examination continued for two days and Joshi was completely floored. Tilak succeeded in proving that the translator gave an incorrect, perverted and distorted rendering of the original articles. After Joshi's cross-examination he was re-examined.

Another witness examined was Inspector Sullivan. He was the officer who had conducted the search of Tilak's Gaikwad Wada in Poona and his bungalow at Sinhagad. The prosecution was allowed to put on record the post-card which Sullivan had seized from Tilak's papers. Tilak raised an objection to putting the post-card on record.

Tilak had been making preparation for his defence for the previous eight or ten days. In the room on the second floor of the High Court he was busy the whole night writing out the speech which he was to deliver the next day. In one corner there were books on a table and some blank sheets of paper. Outside the room stood a European sergeant to watch the under-trial prisoner. Deeply engrossed in his thoughts, Tilak was pacing the room. After one or two rounds he took out a book from the heap and opened it at a certain page, put a piece of paper there, and again began to pace up and down. Again he took out a book, inserted a piece of paper in it, and put it aside. The sergeant complained murmuring that it was half-past one. There was heavy sleep on his eyes. He began to doze. He made bold to tell Tilak to go to bed :

SERGEANT : It is now getting rather late. Sir! Don't you think you should have a little rest now ?

TILAK (assuringly): Why? Are you feeling sleepy? You may please sleep, if you like. I won't abscond!

The police officer went to bed. Tilak was pacing the room, selecting books, inserting pieces of paper in various pages till four o'clock in the morning. He then awoke the sergeant and said: "I have finished my reading! I will now have a little rest. Have you had enough rest ? "He pulled himself together and thanked Tilak sincerely. At five Tilak was fast asleep and was snoring!

III

15TH JULY WAS the third day of the trial. The Bombay Sheriff Dwarkadas Dharamsey, General Knight, and the Russian Consul were present in the Court to witness the trial. The proceedings commenced with the cross-examination of Sullivan by Tilak. The Inspector said that he had been to Sinhagad to search the accused's house. He did not take, he said, any of the accused's men or relatives to Sinhagad. Two cupboards were forced open by loosening the hinges as there were no keys. As the prosecution put the post-card in evidence Tilak also took advantage of that situation by putting in several cuttings as evidence on his behalf thereby even losing his right of reply.

As regards the post-card, Tilak said in his statement which he read that he wished to criticise the Explosives Act. For that purpose it was necessary to collect materials, and the names of the two books in the post-card were taken down from a catalogue in his library, with a view to sending for them in case they could not be found in any of the Poona or Bombay libraries. He then related briefly his views on political reforms which he had advocated in his statement submitted to the Decentralisation Commission in March 1908. He said the article of the 9th June was intended to point out the futility of repressive measures as the sole means of preventing the recurrence of bombs. In support of what was stated above, he produced along with this statement papers as per list annexed. The articles objected to by the prosecution merely embodied his honest convictions and opinions.

"I state that I am not guilty of any of the charges brought against me, and pray that I may be acquitted."

As the accused had put in some papers in making his statement, he was called upon to address the jury first.

Tilak, then, at four in the afternoon, began his defence speech which he took four and a half days to complete. In his speech, he explained the background of his articles, showed how the translations were perverted, dealt extensively with the duties of a jury, the freedom of the Press, and the political situation of India.

He told the jury that the case for the prosecution had been briefly put before them. It was rather vague and the whole responsibility was thrown upon him of replying to every portion of the articles. He did not know on what portion of the articles the prosecution was going to rely; so he had to cover every ground and possibility to detain them longer than he himself would wish to do.

In a case of sedition, he observed, three points were to be considered; the question of publication, the question of insinuations and innuendoes, and the question of intention. As to the publication, he took upon himself the full responsibility for the publication of the articles complained of. On the question of insinuations and innuendoes he would address them later on, but he might mention that in this case the inferences of insinuations and innuendoes were being drawn not from the original words used by the writer, but from the perverted form in which the articles had been translated from Marathi. It was unsafe to draw inferences from the translations such as were put before them. As to the question of intention, the only evidence adduced by the prosecution on the point was the post-card. The question of intention was the main question in this case, and he hoped to show that on reading the articles by themselves they could not form any judgment as to his guilt or innocence.

The *Kesari* was read only by Marathi-knowing people, and not read all over India. They had not to judge what effect the articles would produce on them or him or upon the people of Bengal, but upon the minds of the readers of the *Kesari* and that too solely from the fact that the words complained of had particular meanings and the sentences conveyed particular insinuations.

In England, Tilak proceeded, English juries drew their conclusions not merely from the character of the writing itself, but from all the surrounding circumstances. The prosecution ought to have shown by substantial proof in this case that the writer had exceeded the limits of fair criticism. If the jury found that his intention in writing the articles was to reform Government, it was no sedition. They might not agree with his views. The question before them was not that of views, but of good or bad intention.

If after considering all the circumstances they honestly came to the conclusion that there was an attempt made as mentioned in the sections, they might find him guilty. He did not ask them for any mercy or grace. He was prepared to stand by the consequences of his acts. He was not going to tell them that he had written the articles in a fit of madness. He had written them in the honest belief that it was his duty at that time to write in that way and that it was in the interests of the public as well as of the Government that he should do so.

He was not a *persona grata* with the Government. He submitted that that was no reason why he should not have justice done to him. They might be aware that in England juries had returned verdicts, even against the opinions of the judges. Government policy was quite distinct from the principles of law and the principles of justice. It was not a question of convenience or expediency, but it was a question of justice, pure and simple.

The prosecution had failed, he continued, to show that the articles actually had the effect of exciting feelings of disaffection against Government, and, therefore, so far as that part of the Section 124A was concerned he was entitled to an acquittal with regard to the part of the Section which related to 'Attempt'. He quoted the case of the Dean of St. Asaph who was tried in 1792 in England before Mr. Justice Butler. The jury there returned a verdict of guilty of publication only and not guilty of sedition. The judge refused to take that verdict and convicted the accused. That was considered a wrong judgment.

Happily for India the law was the same here. He was glad that the case had been brought to Bombay and was being tried by a jury. The function of a jury was to stand between arbitrary power and the liberty of the people. In Britain it was properly exercised. India was now on the threshold of a great constitutional struggle between the bureaucracy and the people, and he asked the jury to give the people the same support as the English jury gave the people at home a hundred years before.

Turning to the bomb outrage, he said that it occurred at the end of April in Bengal and as it was the question of the day, he considered it his duty as a journalist to press upon the attention of the Government the causes of it, irrespective of the question whether the times were disturbed or peaceful. There could be no two opinions that the Muzaffarpur incident was a very deplorable one. He did not say this then. He said it at the time, and the very heading of the article, "Country's Misfortune", showed that he condemned the event as a misfortune.

What were the causes and how to prevent the bomb explosions was the question.

The Anglo-Indian newspapers such as the *Times of India*, the *Pioneer* and the *Englishman* urged on the one hand that the bomb explosion was the outcome of the agitation carried on by the native gentlemen in different forms and on the other maintained that the Congress leaders spoke moderately in Councils and vigorously outside those bodies.

He was bound to protest against such comments. His view was that if they wanted to stop bombs it would not do to put down the agitation of the Congress, but that they should put down the bureaucracy and reform it. The struggle was between the pro-bureaucracy Party and the pro-Congress Party. An attempt was made in the Anglo-Indian press to show that it was a conflict between the races. The view of the Indian publishers was that it was not so. He quoted an extract from the *Pioneer* of 7th May 1908 which referred to the bomb explosion in Bengal and which suggested that a wholesale arrest of the acknowledged terrorists in a city or district should be made and at the next repetition of such an offence ten of these should be shot for every life sacrificed; that would, the paper said, soon put down the practice. Tilak said that the *Pioneer* recommended a wholesale slaughter of the innocents. To counteract the effect of such mistaken writings he wrote those articles. Were they to be considered guilty of sedition if they wrote in equally strong terms? That fact, he observed, should be borne in mind which had provoked the controversy.

As regards the article of 12th May, he said that a struggle between the people's Party and the Bureaucracy was going on in the hope that they would get what they asked for and as the cause was righteous they were bound to succeed. Referring to the article of 19th May, he said it was sober and more calmly written than that of the *Pioneer*. Nobody had taken steps against the *Pioneer*. The article was to tell the Government that while they should deal with the bomb outrages with a strong hand, the only way to prevent such occurrences was to reform the administration.

Tilak then alluded to his comments on bombs and said that in commenting on bombs and the military powers of India, he had not tried to deride the military power of the Crown, which was great; but he had tried to show that the passage of the Explosives Act would not suffice to put a stop to the outrages, but that the people should be given some rights in the administration of the country.

He had said that the knowledge of making bombs had come to the notice of the people, and he had therefore considered the question from the material as well as the intellectual point of view.

Coming to the post-card found in his room during the search, he said it had been photographed, and he would be surprised if it had not been sent home for the inspection of Lord Morley.

He then referred to an important point. His criticism was against the bureaucracy. Bureaucracy was not a class. It could not be both a Government and a Class of His Majesty's Government.

"I can trace a great struggle between the people on the one hand, and a mighty bureaucracy on the other; and I ask you to help us, not me personally, but the whole of India. I am now on the wrong side of life and for me it can only be a matter of few years, but future generations will look to your verdict and see whether you have judged wrong or right. The verdict may likely be a memorable one in the history of the freedom of the Indian Press. ... If at least one of you would come forward and say that I was right, it will be a matter of satisfaction to me; for I know, that if the jury are not unanimous in England, another trial takes place. It is not so here, but it would be a moral support upon which I would rely with great satisfaction. I appeal to you, not for myself, but in the interest of the cause that is sacred and I doubt not, gentlemen, that; He, before whom all of us will have to stand one day and render an account of our actions, will inspire you with the courage of your convictions and help you in arriving at a right decision on the issue involved in this case."

IV

TILAK FINISHED HIS defence on the afternoon of June 22. His defence speech lasted for twenty-two and a half hours. Then Branson, Advocate-General, replied in a satirical, offensive manner. In a four-hour speech he said Tilak had confounded motive with intention and that his contention that the Jury were the Judges of both law and fact was absurd, fiddle-sticks! He said Tilak had tried his best to throw all the dust he could collect, even in that monsoon weather, into the eyes of the jury on this point. Tilak could not be allowed to say now 'of course I wrote sedition and meant affection'. He said the accused had a fair and impartial hearing and to the fullest extent. As regards the translation, he said the alterations or amendments did not alter the general tenor and character of the article. In one of the articles it was stated that the bomb was more than a form of knowledge; "it was a kind of witchcraft; it was a charm or amulet."

He quoted the article of 2nd June in which the *Kesari* had remarked: "Considering the end and the means, the Bengalees must be given greater commendation. Considering the matter from the point of view of daring and skill in execution the Chapekar brothers took a higher rank than the members of the Bomb Party in Bengal." He therefore said that he was satisfied that Tilak's own language carried with it his own condemnation and conviction.

Concluding his speech, he said that he had intended to avoid the language of passion. But having the misfortune to sit through these ravings from morning to morning he could not help it. So he declared himself to be ready to stand by any rebuke His Lordship might offer him.

The Judge thought it desirable to finish the case that night. So he summed it up in lamplight. The learned judge observed that no speaker or writer had any right to attribute to Government any dishonest or immoral motive. He asked the jury to accept all the accused's corrections, and then judge if the sentiments of the article were different from the sentiments in the original translation. They must judge the intention of the article from the article itself. Turning to the post-card, he said they should not pay too great attention to it. If what he said commended itself to them, well and good; if not let them reject it by all means.

The jury retired for consideration at three minutes past eight. Mr. Justice Davar also went inside. It is said that he had received a telegram from Minto asking about the decision. At this moment he wired back to Minto " Defence grave, depending Jury." [4] This was intercepted by a revolutionary serving in the telegraph office. In dim gas light there was breathless silence. Everybody was anxious to hear the decision. In the meanwhile Dadasaheb Khaparde and Tilak's chosen friends had tea in the company of Tilak. All were down in the mouth. Tilak broke the silence. He said to Khaparde: "Dadasaheb, from the ominous surrounding I have

---

4 Bhat, Dr. V. M., *Abhinav Bharat*, p. 113.

a premonition that transportation is in store for me. This may prove to be the last tea we take together." Those who fight for a noble cause with an untiring and undivided devotion can alone have the courage to utter such words in the face of impending disaster and ruin!

The jurors returned at twenty minutes past nine after a deliberation extending over an hour and a quarter and announced the majority verdict of guilty on all charges. They were divided in the proportion of seven to two. The European jurors returned the verdict of guilty, the two Parsees returned the verdict of not guilty.

The Advocate-General then said he proposed to put up the accused on another charge of a previous conviction for sedition. The accused would have to plead yes or no and if he denied it he had papers to prove it, and the jury would decide. Tilak replied that as it was not specified in the first charge under Section 75 it was not admissible for the purpose of enhancing the punishment. He, however, admitted the previous conviction.

In reply to the Judge's question whether he had anything to say before sentence was passed, Tilak said: "All I wish to say is that in spite of the verdict of the jury, I maintain that I am innocent. There are higher powers that rule the destinies of men and nations; and it may be the will of Providence that the cause which I represent may prosper more by my sufferings than by my remaining free." [5]

These were the words of a leader of the people, a maker of a nation, solemn, firm, serene and undying, symbolic of the man who had been waging a relentless war for the liberation of his motherland.

Then the Judge, delivering the judgment, said: "It is my painful duty to pass sentence upon you. I cannot tell you how painful it is to me to see you in this position. You are a man of undoubted talents and great power and influence. Those talents and that influence, if used for the good of your country, would have been instrumental in bringing about a great deal of happiness for those very people whose cause you espouse. Ten years ago you were convicted and the Court dealt most leniently with you and the Crown dealt still more kindly with you."

"It seems to me," announced His Lordship, "that it must be a diseased mind, a most perverted intellect, that could say that the articles, which you have written, are legitimate weapons in political agitation. They are

5 The Government of Bombay has inscribed these memorable words on a tablet which is fixed outside the Court Room wherein the historic trial took place.

seething with sedition, they preach violence; they speak of murders with approval and the cowardly and atrocious act of committing murders with bombs not only seems to meet with your approval, but you hail the advent of the bomb into India as if something has come to India for its good. As I said it can be only a diseased and perverted mind that can think that bombs are legitimate instruments in political agitations. And it must be a diseased mind that could ever have thought that the articles you wrote were articles that could have been legitimately written."

"Your hatred of the ruling class," declared the Judge, "has not disappeared during these ten years. And in these articles, deliberately and defiantly written week by week, not as you say, on the spur of the moment, but a fortnight after that cruel and cowardly outrage had been committed upon two innocent Englishwomen, you wrote about bombs as if they were legitimate instruments in political agitations. Such journalism is a curse to the country. I feel much sorrow in sentencing you. I have considered most anxiously in the case of a verdict being returned against you, what sentence I should pass upon you. I have decided to pass a sentence which I consider will be stigmatised as what is called 'misplaced leniency'. Having regard to your age and circumstances, I think it is most desirable, in the interests of peace and order and in the interests of the country which you profess to love, that you should be out of it for some time. I pass a sentence of three years' transportation under each of the first two charges, the sentences to run consecutively. You would have thus six years' transportation. On the third charge I do not think I will add to your trouble any additional period of imprisonment. I, therefore, fine you one thousand rupees and direct that with reference to the fourth charge you are discharged."

The Judge servilely served his imperialist masters in his own slavish manner! Tilak went down in history as one of the makers of the nation, and posterity is sorry that a man with so servile and diseased a mind as Davar should have sprung from the stock that produced great stalwarts like Dadabhai Naoroji and Pherozeshah Mehta. However, forty-eight years later when the nation celebrated Tilak's birth centenary, Chief Justice Chagla of the Bombay High Court, while unveiling the plaque, as mentioned above, on the wall of the very Court in which Tilak was twice sentenced for sedition, pronounced the inevitable verdict of history on Tilak. He declared that the convictions were a flagrant denial of substantial justice. Tilak was sentenced because he loved his country more than his life or liberty. He added that they were making atonement for the suffering caused to a great and distinguished son of India and were removing the disgrace that tarnished "our record".

To resume. As soon as the sentence was pronounced and the Judge left the Court, police took charge of Tilak. While they were coming downstairs they came across Davar, Bar-at-Law, who had appeared for Tilak in the lower Court. He was coming upstairs in a hurry as his father had not come home at the usual time. When Davar the junior saw Tilak in the custody of the police, he turned his face for shame. Tilak saw this and he begged permission of the police to have a chat with the junior Davar. He consoled him, "Don't be nervous and sorry. You did your best to help me in the lower Court. I realise your difficulty and can understand why you could not be helpful in the High Court. Six years is not a long period. It will end and we will meet again."

A large portion of the crowd that had gathered outside the High Court thought that the case could not be concluded that day and had left. But when news spread that judgment was to be delivered that night many rushed back to the High Court and waited anxiously to have a glimpse of their leader in the dark rainy night, in the muddy streets. News had come that a steamer was ready in the harbour, and so people guessed that Tilak would be sent to the Andamans. A special train was ready at the Victoria Terminus. But Tilak was taken in a car to Colaba station of the B.B. & C.I. Railway.

Lord Morley and Lord Minto were watching the trial anxiously and conveying their reactions to each other. At first Morley informed the Viceroy that although his breakfast had doses of bitter in it those days in the shape of telegrams about Tilak's trial in the morning papers, he hoped the sentence would be heavy enough to produce a good deal of exasperation in the Mahratta mind and to make the Moderate game harder to play. He said he had read the two articles, but they were not at all so bad as to make a prosecution inevitable. Minto informed Morley on July 23 that he heard late in the previous night of Tilak's conviction and hoped that the sentence of six years' imprisonment would have an excellent effect, and referring to the Bombay riots he said that Bombay was touchy to a degree! On August 5 he again wrote to Morley that they could not have possibly afforded not to prosecute. He believed that the effect of the sentence would be excellent; but Minto could not help admitting to Morley that "there is no

6 Mary Countess of Minto, *India, Minto and Morley*, pp. 246-47.

doubt whatever as to the part Tilak has played. He is recognised throughout India as the arch-leader of sedition. There is ample evidence to prove it. His story is very different from that of Lajpat Rai."[6] Morley was of the opinion that the sentences passed on Tilak and others were monstrous.

Morley, however, sharply remonstrated with Sir George Sydenham Clarke as he feared that the mischief that would be done by Tilak's sentence would be dangerous, and later he issued orders instructing the Local Governments to refer such matters to the Government of India before they launched any political prosecution. Sir Michael O'Dwyer writes that Morley regarded this prosecution of Tilak as a mistake and likely to make Tilak a martyr.[7]

With the transportation of Tilak, the Anglo-Indian newspapers heaved a sigh of relief. Their mouthpiece, the *Times of India*, Tilak's inveterate enemy, was full of joy! It said Tilak's was a fair trial, the sentence was just and merciful, and he was rightly found guilty. Referring to the statement of Tilak that he was engaged in the work of constitutional reforms and fighting for the liberty of the press, the *Times of India* declared that "no greater nonsense was ever talked in a Court of Justice!" It further observed that Tilak had deliberately chosen his path to preach hatred of the ruling race, disaffection against Government, contempt of authority. He thereby brought himself within the operation of law, as would all who followed in his footsteps, it concluded.

The Times, London, in an editorial, observed: "The real importance of Mr. Tilak's conviction lies in the fact that he is the acknowledged and undisputed leader of the Extremist movement in India!" "Yet Mr. Tilak remained," *The Times* went on, "at the moment of his conviction the most conspicuous politician in India, and among large sections of the people he has enjoyed a popularity and wielded an influence that no other public man in the dependency could claim to equal." The editorial recalled that the Extremist movement was almost entirely Tilak's conception, remembered that the wrecking of the Congress was due to his personal intervention, said that his Shivaji movement was a potent cause of unrest, and then observed, "But the agitator who professes to be fascinated by the charm of patriotic bombs, must not complain if he is given an opportunity of revising his beliefs in the seclusion of the Andamans."

7 O'Dwyer, Sir Michael, *India As I Know* It, p. 145.

The *Manchester Guardian* observed: "Sir George Sydenham Clarke, in deciding upon the arrest of Mr. Tilak, has doubtless realised that the Government could not consistently prosecute the smaller fry without striking at the most powerful revolutionary in the country, a man by comparison with whom such persons as Bepin Chandra Pal and even Lajpat Rai are inconsiderable."

The correspondent of the *Daily News*, London, described Tilak as the ablest, subtlest and most powerful leader and the high priest of extremist Nationalism.

The *Scotsman* remarked that the closing of the markets was perhaps of graver import than the riots and added that the feeling was certainly proof of the supreme popularity of the man.

In a true estimation of Tilak's work, Henry Cotton said: "Prior to his arrest, Mr. Tilak was but the leader of a party. He is now a national martyr and a popular hero."

Yet a glowing tribute came from Keir Hardie: "There is no man in India," he wrote in his *Labour Leader*, "who has such a hold upon the working class as Mr. Tilak, and the result of his conviction will be more far-reaching than that of any single individual which has yet taken place. His life-history has been a record which makes him out as one of those men of whom most nations are proud."

The Indian Nationalist papers vehemently attacked the Government for its outrage against the freedom of the press, and all swore that they would carry out his message into action.

The *Indian Spectator* observed: "Labouring under the dead weight of all possible adverse circumstances, Mr. Tilak presented his own case to the jury in a manner which has evoked universal admiration in the country. He has by his powerful address vindicated the right, such as ought to exist, of the liberty of the press in this country, for which all lovers of national progress ought to feel grateful to him. Mr. Tilak's dauntless courage in rising superior to his surroundings and subordinating self-interest to the country's cause, are the rare qualities of an ardent patriot."

The revolutionary paper *Kal* observed : "If the Hindus are to consider Tilak guilty because a British Court of Justice has condemned him, Christians will have to foreswear Christ because He was crucified by a Roman Court. There is no sense in saying that Tilak was sentenced according to law. There was mockery of justice, not justice."

But the most pathetic bewailing came from the *Bande Mataram*. Recalling his brilliant address to the jury, which would forever enrich our patriotic literature, was not meant for his own defence but only to put heart in his countrymen, the *Bande Mataram* avowed. "Go, Tilak, wherever you may be sent to crush your body. Your example will hover around us all unimprisoned and unexiled. The canker of the chains will not only eat into your limbs but also into every heart of the country to stir it up to its duty. Nearer the God, nearer the fire. He places his good soldiers in the very thick of the battle. You have fulfilled your mission. You have taught your people to bear tortures rather than deny their country, you have startled the deep slumber of false opinions, you have thrilled a pang of noble shame through callous consciences. And into the next age, if not into your own, you have flashed an epidemic of nobleness. What else have patriots, heroes and martyrs done ?"

Six months before Tilak's trial Dr. V. H. Rutherford, who was then a Member of the British Parliament, had an opportunity of meeting a bureaucrat in India and the following conversation had taken place between them :

BUREAUCRAT: What do you think of Tilak ?

DR. RUTHERFORD: I think he is a great patriot, rightly fighting for his country's freedom.

BUREAUCRAT: Gokhale and the Moderates we do not fear, but Tilak and the Extremists are a danger to British rule, and we mean to hate Tilak.

"This reveals," observes Dr. Rutherford in his reminiscences of Tilak, "how fear and vindictiveness mingled in the minds and administration of alien bureaucrats." [8]

The Moderate leaders like Pherozeshah Mehta and Gokhale sat unconcerned. Gokhale was then in London in connection with the proposed reforms. When Morley told him that asking for Colonial Self-Government for India was merely to cry for the moon and safely added that the fur-coat of Canada's constitution would never suit the actual conditions of the historical, cultural and psychological climate of India. Gokhale was asked by the Indian revolutionaries in London to preside over the meeting held to protest against the transportation of Tilak. He refused to do so, nor did he himself hold any meeting. Moreover some of the Moderates in Poona distributed sweetmeats! Some of them, said the Governor, Sir

8 *Reminiscences and Anecdotes about Lokamanya Tilak*, Vol. Ill, p. 102.

9 Sydenham, Lord, *My Working Life*, p. 223.

George Clarke, although gave him no public support, welcomed in private the action taken by him against Tilak.[9] The Revolutionaries in Maharashtra working in the post office of Bombay intercepted a message from Lord Morley wired to Minto saying "G. K. says Savarkar and Bapat are in close contact with Tilak." "Keep watch on the activities of Savarkar." Mr. Savarkar mentioned in this message was Babarao Savarkar, Veer Savarkar's elder brother.

Much is made of this telegram. It may be that Gokhale might have casually referred to the names of the revolutionary leaders and Morley must have taken a cue from it. The revolutionaries in London were enraged at Gokhale's indifferent attitude to Tilak's arrest, and they were going to kill him, but Savarkar who said that revolutionary methods were to be adopted in the case of outsiders and evolutionary in that of one's own countrymen, dissuaded his followers from the misdeed. Since then Gokhale's life stood in danger in Maharashtra as some of the over-enthusiastic young followers of Tilak wanted to get rid of him; but Gokhale's innocence par excellence overpowered their merciless hearts.

CHAPTER XVIII

Prison Philosopher

I

THE TRAIN CARRYING Tilak started from Colaba station. The police party escorting Tilak did not know its destination. Tilak was fast asleep and awoke in the morning at seven o'clock when it had stopped at the Sabarmati station. July 23, 1908, was his fifty-second birthday and if nobody from his lieutenants could be present on that day to greet and felicitate him, the Collector of Ahmedabad District was present! He took him to Sabarmati Jail.

By midnight the news of the dreadful sentence on Tilak spread in every nook and corner of the city of Bombay. The news fell on their ears like a fire on the prairie.

The morning of 23rd July brought with it unrest all over Bombay city which soon turned into a battle-field. Government officers tried to send the mill-hands to work, but textile workers were enraged at this and a fight began in the streets between the police and the workers. Their leaders were called to the Secretariat and castigated. Police opened fire and about seventy persons were injured, and for some time military batches were posted at certain danger zones in the mill area. For six days there was a complete strike, all the eighty textile mills, Railway workshops and markets being closed! Bombay sank into sorrow and it reminded people of Ayodhya sobbing for the exiled Rama. This strike of the textile workers was considered the political action of the Indian proletariat, and it was hailed by Lenin at the time as a portent of the future.

In the police firing fifteen workers were shot dead; thirty eight were wounded seriously. In order that peace should be restored speedily, the Governor paid visits to hospitals to inquire after the wounded and presented a gift to a worker's daughter who had been wounded in the firing. After peace was restored, the workers who were under arrest were sentenced to different terms extending from six months to one year. Baptista presided over a meeting called to felicitate Tilak on his fifty-second birthday. Government thought it was not quite proper for a Justice of the Peace of the Town and Island of Bombay to preside at the birthday celebration of a patriot who was serving his term in jail, more so since his incarceration had caused bloodshed in Bombay. The result was that a week before the expiry of his term of office, Baptista's name was removed from the Bench of Justices of the Peace by Sir George Clarke—afterwards Lord Sydenham. "The Lord hath given, the Lord hath taken away. Blessed be the name of Lord Sydenham," exclaimed Baptista.

Patriot Joseph Baptista, a young Christian Nationalist barrister, showed unique courage in appearing for Tilak in the Court. For his spirited and nationalist views he had to suffer a lot, and Baptista became known as Uncle Baptista. People also retaliated in their own way. Branson, who refused to conduct Tilak's case, was, in the words of his son, boycotted by Indian clients. He lost the greater part of his income. After his death his son represented the facts to the Government of India, who "gave my mother a handsome donation to make up for the loss", and Branson's wife was thus sent back to England.

Tilak's nephew and his son-in-law saw him at the office of Sabarmati Jail on July 29, when he was in his ordinary dress. He was given food which was served to ordinary criminals in jail. That wretched diet took away 10 lbs. within ten days and the Jail Superintendent changed his diet, giving him 2 lbs. of milk and two ounces of ghee, wheat-bread and rice every day.

Baptista saw Tilak in Sabarmati Jail. The jailor had kept only one chair in the room. "I offered it," said Baptista, " to Tilak." "Oh no," said prisoner Tilak, "it would make you a standing counsel in a double sense!" So they both sat on the floor. Tilak insisted that no point should be made of the severity of the sentence of six years' imprisonment. " Most likely," he said to Baptista, "I will give them the slip long before six years unless God in his design has work for me on earth."[1]

Like his leader and master, N. C. Kelkar, editor of the *Mahratta*, came into trouble. He wrote an article on the judgment of Justice Davar

1 *Reminiscences and Anecdotes about Lokamanya Tilak*, Vol. II, p. 503.

and was tried for contempt of Court. He was sentenced to fourteen days' imprisonment, was fined twelve hundred rupees and was to be kept in prison till he tendered an unconditional apology to the Court. He was released after fourteen days when he tendered an apology to the Court!

An appeal for a Defence Fund was made over the signatures of N. C. Kelkar and K. P. Khadilkar, and it was decided to fight out the Tilak Case to the end. An application was made on August 7. On August 18 the Full Bench of the High Court admitted the application. Joseph Baptista and Dadasaheb Karandikar appeared for Tilak instructed by Solicitor Raghavayya. On September 2 Baptista argued the case and Robertson, who appeared for the Government, replied to the points raised by Baptista. The decision of the High Court was that the third charge should be waived, and the fine should be refunded to the prisoner. Accordingly it was refunded. On August 15 Dadasaheb Khaparde had already left Bombay for London to make arrangements for an appeal to the Judicial Committee of the Privy Council. On September 8 Government declared that they had commuted the sentence into one of simple imprisonment.

The Government resolution about the commutation of Tilak's sentences must have reached the Jail Superintendent about the 10th September. But Tilak was not informed about it; along with it were perhaps the orders for the removal of Tilak to Mandalay Jail. So on the night of September 13 the gaoler came to Tilak's cell, unlocked the door, and took Tilak to the jail office. There Tilak was asked to put on his usual dress—dhoti, flowing coat, red turban and red shoes. A special train was ready outside the jail. Tilak was asked to board it in the company of a special police party consisting of Muslims only. A Gujarati Brahmin prisoner was also taken with him as a cook for Tilak. All the doors and windows of the train were shut up. None in the train knew where they were going. The next morning the train reached Bombay, and the party was taken to a steam-launch and thence to the s.s. *Hardinge* which was waiting in the Bombay Harbour for the arrival of the illustrious prisoner.

Tilak was put in a room on the lower deck, and the Gujarati cook in another. For some time, twice a day Tilak was taken to the upper deck for fresh air. The s.s. *Hardinge* reached Rangoon on September 22. News of Tilak's expected arrival had leaked out in Rangoon, and about two thousand people had assembled to have a glimpse of the great man. Outside the harbour a special train was kept ready. The party got in and the next morning the train reached Mandalay. The police party handed Tilak over to the jail authorities and returned. The Jail Superintendent Captain Greig had made arrangements for Tilak's dwelling in a two-room cell separated from the other cells of a jail house in the Mandalay jail compound.

The cell measured 20 X 50 and its immediate isolated compound measured 130 X 50 in which Tilak was allowed to move freely in the daytime. In the compound there were mango and other trees. For some days in the beginning there were other prisoners in the cell, but they were removed to different cells, and Tilak was left alone. Nobody was allowed to enter that compound, and when visitors came the jailer accompanied them. The jailer personally locked the room and the compound at six o'clock in the evening and opened it in the morning at six. At night two earthen pots were kept in the cell for urine and other purposes.

There Tilak was allowed to have his food cooked by the Gujarati Brahmin convict who had been brought along with him from Sabarmati Jail. He was placed at Tilak's disposal. This convict was sent back after a month or two, and a Maharashtrian Brahmin convict by name Vasudeo Ramrao Kulkarni from Yeravda Jail was brought to cook his food. This man who had never seen Tilak in India served him devotionally. He paid close attention to Tilak's health and regarded the service of the great man as a rare opportunity. For some days he had to cook Tilak's food in the common kitchen of the jail.

Tilak's cell had a table, a chair or two, two cupboards for books, an arm-chair, an iron cot, one or two pots, bedding and a lantern. He was allowed to wear his usual dress, and when he was permitted an independent kitchen for himself, he was given a room on the first floor for it. He was allowed to buy utensils for the kitchen at his own cost.

Tilak changed his routine. Destiny had given him a respite which the Government called transportation. Usually at home he used to get up late because he went to bed very late. But now there was no bustle, hubbub or the hurry of a political life. He got up early, washed his mouth, chanted some Sanskrit stanzas and sat in his bed in meditation with closed eyes for an hour or so.

After going to the lavatory in a tin shed where two earthen pots were kept, he cleansed his teeth with ash. Then he had a cup of tea and busied himself with reading or writing till nine o'clock. After nine he came downstairs for his bath which was a long pleasant affair and rather a luxury. Tumblers full of clean hot water came one after another, the fingers rubbing all muscles and joints of the body for an hour or so.

With a pinch of ash dabbed on the forehead, he took his meal sitting on a wooden seat in the orthodox Brahmin manner, sprinkling water, and as he had now ample time, even muttering the *Gayatri mantra*. Wheat-bread or rice was taken alternately at every meal with a little *dal*. He was allowed to have *pickles* and *papad* from Poona. He, however, never uttered a word of displeasure if any of the dishes were spoiled. When the cook trembled at the thought of a mistake in cooking, Tilak too exclaimed that he had no idea about it, and so there was no necessity, he said, for regret or repentance!

In the afternoon a glass of lemon juice, milk or fruit, followed by a talk with the cook when Tilak used to tell stories and the cook was charmed with his art of story-telling which he did like a religious preacher. He sat in the arm-chair and chewed betel-nut, his mind roaming in the regions of the poles, hunting with primeval Aryan warriors in the *Rigveda* and enjoying the super-glory of the Aurora at the Pole-star. Then again reading or writing and at five the second meal or supper, and at six the room was locked from outside and the compound too. Then again stories conveying general knowledge were narrated to the cook when passages from history, scriptures and sacred books were cited.

That was followed by writing or reading near the lantern for an hour or so. At the time of going to bed, he washed his face and feet, and spent an hour or so again in bed in meditation. When he was absorbed in his thoughts he became oblivious to the surroundings, and the cook asked him what he was always revolving in his mind. He told him that the cell was his university, the books were his professors, the jailer was his watchman, and the cook his playmate! As he was suffering from diabetes, he did not allow himself to be shaved by the jail convicts who had learnt the art of the barber. He made arrangements to bring a barber from the town and paid him one rupee for shaving his head. He was allowed to write a letter once a month and to receive once a month one envelope in which the number of letters was so much a point for objections. Once in a quarter of a year he was allowed to interview his relatives or friends with the previous permission of the jail superintendent.

II

THE THOUGHT OF release was uppermost in Tilak's mind for over six months. On reaching London, Dadasaheb Khaparde strove to secure the release of his friend and leader in every possible way. In the meanwhile Dadasaheb

Karandikar reached London with the papers of the case. In November 1908 Tilak instructed Khaparde to refer to the trial of the Irish leader O'Connel, who was tried for sedition about 1844. There was some defect in the selection of the number of the jury, and on a petition to the House of Lords they reversed the orders of the Court and acquitted O'Connel. He, therefore, asked Khaparde to stress the point of selection of the jury and the definition of the word 'attempt'.

Meantime some Members asked questions in the British Parliament. Dr. Rutherford appealed to Government to recommend to the King to extend clemency to Tilak in view of the position he held in the Indian nationalist movement. Keir Hardie wanted Tilak's articles to be published as Parliamentary papers. A. Lipton questioned the composition of jury. F. C. Mackarness inquired whether an appeal could be made against the sentence. T. S. Buchanan, the Under-Secretary of State, replied that the Judicial Committee of the Privy Council might give special leave to appeal. He said 'No' to Keir Hardie and Dr. Rutherford.

In the second week of February 1909, Khaparde succeeded in filing an application in the Privy Council, and hearing the long expected telegram 'filed' direct from London, Tilak was glad that the machinery was put in motion. Tilak was hopeful of success and thought that there would be no difficulty about 'admission' which was the second stage. He, therefore, instructed Khaparde to telegraph to him direct the result of both admission and the final hearing.

Tilak instructed Khaparde to lay emphasis on the point that he had been distinctly prejudiced by the amalgamation of the cases; and that was the sole object of the Prosecution in getting the cases or charges amalgamated. The least that he expected was, he said, a 'new trial'. "However," he said, "you must keep ready the second string to your bow—I mean 'petition to Parliament', if the result of the Privy Council appeal be unfavourable."

Khaparde approached Sir Rufus Isaacs, afterwards Lord Reading, to plead the case in London. He was then a leading lawyer in England who afterwards became Lord Chief Justice of England and then Viceroy of India. He kept the brief for two months and returned it. That was a pointer. During the 1897 trial Mr. Asquith was Tilak's counsel in the Privy Council and *The Times*, London, had criticised him for accepting Tilak's brief.

The Privy Council, however, declined to grant leave to appeal and rejected the application on March 3, 1909. Tilak was informed about it by a cable. Tilak exclaimed : "The judicial door is thus finally closed against me!

"He wrote to Khaparde that the returning of the brief by Sir Rufus Isaacs was itself ominous. He recalled to Khaparde how *The Times*, London, had taken Asquith to task for accepting his brief, and observed: "Sir Rufus Isaacs might perhaps have been actuated by some such apprehensions or he may have personally known or guessed the temper or inclination of the Court." He, therefore, wrote to Khaparde that he should try a petition to the House of Lords, and then return to India, leaving Mr. Dalgado or Mr. Parikh in charge of the matter.

In May 1909 he again wrote to Khaparde that he did not think that a motion in Parliament could do him any good. A petition to the House of Commons would only serve as a basis for questions. Khaparde was of the opinion that a petition to the King or the Premier would be of greater use. "It is no longer," he observed, "a question of law and justice, but of time and expediency or what they call policy; and we cannot expect any immediate result." In his next letter he asked Khaparde that efforts for his release should be made on the remaining two grounds: equitable and humanitarian, the legal ground being already tried."

As regards the point of Equity he suggested that the Civil Rights Committee should take up his cause on that ground. He said he still believed that if he had an Indian jury he should have been acquitted. If every European British subject in India could claim a European jury why could he not have an Indian jury even in a Court of Sessions in a trial for offences against the State? That could be the equitable ground, because though the letter of the law was not violated, the law itself was inequitable.

The third ground was the severity of the sentence or what he called the humanitarian ground. It was true, he said, that the Government of Bombay had toned down the severity of the sentence by commuting it into simple imprisonment. "But still," he added, "taking into consideration the actual nature of the offence and my age, position in the society, I believe that anybody will still consider the punishment to be a harsh one though Mr. Justice Davar characterized it as lenient. It is on this ground that an appeal for mercy can be made by those who think the punishment to be too severe for a man of my age." [2]

If the Government put any conditions for his release, he said, he could not hesitate to accept the conditions if they were the same as those offered

2 *Reminiscences and Anecdotes about Lokamanya Tilak*, Vol. Ill, p. 164 (English Section).

to him in 1898. He would never accept a condition imposing restrictions on his public activity. That was inconsistent with all his antecedents. "In fact," he wrote in a touching tone, "I shall be undoing my life's work thereby."

For a few years' personal comfort he said he would not accept effacing himself from public life. He would rather like to be in jail for that period than be out a disabled man. He did not wish release at any cost. Several men, he proceeded, suffered in the past for the expression of their honest views and if it was destined that he should be one of them nobody could prevent it.

He gratefully admitted that whatever might be the result of Khaparde's work, Khaparde had discharged his duty to a friend. The question should be kept persistently before the eyes of the Government and the public in different ways. "They have allowed all the books I wanted and I spend my time in reading with a view that I shall be able to write out the books, which, you know, I have designed out long ago."

He wrote to Khaparde to convey his regards to Mr. Swinny, the editor of the *Positivist Review*, and to Keir Hardie.

During the first year, Tilak's health was not affected. His normal weight was 130 lbs. It was 126 lbs. at Ahmedabad. He lost 8 lbs. during his journey from Bombay to Mandalay, and it was steady at 124 lbs. The climate of Mandalay was not as cold as that of Poona. His gums gave him pain. There was pus and bleeding. His fingers became numb. He tried even homoeopathic medicines which Dr. Gadre of Poona had prescribed. Dyspepsia, diabetes and hernia were the other ailments he had to fight.

III

THERE WAS NO change so far as the jail life was concerned except that he was removed to Meiktila Jail from the 19th June when cholera broke out in Mandalay. He was taken out in a motor-car which was watched by European sergeants standing on either side of the road from the jail to the station. He told Lieutenant Fennell, who took him to Meiktila, that no foreigner had a right to rule India and so on his release he would recommence his preaching and teaching against the British and devote his life to getting the British turned out of the country. He admitted that the departure of the British would be followed by years of bitter warfare, but one race or one religious body would conquer and would rule, and India would be for better or for worse ruled by her own sons.[3]

3 Source Material for A *History of the Freedom Movement in India*, p. 281.

Although they took every precaution to shut Tilak out from the public view, the news of his removal had spread, and a vast crowd cheered him as he entered the railway station at Mandalay. At Meiktila shouts of " Tilak Maharaj-ki-Jai" greeted him at the station.

Somehow the word Maharaj attracted the attention of the new jailer and he, perhaps in a jeering or jolly mood, inquired of Tilak the name of the State over which he ruled! Tilak said with a smile : "When I am not the master of my person how can I be a ruler of a State ?" Tilak was in Meiktila Jail for about two months, and then he was removed back to Mandalay Jail on September 9, 1909.

Upto this time Tilak had a ray of hope that something might turn out in his favour, and he would be released. But now he wrote to his nephew Vidwans that he would not be released till the completion of his full term of transportation. Yet he cheered up his wife that they should all patiently face the unfavourable times with hope and courage. They were grappling with misfortune, and if they patiently and boldly held out they would surely come out successful in the end. As a practical step he now decided to make a Will. The gums exuded pus and troubled him. Yet the tranquillity of his mind was not disturbed. He gave detailed instructions regarding the proposed repairs to the tomb of Shivaji.

He was very particular about the studies of his children and asked his nephew to arrange for a tutor. He wrote that he would like even Kelkar to find some time to look after their studies. He asked Vidwans to look after the studies of Jagannath Maharaj. But the most gnawing anxiety he felt was about the health of his wife. She too was suffering from diabetes, and her health was impaired. From the cell he suggested some medicines which he had tried himself.

Tilak prepared his Will in jail as a precaution. But he asked his nephew to deal with court matters in his name as far as possible, although he had passed a deed vesting his powers in him to look after the press and papers.

Tilak utilised the enforced leisure for reading, and the scholar in Tilak began to play his role in the hermitage. He was not allowed to read newspapers and magazines of any kind. He could read books which required the approval of the jail authorities. The scholar was allowed to have full play, and orders from Mandalay cell came home one after another for books and more books. He asked his nephew to take proper care of the home library and instructed him not to lend books as far as possible. When he asked for a book and if it was not found, he wrote back pointing out the exact place where it could be found.

Among the books Tilak asked for during the first year were the Bible, Sanskrit-English Dictionary by Apte, *Sociology* by Spencer, Rousseau's *Social Contract, Fundamental Principles of Positivism, Prince* by Machiavelli, *Government of Dependencies* by Lewis, Voltaire by Morley, Tukaram's Gatha, *Dasbodh* by Ramdas, *Essays on Vedantism* by Shreepati, Volumes of *Historians—History of the World Series,* Leslie Stephen's Work on Ethics, and several others. This list shows the type of reading he was engrossed in.

The second year 1910-11 was very important from the point of view of his life. In November 1909 he submitted his petition to the Secretary of State for India through the Government of Bombay, but it was returned to him as it was, it said, not properly addressed. So in December 1909 he sent it to his London Solicitors with a request to move further in the matter and advised Khaparde to leave London entrusting the matter to his solicitors and friends. If the Secretary of State did not do anything, he said, there was no hope of his doing anything afterwards. Sir William Lee-Warner and the Secretary of State remonstrated with the Government for not forwarding Tilak's application. The Governor said he felt the snub keenly!

By December 1909 he completed the course of French Grammar and asked for a German Dictionary and a German Grammar. He wanted to study the views of Western scholars on Indian philosophy, especially their views on the *Gita*.

As the summer climate of Mandalay affected his health, he appealed to the Bombay Government in April 1910 to remove him to any place like the Andamans which was cooler than Mandalay. But his appeal was turned down.

Tilak was anxious about the health of his wife. He said she should at least for his sake go to Sinhagad for rest. He asked for the progress books of his sons and hoped that lieutenants Kelkar and Khadilkar would pull together and co-operate with each other. He once again asked his nephew to take care of his Home Library. He enquired of his nephew whether a certain young man had secured a job or not, noted the news about the deaths of acquaintances and colleagues with a sad heart, and expressed joy at the success of his son-in-law Sane, who obtained a Ph.D. degree in Germany.

In August 1910 he read the famous work by Weber. His joy was indescribable. He expressed it by saying that a part of his sentence was thus usefully utilised.

While he was enjoying the divine pleasure of conversing with great sages and thinkers of the past ages, he received buffets of misfortunes. The party of Bala Maharaj, although defeated at the Court of the First Class Judge at Poona, had filed an appeal in the High Court from that judgment. After a long delay the case came up before Mr. Justice Chandavarkar and Mr. Justice Heaton for hearing in the Bombay High Court. M. R. Jayakar appeared for Bala Maharaj, and for Tilak, Khaparde and others, the respondents, appeared D. A. Khare, S. R. Bakhale and R. P. Karandikar. The learned Judges observed in their judgment delivered on September 23, 1910, that some statements made by Tilak in his deposition and in his affidavit varied, and they took the view that Tai Maharaj had accompanied Tilak to Aurangabad because she was in a way forced against her will to do so. Quoting Tilak's statement that ' I told her that according to the will we had the matter (of her maintenance) within our discretion', they observed that there were misleading statements and half truths, and she was led to believe that she was legally subject to the control of the executors of her husband's Will.

The adoption of Jagannath Maharaj by Tai Maharaj was not valid because it was brought about through undue influence exercised over Tai Maharaj by both Tilak and Khaparde. It was shocking news, and Tilak was greatly distressed and surprised by the decision of the Court. He said he was prepared for the worst and must patiently fight out the case till the end.

Khaparde returned to India and he saw Tilak at Mandalay Jail on October 21 and 22 in the presence of the new Jail Superintendent Captain Tarapore. Khaparde embraced his leader and his eyes got dim with tears at the sight of the caged lion. They talked about Tilak's health and about Tai Maharaj's case decided by the Bombay High Court. Tilak furnished Khaparde with notes on the appeal to be preferred to the Privy Council. Khaparde, a charming gossip and story teller, in his most humorous style of conversation captivated the Jail Superintendent. He skilfully reviewed before the Jail Superintendent the full details of the efforts he had made and the work he had done during the past two years for the release of Tilak and the Reforms Scheme which was being prepared by Morley and Minto, so that Tilak might hear the details and history of the case more closely. Tilak talked about the education of his children and the health of his wife and expressed his grief over the death of Khaparde's mother. The jailer showed Khaparde and V. G. Vijapurkar the cell of Tilak from a distance. Tilak described this visit of Khaparde as an incident in a dream. It was so refreshing and so short! He noticed that the stream of humour in Khaparde, though full, was not flowing as usual.

Sufferings and sacrifices are modes of perfection and life in the hermitage unfolds its sacredness. Tilak started on November 2, 1910, writing the *Gita-Rahasya*. By the end of March 1911 he had finished that work. He wrote home that he had finished the work and that the title of the work was *Gita-Rahasya*. He said that some of the interpretations were independent and absolutely original, and were coming before the public for the first time. The central idea of the book showed how the Indian religious philosophy could be applied to the solution of ethical problems. He said that his line of thinking was like the one followed by the English Philosopher Thomas Hill Green in his work *Prolegomena to Ethics*.

In his view the *Gita* was a work on ethics—not utilitarian, nor intuitional but transcendental morality. He said he had compared the philosophy preached in the *Gita* with the Western philosophy, both religious and ethical, and proved that the Gita philosophy was not inferior in any way to the Western philosophy. The most difficult part of the book, the *Gita-Rahasya*—essence—had been completed and the translation of the *Gita* in Marathi was being made. The book contained 15 chapters with an appendix devoted to a critical examination of the *Gita* as part of the *Mahabharata* and discussing its age. It would fill, he said, about 350 pages. The translation of the verses which he was to append to it, he completed later by the end of March 1911. Thus Tilak realised his ambition which he had been cherishing for the past twenty years.

Modern Indian literature, especially its bright part, is much indebted to British tyranny over India. It made India richer in one way. By sending Tilak, Savarkar and later Nehru to gaol, Government inspired these great men to write great works. Tilak's *Gita-Rahasya* and the autobiography of Nehru have attained world-wide publicity, and though equally important are *Kamala* and *Gomantak*, parts of the epic planned by Savarkar, they could not gain world-wide publicity as they are in Marathi. In his letter of July 3, 1911, Tilak referred to the *Bhagwat Gita* by Brook and said it was true that Brook had anticipated him to a certain extent, especially in maintaining that the *Gita* taught Karmayoga! But his work was desultory and mystic, whereas his own was exhaustive, scientific, philosophical and critical. Concluding his letter, Tilak observed that according to him "Karmayoga in Sanskrit includes what modern writers call ethics and that the *Gita* was the ethics of Vedanta—a science by itself. There are some schools who think that Vedanta has no ethics but this is an error; and, I have tried to expose it by comparing the ethics of the *Gita* with the ethics of Mill, Spencer, Martineau, Butler, Sidgwick and others."

In August Myran Phelps visited India and paid a visit to Tilak's residence. He was an admirer of Aryan civilisation. He paid tributes to Tilak and said, "That great man's world-wide fame and his antiquarianism brought me here, especially to this part of the country. Your holy land has ever produced great men among whom we reckon Mr. Tilak. Men like Tilak are born for the world's progress and not merely for their own land." There was a rumour that Tilak might be released in November on the occasion of the Delhi Darbar. He said there was no hope for his release till the completion of his term ; but if his name appeared in that lottery he would welcome it. He had a mind to write some books on Hindu religion and general politics, Vedic Chronology and an English book on the fundamental principles of the Integral Calculus.

In October he had fever for five days which reduced his weight by 7 lbs. He had a similar attack of fever in October 1909, and the front teeth fell making a wide gap in his mouth.

January 1912 dawned and he said there was now a ray of hope for his release. After the Delhi Durbar, a secret meeting was held in Calcutta. It was attended by the Viceroy, Governors and Councillors. When the King-Emperor asked the members of the meeting what gift he should announce for India, Sir Gangadhar Chitnis of Nagpur suggested that the release of Tilak would be a welcome gift to the people. The suggestion appealed to all. At that meeting the King-Emperor himself narrated a story about Tilak's popularity in London. But Lord Lamington, the arch-enemy of Tilak, privately supported by some of the Moderate politicians in the Presidency, intervened and the King-Emperor gave up the question of the release of Tilak.[4]

Tilak felt glad to note that his wife's health was somewhat better. Diabetes began to cause anxiety to Tilak. So he reverted to his old diet. In February 1912, he submitted another petition to the Bombay Government, praying that he might be given the benefit of remission which an ordinary

4 S. V. Bapat in *Tarun Bharat*, 28 July 1957.

prisoner got and should be released as an act of mercy; especially as he was then 56 years of age and subject to diabetes. He instructed his nephew to ask Khare whether he could personally do something in the matter of his release. But he was informed early in June 1912, that the Governor-in-Council was unable to accede to his prayer. In April 1912 he sent a criticism of Prof. Radhakrishnan's article which had appeared about that time in the *Madras Review*.

IV

THE HEALTH OF Tilak's wife Satyabhamabai had now been completely shattered. Diabetes had full sway in her body. She must have been sorely disappointed by the rumours of her husband's release. Since the transportation of her husband she had kept rigidly to her house. She shut herself up in the kitchen, in the lonely room reserved for worship and in the lying-in-room. She spent most of the day in meditation and worship. On rare occasions she relieved her mental burden by having an aimless walk in the compound. She lived on milk, buttermilk, bananas, mangoes, guavas and other Indian fruit. She had given up her usual dress and wore plain saris, glass bangles and her marriage locket, the most precious possession of a Hindu married woman. She looked like a *sanyasini* and the lines of her irreparable sadness went on deepening. At last she died on June 7, 1912.

They had been married forty-one years. Tilak lost his life's better-half, true partner, real companion. Confined to the kids and the kitchen, she could not participate in her husband's public activities and even could not be present on the great occasions in his life. To be a life's companion of a great man is a task onerous and difficult and fraught with dangers too. This dutiful wife silently faced all dangers and difficulties with fortitude, and sad, shrunken and careworn, she at last succumbed to the disease.

A telegram was sent to Tilak informing him about her sad demise. "Your wire," wrote back Tilak describing one of his rare moments of grief, to his nephew Dhondopant Vidwans, "was a great and heavy blow. I am used to take my misfortunes calmly, but I confess that the present shook me considerably. According to the beliefs ingrained in us it is not undesirable that the wife should die before her husband. What grieved me most is my enforced absence from her side at this critical time. But this was to be, I always feared it, and it has at last happened. But I am not going to trouble you further with my sad thoughts. One chapter of my life is closed and I am afraid it won't be long before another will be."

"Let her last rites be duly performed and her remains sent to Allahabad or Banaras or any other place she might have desired. Carry out literally all her last wishes, if you have not done so already. The task of looking after the physical and intellectual development of my sons falls on you now with greater responsibility; and I shall be still further grieved if I were to find it not properly attended to. I believe Mathu and Durgi are still there. They as well as Rambhau must have keenly felt the bereavement especially at a time when I am away. Console them in my name and see that Rambhau and Bapu do not get dejected. Let them remember that I was left an orphan when I was much younger than either of them. Misfortunes should brace us up for greater self-dependence. Both Rambhau and Bapu should take a lesson from this bereavement and if they do that I am sure God will not forsake them. See that their time is not lost in useless grief. The inevitable must be faced boldly."

"As regards her things and valuables make a list thereof, and keep them with you under lock and key till my release or till you next hear to the contrary from me, in the meanwhile. Above all face the situation courageously yourself, for there is no one else on whom the children can depend in this critical state. May God help you all is all that I can wish and pray for from this distant place."[5]

When the Bombay Government rejected his application, Tilak wrote home in the first week of July 1912, that Destiny was bent upon ruining him in various ways. Yet he observed that he would again represent his case to the King-Emperor; what the decision would be was a foregone conclusion. He said he was not tired of making petitions; the Government was not tired of turning them down!

At the end of the fourth year his weight was 123 lbs., but the output of urine was 80 ounces per 24 hours. He asked his nephew to bring his children to Mandalay to see him. The thought uppermost in his mind for the time being was no other than the education of his children. In August 1912 he submitted his petition to the King-Emperor for his release in which he prayed that the unexpired portion of his sentence might be remitted. In March 1913 the Secretary of State for India disposed it of saying that he was unable to advise His Majesty to comply with the prayer thereof. Tilak was disgusted with the preparation of satu food. In ordinary course

5 *Reminiscences and Anecdotes about Lokamanya Tilak*, Vol. III, p. 155 (English Section).

he would have been given a remission of about a year had the sentence been not commuted, but Government was not prepared to show an iota of sympathy to Tilak. Yet his reading was going on. The books he asked for were *Life of Buddha* by Oldenburg and the *Gita* by Thompson. He asked his nephew to convey his best regards to Prof. Radhakrishnan. In April he asked for some seeds of vegetables. About this time a poor Dhangar from Maharashtra forwarded his case papers to Tilak and requested him to favour him with an application to the High Court. Tilak asked his relatives to direct that man to Khaparde.

The Indian world had not forgotten Tilak, its deliverer. The native princes silently, saints softly, paupers proudly, and leaders in India and litterateurs from foreign countries sympathetically, made enquiries about his health. His great political opponent Sir Pherozeshah Mehta, although he differed from Tilak in his political views, said in an appreciative mood that so long as Maharashtrian youth did not forget the spirit of Shivaji and Tilak, they would solve the problcm of Swaraj.

In May 1913 the motherless boys Rambhau and Bapu went to see their father with Dhondopant Vidwans who was the manager of Tilak's papers and property. Dhondopant had seen Tilak at Mandalay Jail twice or thrice. In Mandalay they took their lodgings at the house of one Jamnadas Umedchand Jhaveri. At noon the two sons accompanied the nephew of Tilak to the office of the jail. The boys' eyes were fixed on the entrance by which their father would enter the office. A few minutes after he came. He was walking as usual, but suffered for want of strength. The dress was full of wrinkles and it was untidy. The red turban and the red shoes were at the proper places to complete the picture. The father rushed to them and the children ran to him, and he clasped them to his bosom. The eyes of the Superintendent of the jail became wet. After a talk with his nephew Vidwans, he took his sons to his cell with special permission. A warder accompanied them. The children climbed up the staircase to see the cell where the lion was caged. He showed them his note-books and the manuscript of the *Gita-Rahasya*. The Brahmin convict, his cook, brought them tea and the children drank it in a small round tin. Tilak used to drink tea from the tin. The boys were there for about twenty minutes. He then offered them a little betel-nut, patted them on their backs, embraced them again and the children left the cell.

On August 28, 1913, he had a third attack of fever. It reduced his weight by 6 lbs. In November 1913 he advised his young son to get inoculated if he was afraid of the plague. Fear makes a man vulnerable to a disease. So he asked him to get inoculated. In December 1913, his weight rose to 128 lbs.

Tilak had now come to the end of his transportation. Five months more and he would be released. Diabetes harassed him, but diet had checked the disease. All the eatables and good rice were used for the cook who served him faithfully. When the time for Kulkarni's release came he was not willing to leave him and asked Tilak to write his application for allowing him to stay with him. But his request was not granted.

Tilak had secured him some concessions and relief, and the poor fellow left for his native place with a heavy heart. When he reached Yeravda, he was released and was strictly forbidden to visit Tilak's residence. He went to his native place in Satara District and soon returned to Poona. He saw Tilak's relations at Gaikwad Wada, showed the teeth Tilak had given him as a sign of his trust in him, and related to them how Tilak was passing his days in Mandalay Jail.

Another Brahmin convict was now brought to cook his food. Tilak was now habituated to all surroundings. Even sparrows kept him company in the room. Birds were eaten in Mandalay Jail without even being cooked. So the Jail Superintendent and all were surprised to see the sparrows hovering around Tilak.

On the whole the jail authorities gave him good treatment, treating him as a first class prisoner. Except cutting some parts of his letters which contained, according to them, objectionable matter, they did not harass him. The Lieutenant-Governor of Burma paid a casual visit to the jail and had a formal talk with Tilak. He must have stared at the Napoleonic figure who had turned the soul of India against the rule of Britain! Subhas Bose narrated in his reminiscences of Tilak that, because one officer had omitted the prefix "Mr." while addressing Tilak, the old lion "in a rage went for the official".

The last book Tilak asked for was perhaps the *Life of Buddha* by Prof. Seland. The cell library had now about four hundred choice books, the names of which indicated the power and range of the intellect that digested them! He had planned writing a book on Vedic chronology and had completed the first two chapters of the work, but he could not finish it. These two chapters together with the bibliography and synopsis of the unwritten chapters were published in 1925 in a book called *Vedic Chronology* and *Vedang Jyotish*, the Vedang Jyotish being his unpublished essays. In one of his jail note-books he had jotted down a list of books he had contemplated writing. They were:

(1) History of Hindu Religion.

(2) Indian Nationalism.

(3) Pre-Epic History of India.

(4) The Shankar-Darshan (Indian Monism).

(5) Provincial Administration.

(6) Hindu Law.

(7) Principles of Infinitesimal Calculus.

(8) Bhagwat-Gita-Rahasya-Ethics.

(9) Life of Shivaji.

(10) Chaldea and India.

Early in May 1914, Tilak packed off his library and sent it home through the jail authorities. On the morning of June 8, 1914, at eight o'clock the Jail Superintendent came to his cell and asked him to make ready for departure. At once he was handed over to the police from Rangoon. They came in a motor-car to the station where a special bogie was ready for the party. He left the gaol and left behind the lemon trees which he had planted in his compound to keep alive the sweet odour of his existence!* As soon as a station came in sight they shut the doors and windows of the bogie. He was asked to wear a cap till they reached Rangoon and from Rangoon he was to wind a scarf round his head. He was not allowed to wear his famous turban. Next morning the party was asked to get down at one station short of Rangoon.

On board the ship Tilak saw the police from Poona. The steamer would have reached earlier, but it reached Madras on the morning of June 15, 1914. A special bogie was attached to the train. The train left immediately and came near Poona on the night of the 16th June. At Hadapsar station Tilak was asked to get down. The ticket collector asked for the ticket at the gate and Tilak pointed to the police officer. The Deputy Police Superintendent of Poona was present at the station. The party got out of the station. The two cars passed the road which leads to Yeravda Jail. Tilak knew now that they were taking him home. The police van that was going ahead turned back, and the motor-car that carried Tilak went to his Gaikwad Wada. It

---

* A Hall has now been built in Mandalay Jail in memory of this illustrious prisoner.

was now 2 a.m. Guider, the police officer, told him that Government was kind enough to remit the remaining sentence. Tilak asked him to convey his thanks to Government for the act of kindness! The watchman, who neither recognised his master nor had any idea of his release, was bewildered and would not open the gate of Gaikwad Wada. He ran to Vidwans, who was asleep in the Wada. He instantly recognised Tilak and there was all joy, but at the first step in the compound Tilak's thoughts must have mingled with the sad memory of his wife's death!

CHAPTER XIX

Moderates Make Way

I

THE NEWS SPREAD throughout Poona and crowds of people ran to Tilak's residence. All furniture and curtains were removed from the halls on the first floor, and mattresses were spread. Tilak sat in the middle of the hall against a pillow with his sons by his side. In a few minutes the hall was packed to capacity. Admirers and followers came in one by one, fell prostrate before him or put their heads at his feet, moved aside and sat down nearby. There were heaps of fruit and garlands and sweetmeats. They talked till four o'clock in the morning. Tilak told Sardar Balasaheb Natu that of all the things he most resented was the solitary confinement.

At four the people went home. For a week they went to his residence to have a glimpse of their leader. Telegrams were sent to important leaders of the Nationalist Party all over India.

Tilak invited his lieutenant Kelkar to dinner and learned from him and from others about the political situation in India. What was the condition of India when Tilak arrived in Poona from Mandalay? Almost all parties were paralysed. The removal of Tilak's towering personality, Aurobindo's protracted trial, and the arrests and imprisonment of several nationalist editors in Maharashtra and Bengal unnerved the Nationalist Party. It broke down, and the country sank into dismay. The transportation of Veer Savarkar in 1910 to the Andamans gave a setback to the revolutionary forces in India and particularly in Maharashtra. The *Rashtramat* had been muzzled in 1910. The arrests, transportations and deaths on the gallows of several revolutionary leaders in Bengal and Maharashtra resulted in the break-up of the revolutionary forces in Bengal and Maharashtra. There was a lull all over India and repression reigned supreme. The Seditious Meetings Act, the Press Act, the Criminal Law Amendment Act, all had suppressed and gagged the freedom of the press and platform. Books were proscribed. Articles, poems and pamphlets concerning the national movement were banned, national schools were forced to close down. In June 1910 the Samartha Vidyalaya had been declared an unlawful institution.

Moreover those leaders who could not be imprisoned went into voluntary exile. Lala Lajpat Rai resorted to self-imposed exile. So did B. C. Pal. They both went out of India. Aurobindo Ghose, who was acquitted after a year's trial, got a glimpse of a bright new horizon, and a new flood of light burst upon him. He felt secure in the hands of God, and in April 1910 he escaped to Pondicherry in quest of God! The partition of Bengal against which the Bengal leaders and revolutionaries had valiantly fought had been annulled, but Lord Curzon is said to have remarked that, Hindus who were ringing the bells would wring their hands in future. Bombs and Tilak's transportation had forced the Morley-Minto Reforms in December 1908. But it is not known whether Tilak realised the danger to Indian unity arising out of the communal division laid down in those Reforms. Although the democrat and liberal philosopher in Morley was vacillating and the policy of counterpoise and the fear of a Muslim rising dominated Minto's mind, Gokhale, who wanted to favour minorities with special separate representation, was a leading party to communal electorates. But Tilak also acquiesced in it inasmuch as he, two months after his release, hailed the Reforms as a mark of growing confidence between the people and the Government. The Morley-Minto Reforms introduced a vicious element of communal electorates into the body politic of India. Minto had then issued a circular letter to all Native States seeking their co-operation in annihilating the seditious movement which was dangerous to both, as he believed that the movement had its stronghold in the Native States.

The Moderates were leaders without followers. The Congress session was held in 1908 at Madras where Gokhale had prevented any discussion on boycott, deportations and partition. At Lahore the Congress session was to be presided over by Pherozeshah Mehta in 1909, but he did not go to Lahore as he perhaps expected trouble from the Nationalists. In 1910 Gokhale took up the responsibility of the health of Sir William Wedderburn, and it was at the instance of Gokhale that Wedderburn came to preside over the Congress session at Allahabad. Then in 1911 the Congress session was held at Calcutta and in 1912 it was held at Bankipur which was attended by Gokhale and about 250 delegates, but on account of ill-health he could not attend the Congress session in 1913. Pherozeshah Mehta had been to England in 1910, and he returned in February 1911. He did not attend the Congress sessions in 1912 and 1913. A. O. Hume, the Prometheus of the Congress, passed away in 1912. This was the sad state to which the Congress had been reduced!

The citizens of Poona decided to congratulate Tilak on his safe return. A public meeting was held at the Sarvajanik Sabha on June 21, 1914, under the presidentship of Annasaheb Patwardhan, and a resolution was passed declaring that Tilak be felicitated at his home the next day on behalf of the people of Poona.

The next day a meeting was held at Gaikwad Wada. Many of Tilak's lieutenants attended it. Representatives and leaders of the Nationalist Party from Nagpur, Satara, Nagar, Khandesh, Akola and Bombay garlanded Tilak on behalf of their branch organisations. Prof. S. M. Paranjpe, who had undergone rigorous imprisonment for sedition for 19 months, said he was garlanding Tilak on behalf of the patriots who could not be present at the function.

Thanking the people for the honour done to him, Tilak said, "When after six years' absence, I return and begin my acquaintance with the world, I find myself in the position of Rip Van Winkle. I was kept by the authorities in such rigorous seclusion that it seems that they desired that I should forget the world and be forgotten by it. However, I have not forgotten the people, and I am glad to notice that the people have not forgotten me. I can only assure the public that separation for six long years could not diminish my love for them and that I am willing and ready to serve them in the same capacity as I did six years ago, though, it may be, I shall have to modify the course a little."

This declaration set at rest the rumours that Tilak was going to abandon the exacting and exhausting field of politics for the peaceful pursuits of literature in the evening of his life. It was the wishful thinking of his enemies. There were some well-meaning advisers, like his son-in-law Dr. Sane, who, with a break in their voice, would entreat him to turn to the quiet work of literature, and earn lasting renown in it. "Works of literature and philosophy," Tilak maintained, "are not the primary needs when the country is rotting in slavery. They are to be followed in times of leisure or in jail. To turn to other pursuits, leaving the nation in political servitude, is to show the weakness as did Arjun on the battle-field."

To one leader of his party Tilak said that somebody must do the work which he was doing. That work served to some extent as a brake to the unbridled actions of Government. If none agitated, the British would rule as they liked. To another person he said if he was not to strive for the welfare of his people in his honest way, then it was better to die in jail. He did not attach any importance to personal salvation or glory. When men around were hungry, harassed and crying for liberty, it was a sin to sit in a corner and be engrossed either in the songs of eternity or in personal elevation. To turn one's back on personal renown and to choose, at whatever cost, the service of the nation, was a great sacrifice, he added.

Government did not like that people should come in contact with Tilak in any way. They wanted to break off the relation of the moon with the sea. So ludicrous was the attempt! Yet they gave practical shape to their vindictiveness. On June 26 Government issued an official circular proclaiming a boycott of Tilak and declaring that until Tilak showed by overt acts that he had altered his views and intended to modify his propaganda, he must be looked upon as the enemy of the British Government. They installed two Police Chowkies in the neighbourhood of his house and kept rigorous and close surveillance on him. Visitors to his house were openly accosted, and they were compelled to give their names. Under special circulars managers of recognised schools were informed that students should not be allowed to associate themselves with Tilak in any way or to pay visits to his residence. Jagirdars, inamdars, watandars, title holders, Government servants of all grades, Government pensioners and teachers, and persons employed in or connected with recognised educational institutions, were prohibited from keeping contacts with Tilak and warned that their association with Tilak would be looked with grave dissatisfaction and would be marked by such punishment as the Government might consider suitable in each case.

Those who never had any contact with Tilak, but went along the road near his house, naturally abandoned that road; but those who never curried favour with Government and were indifferent to their orders boldly entered Tilak's Wada. One such leader was Belvi from Belgaum. He met Tilak in Poona and returned to Belgaum. On his return to Belgaum, the Collector of the District tried to snub him; but the self-respecting and spirited lawyer and leader in Belvi told him fearlessly that the Collector was not dealing with an ordinary man. He was a Member of the Legislative Council, and it was not the Collector's business to draw his attention to any order or law!

Nationalist leaders were eager to know about Tilak's health and his future plans, and so there were anxious inquiries from all parts of the country. Motilal Ghose, who considered himself to be fourteen annas on the other side of the world and two annas on this, wrote to Tilak, his "Dear beloved friend", expressing his doubt as to whether he would be able to see Tilak with his mortal eyes; for he had found it stated in the papers that Tilak was going to England and intended to pass several years in Europe. So he said he must bid farewell and hoped that he would meet him in the land of butterflies where they both would be free as air and dance in joy and suck sweet honey, snapping their fingers at the police and the C.I.D. and the Sandhursts and the Davars. He was glad to hear that Tilak had written some valuable books during his imprisonment and added that there they saw the loving hand of God in their misery.

Tilak grew indignant at this harassment and unjust attitude of the Government. He wrote at once to Keir Hardie, drawing his attention to this harassment and political vendetta. Keir Hardie referred the matter to the Secretary of State for India. Tilak also wrote directly to the Secretary of State for India. Motilal Ghose, too, complained to the Central Government of this harassment; but it upheld the stand taken by the Provincial Government, stating that it had rightly taken steps to keep Tilak's behaviour under observation. There was another shameful side to this picture. The Kolhapur State, which seemed to have lost the soul of Shivaji and echoed helplessly its British Master's voice, issued on July 22, a similar proclamation prohibiting its subjects from having any connection with Tilak who was carrying the message of Shivaji to the people to rise against slavery.

II

In the meanwhile war broke out on August 4, 1914, and naturally the British Government was in no mood to make enquiries or remonstrate with the Bombay bureaucrats. Tilak must have been very happy that he was free to take advantage of the situation that arose out of the war. A thought crossed his mind that had his term of transportation not come to an end before the outbreak of the war he would have been detained in the prison on some pretext or other! Tilak was seeing how the land lay. He knew from his secret sources about the activities of Indian revolutionaries, who were struggling in Europe for the emancipation of India. He, therefore, thought it a matter of expediency and policy to co-operate with the Government whenever possible, and allow himself to work unhampered believing that England's difficulty was India's opportunity for snatching political reforms. With this end in view he issued a statement on August 27, which was a counter-statement to the Government proclamation. At the outset he described the Morley-Minto Reforms as a marked increase of confidence between the rulers and the ruled, and a sustained endeavour to remove popular grievances.

Then he referred to Chirol's book *Indian Unrest* in which the author had interpreted "my actions and writings as a direct or indirect incitement to deeds of violence or my speeches as uttered with the object of subverting the British Rule in India." Refuting these 'nasty and totally unfounded charges', Tilak declared: "That has never been my wish or my object. I may state once for all that we are trying in India, as the Irish Home rulers have been doing in Ireland, for a reform of the system of administration of Government, and not for the overthrow of Government; and I have no hesitation in saying that the acts of violence which have been committed in different parts of India are not only repugnant to me, but have, in my opinion, only unfortunately retarded to a great extent, the pace of our political progress. Whether looked at from an individual or from a public point of view they deserve, as I have said before on several occasions, to be equally condemned."

"It has been well said," Tilak further observed, "that British Rule is conferring inestimable benefit on India not only by its civilized methods of administration, but also thereby bringing together the different nationalities and races of India, so that a united Nation may grow out of it in course of time. I do not believe that if we had any other rulers except the liberty-loving British, they could have conceived and assisted us in developing such a national ideal."

"England, as you know, has been," he concluded, "compelled by the action of the German Emperor to take up arms in defence of a weaker state. At such a crisis it is, I firmly hold, the duty of every Indian, be he great or small, rich or poor, to support and assist His Majesty's Government, to the best of his ability." [1]

The Anglo-Indians and other pro-British politicians in India heaved a sigh of relief and appreciated the attitude of Tilak with an inward serene satisfaction that he had at last come round. This statement, however, came

1 Statement, 27 August 1914.

as a disappointment to his lieutenants and followers, and some of them openly said that Tilak had become a Moderate by rejecting his avowed extremism. Some Moderates in Poona bleated that Tilak had at last said ditto to the statement purported to have been prepared by the Government. They chuckled over the helplessness of a mighty patriot of his day who had issued it as a matter of statecraft!

After Tilak's incarceration, the Congress Continuation Committee led and formed by his lieutenants had tried to hold a separate Congress at Nagpur in December 1908. Kelkar had opposed the idea of a separate Congress. Government prohibited them from holding the Congress at Nagpur, and the Tilakaites drew in their horns. These were the lieutenants who said that Tilak had become a Moderate! Tilak's other lieutenant Khadilkar, no doubt, wrote brilliant and matchless plays like the *"Killing of Kichak"* which the Government had proscribed and Chirol criticized, but in active politics he had done nothing. When he presented Tilak with a set of his new plays, the leader put it aside and asked him whether that was the political work he had done during his absence. On his release Prof. S. M. Paranjpe also could not give any lead to the Party. Times were very dangerous, and oppression and repression reigned supreme. Tilak silenced these well-meaning advisers by telling them that owing to their inaction and failure to give a lead to Maharashtra he had to eat humble pie. Had they kept up the struggle it would have been possible for him at that juncture to take advantage of the situation created by the war and to raise the banner of revolt in India.

Tilak, however, expressed his satisfaction at the great service rendered by Kelkar in keeping intact the *Kesari* which was in fact no mean achievement in those days of repression.

The shrewd Mahratta tactics shown by Tilak in issuing the statement had the desired effect. Shivaji also had once written an appealing letter to Aurangzeb to bring pressure on the ruler of Bijapur to release his father Shahaji. That was not a policy of surrender. It was a tactical move. Government removed the police chowkies and the watch, and Tilak became free to move and work.

As regards the denouncement of the revolutionaries, he had done it not from the bottom of his heart. It was a fact that he did not regard the revolutionaries as political untouchables. His relations with them were god-fatherly and cordial. His relentless struggle against British rule, his noble sacrifice, his long sufferings and his fiery pen had greatly influenced the young revolutionary leaders.

Subsequent to this statement when mischievous persons said that Tilak had gone Moderate he asked them to go to the Moderates and ask them whether they would employ young men like P. M. Bapat and Dr. V. M. Bhat who had suffered imprisonment for revolutionary activities. It was also well known that Tilak helped the relatives of the revolutionaries and spoke of them very sympathetically.

One more point is worth mentioning here. The Moderates treated the revolutionaries as political lepers. The *Modern Review* had explained brilliantly the position and role of the revolutionaries and replied in a balanced manner to these honourable armchair politicians. The British statesmen's policy in asking Indians to rally round the Moderates had a very deep meaning. In fact they did not like the soft-tongued Moderates either, but because Tilak had the moral backing of the revolutionary forces, British statesmen loathed him unremittingly and preferred to talk and deal with the Moderates. This was the real object behind the vindictive attitude of the Government to Tilak.

Tilak was now seriously thinking of picking up the threads of his last compromise move in fusing the two arms of the Congress. Before his arrest in June 1908, he had set up a Congress Continuation Committee with that object in view. To think of politics again after thrice undergoing such rigorous gaol hardships was no easy thing. It showed the grit, iron will, and unflinching aim of the Mahratta rebel to which statesmen like Nevinson had testified. Almost all of Tilak's first-rate colleagues like Aurobindo Ghose, Lala Lajpat Rai and B. C. Pal had receded into the background. Tilak alone could keep to the battlefield. Politics had now gone beyond the reach of the armchair politicians. Surendranath had relapsed into inactivity after the Delhi Darbar in 1911, Mahatma Gandhi, Jawaharlal Nehru and Sardar Patel had not then appeared on the political horizon. Tilak was now almost alone to resume the role of a nationalist leader and to give a lead to the country. He must first repair the ship of the Congress. The Chitpavan rose from his ashes of sufferings and like Parashuram, Tilak stood again for war.

The observations made in this respect by Sir Michael O'Dwyer in his book *India As I Know It* are worth noting. "The reason for the undoubted pre-eminence of the Mahratta Brahmins," states he, "in the political movement of the last thirty years, whether a Moderate such as Gokhale or an Extremist such as Tilak, is to be found in their history." "The Mahratta Brahmin," he proceeds, "is the only class among the Hindu intelligentsia that had behind it the tradition of two centuries of almost independent rule. That gives them an experience and the outlook on politics far more real than of the subtle but shallow Madrasi, the fervid but frothy Bengali, the eloquent but unconvincing Pandit of the Ganges valley, none of whom have behind them any tradition of the Swaraj which they so glibly claim as their 'birth-right'."[2] This opinion is quoted here just to show how the unflinching courage and political realism shown by Tilak at this juncture were true to the Mahratta spirit; one may not at all agree with Sir Michael O'Dwyer's remark as to the Bengali, Madrasi or the Pandit brethren.

It was now possible that Tilak would go out for delivering speeches during the Ganesh festival which was drawing near. The District Magistrate of Poona, therefore, issued orders prohibiting the singing of songs at public places without the previous sanction of the Government, the shouting of "Jais" to anyone except the Ganapati, displaying the pictures of the men who were convicted of sedition, honouring such men or their relatives during the festival, and forbidding any man to address the processionists at intervals on the way.

This was an indirect check on Tilak. And as if this was not enough, the District Magistrate wrote on August 26 to Tilak desiring him not to take part in the procession on the day of the Ganapati immersion. Tilak accepted this as it was asked for under special circumstances. Tilak delivered four speeches at Gaikwad Wada during the Ganesh festival on the *Gita* and its message, and declared his re-entry into public life.

The manuscript of his *Gita-Rahasya* was returned to Tilak by the Government at this time, after being examined by a Shastri! It was not in vain that Chirol had written in his book that *Bhagvad-Gita* was impressed into the service of sedition! *Gita-Rahasya* was the combination of the *Gita* and *Tilak*! They thought that Tilak must have turned the *Gita* philosophy into a philosophy of relentless action. So it must have been dissected and examined by both philologists and pathologists! On receiving the manuscript, Tilak began to prepare the press copy of the *Gita-Rahasya*.

The question of compromise between the two sections of the Congress received a fresh stimulus on the release of Tilak. Mrs. Annie Besant had just then appeared on the scene as a political leader. From her earliest

---

2 O'Dwyer, Sir Michael, *India As I Know It* (1885-1925), p. 160.

womanhood she was hailed in England as the finest platform orator of her generation. She was a person of great power and capacity of mind and a tireless worker, a person born to lead and serve. She had moved from Atheism to Theosophy as she travelled from one continent to another each time subordinating the first god to the new one. She had propagated Atheism under the influence of Bradlaugh, Evolution under the influence of Edward Aveling, Socialism under Bernard Shaw and Theosophy under Madame Blavatsky.

Intensely proud of India's glorious cultural heritage, Besant came to India, rendered a great service in various fields, and she now entered upon a political life. She thought it desirable to fuse the two wings of the Congress and make it a powerful weapon for use in the fight for the rights of the people. So she wrote to Tilak, and in a month or two the correspondence developed to the stage of proposing an interview between Tilak and Besant. Gokhale's health was collapsing. Pherozeshah Mehta's health was broken. But Mehta was deadly against the entry of Tilak's firebrands into the Congress. Tilak in his heart of hearts knew the importance of the Congress as a rallying point.

It was about this time that Srinivas Sastri introduced a Bill in the Madras Legislative Council. It recommended post-puberty marriages. As usual Tilak made a violent attack on it and its mover! On another occasion he had a discussion on a similar topic or perhaps on the Bill with the sub-editor of the *Mahratta*, V. M. Joshi. He told him that he would send the note to him on the topic and when Joshi went to him and asked for it, Tilak stormed at him as if Joshi were the promoter of the Bill! Later the Sastri Bill sank into the din made by World War I. After the Surat embroglio, the Congress creed, constitution and rules of the conduct of its meetings had been so framed by the Moderate leaders as to exclude the Nationalists becoming members of the Congress. What Tilak objected to most was that the old practice of electing delegates at public meetings was set aside and the election of the Congress delegates was completely and exclusively put in the hands of the Moderate associations. Tilak, therefore, said that the only course that could bring the Nationalists in the fold of the National Congress was so to amend Article XX of the constitution of the Congress as to enable them to elect their delegates at public meetings or at meetings of the Nationalist associations like the Sarvajanik Sabha.

Tilak issued on November 26, 1914, a circular letter to his party-men asking for their opinions on the proposal for a compromise with the

Moderates. He informed them that Mrs. Besant and Subba Rao, the Joint Secretary of the Congress, were coming to Poona to meet Gokhale and himself to discuss certain proposals for holding a united Congress. He expressed a hope that the desired amendment might take place that year, especially as the President-elect Bhupendranath Basu was in their favour.

Meanwhile Gokhale returned to India on November 29, 1914, after his stay in England for over six months in connection with the work of the Public Commission of which he was a Member.

Mrs. Besant and Subba Rao went to Poona not on the appointed day, but on December 7. She met Gokhale, who was agreeable to modifying Article XX of the Congress Constitution. She then came to Tilak who was waiting for her with his other party leaders like Khaparde, Dr. Moonje, Kelkar, Paranjpe and Karandikar. The talks began, but Dr. Moonje intervened and asked Besant whether she had a sanction from Mehta behind her. She replied in the negative. Dr. Moonje then said that it was useless to continue the talk. Besant felt offended, and she left. Tilak was displeased with Dr. Moonje at the way he talked with Besant. Dr. Moonje at once tendered an apology. Tilak, however, told Subba Rao that he intended starting a Home Rule League and keep voicing the demand for Swaraj, and that he would make efforts to bring a Home Rule Bill in Parliament.

Tilak, Khaparde and Moonje then went to the Servants of India Society to meet Mrs. Besant. On the way Dr. Moonje jokingly said to Tilak, "Balwantrao, be careful, there is danger of your meeting with constitutional and political treachery!" Tilak replied readily, "I am not born to meet constitutional and political death at the hands of a man like Gokhale!" Besant and Tilak had a talk. Tilak met Gokhale. He inquired after his health. Besant then took a draft of the resolution to be moved in the Congress during its session, which was to be held in the last week of the month, and left Poona for Madras. When someone asked Tilak what he should say to Mrs. Besant while bidding her farewell, Tilak said, " Tell her, for achieving Swaraj for India I would, if occasion demands, bow down to or fight the enemies of our country!"

Subba Rao saw Pherozeshah Mehta in Bombay and then again saw Gokhale at Poona. Mehta did not approve of Gokhale's talks with Tilak. Maybe, goaded by this pressure or maybe due to a change in policy, Gokhale decided again to have a talk with Tilak on the subject. So in the same week Gokhale paid a return visit to Tilak and during the talk tried to impress upon him the desirability of his not entering the Congress as he thought Tilak and the Moderates would not hit it off together. Tilak told Gokhale that the Congress was not the property of any one Party. It belonged to the nation. He would prepare the country first and then capture the Congress. Then Gokhale inquired after Tilak's health. He was himself a patient of diabetes and suggested to Tilak to apply Rasinol ointment to the pimples on his head. Tilak used it to the end of his life.

Meantime Gokhale wrote a letter on December 14 to the President-elect, Bhupendranath Basu, saying that to heal the breach in public life he was prepared to so relax the rigidity of the rules as to make them less humiliating to his countrymen, but his hope had been shattered the previous week, for Tilak had told Subba Rao frankly and in unequivocal terms that though he accepted the position as laid down in what was known as the Congress creed he did not believe in the present Congress, which rested on association with Government where possible, and opposition to it where necessary. In place of this he wanted to substitute the method of opposition to Government pure and simple within constitutional limits, in other words a policy of Irish obstruction.

Gokhale further said: "Tilak wants to address only one demand to the Government here and to the British public in England, viz. for the concession of Self-Government to India, and till that is conceded, he would urge his countrymen, to have nothing to do with either the public services or Legislative Councils and Local and Municipal Bodies. And by organising obstruction to Government in every possible direction within the limits of the laws of the land, he hopes to be able to bring the administration to a standstill, and compel the authorities to capitulate. This is briefly his programme." [3]

IV

THE SESSION OF the Congress was held at Madras in December 1914. Tilak was requested by Mrs. Besant to attend the Congress. She had even expressed in her *New India* a desire that the Chairman of the Reception Committee should invite Tilak to attend the Congress at least in the capacity of a guest. Tilak could not afford to be a mere spectator and waste his time. So he did not go to Madras. At the meeting of the Subjects Committee Bhupendranath referred to Gokhale's letter and said that Tilak insisted upon boycott of Government. Besant was nonplussed. She wired to Tilak:

3 Mody, H. P., Sir *Pherozeshah Mehta*, pp. 654-56.

"Moved amendment Debate adjourned. It is said by opponents you favour boycott of Government. I say you do not. Wire which is truth (Reply prepaid)." Tilak replied: "I have never advocated boycott of Government. Prominent Nationalists have served and are serving in Municipalities and Legislative Councils and I have fully supported their action both privately and publicly." Perhaps the expression "never advocated boycott of Government" is to be read in the context of the foregoing talks!

And the controversy over Gokhale's letter to Bhupendranath started bitterly. Tilak said that Gokhale had stabbed him in the dark and challenged him to publish his letter to Bhupendranath. It was reported that he was about to resort to his usual weapon of taking legal proceedings against Gokhale.

Gokhale stated that he had gathered from Tilak's talks with Subba Rao that Tilak's old policy was unchanged. Because it was not possible for him to go to the Congress he had written a private letter to Bhupendranath saying that he was completely disappointed of Tilak's attitude. Gokhale issued a statement on February 6, stating that he had shown that letter to Tilak's friend Prof. Vijapurkar, who was present during Subba Rao's interviews with Tilak and who had assured him that his statement of Tilak's position in the letter was quite correct. Neither Bhupendranath nor he himself, added Gokhale, had used the expression 'boycott of Government'. He said he was not bound to publish the private letter but he was willing to show it to Tilak or to any of his authorised representative.

Upon this Tilak replied to Gokhale that Babu Bhupendranath was said to have asked for a modified copy of the confidential letter in order that the same might be freely used. But before the second letter of Gokhale reached Bhupendranath, he had shown the first letter to some of his Bengali friends to justify his own stand. Tilak, therefore, said that Gokhale owed it to himself and to him (Tilak) to publish his letters, so that the public might, after his reply to the letters, form their own judgment. It is said that Tilak was in possession of the copies of Gokhale's two letters[4] to Bhupendranath Basu. Motilal Ghose had sent, it is said, a copy of the letter through one Shastri of Poona, who happened to be in Calcutta at that time.

Tilak also published a reply in the *Kesari* of the 9th February 1915, saying indignantly that the funeral pyres of Gokhale and Tilak were as good as ready at the crematory and challenged Gokhale to publish his letter to

---

4 *Reminiscences and Anecdotes about Lokamanya Tilak*, Vol. I, p. 411.

Bhupendranath. Gokhale published a reply next day in the *Dnyanprakash* to the effect that he did not publish the letter as he thought that it would harm the cause of the country. He was rolling in his bed with a malady, and he had to prove his stand by publishing his letter. Whether or not Tilak had said during the talks that boycott of Government should be resorted to, it was Gokhale's responsibility to publish his letter. Gokhale wrote to Subba Rao: " The *Kesari* in particular has been pressing the accusation against me with a virulence of which I can give you no idea. I have carried forbearance to its extreme limit and it is impossible for me to keep silence any longer." [5]

It is not conclusively proved that Gokhale had written two letters to Babu Bhupendranath. The one quoted in Sir Pherozeshah Mehta's biography has been cited above. Tilak did not publish the copy of the letter because thereby the man who had brought that letter from Bhupendranath would have been betrayed, or perhaps it might not have been very helpful to Tilak or to both! A great man commits a great mistake once in his life, and Gokhale might have done it at this time: for all this smoke was not without fire!

Gandhi had just then returned 'to India, and he had come to Poona to meet his Guru Gokhale. There was a suggestion that he should join the Servants of India Society. Gandhi learnt that Tilak had written a very violent article in the *Kesari* denouncing Gokhale. He, therefore, saw Tilak and expressed his resentment at it. Tilak said it was a reply to Gokhale's men who had written against him several articles whereas he had written only one! When the man with the turban, blanket, and sandals went out, Tilak remarked: "Oh! he is a seasoned missionary!" This was Gandhi's first encounter with Tilak after returning from South Africa!

Tilak was busy at Sinhagad preparing the manuscript of his new book the *Gita-Rahasya*. On his arrival from Mandalay, he had intermittent attacks of fever, and his health had not fully recovered. His head had some black spots caused by the application of acid to pimples which he got as a result of diabetes.

Gokhale's sustaining power was yielding. He could not get over the shock. He could not attend the meeting held at the Servants of India Society to honour Gandhi, the hero of South Africa! On February 17, he completed his Reforms Scheme and sent its copies to the Aga Khan and Sir Pherozeshah Mehta.

---

5 Parasnis, Prof. S. R., *Namdar Gopal Krishna Gokhale* (Marathi), p. 148.

Gokhale at last succumbed to his illness on February 19, 1915. With his death a great statesman was removed from the scene of Indian politics. Curzon had said that Gokhale was a foeman not unworthy of his steel and that he was the ablest Indian he had come across. Minto said he had the highest respect for Gokhale, the leader of the Opposition in the Central Legislative Council. A graduate at eighteen, a professor at twenty, an editor at twenty-four, a joint secretary of the Provincial Conference at twenty-five, President of the Congress at thirty-nine and founder of the Servants of India Society, Gokhale, a poor Brahmin lad, rose from a humble rank to the top of the ladder of eminence by dint of his patient industry, spotless sincerity, unsullied character and selfless service.

In his day Gokhale the patriot with his sweet reasonableness played an important role in discussing reform proposals with the British statesmen, impressing on them that if they did not introduce reforms the Extremists would have their way, and confusion, danger and ruin would follow. He was a parliamentary orator; but his practice of sending his points on budget in advance to the Member in charge of the budget hardly befitted any parliamentary opposition, if in a parliamentary system the Government has to be kept on the anvil. A great gentleman in politics, Gokhale, devoted to spiritualizing politics, was thus sometimes the victim of his Utopian ideals.

Tilak hurried back to Poona from Sinhagad to attend his one-time colleague's funeral. To many this gesture was a surprise. Addressing at the cremation grounds the people who unwittingly cheered him, he paid eloquent tribute to Gokhale and said, "This is not a time for cheers. This is a time for shedding tears. This diamond of India, this jewel of Maharashtra, this prince of workers is laid to eternal rest on the funeral ground. Look at him, and try to emulate him. Everyone of you should place his life as a model to be imitated, and should try to fill up the gap caused by his death; and if you will do your level best to emulate him in this way, he will feel glad even in the other world."

A few days after the demise of Gokhale, Tilak called some young men to his place and urged them to take to politics, not to continue the quarrels of Gokhale and himself, but to keep up the tradition of service, sacrifice and leadership of Poona.

About this time Tilak received a message from some Indian revolutionaries who were then in Germany. They had also sent him about sixty diamonds with a Maharashtrian Brahmin. Tilak, a shrewd, selfless and cautious man that he was, did not touch them and sent them to his lieutenant Gangadhar Deshpande to be utilised for patriotic purposes. Thereupon Deshpande met Tilak in Poona and asked him what he should do with the diamonds. Tilak asked him to utilise them in undermining the loyalty of some of the important army officers of the Maratha Infantry stationed at Belgaum. As Deshpande found the task very difficult he sent the diamonds to Kaka Patil at Thana. He as well as Govindrao Yalgi disposed of the diamonds and at the instance of Tilak money was handed over to the man who had risked his life in bringing the diamonds from Germany.[6]

Tilak had a confidential talk with Chidambaram Pillai who had been called by him to Poona. Pillai reached Poona on the night on which Gokhale died. Tilak discussed with Pillai the European War. The secret message from the revolutionaries had forewarned that certain occasions would arise during the course of the War, and Indians should do certain things on those occasions. They discussed for two or three days the advisability, possibility and the probable result of their carrying out the terms of the message. Concluding the discussions, Tilak said that the occasions referred to in the message might not arise, as there were several complications in Europe in connection with the War.[7]

In the last week of March Tilak achieved one of the most important triumphs of his life. The Bombay High Court had delivered judgment against the adoption of Jagannath Maharaj in the Tai Maharaj Case. On an appeal to the Privy Council which was made about two years before, the Privy Council quashed on March 26, 1915, the decree of the Bombay High Court and restored the judgment of the sub-judge! Referring to the statement made in Sir Chandavarkar's judgment that Tilak and others had conspired together to give false evidence, their Lordships said that they did not think that one word of it was justified by the evidence in the case! They added that the conclusion come to by the learned Judges of the Bombay High Court was entirely unwarranted on the facts. It was not a revision. It was a rebuke, severe and scathing! Tilak was happy that he had at last won the case after a long-drawn-out struggle which taxed his purse and brains for over fourteen years. It was a great victory vindicating his character, a final blow to the Government which had been cherishing an evil desire

6 A note prepared by H. M. Joshi, Research Officer, Maharashtra State Committee for History of Freedom Movement in India.

7 *Reminiscences and Anecdotes about Lokamanya Tilak*, Vol. II, p. 135 (English Section).

to damage the reputation of Tilak, and was rightly a great occasion for jubilation to his followers and admirers.

Tilak now thought it a proper time to consolidate and organise his Party and then enter the Congress as an organised Party. At first he called on April 20 a meeting of the leading members of his Party at the Sarvajanik Sabha in Poona and formed the Reception Committee. The Conference of the Nationalist Party met accordingly at the Kirloskar Theatre in Poona, on May 8, under the presidentship of Joseph Baptista whose noble patriotism and selfless service in the cause of India was highly appreciated by the Nationalists all over India. Baptista impressed upon the Conference the need for the formation of a Home Rule League and of constant propaganda in London.

Gangadharrao Deshpande moved a proposition that Veer Savarkar and all other political prisoners should be released. There was violent opposition, and a delegate threatened to oppose the resolution in the open session. Tilak intervened and told Deshpande to wait for some time till the man who opposed that resolution had got inured to the methods of the Party. So Deshpande withdrew his proposition. At this Conference Tilak formally moved a condolence resolution on the death of Gokhale and said, "I feel sadness and sorrow more keenly than others, because I was in part responsible for introducing Gokhale into the field of politics, a field in which that zealous and sincere worker lost his life."

"No man can better know," observed the great obituarist in Tilak, "than I do Gokhale's qualities of head and heart; his zeal for the country's cause, his sincerity and single-mindedness, his determination to take to the end the task he undertook. It is a misfortune that India cannot boast of many such men." The Conference appointed a committee consisting of Tilak, Baptista and Belvi to negotiate with the Moderates a compromise with regard to the entry of the Nationalists into the Congress.

Early in May Tilak presided over the meeting of Bharat Itihas Sanshodhak Mandal, which had been started long before. He said he had joined it as knowledge of the history of a nation was essential to those who struggled for its prosperity.

V

THE PRINTING OF the *Gita-Rahasya*, *The Hindu Philosophy of Life*, *Ethics and Religion* had been already begun, and it was now coming to an end. Tilak went to the Press every morning to see that the work was being done properly. He had tried his utmost to secure *Swadeshi* paper for the book. The Magnum Opus of Tilak at last saw the light of day in June 1915. Tracing the origin of the thought that made him write the book, he said, "When I was quite a boy, I was often told by my elders that strictly religious and really philosophic life was incompatible with the humdrum life of every day. One could not serve two masters, the world and God. In my boyhood I was also told that the *Bhagvat Gita* was universally acknowledged to be a book containing all the principles of philosophy of the Hindu religion. I thought if this be so, I should find an answer in this book to my query."

"The conclusion," he said while explaining his stand, "I have come to is that the Gita advocates the performance of action in this world even after the actor has achieved the highest union with the Supreme Deity by Jnana (knowledge) or Bhakti (devotion)." "Jnana-Yoga," he said, "and Bhakti-Yoga are both subservient to the Karma-Yoga preached in the *Gita*. If the *Gita* was preached to desponding Arjuna to make him ready for the fight—for the Action—how can it be said that the ultimate lesson of the great book is Bhakti or Jnana alone? In fact, there is a blending of all these Yogas in the *Gita*; and as the air is not oxygen or hydrogen, or any other gas alone but a composition of all these in a certain proportion, so in the *Gita* all these Yogas are blended in one." [8]

Speaking on the message of the *Gita*, he again observed that the law of duty has been the sacred heritage of India from times immemorial and that the goal of life should not be meditation alone. "No one can expect," believed he, "Providence to protect one who sits with folded arms and throws his burden on others. God does not help the indolent. You must be doing all that you can to lift yourself up, and then only you may rely on the Almighty to help you. You should not, however, presume that you have to toil that you yourself might reap the fruit of your labours. That cannot always be the case. Let us then try our utmost and leave the generations to come to enjoy that fruit. Remember, it is not you who had planted the mango-trees the fruit whereof you have tasted. Let the advantage now go to our children and their descendants. It is only given to us to toil and work. And so, there ought to be no relaxation in our efforts, lest we incur the curse of those that come after us. Action alone must be our guiding principle, action disinterested and well-thought out."[9]

8 Bal Gangadhar Tilak: *His Speeches and Writings,* pp. 231-34.

9 *All about Lokamanya Tilak*, pp. 578-79.

"The *Gita* was not preached," Tilak wrote in the preface to the book, "either as a pastime for persons tired out after living a worldly life in the pursuit of selfish motives, nor as a preparatory lesson for living such a worldly life, but in order to give Philosophical advice as to how one should live his worldly life with an eye to Release (Moksha), and as to the true duties of human beings in the worldly life."

In short, this great work seeks to establish that a life of action after proper self-realization and not a life of renunciation is the aim of human existence and that a life of renunciation is not preached by the *Gita* but a life of action. It also seeks to establish that the teaching of the *Gita* is based on a proper realization of the mutual relationship between the human being and the universe.

The book was written in Marathi. The first edition was exhausted in a month. The second was issued in September 1915. This commentary on the ancient Sacred Book of India placed Tilak in the galaxy of Shankaracharya, Madhavacharya, Vallabhacharya and Ramanujacharya. Dr. Radhakrishnan, rightly remarked in a review of Tilak's great work that " the scholastic commentators have used the *Bhagvat-Gita* in the interests of their own metaphysical and religious views and twisted out of its shape the true message of the *Gita*. Mr. Tilak attempts to restore the natural sense of the *Bhagvat-Gita* by making Karma-Yoga its central secret." [10]

The book has enriched Marathi. Tilak provided the Marathi language with technical terms, the coining of one word often taking him two days. It is a work compounded of philosophy, logic, art and style. A great book always reflects the personality of its author, and Tilak's personality pervades this work. Another charming feature of the work is the marvellous fusion made in it of the choice stories full of the essence of ethics and politics from the *Mahabharata*. Tilak was not a mere philosopher. He was both a philosopher and a politician! He wanted to give a blow to the popular belief that had been inured to escapism for centuries, escapism on which had been nurtured barren speculations on the other world.

Although Tilak had declared that he had no theory of his own for which he sought any support from the book and that he had no reason to twist the text to suit his theory, some of his critics held that he wrote it in defence of his political philosophy which preached ' tit for tat'. When off his guard, he once, admitted that one of his objects in writing the book was

10 Ibid, p. 636.

the propagation of his political views. Indeed he expressed his opinion that every commentator on the *Gita* had interpreted it to suit his own metaphysical system![11] If Tilak thought it proper to impress the *Gita* to suit his times, why he kept unchanged the original ideas in the *Gita* about the caste system was another objection raised by others! Some think that the interpretation Tilak put on the words 'Dharma' and 'Yoga' is not correct. According to some critics the *Gita-Rahasya* is not so profoundly critical and original as is Garbe's *Introduction To The Bhagvat-Gita*. The *Gita-Rahasya* reflects the heart of a faithful devotee and the erudition of the great author, but lacks the historical perspective through which an ethical problem of a given time must be judged.

Tilak wrote this commentary on the pattern of old commentaries using the terminology of metaphysics to explain worldly problems. In political discussions Tilak adopted the Western system of discourse, but in his commentary on the *Gita* he followed the Indian system. Had he adopted the Western system, his work would have developed into a magnificent epitome of philosophy in the modern world. Yet the most vital objection raised to his theory of Karmayoga is that Tilak accepted the absolute non-dualism of Shankaracharya and engrafted on it a dissimilar and uncongenial theory of Karma, the logical conclusion of *advaita* being sanyasa, absolute renunciation.

Every chief of a sect in philosophy, said Voltaire, has been a little of a quack. And the philosopher in Tilak, like Tilak the politician, could not escape such criticism. One more point is to be noted concerning the book. Tilak, like Yudhishthira who bowed before Bhishma just before the Mahabharata war began, bowed to Shankaracharya and then fought an intellectual war with him; but the orthodox pundits, who had admired Tilak because he had opposed social reforms, said that the language he used in reference to sanyasins was rather harsh. It seems his opposition to Shankaracharya's viewpoint had been formulating since 1893. M. R. Bodas, who was then editor of Tilak's *Kesari*, wrote a series of articles defending Shankaracharya's philosophy, and Bodas had to resign as his boss differed from him.[12]

Whatever the critics say, the fact cannot be denied that among the various commentaries on the *Gita*, Tilak's work occupies a place next to

11 Edited by Kelkar, N. C., *Nibandhakar Tilak*, p. 16.

12 Bodas, M. R., *Shankaracharya Ani Tyancha Sampradaya* (Marathi), p. 105.

that of Shankaracharya, and although not belonging to the superb class of Dnyaneshwar's *Dnyaneshwari* and *Tukaram's Gatha*, it will be regarded as one of the peaks of the Marathi literary world!

Tilak showed much interest in the historic role Gandhi had played in South Africa and he paid tributes to the service of Gandhi at the meeting held in Bombay a few days before to congratulate the hero. Now Gandhi was congratulated in the Sarvajanik Sabha and at the Kirloskar Theatre in July. It was during this visit that Gandhi acted as an intermediary between the Moderates and Tilak. He tried to persuade Tilak to accept the creed as formulated in article No. 1 of the Congress and added that Tilak would be doing a national service if he surrendered himself completely.[13]

In September 1915, Tilak made a very important contribution to Indian research. He wrote an article in the *Sanskrit Research* (Vol. I, No. 2) in October 1915 on "a missing verse in the *Sankhya-Karikas*" explaining how it should be reconstructed and restored from the data he had collected and why. Tilak studied patiently the French translation of the Chinese commentary on the Sankhya-Karikas, Gaudapada's Bhashya, and H. A. Wilson's edition. He got this idea from the notes H. A. Wilson had given in his work on Sankhya-Karikas. He put down one by one all the verses that were carried down from A.D. 400 and spent his leisure hours on them. One day while he was tossing in his bed with his thoughts on the missing Karika, the solution flashed across his mind. When he found out the clue, he could not sleep for joy the whole night! It was the divine joy of a scholar! Tilak took his cue from certain words in the commentaries and their import in Sankhya philosophy, and, putting all the facts together, he concluded: "We are led to infer that originally there was one verse between the 61st and the 62nd (in Wilson's edition)!". This article was later on published along with his article on "Chaldean and Indian Vedas" in the book *Vedic Chronology and Vedang Jyotish*. The missing verse according to Tilak was:

"Karanam Ishvaram eke Purusham Kalam pare Swabhavam va, Prajah Katham nirgunato vyaktah Kalah swabhavas cha."

It was a probe in the evolution of Indian philosophy!

By this time Tilak had decided to prosecute Sir Valentine Chirol for the defamatory attack he had made on his personality in his book *Indian Unrest*. The book contained the articles which he had contributed to *The Times*, London, in 1910, from India where he was sent as its representative

13 *Letters of Lokamanya Tilak*, edited by Vidwans, M. D., pp. 266-69.

to study the revolutionary movement. Chirol toured throughout India and came to the conclusion that Tilak had been the most dangerous pioneer of disaffection and the father of Indian Unrest. The special interest shown by *The Times*, London, in Indian affairs was, however, a sequel to the special articles contributed to it by C. A. Kincaid, who had served in the Bombay Province. Kincaid wrote these articles at the instance of Sir William Lee Warner, the senior Member of the Council of the Secretary of State, to hustle Morley into consenting to Press Act Bill mooted by Minto. These articles were attributed to Chirol who was then the editor of the foreign department of *The Times*!

To Tilak the most objectionable thing was that Chirol interpreted his actions and writings as a direct or indirect incitement to deeds of violence, and some of his remarks on Tilak's personal character were based on the judgment of Mr. Justice Chandavarkar. But that judgment had been quashed and Tilak's character had been vindicated. So he decided to teach Chirol a lesson for his insinuation against him in his book. He served a notice on Sir Valentine Chirol, the author of *Indian Unrest,* through his London Solicitors, Messrs. Downer Johnson, claiming damages for libel and for an injunction to restrain publication of the defamatory matter. At the beginning there was a move for a compromise, and the solicitors of *The Times*, London, in which Chirol's articles had appeared, met the solicitors of Tilak. They showed their readiness to correct some mistakes in Chirol's book and to append some important notes to it. But at a later stage the talks broke down, and a regular suit for defamation was filed in the Court in London in November 1915. It is interesting to note that the Legal Adviser of Government had opined that Sir Valentine had defamed Tilak in his book!

Mrs. Besant, who had by now developed into a great political force, declared in November 1915 to start an agitation for Home Rule. She proposed starting a similar agitation also in England. She said it would act as a supplement to the Congress. The Moderates in Bombay did not like Besant starting another political institution. They attacked her as they had previously attacked Tilak. Their papers said that she was ambitious and emotional! Despite this she made a whirlwind tour and preached her gospel of Home Rule to the country.

Pherozeshah Mehta, who was deadly opposed to the re-entry of the Nationalists into the Congress, invited the Congress of 1915 to Bombay. He was determined to foil the attempts of other leaders in making a compromise with Tilak. He wanted to save the Congress from the influence of Tilak. He condemned the compromise as mischievous. He stormed, he raged, he railed at the idea of a compromise! So this old giant was in search of an eminent man who could say ditto to him. He found one in Sir Satyendra P. Sinha. Sinha declined at first. Mehta wired back: "You dare not refuse." And he accepted the invitation to preside over the Congress.

But everything under the sun has an end. Destiny removed Pherozeshah Mehta. This great statesman and patriot and one of the makers of modern Bombay died on November 5, 1915, a few weeks before this Congress was held. Sir Pherozeshah Mehta was born on August 4, 1845, in Bombay, and was brought up in Bombay. A brilliant and aspiring student, he was called to the Bar in London, became an eminent legal celebrity, stormed the Council, the Bombay Municipality and the Assembly, dealt with the British officers in a self-respecting manner, returning argument for argument, invective for invective, and ridicule for ridicule. His imposing personality dominated Indian public life for over two decades. His name had had a tremendous influence on the Britishers. When their Royal Highnesses Prince and Princess of Wales, landed at Bombay in 1905, Her Royal Highness asked Mehta to sign his name in her autograph book!

Some three or four months earlier Tilak had been to Pherozeshah to inquire after his health when the latter was taking a rest at a place near Poona. Tilak kept the tonga at a distance, so that Mehta might not be disturbed by the rumble of the vehicle. Mehta felt sorry that Tilak had walked a long distance and not brought the tonga nearer to his bungalow; for Tilak, too, he said, was very much pulled down.

The Congress session met in Bombay under Satyendra P. Sinha, afterwards Lord Sinha. He sang the swan-song of the Moderates. The amendment to the Congress constitution was accepted by the Bombay Congress, and this brought about the union between the two wings of the Congress. Mrs. Besant wired to N. C. Kelkar the decision of the Congress.

The wound inflicted in 1907 at Surat was thus healed in 1915 in Bombay. When the next split came, it was the Moderates who went out of the Congress, assuming a new appellation, the Liberals. While the Congress session was going on in Bombay, Tilak called an urgent meeting of his Party leaders. Five hundred leaders attended the meeting held in Poona, and a committee was appointed under Khaparde to take steps for the foundation of a Home Rule League.

CHAPTER XX

"Home Rule is My Birth-right"

I

TILAK NOW DECIDED to launch propaganda for Home Rule. He wrote articles on this subject in December 1915 and afterwards, explaining to the people what he meant by it. Tilak perhaps preferred this expression, because it was a parliamentary, legal term. He purposely dropped out the term 'Self-Government' or 'Swaraj'. One of the causes that led to the battle of Surat was the definition of the words 'Swaraj' and 'Self-Government', because Gokhale and the other Moderates meant Self-Government within the British Empire. Tilak wanted to keep the word Swaraj undefined, because Pal and Aurobindo had voiced absolute political independence as the goal of the Congress, and he wanted to maintain unity among the Nationalist leaders from Bengal and Maharashtra. Home Rule was perfectly legal and implied all those terms! He had deputed Kelkar to Calcutta to feel the pulse of the Bengal leaders and pave the way for the unification of the Congress. Kelkar had interviewed also the leaders of the U.P. So Tilak called all the leading men of his Party in February 1916, and after full discussion he convinced them of the correctness of the step he was going to take. They decided to join the Congress. But they planned to make a declaration accordingly at a conference of the Party. So a Provincial Conference was convened at Belgaum in the last week of April 1916.

Meanwhile Chirol's written statement was filed on March 3, 1916, in the Bombay High Court. Witnesses on both sides were examined and documents and exhibits were recorded before a Commission. Tilak was not permitted to inspect certain documents. It is very surprising that Shri Shahu Maharaj of

Kolhapur secretly supplied Tilak with confidential letters issued to him by Government and helped Tilak's Counsel to floor the Home Secretary![1]

Meanwhile, in a conciliatory mood, Tilak attended a meeting which was held in Poona, on March 26, 1916, at the Kirloskar Theatre. The object of the meeting was to present the retiring Governor-General Lord Hardinge with an address on behalf of the citizens of Poona and Poona District for his sympathetic attitude towards Indian aspirations and his efforts for their advancement. Tilak's lieutenant Khadilkar moved the main resolution. Seconding it, Tilak said it was after twenty-five years that such an occasion had arisen. They had a good Viceroy in Lord Hardinge after Lord Ripon. It may be recalled here that in December 1911 at the time of the Delhi Durbar, Ras Behari Bose and his friend had thrown a bomb at Lord Hardinge, and he was seriously wounded! Tilak had genuine sympathy for Lord Hardinge. That was seen three years later when he told a revolutionary during his discussion on their work that had they thrown a bomb at General Dyer people would have appreciated it, but it was bad that they threw it at a good-intentioned Viceroy like Hardinge.

In conformity with the Poona decision a Reception Committee was formed, and D. V. Belvi was elected its Chairman. Both the Moderates and the Nationalists were now eager to win over Gandhi to their side. Kaka Kalelkar wrote to Gandhi to attend the Belgaum Conference. The Moderate forces tried to persuade Gandhi not to attend the Conference. Gandhi gave up the idea of joining the Servants of India Society whose committee members had differences of opinion over the nomination of Gandhi! So he was about to start his Satyagraha Ashram. Gangadharrao Deshpande sent another reminder to Gandhi, and he wired back saying that only death would prevent him from going to Belgaum. He went to Belgaum.

Nationalist leaders went to Belgaum to attend the Conference. Gandhi, Khaparde and Tilak had a discussion, and after the talk Gandhi went out. Gangadharrao Deshpande asked Tilak about the views of Gandhi. Khaparde intervened and said, "He does not belong to our Party." Tilak did not pass any remark. He knew the power of Gandhi who had shaken the British Government in Africa. Gandhi, however, refused to be a delegate to the Conference. D. V. Belvi and D. V. Gokhale saw Gandhi and requested

---

1 Thakare, Prabodhankar, in *Marmik*, 1 March 1964.

him in the name of Tilak to be a delegate so that the delegates would have an opportunity to know his views. He agreed.[2]

Before the Provincial Conference commenced, the Home Rule League was founded at Belgaum on April 28, 1916, and Kelkar was elected its General Secretary. The Home Rule League accepted the creed of the Indian National Congress.

The Provincial Conference of the Nationalists met under the Presidentship of Dadasaheb Khaparde on April 29, 1916. Some young leaders were against joining the Congress. On the previous night of the session they held a private meeting, and by an overwhelming majority decided to oppose the report submitted by the Committee of Tilak, Baptista and Khaparde. Tilak was informed of this decision. Dr. Moonje made bold to tell Tilak that just as Parashuram and Krishna were defeated after the mission of their life was over, so Tilak would be defeated on his joining the Congress. Yet he told Tilak that he believed in his sagacity and promised him not to oppose him in the open session.

It was the confirmed opinion of Tilak that no other party but the Congress would be the proper institution for the national struggle. So the next day when he submitted the report recommending to the Nationalist Party to join the Congress, he asked some young leaders whether any of them wanted to oppose the report. Who was to bell the cat ? None came forward. Tilak had prepared his speech very carefully and spoke in English, so that there might not be any chance for misunderstanding. The Conference accepted the report submitted by the Committee of Tilak, Baptista and Khaparde, recommending their entry into the Congress. They passed a resolution appealing to the Government to release all political prisoners and another on the need for the preparation of a memorandum on the Home Rule demand. When just after this resolution the *Times of India* declared that Tilak had captured the Congress by this resolution, Dr. Moonje admitted his mistake! At this Conference Tilak, supporting the Loyalty resolution, appealed to the Government to repeal the Arms Act which had eaten into the vitals of the country. Its repeal would gladden the hearts of the millions and would make them, he concluded, powerful enough to come to the rescue of the empire in the hour of its need.[3]

---

2 *Reminiscences and Anecdotes about Lokamanya Tilak*, Vol. II, p. 182.

3 Bal Gangadhar Tilak: *His Writings and Speeches,* published by Ganesh & Co., Madras, p. 410.

The Conference over, Tilak made at Belgaum some speeches on Home Rule which resounded throughout India. "To put it briefly, the demand that the management of our affairs should be in our hands is the demand for Swaraj." "We want to remain," said he, "under the sway of this rule. But we do not want the State Secretary who has been created a son-in-law. We want at least our men, men elected by us, in his council. This is the first reform that must be made." "I again say, if the nation is to get happiness, if the thousands of complaints that have arisen today are to be removed, then, first of all, change this system of administration. Complaints about forests, complaints about Abkari, complaints about the Kulkarni Vatans have arisen because the authority is not in our hands. To state it in slightly changed words—because we do not have Swaraj. That we should have Swaraj for us is at the root of our demand. We need not then dance to anybody's tune. The demand for Swaraj has nothing to do with sedition."

"The effect of the action," he concluded, "may not be obtained in my lifetime, perhaps I may not be benefited by it. But this action must have its fruit. I am sure that by the grace of God your next generation will not fail to obtain the fruit of this work, though it may not be obtained in your lifetime."[4]

Tilak was informed by some sources that Government was thinking of taking action against him for his speeches on Home Rule!

He returned to Poona via Satara where the citizens presented him with an address.

Tilak and Besant delivered lectures on Home Rule during the Shivaji celebrations in Poona. The day she made the speech in Poona, a security of two thousand rupees was demanded from her paper *New India*. The Press Act was enforced rigorously to nip the Home Rule movement in the bud. Securities were demanded especially from Nationalist papers like the *Maharashtra* of Nagpur. After a few days the security deposited by Mrs. Besant was forfeited.

After having rest at Sinhagad, Tilak went to Nagar to attend the session of the District Conference. There he addressed a meeting on Home Rule on May 31, 1916. Declaring that the British administration was as a matter of fact alien, and there was no sedition in calling them so, he observed: "By alien I do not mean alien in religion. He who does what is beneficial to the people of this country, be he a Mohammedan or an Englishman, is

---

4 Bal Gangadhar Tilak: His Writings and Speeches, pp. 104-133.

not alien. The King's duty is to do all those things whereby the nation may rise, prosper and become the equal of other nations. That King who does this duty is not alien. My opinion is that whatever be the Government, whether British or any other, it has, as Government, a sort of duty to perform. Government has a sort of religious duty to perform; a sort of responsibility lies on its shoulders. I say that when a Government evades this responsibility it is no Government at all."

"The meaning of Swaraj," explains Tilak shrewdly, "as stated above is the retention of our Emperor and the rule of the English people, and the full possession by the people of the authority to manage the remaining affairs. This is the definition of Swaraj."

He particularly mentioned in his Home Rule speeches the exorbitant salaries of the Government Officers. "The Viceroy who comes to govern India," he proceeded, "gets twenty thousand rupees a month while the Prime Minister of England gets five thousand rupees. He who has to live in England and manage the affairs of the whole Empire gets five thousand rupees, while he who carries on the administration of India here gets twenty thousand rupees. Why so ? This is because the latter is managed at the cost of others. (Cheers.) This is India. Go and eat." [5] "There is no other remedy," he concluded, "than that the power should pass into the people's hands and rest in the hands of the people." [6]

On June 1, 1916, Tilak delivered another speech on Home Rule. He told the people that if they did not attain Swaraj, there would be neither industrial progress nor any kind of education useful to the nation, either primary or higher. He further declared that it would be seen from the condition of the whole of the world that England would have some day or other to bestow liberty on the provinces and countries forming parts of the Empire under her control.

Tilak said that in the reorganisation of Swaraj, India might be divided into separate states, according to languages. The foreign policy might be kept in their hands by the rulers. He asked them to say resolutely that they wanted what was theirs. "What is there," he said, "to fear in saying that you want Swaraj ?" That was a lawful way. The Goddess of Liberty would descend from above if the people showed a firm belief in their goal and showed unflinching courage. He asked the people to take what would be

5 *Bal Gangadhar Tilak: His Writings and Speeches*, pp. 138-52.

6 Ibid.

given and to ask for more. They would not be benefited by England going away and Germany coming in her place. He appealed to the businessmen for funds. He told them that the Congress assembled only once a year and then they had to wait till the next year. But the object of the Home Rule League was to work all the year round. That was a work for the protection of religion and for the protection of the cow. That was the work of the nation and political progress. If the sons of the cow would not care about that, then they would have to be called bullocks, as the sons of the cows were called.[7]

In the middle of June Tilak addressed a meeting during the Shivaji festival and said that the fears of Mohammedans that they would be ill-treated if Swaraj were granted to India, were groundless. On July 2 he addressed a meeting held at Wilson College Hall to commemorate the twentieth death anniversary of Agarkar. R. P. Paranjpye presided over the meeting. Tilak impressed upon the minds of the audience Agarkar's spirit of self-sacrifice and his great selfless services to the cause of education and said that the social reformers could not digest the whole of Agarkar's philosophy, especially its political message. He therefore asked the admirers of Agarkar to remember that Agarkar was also a bold advocate of political rights for the people.

II

TILAK WAS COMPLETING his sixtieth year on July 22, 1916. So his friends, admirers, followers and lieutenants planned to celebrate his Diamond Jubilee all over the country with great pomp. Tilak had become the first all-India leader in the Congress movement, and there was no other leader of his standing and sacrifice in the country. His friends had been gathered to their forefathers. Many of his colleagues, Chiplunkar, Agarkar, Apte, and Namjoshi, had all departed this life. His life had been a story of long sufferings and persecutions, an undying devotion to the cause of the nation and an unflinching will. So great was the enthusiasm that though N. C. Kelkar sponsored, just a week or two before the celebration, a move to present the great stalwart of Indian freedom with a purse of a lac of rupees on the occasion of his sixty-first birthday, the organizers succeeded in collecting the amount before the day of the celebrations.

---

7 *Bal Gangadhar Tilak: His Writings and Speeches*; pp. 143-200.

On the morning of the 23rd July 1916, Tilak went to Annasaheb Patwardhan to seek his blessings. Annasaheb was a revolutionary in his youth and had turned a sanyasin in his later life. Tilak's respect for this spiritual patriarch was boundless. Religious rites were performed at Tilak's Gaikwad Wada and in some temples in Poona, grain was distributed to the poor, and food and fruit and other articles were sent to hospitals for patients.

A large number of admirers and party-men from the mofussil came to attend the function with pride and presents. Those who could not attend the rare festivities, celebrated the day in their villages or towns. They were happy that such a day should have dawned in the life of Tilak who had been subjected by foreign rule to hardships and sufferings. But the spiteful Government was ready to deprive the function of its grandeur and the people of their great joy. A police officer came to serve Tilak with a notice from the District Magistrate calling upon him to show cause why he should not be bound over for good behaviour for a period of one year in a sum of twenty thousand rupees in his own recognizance and in two securities of ten thousand rupees each. The trouble had arisen over Tilak's speeches on Home Rule at Belgaum and Nagar! This was a birthday present from the Government! When Tilak was informed about the arrival of the officer he said with a smile that he was glad that the Government should offer him a present on the auspicious day. He exclaimed, "New year! New danger! "The police officer felicitated him on his birthday. Tilak was a man who took victory and defeat, pain and pleasure, in a spirit of resignation. He signed the papers and accepted the notice. Under the notice he was required to attend the court on June 29, 1916, and the police officer could have waited for a day more to serve the notice. But those were the days when British bureaucracy dominated the British statesmen. The little daughter of the police officer had sent Tilak a postcard and intimated to him that her father was going to come to his house to serve a notice on him.

Nevertheless, the birthday celebration was performed with great dignity and pomp in the evening at Gaikwad Wada compound. An address was presented in a silver casket to Tilak and glowing tributes were paid for his courage and sacrifice, and a purse of a lac of rupees was presented to him in appreciation of his great services to the nation. Representatives from Karnatak, Berar, Gujarat and Bombay City were present among the crowd that had thronged the compound. Some persons presented him with clothes, turbans, rings, currency notes and other things. Tilak's friend

D. A. Khare was happy and proud of his friend's great achievement and great fame, his courage and industry. Gangadharrao Deshpande said that Tilak's philosophy was nothing but doing one's duty with one's might in disregard of dangers.

Then Tilak rose to reply. He was touched with the great regard and honour the people showered on him. Life from the student days to transportation must have moved before him in a panorama. "Memories of storm and stress," he slowly said, "rather than a comparative happiness rise before my mind's eye." Those brave patriots like Chiplunkar, Agarkar, Gokhale, Apte, Kelkar and Namjoshi with whom he had started his public life had left him in the middle, and he remained to represent them. Looking into the future, he said with firm conviction, "After completing sixty years, one's mind cannot but be filled with misgivings, and with declining strength one is apt to feel less hopeful. But I devoutly hope that God may grant me life and courage to add, with your support, to whatever work of public good I have done."

"I do not know," he said with humility, "what I can do with the money. I do not want the purse for my own sake, nor would it be proper for me to accept it for personal use. I can only accept it in trust to spend it in a constitutional way for National work after adding my own mite to it."

The celebration was over, and the proceedings of another trial commenced. There were new officers, new governors, new circumstances at every trial of Tilak; but Tilak was Tilak to every officer, a terror, a threat!

Tilak was now to make all the preparations. This time no English barrister! The lawyer had to defend the right of Home Rule. So no English barrister would have done the work more zealously than an Indian barrister. So Tilak's eyes turned to Jinnah. N. C. Kelkar went to Bombay and saw Jinnah. He accepted the brief. The hearing commenced in the Court of the District Magistrate of Poona on August 2, and was postponed to the 7th August on which day it commenced again. Binning, Counsel for the Crown, dubbed Tilak's declaration of loyalty a mere cloak to defend himself from the clutches of the law. Jinnah, Baptista, Karandikar, Bakhale, Erulkar and Kaka Patil appeared for Tilak. Tilak was examined. In his examination he told the Court that his object was to explain to the people what Home Rule meant. Jinnah argued the case. The District Magistrate said that the effect of Tilak's speeches as a whole had on his mind was that Tilak wanted to disaffect his audience towards the Government. The District Magistrate, Hatch, therefore, under section 108 of Criminal Procedure Code, directed

Tilak to enter into a bond for a sum of twenty thousand rupees with two sureties each in the sum of ten thousand rupees to be of good behaviour for a period of one year. Tilak signed the bond and tendered Trimbak Hari Avate and Ganpat Vithoba Morval as his sureties.

The *Times of India*, ever ready to attack Tilak, seized this opportunity and wrote an editorial in its issue of the 15th August 1916. It said with imperial dignity: "We have not published these speeches because we have no intention of allowing our columns to be used for the wider dissemination of seditious writings." It pointed out that the King was held up by Tilak to shadowy respect; the King's Government was made the subject of every species of abjuration and abuse. "If Mr. Tilak," observed the *Times of India* with the air of a judge "who is sixty years old and has been in politics for the greater part of his life, has not learnt wisdom now, then it is absolutely necessary for the administration to put restrictions on his political activities."

Tilak filed an appeal in the High Court at Bombay against the decision of the Poona District Magistrate. Mr. S. R. Bakhale appearing for Tilak told the Court that the lower court had misconstrued the effect and scope of Tilak's speeches at Belgaum and at Nagar in connection with the Home Rule League. Tilak's main object was to bring about a change in the system of the Government of India only by an amendment of the Government of India Act and his speeches fell within the second explanation to Section 124A of the Indian Penal Code. His speeches were mere comments expressing disapprobation of the machinery used or employed in the administration of the country with a view to obtaining its alteration by lawful means; the object of the speeches was not to criticise the Government established by law.

III

THE COURT ADMITTED the appeal. The hearing of the appeal in the High Court before the Hon'ble Mr. Justice Stanley Batchelor and the Hon'ble Mr. Justice Shah commenced on November 9, 1916. M. A. Jinnah with Joseph Baptista, D. S. Erulkar and Bakhale appeared for the appellant. M. R. Jardine with D. B. Binning, Strangman and others appeared for the Crown.

Mr. Jinnah submitted that the section contained the words Government established by law in British India. In other words, Government in the abstract and not in the concrete form. He therefore told the court that Tilak's speeches were directed to the part of the civil service which formed a part of the bureaucracy of the whole system. He attacked only the bureaucracy that had the monopoly of power and were not responsible to the people. His object was to convince the people that the Home Rule League was a step in this direction, and he wanted people to become its members. His speeches, stated Jinnah, thus conclusively showed that he had no intention of spreading disaffection towards Government established by law in British India. Jardine, Counsel for the Crown, said that Government meant persons who had the power to carry on the Government.

Mr. Justice Shah questioned: Take a concrete case, say of the Forest Department, or the Civil Service. Would you say that Government is criticised if that department is criticised?

Mr. Jardine: I should certainly say so.

Mr. Jardine said that Tilak charged that it was an alien Government and was deliberately trying to impede the development among the people, and that he referred from time to time to the slavery of the people. This could not be disinterested criticism although the speeches were not an attack upon His Majesty and the Houses of Parliament.

Delivering judgment on November 9, 1916, their Lordships opined that the speeches complained of by the Crown were not of a seditious character within the meaning of section 124A of the Indian Penal Code as they could not be said to be such as to excite hatred or contempt or an attempt to create disaffection towards the Government established by law in British India. They therefore set aside the order of the District Magistrate of Poona.

Mr. Justice Stanley L. Batchelor considered that the aim of Tilak's speeches was reasonably clear. In contending for what Tilak described as Swaraj, said the Judge, his object was to obtain for Indians an increased and a gradually increasing share of political authority and to subject the administration of the country to the control of the people or the peoples of India. "In my opinion," he observed, "that advocacy is not *per se* an infringement of law, nor has the learned Advocate-General contended that it is."

His Lordship, however, desired to guard himself from being supposed to say that the advocacy of "Swaraj" was in all cases permissible, for the word "Swaraj" had a dozen different meanings in the mouths of as many speakers. This was indeed a great victory for Tilak who evoked the justification of his goal from the High Court which had condemned him in 1897 and in 1908.

Tilak was in Bombay. He attended the Court on the day on which the Court delivered the judgment. Jinnah shook hands with him and congratulated him on his victory. A small function was held in Patel's chamber, and Tilak was honoured by his friends and admirers in the High Court. All were happy except the *Times of India*. It had, in consternation, to announce the next day that in the opinion of the District Magistrate the speeches were seditious. The High Court, however, took a different view, and therefore "in the light of this exposition of the law as applied to the speeches, the deductions based on the decision of the Magistrate, which we regret having made in the issue of the 15th August, must be unreservedly withdrawn."

Those who were hesitating to enrol themselves as members of the Home Rule League now immediately became its members. The Home Rule Movement now became a legal demand! While the hearing of the case was going on, N. C. Kelkar as the Secretary of the Home Rule League had opened an office in Poona, but not more than fifteen persons turned up to enrol themselves as members!

Meantime, Tilak had addressed in the first week of September two meetings during the Ganesh festival and replied to the varied criticisms of his *Gita-Rahasya*. He had addressed a Paisa Fund meeting in Bombay on October 1, 1916, and made a moving appeal to the people to contribute to the Fund that was being utilised for small-scale industries. He had also attended the Provincial Conference held at Ahmedabad in October 1916, under the presidentship of Jinnah, who declared that the distinction between the Moderates and Extremists had already disappeared. They were now all nationalists. Tilak was accorded a grand reception. Speaking at the Conference, he appealed to the people to support the Memorandum submitted to H.E. the Governor-General of India by nineteen non-official Members of the Central Legislative Council regarding post-war Reforms. The Conference was attended by R. P. Paranjpye, Srinivasa Shastri and V. J. Patel. This was the first Provincial Conference attended by both Parties after the Surat fight.

Although the bureaucrats were humiliated in the High Court, they did not sit silent. They caught an opportunity to trap and trouble Tilak while he was on some business at Gadag, a town in the Dharwar District. The local leaders had arranged for a reception. But the Collector and District

Magistrate of Dharwar, D. G. Turner, who happened to be at Gadag, issued orders prohibiting Tilak from delivering any speech. The Mamlatdar demolished the platform erected for the function by the local leaders. The local leaders met Tilak just before the time of the meeting. Tilak said he would attend the meeting. When Tilak reached the place, the Mamlatdar served him with the order. Tilak the lawyer told the Mamlatdar that the orders of the District Magistrate had not put a ban on the reception. So he was allowed to make a brief speech in reply to the reception. Tilak did so, and deprived the European District Magistrate of his laurels!

IV

DURING THE LATTER part of 1916 the Home Rule Movement claimed Tilak's time. C. Y. Chintamani, Srinivasa Sastri, Surendranath Banerjee, all at different conferences and meetings declared their opinion in favour of Swaraj or Home Rule and said after the War was over it should be conferred on India. Mrs. Besant's voice echoed in India. She wanted a dynamic political body and organised an auxiliary Home Rule League in London on June 12, 1916, and on September 1, 1916, her Home Rule League in India was founded in Madras. She now raged a waging and tearing campaign for Home Rule. Baptista came forward with a scheme for Swaraj. The Bombay Moderates published their scheme. Sir Krishna Govind Gupta, who arrived in Bombay as the representative of the London Congress Committee, opined that there was a great need for propaganda for Home Rule in London. All these schemes and points of view were to be considered. The sky reverberated with the slogan "Home Rule".

In November Tilak was elected a member of the All-India Congress Committee by the Bombay Provincial Congress Committee along with fourteen other members. However, the efforts of Tilak in affiliating the Sarvajanik Sabha with the Bombay Provincial Congress Committee were unsuccessful.

And on December 23, 1916, Tilak started by a special train for Lucknow from Bombay, accompanied by his admirers and party leaders and delegates. This was the first time that a special train was arranged by political leaders to carry delegates to the Congress. The platform was filled to capacity. The compartment occupied by Tilak was decorated by his admirers with flowers and bunting. And amidst thundering cheers Tilak started, like a conqueror, to attend the Congress, the Congress for the strength and organisation of which he had been struggling ever since 1895 and which he could not attend for the last eight years!

En route to Lucknow, people held receptions at Kalyan, Nasik, Manmad, Bhusawal, Chalisgaon, Bhopal, Bina and Jhansi stations greeting Tilak with 'Jais', serving the party with light refreshments, tea, fruit and meals. The *Times of India*, Bombay, warned the Moderates that Tilak was going to capture the Congress. Several public workers, old and new, took a hungry glimpse of "Bhagvan Tilak", "Mahatma Tilak" who was old and who had returned after six years' transportation. In the severe cold nights of December, old men, women and children waited at different stations for the arrival of the train by which their great leader was travelling.

The special train reached Kanpur on the morning of December 25, 1916. Tilak was accorded a warm reception, and then the train reached Lucknow at noon. A vast crowd was awaiting the arrival of the train which was behind time. A thundering ovation was accorded to 'Bhagvan' Tilak. The Reception Committee wished that Tilak and his party should straightway motor to the camp. Young leaders and volunteers bubbling with enthusiasm wanted to take Tilak in a brougham drawn by themselves. So someone punctured the tyres of the motor-car, and he was made to sit in the horse carriage. But after a few minutes the horses were let off, and the volunteers drew the carriage! At some distance Malaviya came to meet Tilak. He was asked by the people to occupy a place by Tilak, and the procession reached its destination. Tilak and his party reached their lodgings at Chedilal Dharmashala. He bowed to the people and said that the Home Rule Flag would be flown the next day in their ' lucky' city.

Next morning Tilak saw Pal, Surendranath, Ambikacharan, Jinnah and Mrs. Besant. Tilak found it difficult to move forward. The route from the Dharmashala to the Congress pandal was transformed into a standing procession!

The special features of the Lucknow Congress were the return of the Nationalist Party, the presence of Tilak and the scheme of reforms to be jointly submitted by the Hindus and Muslims. That scheme afterwards became known as the Lucknow Pact. At the joint conferences of the Muslim League Council and the Congress Executive at Allahabad in April 1916 and in Calcutta in November 1916 the scheme was considered and was completed in almost all its details, except the quotas of the Punjab and Bengal in respect of Muslim representatives in the legislatures which were to be settled during the session of the Congress. This was done before Tilak could be a member of the All-India Congress Committee.

On the eve of the Congress the Secretariat of the U.P. Government issued a warning to the Reception Committee against any spirit of sedition in the Congress speeches, and a copy of the letter was served upon Ambikacharan Mujumdar, the President-elect, and another through the Government of Bengal.

On December 26, 1916, the session of the Congress commenced. The pandal was packed to capacity. There were about twenty-three hundred delegates and thrice as many visitors. Leaders entered the pandal and took their seats, and when, to quote Sir Valentine Chirol, Tilak in company with Besant stepped on to the platform for the first time since his six years' transportation to Mandalay, they were both acclaimed almost like incarnations of the deity! The Chairman of the Reception Committee, Pandit Jagat Narayan, expressed great joy at the return of the Nationalists to the Congress and the participation of the Muslims in the Congress.

The Congress President proudly declared that the United Congress, which was buried in the debris of the old French Garden at Surat, was reborn that day in the Kaiser Bagh of Lucknow. Referring to Tilak, he said, "I most cordially welcome Bal Gangadhar Tilak, Motilal Ghose and other brave comrades, who separated from us at Surat and have been happily restored to us at Lucknow. I rejoice to find that they are after all 'of us' and 'with us' and let us hope never to part again." He also referred to the recent proceedings which were instituted against Tilak by the Government, and regretted that it was ill-advised in taking them at a time and under circumstances where its action was liable to be misconstrued. In the evening Tilak attended the joint conference of the All-India Congress Committee and the Muslim League. In one of his speeches on that day he said, "We are entitled to the possession of the whole estate at once. If we allowed you to share in that possession, it was in the hope that you would clear off. You must acknowledge that we are the masters."

Next day the members of the Subjects Committee were to be elected at a meeting by the delegates of each Province. As the compromise move had failed, names were placed before the house in pairs, one Nationalist and one Moderate; and in every case it was the former that was elected. Gandhi then more or less was inclined to the Moderates; and when his name was pitted against a Nationalist, he was voted down; but Tilak declared that Gandhi was elected!

When the draft of the proposed Congress-League Scheme came up for consideration before the Subjects Committee, a storm raged over it. Pandit Madan Mohan Malaviya had promised some Hindu leaders who were against the scheme that he would hold a huge demonstration against the Congress if it surrendered to the Muslims. The Moderates had lost the initiative, and the only organised party in the Congress being under Tilak, he was determined to carry the scheme through. "When angry speakers were foaming on all sides," wrote C. S. Ranga lyer, the then editor-in-charge of the *Advocate*, in his reminiscences of Tilak, "he was calm as a rock. The leader of Maharashtra who was the most religious, the most learned in the *Vedas* and among the most orthodox of the Hindus would not listen to any arguments against the Pact. Not that he was enamoured of it himself, but if it would satisfy the Muslims, if it could bring them to the Congress, if it could replace their extra-territorial patriotism by Indian Nationalism, the agreement was worth reaching. Lokamanya Tilak's attitude was the deciding factor in the Hindu-Muslim settlement, the last word on the subject so far as the Hindus were concerned." [8]

V

IT HAD BEEN the impression of many that Tilak was anti-Mohammedan, that his Shivaji and Ganapati festivals were started by him to counteract Muslim aggressiveness and to intimidate them. He wanted to take advantage of the war situation and was eager for a compromise to present a united demand to the British. He, therefore, wanted to win the support of the Muslims to the Congress and sought the co-operation of leaders like M. A. Jinnah, who was according to him a genuine Nationalist Muslim of his day. Tilak was criticized for granting sanction to the anti-national and anti-democratic separate electorates. Moonje and Sapru opposed him. On the morning of December 29, he told D. G. Dalvi, a Bombay delegate, that if the latter had studied the history of India carefully he would remember that the Hindu had overthrown Muslim rule twice and would do so again if such a situation arose. But in the existing circumstances, he added, there was no go but to avoid a triangular fight and win over the Muslims to the national struggle to drive away the Britishers.[9]

When Tilak rose to speak on December 29, in the open session, on the Self-Government resolution, the twenty-three hundred and odd delegates

---

8 *Reminiscences and Anecdotes about Lokamanya Tilak*, Vol. II, p. 564.

9 D. G. Dalvi in the *Vividhavritta*, Bombay, 22 July 1956.

and thrice as many visitors gave a thundering ovation to their great leader! At the outset Tilak observed, "I am not foolish enough to think that this reception is given to my humble self. It is given, if I rightly understand, to those principles for which I have been fighting, principles which have been embodied in the resolution I have the honour to support. I am glad to say that I have lived these ten years to see that we are going to put our voice and shoulders together to push the scheme of Self-Government. We are now united in every way in the United Provinces."

Referring to the opposition to the Congress-League Scheme, Tilak said, "It has been said that we, Hindus, have yielded too much to our Mohammedan brethren. I am sure, I represent the sense of the Hindu community all over India, when I say that we could not have yielded too much. I would not care if the rights of Self-Government are granted to the Mohammedan community only. I would not care if they are granted to the Rajputs. I would not care if they are granted to the lower classes of the Hindu population. . . . Then the fight will be between them and another section of the community, and not, as at present, a triangular fight."

"The British tell us," he proceeded, "that we the descendants of the Aryans are not the original owners of the soil. We Aryans took the country from the Aborigines; the Muslims conquered it from the Aryans, and the English conquered it from the Muslims. Hence the English are the guardians of the Aborigines. Well, I agree to this and ask the English to go away delivering the possession to Bhils, Gonds and Adi-Dravids. We will gladly serve the original owners of the soil." At this the whole pandal rocked with laughter and cheers. When after explaining further he said in his natural husky voice, "Home Rule is, my birth-right and I shall have it,"[10] the whole pandal resounded with one resonant voice. After Tilak's speech Baptista and Mrs. Besant spoke on the resolution, and it was carried. Tilak then had a talk in the President's tent with Surendranath Banerjee and Rash Behari Ghose.

On the evening of December 30, a meeting was held at the pandal of the theosophical convention near Aminabad High School. The meeting was attended by over one thousand Home Rulers. It showed that the Moderates were now vanishing from the Congress platform. Besant delivered one of her best speeches, at the meeting. Tilak too delivered an effective speech. "There is a feeling among the Hindus," he said, " that too

---

10 *Reminiscences and Anecdotes about Lokamanya Tilak,* Vol. I, p. 479.

much has been given to the Muslims. As a Hindu I have no objection to making this concession. When a case is difficult, a client goes to a lawyer and promises to pay him one-half of the property if he wins the case. The same is the case here. We cannot rise from our present intolerable condition without the aid of the Muslims. So in order to gain the desired end there is no objection to giving a percentage, a greater percentage, to the Muslims. Their responsibility becomes greater, the greater the percentage of representation you give to them. They will be doubly bound to work for you and with you, with a zeal and enthusiasm greater than ever. The fight is at present a triangular one."

"History and reason," he continued, "are against the difficulties created by the bureaucracy, and we must triumph in the end. Be prepared to say that you are a Home Ruler. Say that you must have it and I dare say when you are ready you will get it. There is nothing anarchical in this demand."

"Home Rule," he concluded, "is the only remedy. Insist on your rights. India is your own house. Is it not? (cries of Yes!). Then why not manage it yourselves ? (cheers). Our domestic affairs must be in our hands. We do not want separation from England."

Tilak's scheme for the appointment of special working committees came up for consideration, but oddly enough, the President ruled it out!

Tilak attended the Hindu Mahasabha session and addressed the delegates of the Hindu Mahasabha who were displeased with Tilak for having conceded separate representation to the Muslims and that too in a greater proportion than was just.

He attended also the session of the All-India Muslim League. On December 31 the Muslim League ratified the Congress-League Scheme which afterwards was called the Lucknow Pact.

The Muslim League on behalf of the Muslims agreed to the demand for Swaraj, and the Hindu leaders in the Congress headed by Tilak agreed to separate electorates for the Muslims and weightages in the bargain. If the Muslim League ratified the pact on behalf of the Muslims, whom did the Congress represent? Thus Tilak gave a national sanction to the anti-national separate electorates and the separate political entity introduced by the Morley-Minto reforms and a national recognition to the Muslim League as the accredited spokesman of the Muslims. It is history that after Tilak's death the Lucknow pact proved to be a rift in the lute. Tilak's subtle intellect could not foresee it!

The Lucknow Pact laid down that one-third of the Indian elected Members in the Central Legislature should be Muslims elected by separate Muslim electorates.

On December 31 Tilak drove to the Royal Hotel in Lucknow and saw Miss MacLloyd of the Ramkrishna Mission. He decided, with the help of Malaviya, Surendranath and Jinnah, to launch a vigorous Home Rule campaign and left Lucknow for Kanpur.

Accompanied by his colleagues Khaparde and Belvi, Tilak reached Kanpur on January 1, 1917. Kanpur was richly decorated, and Tilak was honoured at every turning in the city in the Hindu fashion by women with *arti*. At the parade ground Tilak addressed in English a meeting of twenty thousand people. He was presented with an address written in Sanskrit. At the outset he said that he was very sorry that he could not speak in Hindi, although he was one of them who held that Hindi should be the *lingua franca* of India in future. Khaparde gave in Hindi the gist of Tilak's speech. During the course of his speech Tilak said that Hindus believed in the Four Varnas, but the conception of that Chaturvarnya was based on merit and not on birth.

Turning to politics, Tilak said that Home Rule was nothing else but to be masters of their own houses. Prayer meant cultivation of mind. He asked them to pray for Home Rule. "It is no use praying merely for nothing. God does not want prayer for Himself. God does not want praise from you," he added. Tilak then went to Calcutta to meet ' Motibabu' who regarded Tilak as his younger brother. He was staying with Motilal. Bepin Chandra Pal and the editor of the *Sandhya* had a talk with Tilak. He met Mrs. Besant also in Calcutta. The Maharaja of Darbhanga expressed a desire to meet Tilak. Therefore he saw him along with Khaparde and Motilal Ghose. They discussed Varnashram-Dharma and the caste system.

CHAPTER XXI

Home Rule Movement

I

ON HIS WAY back to Poona, Tilak visited Nagpur, Yeotmal, Akola and Murtizapur. At Nagpur Tilak delivered a speech on Home Rule in the theatre at the Chitnavis Park under the presidentship of Dr. Gour. The speech was very effective, and the audience was greatly impressed. At the end of the meeting the crowd swelled, and Tilak had to go out by a private door of the theatre. The stress told upon Tilak's health.

Then the party reached Amraoti which was decorated and illuminated in honour of Tilak's visit. At the Jog Square, several institutions including the Depressed Classes Committee honoured him. Tilak spoke for about twenty minutes. He told them that the goal was settled at Lucknow by leading men of all parties and creeds. It was Home Rule or Swaraj. Everyone should ask boldly for Swaraj. The ideal of Home Rule for India was held legal. To preach it was no sedition.

At Yeotmal, he was accorded an enthusiastic welcome and was presented with an address. Replying to the address, he said that the word Swaraj had a limited meaning that day. He said it was right to have Home Rule but it was a historical and a European way of putting it.[1] He observed that Home Rule was Dharma; and just as they could not separate heat from fire, so they could not separate Home Rule from them. After the functions and speeches, someone said to Tilak that he had captured the Congress. Tilak replied calmly that for that he had given his blood and added that now that he had captured the Congress the time for the real test had come. He was old and his hopes were hovering around the youth of the nation.

1 *Bal Gangadhar Tilak: His Writings and Speeches*, p. 230.

At a public meeting in Akola, Tilak observed that Government said that the leaders should ask for Home Rule as much as they liked, but they should not criticize the bureaucracy. It was like asking a man to eat a fruit without biting it, he said!

When Tilak reached Poona he fell ill. A pensioner (acquaintance of his) suggested that he should now retire from politics. Tilak replied that just as the pensioner had handed over charge to somebody before his retirement, so he wanted to hand over the charge to somebody. Working day and night for the cause had now become a habit with him. Indeed it is true that men achieve greatness on account of their untiring work. Somebody told him that Besant worked for about twenty hours a day. Thereupon Tilak said: "Greatness is achieved and retained by untiring work!"

In spite of his ill health, Tilak convened a meeting of the Home Rule League in the last week of January 1917 and reviewed its work. Shortly afterwards Tilak addressed a meeting at the Kirloskar Theatre when he said that if Swaraj was granted to India, the Indians would fight to defend the British Empire. In the first week of February, Annasaheb Patwardhan thc patriarch died. Tilak walked eight hours with the funeral procession without taking a drop of water! When his nephew Vidwans insisted on his eating a little and taking a glass of water, he said he could not bear the idea of leaving the deceased for a moment. Food was available every day; but the sage would never be seen again! His estimate of Annasaheb Patwardhan was very high. It was his opinion that had Patwardhan been born during the days of Vijaynagar Kingdom, he would have been Madhavacharya; or if Poona had been Paris of the medieval times, he would have been Cardinal Richelieu. There was much of gratitude and glorification in this tribute paid to an elder who had boundless sympathy for Tilak's political work.

Tilak, who was studying the war situation, knew that the supremacy of England over the seas was endangered by the German submarines and mines. Warfare was quite revolutionized by new types of aeroplanes, long-range guns, and other dangerous weapons. It meant that the Government required lacs of soldiers to fight the Germans. This compelled the Britishers to revise their militarisation policy. Tilak therefore thought that in seizing that opportunity the Indian youth would serve the King, Empire, and country too. On February 1 Tilak addressed a meeting at the Kirloskar Theatre, Poona, and protested against the Indentured Labour System in the Fiji Islands.

On February 17, 1917, a meeting was held in Poona for impressing upon the youth the necessity of joining the army. The president of the meeting was R. P. Paranjpye. He expressed satisfaction at the announcement made by the Viceroy regarding the intention of the Government to enrol Indians in their units in the Defence of India Force for general military service in India for the duration of the War. Tilak appealed to the youth to join the army for military training. He said they should not think that life in the military was a waste. Whatever the hardships and however unsatisfactory the conditions for military service might be, it was in the interests of their country that they should learn modern warfare. To him it was a sacred duty to become a soldier to defend the Motherland. If they were not prepared to defend the country, why they should talk of Swaraj, he asked. As regards the inferior posts the Indians were given in the military, the question would be taken up, he concluded.

While Tilak was thus making a speech in favour of militarisation of the Indians, the Indian Government was restless over the safety of the Punjab Province! Lord Hardinge describes the condition of the Punjab, "The internal situation in the Punjab had grown menacing, owing to the anarchists, realising our military weakness owing to the depletion of our troops."[2] The Maharaja of Nepal sent 6,000 men to suppress the revolutionaries.

Owing to the incursion of seven hundred revolutionaries of the Gadhar Party from America there was terrible unrest in the Punjab. Several of them fell fighting, many of them were transported, and some went underground. A Maharashtrian revolutionary Pingle was arrested with ten loaded bombs inside the lines of the 12th cavalry at Meerut. At the same time a conspiracy was discovered to rob the armoury and magazines of certain regiments at Lahore, Rawalpindi and Ferozepur.[3] Naturally the Government was taking precautions not to add fuel to the fire of the revolutionaries in the Punjab by allowing Tilak's volcanic personality to enter it.

The Government had information that Tilak was intending to make a Home Rule tour of the Punjab. The Punjab Government therefore issued a notice under the Defence of India Consolidation Rules, 1916, prohibiting Tilak from entering the Punjab. The notice was served on

---

2 Lord Hardinge's Memoirs in the *Times of India,* 4 July 1948.

3 Ibid.

Tilak on February 17, after the above-mentioned meeting was concluded. A similar notice was served on Tilak by the Commissioner of Police, Delhi, prohibiting him from entering the city of Delhi. Government had no faith in him. They knew each other well.

Tilak reiterated his views at a meeting in Bombay on March 2, where he said that when men with military training would be seen in different walks of life, it would have some sort of good effect upon the policy of the Government. The result of his powerful appeal was that about eight hundred young men came forward and enlisted their names for joining the military.

Immediately Tilak left for Calcutta to attend the meeting of the All-India Congress Committee. Gandhi, Samarth, Prof. Kale and Deodhar were in the same train. At the meeting the personnel of the delegation to be sent to London was discussed and settled. Calcutta was chosen as the venue of the next Congress. Tilak, accompanied by Motilal Ghose, paid a visit to the Karlekar's Circus whose performances had been going on in Calcutta. At the instance of the proprietor who garlanded Tilak and the guests, Tilak made a speech and requested Motilal Ghose to present a Gold Medal to the proprietor offered by the Maharashtra Club of Calcutta.

Tilak returned from Calcutta hurriedly and went to Chikodi to attend the Belgaum District Conference. There he appealed to the youth to join the military. He said if he were in power he would have made education free and compulsory. In olden times saints spread education through their preachings, and Kings did not take it up. But under the British regime the Government were not educating them, and, on the contrary, they did not grant them political reforms, because people were not educated. He appealed to the people to shed fear and be brave enough to say that they demanded Home Rule. Secret police always accompanied the Viceroy or Governor also. If they accompanied them, they should be regarded as their protectors. The demand for Swaraj was to be placed before the bar of the British people. The demand was voiced unanimously. Formerly British leaders asked Gokhale, "Oh, but what about the Mohammedans ?" That question was solved. People who thought they would attain salvation if they died at Pandharpur, he concluded, should regard death in the cause of freedom as a sure passport to salvation.

At another meeting at Chikodi he told the people that they should help the Government, but they should put money into the boxes of the

Government with a slip attached to it saying that they expected in return Home Rule!

From Chikodi Tilak was taken to Nipani. There he protested against his being styled as 'Mahatma Bhagwan Tilak'. He asked them to stop that fad. What he knew he told the people. He did nothing extraordinary. He appealed to the citizens to join the military. During Peshwa Rule the Desais at Nipani could raise a battalion in one day. But their present condition was very pitiable. Citizens fled at the sight of a recruiting officer. That was the pitiable state to which they had been reduced by the British Government. It neglected also the Nipani tobacco and imported it from Egypt, he added.

The Provincial Conference met at Nasik in May under the presidentship of Srinivasa Sastri. Speaking at the Conference, Tilak said that the mission of the Home Rule League was not to propagate social reforms or industrial reforms, but to propagate the rights of Swaraj, Home Rule. The object of the Madras Home Rule League and that of his Home Rule League were not different. He said that the spirit behind the Home Rule movement was eternal and indestructible. Soul meant God, and mind would not rest till it got identified with Him. If one body was worn out, the soul would take another. No weapon could cut the spirit, no fire could burn it, no water could wet it, no wind could dry it. "We will follow," he declared, "Shri Ramchandra in obeying the order of our father the Congress. We are determined to make efforts to get this resolution enforced even if the effort leads us to the desert, compels us to live incognito, makes us suffer hardships and even if it finally brings us to death I"[4]

The Conference passed, after a hot discussion between the Moderates and the Nationalists, a resolution demanding the release of political prisoners like the Savarkar brothers. The Social Conference also held its session at Nasik. M. R. Jayakar presided. At the instance of M. R. Jayakar and G. S. Pradhan, Tilak attended the Social Conference causing considerable surprise among his followers. Addressing the Conference, Tilak put forth his stock argument that he could not take part in the Social Conference because he acted on the principle of division of work.

After the Conference was over, Tilak visited Shirdi with Khaparde to pay his respects to Sai Maharaj. Looking at Tilak, in a saint's mystic accent, Sai Maharaj said: "People are bad. Keep yourself to yourself."

---

4 *Bal Gangadhar Tilak: His Writings and Speeches*, p. 243.

II

In May 1917 Government declared by a resolution that the militarisation movement failed because the Indian leaders were not co-operating. Just then Lloyd George told the Irish leaders that he was thinking of granting them Home Rule. The main object behind this announcement was to prejudice Lloyd George and other British statesmen against Indian leaders and make them put off the Indian demands. Being disappointed at the stand taken by the Muslims, the Indian Government now tried to set the non-Brahmins and the Indian States against the Indian movement for Swaraj and tried to suppress the Home Rule movement which had outshadowed the Congress. They arrested on June 15, 1917, Mrs. Besant and her two lieutenants G. S. Arundale and B. P. Wadia and interned them at Ootacamund. These three persons were prohibited from writing new or re-publishing old articles or books, and from corresponding with anyone. Securities deposited for Besant's press and paper were forfeited.

But this gave an impetus to the Home Rule movement, all leaders like Jinnah, Chintamani, Surendranath joining the Home Rule League. Sir Subramania lyer, who was a retired Chief Justice, wrote to President Wilson protesting against the internment of Besant and declaring that it was the attitude of the bureaucracy that was coming in the way of militarisation. When Lord Chelmsford met Sir Subramania in Madras, the Viceroy stormed at him for his move!

As regards the non-Brahmin movement, Tilak said that a time would come when they too would be disillusioned; for God would not be able to satisfy them for all times. When that took place, they would join the battle for Swaraj.

Tilak declared in an article in the *Kesari* that the only way to settle the Indian problem was a proclamation by the British King declaring that the ultimate object of the British Government was to grant Swaraj to India, that the first step after the War towards that end should be taken immediately, and that India would be raised to the status of a self-governing member within the Empire.

Dadabhai Naoroji the great pioneer, patriot and the Grand Old Man of India, died in Bombay on June 30. Tilak joined the funeral procession of the great patriarch whom he had praised as a Mahatma. Tilak now wanted to take advantage of the war situation and to push ahead the demand for Swaraj. He therefore sent Joseph Baptista to London on July 14, 1917, to propagate the idea of Home Rule for India, as far as possible on the basis of the Congress-League Scheme.

The All-India Congress Committee and the Muslim League Committee met at Bombay in the last week of July 1917, and they passed a resolution demanding the release of Besant and the Ali brothers. Meetings were held all over India for the release of Mrs. Besant and the Ali brothers. The Home Rule League of Madras bounced with enthusiasm and courage. It awarded medals to those who suffered jail for the cause of the nation. Sir Subramania Iyer sent such a special Golden Medal to Tilak and wrote to him to accept the Award which he so richly deserved. The Award bore an inscription of a Lock with two letters "F.I." meaning Fellowship of the Interned. The British Government was now compelled to pay adequate attention to the Indian problem. Depressed by the war reverses, pressed by the Indian Home Rule Movement, and oppressed by the Indian revolutionary forces, the British Government proclaimed on August 20 through Montagu, the Secretary of State for India, Britain's policy of gradual development of self-governing institutions with a view to progressive realisation of responsible Government in India as an integral part of the British Empire.

On September 17, Tilak attended at Satara the 60th birthday celebration of his lieutenant and lawyer Dadasaheb Karandikar. On the previous day, Besant and her lieutenants were released, and people expressed satisfaction at this. On October 3 Tilak addressed a meeting in Bombay demanding the release of the Ali brothers. While Tilak was in Bombay, the leaders decided to send a public memorandum to the British Government demanding Swaraj, and the work of obtaining signatures of the people to the Congress-League Scheme was begun by all Home Rule Leaguers. This was the suggestion of the practical politician in Gandhi who had shaken the Bihar bureaucracy in April 1917, by his fight for the tenants slaving in the indigo fields in Champaran. In September 1917, the Bombay Provincial Congress Committee passed a resolution on passive resistance when Tilak spoke strongly in support of it.

The All-India Congress Committee and the Council of the Muslim League met on October 7, at Allahabad, and the question of passive resistance was dropped, Besant herself being against the idea. This was a great disappointment to the young leaders. The first meeting of the All-India Congress Committee and the Council of the Muslim League, therefore, decided upon sending an All-India Deputation to the Viceroy and the Secretary of State for India with a reasoned representation in support of the Congress-League Pact.

Tilak addressed two meetings at Allahabad preaching the doctrine of Home Rule and added that the British Democracy had clearly seen that there was much force in Indians' cry for freedom and that they would still hear the cry. Therefore it was time to place their demands before Montagu, who was expected to visit India shortly, more forcibly than the bureaucracy. The ideal and the demand of the Home Rule League and those of the Congress were the same.

From Allahabad Tilak went direct to Pandharpur to attend the Sholapur District Conference, and next week presided over the conference of astronomers who were making efforts to reach a decision on the reformation of the almanac.

On his return to Poona from Pandharpur, Tilak attended a tremendous meeting which was held at Shaniwar Wada in Poona, under the auspices of the Maratha Rashtriya Sangh, to support the Congress-League Scheme. It was predominantly attended by non-Brahmins of different castes, as also the Brahmins. One leader of every community spoke. Tilak, who wanted to win the support of the non-Brahmins to the Congress-League Scheme, had agreed to speak on behalf of his Brahmin community and he shrewdly made a speech appropriate to the occasion. Addressing the meeting, he said that India did not want the old system of Swaraj. She wanted to establish her Swaraj on the Western pattern. The caste system brought on the British Raj over India, and if the past dissensions continued they would be ruined under Swaraj also. Under pressure of circumstances, politicians sometimes speak what they never mean. That there was a slight departure from his policy and not a divergence from Tilak's social philosophy can be seen from his further speeches on this subject. He would not parry the question at this meeting, and so he, so to say, played to the gallery.

Tilak attended, in the first week of November, the Provincial Conference at Godhra which was held under the presidentship of Gandhi. The special feature of Gandhi's speech was that among other things for qualifying themselves for Swaraj he said that the Hindus should remove untouchability.

Again a meeting of the Home Rule League was held under the presidentship of Gandhi. It was a unique meeting. Gandhi was its president and Tilak was the speaker, and the subject was Swaraj. Tilak said that by Swaraj he meant that power should be vested in the people. People were no longer prepared to put up with Governors who were busy laying foundations of buildings. A strong wave of democracy was passing all over the world. All the world over Self-Government was on the anvil, and Indians could not be expected to sit idle. Tilak and Khaparde did not attend the Social Conference called "Sansar Sudhar" which was held at the same place. When asked why they did not attend it, Tilak evasively said that his wife was, dead, and his Sansar had ended long before. He sarcastically added that Dadasaheb too, was an old man, and it was not necessary to reform his "Sansar"!

On his way back to Poona Tilak paid a visit to Surat where he was accorded a great ovation. It was a mammoth meeting, and Tilak had to address the people from six different platforms, moving from one to the other; Khaparde followed translating his speeches in Gujarati.

It was during this week that a memorial was presented to Lokamanya Tilak, 'Mataji' Annie Besant and Maharaj Dwarkadas in Bombay on behalf of the Untouchables of Bombay, in which the supplicants prayed that the Bombay Hindu temples should be thrown open to the untouchables, who also were Hindus. Needless to say, Tilak gave no response to it. He was a political leader, and he had nothing to do with such problems that clamoured for social justice and equality.[5]

About the middle of November Tilak attended the Belgaum District Conference held at Athni, at which he made an offensive speech and provoked a wave of angry protests from non-Brahmins all over Maharashtra. In the course of that speech he said that councils were not parade grounds for castes and communities; so only men of political understanding and acumen should be elected by the voters. In an unguarded moment or under an unfortunate provocation he asked the audience contemptuously whether the tailors had to use scissors, Kunbis to handle the plough, and the Banias to hold the grocer's pair of scales in the Legislative Councils! [6]

III

MONTAGU CAME TO India. When he landed at Bombay, Tilak sent him a telegram, welcoming him to India. Montagu began from, the 17th November 1917 to interview the Indian Parties and institutions as regards their views on political reforms. The restrictions on Tilak's visit to Delhi

---

5 The *Hindu Missionary*, 7 January 1918.

6 *Tilak-Paranjpye Controversy*, p. 6; also Jawalkar, Dinkar S., *Deshache Dushman* (Marathi), p. 4.

and the Punjab were temporarily waived, as he was invited to place before Montagu the views of his Home Rule League. Tilak went to Delhi. He travelled, of late, first class, so that he might get a little rest and be free from unnecessary talks with fellow travellers and admirers. Tilak and Besant led the deputations of the Home Rule Leagues and met Montagu in Delhi on November 26. At the time of the interview with Montagu, Tilak wore brand new shoes and had put on his best clothes. He said he was a Mahratta and must maintain the dignity and decorum of the Durbar! But it seems he had kept his shoes outside the Hall as Montagu describes him as clad in white with bare feet. Tilak told Montagu that he would accept what the British Government gave and would fight for further reforms. On the same day the Congress and the Muslim League deputations waited on Montagu.

What was the impression created by Tilak upon Montagu ? Montagu told C. Y. Chintamani that he had read the full record of Tilak's opinions and activities and come to the conclusion that there was only one genuine extremist in India, and that was Mr. Tilak.[7] In his diary Montagu describes Tilak as 'the great Tilak' "who probably has the greatest influence of any person in India and who is very extreme. His procession to Delhi to see me was a veritable triumphant one. He was really the author of the Congress-League Scheme, and although he did not impress me very much in argument, he is a scientific man of great erudition and training." When Besant stepped forward to garland the Viceroy, Chelmsford, he took the garland in his hands. Tilak garlanded Montagu, but the latter feared that if it was known outside they would say that he was garlanded by a man who had served a penal servitude and was connected by his newspaper writings with the murder of an Indian official! [8]

On his way back Tilak was compelled to get down at Agra; The Vice-President of the Home Rule League lifted him up bodily and carried him across the station. They took him out in procession, and students drew his carriage. At night Tilak and his party were brought back to the station, and they returned to Poona.

Montagu showed no regard for Mrs. Besant. He noted in his diary that she had broken her pledges. What those pledges were no Indian leader knew. After the interview with Montagu she said: "We must support Mr.

7 Chitamani, C. Y., *Indian Politics since the Mutiny*, p. 82.

8 Montagu, E. S., *An Indian Diary*, pp. 59-61.

Montagu." Lord Chelmsford shunned Besant. He had turned down her appeals for an interview. The memorandum containing the Congress-League Scheme was submitted to Montagu with the signatures of a million people.

In the last week of December 1917, Tilak went to Calcutta to attend the Congress session which was held under the presidentship of Mrs. Besant. He was accorded a royal reception and taken in procession which was a mile and a half in length and was headed by bands and banners. When he entered the Congress pandal the whole assembly got up and cheered Tilak. Mrs. Besant delivered a very brilliant address which was an elaborate thesis on India's Self-Government. At the Subjects Committee of the Calcutta Congress the question of the formation of provinces on the basis of languages was keenly discussed. Even Gandhi thought the question might await the implementation of the Reforms, but Tilak saw the point, namely, that Linguistic Provinces were an essential condition pre-requisite for real Provincial Autonomy. After two hours' discussion the principle was accepted.

In the open session Tilak supported the resolution on Self-Government and warned the Congress and the country against accepting any scheme other than the Congress-League one. Some leaders were influenced by the scheme of Mr. Curtis, and so he had to put them on their guard. Tilak moved the resolution demanding the release of the Ali Brothers. They were arrested first and the reasons were invented afterwards. He said that those reasons were illusory and fallacious and unjust. Pointing to the mother of the Ali Brothers, Tilak said : "I pray to God that we may have many more mothers like her in this country."

On his return journey Tilak got down at Nagpur and attended the Kirtan Sammelan where a public reception was held. He was suffering from pain in his leg. Then Dr. Moonje came and took them to Itwari in a motor-car. The city was decorated, and flowers and garlands were offered to Tilak at many places.

IV

ON HIS ARRIVAL from Nagpur Tilak attended in the last week of January 1918 the Poona District Conference at Lonavla at which M. R. Jayakar presided at the instance of Tilak. Jayakar was quite impressed with the affable charm and sweetness of Tilak who wanted to win over young men to the freedom movement of India. Tilak asked Jayakar to commit in his presidential address Maharashtrian politicians to the acceptance of the Montagu-Chelmsford announcement despite its deficiencies, but with proper criticism.

At Lonavla, Karmaveer Shinde had a discussion with Tilak on social reforms. Tilak was planning to take a deputation to London to plead the cause of Home Rule for India in England, and so he wanted funds. He tried to win over able men like M. R. Jayakar to his side to go on deputation to London, but his efforts were not successful. His literary warfare and his defence of social reactionaries had estranged many of the enlightened eminent men of his day. Tilak then decided to make a tour of the Central Provinces and Berar. The tour is known as the Home Rule Tour. He chose for the collection of funds that part of Maharashtra from which most of his lieutenants Khaparde, Paranjpye, Moonje and Aney hailed.

The programme was planned with every possible detail having regard to the routes and rivers, places and personalities, meetings and conferences. The tour began from Bombay on February 5 and lasted till February 24, 1918. From morning till eleven o'clock at night, except one or two hours at noon, Tilak was either in a motor-car or on the platform at some function or other. People showed tremendous enthusiasm. The leader of a certain village informed those who chalked out Tilak's programme that if his village were dropped out from the programme and Tilak did not pay a visit to his place, the people of the village would regard their village as a place of heaps of ruin. Villagers cleaned the squalid places and slums; towns were decorated; cities displayed arches and buntings at their main centres. Where mud, rocks or water stood in the way as obstruction to the passage of the motor-car, the people laboured hard to remove these obstructions, and at one place the villagers built up a temporary bridge of sand over a river!

At the places which could not be visited for want of time or for want of car-roads, the people waited in the hot noons or in the cold nights on the outskirts of the village with flowers and fruits, to catch a glimpse of the great leader. If it was a dark night, people would light heaps of hay and dry leaves and welcome their leader. They ran towards his car, touched it as it was not possible for all to touch his feet, smeared the dust from his car on their foreheads! Tilak's leg was paining, and he was suffering from diabetes. So it was arranged that he should put his hands forward, but people would not listen! At the time of planning the tour it was agreed that he should travel for only about three or four hours a day and deliver only one speech; but these terms could not be observed even for a day.

Civic addresses at different places were presented to Tilak; purses were given at many places, the amounts ranging from five hundred to seven thousand rupees. One man transferred his insurance policy to the Home Rule League; women handed over to Tilak their savings; a Jain gave his locket to Tilak as a blessing of God! Some villagers gave small purses of a few rupees with their blessings. Tilak visited during his tour Malkapur, Buldhana, Khamgaon, Nandurbar, Jalgaon, Akola, Washim, Murtizapur, Chanda, Wardha, Nagpur and Bhandara.

From Bhandara, Tilak again returned to Nagpur. He had sent a telegram to the Delhi Police Commissioner requesting him to relax for a while the ban on his entry into Delhi, as he wanted to attend the All-India Congress Committee meeting there. Then he sent wires also to the Viceroy and to the Home Member for permission to attend the meeting of the All-India Congress Committee. Even Khaparde interviewed the Viceroy, but he said that he would not interfere with the orders of the Local Government. Moreover Tilak's visit, he added, would hamper the recruiting work. Tilak received a reply from the Viceroy in the negative.

Tilak then left Nagpur for Bombay by train. On his way back he visited one or two places, and the last speech he delivered was at Bhusaval. He returned to Bombay on the morning of February 24, 1918.

During this tour Tilak impressed upon the people the necessity of joining the military forces in the interests of the nation and for their future betterment. He had expressed in one of his previous speeches that if the young men did not join the army, he would abandon the agitation for Home Rule as useless. He was even prepared to send his eldest son as a recruit. His son indeed had joined some recruiting agency, but he was sent back. Yet the bureaucrats could not bring themselves to believe that Tilak was preaching militarisation without any ulterior motives. The Deputy Commissioner of Yeotmal informed the local Home Rule League Office that the Government would not allow Tilak to make discouraging speeches on militarisation. If he did not want to support it from the bottom of his heart, he grumbled, he should not open his lips. Government was suspicious not only of Tilak's attitude towards the war, but also that of Besant. It was alleged that she had been a hireling of the German Government.

Tilak travelled over two thousand miles and collected about fifty thousand rupees. With his old, weakened, ailing body he undertook the tour and delivered thirty-two speeches. "People cannot possibly realise," he once said, "that I feel so weak. When the moment comes I make a speech. But the body is all the while under the strain. The speech over, I return from the crowds and sleep over my fatigue. Only my will to live sustains me."

On his return to Poona, Tilak presided over a meeting which was addressed by Besant on March 6, 1918. Replying to the Government charges, Tilak said that the Home Rule Leagues were in favour of the policy of recruitment. Joining the military was not done for the meagre salary of Rs. 15 or 16, but for the protection of the British Empire. If Government said that these things would ultimately lead them in the direction of Swaraj he would raise an army of twenty-five thousand men in Maharashtra alone.

The Congress was not willing to send its deputation to London until Montagu's Report was out. A special session of the Congress had pronounced India's verdict on it. According to Tilak and Baptista, who was then in England, that was the time to appeal to the British public and politicians to consider the problem of India. So Tilak as also Mrs. Besant decided to take their Home Rule League deputations to London. It was declared that Tilak would sail in the first week of April 1918 via Colombo. Those were the days when passports were not easily granted, and the voyage also was risky. When someone said that the voyage was not safe in those days, Tilak would say he was determined to go and besides when persons like the Viceroy undertook the voyages why should he not? Tilak had another important item of work in London. The hearing of the case against Chirol was to begin in London. For that he wanted money. So he mortgaged his property including Gaikwad Wada which stood in the name of his son Rambhau Tilak. He told his colleagues in confidence that if he lost the Chirol case he would retire for one year to Sinhagad from public service and pay his debts by writing books.

On the eve of Tilak's departure to London, he paid a flying visit to Kalyan, Thana, Bhivandi and Panvel where his admirers and followers substantially contributed to his Home Rule Fund. Then he paid a visit to Satara. There he was presented with a big purse.

Although very busy making preparations for the voyage of the deputation, Tilak wrote just at this time a thought-provoking preface to the biography of Gandhi written by Mrs. Avantikabai Gokhale, in which he observed that the path of passive resistance discovered by Gandhi and sanctified by his penance had great potentialities although it was difficult for one to say, he added, whether it could be followed on all occasions even if justifiable, or whether it would be effective everywhere. He opined that Gandhi's life was instructive and exemplary because of his moral stature and spiritual power which great men attain by practice of penance and utter selflessness.

The day of Tilak's departure from Poona dawned. Poona was full of enthusiasm. Several programmes were arranged in his honour. Many parts of the city were decorated with arches and flowers. In the temple of Omkareshwar he received the blessings of the Poona Shastris. Tilak said that the abode and blessings of God would be there where the protection of the good and destruction of the wicked was going on. If an organisation did not do this type of work and yet installed an image of God in its office, God's abode would not be there. In a moving poem Ram Ganesh Gadkari, the front rank play-wright of Maharashtra, appealed to Tilak to bring back Shivaji's sword Bhawani which was believed to be in the London Museum. The main farewell meeting was held at Reay Market in Poona where Tilak was presented with a purse, an address and dress. Replying to the address, Tilak said he would counteract the anti-Indian propaganda of Lord Sydenham in London. He appealed to the people to keep up the agitation for Home Rule and extend their solid support to him when he would be in England. The Sarvajanik Sabha, too, bade him farewell.

CHAPTER XXII

Mission to England

I

TILAK LEFT POONA on the night of March 23. The procession started from his house by the light of some 150 gas-lamps and reached Poona station. There vast crowds bade him farewell. Tilak said to someone that he was going for *Lankadahan* and bringing back Sita, the Goddess of Liberty, and in the meanwhile they should keep the soldiers ready. In Bombay, Tilak was presented with purses and addresses in different localities by merchants, doctors, Shastris and mill-hands. The mill-hands held the function on behalf of forty mills. At Dana Bunder a leaflet with the autograph of Tilak was put to auction, and it fetched five hundred rupees.

In Bombay, Tilak was disposing of smaller items of work, writing notes, letters, and signing authority deeds. Just on the eve of his departure, Shri Jagannath Maharaj came to him and requested him to look into the accounts and to receive back the expenses which Tilak had incurred on the civil suit of his adoption. Tilak said that he treated him as his son; but since Shri Jagannath Maharaj insisted on his receiving the money, he told him that he had spent Rs. 60,000. He, however, wished Shri Jagannath Maharaj to give him a certain piece of land worth Rs. 30,000, as he wanted to donate it to the S.P. Mandal for erecting a building for its New Poona College, and since he regarded him as his third son, he had waived his claim on the other half of the money. In the course of his talk Tilak revealed to Jagannath Maharaj how he had obtained Government papers for the preparation of the Chirol case in the night, and how in the day-time they were kept in their proper places in Government offices.

On March 24, 1918, the All-India Depressed Classes Conference was held under the presidentship of Shri Sayajirao Gaikwad, the Maharaja of

Baroda. Tilak attended and addressed the Conference. He said: "God is for all. Taint finds no room in the eyes of God, why should we then recognise it? It is a sin against God to say that a person is untouchable, who is not so to God Himself and if God were to tolerate untouchability I would not recognise Him as God at all. I do hold that the Untouchables must cease to be Untouchables. This is a matter only of social usage and the social usage must change. In some old days the autocracy of the Brahmins created this usage! I do not deny that. It is a disease and it must be removed. Many ask me what I am prepared to do personally in this behalf. I answer it is not my work. I cannot undertake to do many things. My brain is not capable of leading many movements. I have perfect sympathy for such movements and undertakings."[1]

A manifesto declaring that its signatories would not observe untouchability in their day-to-day life was issued the same day by the leaders of the Conference, but Tilak refused to sign it! He did this, it is said, on account of pressure from his lieutenants. In social matters he was a follower of his followers! Tilak had told Karmaveer Shinde, the convener of this Conference, that he would attend it in his personal capacity and not as the editor of the *Kesari*. The policy of Tilak's *Kesari* in those days was to observe studied silence on such speeches of Tilak, so that those, so alleged Tilak's opponents, might not disturb his orthodox lieutenants and followers, and those commitments might not be cited against him by his opponents! Commenting upon this speech, R. P. Paranjpye said that Tilak and his party had contemptuously kept silence for years on this question, and as Tilak was not willing to wield his influence over his followers to remove untouchability, the foregoing speech of Tilak was nothing but a solitary declaration made with the object of strengthening his position before the Labour Party of England. Another point must be borne in mind that Gandhi had an untouchable family in his Ashram. As regards Paranjpye's remark, it may be noted that during Tilak's stay in England, Colonel Wedgwood, British Labour leader, did mention to Tilak in London that Indian Legislative Assemblies should pay more attention to the welfare of the Untouchables and backward classes and added that much depended upon how they would treat those lower classes!

As regards his non-advocacy of the removal of untouchability, Tilak observed, a few months later, that in America no thinking men would ignore

1 *The All-India Anti-Untouchability Movement*, p. 22.

the other work of any American statesman simply because he declined to take a prominent part in the emancipation of the Negroes in the United States. The point was whether it was a fact that Tilak had never expressed views favourable or unfavourable on any problem unless he was prepared to do actual propagandist work in connection with that particular problem. His signature would have greatly helped the cause of the Untouchables. But it was unfortunate that he should have stuck to his orbit of tradition. Evidently the reason he put forward for his refusal to sign the manifesto was not justifiable. And that justification was rendered more vulnerable and tragic when it is observed that he had advised the Shankaracharya, Dr. Kurtkoti, not to accept the presidentship of this anti-untouchability Conference because, he said, it was improper for a religious head to do so until the people were themselves prepared to welcome such a change in society!

The second annual session of the Home Rule League was held in Bombay on March 26, at French Bridge. It was attended by about 7,000 delegates. Khaparde, B. C. Pal and Tilak delivered brilliant speeches at the session. About fourteen hundred telegrams supporting Tilak were received by the Reception Committee.

During his stay in Bombay Tilak had sent a cheque for fifty-thousand rupees to Tagore with a special messenger. Tagore was then planning a tour of Europe. Tilak thought that if Tagore did something to push ahead the mission of India, it would be a great help to India. There was no condition attached to the money. "Tilak did not want my help," Tagore said later, "for any propaganda which he himself was pursuing at that moment for the benefit of his country. He wanted me to be true to myself and through my efforts to serve humanity, in my own way to serve India. I felt that this proposal from Tilak carried with it the highest honour that I had ever received from my countrymen. I do not know if I was worthy of it, but it revealed to me the greatness of Tilak's personality which deeply impressed my mind."[2] Tilak's favour would have provoked the frown of the Government, and the poet must have shrewdly declined.

On the night of March 27, people went in a procession to Bori Bunder station to give a send-off to the Home Rule League deputation consisting of Tilak, G. S. Khaparde, B. C. Pal, N. C. Kelkar and R. P. Karandikar.

2 *Reminiscences and Anecdotes about Lokamanya Tilak*, Vol. II, p. 608.

They started by the Madras Mail, receiving ovations at various stations enroute to Madras.

After breaking their journey at Bijapur, Tilak and his party reached Madras where he and the other Home Rule League leaders were accorded receptions at different places in the city. The members of the Mahajan Sabha, the Madras Provincial Congress Committee, the Home Rule League, and the Madras Presidency Association presented Tilak with a joint address, and a hearty welcome. The main speech was delivered by Sir Subramania lyer. Times had changed, Tilak said in reply to the address, and Responsible Government had now become the necessity of the hour, the necessity of the Empire, and the safety of the Empire.

On their way to Colombo Tilak was cheered with cries of "Tilak Maharaj-ki-jai" at every station even at dead of night and at dawn! At Egmore, he told the Deputy Commissioner that under Swaraj Government he would be promoted to the post of the Commissioner. He would not rot as a Deputy Commissioner. Mrs. Besant gave the Deputation a dinner party at Blavatsky Gardens where tables were laid out under a banyan tree which was illuminated with electric lights, and the whole scene looked like a fairy land. Replying to the reception, Tilak said that times had changed and a man who did not change his opinion with the times was sure to lag behind. He, too, formerly was not so much in favour of a deputation, but now he saw it was the best time to urge India's claim on the ground of liberty and right as well. "No doubt," he said, "I had said that Home Rule is our birth-right, but birth-rights are not always recognized; you must work for them." At the first address offered by the Mahrattas and Andhras of Madras he said that he was one of those who held that the development of India would be much facilitated if vernaculars were developed and if provinces were redistributed according to languages. Leaving Madras on the 31st March, they reached Colombo on the morning of 2nd April.

At Colombo the Indians and Ceylonese held a reception in honour of Tilak and the deputation. Welcoming the deputation, the *Ceylon Daily News* in its editorial observed: "We extend a hearty welcome to the members of the Indian Home Rule deputation who are visiting Ceylon on their way to England. They are going to England to present to the English people India's case for a more honoured place among the nations of the Empire." The paper blamed the railway authorities and the Inspector General of Police.

At the Criterion Theatre Tilak delivered a lecture on "Buddhism in Hinduism" under the presidentship of Sir P. Arunachalam. Admission was by tickets, and the proceeds of about one thousand rupees were donated to the Anderson Memorial Fund. Anderson was a popular Governor of Ceylon.

Introducing Tilak to the audience, Sir P. Arunachalam told them that Tilak was an educationist, a scholar, a journalist and a politician, and added, "It was a rare privilege to listen to a scholar of his distinction and to see in the flesh one whom all India reveres as among the noblest of her sons." "It was an acknowledged historical fact," said Tilak speaking on the subject, " that the Vedic religious worship and philosophy preceded Buddhism. Buddhism was not entirely a new religion. Much of it was based on the Vedic religion. In Buddhism the rituals were dispensed with. There was also this difference: while in Vedic religion one found the existence of the soul and of an absolute Almighty distinctly formulated, Buddhist religion dispensed with that maxim. It, however, did not deny the existence of the soul directly, but said 'what have we to do with all these?' The Buddhists confined themselves to the practical work of spiritual and moral development." Why Buddhism commended itself to Christians was, Tilak observed, the fact that it was a rational religion based on reason rather than on simple faith. "To look upon Hinduism and Buddhism, as two different religions," said Tilak, "was a mistake. Ethnologically, geographically and historically they had much in common. Buddhism therefore should be regarded as reformed Hinduism."[3]

B. C. Pal also delivered speeches on the 'Call of the Empire and Social Service'. The leaders were busy. They purchased some articles which they could not buy in Bombay for want of time. All their luggage was ready. Even Tilak had hurriedly dictated his Will to Vidwans and signed it. But all of a sudden news came that the steamer that was due on April 5, would not reach Colombo till the 23rd April. They decided therefore to go by the *Lancashire*. But the Colonial Secretary's office in Ceylon wrote on the 12th April to Tilak that the War Cabinet had finally decided "that your party should not be allowed to proceed to the United Kingdom," and asked the delegation to hand over their passports to his office for cancellation. Yet Tilak wired to the British Premier on April 16, "The Premier's stirring message to India and the Viceroy's hearty response are entirely in accord

3 The *Mahratta*, 3 August 1945.

with Indian sentiment! But the youths, whether Irish or Indian must be made to feel that they are not fighting to establish a principle abroad which is not applied to them."

On the same day Tilak wired to the Viceroy inquiring whether the ban applied to him and his legal advisers also who were proceeding to England for the libel action which he had brought against Sir Valentine Chirol. The Viceroy informed Tilak that there was no prospect of his case coming up for a hearing just then, and added that postponement, if necessary, could be granted. Montagu has thrown light on this episode and made it clear that it was the British Government and not the Viceroy that was responsible for the cancellation of the passports. "The fact was that the Home Department, without reference to the Viceroy, sent home a telegram containing a black picture of Tilak's antecedents and probable activities." The Home Government were nervous and they cancelled the passport given by duly authorised authority without consulting him. Montagu further observes: "I drafted for the Viceroy a telegram of protest which was ultimately sent, with a request for reconsideration. It has failed."[4] The Home authorities refused passports on the ground that such a proceeding would be improper when Britain was waging a great war and was confronted with a crisis which called for supreme concentration of national effort.[5]

The news of the cancellation of the passport spread everywhere in India. Gandhi wired to Tilak requesting him not to disobey Government orders! It may, however, be noted that Dr. Nair of Madras was allowed to go to England ostensibly on grounds of health.

II

So, KEENLY DISAPPOINTED, the deputation left Ceylon for India. On the return journey, Tilak delivered a speech at Madras on April 21, 1918, wherein he criticized the Viceroy's move for a War Conference which was due to be held at Delhi on April 26, 1918. The Home Rule delegation returned. During the return journey Tilak's clothes were stolen because the thief did not know that they were not more valuable, perhaps than his own! Tilak addressed meetings in Bombay and Poona where he expressed similar views on the proposed War Conference. Khaparde and Gandhi attended the War Conference convened by the Viceroy, but Gandhi told the Viceroy that unless the latter sought the co-operation of Tilak, Mrs. Besant, and the

4 Montagu, E. S., *An Indian Diary*, pp. 345-46.
5 O'Dwyer, Sir Michael, *India As I Know It*, p. 380.

Ali Brothers it was not possible for him to get co-operation of the people in his war efforts. Gandhi left the meeting, but he again attended it after an interview with the Viceroy. Khaparde tried to move the Home Rule resolution at the War Conference, but it was throttled, and it could not appear on the agenda.

Writing about this Conference, Montagu observes: "With regard to Tilak, if I were the Viceroy I would have had him at Delhi at all cost. He is at the moment probably the most powerful man in India, and he has it in his power, if he chooses, to help materially in war effort."[6] Montagu also wrote that from a speech of Tilak he concluded that Tilak would not accept the proposals. He would be the leader of the Opposition.

About this time Joseph Baptista wrote from London that in order to facilitate the mission of India in London, Tilak must be elected president of the Congress, a labour party must be started in India on the model of the British Labour Party, and financial aid must be given to the British Labour Party at the time of election.

In the first week of May 1918 the All-India Congress Committee met in Bombay. Tilak and Gandhi attended it. The Committee passed a resolution expressing their disappointment at the Viceroy's policy of dropping out the names of Tilak, Mrs. Besant and the Ali Brothers from the panel of the Conference. In Bombay at a party held to welcome back the delegates from the Delhi Conference, Tilak criticized the Viceroy for disallowing Khaparde's resolution on Self-Determination. He said that the Indians would fight for their motherland and not in order that the bureaucracy might enjoy power in India permanently. On June 10, 1918, the Government of Bombay also convened a War Conference at the Town Hall in Bombay. Among the invitees were Tilak, Gandhi, Jinnah and Kelkar. Tilak had informed the Secretary of the Governor that he was going to speak at the Conference.

On the previous night, Gandhi and Tilak had a discussion. During the course of the discussion Gandhi said that Tilak's methods were devilish.[7] Tilak replied that if Gandhi had undergone the tribulations and trials he had, the latter would have been more devilish than he was. He added that Gandhi would go ahead of him after undergoing more trials![8] While saying

6 Montagu, E. S., *An Indian Diary*, p. S81.

7 *Reminiscences and Anecdotes about Lokamanya Tilak*, Vol. I, p. 413.

8 Ibid.

goodbye to Gandhi on the staircase, Tilak patted him on the back. It was quite a familiar talk. Gandhi was to make a speech at the Conference pledging unconditional support to Government, but at the instance of Tilak he changed his mind. He wrote to the Governor's Secretary that as men like Tilak were not included on the Manpower Committee, there would not be a truly national response, and so he expressed his unwillingness to make a speech at the Conference.

The Conference began under the chairmanship of H.E. Lord Willingdon, the Governor of Bombay, on June 10, at the Town Hall, Bombay. Expressing loyalty to the Government, Tilak said in his speech that Indians would lay down their lives for defending India, but defence and Swaraj were interlinked. Lord Willingdon interrupted him. Tilak returned to his seat. Kelkar tried to speak, but he, too, was gagged. So Tilak, Kelkar, B. G. Horniman, Jamnadas Dwarkadas, and S. R. Bomanji silently walked out. Jinnah did not vote when resolution No. 2 was put to vote. As a result of this walk-out the Chief Secretary of the Bombay Government was thinking of interning Tilak in Burma, Horniman at Aden and Jamnadas Dwarkadas at Larkhana and opined that Kelkar need not be interned.[9] Jinnah later on avenged the insult when he routed a proposal for raising a public memorial to Lord Willingdon for which the latter never forgave him.

Soon after the War Conference, Tilak told Gandhi at a meeting in Bombay on June 16, 1918, that Government was not sincere about their military policy. If they were sincere and granted commissions to Indians, he would recruit five thousand youths; if he failed to do so he would pay Government fifty thousand rupees. He sent a currency note worth the amount to Gandhi. Such was the leader in Tilak!

Yet Gandhi who, two years later switched on to the role of an apostle of non-violence, was now striving vigorously to make India offer all her able-bodied sons as a sacrifice to the Empire. His view was that not to help the Empire was to commit national suicide! On June 23, 1918, he issued from Nadiad his famous appeal to the people of Kaira in particular and of Gujarat in general, "If we want to learn the use of arms with the greatest possible despatch, it is our duty to enlist ourselves in the army. There can be no friendship between the brave and the effeminate. We are regarded as a cowardly people. If we want to become free from that reproach, we should learn the use of arms. The easiest and strongest way therefore to

---

9 *Source Material for A History of the Freedom Movement in India*, Vol. II, p. 701.

win Swaraj," he declared, "is to participate in the defence of the Empire. If the Empire perished, with it perish our cherished aspirations. Some say that if we do not secure (political) rights just now, we would be cheated afterwards. The power acquired in defending the Empire will be the power that can secure these rights."[10] The co-operation Gandhiji offered was unconditional; the co-operation Tilak offered was responsive!

On June 22, 1918, Tilak declared again at a meeting in Poona that if the Indians were to remain slaves in India, it mattered little whether they joined the army or not. So Government served him with a notice on July 31, prohibiting him from making a speech in any district without the permission of the District Magistrate; and in Bombay not without the permission of the Police Commissioner. This gagging of Tilak adversely affected the recruiting in Maharashtra, and Gandhi also felt hampered in his recruiting work in Gujarat.

About this time, copies of the Montagu-Chelmsford Report were circulated by Government to newspapers for criticism. Tilak received a copy on July 7. He went through it till the evening, and the next day he published an article in the *Kesari* under the caption "A Sunless Morning". The idea of the heading struck him from the expression 'Hamlet without the Prince of Denmark'. Because Tilak described the scheme as quite useless and unacceptable, Chirol said that in vain Mr. Montagu allowed himself to be garlanded by Tilak. Tilak said they were Montagu-Curtis Reforms and not Montagu-Chelmsford Reforms. Mrs. Besant declared that the scheme was unworthy to be offered by England or to be accepted by India. Sir Subramania Iyer advised his countrymen not to touch the narcotic that was offered to them.

In the meanwhile the Sedition Committee, which was appointed by Government in December 1917, to investigate and report on the nature and extent of the criminal conspiracies connected with the revolutionary movement in India and to advise as to legislation to enable Government to deal effectively with them, worked under its President, Mr. Justice Rowlatt, in camera at Lahore and Calcutta, and presented its report to Government in April 1918. This Report was published in July. It displayed Tilak to the British public as the chief leader of the Chitpavan press and conspiracy. It observed that Tilak nourished the Brahmin youths on his inflammatory writings and incited them to strike a blow for independence

10 Athalye, D. V., *The Life of Mahatma Gandhi*, p. 162.

and end the alien rule by violence, disregarding the limitations of the Penal Code. Every seditious act, every political murder was attributed to Tilak's revolutionary writings.

A special Congress session was held on August 29, near Marine Lines, Bombay, to consider the Montagu-Chelmsford Reforms. The Moderates parted company, changed their Party name to Liberals and started the Liberal Party to work out Reforms. Mrs. Besant, Tilak and Pandit Malaviya tried to dissuade the Moderates from separating from the Congress, but to no purpose! Tilak attended the Congress session. V. J. Patel was Chairman of the Reception Committee. At the Subjects Committee meeting, Tilak chastised a young flamboyant politician roundly. When he called him a child in politics, the young man complained; and President Husan Imam said that it was an honour for anybody to be styled by Tilak as a child in politics.

In the open session Tilak, speaking on the main resolution on the Reforms, said with a bang on the table that the enemies of the Congress who had predicted that by the end of September the Congress would be nowhere were thoroughly disappointed. It would be absurd to tell the British people that they had rejected the scheme. The Montagu-Chelmsford Report was a beautiful, very skilful and statesmanlike document. "We asked for eight annas of Self-Government," he observed, "the Report gives us one anna of Responsible Government and says that it is better than the eight annas of Self-Government." Take half a loaf than have no loaf at all, was Tilak's motto in politics. The resolution on the Reforms proposals declared that the Reforms were disappointing and unsatisfactory and suggested some modifications. The Congress asserted its fitness for Swaraj and denounced the Rowlatt Committee Report and its recommendations.

After the Congress session was over, Motilal Ghose, B. C. Pal and C. R. Das went to Poona. The Government order prohibiting Tilak from making public speeches continued. Still Tilak sat on the platform at the time of the meetings which were addressed by the great sons of Bengal.

At this time Vithalbhai Patel, a front-rank leader of the Congress, gave notice of his intention of introducing in the Central Legislative Council his Hindu Marriage (Validity) Bill which sought to make inter-caste marriages valid among the Hindus. Although Patel was associated with the Tilak group of politicians in the political struggle, he differed from them radically on social views. Long before, he had declared that he was no believer in the caste system of Hindu society, and it was his "firm conviction that as long as Hindus will remain a caste-ridden people there is very little prospect of their rising in the present-day civilization and of their occupying an exalted position amongst the nations of the world." The Bill was his first attempt in the direction of the annihilation of the caste system. The Bill had just been published and was being discussed by the newspapers and by leaders at public meetings all over India. It provoked the whole ranks of social conservatives, orthodox and reactionaries.

Srinivasa Sastri favoured the Bill; Sir Tej Bahadur Sapru upheld it. As was their wont, Pandit Malaviya and other semi-orthodox leaders came forward to oppose it. Tilak, who had so far opposed all the social reforms, gave vent to his opposition to the Bill through an editorial of *Kesari* emphasising that the issue of such a marriage should not be allowed to inherit property backward lineally or collaterally through the father. Later, Tilak justified his opposition to the Bill by saying that he did it on the ground of the economic law of succession. The supporters of the Bill said that Government should remain neutral, and the elected members should decide it. A few days later the *Kesari* voiced its master's views that the Bill aimed at striking at the root of Hinduism and especially at the root of the Brahmin caste, and therefore appealed to Government to use its official 'votes to throw the Bill out'. Lajpat Rai, then in America, wrote that it was with a sense of shame and humiliation that he had read of the opposition to Patel's Hindu Marriages Bill. He further said that the opponents of the Bill, who urged the rejection of the Bill in the name and interest of Hindu Dharma, were poor champions of Hinduism. "Political democracy," Lajpat Rai concluded, "is a myth unless it is based on social and economic justice." The Bill, however, was deferred till the reformed Councils came into existence. And it was lost in the uproar of Non-Violent Non-Co-operation Movement.

III

THE ROWLATT COMMITTEE Report was given wide publicity in England and India and then Tilak was granted a passport to go to London on the express condition that he and his lawyers accompanying him would not do any kind of political work or make speeches in England. Tilak came to Bombay on the morning of 20th September. On September 23, the National Union gave a dinner at Sardar Griha in his honour. With his mouth gagged, Tilak left Bombay on September 24, for London by *s.s. Japan* accompanied by R. P. Karandikar, Wasukaka Joshi, and Ganpatrao Namjoshi his attendant.

Besant and other Home rulers were present at the Docks to give him a farewell.

When Tilak started for London, influenza was raging in India and in Europe. Besides, German submarines were playing havoc in the seas. Naturally anxiety was felt by people for Tilak's health and safety. At first Tilak did not use his trousers and coat and boots on board the ship but stuck to his native dress. He passed nights lying in bed but absorbed in thoughts. Tilak often lay dangling his toe from the bed as was his wont since his youth! In the morning he had a cup of tea with one or two biscuits. At ten o'clock meal followed. Govindji Vasanji of Bombay had given him some victuals. He would take pickles, puri, vegetables, milk, custard. Food was cooked by Namjoshi, his attendant. Sometimes a European passenger would come for a chat with Tilak.

At Aden, the Indian passengers were not allowed to get down. Here Tilak received a wire informing him that the Congress had elected him President of the Delhi session which was to be held in December 1918. He thanked the Reception Committee, but declined the honour. Among Tilak's papers there were some regarding the case of the Savarkar brothers. Tilak said sadly to himself that those two men, who strove for the welfare of the country, were suffering unimaginable hardships. Instead of being subjected to such unbearable sufferings they would have regarded it a blessing had they been shot, he added.

Tilak was still wearing a dhoti. The passengers looked at him with an inquisitive eye, and the chief engineer asked Namjoshi whether Tilak had suits or not. Namjoshi replied that his master had many. Tilak now began to put on trousers and boots for some time every day. He did not touch a hat. Neckties he did not use. On his return from Mandalay in 1914, he one day entered the room of his eldest son and when he found a hat there, he threw it out of the window! He now wore boots, trousers and a long woollen coat. He kept his Poona-turban on! He abandoned the big scarf. He was of the opinion that he should not waste his time wearing a dress that would excite the curiosity of men in England and waste much of his time in excitement and novelty.

At Port Said, the steamer halted for three days. There was a signal for an emergency rehearsal. The passengers were surprised to see that Tilak jumped into the life-boat, took it away and brought it back pulling the oars with the energy of a youth. As the steamer approached the war zone, the thundering of guns were sometimes heard. There were about twenty steamers and the *s.s. Japan* was in the centre befitting the dignity of the Chief of India! Surrounded by submarines and warships and aeroplanes hovering over it, the convoy started! Tilak reached London safely on October 30, 1918. Baptista had made all arrangements at 10, Howley Place, Maida Vale, a house rented for him. When they reached the house, Baptista embraced him like a younger brother!

A man of simple habits, Tilak did not find it difficult to adapt himself to the English environment without offending the English or losing his self-respect. Maida Vale, the place of his residence, was in the west of London. There, an Irish family named McNalty were engaged to look after him. That Irish family consisted of three members, the husband, wife and their daughter Sheila. The lady learnt how to prepare and cook puris of satu on which Tilak lived on account of diabetes. Tilak took his meals at table, sometimes with sodawater or ginger! The next day of his arrival, Tilak fell from his bed and Baptista said that it was a sign of his infancy in England!

Tilak knew English etiquette from his interviews with and visits to Europeans in India. When he was invited to dinner such occasions were very few—he ate only fruit and did most of the talking. Sometimes he shaved himself without waiting for a barber. As soon as he returned to his lodging, he threw off his trousers, boots and coat! He had minutely studied the map of London from a guide. Yet Tilak's movements caused anxiety to his colleagues. His failing eyes were strained for want of spectacles, which he did not use to the end of his life; his weak legs and the heavy traffic, sometimes caused his attendant anxiety. When he crossed the road, he sometimes stopped the cars himself and crossed the road! On seeing him do so, Baptista would say to him, "You are a nuisance to the Indian Police and here too you are harassing the British Police!" When someone said that he would meet with an accident if he was not more careful, Tilak replied that he was not born to die in a motor-car accident in the street!

When Tilak found time he paid visits to George Lansbury, the Labour leader, and to old Hyndman, the Socialist leader. Another attraction for him was Thomas, the librarian of the India Office. He saw England that came into his view whenever he moved out for his interviews or on other business. He must be one of the rare visitors who lived in England for a little over a year and yet saw the fewest parts of England! He employed a lady to copy down some extracts from the ancient Syrian and Chaldean literature. Thomas took him to a professor who was an authority on the Syrian language. The poverty of the learned man was as great as his learning! During the discussion, the tea became cold and the professor's mother-in-law had to remind both the scholars of the tea! Whenever he saw Indian youths with English wives, Tilak felt very sorry for them. He said if youth fell victims to passion the nation's cause would suffer for want of workers. Whenever he saw well-to-do Indians in England he asked them to serve the cause of the nation which needed their help.

Socialist leaders visited him. There was no interference now from the secret police as they performed their work intelligently. But Tilak said to his attendant that he always liked to have a talk with the secret police because from his talks with them he read the mind of the Government. He told his attendants that from one of the C.I.D. men he had come to know that his conversation with Savarkar at Nasik was on the Government's record!

Within a fortnight of Tilak's arrival in London, the British people, after months of rabble and ruins, desolation and despair, gave themselves up to the rejoicings of Peace Day. The practical politician in Tilak wrote to the British Prime Minister, Mr. Lloyd George, requesting him to convey his loyal homage and joyful greetings to their Majesties. He requested the Indian Government and the British Government through his solicitors not to publish, till the decision of the Chirol case, the Rowlatt Report in England some of the passages in which were damaging to his reputation. He got the restrictions on his political work removed. Baptista had started the Home Rule for India League with George Lansbury as its President and other Labour leaders as its office-bearers. Just then elections were to be held in Britain. On the eve of the elections, Tilak flooded the British electorate with important pamphlets on India. The self-determination pamphlet was full of cartoons. Written in a moderate tone, it visualized a federation of nation states to form the United States of India with Provincial Governments and a Central Government, responsible and democratic. This pamphlet had captured the imagination of some British worthies. Hyndman, the father of the British Labour movement, supported India's right to self-determination.

On inquiry Tilak learnt that the London Congress Committee was not in harmony with the aspirations of the Congress; its spokesmen like Polak and its mouthpiece *India* were opposed to the views of the Indian National Congress. It did not publish any of the resolutions of the Indian National Congress. He decided to change its policy. Tilak contributed to the Labour Party Funds a sum of Rs. 15,000 on condition that the Labour leaders would lend their support to the Indian cause, but he was disappointed as there was a Tory landslide in the general election. The Delhi Congress, which met in December 1918, included Tilak's name along with Gandhi's in the Congress delegation to the Peace Conference. Mrs. Besant was defeated, and she felt that her defeat over her suggestions that Provincial autonomy should be put in operation after 5 years, was due to the non-co-operation of Tilak's men. Pandit Malaviya, it is important to note, the President of the Congress in place of and in the absence of Tilak, did not make any reference to Tilak in his presidential address!

Tilak was probing the chances of his success in the Chirol case. The solicitors and the lawyer Sir John Simon were not very hopeful. He was told that none would like the utterances against the British Government which Tilak had made twenty years before. There was hardly any chance of success. So Tilak now fully realized that his original object in winning a decision of an English Court to stop the circulation of the libel all over the Empire would not be gained. Yet he insisted that the proceedings must go on. Sir John Simon, it is said, was one day even thinking of returning the brief. On the defence side was England's formidable lawyer Sir Edward Carson who had annihilated men like Oscar Wilde! Carson was an Irish Home Ruler, and Sir John was a leader of liberal political view and a legal celebrity of his day.

The Indian Government had deputed A. Montgomery, as a special officer to assist Chirol in preparing the defence, for the Government of India also feared that if Tilak succeeded in the case, it would have to face a similar action. It is interesting to note that this special officer appointed to ascertain the facts and evidence from the point of view of the defence, had opined objectively that the prospects of success of the defendant were not fair, and that success depended upon how the court viewed the case.

IV

THE HEARING OF the Chirol case commenced on January 29, 1919, before Mr. Justice Darling and a special jury. Tilak had to spend £400 every day. The libels complained of were six in number. That Tilak had started cow-protection societies to insult and provoke the Muslims; that he started the gymnastic societies with the Natu brothers in order to turn the British out of India; that Tilak used the newspapers for the purpose of blackmailing unwilling subscribers with the lash, and his gymnastic societies sometimes resolved themselves into juvenile bands of dacoits to swell the coffers of

"Swaraj", that he was the real author of the murders of Rand and Jackson and that the proceedings in the Tai Maharaj Case showed that he was not even a man of common honesty.

Sir John Simon's address to the court was a long affair lasting several hours. He explained that Tilak was not concerned with the allegations made in the six libels. At the end of it, Sir John Simon said: "I will call Mr. Tilak into the witness box. You will hear him, I have no doubt, under the cross-examination of my friend, Sir Edward Carson, and no man can possibly have to undergo an experience more severe." Then Mr. Spencer made the examination-in-chief of Tilak.

The following are some of the important extracts from the examination-in-chief and cross-examination of Tilak :

MR. SPENCER : Did you belong to any cow-protection Society ?

TILAK : No. I did not. I am not a member, nor a supporter of them, and I have never subscribed to them.

MR. SPENCER : Have you ever advocated the immediate and, if necessary, violent emancipation of India?

TILAK : No, not emancipation. If it means acquisition of greater rights I do, but if emancipation means complete freedom from British Rule I do not.

MR. SPENCER : Have you ever advocated the use of violent means?

TILAK : Never.

MR. SPENCER : Had you ever heard of Chapekar at all before this murder?

TILAK : No.

During the examination-in-chief of Tilak, Sir John Simon referred to the date of the killing of Afzulkhan and said it was about the battle of Boyne and whispered, "not the second battle of the Boyne" in which constituency Carson had been defeated! "Which was not as recent" Carson retorted, "as the Battle of Walthamstow" in which constituency Simon had suffered defeat!

SIR EDWARD : The question is, can you point to me anything in Sir Valentine Chirol's book which is more severe upon you as a criticism than what the learned judge says in that passage that I have just now read ?

TILAK : Yes, I can.

SIR EDWARD : What is it ?

TILAK : It is the actual connection with the fact. I do not complain of opinion; any man may have any opinion of my conduct. I complain of being connected with these murders by a particular series of facts as stated in Chirol's book.

SIR EDWARD : What science you used to teach ?

TILAK : That which is useful for pupils—physics, mechanics, astronomy.

SIR EDWARD : Chemistry ?

TILAK : No.

SIR EDWARD : Picric acid ?

TILAK : I am not a proficient man. It was never a study I taught.

SIR EDWARD : You know what picric acid is used for ?

TILAK : Yes, from papers.

SIR EDWARD : Havc you not said so in your own paper ?

TILAK : Yes.

SIR EDWARD : If a man thinks the law is not good, he must break it ?

TILAK : If the law is broken you have to withstand the punishment. That is what we call passive resistance.

Then Carson asked Tilak a number of searching questions about Veer Savarkar's book Mazzini which was dedicated to "Lokamanya Tilak and Lokamanya S. M. Paranjpe "and asked him whether the Savarkars were dangerous people. Tilak replied that they were not dangerous but hot-headed at that time; but he had advised them to work on constitutional lines.

SIR EDWARD : Were you trying to create disaffection ?

TILAK : Certainly not.

SIR EDWARD : That you would not like to do ?

TILAK : No. I have never done it and I do not like to do it.

SIR EDWARD : You have been convicted twice of it ?

TILAK : Yes, a man can be convicted, but it does not mean that he is guilty.

SIR EDWARD : But rulers who exercise unrestricted power must always remember that there is also a limit to the patience of humanity—was that the British Government you were referring to there ?

TILAK : It is for all despotic rulers.

Then a sparring match between Carson and Tilak followed.

SIR EDWARD : Was the partition of Bengal the cause of all this bomb throwing?

TILAK : Yes, I think so.

SIR EDWARD : Setting up the partition of Bengal was the cause of bombing ?

TILAK : Exactly as in the case of Ireland and Ulster.

SIR EDWARD : Never mind Ulster. Ulster will take care of itself. You will not gain anything by trying to introduce personal matters into the case.

TILAK : I am not introducing personal matters into the case. You will find Ireland quoted in the articles.

Carson further asked Tilak whether the revolutionaries who were hanged were all Chitpavan Brahmins.

SIR EDWARD : Were you not the leader of the Chitpavan Brahmins?

TILAK : I am a Chitpavan Brahmin. I cannot denounce my own caste.

SIR EDWARD : Were you not the leader of them ?

TILAK : I am the leader of the whole people, not the Chitpavan Brahmins. There is nothing in that.

SIR EDWARD : At Nasik, how many men were transported for life for being engaged in the conspiracy of murdering this man Jackson ?

TILAK : I do not know how many. I would look into the papers and see.

SIR EDWARD : Did you never inquire ?

TILAK : No, I do not believe it is correct. It is a false theory and the outcome of a diseased brain.

SIR EDWARD : That is what the judge said about you.

TILAK : And he judged wrong. I had no opportunity to reply.

SIR EDWARD : England has come into existence to parade as political power before the people of other nations who are its equal in order to make them suffer the miseries of slavery. Is that your view ?

TILAK : If you keep a Dependency always in a state of dependency, it means that.

SIR EDWARD : Is that your view ?

TILAK : Yes. It means that. That is my answer, and that is my view.

SIR EDWARD : Is that your opinion that 'great men are above the common principle of morality' ?

TILAK : Yes, a superhuman man is not bound by it.

SIR EDWARD : What do you mean by a superman ?

TILAK : A great man.

MR. JUSTICE DARLING : Do you believe if you were to eat English sugar you would get the plague ?

TILAK : It may be plague or anything.

MR. JUSTICE DARLING : Do you think that if you eat English sugar you might lose this action ?

TILAK : That is carrying it too far.

SIR EDWARD : English law is a foreign thing to you ?

TILAK : It is not said here that an English law is a foreign thing.

MR. JUSTICE DARLING : And Sir John Simon is not a swadeshi lawyer either?

TILAK : We are speaking of articles in ordinary use.

Then another passage-at-arms took place.

SIR EDWARD : You have told me already. Who is V. M. Bhat ?

TILAK : One of the Nasik men belonging to the *Kesari*.

SIR EDWARD	:	Was he convicted also of waging war against the King?
TILAK	:	Afterwards.
SIR EDWARD	:	Is he in your employment still ?
TILAK	:	I do not know yet, but I think he is. I am here now.
SIR EDWARD	:	Do not be ashamed of it!
TILAK	:	I am not ashamed of anything. When members convicted sit in Parliament, why should I be ashamed of him?

Carson then quoted one extract after another:

SIR EDWARD	:	Is it seditious ?
TILAK	:	No, it is legitimate criticism.
SIR EDWARD	:	Well what language do you really consider seditious?
TILAK	:	Quotations from your orations on the Irish Home Rule.

Sir Edward Carson was completely floored. It was a battle of giants!

lan Colvin, biographer of Carson, describing the fight between Tilak and Carson observes that as Carson traced the connections between Tilak's writings and the murders of Englishmen which followed them, an almost terrifying change was observed to come over the witness (Tilak). He leaned forward, his face convulsed, his fingers clutching the frame of the witness box. Carson, as he afterwards said, had an uncomfortable feeling that Tilak was about to spring at his throat. But, adds lan Colvin, nothing happened.[11] lan Colvin has described this scene with a view to making Carson stand out in bold relief against Tilak. Tilak must have felt keenly the helplessness of the situation in which circumstances had put him.

Sir Valentine Chirol was put in the witness box. Carson's colleague conducted his examination-in-chief. But he also had a gruelling experience at the hands of Simon!

Lord Lamington, the former Governor of Bombay, Sir Richard Lamb, the former Collector of Poona, and Sir Edward Giles, ex-Director of Instruction, were examined and cross-examined.

11 Colvin, lan, *The Life of Lord Carson*, pp. 370-71.

Then Sir Edward Carson opened his defence speech with his forensic skill saying that Tilak was a man who had been twice convicted of sedition. If the defendant was right in saying that these were the results of the plaintiff's teachings, what became of the rest of the charges? The remaining libels were trifles, he observed.

Concluding his address, Carson said, "If he deserves a verdict at your hands give it to him, if it is right, if you think he deserves it. But I am bound to put to you the importance of this case from the public point of view. You are really asked, and that is the object of his coming here, to set him up in India as a man who can continue the course of action which he adopted in his press, and that he has a right, notwithstanding these decisions of the judges out there in his cases, to do it with impunity. I need hardly remind you of the far-reaching effects of such a verdict as that on the peace of the Government of India and on the difficulties of the white officials out there who do their duty so well to the country."

Sir John Simon, making a brilliant reply, said that the question before the jury was whether Sir Valentine's book contained matter defamatory to the plaintiff. The question was not whether he had published seditious articles, whether his criticism of Government was violent, whether he had friendships with this or that person. He appealed to them to be fair and valiant. He pointed out to the jury how Carson, the burden of whose song in defence was that Tilak's inflammatory writings led to the murder of Rand, avoided referring to the murder of Jackson because Tilak was then at Mandalay. Summing up the case, Mr. Justice Darling also showed his leanings to the defendants. He declared that he had not tried a more serious case having regard to its possible public consequences. The burden of his summing up was that 'that was sort of a man who came to the jury for damages!' and hinted that Tilak's character was not above reproach. He further pointed to the jury how Sir John Simon was pressed to say that in many respects the character of the plaintiff was far from being above reproach.

Thus Sir Edward Carson and Justice Darling worked on the fears of the jury, and after a hearing lasting eleven days, on February 21, the jury returned a verdict for the defendant. When the jury gave the verdict, Tilak came down the steps into the big hall of the Court room, supported by two of his colleagues, and exclaimed: "This sort of justice I could have obtained in India." He immediately drove to his residence with Baptista, in sad silence. "Till midnight," writes Baptista, "we sat silent and then went to bed. The next morning he was in my room as if nothing had happened."

Tilak had to spend £400 every day as fees and the lawyers on some plea or other insisted on being paid every day. The fees for studying the brief amounted to £3,000! Tilak had chosen the British Court because he thought that the British Court would not do him an injustice at least while the War was on. When the War had come to an end, Tilak told Karandikar, his legal adviser, that there was then little hope for success in the case! People expressed different opinions on the case. Tilak's opponents styled it an inconceivable folly on the part of Tilak. Some friends called it a blunder. Shortly afterwards Sir Valentine Chirol said to a representative of the *Observer*: "I have also the satisfaction of being able to look upon a long professional career in which my work has, I think, never challenged any serious hostility except from two distinguished individuals, one of them this Mr. Tilak, and the other the German Emperor. The juxtaposition of these two names is not, perhaps, so far-fetched as it may sound."[12]

After the decision in the Chirol case all Tory papers and Tory leaders like Sydenham opened a campaign of vilification against Tilak, and however Tilak's admirers like Edgar Wallace tried to counteract it, the edge of its violence did not become blunt!

Two days after the decision of the Court, Tilak wrote to his nephew from London, "We have lost our case against Chirol. There was as you know no evidence to prove the charges. But the judge made a monstrous charge to the jury, ignoring the difference between political and private character as suggested in Carson's arguments." Stating that the liability had amounted to £14,000, he cheered up his nephew saying that he would meet the situation as he had been doing hitherto, bravely and calmly.

"The jury and the judge," he continued, "looked upon it as a Government case and Mr. Montgomery was watching the case in Court openly on behalf of Government; in other words he was assisting Chirol. All went on the theory that if Tilak succeeded, it would be a disaster for Government. The London *Times* actually says so."[13]

In a letter written to D. V. Gokhale, his assistant editor, he said there were very few chances of success in appeal. The times had changed and under the existing circumstances there was hardly any chance of getting a

12 The *Times of India*, 30 March 1919.

13 *Reminiscences and Anecdotes about Lokamanya Tilak*, Vol. III, pp. 228-29.

judge or jury to consider the question independently of politics. He said he was not dejected. He was too old a hand to be upset even if the heavens were to fall down. "I would rather utilize the fall of the heavens for my purpose than be dismayed thereby," he averred with a growl.

When this shocking news reached Tilak's colleagues and followers, they were moved by the tragedy their leader was plunged into. They started collecting a fund to defray the expenses of the case and in spite of Tilak's appeals to the contrary they did it successfully; and by August 1919 the collection amounted to two and a half lacs of rupees. At one of the meetings held in Bombay on May 30, 1919, to support the collection of the fund, Gandhi supported it saying that although his methods differed from those of Tilak he had high regard for his sacrifice and learning. He wished Tilak were a satyagrahi! Prof. S. M. Paranjpe replied that because Tilak was a satyagrahi he fought out his case to the bitter end!

V

TILAK SENT BACK Baptista and Karandikar to India. He then turned his mind to political work. He was invited to a tea-party given by the British Indian Society. A comic incident happened on that occasion. Tilak was introduced to Lord Sydenham, Ex-Governor of Bombay, who had been opposing the Indian Reforms. Lady Sydenham looked furious because her husband talked to Tilak who was once a convict!

Tilak brought sufficient pressure to bear upon the paper *India*, got his short notes and articles published as advertisement in the British newspapers. Only George Lansbury's weekly *Herald* published them free. British Politicians thought that Tilak was a great bellicose demagogue, with stilettos in hands. But they found a fragile philosopher appealing to reason and history! They were quite impressed with his patience and forbearance, his vast knowledge, his simple life. Tilak now began to address meetings at different places and in order to be able to cope with those activities he called his lieutenant and colleague Kelkar to London. At one such meeting the labour leaders Lansbury, Rutherford, and Colonel Wedgwood, supported his stand. At Cambridge Tilak asked the Indian students to prepare themselves for national service and not to accept jobs under foreign rulers. Subhas Bose was one of the students.[14]

14 Das Gupta, Dr. Hemendranath, *Subhas Bose*, p. 153.

In the meanwhile Gandhi was preparing the country for a non-violent struggle against the Government of India over the Rowlatt Act. Government had, on publication of the Rowlatt Report, introduced two Bills called the Rowlatt Bills in the Central Legislative Council embodying the Rowlatt Committee's recommendations. These Rowlatt Bills were passed by the Central Legislative Council on the 18th March 1919 despite Indian public opinion, and therefore Gandhi decided to inaugurate satyagraha with a fast! A new idea! On April 6, 1919, country-wide demonstrations were held, and Gandhi began a new chapter in the history of India. Serious disturbances took place at Viramgam, Nadiad and Ahmedabad; on April 15, 1919, Martial Law was proclaimed at Lahore and Amritsar; and General Dyer massacred innocent Indians in the Jallianwalla Bagh at Amritsar. Government passed orders on Gandhi, prohibiting his entry into the Punjab and Delhi. Tilak held a meeting in London to protest against the Rowlatt Act, and a few days later said in reply to a letter from Dr. D. D. Sathye, a leader in Bombay, that he himself had already written that "we should fully support Mr. Gandhi."

On April 28 Tilak's left ankle was sprained, but it became all right after some days! His eye-sight and hearing were fast failing. He had prepared a representation to be submitted to the Peace Conference on behalf of India, but the India Office returned it to him. He, therefore, applied for permission to go to Paris. On being refused a passport to go to Paris for the Peace Conference, Tilak sent a memorial, which was drafted by Baptista, to M. Clemenceau, Premier of France and President of the Peace Conference, claiming that[15] "with her (India's) vast area, enormous resources, and prodigious population she may well aspire to be a leading power in Asia, if not in the world. She could therefore be a powerful steward of the League of Nations in the East for maintaining the peace of the world and the stability of the British Empire against all aggressors and disturbances of peace whether in Asia or elsewhere."

Tilak came to know that his letters had reached President Wilson and Mr. Clemenceau. Edgar Wallace, who had been to Paris, told him that they had received it! Tilak had also received a formal acknowledgment of his letter from the Secretary of President Wilson saying that the question of self-determination of India would be taken up in due course of time by the proper authorities. But that acknowledgment was kept a secret! As regards

---

15 *Great Men of India*, published by the Home Library Club of Times of India, p. 260.

the result of this memorial, he wrote to D. V. Gokhale that the Peace Conference might not or could not openly and officially take up the Indian question but even a suggestion from the Conference—a hint—would be of great value. Tilak, however, had lost hope about it. He made a very impressive speech at a meeting at the famous Caxton Hall. His left leg was paining, and he could not move; but the enthusiasm of the audience was so great that he chose to strain his leg rather than disappoint the audience and saved the organisers of the meeting from an embarrassment. At meeting after meeting he denounced the Rowlatt Act, and the labour leaders at their Hyde Park rally on May Day called for the annulment or abrogation of the Rowlatt Act. Kelkar and Vithalbhai Patel reached London in the last week of May 1919, and the Congress deputation also arrived there. They captured the paper *India* from Polak, and Kelkar was appointed joint editor with Miss Normanton.

Khaparde and Mrs. Besant and the Liberals' deputation also reached London. Tilak tried to establish a united front of all the parties on the basis of a common formula of demands. When Besant, who had expressed sharp disagreement with the Tilak group in India, came to London, Tilak went to receive her at the station although his colleagues felt he was compromising himself by doing so. Tilak told Satyamurti and others that he should subordinate his personal feelings to the country's welfare.[16] Tilak, therefore, tried his best to seek her cooperation. But she complained that Tilak was at the bottom of the insults heaped upon her by Khaparde. Tilak also visited Oxford, Cambridge, Birmingham, Bristol, and some places in Scotland, explaining the demands for immediate Self-Government put forth by the Congress and emphasizing the miserable condition under which Indian peasants and labourers had been perishing with disease, poverty, illiteracy and hardships. Thus he had prepared the spade-work for all future deputations in the same cause.

There were five deputations. The Congress deputation, the All-India Home Rule League deputation, the National Home Rule League deputation, the non-Brahmin deputation and the Liberals' deputation. The Joint Parliamentary Sub-Committee under the Chairmanship of Lord Selbourne interviewed Besant, Vithalbhai Patel and Tilak. Besant represented her League, Tilak his, and V. J. Patel and V. P. Madhav Rao, ex-Dewan of Mysore, the Congress. But at the time of Tilak's interview,

16 S. Satyamurti in *Reminiscences and Anecdotes about Lokamanya Tilak*, Vol. I, p. 486.

Lord Sydenham and other old and young reactionaries left the hall. Tilak was not examined. He only submitted his statement. Dr. P. J. Mehta, A. Rangaswami lyengar, Syed Hassan Imam, B. G. Horniman and Dr. Sathye were also members of the Congress deputation. The Independent Labour Party passed a resolution at their annual session in Glasgow, supporting self-determination for India.

The Montagu Bill came up before Parliament. Mrs. Besant, despite opposition from Patel and Tilak, supported the Bill. But Mehta and Patel could not get it modified as they wished. This led to an estrangement between Besant and the Congress group. Lajpat Rai and Hardikar were then putting the Indian view before the American public. Tilak sent money from London to Lajpat Rai for his propaganda through a theosophical friend of Besant.

At Calcutta, the All-India Congress Committee met in June 1919 and decided Amritsar as the venue of the next Congress. Tilak now decided to return to India, and he and his party-men left London on November 6, 1919, so that they might be able to attend the Amritsar session of the Congress. Tilak had purchased a second-hand machine for his Press. He had been elected by the Bombay Labour Unions to attend the Washington Labour Conference, but he could not go to America. Mentally very active on the platform, Tilak showed himself a man of realism while dealing with hard facts, and overcame obstacles with diplomacy. A strict vegetarian, he lived a frugal life. He kept himself in touch with affairs at home, at the Paris Peace Conference, in America, and in England.

Tilak was about thirteen months in England. He had created by his tongue and talents a favourable impression upon British men of learning and politicians who came in contact with him. He was mainly responsible for the support of the Labour Party in putting forward before the Joint Parliamentary Committee and the British Parliament the Congress point of view on Reforms. Yet at all public meetings he had scrupulously avoided advocating separation of India from the British Empire! He appealed for the self-governance of India within the Empire. Yet a British Cabinet Member said to a student from Ceylon: "There is only one Indian whom we cannot win over by any sort of influence or inducement and that is Mr. Tilak; all others, we can influence more or less."[17] Tilak had met George Bernard Shaw, and also Lord Shaw the President of the Privy Council, the

17 *Reminiscences and Anecdotes about Lokamanya Tilak*, Vol. Ill, p. 9.

latter acclaiming Tilak the great man of India. The London Secret Police report observes that "Tilak has the strongest hope of the deliverance of India by the Bolsheviks and was delighted with the Afghanistan imbroglio and Amritsar riots."[18]

On board the *s.s. Egypt* he had a talk with S. Satyamurti. He told him that he felt no necessity of performing any *Prayaschitta* since he had not gone to England for his own selfish purpose, but a few days later he changed his mind and did perform it in Poona. On the deck Tilak delivered a speech for the European passengers one of whom said, "What Indian politics has gained in Tilak, scholarship and research have lost." When Satyamurti asked his opinion on Reforms, Tilak quoted a verse of Bhartrihari: "Gods did not stop their struggle till they got nectar. Brave men do not give up the struggle till they attain what they want." When Tilak landed at Bombay on November 27, a vast crowd received him with loud acclamation at the Ballard Pier. They rejoiced at welcoming back their leader who had returned hale and hearty.

In the evening Tilak was presented with an address at a public meeting in the compound of Shantaram's Chawls under the presidentship of Baptista. Another address presented to him at this meeting was by the Home Rule Club, Dadar. Tilak advised the people to accept whatever was offered by the British Government and strive for further reforms. He said he was sorry that he was not there to participate in the satyagraha when Gandhi launched it against the Rowlatt Act.

18 *Source Material for a History of the Freedom Movement in India*, Vol. II, p. 195.

CHAPTER XXIII

Last Days

I

On his return to Poona, on December 1, 1919, Tilak was welcomed like a prince. The Poona Municipality made history by presenting an address to Tilak, a non-official, and to N. C. Kelkar also who was for some time its first elected President. On December 7 the citizens of Poona presented Tilak with an address. The Moderates of Poona and the non-Brahmin leaders wanted to oppose it, and so they declared that the address proposed was not on behalf of all the citizens. It was decided that the opponents should sit at the place reserved for them on the occasion and should have their say. But the big guns of the opposition did not turn up. Mr. Shivaram Janba Kamble, a young leader of the Depressed Classes in Poona, and Madhavrao Patwardhan, a black-capped youth, boldly voiced the opinion of the opponents. Kamble said that if Tilak was willing to have an inter-caste dinner he would not oppose the address. As a result of this muddle a bitter controversy raged between Tilak and R. P. Paranjpye when the latter complained of the invective which Tilak described as a gun of a longer range used in political warfare.

At a meeting held on November 29, 1919, behind the Elphinstone Mills, under the presidentship of Mavji Govindji, workers of Bombay presented an address to Tilak whom the Bombay Labour Unions had elected to represent India at the Washington Labour Conference. In his reply Tilak said that to work was a blessing. Comparing the labour class in England with that in India, he said that it was better to increase the happiness of the labourer than his wages and that a man's pay must be proportional to his expenses. He said the Government was draining wealth out of the country, reducing them all to labourers. He explained to them that he could not attend the Washington Labour Conference, because he would have been required to go as an assistant to Mr. N. M. Joshi of the Servants of India Society who attended that Labour Conference as the nominee of the Government. He said that the message of the labouring classes of England was that they should form Trade Unions, and the stronger they were, the sooner they would obtain their rights. Then he emphasized the point that it was the duty of the Government to provide every worker with work. He referred to the strikes in Ahmedabad and told them that Gandhi struck thrice and got what the workers wanted. He appealed to the workers to get rid of the bureaucrats, whom some called white Brahmins. He was proud, he went on, that he was a black Brahmin with a white heart and not a white one with a black heart. No one could be, he concluded, a true Brahmin, Kshatriya, Vaishya or Shudra whose heart was black.[1]

One point about the Labour Movement which Tilak visualized must be made clear. He said he did not wish to set labour against capital in India. "I would certainly organise labour, but I would do it, on the basis of social welfare." By that he meant providing them with employment insurance, hospitals, entertainment rooms, savings and co-operative credit societies.[2]

On December 17 Tilak reached Madras. There he was presented with public addresses under the presidentship of the editor of the *Hindu*, S. Kasturi Ranga Aiyangar, at Triplicane Beach. The address presented by the non-Brahmin Party was a special feature of the function. Replying to the addresses, Tilak said that the world was passing through a stage of reconstruction, a stage of unrest, a transition, the end of which was to be the establishment of freedom and democracy all over the world. He said there was a rumour in India that Tilak had grown a Moderate in the English climate. He added that he did not care whether he was called a Moderate or an Extremist so long as he stuck to the Congress scheme and did not in any way fall behind the Congress goal. He added that he was surprised to hear while in England about the Scottish Home Rule League. He told the British public that in those days of electric lifts they did not go up step by step to the second floor. He had declined to answer in England the question whether he accepted the Reforms or not. It was for the British Parliament to accept the Congress scheme.[3] It may be pointed out that Tilak sometimes called himself an animated Moderate. It is just like saying that a tiger is an animated cat!

1 *Source Material for A History of the Freedom Movement in India*, Vol. II, pp. 317-19.
2 *Reminiscences and Anecdotes about Lokamanya Tilak*, Vol. I, p. 81.
3 *All about Tilak*, pp. 595-610.

Tilak returned to Poona and then started in the last week of December 1919 by a special train for the Amritsar Congress. On the way to Amritsar they learnt of the Proclamation of H.M. the King Emperor. In consultation with Kelkar and Baptista he sent a telegram from Gangapur railway station addressed to the King Emperor through the Viceroy and Mr. Montagu. The telegram said: "Please convey to His Majesty grateful and loyal thanks of Indian Home Rule League and the people of India for Proclamation and amnesty and assure him responsive co-operation." The phrase 'responsive co-operation' was coined by Baptista. This telegram created a sort of consternation in the minds of Tilak's party-men like C. R. Das. They were displeased. Tilak, who had been a lifelong non-co-operator with the Government which called him its arch-enemy, was now considered to have become a Moderate! Tilak reached Amritsar, and as usual a big procession was taken out.

The Amritsar session of the Congress was the biggest one held upto that time. The President was Pandit Motilal Nehru. It was attended by thirty-six thousand people of whom six thousand were delegates and twelve hundred tenant-delegates. Pandit Motilal Nehru said that the Congress assembled in deep mourning, and, referring to the Jallianwala Bagh atrocities, he said that if the ordinary rights of human beings were denied to Indians, then all talk of reforms was a mockery. He referred to the withdrawal of the order which prohibited Tilak from entering the Punjab Province. The President added that all would join with him in offering a most cordial welcome to Tilak after his arduous labour in England for the cause. The main resolution proved to be a battle royal. C. R. Das moved a resolution which declared that the reforms were inadequate, unsatisfactory and disappointing.

The irony of the situation was that Gandhi, Malaviya, Sastri, Mrs. Besant and Motilal Nehru were for working the reforms and offered co-operation to Government. Das was for rejecting the scheme. He was an out and out non-co-operator. Gandhi was then an apostle of co-operation. Tilak wanted to work out the scheme with responsive co-operation; but was for declaring that the Reforms were disappointing and inadequate. Thus he was a responsive co-operator. Gandhi moved an amendment suggesting omission of the word 'disappointing' and adding to the resolution of Das a fourth paragraph. His amendment contained the phrases "Congress begs loyally to respond", and "'warmest' thanks to Montagu". This amendment was hotly discussed.

The party led by Mahatma Gandhi said that the Congress should not say that the Reforms were disappointing; for he feared that the people would not show interest in them. Tilak said that the people should know that they had to fight for further Reforms.

Speaking on the resolution, Gandhi said, "If Tilak Maharaj tells you that we are going to make use of the Reforms Act as he must, and as he has already told Mr. Montagu, as he has told the country that we are going to take the fullest advantage of the reforms, then I say, be true to yourself, be true to the country and tell the country that you are going to do it. But if you were to say, after having gone there, you will put obstruction, say that also. But on the question of propriety and obstruction, I say, Indian culture demands that we shall trust one who extends a hand of fellowship."[4] Gandhi added that they should co-operate by accepting the reforms and not say one thing when they meant another. This main resolution was discussed for three days. On the fourth day the delegates were leaving Amritsar. Some of the Maharashtrian delegates had even left for the station. When Tilak saw that no compromise was reached and voting was inevitable, he sent word to his men to come back. They all returned from the station. Then the leaders arrived at a compromise. The original resolution as proposed by Das with Gandhi's amendment shorn of the expressions "begs to loyally respond" and of the word "warmest" from thanks, was passed.

The Amritsar Congress witnessed the eclipse of Mrs. Besant and the emergence of the power and personality of Gandhi, who had by now developed into a challenging force! Yet Gandhi said that his participation in the Congress proceedings at Amritsar was not his real entry into Congress politics! The session was quite thrilling. Most of the Punjab leaders and the Ali Brothers had been released, and they all rushed straight to the session and were enthusiastically cheered.

The session over, Tilak addressed a Home Rule meeting under the presidentship of Dr. Kitchlew. Tilak told the audience that he had insisted on incorporating the words 'disappointing and inadequate' in the resolution, because when contentment and satisfaction prevailed progress came to an end! Tilak then returned to Poona.

The proceedings of the Amritsar Congress, which was dominated by Tilak, left Pandit Malaviya and Gandhi very unhappy. The first open clash with Tilak weighed heavy upon Gandhi's mind. Writing about this session

---

4 Tendulkar, D. G., *Mahatma*, Vol. I, p.

in his *Liberator* Swami Shraddhanand observed that these two leaders were then thinking of 'purging the Congress of its diplomatic and crooked policy'. Malaviya wanted Shraddhanand to go out of the Congress with himself and Gandhi and to work for the reform of the Congress.[5] It seems that Gandhi was arranging his forces against the formidable leadership of Tilak.

So immediately after the Amritsar Congress where Gandhi said that Tilak should not say one thing when he meant another, he joined issue with him in *Young India*: "For as party formation progresses, we suppose it would be considered quite the proper thing for party leaders to use others as tools so long as there are any to be used. Care will have therefore to be taken rather to purify our politics than for fear of being used as tools to hesitate to take the right course. Lokamanya Tilak represents a definite school of thought of which he makes no secret. He considers that everything is fair in politics. We have joined issue with him in that conception of political life. We consider that political life of the country will become thoroughly corrupt if we import Western tactics and methods."

Tilak's reply to this article of Gandhi appeared in *Young India* of 28th January 1920, and is given below:

"I am sorry to see that in your article on 'Reform Resolution' in the last issue you have represented me as holding that I considered everything fair in politics. I write this to you to say that my view is not correctly represented herein. Politics is a game of worldly people and not of Sadhus and instead of the maxim: 'One should conquer anger by opposing it with tranquillity, non-anger' as preached by Buddha, I prefer to rely on the maxim of Shri Krishna: 'My response to the devotees is in perfect harmony with the manner of their approach.' Both methods are equally honest and righteous, but the one is more suited to this world than the other. Any further explanation about the difference will be found in my *Gita-Rahasya*."

Gandhi's rejoinder to Tilak was as follows:

"With deference to the Lokamanya I venture to say that it betrays mental laziness to think that the world is not for Sadhus. The epitome of all religions is to promote Purushartha, and Purushartha is nothing but a desperate attempt to become a Sadhu, i.e. to become a gentleman in every sense of the term. Finally, when I wrote the sentence about everything

5 Swami Shraddhanand: *The Liberator*, 8 July 1926.

being fair in politics according to Lokamanya's creed I had in mind his oft-repeated quotation 'tit for tat'. To me it enunciates bad law. I shall not despair of the Lokamanya with all his acumen agreeably surprising India one day with a philosophical dissertation proving the falsity of the doctrine."[6]

It is crystal clear from the foregoing letters how Tilak writes with dignity and tranquillity, how Gandhi charges his formidable adversary with mental laziness and praises his acumen in the same breath. Although the bitterness is couched in moral clothing, yet the human heart of Gandhi, the great man, reveals its inside. He is damning his adversary with faint praise!

Gandhiji, however, did not come out successful in this controversy. Tilak said, "Politics is a game of the worldly people and not of sadhus." Gandhi put a wrong interpretation on Tilak's remarks when he said: "Sadhus have no place in this world! "Tilak suggested that sadhus ought not to pollute themselves by contact with the worldly game of politics. However high on the moral plane a man might be it would be impossible for him to achieve the desired goal in this matter-of-fact world without sacrificing at some stage his saintliness, but in so doing the object of the saintly man ought to be selfless. This is what Tilak meant. This was Tilak's guiding principle. It is history that the politician in Mahatma Gandhi himself could not be an exception to this.

II

TILAK WELCOMED BACK V. J. Patel, Dadasaheb Khaparde and Dr. Sathye, who returned to India, and on the 30th January 1920, at Shantaram's Chawls, Bombay, he presided over a meeting held to honour the Ali brothers. He was unwell, so he could not make a speech; but he said he was offering fine garlands to the Ali brothers with a fine heart. Tilak said the Ali brothers were the staunchest and the boldest adherents and advocates of Hindu-Muslim Unity. Although the people in Bombay, he concluded, had given them a rousing welcome on the previous day, they were again honouring them as there was pleasure in repeating pleasurable things.

Just then Poona was greatly agitated over the question of free and compulsory education for boys and girls. The Tilak Party favoured compulsion for boys only on the ground of shortage of funds and the Moderates and non-Brahmins held almost fifty meetings during the fortnight

6 *Young India,* 28 January 1920.

voicing their demand for compulsory education for both boys and girls. The Retrenchment Committee appointed by the Poona Municipality had shown how compulsion could be extended to both boys and girls without impairing the efficiency of education and without raising taxation. Every day since February 2, public meetings had been held under the guidance of Ramabai Ranade, widow of the late Mr. Justice Ranade, voicing the demand for extension of compulsory education to girls also.

Tilak came forward to support the view of those who wanted to exclude girls from compulsory education. Meeting after meeting was held, and on Sunday, 8th February 1920, an important meeting was held at which several amendments in favour of girls' education were moved. Principal Paranjpye, Prof. Kanitkar and some non-Brahmin leaders spoke urging compulsion for the education of girls also. Two ladies, who spoke at the meeting, were heckled and insulted. Tilak got up to support the views of his Party and to explain why girls should be excluded. The audience was so exasperated by the insults offered to the lady speakers that when Tilak got up to support the view that girls should be excluded from compulsory education, cries of 'shame' filled the whole place, and rotten eggs and bhajias were thrown at him. The meeting was dissolved, and Tilak had to be taken to his residence under police escort.[7] The lion-tamer was now attacked by rats!

During February, Tilak was busy with the reform of the Hindu Calendar. He presided over the Astronomical Conference at Sangli on February 16, 1920. In the third week of February 1920, he completed the work of reforming the Hindu Calendar, which he had sponsored years earlier. The public meeting addressed by Tilak at Sangli too ended in pandemonium. He was overjoyed at the success of the Conference, and so on his arrival at Poona he wrote to Khaparde that Keropanti Ayanansh had been adopted at the Sangli Jyotish Conference almost unanimously and that the future Panchanga would be prepared accordingly. It must be noted that Tilak, who lashed at Ranade, Bhandarkar and Telang and crushed down social reformers for causing a split in society by wounding the feelings of the majority, now himself sponsored a new almanac which caused a split in society. According to the new almanac the Brahmin followers of Tilak sometimes celebrate Diwali a month earlier than the majority of the Hindus who do so according to the old almanac!

---

7 *The Bombay Chronicle,* 11 February 1920.

Just after this Astronomical Conference, Tilak went to Bombay to receive Lala Lajpat Rai, who arrived on February 20, 1920, from America. Two meetings were held at Shantaram's Chawls, one on the 20th February on behalf of the citizens and the other on the 21st February on behalf of the Students' Committee of Bombay. Tilak spoke on both the occasions. Tilak, who feared Lajpat Rai being influenced by Gandhi, must have felt happy to hear him declare at the first meeting he addressed on his arrival that the dawn of a new spirit had come and that they should utilize the Reforms to the fullest extent. Lajpat Rai added that he did not intend to boycott them. At the second meeting also Tilak presided. The students' leader S. A. Dange eulogised the services of Lajpat Rai in the domain of education, laying emphasis on the fact that they had a noble example in the guest. In the introductory speech Tilak said that it would be very curious for him to begin by thanking the bureaucracy, who, though not doing any other service to India, had at least manufactured patriots of Lala Lajpat Rai's stature by giving him an opportunity through his exile, voluntary or involuntary, to study the administration of different countries and to carry on propaganda work there. Good qualities in a man were often brought out by persecution, he added. The fire through which Lajpat Rai had passed his days showed to the whole world what stuff he was made of. Lajpat Rai was still a missionary both in religious and in political matters.

Replying to the address, Lala Lajpat Rai said that though he had not suffered one hundredth part of what his friend—a noted convict (laughter) Lokamanya Tilak had suffered—perhaps the ordeal was still in store for him—he had never been depressed by the prospect of being imprisoned. At the end of the meeting Tilak advised the students to follow Lalaji in his footsteps. It was not so much a matter of so-called education as a question of character. The existing system of education was only manufacturing good Government servants and good subordinates 'Good Cows,' said Lajpat Rai—for the bureaucracy. It was not so in any independent country such as England, France and America, he concluded.

During the same week Tilak delivered as President of a meeting one of the important speeches in his life. In it he dwelled upon Vedanta, the League of Nations and Bolshevism. The occasion was the birthday anniversary celebration of Ramakrishna Paramahamsa in Poona. Tilak exhorted the audience to give up the spirit of imitation and to realize the truths of the Vedanta, which, he said, alone could save India and the world. It alone would give India a sound spiritual basis for the reconstruction of society in that new era. Describing Ramakrishna Paramahamsa as one of the saviour sages of India, he remarked it was a pity that it was the Americans who discovered Vivekananda and his Guru for India, because India had lost the faculty of recognising her heroes, and was under the hypnotism of the West.

Talking of the "Bolshevik peril", he observed : "India need have no fears. Bolshevism preaches equality of all and nobleness of manual labour. We have already these doctrines in a more refined and truly spiritual manner. Bolshevism, as it is preached in the West, cannot succeed in India. Let us stick fast to our Vedanta and all our desires shall be fulfilled. With and through Vedanta alone the regeneration of India is and would be possible and assured."[8]

As regards the League of Nations, he observed that with its doctrine of self-determination it was a noble thing. But because Europe was not spiritualised by Vedanta, it had become a body without a soul and become a farce.

Shortly after this Tilak attended a conference at Junnar. There he was presented with an address by the Municipality; but at the Conference and at some other places Tilak had to face opposition from a group of Liberals and non-Brahmin politicians. On March 5, 1920, the Belgaum District Conference met at Sankeshwar where some non-Brahmins opposed the address to be presented to Tilak on behalf of two Talukas, Sankeshwar and Hukeri.

Tilak's opposition to Sastri's Marriage Bill, his support to the orthodox in opposing Patel's Bill, when in recent years the backward classes began to claim communal representation, his asking in an irritated mood at a meeting in Athani whether they had to handle the plough or hold the grocer's pair of scales in the Legislative Councils,[9] and his opposition to compulsory education being extended to girls by the Poona Municipality, incurred the displeasure of many and angered many from those ranks. Their angry attitude to Tilak was utilized by the Moderates for their propaganda, thus adding weight to the opposition.

Replying to the address presented by the people of the two Talukas at Sankeshwar, Tilak said that he appreciated the independence and the spirit of the two non-Brahmin young leaders who opposed the address.

---

8 The *Bombay Chronicle*, 8 March 1920.
9 Paranjpye, R. P., *Young Liberal Series No. 4*, p. 6.

He said those were the days of democracy when all communities should come forward to put their views before the public, but he hoped that the non-Brahmins would show a similar spirit and courage in opposing the Government also. If the country's cause, he continued, demanded it, he was ready to dine with the Untouchables as a Brahmin did in Shivaji's times. He reassured them that political freedom should be achieved first and social reforms should not impede political progress. He was engaged only in political organisation and could not spare time, he added, for social questions. The woes of the people were the result of Government policy, and if the Government were to hand over full Self-Government to the non-Brahmins he would be glad!

Opposition to Tilak was also voiced at this juncture at a meeting which Tilak addressed in a mill locality in Bombay near Prabhadevi. All these men who had never moved their little finger against their slavery made, it is evident, much of Tilak's unfortunate Athani speech, and the Moderates—now called the Liberals—and the non-Brahmins joined hands not to oppose a foreign Government, but their political liberator. Nevertheless it can be said that those attacks on Tilak's social views at public meetings, though on a small scale, indicated that society was moving towards a change.

The opposition sponsored by the non-Brahmins agitated Tilak's mind. So in order to pacify these forces he addressed a meeting under the auspices of the Gopal Club at Poona and explained his views on the problem. He said, *inter alia*, "It is the British policy and not the influence of Brahmins that has thrown the non-Brahmins into the background. They are thus made backward by the policy of Government. The Brahmins as clerks became the literate class and they found that nothing short of Self-Government would mend matters. The Brahmins did not demand Self-Government for themselves. They demanded it for all. They knew that the society was disorganised by caste distinctions, but it was the political emancipation and not the social emancipation that was urgently and immediately necessary to save India which was grovelling in abject poverty and misery."

"Are interdining and intermarrying such pressing questions that I should put the all-important question of Self-Government into the background ? If anybody would win Swaraj for my nation, then I am ready to interdine with any man, no matter of whatever caste, creed or colour he may be."

"The non-Brahmins must again remember that abolition of the caste was tried by Buddhists, but they failed in it. We therefore cannot hang our problem of Self-Government on this peg of the abolition of caste which would require perhaps centuries to come. Self-Government is dawning and you will be free and prosperous like kings. When we will win Self-Government there will be time enough for us to adjust social relations. I know they require drastic changes. I do not defend the past. But also I cannot forget the present. The present requires all our energies. Let us, therefore, walk shoulder to shoulder and march ahead on the road to freedom and prosperity."[10]

Tilak's views that he would interdine with any man whatever his caste or creed, if he won freedom, evidently suggested a benevolent and patronizing attitude towards those who clamoured for social justice and social equality.

It is no wonder then that Samuel Damle who had just been reconverted to Hinduism was not allowed to dine in the company of Tilak when he dined at a party with a number of Brahmins at the Sardar Griha in Bombay.[11] Damle was originally a Brahmin but on his conversion to Christianity he had lost his caste. So he was a red rag to the orthodox Brahmins. Here too Tilak did not follow Shivaji who gave his daughter in marriage to the son of Bajaji Nimbalkar after Bajaji's conversion from Islam to Hinduism. If the social reformers could not digest the whole of Agarkar's philosophy, Tilak too could not digest the whole of Shivaji's ideology.

That is why Tilak's critics and opponents said that the Tilakites, who were the vanguard in politics, were reactionaries in social matters. Even Tilak's colleagues like Lala Lajpat Rai reiterated this view as late as April 1927,[12] saying that Tilak's social views were reactionary. The manifesto of Tilak's Democratic Swaraj Party was just then on the anvil. The highest value conceived by the democratic ideal is the worth and importance of the individual. And so Democracy is defined as being free from discriminations, prejudices, privileges, hatred and superiority. Yet Tilak was called, perhaps vaguely, a democrat much more on account of the latitude he allowed to his colleagues in discussions and the compromising attitude he showed during the Congress debates, than for his views on Democracy.

On persistent invitation from the people in Sind, Tilak now decided to tour that Province. He reached Delhi on March 20, 1920. This was the first time that Tilak was going to Delhi after the ban on his entry there was

10 *The Hindu Missionary*, 29 March 1920.

11 Ibid., 29 December 1919.

12 *Brahman-Brahmanetar*, 16 April 1927.

lifted. People therefore gave an imposing reception to the "Poona King", "Bhagwan Tilak". He was presented with an address. Then accompanied by Khaparde and Pal he went to Ajmer where the streets were decorated with flags and flowers. Tilak was honoured in a Mosque at Ajmer.

Then the Sind tour began. Tilak reached Hyderabad and was received there like a king. He was presented with a purse at Shikarpur. At Sakkar he delivered a speech, and the proceeds of the meeting were contributed to the Jallianwalla Baug Fund. People at Sakkar also presented him with an address. On March 29, 1920, the Hindus and Muslims of Karachi took out procession with their flags simultaneously flying over the carriage in which Tilak was sitting. The Muslim League, the Congress Committee and the Students' Federation presented him with addresses. Tilak then visited Mirpurkhas, Tandoja and Koti and returned to Hyderabad on March 30.

From Hyderabad he went directly to Sholapur to attend the Provincial Conference which was held under the presidentship of N. C. Kelkar. Mrs. Annie Besant was present. On the first day there was some disturbance, and stones were thrown at the Conference. There were a few brawls. There.was opposition from Besant to the main resolution which Tilak had supported. The resolution recommended to the people that they should elect in the ensuing election those persons whose allegiance to the Congress was beyond all question. She moved an amendment saying that the 'best men' should be elected irrespective of their parties. But she was defeated. She could not reverse the verdict of the Amritsar Congress. One point is worth mentioning. Kelkar had put a time-limit for every speaker. He rigidly enforced it against Tilak also! Walchand Kothari, R. P. Paranjpye and B. S. Kamat were the three leaders who opposed Tilak. For the disturbances at this Conference Tilak vehemently attacked Paranjpye in the *Kesari*, denouncing him as a Pashupal, a keeper of the menagerie! The boomerang of brute force was now recoiling on Tilak, its master!

III

IN APRIL THERE arose a controversy between Mrs. Besant and Tilak. She had issued an appeal on April 7, 1920, requesting the All-India Committee of the Congress to dissociate themselves, as men of honour, from the utterances of V. J. Patel and Dadasaheb Khaparde, so that they might not share in the disgrace of their methods. She complained that Khaparde had 'shamelessly' insulted her by calling her Putana, the Rakshasi, the treacherous, but unsuccessful murderess of Shri Krishna, and that Khaparde had falsely charged that she had worked in England against the Congress Deputation. She added in her appeal, "Tilak has put into my mouth at the same meeting words which I never spoke, but as he laid down in his speech at Amritsar after the Congress, the general theory that the use of falsehood is justifiable against a political opponent, it is not worth while to refute any particular untruth he may utter."

Tilak took upon himself the responsibility of replying to Mrs. Besant as V. J. Patel had just then left for England on April 14 on a mission entrusted to him by the All-India Congress Committee. Tilak issued a statement on April 16, 1920, vehemently refuting her accusations. "I thank Mrs. Besant," concluded Tilak, "for not further pouring vials of her wrath on my head; but I must say that she has, to use her own words, shamelessly, misrepresented me in this behalf. I have always maintained and do maintain that diplomacy, and not necessarily the whole truth, is expected from a statesman, and this view is sanctioned both by Eastern and Western ethical writers. I am, therefore, not ashamed to own it, for I stand in good company." [13] Tilak had been similarly accused of such a breach in his political conduct by R. P. Paranjpye also. While counting votes at a meeting of the Provincial Congress Committee in Bombay it was found that there were some omissions and mistakes wilfully committed. There were appeals for recounting the votes. The atmosphere was full of heat, and passions were roused. Enraged at the trick, one Moderate leader said he was sorry that people did not observe morality in politics. Tilak was sitting by. He shot back: "What has morality got to do with politics?" Upon this R. P. Paranjpye sprang up to his feet and answered back : "The day I find that morality is divorced from politics, I shall care a jot for politics and retire from public life."[14]

The foregoing Tilak's reply to Mrs. Besant epitomizes his conduct in political affairs. A man of peerless private life with straightforward dealings, Tilak was severely criticized by his opponents for this doctrine which he said he followed in political affairs solely for the sake of the welfare of his people! Gandhi protested to Tilak for stigmatising Mrs. Besant as Putana and told him that she was doing her work in her own way honestly. Tilak replied that Putana also did it in her own way honestly to kill Krishna![15]

13 *All about Lokamanya Tilak*, published by B. G. Paul 8c Co., p. 308. 28

14 Quoted by T. V. Parvate in My *Interviews with Eminent Men* (Marathi), p. 22.

15 G. V. Ketkar in *Reminiscences and Anecdotes about Lokamanya Tilak*, Vol. I, p. 26.

On April 20, 1920, Tilak published the Manifesto of the Congress Democratic Party which he wanted to found. Before its publication it was also seen and approved by Gandhiji. The Manifesto was based on loyalty to the Congress and faith in democracy. "The Party believes," it continued, "in the integration or federation of India in the British Commonwealth for the advancement of the cause of humanity and the brotherhood of mankind, and demands exclusive right of fashioning the form of Government determining the most appropriate constitution for India and proposes to work the Montagu Reforms Act for all it is worth and for accelerating the grant of full Responsible Government." The Party advocated the removal of all civic, secular or social disabilities based on caste or custom, but it did not feel any need for pledging protection to the agricultural tenants against the money-lenders. Tilak wanted to get that Manifesto approved by the session of the Calcutta Congress which was to be held soon.

Referring to this promise of removal of civic, social or secular disabilities, Gajananrao Vaidya, a leading social reformer and Hindu Missionary, observed in the *Hindu Missionary* : "But he (Tilak) writes as a politician par excellence! During his life he has held up to scorn all social reforms. His words today can't inspire confidence in those for whose benefit they are meant. He has never befriended any social sufferers. He is very good as a politician; and in the decline of his life it is not possible for him to surrender his popularity and championship to unpopular causes. By his temperament he is not fitted for that kind of work." This was the general opinion held by thinking men outside Tilak's Party, and many of them were admirers of Tilak the political leader.

Shortly afterwards, on May 22, Tilak was presented with a purse of three lacs of rupees at a public meeting in Poona under the presidentship of his friend Dr. Nanasaheb Deshmukh. Gratefully thanking the people on the occasion, Tilak said that he had decided to work out the Reforms. Council entry was one of the items of work they would have to attend to. He impressed upon the minds of his followers the significance of propaganda in England and the necessity of putting their views before the League of Nations. He gratefully acknowledged the debt of his gratitude to the people and said through that purse they had purchased him.

In the last week of June he attended a meeting of the All-India Congress Committee at Banaras. At this meeting Gandhi proposed that the Congress should recommend to the country a programme of non-co-operation without further delay, as a protest against the Turkish Peace

Treaty and the decision of the Government in respect of the Punjab affairs. But the Committee postponed it till the special Congress met at Calcutta. Shaukat Ali requested Tilak to attend the meeting of the Council of the All-India Muslim League, which was held at Allahabad to discuss the Khilafat question. Tilak told him that he would not attend any meeting except that of the Congress to decide questions of National policy. He told Shaukat Ali that his idea was that Muslims themselves should take the initiative in the matter, and it was for the Hindus to support them in whatever decision they would arrive at. He addressed two meetings at Banaras. On his return journey he stayed for two days at Jubbulpore, where he delivered a speech at the Town Hall.

Tilak performed in May 1920 the marriage ceremony of his second son Shridharpant who was in the senior B.A. Class. His eldest son Rambhau was a medical student. He refused to go in for marriage at that juncture and ultimately died unmarried in 1955. Shridharpant was a promising youth with progressive views. Unfortunately he ended his life in a tragic manner in 1928. He had two sons Jayant and Shrikant. Jayantrao has the proud distinction of occupying the editorial chair of his grandfather and is now coming to the forefront in Maharashtra as editor, leader and legislator.

Just before the celebration of Shridharpant's marriage, Tilak performed *Prayschitta* for having crossed the seas! Many said that this reflected discredit on Tilak. Many pitied him for having bowed down to the Poona orthodox.

The shrewd politician in Tilak was now thinking seriously over the social and political changes. The needs of the society, the mood of the people, and the methods of the freedom struggle coming up with the emergence of Gandhi in Indian politics, were changing fast. So he told Khadilkar that he would not accept the presidentship of the Congress session at Calcutta as was being planned by his opponents. He said he would have to work hard during the Calcutta Congress to avert the rift among the Congress leaders on the question of non-co-operation. He said he would perhaps go to England. He expected that Gandhi's movement was likely to spread, and in that case Gandhi and he would be put in jail. And at the time of compromise instead of granting full reforms the Government would pacify the people by releasing Gandhi and himself.[16]

16 Collection of K. P. Khadilkar's Writings, Vol. II, p. 150.

The news about his proposed visit had also appeared in the *Hindu Missionary*, Bombay. The editorial note said, "We hear that Lokamanya Tilak is proceeding to England soon. His continued presence there for a few years will do immense good to India. We only hope that he will speak not only on politics, but also at centres of learning on the Aryan civilization and ancient Indian civilization. His lectures on *Gita* will attract the scholars of England not only to the greatness of India but to the ability of the great son of India."[17] Tilak had told Vithalbhai Patel about his intention to establish Information and Publicity Bureaus not only in London, but also in Paris, New York and Tokyo. He had also an idea of establishing an Indian News Service Agency between India and the important civilized countries of the world. When Patel once asked him how far the foreign propaganda would help India, Tilak replied that he never believed that India's salvation would come from outside, but he added that a favourable opinion of the civilized world towards Indians' aspirations would be a valuable asset to India's struggle for freedom, and therefore Indian leaders could not afford to neglect world opinion except at their peril.

It was now the middle of June 1920. One of Tilak's staunch lieutenants Achyut Balwant Kolhatkar had turned a bitter critic in connection with the accounts of the Tilak Purse Fund. He had made serious allegations against Tilak's lieutenants Kelkar, Nanasaheb Deshmukh and Annasaheb Nene. He wrote an arrowy article on this subject in his paper *Sandesh*, holding Tilak to ridicule. So with great reluctance Tilak took up his fiery pen that flourished and flowed with combativeness and burst forth upon Kolhatkar like a bomb-shell, smashing the fort of his arguments to pieces. This was the last time Tilak took up his pen to put an end to an acrid controversy.

IV

TILAK WENT TO Bombay on July 12 in connection with the last act in the Tai Maharaj Case. As the Kolhapur ruler would not allow Jagannath Maharaj to take possession of his property at Kolhapur, he had made an application to the Bombay High Court. That application was to come up before the High Court on July 14. So Tilak worked hard to prepare a statement for the use of counsel. Tilak had been indisposed for the previous two months. He had intermittent malarial fever. The application was heard on July 14 by the Judges, but the judgment was reserved. So Tilak had to extend his stay in Bombay.

---

17 *The Hindu Missionary,* Bombay, 5 January 1920.

While Tilak was thus busy with the proceedings of the case, Gandhi and Shaukat Ali met him. Gandhi observed in his reminiscences of Tilak, "About Hindus and Mussalmans he said, turning to the Maulana, 'I will sign anything that Gandhi suggests, because I have full faith in him on the question.' About non-co-operation, he significantly repeated to me what he had said to me before. 'I like the programme well enough, but I have my doubts as to the country being with us in the self-denying ordinance which non-co-operation presents to the people. I will do nothing to hinder the progress of the movement. I wish you every success, and if you gain the popular ear, you will find in me an enthusiastic supporter.' Tilak added that if the Muslims boycotted the councils he and his party would follow suit!"[18]

The details of the foregoing discussion between Tilak and Gandhi will not be complete unless its other side, which Gandhi has not narrated, is given here. Tilak said to Gandhi, "I consider an armed revolt also constitutional. The only difficulty is, at present it is not possible. If anyone were to assure me that armed revolt would be successful to the extent of even eight annas in the rupee, I would start the revolt, trusting God to give success to the extent of the remaining eight annas. But today to the extent of even four annas we are not prepared and there is no certainty."[19]

Tilak was sceptical of the success of satyagraha. A few days before he had told Ajgaonkar, an eminent Marathi author, that up to that moment, he had thought that Gandhi was a Jain, and because Gandhi was a Jain his teachings were tinged with Jain religion, non-violence, satyagraha, fasting, etc., which were more in keeping with Jainism than Hinduism. But these means were of no use in politics which required to change its attitude from time to time. He further said that exalted religious principles or abstract doctrines about truth were not of much value in the existing political game. Satyagraha would have the least effect upon the rulers and even hartal would lead to bloodshed when the officers would try to break it.[20]

Tilak was sceptical also of the Khilafat movement which the Hindu leaders had supported in order to win the friendship and co-operation of the Muslims in the national struggle. He wanted the national movement to be kept entirely from all contamination with any theological or foreign political

18 *Reminiscences and Anecdotes about Lokamanya Tilak*, Vol. I, p. 514.
19 Ketkar, G. V., in *Reminiscences and Anecdotes about Lokamanva Tilak*, Vol. I, p. 26.
20 *Reminiscences and Anecdotes about Lokamanya Tilak*, Vol. I, p. 315.

questions. He foretold that the Hindu leaders would be disillusioned, and ultimately they would find that they had deceived themselves and not the Muslims who were very shrewd at diplomatic negotiations. He was of the opinion that the co-operation of the Muslims should be sought on the broader national question of Swaraj by offering them special privileges and added : "Never seek to introduce theology into our politics." [21]

Tilak sometimes said that he wanted to hand over charge to someone, and these words indicated what was going on in his mind! Would Gandhi step in? Tilak and Besant joined hands, would Tilak and Gandhi do so? They both belonged to the masses. Both were short in stature, thin in build, muscular and simple in appearance, simple in habits. Both were ascetics and altruists. Both were lawyers. But Gandhi had conducted cases in court; Tilak never practised law. Both had phenomenal energy and were fearless. Both were simple, effective speakers. Both had appealed to the masses. Both had tried to help recruitment, but Gandhi was a holder of the Kaiser-I-Hind Medal conferred on him by the British Government for his meritorious service during their wars. Gandhi was respected both by the Government and by the people. Tilak was the most hated man in India by the bureaucrats, feared by the Moderates and suspected by the Muslims.

Gandhi was called Mahatma. Tilak was called Lokamanya. The models for Gandhi were Christ and Lord Buddha; the model for Tilak was Lord Krishna. Both loved the *Gita*. But their methods differed. Gandhi would say, "My method is not Tilak's method." Tilak made people fearless and self-respecting. Gandhi turned the people against the Government. Tilak said he worked within the law. Gandhi said he wanted to break oppressive laws. Tilak touched on the problem of the Untouchables when it was inevitable. Gandhi had in his Ashram an untouchable family! Both believed in the Chaturvarnya. Tilak had opposed the age of Consent Bill; Gandhi had said that any sensible legislation in the direction of raising the age of consent would have his approval. Gandhi assessed more correctly the urgent necessity of the removal of untouchability, of women's education, of improving the lot of the working classes, and the necessity of a just solution to the grievances of the non-Brahmins. The moral courage of both was supreme. Tilak was a scholar statesman; Gandhi an ascetic statesman. Gandhi's father was a statesman, a Dewan. Tilak hailed from

---

21 *Reminiscences and Anecdotes about Lokamanya Tilak*, Vol. Ill, p. 127 (English Section).

the Chitpavan Brahmin community having a tradition of politics and public service! Gandhi enriched the Gujarati language, Tilak enriched the Marathi language. Both were journalists, and men of mission.

But would Gandhi step in? A leader holds the leadership of a nation so long as his qualities and message meet the need and mood of the people. The ambivert in Tilak had rightly sensed that this was the time for a change. A man who had towered in the forefront of politics and played so decisive and cardinal a part in the affairs of his nation would have found it rather difficult to reconcile himself or to gravitate to Gandhian methods of non-violence and a jail-courting programme! So the thought of leaving India for England was floating across his mind; perhaps to allow the Gandhian movement to have its full sway!

V

TILAK WAS STILL in Bombay. On July 20 Tilak had a drive with Diwan Chaman Lal. After two hours he returned. He told his grandson Gajananrao Ketkar that he was feeling feverish and went to bed. Fever set in. Next day he ran, high temperature. The last word on the Tai Maharaj Case was said in the High Court. He won the case and thus brought to a successful conclusion the affair of the Tai Maharaj Case and fulfilled the promise he had given to Baba Maharaj in 1897. S. R. Bakhale, one of his counsel, came direct from the Court and informed him that the Court had decided the case in his favour. He asked him to bring a copy of the judgment next day. Bakhale brought it, but Tilak's fever had not yet abated. So Tilak asked his attendant to put it into a cupboard! The last word on this case was said after nineteen years! Such a prolonged, tedious and taxing affair had it been for Tilak and Kelkar, his colleague and biographer, was led to remark in his autobiography that if at all Tilak preferred to live the same life over again, he would pray that he should not come across a friend like Baba Maharaj! That day congratulations on his sixty-fourth birthday flowed in a stream of joyous and laudatory messages from every part of the country. It was thought at the time of the first medical examination that it was the recrudescence of the malarial fever, but on a second examination it was found that he had developed pneumonia. For the next three days there was no change either for the better or for the worse. Dr. Sathye and Dr. Gopalrao Deshmukh were attending him.

For a week Tilak put up a brave fight with the malady. He got angry with his sons for coming over to Bombay! He cracked jokes with his daughters, who had come down to Bombay to look after the health of their Dada, saying that they were very fond of the father's place. When his nephew asked him if he wanted to say anything about his affairs, he said, "I am not going to die for another five years; be sure of that. The critical period is over! "On Wednesday morning, July 28, the temperature was normal and pulse regular. But from July 29, his health became extremely critical, the temperature going down and becoming sub-normal. The body that had been suffering from diabetes over fifteen years now could not react to medicine. Tilak became delirious and became unconscious. He continued in that state more or less for three days. In his drowsiness he did not talk of domestic matters; he talked of the Punjab affairs.

At night he murmured during the momentary recovery which so often precedes death. "This happened in 1818 and this in 1918. A hundred years' history—what a life of servitude!" The last words uttered by him were: "Unless Swaraj is achieved, India shall not prosper; it is required for our very existence!" Such great thoughts do not come to men suddenly. They are ingrained in their blood, bones and brain. The life of England's great Premier, William Pitt the Younger, provides an analogous example. When he was about to yield his breath he said, "Oh! my country! how I leave my country!" This indicates how Pitt had been at one with the struggle of England, and the last words uttered by Tilak show how Tilak had been at one with the struggle of India!

As said above, the condition of Tilak's health became precarious since the morning of the 29th July. A stream of visitors came with soft steps inquiring after his health and walked out with heavy hearts. A large crowd continued to stand anxiously near the Sardar Griha. The staircase was packed with large crowds anxious to get some news. In the evening the crowds grew so large that the gates of the lodge had to be locked. Amongst the visitors were Gandhi, R. P. Paranjpye, M. R. Jayakar, Kamat, Baptista, Jamnadas Dwarkadas and L. R. Tairsee. Nationalist leaders from all parts of the Province arrived in Bombay. Shri Shankaracharya of Karveer Peeth arrived in Bombay, and prayers were offered for Tilak in temples. Mrs. Besant wired inquiring after Tilak's health.

The devotion of the crowds was touching. A Marwari distributed one thousand rupees among the poor. An old man came from Sind just to have a look at the Lokamanya. School children waited at the gates with anxious faces. Bulletins about his health were issued to the press and pasted at the entrance of the Sardar Griha every hour. Anxious crowds scanned them without a word!

On Friday the 30th, Doctors said that his health showed signs of improvement. Jinnah and Sir Narayan Chandavarkar called at the Sardar Griha. Sir Ramkrishna Bhandarkar wired from Poona earnestly wishing Tilak a speedy recovery. Khaparde arrived.

On Saturday night, at ten-thirty, his heart began to show signs of exhaustion and his breathing became hard. The clock struck twelve and August commenced! During the first hour of August 1920 at forty-minutes past twelve, the mysterious power which rules the world stole a march over the unconscious man and carried him away in the presence of his two sons and three daughters, and his colleagues Kelkar, Khadilkar, Dr. Sathye and Dr. Deshmukh. Thus passed away the honoured, respected and beloved son of India. In the drizzling rain people were waiting with anxious faces in the streets. Except the dim lights in the streets darkness reigned supreme. Somebody whispered on the staircase 'departed!' People in the streets were shocked. All theatres and entertainment programmes were deserted!

The lamentable news spread from house to house in Bombay, and people wound up their beds and sat till daybreak, speaking in whispers of the architect of their nation. In the morning people went out of their homes and gathered in thousands before the Sardar Griha. Workers did not go to the mills, the Marwari put aside his account books, the Bania his purse. All vehicular traffic was blocked. At eight o'clock on Sunday morning Tilak's body was placed in a sitting posture on a raised seat in the balcony on the first floor of the lodge so that the people in the streets could see him. Only leaders of note and women were allowed to go inside! Jinnah, Gandhi, Shaukat Ali, Baptista and R. P. Paranjpye came. About eleven o'clock a huge mass of humanity spread down from Dhobi Talao to the end of Carnac Road. The balconies, terraces, roofs, and windows on either side of the streets from where the funeral procession was expected to go were thickly crowded. Two special trains came from Poona and Tilak's followers arrived. Parsees, Muslims, Christians, all came to pay their homage to the man. The Poona leaders wanted to take his dead body to Poona, but the Bombay public did not allow them to do so. Some leading Tilakites took a solemn vow in the august presence of the mortal remains of their great leader that they would not let down his mission and banner.

Tilak's body was seated in a palanquin and at two-fifteen in the afternoon slowly the last triumphal march of Tilak began. It was a mile and a half long procession. Never within living memory had the city witnessed such an impressive funeral. Some of Tilak's Brahmin friends and relations desired that only Brahmins should lift the bier! When Mahatma Gandhi came forward and bent low to lift up the bier, someone tried to obstruct him. Gandhi stood up for a moment and said, "A public man knows no caste." He shouldered the bier, so did Shaukat Ali and Dr. Kitchlew. Pandit Jawaharlal Nehru accompanied the funeral procession.

The air was weeping and there was, as it were, a rivalry between the drizzling rain and the streaming tears of the vast multitude of people! Flowers were showered on the bier with religious devotion while the funeral procession passed by important places. It went along Shroff Bazar, and when it reached Moti Bazar a merchant showered pearls on it. Then it went along Bhuleshwar, Girgaum, Sandhurst Road, and reached the Chowpatty sands at sunset. The Government also bent to the popular will and pressure and granted special permission to cremate Tilak on the sands of Chowpatty.

The pyre of sandalwood was lit up, and Tilak disappeared in body, but the immortal Tilak remained behind. How truly did Shakespeare describe such a man when he wrote:

"Nature might stand up
And say to all the world, this was the Man."

Never before in the history of Modern India was such nationwide grief witnessed. The 1st August had been fixed for the inauguration of the non-co-operation movement by Gandhi although the Congress had not accepted it in principle so far.

Leaders irrespective of party, creed, and caste issued public statements. Meetings were held all over India to mourn Tilak's death. Paying a glowing tribute to Tilak, Gandhi said, "His patriotism was a passion with him. He knew no religion but love of his country. He was born a democrat. He had an iron will which he used for his country. His life was an open book. His tastes were simple. His private life was spotlessly clean. He had dedicated his wonderful talents to the country. No man preached the gospel of Swaraj with the consistency and the insistence of Lokamanya."

"For us," Gandhiji concluded, "he will go down to the generations yet unborn as a maker of Modern India. They will revere his memory as of a man who lived for them and died for them." Sir N. G. Chandavarkar said that Tilak had made his mark in history. R. P. Paranjpye described him as a great son whose great intellect, sacrifice and devotion to the country even enemies acknowledged. Mrs. Besant said that history would record his name among those who won India's freedom. Lala Lajpat Rai, who had reached Bombay a few hours after Tilak's death, said that the sense of loss was the greatest imaginable. Aurobindo described him as the light and incarnation of the Mahratta character. Jinnah called him a selfless patriot and a unique figure. Maulana Hazarat Mohani said that Tilak was greater than and superior to every other leader in every respect.

"His valuable contribution to world-thought will live," remarked the *Independent*, "as long as philosophy and knowledge are not banished from the son of man." The *Amrita Bazar Patrika* described him as the mightiest of the sons of India, the greatest nation-builder of modern India. The *Hindu*, Madras, said that in Tilak was symbolised all that was best and greatest of India's past culture and the greatness of the rich fulfilment of its glorious future. The *Rangoon Mail* characterised him as the hero of a hundred battles. The *Express* said that a prince among men had fallen. The *Morning Post* of London described him as the promoter of disaffection. The *Manchester Guardian* called him an exponent of Indian nationalism. The *Times*, London, represented him as the arch-inspirer of Indian unrest.

Tilak's inveterate enemy, the *Times of India*, Bombay, was relentless even after his death. It observed, "He was a man of considerable intellectual powers. . . . He was a man of courage, enterprise, and unflagging zeal in the propaganda to which he devoted his life. His style would not bear translation. and in Marathi he was a pithy and effective speaker and writer. These talents and energies were, however, devoted to a life of political violence, social reaction, and campaigning terrorism to which we know no parallel in constitutional history." "It is a lamentable record", the *Times of India* concluded, " for a man of his abilities, courage and energy; but such it is."

On August 3, 1920, Tilak's ashes were taken by a special train to Poona. The box containing the ashes was carried in a chariot drawn by four horses. An imposing procession started from the station and after four hours reached Tilak's famous abode, Gaikwad Wada. A grand statue was later erected at the place on the Chowpatty sands in Bombay where Tilak was cremated.

CHAPTER XXIV

End of an Epoch

THUS TILAK, THE Father of the Indian Freedom Struggle, who held the field of politics and public life for over two decades, passed away. What was the secret of his power and unparalleled hold over the people? As thinking men rolled back the years, a panorama of events of three decades passed before their minds, and a train of thoughts must have gripped their minds.

At a time when Indian men of learning were eulogising British rule, the masses had grown lethargic and oblivious of their degradation, and darkness had enveloped India, Tilak appeared on the horizon and infused into the minds of the people self-respect and courage to stand up for their rights.

Before the advent of Tilak into Indian politics, there was no active or popular political agitation or movement worth the name. Men of learning, who were enthralled at the mighty power of the British and Western culture, gathered together during the holidays once a year and returned home after delivering brilliant orations. They never went to the people; people were not in their picture at all, as those men of learning and light sincerely believed in the Divine Dispensation of British rule in India and thought that the moral sense of Britain would bring about the political progress of India. So they had no message for the masses. They never took into consideration the fact that the people were the real source of their strength. People were left to sweat and suffer in hopeless degradation. So Tilak made it the mission of his life, the purpose of his life, the profession of his life, to arouse the people against political slavery and foreign rule.

Tilak appeared on the scene and told the men of learning and light that unless they had the support of the people they would not attain their objective. Tilak was the first leader who boldly declared that constitutional agitation would not by itself have any effect on the British Government.

He, therefore, resolved to organise the people under the banner of the Congress and to make it the real spokesman of the people. It was indeed he who first brought politics and the common man together in India. He inaugurated national festivals and functions to awaken the people to national pride, national self-respect and national honour. He was the first leader to use the word Swaraj[1] as it is understood today, as also the first leader to launch the Swadeshi movement. He started these movements but the old guard opposed them. As he was the first leader to start popular political movement in India, he had to channel his own path, fashion his own weapons and mould the pattern of a political organisation. He did what Shivaji did three hundred years before him. He organised the people and set them on their march. In doing this he had to cross swords with the veteran leaders of his day. For, to fight intellectually with leaders from Ranade and Bhandarkar, the intellectual worthies, down to Pherozeshah Mehta was not an easy path. On one side was the mighty Government, on the other were these stalwarts who believed that petitioning the Government would bring political reforms.

Tilak, therefore, had at every stage to fight the old guard single-handed with arguments, facing their attacks, putting forth fire and brimstone, overpowering their opposition at every session of the Congress. He had to battle against the Government with his pen and press and platform. He had to educate the people to stand up for their rights and to compel the Government to redress their grievances. Naturally he had to bear the brunt of the struggle alone and face the unceasing hostility of the foreign Government, and the wrath of its haughty Empire! The result was that Tilak had to face persecution and prosecution and suffer jail hardships, misunderstanding and calumny such as no other leader except the revolutionaries had till then suffered. He made life in jail for the political leaders in subject India an honourable and unavoidable service. His sufferings made blunt the edge of the hardships of jail life of political prisoners in India, and he served as the leader of sappers and miners in the life of the national army of Swaraj. By his ceaseless actions, his fearlessness, his selflessness, he infused courage into a generation that came forward to follow him, to support him, and to die for the cause of the motherland.

The first requisite for a leader is boldness in thought and action. The second is ability to take quick decisions. The third is fearlessness and

1 Chintamani, C. Y., *Indian Politics since the Mutiny,* p. 58.

the fourth is sincerity of purpose. Tilak possessed all these qualities. When politicians showed lack of grit, courage and frankness, Tilak became impatient with them. His fearlessness was incomparable. It is no exaggeration to say that fear was not a word to be found in his dictionary. He told a British Governor that if he could he would raise the banner of revolt! When a Governor-General was touring India and attending banquets during the days of famines, he fumed at him and regretted that there was no power in people's hands to bring such a ruler to book! He was courage incarnate. His coolness and self-control in times of danger was uncommon; his practical sense was marvellous.

Tilak was a born rebel who wore the rebel robe to the end of his life. As his influence grew, the challenge to the British Government became more active; and he became a terror and a nightmare to it. At every trial his influence spread wider and his personality loomed large on the political horizon of India. The slogan of Swaraj which he gave early in the nineties of the last century came to capture the imagination of the people in 1906. The goal of Swaraj itself was embodied in the Reforms of 1919! And at last the breaker of the Congress, became the maker of the Congress and the architect of the nation. Tilak was not only the first mass leader of India to rise in revolt in Asia against the British Empire, but also the herald of Asian nationalism who inspired the Asian leaders and nations that were suppressed under the iron heel of Western imperialism. Dr. Sokarno, the Indonesian President, testified to this fact when he said during the course of a speech at Bombay that he derived inspiration for their freedom struggle from Tilak,[2] Gandhi and Dadabhai Naoroji. He was the first Indian leader who recognised that no imperialism is altruistic.

Tilak did not make a fetish of non-violence, and although he resorted to militant constitutional agitation, he did not regard revolutionaries as political untouchables. To risk life for the cause of one's own country is the greatest sacrifice one can make; for there is nothing dearer than one's own life. Tilak knew that the revolutionaries were fighting selflessly at the cost of their lives. So he never discouraged or disparaged them. Moreover, Tilak was neither an egregious pacifist, nor an impotent moralist. He had confined his Swaraj movement to the threefold programme of Swadeshi, Boycott and National Education not because he was a believer in the gospel of absolute nonviolence or pacifist idealism; but because he believed that

2 The *Lokamanya,* 12 January 1958.

the Congress organisation was the best weapon for creating universal hatred of the British power and for popularising the idea of Swaraj.

It is true that Tilak never planned a national insurrection like the revolutionary leaders Savarkar and Aurobindo[3] who hoped to start a revolt on the basis of historical experience. But had such a revolution been started by the revolutionaries, one would not be far from truth if one were to conclude that Tilak would have supported it. For he considered an armed revolt also constitutional. He often said that he would join a revolt provided there was any possibility of success. His secret message to Senapati Bapat to send a Bomb Manual, the caustic rebuke with which he goaded Damodarpant Chapekar, the care he took of Balkrishna Chapekar when he was in hiding in the forest of Hyderabad, the explosive remark he made on hearing the news about the transportation of Lala Lajpat Rai, the activities of his lieutenant who strove to set up an ammunition factory in Nepal, and the activities of his followers in Goa in 1915 under the cloak of National Education, were not innocent.

Tilak's relations with the revolutionary leaders were quite cordial and God-fatherly. Naturally, the diabolic thought of breaking up the revolutionary movement and handing over to the foreign Government for capital punishment or deportation the revolutionaries who came to him for help, advice or shelter, could never come to his mind. To Tilak the failure of Wasudeo Balwant must have acted as a warning, and, therefore, he must have chosen the path of an open movement to rouse the people against foreign rule in a constitutional way. And with age and experience must have grown an unflinching conviction upon him that the real power of bettering the condition of the people was the will of the people.

He thus equally loved both sides of the freedom struggle, the revolutionary and the constitutional. Indeed he regarded the revolutionary movement as the plank of the freedom struggle, and he himself galvanized the Congress into a militant constitutional movement.

Tilak had realised the importance of the reorganization of the States in India on linguistic basis. He always thought of Swaraj in terms of the whole nation. He sang the glory of Maharashtra not out of a narrow geographical pride, but because it was easy for him to rouse the patriotic fervour of the Mahrattas.

---

3 Sri Aurobindo on *Himself and on the Mother*, p. 33.

Yet it is unfortunate to note that he never raised his little finger against the existing social order which was sogged with injustice and inequality and misery. Had he assumed at least the role of neutrality as did Dadabhai and Gokhale in matters social, he would have indirectly contributed to the progressive social forces that were working for the reorganization of society on deeper and broader foundations. But instead of widening the mental horizon of the orthodox and helping the development of new social attitudes, he defended the defective and decaying institutions of that old social order with unabated ferocity. Not only did he do this but also he led an active, bitter opposition to the social reform movement and helped the social reactionaries.

Tilak failed to look at the non-Brahmin problem from the angle of social justice and equality, its basic urge for a better social order in a changing age, and the needs of a changing social and economic life. And his talks to the non-Brahmins, which were of a condescending and patronizing rather than democratic nature, amply proved that he could not outgrow, as sometimes great men do, the social barriers under which he was born. It is just like the tragedy in the life of Churchill who fought for democracy and human freedom and yet turned down India's demand for freedom and equality and justice.

This tragic role of Tilak was so disappointing that even his sons, who held progressive views in social matters, jokingly told Tilak that they did not want to be Lokamanya as they thought that their father's title rested much on his orthodox views![4] That is why his official biographer D. V. Tahmankar had to remark that Tilak's opposition to social reform presented a difficult problem. Stating that social reformers were fully conscious of the extraordinary hold he had over the masses, Mr. Tahmankar observes that one word from Tilak would have changed popular hostility to reform into friendly co-operation; but Tilak did not say the word. He, however, struggled to make a sort of defence of Tilak's opposition to social reform till the time of his transportation to Mandalay by putting forth a lame excuse that had Tilak supported Ranade, Ranade could not have supported Tilak in his political stand!

"But this defence," Tahmankar himself concludes, "begins to wear thin after his release and return from Mandalay. We cannot ignore the fact that his sacrifice and sufferings in the service of his country gave him

---

4 Kelkar, N. C., *Gata Goshti* (autobiography), p. 453. 29

such a high position and authority after 1915 that there was no danger of the people misunderstanding his action, if he had cared to come out more openly in support of social reform. Indeed, in the last two or three years before his death, Tilak did speak for social reform and particularly for the removal of untouchability, when he declared that he would refuse to acknowledge God if he thought that he sanctioned the vile practice of treating a section of the community as sub-human. But one is forced to admit that he never felt the same moral fervour and enthusiasm for social reform which he felt for the cause of political independence. This was perhaps partly due, as some critics have claimed, to the narrow religious influences which prevailed in and around Poona." [5]

But the credit for his speech against untouchability was nullified the same day when Tilak refused to sign, along with other leaders, the Manifesto declaring that the signatories would not observe untouchability in their day-to-day life. It must, however, be noted that the reformers failed owing to inaction; and it was true that the non-Brahmins could not rise to the occasion.

Undoubtedly, the nation will ever remain grateful to Tilak for the deathless struggle he launched for the deliverance of his countrymen from political bondage and for the endless sacrifices and sufferings he made in the cause of the motherland. Indeed, he was largely the maker of the Congress movement, and it was he who brought about a mass consciousness and changed the course of history!

A man of iron will, Tilak sometimes met his political opponents half way. It was true that he was more helpful and more generous in private life than he was in politics. But the patriot in him dominated the private man, and he talked with disdain, with rage, using contemptuous epithets about those who sang the glory of the British regime and thus disheartened the people. He spoke daggers and poured bitter and biting ridicule on them. In doing so he often attacked his opponents with a ferocity which often violated all the laws of literary warfare. No other leader in modern India raised as bitter and furious controversies as did Tilak. That is why one of his contemporaries has said of him that he was a good master, a bad colleague, and he found co-operation with equals more difficult than leadership of his followers.[6] Every running river carries stones with it; there is no river

5 Tahmankar, D. V., *Lokamanya Tilak,* pp. 321-22.

6 Chintamani, C. Y., *Indian Politics since the Mutiny,* p. 82.

with clean water. Indeed Tilak had some foibles of his times and place as every great man has. But it may be conceded that his conflicts originated in political necessity rather than in personal animus. Yet those conflicts proved to be the driving power behind the Congress organisation. And though under his lashes opponents reeled and wriggled, not a breath of any scandal ever tarnished his name. So spotless was his private life.

His generosity was patronizing and unending. The guest-chamber of his big house was an abiding abode for men of learning, patriots and revolutionaries with whom he talked as patriots talk to one another in a subject nation. However, it does not redound to his credit that the editors working under him were not suitably paid. He was a simple man but not a simpleton. A cunning flatterer bent upon fooling him and extracting money from him would often be sent back with the wiles of his flattery shorn off. One day a cunning man told him that there was a message in his dream that Tilak would give him five hundred rupees! Tilak silenced him by saying that until he too had a similar message in a dream he would do nothing!

The simplicity of his private life was impressive. He did not care much for his dress. Sometimes when he put on old clothes and went out, his nephew would often bring it to his notice and ask him to change them. Never in his life did he use oil for his head, not to speak of applying it to the body! He had a kind of dislike, for using any oil for the purpose. In his house onions and garlic were taboo. He allowed the believing Hindus to tie charmed amulets to his wrist; he accepted blessings of saints through their devotees. But when people deified him, he said, "What man has done, any man can do." In his old-fashioned home life, there were few occasions when wife and husband were found talking in the front portion of the house! Either Tilak the leader was out, or Tilak the scholar was absorbed in his books. A joke here or a remonstrance there would be heard in the house when there was an occasion for it or leisure! He never cared for money nor kept any accounts. Had he followed the profession of law with his subtle, astute and legal acumen, he would have built up a fortune. But he subordinated everything to the service of the nation. Yet the hundreds of petitions he wrote and the legal advice he gave gratis could have brought in a vast fortune!

An eminent scholar of Sanskrit possessing mathematical and astronomical genius, he could have dominated any assembly of learned men in the world. His vast knowledge made him a ready speaker, a walking encyclopaedia. At many a meeting where subjects like Sanskrit literature and mathematics, astronomy and history, were discussed, Tilak the scholar would often reply to or introduce an eminent scholar. At a meeting in Bombay he spoke on the new research of Sir Jagadish Chandra Bose and Bose declared that he wondered how Tilak could simplify so difficult a subject and explain it lucidly to the audience! Men of learning in the world looked to him for light on the riddles of humanity, and liberators of nations like Lenin watched his stormy career with hope and admiration. He was a rare combination of a great scholar and a great mass leader.

Tilak was a pioneer in the field of Indian journalism, who wrote and conducted his papers in the vernacular, so that the waves of self-respect and national movement might directly reach the people. His lucid, forcible, pure and direct style tremendously struck the readers and burnt in their hearts. It showed how journalism becomes a power in the hands of an astute, powerful man of learning and ability. Equally powerful were his speeches. His hard straight thinking and his plain direct speech were effective. When a man of sincerity speaks, the speech is always effective.

Tilak's writings, his lectures, his methods, his agitations, his movements, were all inspired by the noble mission of Swaraj. A great life selflessly lived, a dedicated life, his easy accessibility to the poor, young and old, his utter disregard for personal safety or comforts, his sufferings in the people's cause, his pure noble private life, his vast learning, his will to persevere were the secrets of his uncommon power and popularity, his wonderful hold on the people who rightly called him Lokamanya 'adored by the people' ever since 1893 and especially from 1900! The title conferred on him by Sir Valentine Chirol that Tilak was the Father of Indian Unrest was a worthy tribute!

How appropriately C. Vijaya Raghavachariar, the Congress President of 1920, paid a tribute to the abiding glory of Tilak when he described him as 'a great son of India whose manhood was a life of selfless suffering in our country's cause in a spirit of dedication rarely surpassed in the annals of national struggles for freedom.' Pandit Jawaharlal Nehru described him as Father of India's Revolution.

Tilak's life was an embodiment of struggles, sufferings and aspirations of the people, and his name a symbol of Swaraj. He was an institution, a school of thought by himself. His energy and will played a magnificent role in destroying British power and prestige in India! Few leaders of his times had such a hold over the people. Therefore, as Gandhi and Aurobindo said, Tilak would go down in history as the Maker of Modern India. His name will stand high along with the liberators of nations like Mazzini, Washington and Dr. Sun Yat-Sen. As long as nations take pride in those of their countrymen who have changed the course of history, so long will Tilak's figure with his swarthy complexion, massive head, awe-inspiring reddish eyes, thick eyebrows, big sprouted moustaches, walking stick or umbrella in hand, scarf over the shoulders, long flowing coat with strings, red turban on head, red shoes on feet below the white dhoti, be gratefully remembered by India as the Father of the Indian Freedom Struggle and the Prophet of Swaraj. He will ever be a fount of inspiration for action, service, devotion and sacrifice to those who struggle to lead humanity to Liberty's altar; and so posterity will proudly sing of him in the noble words of Swinburne:

> "These, O men, shall ye honour,
> Liberty only and these.
> For thy sake and for all men's and mine,
> Brother, the crowns of them shine,
> Lighting the way to her shrine,
> That our eyes may be fastened upon her,
> That our hands may encompass her knees."

Chronology

Year	Important Events
1761	Dhondopant Tilak from the family of Vatandars from Chikhalgaon in Dapoli Taluka of then Ratnagiri District participated in the battle of Panipat.
1778	Keshav born to Dhondopant's brother Krishnaji. Rose to the position of Mamlatdar.
1818	Keshavrao Tilak retired after the debacle of the Peshwas.
1820	Ramchandra, who worked as a surveyor under the new British regime, has a son Gangadhar.
1827	Jyotirao Phooley born.
1841	Gangadhar becomes a teacher first in Malvan, later transferred to Chiplun and Ratnagiri.
1848	Phooley starts schools for untouchables and girls.
	Satyashodhak Samaj set up.
	Gopalrao Deshmukh (Lokahitvadi) writes Shatapatre.
	Mahadeo Govind Ranade, leading light of Sarvajanik Sabha, is one of the founders of the Prarthana Sabha.
	Reformers Lokahitwadi, Mahatma Phooley and Ranade welcomed the new machine age, secular education, the spirit of enquiry and they propagated the abolition of casteism and child marriage and encouraged widow remarriage.
1850	Vishnushastri Chiplunkar, son of Krishnashastri born.
1852	Deccan Association set up in Poona to represent grievances of the Indian people to the British authorities in Bombay.
	Dadabhai Naoroji and others formed the Bombay Association.
1853	Railway begins in India. First train runs between Byculla (Bombay) and Thane.
23 July, 1856	Birth of a boy, named Keshav, after his grandfather; was called Bal. That nickname stuck and was later turned into Balwantrao.
1857	The Revolt.
1861	Bal was sent to school in Ratnagiri.
1864	Bal's thread ceremony.

Year	Important Events
1865	Gangadharpant, Bal's father, appointed Assistant Deputy Educational Inspector in Poona.
1866	Bal's mother Parvatibai dies, Bal brought up by his aunt.
1869	Dadabhai Naoroji founded the Bombay branch of the East India Association.
1870	Sarvajanik Sabha started in Poona by Ganesh Vasudev Joshi alias Sarvajanik Kaka and Sadashiv Gawade.
1871	Bal married to Tapi, daughter of Ballalrao Mahajan of Ladghar. Named Satyabhama.
1872	Passed Matriculation of the Bombay University.
1872-76	A student of Deccan College in Poona, briefly at Elphinstone College in Bombay graduated in 1876.
1876	Famine in Maharashtra; M.G. Ranade helps government through concrete suggestions made by Sarvajanik Sabha.
1877-78	Tilak Studies for his Law degree. Meets Gopal Ganesh Agarkar, then studying for M.A. at the Deccan College.
1878	Vernacular Press Act—suppression of newspapers in Indian languages.
1879	Revolt of Wasudeo Balwant Phadke. Its failure deeply influences Tilak and Agarkar.
1879	Tilak and Agarkar seek Ranade's blessings and approach Chiplunkar.
1879	Wasudeo Balwant Phadke sentenced to transportation for life.
1880	Along with Chiplunkar, Tilak starts the New English School.
1880	Tilak gets LL.B degree.
1880	Sarvajanik Kaka Dies.
1881	Agarkar joins the School.
1881	Kesari in Marathi and Mahratta in English started as weeklies. Agarkar was the founder-editor of Kesari and later Tilak was the editor. Tilak was also the founder-editor of Mahratta.
1881	Tilak gets sanad to practice as a lawyer.
1882	Tilak and Agarkar face trial in the Kolhapur libel Case.
17 March, 1882	Chiplunkar dies
	Tilak and Agarkar sentenced to four months in jail
	Agarkar writes two Marathi books in Jail: *Dongarichya Turungatil 101 Diwas* (Our 101 days in Dongri Jail) and translation of William Shakespeare's *Hamlet*. When released from the jail, they got heroes' reception from Phooley's men as well as Sarvajanik Sabha.

Year	Important Events
1882	The Hunter Commission visits the New English School and lauds its high quality.
January, 1883	The School expands and moves to Gadrewada.
13 February, 1884	Governor Furgusson attends the prize distribution ceremony.
24 October, 1884	Deccan Education Society set up.
1884	Tilak appears for M.A. with Mathematics but fails.
1885	Fergusson College inaugurated.
1885	Bombay Presidency Association founded by Sir Pherozshah Mehta and others.
28 December, 1885	Indian National Congress established at Mumbai, which grew into a strong nationwide political organisation and later turned into an influential political party.
	Second Provincial Conference held in Poona. Tilak made his first important public speech. Tilak along with Namjoshi and Gokhale appointed secretaries of the Provincial Conference to organise its next session.
	An Act of Indemnity was passed saving the Mamlatdars invloved in Crawford case from prosecution and persecution.
13 September, 1886	Interview of the Poona Shastris with H. E. the Governor.
1887	Bipinchandra Pal made his first speech at the Madras Congress.
1888	Lala Lajpat Rai made his first speech at the Allahabad Congress.
1889	Tilak returns to the college. Tilak and Gokhale attend in Bombay the fifth session of the Congress.
1889	Bombay session of the Congress presided over by William Wedderburn. Tilak and Gokhale took active part.
1890	Third Provincial Congress held in Poona. Gokhale places Sitaram Chiplunkar as secretary of Sarvajanik Sabha.
14 October, 1890	Tilak resigns from the Deccan Education Society.
1890	Malbari is able to persuade the Government of India to legislate on raising the age of consent for marriages.
	Tilak puts forth counter proposals. Risley circular creates impediments in the active participation of Justice M. G. Ranade in the affairs of the Congress.
1891	Tilak starts a Law class for the purpose of preparing students for the High court and District Pleaders' Examinations. Tilak invests in a ginning factory in Latur.
1891	A fierce controversy on Age of Consent Bill.
	Despite severe opposition from Tilak and other conservatives the Bill is passed.

Year	Important Events
1891	Bombay Provincial Conference held in Poona. Gokhale resigns from his post as Secretary of the Bombay Provincial Conference.
1892	Swami Vivekanand visits Poona, stays with Tilak.
1892	Aurobindo Ghose passes Cambridge Tripos with distinction.
October, 1893	Tilak submitted his paper on 'The Orion' or 'Researches into the Antiquities of the Vedas' to the Oriental Congress.
1895	Tilak elected to Poona Municipality and also to Bombay Legislative Council.
	Agarkar dies. Tilak supports Shivaji Memorial at Raigad.
July/August, 1895	Tilak party captures Sarvajanik Sabha. Muslim members resign.
	Gokhale resigns secretaryship and establishes the Deccan Sabha. Tilak tries to demolish Ranade and pave the way for the division of National leadership between Moderates and Extremists.
	Eleventh Congress session held in Poona. Tilak engineers to bar Social Conference from the Congress Pandal.
1896	Gandhi meets Tilak with a view to orgainising a meeting on the grievances of Indians in South Africa.
16 November, 1896	Bhandarkar, Tilak, Gokhale and others submit a memorandum to the Government of India on the disabilities imposed on the Indians in South Africa.
1896	Tilak organises Shivaji's birth anniversary at Raigad on a grand scale.
	Tilak invites Swadeshi movement and boycott of foreign clothes.
	Provincial conference held at Karachi.
	Famine breaks out in Maharashtra. Tilak takes up the cause of the farmers.
1897	Tilak attends Calcutta session of the Congress, the Government withdraws the right of Sarvajanik Sabha to petition the Government.
1897	Baba Maharaj dies. Tilak agrees to be an executor of the will of his dying friend Shri Baba Maharaj.
22 June, 1897	Diamond Jubilee of Queen Victoria's rule celebrated all over India.
1897	Plague breaks out in Poona. Chapekar brothers shoot Commissioner Rand. They are sentenced to death.
	Tilak tried for sedition. Released on bail by Justice Budruddin Tyabji.
1898	Widow Tai Maharaj gives birth to a boy, which does not survive.
	Dadasaheb Khaparde, a trustee with Tilak, obtains a probate.

Year	Important Events
1898	Tilak sentenced to Rigourous Imprisonment. Becomes a hero,
	Reads Max Müller's translation of Rigveda.
	Conceives the central theme of the 'Arctic: Home of the Vedas'.
	Released conditionally. Rests at Sinhagad and starts writing 'Artic: Home of the Vedas'
	Visits Madras for the Congress session. Visits pilgrimage centres in South India.
1899	Congress Session is held in Lucknow presided over by R.C. Dutt. Ranade, Gokhale and Tilak travel by the same train to Lucknow.
1899	The two young Chapekar brothers hanged to death for Rand murder.
1900	Tilak sues *The Times of India*, Bombay and *The Globe*, London for defamation.
1900	Tilak along with Wasukaka Joshi visits Rangoon.
1900	Provincial Conference held after a gap of five years in Satara.
1900	Lahore Congress presided over by Justice N.G.Chandavarkar.
16 January, 1901	Ranade dies, Tilak, despite his differences with the Moderates, pays a rich tribute.
1901	Tilak and Khaparde select a boy, Jagannath, who is taken in adoption by Tai Maharaj.
1901	Calcutta Congress, Tilak meets Swami Vivekanand.
1901	Tilak along with Joshi proceeds for Nepal but is stopped at Patna.
	In Nagpur, Tilak gives an outline of his future work '*Gita Rahasya*'.
1902	*Kesari* redesigned with new printing machinery.
1902	Tilak and Tai Maharaj case comes up for hearing. Criminal proceedings against Tilak. Tilak unable to attend Ahmedabad Congress.
1902	Tilak publishes '*The Arctic: Home of the Vedas*' as a sequel to '*The Orion*' or '*Researches into the Antiquities of Vedas*'
1902-3	Tilak endorses a fully operative congress.
1903	Tilak says Vaishnavism and Jainism not much different.
	Tilak attends Provincial Conference at Dharwar, presided over by his friend B.A. Khare.
February, 1903	Tilak's eldest son Vishwanath succumbs to Plague.
24 August, 1903	Tilak sentenced to 18 months rigourous imprisonment.

Year	Important Events
30 September, 1903	Tai Maharaj dies.
December, 1903	Tilak attends Madras session of the Congress.
4 January, 1904	Tilak's sentence reduced to six months.
1904	Tilak acquitted by the High Court.
1904	Tilak refers to Hindutva, leans towards extremism.
1904	Tilak opposes Curzonism.
1904	Tilak defends Paranjpe's *Kal.*
December, 1904	Bombay Congress Session presided over by Sir Henry Cotton.
1904	The extremists who refused to believe in the doctrine of divine dispensation were led by Tilak and supported by Lala Lajpat Rai.
1905	Tilak's youngest daughter married.
1905	Boycott resolution passed at Tilak's instance. A step away from the Moderates in Banaras.
	Gives important speeches at Nagar Pracharani Sabha and Bharat Dharma Mahamandal.
	Tilak praises Asiatic Japan's Victory over European Russia - exploding of the myth of European Supremacy.
July, 1905	Curzon announces the partition of Bengal, comes into force from October 16, 1905.
July, 1905	Shyamji Krishna Varma establishes India House in London to support revolutionary activity.
	Swadeshi movement and boycott of foreign goods launched. Savarkar joins Tilak.
12 August, 1905	Lord Curzon resigns as Governor General.
1905	Tilak on Hinuduism at Banaras.
	Liberal party wins in UK.
	Lord Morley becomes the Secretary of State for India with Tory Lord Minto as Viceroy.
	Agamya Guru sets up Vedant committees in Europe.
	Shivaji festival observed in great style at Raigad.
	Tilak recommends Savarkar to Shymaji Krishna Varma for the Shivaji Scholarship.
	Tilak meets Savarkar for the last time.
	Gokhale elected president of the Congress.
1906	Tilak visits Calcutta and opens Shivaji festival and Swadeshi exhibition.
	First Indian to get tremendous ovation outside his province. Samarth Vidyalaya started in Poona.

Year	Important Events
	Adoption suit decided in favour of Tilak.
1906	Tilak recommends Savarkar's application for Shivaji Scholarship in England.
1906	Tilak addresses Bharat Dharma Mahamandala on Hindu religion.
1906	Pandit Malviya proposes founding of Hindu College.
December, 1906	All India Muslim League founded.
1906	Tilak explores the possibility of military training for Indians.
	Calcutta session - Bipinchandra Pal and the extremists want Tilak as president. Sensing moderates opposition they persuade Lajpat Rai. The moderates persuade Dadabhai Naoroji to come from England. He uses the word 'Swaraj' for the first time from Congress platform.
1906	Aurobindo writes articles in B.C.Pal's *Bande Mataram* and then takes complete editorial control.
1906	Aurobindo becomes first principal of the National College.
December, 1906	Boycott resolution passed.
1906	Extremists come to be known as Nationalist.
1907	The Moderates build up their forces through Provincial Conferences. Bombay Province Conference held after 12 years in Surat.
17 August, 1907	Aurobindo Ghose arrested, tried for sedition, acquited.
	B.C.Pal sentenced for refusing to depose in this case.
28 December, 1907	Surat Congress breaks up as the extremist want Lala Lajpat Rai as President while moderates want Rash Behari Ghose.
1908	Morley Minto reforms.
22 June, 1908	Tilak tried and sentenced to six years transportation.
December, 1908	Congress session in Madras.
1909	Lahore session: Pherozshah Mehta elected president but could not be present.
1909	Tilak's friends try to secure release or at least a fresh trial but the judicial door is finally closed on Tilak.
	They seek relief on grounds of equity and humanitarism.
1910	Tilak reads Weber.
	Khaparde visits Tilak in jail, Tai Maharaj case reopens
	Tilak loses. Appeals to Privy Council.
1910	Savarkar sentenced to transportation for 50 years.
1908-14	Tilak writes 'Gita Rahasya' in Mandalay jail.

Year	Important Events
1910	Allahabad Session, Williams Wedderburn presides.
1910	Home Rule League founded. Bombay Provincial Conference in Belgaum.
1911	Savarkar sent to the Andaman.
1911	Delhi Durbar.
1911	Surendranath relapses into inactivity.
1911	Calcutta Session.
1912	Bankipur Session.
1912	Tilak's wife Satyabhamadevi dies of diabetes.
	Tilak applies for remission of the remaining part of the sentence.
	The petition is turned down.
1912	A.O. Hume passes away.
1913	Tilak has a third attack of fever in jail.
1914	Tilak released and brought back to Poona.
	Tilak put under surveillance by provincial authorities.
	War breaks out in Europe.
	Change in Tilak's strategies. Issues a statement praising civilised methods of administration of the British in India.
1914	Refutes charges made in Valentine Chirol's Indian Unrest as nasty and totally unfounded.
1914	Annie Besant tries to unite the two factions of the Congress.
1915	Gandhi returns from South Africa. Takes issue with Tilak on behalf of Gokhale.
1916	Tilak is sixty. Served with a notice by the District Magistrate Tilak exonerated.
	Tilak attends Provincial Conference in Ahmedabad under the presidentship of Jinnah.
1916	Tilak elected a member of the managing committee Lucknow Congress. Tilak attends after a gap of eight years. Gandhi defeated in election to the subjects Committee. But Tilak declares him elected.
	Tilak and Jinnah reach an agreement on behalf of the Congress and the Muslim League.
1917	Annasaheb Patwardhan passes away.
	Tilak opposes Industrial Labour System in Fiji.
	Tilak and R.P. Paranjapye call on youth to join the army to fight the German.

Year	Important Events
	Punjab becomes volatile with the presence of revolutionaries from the Ghadar party.
	Tilak prohibited from entering the Punjab and Delhi.
	Tilak attends AICC conference in Calcutta accompanied by Gandhi among others.
	Chikodi, Belgaum District Conference and Provincial Conference at Nashik. He supports war.
	Tilak attends Social Conference and explains that he could not attend Social Conference as he believes in division of work.
1917	Provincial Conference in Godhra presided over by Gandhi. Gandhi appeals for removal of untouchability for getting Swaraj.
1917	Montague Declaration.
	Montague visit to India.
	Tilak and Annie Besant lead the Home Rulers in representation to Montague.
	Calcutta Congress under presidentship of Annie Besant. Resolutions on linguistic parties and against untouchability.
	Dr. Ambedkar returns after his days at Columbia and London.
1918	Savarkar deported to the Andamans.
	Samarth Vidyalay declared an unlawful institution.
	Lala Lajpat Rai and B.C.Pal went into self-imposed exile.
	Auroboindo escapes to Pondicherry in search of God.
1918	Tilak's Home Rule tour of Vidarbha. Tilak writes Foreword to the biography of Gandhi written in Marathi by Avantikabai Gokhale.
	Tilak leaves for England via Colombo but has to return as his passport is cancelled.
	Tilak attends the Depressed Classes Conference held under the presidentship of Maharaja Sayajirao Gaikwad of Baroda. Tilak supported anti-untouchability movement in his speech but refused to sign the pledge.
1918	Tilak reaches England for Home Rule Propaganda and to fight the case against Chirol.
	Second Home Rule Conference held in Bombay.
	Tilak sends a donation for Tagore's European tour.
	In Madras, Tilak speaks on Buddhism as reformed Hinduism. Gandhi on war effort.
	Rowlatt Sedition Committee report published. Special session of the Congress in Bombay.

Year	Important Events
	Moderates part Company and start liberal party to work with the reforms.
	Tilak opposes Vithalbhai Patel's Hindu Marriage (Validity) Bill.
1918	Tilak leaves for England from Bombay. Tilak elected president of the Delhi Congress session but declines the honour.
1919	Tilak loses the case. Starts with the support of the Labour Party.
	Rowlatt Bills passed in India.
	Gandhi starts Non-cooperation Movement in India. Jalianwala Baug.
1919	Amritsar session presided over by Motilal Nehru.
1919	Tilak returns to India.
1920	Tilak presides Astronomical conference.
1920	AICC meeting at Banaras. Gandhi recommends a programme of non-cooperation. Decision postponed.
	Tilak declines being considered for presidentship of Calcutta Congress.
	Tilak falls ill at Sardar Griha, Bombay.
August 1, 1920	Tilak passes away the day Gandhi's Non-cooperation movement was to be launched.
1925	After legal battle for over 11 years the Privy Council decides in favour of Tilak in the Tai Maharaj case.

FURTHER READING

English Books

Athalye D. V.: *The Life of Lokmanya Tilak,* Swadeshi Publishing Co., 1921

Athalye D. V.: *The Life of Mahatma Gandhi,* Swadeshi Publishing Co., 1921

Bapat S. V.: *Reminiscences and Anecdotes about Lokamanya Tilak, Vol. II-III*, Poona, 1928

Besant Annie: *'How India Wrought for Freedom'*, Theosophical Publishing House, 1915

Branson Major L. H.: *A Life of Deception: Reminiscences of a Magician,* Robert Hale, London, 1953

Bruce Reverend Henry J.: *The Literary Work of the American Marathi Mission, at the semi-centennial anniversary of the commencement of the Ahmednagar mission*, October 26-30, 1881

Chintamani C.Y.: *Indian Politics Since The Mutiny,* Kitabistan, Allahabad, 1937

Chirol Sir Valentine: *Indian Unrest,* Macmillan and Company Limited, 1910

Colvin Ian Duncan: *The Life of Lord Carson,* V. Gollancz Limited, 1934

Cumming Sir John: *Political India, 1832-1932: A Co-operative Survey of a Century,* S. Chand, 1968

Dange S. A.: *Gandhi Vs Lenin, Liberty Literature,* Bombay, 1921

Das M. N.: *India Under Morley and Minto,* G. Allen and Unwin, London, 1964

Desai Valji Govindji (translated from Gujarati and ed.): Th*e Diary of Mahadev Bhai*, Navajivan Publishing House, Ahmedabad,

Dutta Charuchandra: *Articles,* 1 August, 1952

Ghose Babu Aurobindo: Bal Gangadhar Tilak: *His Writings & Speeches*, Ganesh & Co., Madras, 1922

Hardinge Charles Baron Hardinge of Penshurst: *My Indian Years, 1910-1916: The Reminiscences of Lord Hardinge of Penshurst*, J. Murray, 1948

Joshi H. M.: *History of Freedom Movement in India*: *A Note, Government of India*, 1953

Joshi Pt. Laxmanshashtri: *Hindu Dharmachi Samiksha aani Sarvadharma Samiksha; trans by G. D. Parikh, A Critique of Hinduism and other Religion*, Popular Prakashan Pvt. Ltd., Bombay, 1948

Karmarkar D. P.: *Bal Gangadhar Tilak: A Study*, Popular Book Depot, Bombay,1956

Ketkar G. V in *Reminiscences and Anecdotes About Lokmanya Tilak, Vol. I*, Bapat S. V, Poona, 1925

Khaparde G. S in *Reminiscences and Anecdotes About Lokmanya Tilak*, Bapat S. V, Poona, 1925

Krishna K. B.: *The Problems of Minorities or Communal Representation in India*, George Allen and Unwin Limited. London, 1939

Limaye P. M.: *The History of the Deccan Education Society*, Poona Deccan Education Society, 1935

Masani R. P.: *Dadabhai Naoroji: The Grand Old Man of India*, George Allen and Unwin Limited, London, 1939

Mehta Pherozeshah: *Speeches and Writings of Honourable Sir Pherozeshah Mehta*, The Indian Press, Allahabad, 1905

Mody H. P.: *Sir Pherozeshah Mehta: A Political Biography*, The Times Press, Bombay, 1921

Montagu E. S. and Montagu Venetia (Stanley) (Hon. Mrs.).: *An Indian Diary,* W. Heinemann Limited, London, 1930

Moonje Dr.: B. S. in *Reminiscences and Anecdotes About Lokmanya Tilak*, Bapat S. V, Poona, 1925

Natesan G. A.(ed): *Speeches of Gopal Krishna Gokhale,* Natesan & Co., Madras, 1908

Nevinson Henry W.: *The New Spirit in India, Harper & Brothers*, London, New York, 1908

O'Dwyer Sir Michael: *India As I Know It*, London, 1925

Paranjape: *Young Liberal Series*, 29 March, 1920

Parvate T. V.: *My Interviews with Eminent Men*

Paul & Co. B. G.: '*All About Lokamanya Tilak*'

Prasad Dr Rajendra: *At the Feet of Mahatma Gandhi*, Philosophical Library. New York, 1955

Ranade M. G.: *Essays on Indian Economics*, Natesan & Co., Madras, 1906

Reisner I. M. & Goldberg N. M. (eds), *Tilak and the Struggle for Indian Freedom*, People's Publishing House, New Delhi, 1966

Satyamurti S. in R*eminiscences and Anecdotes About Lokmanya Tilak, Vol. I*, Bapat S. V. Poona, 1925

Shore Honarable Fredrick John: *Notes on Indian Affairs*, J. W. Parkar, London, 1837

Source Material for A History of the Freedom Movement in India, Maharashtra State Gazetteers Department,1958

SriAurobindo on Himself and on the Mother, Sri Aurobindo Ashram, Pondicherry, 1929-1949

Sydenham of Combe Colonel Lord : *My Working Life, John Murray*, London, 1927

Tamhankar D. V.: *Lokmanya Tilak: Father of Indian Unrest and Maker of Modern India*, John Murray, London, 1956

Tendulkar D. G.: *Mahatma: Life of Mohandas Karamchand Gandhi*, Vithalbhai K. Jhaveri & D.G. Tendulkar, Bombay, 1951

Thakare K. S.: *Pandita Ramabai*

The All India Anti-Untouchability Movement

The Collected Works of Mahatma Gandhi, Vol. II: 1960 and 1994, The Publications Division, Ministry of Information & Broadcasting, Government of India

The Indian Nation Builder, Mittal Publications, New Delhi

Tilak Bal Gangadhar: *History of Freedom Movement in India*

Times of India: *Great Men of India, Bombay*

Vidvans M. D.: *Letters of Lokamanya Tilak,* Kesari Prakashan, Poona, 1966

Wasti S. R.: *Lord Minto and the Indian Nationalist Movement*, Oxford, 1964

Wedderburn W.: *Allan Octavian Hume,* T. Fisher Unwin, London,1913

Zacharias H. C. E.: *Remanescente India,* Akashdeep, Delhi, 1989

Marathi Books

Awte, Trimbak Hari: *Brahman va Brahmanetar*, Poona, Indira Press. 1928

Bhat Dr. V. M.: *Abhinav Bharat*, Parchure Prakashan Mandir, Bombay, 1950

Collection of K.P. Khadilkar's *Writings*, Vol. II

Deogirikar T. R.: *Wasukaka Ani Tyancha Kal*

Deshpande Gangadhar: *Mazi Jeevankatha*

Guruji K.A.: *Life of Lokmanya Bal Gangadhar Tilak*

Jawalkar Satyashodhak Dinakarrao: *Deshache Dushman*, Sugawa Prakashan, Pune

Joshi V. S.: *Mrityunjayacha Atmayadnya*, Raja, 1981

Karnataki S. N.: *Dr. Sir R. G. Bhandarkar* Karnataki

Karnataki S. N.: *Namdar Nyaymurti Kashinath Trimbak Telang*, M. N. Kulkarni, Pune, 1931

Kelkar N. C.: *Gata Goshti Arthat Mazhi Jeevan Yatra*

Kelkar N. C.: *Life of Lokmanya Tilak Kelkar*

Kelkar N. C.: *Shankaracharya Ani Tyancha Sampraday*

Khaparde D. B.: *Dadasahebyanche Charitra*

Kulkarni A. V.: *Lokmanya Tilak Yanchi Gelin Atha Varshen*, Indu Prakashan, Bombay, 1909

Mangudkar Dr. M. P.: *Poona Municipality Centenary*

Parasnis Prof. S. R.: *Namdar Gopal Krishna Gokhale*

Sardesai G. S.: *Marathi Riyasat*, Popular Prakashan Pvt. Ltd., Bombay

Savarkar Veer: *Letters from London*

Tilak S. B.: *Maza Vyasang*

Washikar S. S.: *Hindi Rajkaran*

Marathi Press

Bhattacharya Vivek: *The Navakal,* 13 August, 1965

Marmik, 01 March 1964

Bapat S. V.: *Tarun Bharat*, 28 July, 1857

The Kesari: 07 April, 1891

The Kesari: 24 March, 1891

The Kesari: 29 October, 1901
The Kesari: 29 March, 1904
The Lokmanya: 12 January, 1958
The Mahratta: 1 September, 1904
The Mahratta: 24 June, 1906
The Mahratta: 03 August, 1945
Young India: 28 January, 1920

English Press

Shraddhanand Swami: *The Liberator*, 8 July, 1926
The Bombay Chonicle: 08 March, 1920
The Bombay Chonicle: 11 February, 1920
The Hindu Missionary: 07 January, 1918
The Hindu Missionary: 29 December, 1919
The Hindu Missionary: Bombay, 05, January 1920
The Times of India: 13 January, 1891
The Times of India: 29 January 1891
The Times of India: 02 February, 1891
The Times of India: 23 March 1891
The Times of India: 01 November, 1895
The Times of India: 30 March, 1919
Memoirs in The Times of India, 04 July, 1948

INDEX